Performance Assessment in St and Conditioning

CW00765955

It is an essential skill for any strength and conditioning coach to be able to reliably assess the physical performance of their athletes and communicate the results and their implications to performers and coaches, alike. *Performance Assessment in Strength and Conditioning* is the first textbook to clearly and coherently suggest the most appropriate and reliable methods for assessing and monitoring athletes' performance, as well as including detailed sections on testing considerations and the interpretation and application of results.

The book explores the full range of considerations required to reliably assess performance, including questions of ethics and safety, reliability and validity, and standardised testing, before going on to recommend (through a comparison of field- and laboratory-based techniques) the optimal methods for testing all aspects of physical performance, including:

- injury risk
- jump performance
- sprint performance
- change of direction and agility
- strength
- power
- aerobic performance
- body composition.

Closing with a section on interpreting, presenting and applying results to practice, and illustrated with real-life case study data throughout, *Performance Assessment in Strength and Conditioning* offers the most useful guide to monitoring athlete performance available. It is an essential text for upper-level strength and conditioning students and practitioners alike.

Paul Comfort, PhD, CSCS*D, ASCC, is a Reader in Strength and Conditioning and a Programme Leader for the MSc Strength and Conditioning course at the University of Salford, UK.

Paul A. Jones, PhD, MSc, BSc (Hons), CSCS*D, BASES Accred. CSci., is a Lecturer in Sports Biomechanics and Strength and Conditioning at the University of Salford, UK.

John J. McMahon, PhD, CSCS, ASCC, is a Lecturer in Sports Biomechanics and Strength and Conditioning (S&C) at the University of Salford, UK.

Performance Assessment in Strength and Conditioning

Edited by Paul Comfort, Paul A. Jones and John J. McMahon

Routledge
Taylor & Francis Group

LONDON AND NEW YORK

First published 2019
by Routledge
2 Park Square, Milton Park, Abingdon, Oxon OX14 4RN

and by Routledge
711 Third Avenue, New York, NY 10017

Routledge is an imprint of the Taylor & Francis Group, an informa business

© 2019 selection and editorial matter, Paul Comfort, Paul A. Jones and John J. McMahon; individual chapters, the contributors

British Library Cataloguing-in-Publication Data
A catalogue record for this book is available from the British Library

Library of Congress Cataloging-in-Publication Data
A catalog record has been requested for this book

ISBN: 978-0-415-78936-3 (hbk)
ISBN: 978-0-415-78938-7 (pbk)
ISBN: 978-1-315-22281-3 (ebk)

Typeset in Galliard
by Out of House Publishing

Contents

List of figures	vii
List of tables	xii
List of boxes	xiv
List of contributors	xv

Introduction: the role of assessing and monitoring performance   1
MIKE MCGUIGAN

PART I
Testing considerations   3

1 Ethical and health and safety issues   5
STEVE ATKINS

2 Psychological issues during assessment of performance   13
JON RADCLIFFE

3 Reliability, validity and measurement error   23
PETER MUNDY AND NEIL D. CLARKE

4 Standardisation of testing   34
JOHN J. MCMAHON, PAUL A. JONES AND PAUL COMFORT

5 Structured testing vs. continual monitoring   42
PAUL COMFORT, PAUL A. JONES AND W. GUY HORNSBY

PART II
Assessment methods   51

6 Assessment of factors associated with injury risk   53
LEE C. HERRINGTON, ALLAN G. MUNRO AND PAUL A. JONES

7 Vertical jump testing   96
   JOHN J. MCMAHON, JASON P. LAKE AND TIMOTHY J. SUCHOMEL

8 Sprint testing   117
   ROBERT LOCKIE

9 Change of direction and agility   140
   PAUL A. JONES AND SOPHIA NIMPHIUS

10 Strength – isometric and dynamic testing   166
   G. GREGORY HAFF

11 Assessment of power   193
   JASON P. LAKE AND PETER MUNDY

12 Aerobic performance assessment   212
   FRED J. DIMENNA AND ANDREW M. JONES

13 Body composition assessment   240
   CARL LANGAN-EVANS, JAMES P. MORTON AND GRAEME L. CLOSE

14 Combined assessment methods   275
   TIMOTHY J. SUCHOMEL, JOHN J. MCMAHON AND JASON P. LAKE

PART III
Interpretation and application   291

15 Interpretation of results   293
   JEREMY A. GENTLES, W. GUY HORNSBY AND MICHAEL H. STONE

16 Presentation and communication of results   313
   JOHN J. MCMAHON AND PETER MUNDY

17 Application to training   332
   W. GUY HORNSBY, JEREMY A. GENTLES AND MICHAEL H. STONE

Index   354

Figures

3.1   Illustration of reliability and validity.   24

3.2   (A) Difference against mean for jump height, with mean difference (*d*) and *d* ± 2 standard deviations (2*s*). (B) Difference against mean for jump height, with *d*, *d* ± 2*s* and 95% confidence intervals for both *d* and *d* ± 2*s* (grey dashed lines).   28

3.3   Differences depend on the magnitude of the mean (heteroscedasticity).   29

5.1   An example of structured testing for a Premier League soccer team.   43

5.2   An example of a continual monitoring schedule for a track and field thrower.   45

6.1   Factors associated with injury occurrence.   54

6.2   Factors associated with poor neuromuscular control of movement.   55

6.3   Frontal plane projection angle (FPPA) conventions for single-leg squat (a), drop jump landing (b) and single-leg landing (c).   60

6.4   The Landing Error Scoring System (LESS) developed by Padua et al. (2009).   63

6.5   The adductor squeeze test.   75

6.6   A Nordic Hamstring Lower with Nordic breakpoint angle illustrated. Breakpoint is the frame of video at which the athlete can no longer resist the increasing gravitational moment.   79

6.7   The Dynamic Control Profile represents the net joint moment (eccentric knee flexors (KF) – concentric knee extensors (KE)) throughout the full range of motion (0° [full knee extension] to 90° of flexion). The point that the net joint moment crosses zero on the *x*-axis is the angle of cross-over, whereby the moment generated by the knee extensors concentrically supersedes the knee flexors eccentrically (Graham-Smith et al., 2013).   81

6.8   Hypothetical model for determining a cut-off threshold to identify bilateral muscle strength imbalances for a given muscle strength quality in a specific population.   83

7.1   A basic illustration of the vertical force applied by an athlete (grey arrow) to the force platform (grey rectangle) and the equal (in magnitude) and opposite (in direction) vertical ground reaction force applied by the force platform to the athlete (black arrow).   97

7.2   Common considerations given to the set-up of force platforms prior to collecting vertical jump force-time data.   98

7.3   An example of the influence of force-platform sampling frequency (500 Hz [light grey squares] versus 2000 Hz [dark grey squares]) on the countermovement jump force-time record just before and after the attainment of peak force.   99

7.4 A typical countermovement jump vertical force-time (top), velocity-time (middle) and displacement-time (bottom) curve.   107

7.5 Countermovement jump force-time (black lines) and velocity-time (grey lines) curves (top) and power-time (black lines) and displacement-time (grey lines) curves (bottom) for athletes who attained a high (dashed lines) versus a low (solid lines) reactive strength index modified.   113

8.1 A 100-m sprint velocity or speed curve highlighting the start action, acceleration, maximum speed and deceleration phases.   118

8.2 An example set-up for the measurement of a sprint using a radar gun.   122

8.3 The position of the test administrator with the hand-held recording device for sprint testing with a timing lights system. The athlete has been positioned 0.5 m behind the first timing gate.   124

8.4 The Brower timing system set up to record a 20 m sprint.   125

8.5 The Swift Speedlight timing system set up to record a 20 m sprint.   126

8.6 The Fusion Sport timing system set up to record a 20 m sprint.   127

8.7 The two-point, the three-point start (a) and standing split-stance start (b).   129

8.8 A subject falsely breaking the first light beam due to a start line too close to the first gate.   131

8.9 An example 40 m sprint test set up for a four-gate timing system where acceleration (0–10 m interval) and maximum speed (30–40 m interval) can be recorded.   132

9.1 Test set-up for the traditional and modified 505 tests.   143

9.2 Test set-up for the T-test.   144

9.3 The test set-up for the pro-agility test. The athlete should begin from the start line, sprint 4.6 m to the left (black arrow), turn 180° and sprint 9.1 m (grey arrow) to the second turning point and turn 180° and sprint 4.6 m (dashed arrow) back to the centre starting point.   145

9.4 The "L-run" test set-up.   146

9.5 The test set-up for the Illinois test   147

9.6 Test set-up for a video-based agility tests.   154

9.7 Test set-up for a reactive agility test (Sheppard & Young, 2006).   156

10.1 Theoretical relationship between strength and performance.   167

10.2 Common force-time curve measures.   170

10.3 Isometric mid-thigh pull apparatus.   171

10.4 Relationships between performance and strength measures.   173

10.5 Isometric squat apparatus.   174

10.6 Isometric leg press apparatus.   176

10.7 Isometric bench press apparatus.   177

11.1 Constituent components of impulse and their possible interactions.   195

11.2 Example of different jump strategies and the effect on biomechanical variables.   198

11.3 A comparison of (a) force-time, (b) velocity-time and (c) power-time curves and values, calculated using force-time and displacement-time data, during the push press.   199

11.4 A comparison of velocity calculated based on barbell and system centre of mass velocity, during the back squat.   202

11.5 Example of the appropriate processes for assessing power, depending on the equipment available.   205

12.1   Estimates of the aerobic contribution to total energy transfer during the
       ten events of the decathlon.   213
12.2   The concept of a maximal rate of O_2 uptake was first recognised in the
       early twentieth century when Hill and colleagues graphed the peak rate
       of O_2 uptake during discrete running bouts and found that at the highest
       speeds encountered, there was a specific rate beyond which no further
       increase could occur (i.e. a "VO_2 plateau").   216
12.3   A plot of [La⁻] upon completion of 3-minute stages during treadmill
       running at increasing speed.   218
12.4   A plot of the time for which cycling can be sustained against a variety of
       high-intensity work rates.   221
12.5   A plot of [La⁻] every 5 minutes during cycling exercise at a variety of
       constant work rates.   223
12.6   A plot of 30-s average VO_2 values (top panels) during ramp incremental
       cycling (left panel) and a subsequent constant-work-rate verification bout
       each performed to the limit of tolerance (dashed vertical lines).   226
12.7   A plot of 10-s average VO_2 values during ramp incremental cycling.   228
12.8   A plot of the rate of CO_2 production against the rate of O_2 consumption
       during ramp incremental cycling with a work-rate increment of 1 W
       every 2 s.   230
12.9   Identification of the metabolic rate at the GET via the V-slope method
       (Figure 12.8) can be confirmed by studying the responses of minute
       ventilation and end-tidal gas tensions during the incremental test.   230
12.10 A plot of instantaneous power output (top panels) and the rate of O_2
       consumption (bottom panels) for two subjects performing a 3-minute
       all-out cycling test.   231
13.1   Time course of total body mass losses in a male combat sport athlete
       over an 8 week period prior to weigh-in.   249
13.2   Time course of Σ8SKf in a male combat sport athlete over an 8 week
       period prior to weigh-in.   250
13.3   Time course of LM changes measured by DXA in a male combat sport
       athlete over an 8 week period prior to weigh-in.   250
13.4   Time course of FM changes measured by DXA in a male combat sport
       athlete over an 8 week period prior to weigh-in.   251
13.5   Time course of FM% changes measured by DXA in a male combat sport
       athlete over an 8 week period prior to weigh-in.   251
13.6   Walk-on spring dial (left image) and electronic (right image) BM
       weighing scales.   252
13.7   Standing stadiometer (left image) and sliding arm (right image).   253
13.8   Anthropometric tape measure.   254
13.9   The neck girth position.   255
13.10 The relaxed arm girth position.   255
13.11 The flexed/tensed arm girth position.   256
13.12 The waist girth position.   256
13.13 The hip girth position.   257
13.14 The midpoint position between the greater trochanter and the lateral
       condyle of the tibia and the mid-thigh girth position.   257
13.15 The calf girth position.   258

13.16	Skinfold measurement equipment (Harpenden callipers).	259
13.17	The midpoint position between the acromion process and the radial head and the triceps skinfold site.	260
13.18	The biceps skinfold site.	260
13.19	The subscapular skinfold site.	261
13.20	The iliac crest skinfold site.	261
13.21	The suprailiac skinfold site.	262
13.22	The abdomen skinfold site.	262
13.23	The anterior thigh skinfold site with knee flexed at 90° (left image) or extended and supported for participants with reduced skinfold thickness (right image).	263
13.24	The medial calf skinfold site.	263
13.25	The skinfold pinch (left image) and measurement (right image) procedures.	264
13.26	BODPOD ADP unit, calibration cylinder and measuring equipment.	265
13.27	Participant attire for ADP assessment.	265
13.28	Eight-site tetra-polar standing BIA system.	267
13.29	Four-site tetra-polar lead-based BIA system.	268
13.30	Hologic Horizon DXA system and spine phantom.	269
13.31	Hologic Horizon DXA system spine phantom and placement for calibration.	269
13.32	Hologic Horizon DXA system with participant placement.	270
13.33	Hologic Horizon DXA system software scan with regional analysis (left image) and android/gynoid ratio analysis (right image).	271
13.34	Hologic Horizon DXA system software scan results for BMC and BMD (left image) and regional BC analysis (right image).	271
13.35	Hologic Horizon DXA system software printed scan results for regional BC analysis including adipose/lean indices and z-scores.	272
14.1	Athlete force-velocity profiles performing squat jumps with loads at bodyweight, bodyweight + 10%, bodyweight + 20%, bodyweight + 30%, bodyweight + 40%, and bodyweight + 50%.	283
14.2	Longitudinal monitoring of weight-room training load (rating of perceived exertion × session duration) (bars) and RSImod (line) in a Division I collegiate volleyball team during the competitive season.	284
14.3	Longitudinal monitoring of weight-room training load (rating of perceived exertion × session duration) (bars) and time to take-off (line) in a Division I collegiate volleyball team during the competitive season.	285
15.1	Changes in VO$_2$max (ml·kg·min^{-1}), squat jump height (cm) and countermovement jump height (cm) after a detraining period in Team A and Team B.	301
15.2	Changes in 10 m and 20 m sprint times after a detraining period in Team A and Team B.	301
15.3	Number of players by age group.	304
16.1	Two forest plots showing the percentage change (black circles) in 20 m sprint speed for 12 rugby union players between the start and end of pre-season training.	315
16.2	Many data sets can lead to the same bar graph.	319
16.3	Additional problems with using bar graphs to show paired data.	320
16.4	Two example univariate scatter plots.	321

16.5	Two example univariate scatter plots.	322
16.6	Example radar charts for two team-sport athletes.	324
16.7	Example radar charts for one team-sport athlete.	325
16.8	Example radar charts for one team-sport athlete.	327
16.9	A scatter plot of weekly reactive strength index (RSI) values (squares) across an 8-week mesocycle for an individual athlete.	328
16.10	Two example univariate scatter plots.	329
17.1	Fatigue-fitness paradigm.	333
17.2	Graphical illustration of vertical barbell displacement for a clean grip pull from the floor and clean grip mid-thigh pull.	340
17.3	Hypothetical example of increased training concentration as an athlete develops over time.	344
17.4	An athlete preparing to perform an isometric clean grip mid-thigh pull.	347
17.5	An athlete performing static vertical jumps across a spectrum of loads (0 kg, 11 kg and 20 kg).	348
17.6	An example of a training prescription for a weightlifter displaying planned volume loads, training block objectives, testing periods and the upcoming competition schedule.	350

Tables

1.1	Example 3 × 3 risk severity rating system.	9
2.1	Key strategies to ensure valid and reliable testing procedures.	19
3.1	Hypothetical data from a validity study comparing vertical jump height measured by a force platform (FP) and portable jump monitoring device (PJMD).	25
3.2	Output from the hypothetical validity study, including Excel formula.	27
3.3	Hypothetical data from a reliability study comparing a test and a retest of vertical jump height using a portable jump monitoring device (PJMD).	31
3.4	Output from the hypothetical reliability study, including Excel formula.	32
5.1	Suggested repetition maximum testing at the end of selected mesocycles.	46
6.1	Guidance for providing feedback.	56
6.2	Definition of key terms related to validity and reliability of measurement tools.	57
6.3	Normative data for FPPA.	60
6.4	A qualitative screening tool for single-leg loading tasks.	61
6.5	Normative data for horizontal hop tests.	69
6.6	Reported reliability for the adductor squeeze test.	75
6.7	Summary of the key considerations for conducting isokinetic assessment.	77
6.8	Variation of methods to assess reciprocal and bilateral muscle strength imbalance.	82
7.1	An overview of common field-based equipment used to quantify vertical jump performance, including their main benefits and limitations.	100
7.2	Overview of common mean, peak and summed variables derived from vertical jump tests performed on a force platform.	111
8.1	Different sprint testing equipment, the company that produces the equipment, the company or example sale websites, and the approximate costs of this equipment in US dollars. These prices do not includes sales taxes or shipping.	118
8.2	Reliability (intra-class correlation coefficients [ICC]) and measurement error (coefficient of variation [CV]) for popular sprint timing systems over different sprint intervals, and the common sources of error for each system.	120
9.1	Example classification of existing change of direction speed and agility tests.	142
9.2	Summary of the different purposes of COD that may be assessed with underpinning purpose, examples, benefits and limitations.	159
10.1	Common force variables quantified from the analysis of an isometric force-time curve.	168

10.2 Common rate of force development variables quantified from the analysis of an isometric force-time curve.   169

10.3 Maximal strength prediction equations.   180

10.4 Basic considerations for performing isometric tests.   182

10.5 Basic isometric assessment protocols.   183

10.6 Protocols for measuring dynamic muscular strength.   185

10.7 Guidelines for testing common dynamic lifts.   186

11.1 The most common different methods used to calculate back-squat mechanical power output.   197

12.1 General classifications of running economy expressed as the VO_2 cost of running a specific speed and the O_2 cost of running a specific distance.   225

12.2 General classifications of VO_{2max} relative to body mass ($ml \cdot kg^{-1} \cdot min^{-1}$) at a variety of levels of performance for athletes in the United Kingdom.   225

13.1 Sections, compartments and validities of body composition measurement at differing levels. A section may be assessed by a range of measurement methods which have differing compartments and/or validities.   241

13.2 Benefits of lower or higher values in anthropometrical variables for sporting performance.   244

13.3 Sum of skinfold measurements for lower, middle and upper values across a range of differing sports using the ISAK eight-site methodology including bicep, tricep, subscapular, abdomen, suprailiac, iliac crest, mid thigh and medial calf.   246

14.1 Combined assessment methods commonly used to assess athlete performance.   276

14.2 Example athlete dynamic strength deficits and training recommendations.   281

14.3 Example athlete peak power eccentric utilisation ratios and training recommendations.   282

15.1 Daily testing schedule and details.   300

15.2 Performance assessment details of professional baseball players.   303

15.3 Performance assessment details of elite endurance cyclists.   307

15.4 Performance assessment details of rugby league players.   309

16.1 An example of the process undertaken to construct a traffic-light system for the reporting of 16 rugby league players' changes in countermovement jump height between the start (pre) and the end (post) of a power training mesocycle.   317

16.2 An example of a user-friendly traffic-light system for the reporting of 16 rugby league players' changes in countermovement jump height between the start (pre) and the end (post) of a power training mesocycle.   318

17.1 The exercise displacement of eight (five male, three female) competitive weightlifters (Hornsby dissertation data, 2013).   338

17.2 Hypothetical volume load and training intensity (average load) comparison of the clean grip pull from the floor and clean grip mid-thigh pull.   339

17.3 Performance data pre and post strength endurance block.   347

Boxes

6.1   Determining diagnostic accuracy   58
6.2   Single-leg squat task procedure   61
6.3   Single-leg landing task procedure   62
6.4   Drop jump task procedure   63
6.5   Marking criteria   64
6.6   The star excursion balance test (SEBT)   66
6.7   Hop protocols   68
6.8   Glenohumeral internal rotation deficit (GIRD) test procedure   70
6.9   Closed-chain upper-limb test   71
6.10   Hand-held dynamometry methods   73
9.1   COD speed tests: traditional and modified 505 tests   143
9.2   COD speed and manoeuvrability: T-test   144
9.3   COD speed tests: pro-agility   145
9.4   Manoeuvrability test: L-run or three-cone drill   146
9.5   Manoeuvrability: the Illinois test   147
9.6   Agility: video-based reactive agility test (Y-agility tests)   154
9.7   Agility tests: reactive agility test   156
9.8   Use of timing cells for change of direction and agility tests   157
12.1   Testing for the presence of a VO_2 plateau during ramp incremental cycling   227
12.2   Testing for verification of VO_{2max} during ramp incremental cycling   227
12.3   Calculating the VO_2/work-rate slopes below and above GET and the mean response time for ramp incremental cycling exercise   229
17.1   The fitness-fatigue paradigm and preparedness   332
17.2   Considerations for vertical jump testing and training age   343

Contributors

Steve Atkins, PhD, BASES Accred. CSci. CSCS, is the Director of Sport, Exercise and Physiotherapy at the University of Salford. He received his PhD in Paediatric Work Physiology from Liverpool John Moores University in 1997. Steve has been a certified S&C coach with the National Strength and Conditioning Association since 2006 and has worked as an S&C coach with a number of athletes and teams. He has first or co-authored >90 peer-reviewed journal articles in areas as diverse as mountain bike performance, concussion and head accelerations, muscle activation in kayaking and immune function in endurance sports. His current research focuses on concussion profiling in cycling, allied to a strong interest in internal/external loading during sports performance.

Neil D. Clarke, PhD, BASES, CSci, SFHEA, is a Principal Lecturer in Sport and Exercise Science at Coventry University and course director for the MSc in Sports and Exercise Nutrition. Neil is also an accredited BASES Sport and Exercise Scientist and holds Chartered Scientist status with the Science Council. He has over 15 years' experience working with elite and recreational athletes, as well as commercial companies. His areas of expertise and research focus include the effect of nutrition and physiological responses to intermittent activity, with a focus on football. Neil completed his PhD in 2006 in "Strategies for Optimal Hydration and Energy Provision for Soccer-Specific Exercise" and has co-authored >40 peer-reviewed journal articles.

Graeme L. Close, ASCC, PhD, rSEN, fBASES, fECSS, is a former professional rugby league player, and is now a Professor of Human Physiology at Liverpool John Moores University, where he is the programme leader for the MSc in Sport Nutrition. Graeme has published over 100 papers and review articles specialising in sport nutrition. Graeme is the expert nutrition consultant to England Rugby, the Head of Performance Nutrition at Everton Football Club, head of performance nutrition for The European Tour Golf and provides nutrition support to Johanna Konta. He is accredited with BASES, UKSCA and SENr as well as being a fellow of ECSS and BASES.

Paul Comfort, PhD, CSCS*D, ASCC, is a Reader in Strength and Conditioning and a Programme Leader for the MSc Strength and Conditioning course at the University of Salford. He has applied experience across a variety of team sports and is currently consulting with numerous professional sports teams within the Greater Manchester area. Paul is a founder member of the UKSCA, where he is also an editorial board member for Professional Strength and Conditioning and joint editor of its "Professional Insights" column. He has published over 100 peer-reviewed journal articles along with numerous book chapters and is a senior associate editor for the *Journal of Strength and Conditioning Research* and associate editor for the *Journal of Australian Strength and Conditioning*.

Fred J. DiMenna, PhD, CSCS, is an Adjunct Assistant Professor of Movement Sciences at Columbia University Teachers College, USA. He earned his PhD in exercise physiology from the University of Exeter, UK, in 2010. His PhD supervisor was Andrew Jones and his research was in the field of oxygen uptake kinetics. After returning to the USA, he continued to work with the group at Exeter in addition to assuming a position as a Research Associate at the New York Obesity Research Center at Mount Sinai St. Luke's Hospital in Manhattan. He also currently works with researchers at the Lung Institute at the Sheba Medical Center in Israel and the Faculdade de Ciências at São Paulo State University in Brazil. Prior to his PhD studies, DiMenna had a 20-year career as a competitive bodybuilder, including 10 years at the professional level. During his career, he won two drug-free United States titles at the amateur level and was runner-up in the heavyweight class of the 1998 WNBF Pro Natural International as a professional.

Jeremy A. Gentles, PhD, MA, BS, is a sport scientist and Assistant Professor at East Tennessee State University. Dr Gentles's primary academic and research interests include biochemical responses to training, the integration of sport technology in the athlete development process, and injury-reduction strategies in sport. For the last 10 years, Dr Gentles has worked with and coached a variety of youth, advanced and elite athletes in sports such as weightlifting, soccer, basketball, baseball, softball and volleyball, as well as tactical populations. Dr Gentles has given numerous scientific presentations addressing topics such as technology in sport, long-term athlete monitoring, the use of biochemical markers and technology to quantify fatigue in athletes, injury prevention and periodisation. He is also the co-owner/founder of Sportably.com, a web-based team- and athlete-monitoring system.

G. Gregory Haff, PhD, CSCS*D, FNSCA, ASCC, is an Associate Professor at Edith Cowan University, where he is the course coordinator for the Masters of Exercise Science (Strength and Conditioning). Additionally, he is currently serving as the President of the National Strength and Conditioning Association. In 2014, he was named the United Kingdom Strength & Conditioning Association: Strength & Conditioning Coach of the Year for Education and Research. Additionally, in 2011 he was awarded the National Strength and Conditioning Association's William J. Kraemer Sport Scientist of the Year Award for his excellence in sport science research. His research examines various aspects of strength and conditioning, including periodisation and neuromuscular adaptations to strength training.

Lee C. Herrington, PhD, MSc, MCSP, is a Physiotherapist, Senior Lecturer in Sports Rehabilitation, at the University of Salford, where he is programme leader for the MSc Sports Injury Rehabilitation. Lee has a clinical role as technical lead physiotherapist with the English Institute of Sport, leading on issues related to lower-limb injury rehabilitation, and also acts a consultant physiotherapist to a number of premiership and championship football and rugby union clubs. He worked as part of the Team GB medical team at the London 2012 and Rio 2016 Olympic Games. Lee has previously worked with British Swimming, Great Britain women's basketball team, Wigan Warriors and Great Britain rugby league teams along with England Table Tennis and Netball. His research interests are the treatment and rehabilitation of sports injuries, specifically: anterior knee pain; hamstring strain injuries and rehabilitation following knee surgery (principally ACL reconstruction). Lee has published >150 peer-reviewed articles, along with numerous book chapters.

W. Guy Hornsby, PhD, CSCS, USAW Certified National Level Coach, is a teaching Assistant Professor in Athletic Coaching Education (ACE) at West Virginia University. His primary responsibilities involve overseeing ACE's strength conditioning minor and graduate assistant strength and conditioning (S&C) program, which provides S&C to three local area high schools. He previously has held S&C positions within both US collegiate sport and the US military. Additionally, he has held faculty positions at the College of Charleston, Virginia Commonwealth University and Glenville State College. His primary research focus centres on optimising the training process for strength/power-based athletes. Currently, he serves as the NSCA state director and USA Weightlifting (USAW) LWC President for West Virginia. He is a Certified National Level Coach by USAW and the Head Coach of West Virginia Weightlifting.

Andrew M. Jones, PhD, FBASES, FACSM, is Professor of Applied Physiology and Associate Dean for Research and Impact in the College of Life and Environmental Sciences at the University of Exeter, UK. Jones received his PhD in Exercise Physiology from the University of Brighton in 1994, after which he completed a postdoctoral research fellowship in respiratory physiology and medicine at the University of California in Los Angeles. Jones is internationally recognised for his expertise in the following areas: (1) control of, and limitations to, skeletal muscle oxidative metabolism; (2) causes of exercise intolerance in health and disease; (3) respiratory physiology, particularly the kinetics of pulmonary gas exchange and ventilation during and following exercise; and (4) sports performance physiology, particularly in relation to endurance athletics. His recent work has focused on the role of dietary nitrate in enhancing nitric oxide production and in modulating blood pressure, blood flow and muscle efficiency/performance. During his 22-year career in research, Jones has authored >250 articles, served as co-editor of three books and acquired external funding totalling ~£2.5 million. He also serves or has served as consultant physiologist to UK Athletics, the English Institute of Sport, the Gatorade Sports Science Institute and Nike Inc.

Paul A. Jones, PhD, MSc, BSc (Hons), CSCS*D, BASES Accred. CSci., is a Lecturer in Sports Biomechanics/Strength and Conditioning at the University of Salford. Paul earned a BSc (Hons) and MSc in Sports Science both from Liverpool John Moores University and a PhD in Sports Biomechanics at the University of Salford. He is a Certified Strength and Conditioning Specialist (CSCS) with the National Strength and Conditioning Association (NSCA), an Accredited Sports and Exercise Scientist with the British Association of Sports and Exercise Sciences (BASES) and a Chartered Scientist (CSci) with The Science Council. Paul has over 17 years' experience in biomechanics and strength and conditioning support to athletes and teams, working in sports such as athletics, football and rugby, and was a former sports science support coordinator for UK disability athletics. Paul has authored/co-authored >60 peer-reviewed journal articles.

Jason P. Lake, PhD, is currently a Reader in Strength and Conditioning Biomechanics at the University of Chichester, where he teaches on both undergraduate and postgraduate biomechanics modules and coordinates their MSc in Strength and Conditioning. His research attention has focused on the mechanical demands of resistance exercise and vertical jumping, more recently focusing on methods used to assess the force-time characteristics of vertical jumping, the calculation of power output, in addition to consideration of appropriate methods for deconstructing the vertical jump force-time curves. He also continues focus on the mechanical demands of weightlifting derivatives and asymmetry at the foot-floor interface.

Carl Langan-Evans, MRes, BA (Hons), ASCC, is the Head of Strength & Conditioning and Sport Science Support at Liverpool John Moores University. He has been an accredited coach with the UKSCA since 2010 and sports therapist with the IIST since 2012. As a previous international-level Taekwondo athlete, his research is concentrated in the area of weight-making in combat sports, with a focus on both sports physiology and nutrition. Carl has worked with a number of combat sport athletes in the areas of strength and conditioning, nutrition and sports therapy and has operated in these capacities at major championships including qualification events for the London 2012 and Tokyo 2020 Olympic Games.

Robert Lockie, PhD, is an Assistant Professor in Strength and Conditioning at California State University, Fullerton, in the USA. He obtained his undergraduate and honours degrees in Human Movement from the University of Technology, Sydney (UTS), in Australia. Dr. Lockie also completed his PhD at UTS, within research that analysed the sprint technique and strength and power capacities of field sport athletes. He has previously worked at the University of Newcastle in Australia as a lecturer in Biomechanics, and as an Assistant Professor in Biomechanics and Strength and Conditioning at California State University, Northridge, before shifting to his current position at Fullerton. Dr. Lockie has a wide variety of research interests, including: linear speed, change-of-direction speed and agility; strength and power training; post-activation potentiation; performance analysis of different sports, including soccer, cricket, American football, sailing, basketball, rugby union and rugby league; and analysis of law enforcement and tactical populations.

Mike McGuigan, PhD, FNSCA, CSCS*D, is currently Professor of Strength and Conditioning at Auckland University of Technology. Prior to this, Dr McGuigan worked at High Performance Sport New Zealand as a power scientist, as well as previously holding positions at Edith Cowan University in Australia and the University of Wisconsin-La Crosse. Since 2009, he has been the sports scientist/research innovation coordinator for the Silver Ferns. Previously he worked with numerous different sports teams in Australia such as the West Coast Eagles (AFL) and Perth Glory (A-League) and has also consulted to the Australian Institute of Sport and Malaysian Sports Institute as a sport scientist. He is the Associate Editor-in-Chief of the *International Journal of Sport Science Medicine,* Senior Associate Editor for the US *Journal of Strength and Conditioning Research* and Associate Editor of the *Journal of Australian Strength and Conditioning.*

John J. McMahon, PhD, CSCS, ASCC, is a Lecturer in Sports Biomechanics and Strength and Conditioning (S&C) at the University of Salford. He received is PhD in Sports Biomechanics from Salford in 2015 following his research into dynamic muscle-tendon stiffness and stretch-shortening cycle function. John has been an accredited S&C coach with both the National and United Kingdom S&C Associations since 2010 and has worked as an S&C coach across several team sports. John has also co-authored >40 peer-reviewed journal articles relating to athletic performance monitoring and development and he is currently researching alternative methods of analysing vertical jump performance, to better inform training priorities and adaptation.

James P. Morton, PhD, rSEN, is a Reader in Exercise Metabolism & Nutrition at Liverpool John Moores University. His research interest focuses on the role of nutrient availability on modulating training adaptations and performance. He has authored over 100 research publications in the fields of sports nutrition, physiology and metabolism as well as numerous books/book chapters on these topics. James also works in elite sport in both sports physiology and nutrition support roles. From 2010 to 2015 he was the performance nutritionist to Liverpool FC and also specialises in providing nutritional and conditioning support to combat athletes. Since December 2014, James has also acted as Head of Nutrition for Team Sky for the consecutive 2015, 2016 and 2017 Tour de France victories. He is a nutritional consultant to the Northern Ireland national football team. He also directs nutrition-related research projects for the English Institute of Sport (EIS) and is Director of World Class Knowledge for Science in Sport (SiS). He also serves on the editorial board for the *International Journal of Sport Nutrition and Exercise Metabolism* and *European Journal of Sport Science*.

Peter Mundy, PhD, CSCS, ASCC, is the Course Director for the MSc in Strength and Conditioning at Coventry University. Peter's current research and applied support focuses primarily on measurement issues associated with technology, as well as the impactful implementation of technology within practice for diagnostic and monitoring purposes. Alongside this, Peter has experience providing performance support to a range of athletes, from elite professionals to grass roots. Peter was awarded a PhD in Sports Biomechanics by the University of Southampton for his work investigating the effects of external loading on human jumping mechanics. Further, he is an accredited Strength and Conditioning Coach with the United Kingdom Strength and Conditioning Association, as well as a Certified Strength and Conditioning Specialist with the National Strength and Conditioning Association.

Allan G. Munro, PhD, GSR, is a Graduate Sports Rehabilitator, having completed his degree at the University of Salford in 2007. He completed his PhD focusing on the assessment and prevention of knee injuries, in particular the ACL, in 2013. Allan's main interest lies in exercise rehabilitation, particularly of the knee and lower-limb tendinopathies. Allan has worked in rugby union for 10 years as Head of the medical team at Sedgley Tigers. He was recently appointed Lead Sport Rehabilitator for the North of England Counties U-20s squad. He has also worked with England Handball, GB U-20s basketball and Salford Red Devils. Allan currently teaches on the Undergraduate Sport Rehabilitation degree programme at Salford University, following 4 years at the Universities of Bradford and Derby. Allan is also the Vice-Chair and CPD Officer for the British Association of Sport Rehabilitators and Trainers (BASRaT).

Sophia Nimphius, PhD, PCAS-E, CSCS*D, ASpS2, AHPM, is an Associate Professor at Edith Cowan University (ECU) and High Performance Manager for Softball Western Australia. She has published over 60 peer-reviewed articles and five book chapters and is a current Board Member for the Australian Strength and Conditioning Association. She previously served as the Sport Science Manager at Hurley Surfing Australia High-Performance Centre and has been privileged to receive several awards for her contribution to the field such as the 2017 Female Leader in Exercise & Sports Science by Exercise and Sports Science Australia.

Jon Radcliffe, PhD, BASES Accred. CSci., is a Chartered Scientist and a BASES Accredited Sport and Exercise Scientist. Dr Radcliffe currently works at Leeds Trinity

University as a Lecturer in Sport and Exercise Psychology and Sports Coaching, as well as being the Programme Coordinator for Sports Coaching BSc (Hons). Dr Radcliffe completed his PhD at The University of Salford exploring sport psychology within strength and conditioning and has subsequently presented and published a number of papers relating to the use of psychology within strength and conditioning and how such factors govern physical performance.

Michael H. Stone, PhD, FNSCA, CSCS, ASCC, is currently the Exercise and Sports Science Laboratory Director and PhD Coordinator at East Tennessee State University. Prior to joining ETSU he was the Head of Sports Physiology for the USOC. From 1999 through 2001 he was Chair of Sport at Edinburgh University. Dr. Stone's research interests are primarily concerned with physiological and performance adaptations to strength/power training. Dr. Stone is also an adjunct professor at the James H. Quillen College of Medicine. He has authored >200 publications in reviewed journals, two textbooks, and has contributed chapters to several texts in the areas of bioenergetics, nutrition and strength/power training. Dr. Stone was the 1991 NSCA Sports Scientist of the Year and in 2000 was awarded the NSCA Lifetime Achievement Award. He has coached several international and national-level weightlifters (including one Olympian) and throwers in both the United States and Great Britain.

Timothy J. Suchomel, PhD, CSCS*D, USAW-SPC, is an Assistant Professor in the department of Human Movement Sciences and strength and conditioning coach at Carroll University in Waukesha, Wisconsin, USA. During his doctoral studies Dr. Suchomel worked as an assistant strength and conditioning coach and sport scientist at East Tennessee State University. He is a certified strength and conditioning specialist, recertified with distinction through the National Strength and Conditioning Association and a certified Sports Performance Coach through USA Weightlifting.

Introduction

The role of assessing and monitoring performance

Mike McGuigan

Performance assessment is a critical component of athlete preparation. When implemented correctly, assessment of an athlete's physical capacities can provide important information such as identification of strengths and weaknesses, response to training programmes, return to play and ongoing monitoring. Strength and conditioning practitioners and researchers have a wide range of assessment and monitoring tools available for their use. This presents a unique set of challenges for effective implementation and maximising the value of this information for athlete assessment and research. For example, a practitioner needs to know which assessments they should use and how to conduct them correctly in an applied setting. A researcher may need to know which tests are valid and reliable for testing a particular physical capacity. Therefore, it is imperative that both practitioners and researchers have a good understanding of the key principles of performance assessment.

Part One of this book provides the reader with a clear road map of the different aspects of testing. It is important that testing is conducted in a manner that is safe, effective and meaningful. Reliability, validity, ethical considerations and psychological factors are critical factors that are discussed in detail, which should enable readers to fully understand these important concepts. Making decisions about the structure and frequency of assessments as well as the important issue of testing versus monitoring are also highly important for effective practice. These principles are discussed in Part One in such a way that will enable to reader to apply these across the range of assessments included in the book.

A fundamental part of any physical assessment is being able to carry out the particular test so that it provides accurate information. Practitioners and researchers can be confident that by following the guidelines provided in Part Two, they are using methods that are best practice and supported by scientific research. The reader is taken through the various physical components that can be tested, including both field-based and laboratory methods of assessment. Practical applications for these methods are provided, including real-world examples that will allow strength and conditioning practitioners to apply these assessments in their practice. In addition, the application of these testing procedures in research settings is also highlighted. The reader is provided with a thorough review of the relevant research literature for each assessment method. Most importantly, standardised procedures for the key assessments are also presented.

A key feature of this book is the link between theory and practical application. In Part Three, the various approaches that can be used to aid interpretation and application of testing data are highlighted. In particular, the critical skills of presentation and communication are discussed. The often overlooked connection between assessment and training of athletes is explored with real-world, innovative case studies. Another strength of the information in these sections is that it is underpinned by scientific studies to provide strong evidence for the approaches being used.

The editors are to be commended for bringing together a group of researchers with a clear understanding of the link between research and practice. The authors who have contributed to this book are all highly regarded, with many considered world leaders in their particular area of expertise. The reader can be assured that the information contained within the chapters is up to date and best practice for assessment and monitoring of sport performance. Accurate assessment and monitoring of performance are clearly essential in both the applied and research settings. Practitioners and researchers need to know that the testing being used is safe, effective, accurate and meaningful. By closely following the recommendations provided in this book, both practitioners and researchers can be confident that the information obtained from their assessment and monitoring can be used for the ultimate purpose of understanding and improving athlete performance.

Part I
Testing considerations

1 Ethical and health and safety issues

Steve Atkins

Human performance testing provides a unique opportunity to generate a truly evidence-based approach to strength and conditioning. Many practitioners will use laboratory or field-based testing to determine the viability and impact of their innovations in training prescription. A fundamental component of all human testing is to enforce strict health and safety standards. Whilst often perceived to be "bureaucratic" in nature, adherence to the highest standards of health and safety practice is essential in protecting all who take part in our testing.

Whether undertaking maximal or sub-maximal testing, enforcing appropriate health and safety standards is a fundamental responsibility. The concept of "to do what is right" must be at the forefront of thinking when considering who to test, when is best and which methods are most appropriate. Ethics is not a set of rules per se, but a conceptual framework driven by a number of core ethical theories. Doing what is right (Virtue Theory) combines with two further philosophies to create our ethical framework. Establishing the "consequence of our actions" (Utilitarian Theory) and ensuring that "ends should never justify the means" (Deontology Theory) are clearly associated with our duty to minimise, or eliminate, risk when testing. When summarising the key message of these theories, a simple series of "values" should be considered as essential in all testing.

1. Respecting the free choice of all individuals (autonomy)
2. Seeking to do good from our testing (beneficence)
3. Avoiding harmful situations (non-maleficence)
4. Treating people fairly (justice)

Scientists are compelled to undertake their duties in a professional and ethical manner. Aside from adherence to the professional guidelines of their affiliated governing body(-ies), recognition of undertaking safe and effective research and practice is essential. Well-informed, skilled, professionals will positively influence their athletes and ensure scientifically informed testing and resulting practices are best implemented. This chapter will provide a review of the primary considerations associated with the administration of safe and effective performance testing, a fundamental component in training development and prescription. Fitness testing should be considered an integral part of athletic training, with the modality of testing determined by a complete needs analysis. This chapter will also review contemporary perspectives on ethics in laboratory and field testing, allied to a review of pertinent issues relating to risk management, liability and special considerations for different populations.

Creating a safe and effective testing environment

Work undertaken in either a laboratory or field setting presents a number of key challenges in ensuring the health and safety of participants, testers and all who may come into the testing environment. It is an essential component of the practitioner skill set that they are fully conversant with contemporary health and safety practices, and are able to recognise their responsibilities. These responsibilities can be summarised under three core headings:

1.   Duty of care in performance testing
2.   Risk management and assessment
3.   Considerations for different populations

Applying fundamental standards of ethical practice and risk management underpins all health and safety operations. Ensuring that such "ethical" practices are embedded into performance testing is a fundamental consideration for the strength and conditioning scientist. When coupled with appropriate mediation of risk, the duties of the "tester" require skills far beyond basic test administration. The need to operate in a manner compliant with protecting the health and safety of all is explicit in the professional standards and guidelines of many professional organisations (NSCA, BASES, UKSCA, ACSM, NATA). To apply these principles effectively, recognition of the difference between an operational "Standard" versus an operational "Guideline" is needed. Triplett et al. (2009) appropriately describe a Standard as "*a legal standard of care*", incumbent upon all strength and conditioning practitioners. Guidelines refer to recommended practices, designed to assist the continuing improvement of operations. Enforcing strict standards, whilst adhering to more local guidelines, will ensure the safest possible testing environment can be afforded to all. At the forefront of this "safety" is the need to recognise our duty of care.

Duty of care in performance testing

For those involved in performance testing, the need to recognise our professional obligation to "protect all from harm" is vital. This protection extends to both controlling the laboratory or field environment and also ensuring our participants are adequately prepared for the demands of testing. Performance testing is a potentially harmful activity, notably relating to the risk of sustaining musculoskeletal injury through a descending scale of potential risk for outcomes such as cardiac dysfunction, thermal stress and serious injury caused via accident. Absolute risk of cardiac events occurring during testing is low (Riebe et al., 2015) yet it is clear that vigorous exercise is associated with elevated transient risk of such episodes compared to when at rest (Albert et al., 2000). Whilst there is much published research investigating relative and absolute risks associated with maximal testing, such as graded exercise tests using treadmills, less is known as to the risks associated with functional testing of strength and power. Therefore, it is essential that as part of the practitioner's duty of care such risks are outlined and explained fully. This allows for fully informed decision-making to be undertaken by the test participant.

Informed consent is one of the most fundamental ethical processes all testers should carry out with their participants. Obtaining first-person, written, voluntary consent to undertake any form of testing is central to our ethical approval processes (Olivier, 2007). All reputable peer-reviewed journals will seek a formal statement in a methodology that written, informed, consent was given by all participants. This also extends to those who may be unable to provide first-person consent, such as children. In such cases parental or guardian, or recognised witness, approval would also be sought, though the wishes and intent of the primary participant will determine the outcome in all cases. The principle of providing informed consent to undertake testing allows two key ethical dimensions to be resolved:

1. That all participants are "informed" of details of the project, including methods, equipment, data protection and risk management
2. That "consent" implies free, voluntary, agreement to participate in testing (Olivier, 2007)

Full disclosure of all relevant information relating to testing is essential. This also relates to ensuring participants are aware that withdrawal from a project is possible during all stages of testing. Clear and precise communication, at this stage, is important to ensure participants feel empowered and informed.

The duty of care extends to all who are exposed to performance testing, whether directly (participants/testers) or indirectly (visitors). In the UK, common law duty of care is enshrined in the Health and Safety at Work Act from 1974. The guidelines of the act propose that organisations, and by extension individuals in their employment, must do "what is reasonably practicable" to minimise risk and ensure health and safety. The basic principles of the act require that good management and common-sense approaches be used to identify and mitigate risk (Jarman, 2007). Similar concepts are embedded in the Occupational Safety and Health Act (1970) in the United States, whereby the principle of duty of care is a legislative precept. Control of duty of care exists in other nations, and all share similar adherence to the use of common-sense approaches in supporting health and safety. Underpinning the establishment and action of a duty of care is the key principle of risk assessment and mitigation.

Risk management and assessment

Risk management is a proactive process designed to decrease the frequency and severity of injuries, reduce liabilities and minimise subsequent claims (Eickhoff-Shemek, 2001). As an example, the United Kingdom Health and Safety at Work Regulations (1999) explicitly require that risk assessments are undertaken for all activities. Importantly, complete documentation of these assessments should be generated and retained, with updates undertaken as required. A five-step process of risk assessment is advocated by the UK Health and Safety Executive (HSE, 1999), including:

1. Identification of any hazards
2. Determination of harm (how and to whom)
3. Evaluation of risk and review of existing control measures
4. Recording significant findings
5. Reviewing and revising assessments on a regular basis

Similar components are evidenced in risk management standards of practice outlined by a number of professional bodies, notably the National Strength and Conditioning Association (Triplett et al., 2009). Risk assessment should be considered a basic component of fitness testing schedules, and represents a legal requirement. Failure to provide evidence of such risk assessments can lead to serious penalties, including large fines and/or imprisonment.

Whilst not expecting individuals to be experts in the process of risk assessment, there is a duty for all to identify and notify any health and safety shortcomings evidenced in the testing environment. Organisations are required to provide effective, and regular, training for all staff in fundamental risk assessment and management. Where staff are not involved in the process of risk assessment then the outcomes will be ineffective. This may lead to a failure of the individual and organisation to comply with basic legal requirements in that workplace.

The most fundamental principle in undertaking effective risk assessment is the recognition that we can only do "what is reasonably practicable". Many risks can be removed entirely, such as ensuring test equipment is checked for electrical compliance through annual portable appliance testing, yet the "unknown outcomes" associated with equipment failure, allied to potential for human error, will often mean all risk cannot be negated entirely. A practical example is when undertaking maximal or near maximal lifting in novice versus experienced populations. Technical mastery of a lift requires much practice, and the novice lifter athlete may not have the technical aptitude necessary to perform the lift safely. Therefore, mediation of such risks is essential. Where risk cannot be entirely removed, you must reduce it by:

- substituting (wholly or partly) the hazard with lower-risk alternatives
- isolating the hazard from any exposed persons
- implementing control of all identified risks
- using appropriate personal protective equipment

These control measures are not designed to be used in isolation, but as part of a wider risk mitigation process. In addition, when deciding what to implement on a "reasonably practicable" basis, consideration of the following should also be given and recorded:

- the likelihood of the hazard or risk occurring
- the degree of harm from the hazard or risk
- knowledge of strategies to eliminate or minimise the hazard or risk

Identifying, controlling and mitigating risk is an essential skill for all who undertake performance testing. Many systems have been proposed to create a quantifiable measure of risk, and these have been applied in myriad settings ranging from laboratory to business management. Risk severity rating systems are common practice in testing settings. Whilst no single method has been adopted there is clear agreement that effective systems should include recognition of inherent likelihood of risk allied to identifying the perceived consequences of those risks. In simple terms,

Risk = Likelihood × Consequence

Correct application of risk severity rating systems allows the reviewer to identify and manage those actions needed to control risks. Risk severity systems are varied, ranging from rudimentary 3 × 3 to extended 5 × 5 classifications. The 3 × 3 system remains most common in basic risk mitigation practice. Table 1.1 shows an example 3 × 3 system outlined by the British Association for Sport and Exercise Sciences (adapted from Jarman, 2007).

Using a recognised risk severity rating system is good practice when completing risk assessment documents. Recording risk assessments is legally essential. Any record must

Table 1.1 Example 3 × 3 risk severity rating system.

Consequence	
3	Major (death or serious injury)
2	Serious (injuries requiring several days absence)
1	Slight (minor injuries requiring no absence)
Likelihood	
3	High (incident likely to occur frequently)
2	Medium (incident likely to occur occasionally)
1	Low (incident unlikely to occur)
Overall Risk Severity Rating (C × L)	
1 (trivial)	No action required
2 (acceptable)	No formal preventative actions though review of processes and potential improvements should be undertaken regularly
4 (moderate)	Risk should be targeted for reduction within 3–6 months. Testing can proceed
6 (substantial)	The risk must be reduced or eliminated before testing can be undertaken
9 (intolerable)	Risk must be reduced or eliminated. A legal duty to reduce risk is dominant. If risk cannot be managed then testing should not be undertaken

identify that control of risks is "suitable and sufficient" (Jarman, 2007). Failure to record and review risk assessment documentation may place the tester at risk of a liability claim. Whilst no performance testing can ever truly be considered risk-free, our ability to put in place effective risk management strategies is a key factor in both ethical approval and also operation of any research/testing.

Undertaking effective risk assessment requires a very careful examination of three key factors:

1. The testing environment

It is essential that consideration is given to suitable access to/egress from the testing area. This is important if rapid access to or egress from the test area is needed in the event of an incident. Testing environments should be free from trip/trap hazards, with wires/cabling sealed and secured to the floor where possible. Similarly, fire exits must also be fully controlled. The provision of fire and first aid safety, including identification of first aid qualified staff, is also important. Further recognition of suitable access to emergency telephone/intercom resources, needed in the event of an incident, should also be reported. Whilst not a legal requirement, best practice should determine that testing staff are first aid qualified in immediate emergency resuscitation as a minimum. Additionally, access to an automatic external defibrillator should be identified where available.

Each testing method has unique requirements with regard to equipment choice and protocol. Simple attention to risk management, allied to ensuring participants are fully informed of what you propose to do, is essential in creating the safest possible environment for all.

2. Testing equipment

Best practice in risk management should see regular, documented, checks of testing equipment undertaken. This will allow for the latest updates of both software and hardware to be implemented as well as simple "wear and tear" checking. Many types of test equipment have specific requirements for safe operations. Reference to manufacturer instructions should be made when creating both risk assessment and standard operating procedure documents. To support this, up-to-date logs of checks and servicing should be held at all points. This will ensure that test equipment remains current, and all updates and processes are attended to in a timely manner.

In addition to documentary evidence of risk assessment a best practice solution is to ensure a standard operating procedure (SOP) is in place for all test methods. This may be a simple SOP outlining how to use a force plate, to more advanced outlines of capillary/venous blood sampling (including advice on disposal of human tissue samples and sharps). Combining an SOP with ongoing review of risk assessments provides a dynamic method of ensuring health and safety in the testing environment.

3. Readiness of participants to undergo testing

The concept of screening participants for readiness to participate in testing is fundamental. For many years pre-test screening processes have been debated and refined, yet no single standard exists to propose a rubric for adoption by all testing facilities. Central to all pre-test screening is the need to provide recorded "clearance" to undertake testing. This is very much a key component of risk assessment, with the use of appropriate pre-test screening recommended for inclusion in all risk assessments.

Screening should be considered an ethical duty for all test organisations. This implies both assurances as to providing the safest possible environment for all, and also adherence to any required legal obligations regarding risk management. A key component of screening is also to ensure participants are fully aware of the informed consent process when being tested. This requires full detail of any testing to be produced, in the form of a participant information sheet, and be supported by a statement of consent to test. Such information and consent form a fundamental aspect of ethical testing procedures.

All participants must complete a suitable pre-test screening to identify any issues relating to increased risk from undertaking testing (Riebe et al., 2015). The majority of existing pre-participation screening tools focus on a combination of risk stratification associated with cardiac disease, chronic underpinning conditions, musculoskeletal injury or current pharmacological prescription. Tools such as the PAR-Q+ and ePARmed-X+ are prominent, yet have a grounding in assessing readiness for increased physical activity participation or a fitness appraisal. To date, no standardised pre-test screening tool for use in performance testing has been produced. Often, local adaptations of existing PAR-Q, or derivative, screening tools are considered sufficient. Therefore, any pre-test screening should identify likely contraindications to testing, and ensure participants are able to withdraw at any time. It is strongly recommended that any potential contraindications for testing are verified by an external clinician before the participant is allowed to test. Protection of the participant is simply non-negotiable, and a short delay to receive confirmation or approval of readiness to test, from a qualified clinician, is deemed essential.

Whilst performance testing activities can never truly be considered free from risk, the appropriate application of risk assessment and mitigation processes is essential in protecting testers and organisations from any legal liability associated with a claim of negligence. To protect against liability claims it is essential that appropriate documentation is created and available, allied to ensuring appropriate professional and personal liability insurance is in place to cover expenses and damages that may result from any claim against a tester or organisation. Minimum documentation standards must include:

- evidence of public liability insurance held by the organisation
- evidence of personal liability insurance as required
- up-to-date risk assessments
- standard operating procedures associated with performance testing (locally created, and including approach to ethics)
- repository of pre-test screening questionnaires and outcomes

The correct management of such information is essential in evidencing our risk management processes.

Consideration of special populations

Performance testing and research involving different populations is both legitimate and valuable. This may include testing children, those who may have learning difficulties, pregnant women, or certain clinical populations. In some cases, these participants may not fully be aware of the demands of the research to be undertaken, and therefore a more inclusive process of generating informed consent is needed. Often, such populations are classified as being "vulnerable". Protecting a member of a vulnerable population has extended implications for the tester. This will include involvement of parents or guardians or named carers in ensuring participants are fully informed and are able to understand the voluntary nature of the testing they are to undertake.

When working with children a key issue relates to the approximate age when consent can be given. The age at which an individual can be deemed to provide informed consent is relatively consistent. In the United States, there is some variation in state-level legislation regarding the age a child or adolescent can be deemed to provide informed consent, notably relating to the definition of an "age of majority" (Campbell, 2004). Further challenge results from the interpretation of legislature relating to classification of "mature minor" status or "emancipated minors". In all cases, deferring to the "age of majority", commonly 18 years of age for most states, will provide appropriate surety. In the United Kingdom, the age of majority again is stated as 18 years of age. There are, again, some differences in the age associated with a legal basis for consent, notably in Scotland. Best practice remains that younger individuals should continue to seek a parental/guardian counter-signatory when generating informed consent (Williams et al., 2011). Assent, or the process of generating a verbal or written "yes" from participants, should be considered useful. However, this must be supported by the generation of parental/proxy consent, again in the written form.

In addition to completing an informed consent form, appropriate safeguards must be put in place to protect vulnerable participants. Safeguarding is the process by which the vulnerable are protected from abuse or impairment of health and ensuring the provision of optimum life chances (Williams et al., 2011). Information on the promotion of a safe and positive environment for testing, allied to continuing training and awareness of staff to issues relating to working with the vulnerable, is vital. The Sport England (2004) guidelines for child protection in sport provide a simple, yet effective, series of standards when working with such vulnerable populations. These include:

- dressing appropriately
- using appropriate language
- avoiding unnecessary physical contact

Attention to these basic standards should be considered essential.

In summary, the health and safety of our research participants is a combination of processes. These involve risk management and mitigation, ethical review and the process of informed consent. Controlling the myriad factors associated with human performance testing is, at times, almost impossible. By *"controlling the controllables"*, by adhering to standards and guidelines determined locally, the health and safety of participants can be afforded considerable protection. Attending to the requirements of professional bodies, all of whom present their own series of standards and guidelines, will also be essential in mediating risk and enforcing a safe and effective testing environment. Generating simple, yet effective, operational guidelines and documentation is a "best practice" step towards conforming to the requirements of effective health and safety, and also ensuring mitigation of risk.

References

Albert, C.M., Mittleman, M.A., Chae, C.U., Lee, I.M., Hennekens, C.H., & Manson, J.E. (2000). Triggering of sudden death from cardiac causes by vigorous exertion. *New England Journal of Medicine, 343*, 1355–1361.

Campbell, A.T. (2004). Institute of Medicine (US) Committee on Clinical Research Involving Children; B, State Regulation of Medical Research with Children and Adolescents: An Overview and Analysis. In M.J. Field & R.E. Behrman (Eds.), *Ethical conduct of clinical research involving children*. Washington DC: National Academies Press (US).

Eickhoff-Shemek, J. (2001). Distinguishing protective legal documents. *ACSM's Health & Fitness Journal, 5*, 27–29.

Jarman, G. (2007). Health and safety. In E.M. Winter, A.M. Jones, R, Davison, P.D. Bromley & T.H. Mercer (Eds.), *Sport and exercise physiology testing guidelines*. Vol. 1, *Sport testing*. British Association for Sport and Exercise Sciences. Routledge: London.

Olivier, S. (2007). Ethics and physiological testing. In E.M. Winter, A.M. Jones, R, Davison, P.D. Bromley & T.H. Mercer (Eds.), *Sport and exercise physiology testing guidelines*. Vol. 1, *Sport testing*. British Association for Sport and Exercise Sciences. Routledge: London.

Riebe, D., Franklin, B.A., Thompson, P.D., Garber, C.E., Whitfield, G.P., Magal, M., & Pescatello, L.S. (2015). Updating ACSM's recommendations for exercise preparticipation health screening. *Medicine & Science in Sports & Exercise, 47*, 2473–2479.

Sport England. (2004). *Funding support pack: Child protection guidelines*.

Triplett, N.T., Williams, C., McHenry, P., & Doscher, M. (2009). Strength & Conditioning Professional Standards and Guidelines. National Strength and Conditioning Association.

Williams, C., Cobb, M., Rowland, T., & Winter, E. (2011). *The BASES Expert Statement on Ethics and Participation in Research of Young People*. Leeds: British Association for Sport and Exercise Sciences.

2 Psychological issues during assessment of performance

Jon Radcliffe

Within the assessment of sport performance, it is important to ensure consistency between trials to ensure validity and reliability of measures. Chapters 3 and 4 provide detailed discussions regarding reliability and validity and standardisation of measurement techniques, respectively. Clearly, reliable and valid measures are imperative in accurately benchmarking athletes and monitoring the efficacy of training practices; however, psychological factors play an influential role in physical performance. Indeed, Couture et al. (1999) concluded that the attainment of optimal performance requires psychological skills to regulate the physiological state. This supports the notion that sporting prowess is dependent on psychological skills and performance fluctuations are attributable to cognitive factors, with such fluctuations casting doubt on the reliability and validity of performance measures.

Mellalieu and Shearer (2012) advocated it would be beneficial to use particular self-regulatory psychological strategies within strength and conditioning. These consisted of goal-setting, mental imagery, self-talk and techniques to regulate the activation of the athlete. In identifying important psychological strategies recent research (Radcliffe et al., 2013) indicates that certified strength and conditioning coaches consider motivation and confidence amongst the most important psychological factors governing performance, further signifying the importance of such variables for physical performance within strength and conditioning. Furthermore, Gee (2010) has suggested that performance could be considered in absolute terms governed only by physiological and biomechanical factors; however, is more accurately considered in relative terms making reference to the way in which psychological barriers govern performance. This chapter serves to provide an overview of pertinent psychological factors which could influence performance and provide recommendations to prevent such factors impacting testing outcomes.

Self-confidence

Self-efficacy (situational-specific self-confidence; Bandura, 1986) is theorised to be dependent upon four major sources of information. These comprise: vicarious experiences whereby an individual makes comparisons with the performance of others who possess similar characteristics (following the notion of "if he/she can do it, so can I"); verbal persuasion; interpretation of physiological states; and previous experiences (Short & Ross-Stewart, 2010). The most dependable source is derived from judgments of previous experiences and associated perceptions of success or failure (Short & Ross-Stewart, 2010). It is through such a mechanism that performance has been improved via misinformation to minimise the perceived discrepancy between capabilities and task demands. The effect of self-efficacy and perceived task difficulty has been widely examined through the use of strength tasks (Fitzsimmons et al., 1991; Wells et al., 1993; McMahon, 2009; Radcliffe et al., 2014), with manipulated self-efficacy having implications for maximal strength and endurance. Researchers have identified that deceiving individuals into believing the task to be easier than it is has resulted in performance improvements in terms of maximal performance measured using the bench press (Fitzsimmons et al., 1991; Wells et al., 1993), deadlift (McMahon, 2009) and hang power clean (Radcliffe et al., 2014). Consequently, it is apparent that a psychological barrier, governed by performance expectations, exists preventing maximum performance. Furthermore, athletes' self-reported effort expended in the weights room over the course of the off-season has been shown to relate to self-efficacy positively (Gilson et al., 2012), thus suggesting the greater effort applied when the athlete is confident in their ability. However, the original premise of a linear relationship between self-efficacy and performance has been questioned in that excessive levels of self-efficacy (being over-confident) can prove detrimental to performance (Woodman et al., 2010). This was hypothesised to be owing to the additional effort invested in the task due to the perceived discrepancy between capabilities and task requirements. However, in consideration of the work of Woodman et al. (2010) it is important to note that the perceived difficulty was sufficiently high to mobilise the required effort.

Activation and "psyching up"

Activation, a term often used synonymously with arousal, is the psychological and physiological readiness in advance of a given situation. Strategies to increase activation are colloquially referred to as "psyching up", with many athletes engaging with such activities to improve performance (Tod et al., 2003). Furthermore, results of a recent study indicated that "arousal regulation" was a major consideration regarding the psychological skills employed by accredited strength and conditioning coaches, with music and pre-performance routines frequently used (Radcliffe et al., 2015). Music is regarded as an effective ergogenic aid, with tempo and preference being key considerations (Karageorghis et al. 2006; Karageorghis & Priest, 2012).

Academic support for using activation strategies exists with improvements observed in hand grip tests (Shelton & Mahoney, 1978) and the bench press (Tod et al., 2005). Despite the academic attention, and anecdotal accounts of using such strategies, there is relatively scant research focusing on endurance-based exercise and much of the research has used novice performers, with research using experienced athletes (over 4 years training experience) casting doubt on the efficacy of "psyching-up" (McGuigan et al., 2005). This could, however, possibly be due to the use of self-selected internalised preparatory strategies by more experienced athletes. Furthermore, many theories associate performance with activation, including the inverted-U, catastrophe model and individual zones of optimal functioning (Arent & Landers, 2003; Hardy & Parfitt, 1991; Annesi, 1998); however, the curvilinear relationship between activation and performance is mediated by sport type and individual differences; thus, providing collectively effective strategies within a research protocol could be considered challenging.

Presence of others

Social facilitation, or the effect of others on performance, has been identified as a consideration in measuring human performance for over a century (Triplett, 1898). Triplett identified that individuals' performance is dependent upon the presence of others either observing (audience), independently performing a similar task without an element of competition (co-action), or in direct competition. Rhea and colleagues (2003) examined the influence of competition and audience on bench-press performance, identifying that the presence of an audience or competition, compared to a co-action condition, resulted in improved performance. No significant differences were noted between either the competition or audience setting. Such observations have been supported in literature reviews (Bond & Titus, 1983; Strauss, 2002) noting small, but significant, effects; however, small effects are important to appreciate in the context of performance monitoring. An interesting observation concerns the type of task being performed, with significant positive effects observed in simple physical conditioning tasks; however, the opposite was observed in complex skills with higher levels of coordination needed (Strauss, 2002; Bond, 1982). Such findings are consistent with drive theory (Zajonc, 1965) that simple tasks with minimal cognitive investment improve via elevated activation; however, in complex cognitive tasks the increased cognitive burden associated with social comparison and subsequent attentional losses result in reduced task performance (see Strauss, 2002, for review).

The thought of being observed (Rhea et al., 2003) and, importantly, evaluated (Strauss, 2002) has been identified to impact performance, with self-presentation an influential factor. Thus, it is important to consider the impact of the tester and specifically the influence of the gender of the tester on athletic performance. Previously, male athletes have been shown to invest more effort (Worringham & Messick, 1983) and self-report lower levels of perceived exertion in the presence of female testers compared to male testers (Boutcher et al., 1988). Such research is effective in identifying threats to the validity of testing protocols; however, a more recent study identified that the sex of the experimenter did not impact the performance of a maximal voluntary contraction (MVC) of the ankle (Lamarche et al., 2011). Differences in findings could be attributable to the tasks. Specifically, experimenter sex influenced performance in continual endurance-type exercise (running and cycling) whilst the MVC is an acute and maximal movement. Thus, it is possible that there is not the attention afforded to the perceptions of the tester in the short-duration tests which is present in the longer duration activities. Furthermore, as stated by Lamarche et al. (2011), the lack of effect may be owing to the lack of social physique anxiety experienced in the young, active and strength-trained population. Furthermore the study failed to consider the individual's achievement goal orientation. Achievement Goal Theory (Nicholls, 1984) states that individuals are motivated via the drive to demonstrate mastery against self-referenced targets (task-orientation) and the desire to demonstrate competence in comparison to others (ego-orientation). Thus it would appear that, in comparison to athletes with a low ego-orientation, the individuals with a high ego-orientation are more likely to be influenced by social mediators such as competition and audience effects. Encouragingly, at least for short-duration activities with trained individuals, the gender of the tester appears to not impact performance.

Psychological skills

Research findings have evidenced the effect of psychological interventions on variables pertinent to strength and conditioning; for example, research has demonstrated the benefits of using goal-setting (Baker, 2000; Tod & McGuigan, 2001; Gilson, 2010; Weinberg et al., 1985) within a training programme and concluded that the athlete's motivational orientation must be considered within strength training (Fry & Fry, 1999; Gilson et al., 2008) and that the proximity and specificity of goals can directly influence muscular endurance

(Weinberg et al., 1985). As such it is important to try and ensure maximal levels of motivation prior to any testing procedures, with one such method being the use of challenging yet achievable, self-referenced and proximal goals that make use of split goals which segment longer-duration events.

Furthermore, cognitive preparatory strategies such as mental imagery can play an influential role in both longer-term expression of strength and acute testing environments; for instance, mental imagery strategies have been utilised to elicit strength gains over a 6-week period (Lebon et al., 2010). A review of the literature (Mellalieu & Shearer, 2012) identifies that the imagery is influential in both chronic and acute applications, with imagery training resulting in strength gains from muscle groups ranging in size from finger to hip flexors (Ranganathan et al., 2004; Smith et al., 2003). Imagery is a beneficial technique in mobilising effort, enhancing self-efficacy (Feltz & Riessinger, 1990), reducing anxiety and moderating activation states (Mellalieu & Shearer, 2012). Indeed many studies (see Cumming and Ramsey, 2010, for a review) are guided by the applied model of imagery (Martin et al., 1999) in which imagery serves a number of functions to influence skill learning, cognitions and activation. Consequently, whilst imagery interventions have been shown to benefit strength over a period of time, ensuring test-to-test consistency in such skill usage is an important consideration to ensure the acute performance-related benefits do not impact the reliability and validity of assessment procedures.

Self-talk is a covert or overt technique used by performers to direct thoughts. Whilst complex and multidimensional in nature, self-talk is typically considered to serve either motivational or instructional functions. Self-talk has been shown to be effective in increasing performance in activities such as leaping, sprinting, endurance running, throwing and leg extension (Tod et al., 2009; Theodorakis et al., 2000; Edwards et al., 2008). The matching hypotheses suggest that specific self-talk functions benefit particular tasks. For instance instructional self-talk enhances performance via eliciting appropriate movement patterns, whereas motivational self-talk, focusing on the outcome, has proven beneficial in increasing activation levels, heightening confidence and increasing energy expenditure. Comparisons between self-talk functions and performance effects were noted by Edwards and colleagues (2008), demonstrating that motivational self-talk was more beneficial than instructional self-talk in improving jump performance. Within strength and conditioning activities motivational self-talk is considered superior to instructional self-talk due largely to the increases in effort expenditure and activation and without the threats to autonomous movement control possible with excessive instructional technical cues (Hardy et al., 2009).

Coaching cues – attentional focusing

A growing body of work has examined the impact of coaching cues and a performer's focus of attention and subsequent impact on performance (Wulf, 2013). Such research concludes that having an external focus of attention towards movement outcomes rather an internal focus toward one's own body has brought about improvements in stability and balance (Rotem-Lehrer & Laufer, 2007; Laufer et al., 2007; Landers et al., 2005). Furthermore an internal focus of attention has been found to induce greater electromyography activity compared to external (Vance et al., 2004; Marchant et al., 2009), indicating that adopting an external focus of attention may result in increased movement efficiency (Lohse et al., 2010). Related studies have reported improved vertical jump height using an external focus when compared to an internal focus (Wulf et al., 2007,

2010). Similar results have also been demonstrated in the standing horizontal jump, most notably by Porter and colleagues (2010), who saw an average increase of 10 cm when using an external focus (jump as far as possible) when compared to an internal focus (extend knees as rapidly as possible).

Halperin and colleagues (2016) measured the effects of attentional focusing instructions on force production during a mid-thigh pull, using three coaching instructions: a control, "Focus on going as hard and as fast as you possibly can"; an internal focus, "Focus on contracting your legs muscles as hard and as fast as you possibly can"; and an external focus, "Focus on pushing the ground as hard and as fast you possibly can". The results significantly demonstrated that an internal focus hinders performance during a maximum voluntary isometric contraction and therefore supports the constrained action hypothesis (Wulf et al., 2001, 2007). Using a repetitions-until-failure protocol Marchant and colleagues (2011) explored the influence of an external focus (focusing on the bar itself) compared to an internal focus (focusing on the working limbs, i.e. the arms or the legs) when performing the bench press and the back squat. Significantly more repetitions were performed before failure using an external focus of attention.

Recommendations for assessing performance

Clearly psychological factors can cause a reduced relative performance compared to the theoretical physically governed absolute performance. In improving performance the objective should be to minimise the discrepancy between absolute and relative performance; however, during the evaluation of performance it is imperative that such factors accountable for relative performance are controlled, ensuring valid and reliable evaluations. The following section offers practical examples through which psycho-social factors can be controlled in the testing environment.

Self-confidence

Self-efficacy is a key variable governing the extent to which physiological performance can be demonstrated. The previous section identified that athletes can be deceived into lifting more than they have previously; however, this chapter does not serve to promote misinformation as a strategy owing to ethical concerns, risk of injury and threats to coach-athlete relationship; nevertheless it does identify the impact of previous accomplishments on situational appraisal and subsequent performance. Previous accomplishments are the prime source of information on which self-efficacy judgements are made (Short & Ross-Stewart, 2010). As a result an appropriate goal-setting strategy is needed which demonstrates previous achievements, but importantly also that the programmed performance increments are also attainable whilst being proximal (quickly attainable) and appropriately challenging.

The testing environment could be modified accordingly to maximise the impact of vicarious experiences. Strategies would include the pairing of individuals of similar ability and training expertise or observing videos of successful similar performances prior to testing. Verbal persuasion and encouragement from the tester is also an effective source of information for efficacious beliefs. Effective verbal persuasion should encapsulate previous performance as a foundation with impactful statements provided by individuals considered knowledgeable about both the athlete and the task.

Activation and "psyching-up"

The knowledge base concerning activation has shown benefits for novice athletes yet has proven inconclusive with more experienced athletes. This could be owing to individual differences in optimal levels of activation, and skill in using appropriate preparatory strategies. This is further confounded by music, a commonly used activating strategy, being the subject of individual preference regarding its motivational qualities (Karageorghis et al., 2006; Karageorghis & Priest, 2012). As a result it is recommended that in the interest of reliability and validity such variables are controlled and standardised between testing sessions. Thus testing environments should not have music playing and athletes should be instructed to use strategies they would typically use during similar activities.

The presence of others

Performing in front of an audience or in competition has been shown to positively impact performance. It is logical to propose an audience given the performance benefits; however, it is important to ensure that the audience is consistent to avoid changes in levels of evaluation apprehension (Henchy & Glass, 1968) which may arise should different individuals observe. It is also noteworthy that such performance benefits are seen in simple movements and the presence of an audience proves detrimental in the performance of complex tasks. Such a strategy would therefore be inappropriate for complex lifts which have not yet been learnt to the point of autonomous execution. Consequently, owing to the instability of anxiety because of the varying audience or simply the athlete's perception of the audience, a pertinent recommendation would be to minimise the number of observers to ensure reliable valid procedures.

Psychological skills

The use of psychological skills has received an encouraging amount of focus; however, it is beyond the scope of this chapter to offer detailed strategies. Nevertheless, in the context of preserving testing rigour, strategies to prevent environmental distractions would be a pertinent approach. The use of pre-performance routines, whilst serving an activating function, would also occupy attentional capacity and thus reduce susceptibility to external, and uncontrollable, distractions which could vary between testing episodes. It would be recommended that self-regulatory strategies are consistently performed in training and testing settings with a structured and consistent routine established. Such a preparatory routine could be supplemented with the visualisation of successful performance and positive motivational self-talk focusing on the outcome of the movement with reference to previous accomplishments; however, the focus must be on consistency of the preparatory routine.

Coaching instructions

There is a useful body of work examining the use of coaching cues relevant to strength and conditioning. Based on empirical results it would be appropriate to recommend that coaching cues are to be provided consistently across all trials and all athletes, with the aim to promote an external, rather than internal, focus. For instance, a jumper may strive to reach and touch a target rather than being instructed to extend legs as forcefully as possible – essentially, the cues should be oriented towards the effect rather than the affect.

Table 2.1 Key strategies to ensure valid and reliable testing procedures.

Use verbal persuasion, making sure to reiterate previous achievements in preparation for the task.

When testing athletes in a group, the group should comprise athletes who are of a similar standard for the given task and are familiar and confident around one another.

Longer-duration activities should be administered and recorded by the same-gender experimenter on each occasion.

Ensure that the testing environment is consistent and free from distractions either with no music or a consistent, upbeat, athlete-selected playlist.

Athletes should be instructed to visualise the successful execution of the test in preparation for the attempt.

Athletes choosing to use psyching-up techniques should be instructed to use similar strategies in preparation for each testing episode.

Where used, athletes self-talk should be motivational rather than instructional (technical).

Verbal instruction should aim to instil an external focus of attention. This should focus on the outcome rather than the internal causes (i.e. push the bar as forcefully as possible, rather than contract the chest as forcefully as you can).

Athletes should be set agreed, and *appropriately challenging*, goals for the specific test. Use splits for longer-duration activities to ensure the goals are proximal.

With the use of creative instructional cues such an approach is possible for all dynamic tests within strength and conditioning. Also, with technological advances, real-time augmented feedback pertaining to force production would serve as a useful method of maximising performance.

Summary

It is widely acknowledged that there is a natural connection between the psychology and the physiology of an athlete (Gee, 2010) with cognitions and moods directly influencing responses at a physiological level (Bradley & Lang, 2000).

This chapter has sought to identify some of the psychological issues relating to assessment of sport performance. Whilst testing protocols are typically rigorously controlled with considered approaches to the standardisation of testing protocols, often the impact of psycho-social factors is inadequately controlled. The impact of such variables on relevant physical activities has been documented, indicating the neglect of such factors would be at the expense of testing rigour. The recommendations identify strategies to minimise the difference between relative and absolute performance and thus enhance the validity of physiological testing measures and to signpost towards key considerations which, if not controlled, could result in inconsistencies in testing results.

References

Annesi, J.J. (1998). Applications of the individual zones of optimal functioning model for the multimodal treatment of precompetitive anxiety. *Sport Psychologist, 12,* 300–316.

Arent, S.M., & Landers, D.M. (2003). Arousal, anxiety, and performance: A reexamination of the inverted-U hypothesis. *Research Quarterly for Exercise and Sport, 74,* 436–444.

Baker, D. (2000). The effectiveness of goal setting in the strength and power training process. *Strength & Conditioning Coach, 8,* 3–8.

Bandura, A. (1986). *Social foundations of thought and action: A social cognitive theory.* Englewood Cliffs, NJ: Prentice Hall.

Bond, C.F. (1982). Social facilitation: A self-presentational view. *Journal of Personality and Social Psychology, 42,* 1042.

Bond, C.F., & Titus, L.J. (1983). Social facilitation: a meta-analysis of 241 studies. *Psychological Bulletin, 94,* 265.

Boutcher, S.H., Fleischer-Curtian, L.A., & Gines, S.D. (1988). The effects of self-presentation on perceived exertion. *Journal of Sport and Exercise Psychology, 10,* 270–280.

Bradley, M.M., & Lang, P.J. (2000). Measuring Emotion: Behaviour, feeling and physiology. In R.D. Lane & L. Nadell (Eds.), *Neuroscience of emotions.* New York: Oxford Press.

Couture, R.T., Singh, M., Lee, W., Chahal, P., Wankel, L., Oseen, M., & Wheeler, G. (1999). Can mental training help to improve shooting accuracy? *Policing: An International Journal of Police Strategies & Management, 22,* 696–711.

Cumming, J., & Ramsey, R. (2010). Imagery interventions in sport. In S. Mellalieu & S. Hanton (Eds.), *Advances in applied sport psychology: A review.* London: Routledge.

Edwards, C., Tod, D., & McGuigan, M. (2008). Self-talk influences vertical jump performance and kinematics in male rugby union players. *Journal of Sports Sciences, 26,* 1459–1465.

Feltz, D.L., & Riessinger, C.A. (1990). Effects of in vivo emotive imagery and performance feedback on self-efficacy and muscular endurance. *Journal of Sport and Exercise Psychology, 12,* 132–143.

Fitzsimmons, P.A., Landers, D.M., Thomas, J.R., & Vandermars, H. (1991). Does self-efficacy predict performance in experienced weightlifters? *Research Quarterly for Exercise and Sport, 62,* 424–431.

Fry, M.D., & Fry, A.C. (1999). Goal perspectives and motivational responses of elite junior weightlifters. *The Journal of Strength & Conditioning Research, 13,* 311–317.

Gee, C.J. (2010). How does sport psychology actually improve athletic performance? A framework to facilitate athletes' and coaches' understanding. *Behavior Modification, 34,* 386–402.

Gilson, T.A. (2010). Outcomes of confidence in sport training settings. *Strength & Conditioning Journal, 32,* 91–96

Gilson, T.A., Chow, G.M., & Ewing, M.E. (2008). Using goal orientations to understand motivation in strength training. *The Journal of Strength & Conditioning Research, 22,* 1169–1175

Gilson, T.A., Reyes, G.F., & Curnock, L.E. (2012). An examination of athletes' self-efficacy and strength training effort during an entire off-season. *Journal of Strength and Conditioning Research, 26,* 443–451.

Halperin, I., Williams, K.J., Martin, D.T., & Chapman, D.W. (2016). The Effects of Attentional Focusing Instructions on Force Production During the Isometric Midthigh Pull. *The Journal of Strength & Conditioning Research, 30,* 919–923.

Hardy, J., Oliver, E., & Tod, D. (2009). A framework for the study and application of self-talk within sport. In S. Mellalieu & S. Hanton (Eds.), *Advances in applied sport psychology: A review.* London: Routledge.

Hardy, L., & Parfitt, G. (1991). A catastrophe model of anxiety and performance. *British Journal of Psychology, 82,* 163–178.

Henchy, T., & Glass, D.C. (1968). Evaluation apprehension and the social facilitation of dominant and subordinate responses. *Journal of Personality and Social Psychology, 10,* 446.

Karageorghis, C.I., & Priest, D.-L. (2012). Music in the exercise domain: a review and synthesis (Part I). *International Review of Sport and Exercise Psychology, 5,* 44–66.

Karageorghis, C.I., Priest, D.-L., Terry, P.C., Chatzisarantis, N.L., & Lane, A.M. (2006). Redesign and initial validation of an instrument to assess the motivational qualities of music in exercise: The Brunel Music Rating Inventory-2. *Journal of Sports Sciences, 24,* 899–909.

Lamarche, L., Gammage, K.L., & Gabriel, D.A. (2011). The effects of experimenter gender on state social physique anxiety and strength in a testing environment. *The Journal of Strength & Conditioning Research, 25,* 533–538.

Landers, M., Wulf, G., Wallmann, H., & Guadagnoli, M. (2005). An external focus of attention attenuates balance impairment in patients with Parkinson's disease who have a fall history. *Physiotherapy, 91*, 152–158.

Laufer, Y., Rotem-Lehrer, N., Ronen, Z., Khayutin, G., & Rozenberg, I. (2007). Effect of attention focus on acquisition and retention of postural control following ankle sprain. *Archives of Physical Medicine and Rehabilitation, 88*, 105–108.

Lebon, F., Collet, C., & Guillot, A. (2010). Benefits of motor imagery training on muscle strength. *Journal of Strength and Conditioning Research, 24*, 1680–1687.

Lohse, K.R., Sherwood, D.E., & Healy, A.F. (2010). How changing the focus of attention affects performance, kinematics, and electromyography in dart throwing. *Human Movement Science, 29*, 542–555.

Marchant, D.C., Greig, M., Bullough, J., & Hitchen, D. (2011). Instructions to adopt an external focus enhance muscular endurance. *Research Quarterly for Exercise and Sport, 82*, 466–473.

Marchant, D.C., Greig, M., & Scott, C. (2009). Attentional focusing instructions influence force production and muscular activity during isokinetic elbow flexions. *The Journal of Strength & Conditioning Research, 23*, 2358–2366.

Martin, K.A., Moritz, S.E., & Hall, C.R. (1999). Imagery use in sport: A literature review and applied model. *The Sport Psychologist, 13*, 245–268.

McGuigan, M.R., Ghiagiarelli, J., & Tod, D.A. (2005). Maximal strength and cortisol responses to psyching-up during the squat exercise. *Journal of Sports Sciences, 23*, 687–692.

McMahon, J.J., Thomasson, M.L., Barnes, J., Graber, S., Fawcett, T., & Comfort, P. (2009). Manipulation of perception of goal difficulty in weightlifting performance – The performance inhibition effect of precise goal difficulty on weightlifting performance. Journal of Sports Sciences, 27, S118–S119.

Mellalieu, S., & Shearer, D. (2012). Mental skills training in strength and conditioning. In D. Tod & D. Lavelle (Eds.), *The psychology of strength and conditioning*. Abingdon: Routledge.

Nicholls, J.G. (1984). Achievement motivation: Conceptions of ability, subjective experience, task choice, and performance. *Psychological Review, 91*, 328.

Porter, J.M., Ostrowski, E.J., Nolan, R.P., & Wu, W.F.W. (2010). Standing long-jump performance is enhanced when using an external focus of attention. *The Journal of Strength & Conditioning Research, 24*, 1746–1750. 10.1519/JSC.0b013e3181df7fbf.

Radcliffe, J., Comfort, P., & Fawcett, T. (2014). The effect of manipulations of perceived goal difficulty on the execution of the hang power clean. British Association of Sport and Exercise Sciences Annual Conference, 2014. Burton-upon-Trent, United Kingdom.

Radcliffe, J.N., Comfort, P., & Fawcett, T. (2013). The perception of psychology and the frequency of psychological strategies used by strength and conditioning practitioners. *The Journal of Strength & Conditioning Research, 27*, 1136–1146.

Radcliffe, J.N., Comfort, P., & Fawcett, T. (2015). Psychological strategies included by strength and conditioning coaches in applied strength and conditioning. *The Journal of Strength & Conditioning Research, 29*, 2641–2654.

Ranganathan, V.K., Siemionow, V., Liu, J.Z., Sahgal, V., & Yue, G.H. (2004). From mental power to muscle power—gaining strength by using the mind. *Neuropsychologia, 42*, 944–956.

Rhea, M.R., Landers, D.M., Alvar, B.A., & Arent, S.M. (2003). The effects of competition and the presence of an audience on weight lifting performance. *The Journal of Strength & Conditioning Research, 17*, 303–306.

Rotem-Lehrer, N., & Laufer, Y. (2007). Effect of focus of attention on transfer of a postural control task following an ankle sprain. *Journal of Orthopaedic & Sports Physical Therapy, 37*, 564–569.

Shelton, T.O., & Mahoney, M.J. (1978). The content and effect of "psyching-up" strategies in weight lifters. *Cognitive Therapy and Research, 2*, 275–284.

Short, S., & Ross-Stewart, L. (2010). A review of self-efficacy based interventions. In S. Mellalieu & S. Hanton (Eds.), *Advances in applied sport psychology: A review*. London: Routledge.

Smith, D., Collins, D., & Holmes, P. (2003). Impact and mechanism of mental practice effects on strength. *International Journal of Sport and Exercise Psychology, 1*, 293–306.

Strauss, B. (2002). Social facilitation in motor tasks: a review of research and theory. *Psychology of Sport and Exercise, 3*, 237–256.

Theodorakis, Y., Weinberg, R., Natsis, P., Douma, I., & Kazakas, P. (2000). The effects of motivational versus instructional self-talk on improving motor performance. *Sport Psychologist, 14*, 253–271.

Tod, D.A., Iredale, F., & Gill, N. (2003). 'Psyching-up' and muscular force production. *Sports Medicine, 33*, 47–58.

Tod, D.A., Iredale, K.F., McGuigan, M.R., Strange, D.O., & Gill, N. (2005). "Psyching-up" enhances force production during the bench press exercise. *The Journal of Strength & Conditioning Research, 19*, 599–603.

Tod, D.A., & McGuigan, M. (2001). Maximizing strength training through goal setting. *Strength & Conditioning Journal, 23*, 22.

Tod, D.A., Thatcher, R., McGuigan, M., & Thatcher, J. (2009). Effects of instructional and motivational self-talk on the vertical jump. *The Journal of Strength & Conditioning Research, 23*, 196–202.

Triplett, N. (1898). The dynamogenic factors in pacemaking and competition. *The American Journal of Psychology, 9*, 507–533.

Vance, J., Wulf, G., Tollner, T., McNevin, N., & Mercer, J. (2004). EMG activity as a function of the performer's focus of attention. *Journal of Motor Behavior, 36*, 450–459.

Weinberg, R., Bruya, L., & Jackson, A. (1985). The effects of goal proximity and goal specificity on endurance performance. *Journal of Sport Psychology, 7*, 296–305.

Wells, C.M., Collins, D., & Hale, B.D. (1993). The self-efficacy-performance link in maximum strength performance. *Journal of Sports Science, 11*, 167–175.

Woodman, T., Akehurst, S., Hardy, L., & Beattie, S. (2010). Self-confidence and performance: A little self-doubt helps. *Psychology of Sport and Exercise, 11*, 467–470.

Worringham, C.J., & Messick, D.M. (1983). Social facilitation of running: An unobtrusive study. *The Journal of social psychology, 121*, 23–29.

Wulf, G. (2013). Attentional focus and motor learning: a review of 15 years. *International Review of Sport and Exercise Psychology, 6*, 77–104.

Wulf, G., Dufek, J.S., Lozano, L., & Pettigrew, C. (2010). Increased jump height and reduced EMG activity with an external focus. *Human Movement Science, 29*, 440–448.

Wulf, G., Mcnevin, N., & Shea, C.H. (2001). The automaticity of complex motor skill learning as a function of attentional focus. *The Quarterly Journal of Experimental Psychology: Section A, 54*, 1143–1154.

Wulf, G., Zachry, T., Granados, C., & Dufek, J.S. (2007). Increases in jump-and-reach height through an external focus of attention. *International Journal of Sports Science & Coaching, 2*, 275–284.

Zajonc, R.B. (1965). Social facilitation. *Science, 149*, 269–274.

3 Reliability, validity and measurement error

Peter Mundy and Neil D. Clarke

Introduction

Strength and conditioning (S&C) coaches are evidence-led professionals. As such, they are often required to adopt a research-based approach to monitoring their athletes' development. Consequently, it is imperative that S&C coaches have the foundation to critically interpret the scientific literature, as well as ensure scientific rigour within their practice. Therefore, the aim of this chapter is to consider some key concepts and terms, before illustrating with example data sets some appropriate statistical methods to assess concurrent validity and test-retest reliability.

Asking the right questions

Key physical performance indicators derived from performance assessments within S&C are commonly measured using continuous-scale data, such as vertical jump height, sprint speed, etc. As such, numerous techniques and measurement tools have been developed with the aim of identifying more convenient, rapid and cost-effective measurements of these key performance indicators. Therefore, in order to ensure that new techniques and measurement tools are of practical use, we must ask the right questions prior to implementation.

The first question we must ask prior to conducting performance assessments is related to test-retest reliability: "what are the properties of the method?" To answer this, we must consider what the measurement error is, and whether we are willing to accept the level of error in practice. This question becomes particularly important when conducting performance assessment which immediately informs the coaching process (e.g. daily monitoring), or when trying to appraise the findings observed within research. If the change in performance between two testing points is not greater than the measurement error, then we cannot be confident that any change observed is meaningful. Further, we must also ask about how the measurement error is introduced (e.g. differences between times of day, testing venues, instructions, pre-test conditions, etc.). Addressing questions around these properties will allow us not only to standardise, but optimise testing conditions. In doing so, we can further control for measurement error, making measurements more repeatable and increasing our ability to inform the coaching process.

The second question we must ask is related to the concurrent validity: "how does the method compare to others?" To answer this, we must investigate the total error, which can be broken down into systematic bias and random error. Systematic bias means that one method gives values that are higher (or lower) than those from the other method by a constant amount (Ludbrook, 1997), whereas the random error relates to the degree of

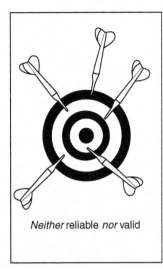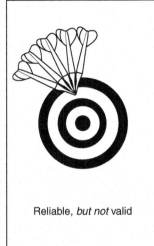

Neither reliable *nor* valid   Reliable, *but not* valid   Reliable *and valid*

Figure 3.1 Illustration of reliability and validity.

random differences that could arise due to inherent biological or mechanical variation, or inconsistencies in the measurement protocol (Atkinson & Nevill, 1998). It is important to emphasise that this is where the two questions become explicitly linked. If either method has poor test-retest reliability due to the aforementioned factors, then considerable random error is introduced, which interferes with the ability to answer the question posed regarding construct validity. Ultimately, answering these two questions will allow us to establish whether the methods are comparable to the extent that one might replace the other with sufficient accuracy (Altman & Bland, 1983).

Conceptually, what has been presented so far is relatively straightforward (Figure 3.1); however, what does pose an issue is the plethora of statistical tests proposed as appropriate for answering these questions. Further, no consensus exists as to the most appropriate statistical test(s), with a number of contradictory limitations reported previously. As these discrepancies have been extensively discussed elsewhere, a comprehensive discussion regarding these limitations is outside the scope of this chapter, and readers will be signposted to further reading throughout. However, within this chapter, we present some of the more commonly used methods within the S&C literature, and appraise them alongside the approaches that we consider to be the most appropriate.

Concurrent validity: "how does the method compare?"

Common practice within S&C is to test the null hypothesis of no difference between the means of two methods. This can be achieved through a paired sample t-test, or, in the case of multiple trials, a repeated-measures analysis of variance. The reported "P value" is the probability that we would have observed mean differences of this magnitude, or greater, if the null hypothesis were true (Batterham & George, 2000). Ultimately, this is seen as an assessment of systematic bias. Using the data within Table 3.1, the portable jump monitoring device (PJMD) resulted in significantly greater jump heights than the force

Table 3.1 Hypothetical data from a validity study comparing vertical jump height measured by a force platform (FP) and portable jump monitoring device (PJMD).

1	A	B	C	D	E
2		FP	PJMD	FP vs. PJMD	
3	Athlete ID	Test (m)	Test (m)	Mean (m)	Difference (m)
4	1	0.38	0.43	0.41	-0.05
5	2	0.32	0.37	0.35	-0.05
6	3	0.38	0.41	0.40	-0.03
7	4	0.33	0.37	0.35	-0.04
8	5	0.42	0.48	0.45	-0.06
9	6	0.38	0.45	0.42	-0.07
10	7	0.40	0.49	0.45	-0.09
11	8	0.45	0.45	0.45	0.00
12	9	0.31	0.36	0.34	-0.05
13	10	0.48	0.53	0.51	-0.05
14	11	0.41	0.43	0.42	-0.02
15	12	0.35	0.44	0.40	-0.09
16	13	0.27	0.34	0.31	-0.07
17	14	0.31	0.36	0.34	-0.05
18	15	0.49	0.50	0.50	-0.01
19	16	0.36	0.43	0.40	-0.07
20	17	0.38	0.43	0.41	-0.05
21	18	0.35	0.40	0.38	-0.05
22	19	0.37	0.39	0.38	-0.02
23	20	0.39	0.40	0.40	-0.01
24	21	0.35	0.41	0.38	-0.06
25	22	0.31	0.36	0.34	-0.05
26	23	0.42	0.45	0.44	-0.03
27	24	0.34	0.41	0.38	-0.07
28	25	0.38	0.43	0.41	-0.05
29	26	0.28	0.33	0.31	-0.05
30	27	0.32	0.35	0.34	-0.03
31	28	0.37	0.43	0.40	-0.06
32	29	0.35	0.41	0.38	-0.06
33	30	0.32	0.37	0.35	-0.05
34	31	0.32	0.36	0.34	-0.04
35	32	0.35	0.43	0.39	-0.08
36	33	0.36	0.41	0.39	-0.05
37	34	0.38	0.43	0.41	-0.05
38	35	0.35	0.35	0.35	0.00
39	Average	0.36	0.41	0.39	-0.05
40	± SD	0.05	0.05	0.05	0.02
41	SD = Standard deviation				

platform (FP) ($P < 0.001$). This suggests that 99 times out of 100, a difference of this magnitude ($-0.05 \pm$ m) or greater would be observed, which indicates a systematic bias between the two methods.

T-tests are often accompanied by 95% confidence intervals, which are intervals constructed that will contain the population mean 95% of the time (Batterham & George, 2000). Such calculations are readily available within most commercially available statistical packages, and using the data within Table 3.1 the 95% confidence intervals were -0.06 to -0.04 m. This suggests that for 95% of observations within our specific population, a difference within this range would be observed. Despite the popularity of the *t*-test, it should not be used in isolation as it provides no indication of random error. It is important to emphasise that observing a significant difference is actually dependent on the amount of random error between tests, with significant systematic bias less likely to be observed if it is accompanied by large amounts of random error (Atkinson & Nevill, 1998). As such, the *t*-test may only be useful for detecting large systematic errors, making it of limited utility when answering our proposed question regarding construct validity.

Another common practice within S&C is to calculate the product-moment correlation coefficient. The correlation coefficient is an index of the goodness-of-fit of a linear regression model to the observed values, which in a vague way is a measure of association (Ludbrook, 2002). However, it has been strongly argued that the correlation is useless for detecting bias, with Ludbrook (2002) demonstrating that a large and significant correlation coefficient value ($r = 0.939$) can coexist with large bias. An alternative approach commonly proposed is the intraclass correlation coefficient; however, this was designed to deal with the relationship between variables within classes, of which measurement tools are not, and has also been strongly criticised (Bland & Altman, 1986, 1990, 1999). Therefore, it is the authors' opinion that the correlation coefficient and the intraclass correlation coefficient are inappropriate to answer the question posed within this section, and will not be discussed any further in the context of validity.

Alternatively, a widely used method within the medical literature is the 95% limits of agreement (LOA). The key principle of LOA is to examine both systematic bias and random error (Altman & Bland, 1983; Bland & Altman, 1986, 1999). In brief, we obtain the differences between measurements by the two methods for each individual athlete and calculate the mean and standard deviation. We can then estimate the LOA as the mean of the differences $\pm$ 1.96 standard deviations. These limits are expected to contain the difference between measurements by the two methods for 95% of pairs of future measurements on similar athletes (Altman & Bland, 1983; Bland & Altman, 1986, 1999). Using the data within Table 3.1, Table 3.2 shows the mean difference is -0.05 m, and the LOA are $\pm$ 0.04 m. These values represent systematic bias and random error, respectively. If the differences within the upper and lower LOA are not of practical importance, then we could use the two methods interchangeably. Table 3.2 shows the upper limit is 0.00 m (mean difference + LOA: 0.05 m + 0.04 m) and the lower limit is -0.09 m (mean difference – LOA: 0.05 m – 0.04 m). Thus, within our example, a jump may be anywhere between 0.00 m and 0.09 m greater than the FP, which is unlikely to be acceptable for informing the physical preparation of an athlete.

It is important to emphasise that LOA are only estimates of the values which would be representative of the population of interest (Bland & Altman, 1986). If you were to conduct the same experiment on a different team, the LOA would be likely to be different. We may want to calculate the standard errors and confidence intervals of both the mean difference and LOA, as this allows us to establish even the most optimistic or pessimistic systematic bias and random error within our desired population (Table 3.2, Figure 3.2).

Table 3.2 Output from the hypothetical validity study, including Excel formula.

1	G	H	I
2		Result	Excel Formula
3	d	-0.05	AVERAGE(E4:E38)
4	s	0.02	STDEV(E4:E38)
5	2s	0.04	H4*1.96
6	d + 2s	0.00	H3+H5
7	d - 2s	-0.09	H3-H5
8	s2	0.00	H4^2
9	n	35	count(E4:E38)
10	t	2.03	TINV(0.05,(H9-1))
11	d SE	0.00	SQRT(H8/H9)
12	d + 95% CI	-0.04	H3+(H10*H11)
13	d - 95% CI	-0.06	H3-(H10*H11)
14	3s2	0.00	3*H8
15	d-2s SE	0.01	SQRT(H14/H9)
16	d + 2s + 95% CI	0.01	H6+(H10*H15)
17	d + 2s - 95% CI	-0.02	H6-(H10*H15)
18	d - 2s + 95% CI	-0.08	H7+(H10*H15)
19	d - 2s - 95% CI	-0.11	H7-(H10*H15)
20	d = difference; s = standard deviation; n = sample size; SE		
21	= standard error; CI = confidence Interval		

As sample size influences standard error, the precision of the observed systematic bias and random error is dependent upon it. As such, if we are to extrapolate findings from research articles to our athletes, we must be critical of the sample size investigated.

As with any statistical test, LOA is not without its limitations, and should be used with caution. Within the literature, the assumptions underpinning LOA are often violated, leading to inappropriate conclusions being drawn. A key assumption underpinning LOA is that the bias and variability are uniform throughout the range of measurements (Altman & Bland, 1983; Bland & Altman, 1986). This assumption is checked by creating a scatter plot of the difference between the methods versus the average of the two methods (although this can also be checked statistically by calculating the rank correlation between the absolute differences and the average) (Bland & Altman, 1999; Nevill & Atkinson, 1997). Within the literature, this assumption check has become synonymous with LOA, with some confusing this plot as the test itself. Figure 3.2 demonstrates a scatter plot of the difference between the methods (FP minus LOA) versus the average of the two methods using the present data set, which satisfies this assumption.

If heteroscedasticity is present (systematic bias and random error are non-uniform throughout the range of measurements, with differences increasing progressively as the average value increases), then the LOA will be too large for certain parts of the range and the systematic bias will be overstated (Figure 3.3). Under these circumstances, both methods' measurements may be log transformed, and if the bias and random error are now uniform, then the aforementioned LOA approach can be conducted (Bland & Altman,

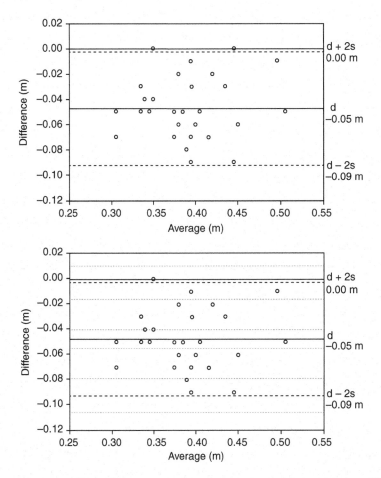

Figure 3.2 (A) Difference against mean for jump height, with mean difference (*d*) and *d* ± 2 standard deviations (2*s*). (B) Difference against mean for jump height, with *d*, *d* ± 2*s* and 95% confidence intervals for both *d* and *d* ± 2*s* (grey dashed lines).

1999; Ludbrook, 2010a). When data are back-transformed, this will give the ratio LOA, which are interpreted as a percentage as opposed to the units of measurement. If transformation does not solve the problem, then regression-based limits of agreement may be calculated; however, this is relatively complex, and readers are referred to Bland and Altman (1999) and Ludbrook (2010a) for worked examples of this. It is important that we understand that the violation of this assumption is the biggest threat to the use of LOA. Further, for alternative, and perhaps philosophically more appropriate statistical analyses (which separately investigate systematic and proportional bias, such as ordinary least-products regression), readers are referred to the extensive work of Ludbrook (Ludbrook, 1997, 2002, 2010b, 2012)

Another common issue is ignoring the data structure and treating sequential measurements as independent observations (Bland & Altman, 1999, 2007). For example, rather than comparing the trial with the highest output, we might use two trials from each athlete in the analysis, doubling the data set from *n* = 35 to *n* = 70. In this instance, the limits of

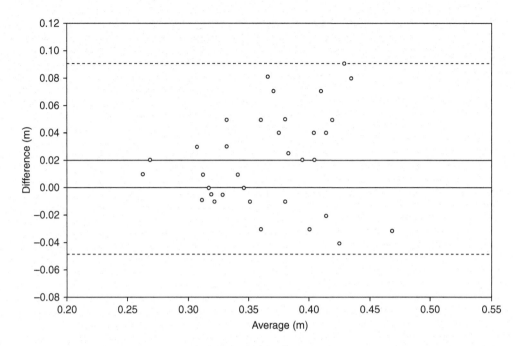

Figure 3.3 Differences depend on the magnitude of the mean (heteroscedasticity).

agreement will probably be too narrow due to an athlete-by-method interaction, whereby repeated observations of an athlete will be scattered around the mean value of all the possible observations by that method, which might be considered the athlete's true value (Bland & Altman, 1999, 2007). Within this scenario, there may both be a bias and a random error for the individual athlete, confounding the outcome (Bland & Altman, 1999, 2007).

Finally, perhaps the most important issue is determining an acceptable systematic bias and random error to inform our choice of performance assessment. Atkinson and Nevill (1998) refer to this process as establishing analytical goals, that is, what the practical implications of a given systematic bias or random error are, and what the S&C coach is willing to accept in practice. This should be a practice-based decision related to underpinning theory; statistics alone cannot really answer this question (Bland & Altman, 1999). Further, to ensure that this decision actually informs practice, and we do not simply accept the measurement error we are presented with, it should be made a priori.

Test-retest reliability: "what are the properties of the method?"

If poor concurrent validity is observed, it may be due to the test-retest reliability of either performance assessment. As such, once concurrent validity has been established, we must then establish the test-retest reliability. This allows us to identify whether or not the poor agreement is a consequence of poor repeatability within either method (Bland & Altman, 1999). Perhaps more importantly though, in order to effectively direct the physical preparation of an athlete, then we must establish the measurement error of a given performance assessment, which will allow us to identify whether or not a change in measurement represents a real change in an athlete's performance. If we measure an athlete's jump height using the PJMD before and after implementing a physical preparation programme, and the change in performance is within the measurement error, then it is unlikely that the physical preparation programme has had the desired effect. Ultimately, the greater the measurement error observed, the greater a change in performance required to be confident a change has been observed.

Calculating the within-subject standard deviation (SD_{ws}) provides an index of measurement error which allows us to make a simple, meaningful and practical interpretation regarding the observed change. In brief, the SD_{ws} will identify the "true" average value over all possible measurements, with all repeated measurements varying around the "true" value due to measurement error (Bland & Altman, 1996a). From a practical perspective, was the output observed during the performance assessment greater than the natural variation (caused by the biological variation of the athlete and/or the variation of the measurement process) of the performance assessment? Essentially, did the athlete get better (or worse), or not? It is important to note that the SD_{ws} is also referred to as the standard error of measurement, as well as the typical error of measurement (which is perhaps more common in S&C) (Hopkins, 2000).

To estimate the SD_{ws}, we need at least two measurements for each athlete. To get the common SD_{ws}, we take an average of the variances, which are the squares of the standard deviations (Bland & Altman, 1996a). Using data within Table 3.3, Table 3.4 shows the mean within-athlete variance is 0.00 m, so the estimated SD_{ws} is 0.01 m. Therefore, in this example, we know that a change in jump performance of 0.01 m is likely to be an actual change in performance. However, it is also important to note that the current example only really tells us about changes required in performance within a single session. Alternatively, if the assessment had been performed 24–72 hours later, under the same conditions, we could then calculate the between-session SD_{ws}. This is imperative for adopting a research-based approach to monitoring an athlete's development, as within-session and between-session test-retest reliability is not always the same due to changes in biological variability.

Readers should be cognisant that the SD_{ws} has previously been calculated in several other different ways (Atkinson & Nevill, 1998; Hopkins, 2000). If we collect more than two trials on each athlete, a more robust way is through using the analysis of variance method, with athlete as the factor, as then the SD_{ws} can be estimated from the square root of the residual mean square (Batterham & George, 2000; Bland & Altman, 1996a). However, regardless of the method used, SD_{ws} only has a coverage probability of approximately 68% (Atkinson & Nevill, 2000). For a coverage probability of approximately 95%, we can use $1.96 \times \sqrt{2} \times SD_{ws}$ or $2.77 \, SD_{ws}$, which is referred to as the repeatability coefficient (also referred to as the smallest detectable difference, among other names), which is comparable to the LOA approach reported in the previous section. The LOA correspond to the interval $-2.77 \, SD_{ws}$ to $2.77 \, SD_{ws}$. Table 3.4 shows the SD_{ws} is 0.01 m, whereas the repeatability coefficient and the LOA are both 0.03 m. In brief, the difference between the two statistics is that the LOA represents a reference interval for test-retest variability whereas SD_{ws} represents a reference interval for "true" score error (Atkinson & Nevill, 2000). As such, the authors' promote the use of either approach, as long as the reference range is reported, the underpinning assumptions are satisfied and we understand the underpinning theory as to why we may employ either (Atkinson & Nevill, 2000; Bland & Altman, 1999).

As with any method, the SD_{ws} is not without its limitations. Often, the SD_{ws} is proportional to the mean, that is, variability increases with magnitude (Atkinson & Nevill, 1998; Bland & Altman, 1996b, 1999; Hopkins, 2000). As discussed in the previous section, this can be checked visually or by calculating the rank correlation coefficient between the mean

Table 3.3 Hypothetical data from a reliability study comparing a test and a retest of vertical jump height using a portable jump monitoring device (PJMD).

1	A	B	C	D	E
2	Athlete ID	PJMD			
3		Test 1 (m)	Test 2 (m)	Mean (m)	SD (m)
4	1	0.43	0.44	0.44	0.01
5	2	0.37	0.37	0.37	0.00
6	3	0.41	0.38	0.40	0.02
7	4	0.37	0.37	0.37	0.00
8	5	0.48	0.48	0.48	0.00
9	6	0.45	0.44	0.45	0.01
10	7	0.49	0.49	0.49	0.00
11	8	0.45	0.44	0.45	0.01
12	9	0.36	0.37	0.37	0.01
13	10	0.53	0.53	0.53	0.00
14	11	0.43	0.43	0.43	0.00
15	12	0.44	0.44	0.44	0.00
16	13	0.34	0.31	0.33	0.02
17	14	0.36	0.36	0.36	0.00
18	15	0.50	0.45	0.48	0.04
19	16	0.43	0.43	0.43	0.00
20	17	0.43	0.43	0.43	0.00
21	18	0.40	0.40	0.40	0.00
22	19	0.39	0.38	0.39	0.01
23	20	0.40	0.40	0.40	0.00
24	21	0.41	0.41	0.41	0.00
25	22	0.36	0.36	0.36	0.00
26	23	0.45	0.43	0.44	0.01
27	24	0.41	0.39	0.40	0.01
28	25	0.43	0.41	0.42	0.01
29	26	0.33	0.33	0.33	0.00
30	27	0.35	0.34	0.35	0.01
31	28	0.43	0.43	0.43	0.00
32	29	0.41	0.41	0.41	0.00
33	30	0.37	0.37	0.37	0.00
34	31	0.36	0.35	0.36	0.01
35	32	0.43	0.43	0.43	0.00
36	33	0.41	0.42	0.42	0.01
37	34	0.43	0.45	0.44	0.01
38	35	0.35	0.37	0.36	0.01
39	Average	0.41	0.41	0.41	0.01
40	± SD	0.05	0.05	0.05	0.01
41	SD = Standard deviation				

Table 3.4 Output from the hypothetical reliability study, including Excel formula.

1	G	H	I
2		Result	Excel Formula
3	SDws	0.01	SQRT(SUMSQ(E4:E38)/COUNT(E4:E38))
4	SDws x 2.77	0.03	H3*2.77
5	1.96 x √2 x SDws	0.03	1.96*SQRT(2)*H3
6	CV65%	2.46	(H3/D39)*100
7	CV95%	6.82	(H4/D39)*100
8	SDws = Within-subject standard deviation; CV = Coefficient of variation		

and the absolute differences (Bland & Altman, 1996b). As such, common practice within S&C is to express the SD_{ws} as a percent of the mean, which is commonly referred to as the coefficient of variation (CV). A crude method is to simply divide SD_{ws} by the "grand mean" (Atkinson & Nevill, 1998; Batterham & George, 2000). Table 3.4 shows that the CV68% is 2.46%, whereas the CV95% is 6.82%. However, perhaps a more appropriate method is to follow the previously described analysis of variance method on log transformed data, with readers referred to Bland and Altman (1996b) and Batterham and George (2000) for worked examples. Finally, as discussed at the end of the previous section, changes in performance must be based on analytical goals, as opposed to arbitrary cut-off points (e.g. 5% CV) (Atkinson & Nevill, 1998).

In terms of analytical goals relating to test-retest reliability, the previous approach can relate to both a 68% and 95% certainty of observing a change in output of a performance assessment. Therefore, in the present example, if an athlete improves their jump height by 0.01 m or 0.03 m following a physical preparation programme, we can be 68% or 95% confident that the athlete's performance has changed. However, whether or not this change means our athlete has improved in comparison to an equivalent level of athlete (e.g. someone competing for their position within the team) is not clear. Put simply, although the change was real, did it actually mean anything?

Previously, it has been argued that a change of greater than 0.2 of the between-subject standard deviation represents the smallest worthwhile change within a given population (Hopkins, 2000; Hopkins et al., 1999). However, caution must be given to the population used, as both the SD_{ws} and the smallest worthwhile change are population-specific, and in certain cases we may not have data on meaningfully comparative athletes for our performance assessment. Using the data within Table 3.3, the smallest worthwhile change would be 0.01 m. Therefore, if our athlete improved by 0.01 m, we would be 68% confident that the athlete had observed a real change, which was meaningful. Conversely, if our athlete improved by 0.03 m, we could be 95% confident that the athlete had observed a real change, which was meaningful. However, ideally measurement error should be smaller than the smallest worthwhile change (Hopkins, 2000), as otherwise it is argued that we cannot measure our athlete with enough sensitivity to identify the smallest meaningful change within their performance. For a more comprehensive worked example, readers are referred to Chapter 16.

References

Altman, D.G., & Bland, J.M. (1983). Measurement in medicine: The analysis of method comparison studies. *The Statistician, 32*, 307–317.

Atkinson, G., & Nevill, A. (2000). Typical error versus limits of agreement. *Sports Medicine, 30*(5), 375–381.

Atkinson, G., & Nevill, A.M. (1998). Statistical methods for assessing measurement error (reliability) in variables relevant to sports medicine. *Sports Medicine, 26*(4), 217–238.

Batterham, A.M., & George, K.P. (2000). Reliability in evidence-based clinical practice: A primer for allied health professionals. *Physical Therapy in Sport, 1*, 54–61.

Bland, J.M., & Altman, D.G. (1986). Statistical methods for assessing agreement between two methods of clinical measurement. *Lancet, 1*(8476), 307–310.

Bland, J.M., & Altman, D.G. (1990). A note on the use of the intraclass correlation coefficient in the evaluation of agreement between two methods of measurement. *Computers in Biology and Medicine, 20*(5), 337–340.

Bland, J.M., & Altman, D.G. (1996a). Measurement error. *BMJ: British Medical Journal, 312*(7047), 1654–1654.

Bland, J.M., & Altman, D.G. (1996b). Measurement error proportional to the mean. *BMJ: British Medical Journal, 313*(7049), 106–106.

Bland, J.M., & Altman, D.G. (1999). Measuring agreement in method comparison studies. *Statistical Methods in Medical Research, 8*(2), 135–160.

Bland, J.M., & Altman, D.G. (2007). Agreement between methods of measurement with multiple observations per individual. *Journal of Biopharmaceutical Statistics, 17*(4), 571–582.

Hopkins, W.G. (2000). Measures of reliability in sports medicine and science. *Sports Med, 30*(1), 1–15.

Hopkins, W.G., Hawley, J.A., & Burke, L.M. (1999). Design and analysis of research on sport performance enhancement. *Medicine and Science in Sport and Exercise, 31*(3), 472–485.

Ludbrook, J. (1997). Comparing methods of measurements. *Clinical and Experimental Pharmacology and Physiology, 24*(2), 193–203.

Ludbrook, J. (2002). Statistical techniques for comparing measurers and methods of measurement: A critical review. *Clinical and Experimental Pharmacology and Physiology, 29*(7), 527–536.

Ludbrook, J. (2010a). Confidence in Altman-Bland plots: A critical review of the method of differences. *Clinical and Experimental Pharmacology and Physiology, 37*(2), 143–149.

Ludbrook, J. (2010b). Linear regression analysis for comparing two measurers or methods of measurement: But which regression? *Clinical and Experimental Pharmacology and Physiology, 37*(7), 692–699.

Ludbrook, J. (2012). A primer for biomedical scientists on how to execute model ii linear regression analysis. *Clinical and Experimental Pharmacology and Physiology, 39*(4), 329–335.

Nevill, A.M., & Atkinson, G. (1997). Assessing agreement between measurements recorded on a ratio scale in sports medicine and sports science. *British Journal of Sports Medicine, 31*(4), 314–318.

4 Standardisation of testing

John J. McMahon, Paul A. Jones and Paul Comfort

Introduction

This chapter provides an overview of the factors regarding standardisation that should be considered when designing and conducting fitness testing and when subsequently analysing the resultant data, to ensure accurate, valid, reliable and comparable data. Specific examples of how the main factors for consideration apply to commonly utilised fitness tests are provided throughout. The information presented in this chapter should, therefore, provide practitioners with guidance regarding standardisation of their testing procedures and data analysis techniques to ensure that any observed changes are real and not due to errors from testing and data analysis. As such, these practices should be consistently applied to the testing procedures described in Part 2 of this book.

When to test

Fitness testing should, ideally, initially take place at the beginning of the pre-season training cycle as the results of testing conducted at this time point provide a baseline of fitness data which will inform this initial training block (based on identified strengths and weaknesses), and serve as a reference point for data collected as part of further fitness testing sessions conducted throughout the remainder of the season. The same fitness test/testing battery should initially be conducted twice (typically interspersed by a 2–7-day gap) at the beginning of pre-season to establish the measurement error of each test (and the athlete or squad tested where appropriate). This will inform the practitioner of what a meaningful change in each tested fitness parameter would be for a given athlete or squad of athletes and thus will help the practitioner to identify "true" changes in a particular test score in subsequent fitness testing sessions. If it is not appropriate or feasible to test the athlete(s) twice in fairly quick succession (2–7 days), and thus for athlete/squad-specific test measurement error to be established, practitioners should refer to published (preferably subject-specific) test measurement error values to help identify meaningful changes in performance (discussed in detail in Chapter 3).

After testing at least once at the beginning of the pre-season training cycle, the scheduling of subsequent fitness testing sessions will vary from sport to sport, depending upon several factors such as the duration and scheduling of the season, but generally practitioners should at least aim to re-test athletes again at the end of the pre-season training cycle so that athletes' level of preparedness for competition can be benchmarked against both published/squad normative data and the fitness test results gathered at the onset of the pre-season training block (i.e. to ascertain the magnitude of improvement/decline in each assessed fitness quality). Preferably, fitness testing will take place at some point within the competitive season (particularly for sports whose season includes a break from competition) to assess the physical demands of competition on the athletes' fitness characteristics. If this is not possible then an alternative solution is to select one or two key fitness tests (e.g. the vertical jump) to conduct on a frequent basis as part of continual athlete-monitoring procedures (see Chapter 5 for a more detailed discussion).

Although scheduling of fitness testing throughout the season may vary between sports, it should be conducted when athletes are rested (i.e. sufficient time (~48 h) must have lapsed post the last match/intense training session) (see Chapter 5 – "Structured testing vs. continual monitoring"). Importantly, when periodic fitness testing does take place, athletes should be tested at approximately the same time of day to account for circadian rhythms, which impact several physical and morphological qualities such as muscle strength (Gauthier et al., 2001) and tendon stiffness (Onambele-Pearson & Pearson, 2007; Pearson & Onambele, 2006). The time of day also influences aerobic contribution to energy production, with better 30-second Wingate test performances (increased power and oxygen uptake) noted in the afternoon versus the morning (Souissi et al., 2007), suggesting that it may be wise to assess aerobic performance in the afternoon. Alternatively, it was more recently suggested that athletes should attempt to coincide training times with competitive performance times (Hayes et al., 2010), thus it might be prudent to adopt the same approach with fitness testing scheduling where possible. If this is not feasible, as long as the time of day is standardised circadian rhythms should not affect comparisons between testing sessions.

Equipment selection

Ideally, the gold standard equipment for testing a particular fitness quality should be used where possible; however, this may be unrealistic from both an accessibility and time perspective for many practitioners. An example of the latter is that although some practitioners working with a team sport may have access to expensive direct gas analysers for measuring maximal aerobic capacity, it would take a long time to assess a full squad using such methods and may therefore be impractical. Instead, practitioners should consider using alternative equipment that has been validated against the currently considered gold standard equipment when access to the latter is either impossible or unrealistic. In reference to the previous example, basic equipment such as cones, a measuring tape and an audio device could be used to conduct the Yo-Yo Intermittent Recovery Test (YIRT) or the Multi-Stage Fitness Test (MSFT), which have both been shown to provide a valid, field-based alternative to direct gas analysis (Krustrup et al., 2003; Ramsbottom et al., 1988) (Chapter 12).

In terms of quantifying vertical jump height, a force platform is considered to be the gold standard equipment (García-López et al., 2013), particularly when using the take-off velocity method (Moir, 2008), but force platforms may be inaccessible for some practitioners due to their general cost. In recent years, however, many cheaper alternatives (which calculate jump height using the flight time method) have been validated. For example, photoelectric cells have been shown to yield similar jump height values to those attained using a force platform (García-López et al., 2013; Glatthorn et al., 2011). Jump mats have generally been shown to yield inaccurate but reliable measurements of jump height (García-López et al., 2013; McMahon et al., 2016; Nuzzo et al., 2011), meaning that their values can be easily and correctly converted through published equations (García-López et al., 2013; McMahon et al., 2016). It is worth taking into consideration that the accuracy of jump height values attained from jump mats depends on the type of jump being performed and the level of performer, with lower accuracy seen for short contact jumps such as the drop jump (Kenny et al., 2012) and for athletes who can jump very high (Whitmer et al., 2015).

It must be noted here that the flight time method of calculating jump height is prone to errors when compared to the take-off velocity method (Moir, 2008) due to, for example, tucking of the legs during the flight phase, and so standardising the instructions given to athletes regarding the flight phase of the jump is especially important when assessing jump height in this manner (see Chapter 7 for additional detail). If using the take-off velocity method of estimating jump height via the integration of force-time data, other considerations such as appropriately establishing the athlete's bodyweight and using criterion thresholds to determine the different phases of the jump come to the fore (again, see Chapter 7 for additional detail). The important point here is that testing should consistently use the same equipment and methods of analyses to ensure that the data are comparable (McMahon et al., 2017a), especially if athletes (e.g. national squads) are being monitored while training on a de-centralised programme across cities/states/countries.

Although gold standard equipment can provide more detail about a particular fitness characteristic, in reality, the type of equipment selected by practitioners to test specific fitness qualities depends upon accessibility, feasibility and affordability. Whether using gold standard equipment or validated alternatives it is vitally important to understand the associated measurement error to allow accurate decisions to be made regarding training adaptations. As some validated equipment alternatives of a similar cost have larger measurement error than others, it would be prudent to choose the alternative equipment that has the highest degree of accuracy.

Another important consideration when selecting equipment for testing certain fitness characteristics is sampling frequency capability. For example, if assessing vertical jump height using a force platform, it has been suggested that a minimum sampling frequency of 1000 Hz should be used (Owen et al., 2014; Street et al., 2001). On the other hand, a sampling frequency range of 500–2000 Hz had no meaningful effect on force-time variables assessed during the isometric mid-thigh pull (Dos'Santos et al., 2016). Alternatively, it has been recently suggested that the minimum sample frequency of linear position transducers for yielding quality movement velocity data is 25 Hz and that sampling above this frequency does not improve recording precision and may, if an excessively high sample frequency is selected, have adverse effects on data quality (Bardella et al., Publish ahead of print). In such instances, additional factors such as data-smoothing techniques (type of filters/cut-off frequencies etc.) and how to standardise these may then also require consideration. Each of these factors should be considered in order to inform the best equipment choice for a given purpose and budget. Where possible, analysis of unfiltered data may be the best option.

Standardising protocols

Another very important factor to consider as part of the fitness testing process is the standardisation of protocols for the test(s) to be conducted, as this will affect the reliability, variability and comparability of the data collected. For dynamic strength tests, the standardisation required might be as simple as ensuring correct barbell placement (e.g. high or low barbell position in the back squat; Wretenberg et al., 1996), the range of motion (e.g. squat depth) is consistent (Bryanton et al., 2012) and athletes put in a maximal effort. The latter point is, indeed, a requirement of all maximal tests. Additionally, the rest period prescribed between trials may also affect the results gathered. For example, during one repetition maximum (1-RM) back squat testing, there were no significant differences in the ability to lift a maximal load when subjects were given 1, 3 or 5 minutes' rest between lifts (Matuszak et al., 2003), although a greater percentage of the subjects lifted successfully after the 3- versus the 1-minute rest period (94 versus 76%), suggesting that a minimum of 3 minutes' rest should be prescribed between 1-RM attempts. Therefore, adequate and *standardised* test-specific rest periods should be prescribed between recorded trials in order to improve test accuracy.

For jump tests, there are many factors that need to be standardised in order to glean consistent data. For example, when jump testing it is important to consider whether or not athletes are permitted to swing their arms, as this has been shown to augment jump height (Hara et al., 2006, 2008; Walsh et al., 2007) but slightly reduce measurement reliability (Hara et al., 2008; Markovic et al., 2004). Also the range of motion (e.g. countermovement or starting depth) (Gheller et al., 2015; Kirby et al., 2011; McBride et al., 2010), movement/contact time (Arampatzis et al., 2001; Walsh et al., 2004) and, as previously mentioned, tucking of the legs during the flight phase (Kibele, 1998), which can all be influenced by coaching cues, will influence the resultant jump height and associated force-time variables (see Chapter 7).

Sprint testing typically has even more methodological factors than strength and jump testing that need to be standardised. For example, the accuracy of sprint times recorded by electronic timing gates will depend upon the height at which they are set up (Cronin & Templeton, 2008; Yeadon et al., 1999), the starting distance from the first beam (Altmann et al., 2015; Haugen et al., 2015) and the starting stance (Frost & Cronin, 2011; Frost et al., 2008; Johnson et al., 2010). Indeed, the type of electronic timing gate used (e.g. single- versus dual-photocell) can also influence the accuracy of resultant sprint times, with dual-photocell electronic timing gates usually leading to more accurate results (Earp & Newton, 2012; Haugen et al., 2014). Single-photocell electronic timing gates can yield reliable sprint times within and between sessions, however, if the aforementioned factors are standardised (McMahon et al., 2017b). Thus, the standardisation of sprint testing protocols can relate both to the equipment setup and to the instructions given to the athlete (see Chapter 8).

Testing order

The order of testing is largely dictated by the amount of recovery required following a given test and so usually baseline measurements of height, mass, body composition and range of motion would be performed first, followed by skill- and/or speed-based tests (jumps, change of direction/agility and sprints), then maximal strength tests (dynamic or isometric) and finally muscular endurance and/or aerobic capacity tests. In reality, the order of fitness testing will depend upon time/equipment availability and the number athletes being tested and so a "round-robin" approach might be adopted by practitioners when larger groups of athletes are being tested in a single session. If this is the case, then the testing order for a given athlete should remain the same in subsequent testing sessions and, ideally, the aerobic capacity tests should be performed last by all athletes. The latter is much more feasible when the YIRT or MSFT is conducted in a large space, allowing several athletes to be tested at the same time.

This is also an important point to consider if a full battery of testing is conducted at the start and end of pre-season and then an abbreviated testing battery is used, resulting in an altered sequence and potentially reduced fatigue, during the rest of the season. In such situations, it is important to ensure adequate rest and recovery between tests during pre-season, to minimise any influence of cumulative fatigue, which is likely to be reduced during abbreviated testing batteries.

Data analysis

After all testing has been completed, at least some (if not most) of the data will need to be processed as much equipment/software does not provide instantaneous results. Like the testing protocols, the way in which data are analysed post-testing will also greatly influence the accuracy, reliability and variability of the results. Vertical jump force-time data are probably the main type of commonly collected data where the analysis varies most between published studies (Eagles et al., 2015) and, most likely, in practice and thus the standardisation of force-time data analysis is of paramount importance to allow for accurate interpretation of these data. For example, when analysing vertical jump force-time data, as can be done in Microsoft Excel (Chavda et al., 2018), the method of determining bodyweight and the thresholds used to identify the onset of movement and the instants of take-off and touch-down will greatly influence factors such as jump height and reactive strength index modified, in addition to variables calculated through forward dynamics procedures such as velocity and power (Eagles et al., 2015; Owen et al., 2014; Street et al., 2001). Additionally, correctly identifying the beginning and end of the braking (if a countermovement is included) and propulsive phases of the vertical jump is important for ensuring correct calculations of several variables in each of these phases (McMahon et al., 2018), including mean and peak force, time to peak force, rate of force development and impulse (see Chapter 7).

As for the vertical jump, the method of determining bodyweight and the thresholds used to identify the onset of force production when analysing isometric mid-thigh pull force-time data also requires consideration (Dos'Santos et al., 2017). Analysing rate of force development attained in the isometric mid-thigh pull at predetermined time bands rather than as an average between the onset of force production and peak force has also been shown to be superior from a reliability perspective (Haff et al., 2015), which further justifies standardisation of the analysis of force-time data for specific tests (see Chapter 10).

To conclude, the standardisation of data analysis is very important and must be applied consistently within and between testing sessions. Where possible, the criterion method (e.g. Owen et al., 2014) for analysing a particular data set should be applied. If a criterion method has not yet been established for analysing a given data set or if certain equipment is used that provides instantaneous results via undisclosed data analysis methods, then practitioners should at least be consistent and transparent with their data analysis procedures. When comparing data collected through fitness testing batteries to the normative data from published studies, practitioners should pay particular attention to the methods of data analysis employed in those studies before forming their conclusions. Another point to consider is the normalisation of strength and kinetic data for body mass (or employ other appropriate scaling techniques) before comparing these results between sessions and athletes, and to published studies, as these data in particular are largely influenced by an athlete's size.

References

Altmann, S., Hoffmann, M., Kurz, G., Neumann, R., Woll, A., & Haertel, S. (2015). Different starting distances affect 5-m sprint times. *The Journal of Strength & Conditioning Research*, 29(8), 2361–2366.

Arampatzis, A., Schade, F., Walsh, M., & Bruggemann, G.P. (2001). Influence of leg stiffness and its effect on myodynamic jumping performance. *Journal of Electromyography and Kinesiology, 11*(5), 355–364.

Bardella, P., Carrasquilla García, I., Pozzo, M., Tous-Fajardo, J., Saez de Villareal, E., & Suarez-Arrones, L. (Publish ahead of print). Optimal sampling frequency in recording of resistance training exercises. *Sports Biomechanics.*

Bryanton, M.A., Kennedy, M.D., Carey, J.P., & Chiu, L.Z.F. (2012). Effect of squat depth and barbell load on relative muscular effort in squatting. *The Journal of Strength & Conditioning Research, 26*(10), 2820–2828.

Chavda, S., Bromley, T., Jarvis, P., Williams, S., Bishop, C., Turner, A.N., Lake, J.P., & Mundy, P.D. (2018). Force-time characteristics of the countermovement jump: Analyzing the curve in Excel. *Strength & Conditioning Journal, 40*(2), 67–77.

Cronin, J.B., & Templeton, R.L. (2008). Timing light height affects sprint times. *The Journal of Strength & Conditioning Research, 22*(1), 318–320.

Dos'Santos, T., Jones, P.A., Comfort, P., & Thomas, C. (2017). Effect of different onset thresholds on isometric mid-thigh pull force-time variables. *The Journal of Strength & Conditioning Research, 31*(12), 3463–3473.

Dos'Santos, T., Jones, P., A, Kelly, J., McMahon, J.J., Comfort, P., & Thomas, C. (2016). Effect of sampling frequency on isometric mid-thigh pull kinetics. *International Journal of Sports Physiology and Performance, 11*(2), 255–260.

Eagles, A.N., Sayers, M.G.L., Bousson, M., & Lovell, D.I. (2015). Current methodologies and implications of phase identification of the vertical jump: A systematic review and meta-analysis. *Sports Medicine, 45*(9), 1311–1323.

Earp, J.E., & Newton, R.U. (2012). Advances in electronic timing systems: Considerations for selecting an appropriate timing system. *The Journal of Strength & Conditioning Research, 26*(5), 1245–1248.

Frost, D.M., & Cronin, J.B. (2011). Stepping back to improve sprint performance: A kinetic analysis of the first step forwards. *The Journal of Strength & Conditioning Research, 25*(10), 2721–2728.

Frost, D.M., Cronin, J.B., & Levin, G. (2008). Stepping backward can improve sprint performance over short distances. *The Journal of Strength & Conditioning Research, 22*(3), 918–922.

García-López, J., Morante, J.C., Ogueta-Alday, A., & Rodríguez-Marroyo, J.A. (2013). The type of mat (contact vs. photocell) affects vertical jump height estimated from flight time. *The Journal of Strength & Conditioning Research, 27*(4), 1162–1167.

Gauthier, A., Davenne, D., Martin, A., & Van Hoecke, J. (2001). Time of day effects on isometric and isokinetic torque developed during elbow flexion in humans. *European Journal of Applied Physiology, 84*(3), 249–252.

Gheller, R.G., Dal Pupo, J., Ache-Dias, J., Detanico, D., Padulo, J., & dos Santos, S.G. (2015). Effect of different knee starting angles on intersegmental coordination and performance in vertical jumps. *Human Movement Science, 42*, 71–80.

Glatthorn, J.F., Gouge, S., Nussbaumer, S., Stauffacher, S., Impellizzeri, F.M., & Maffiuletti, N.A. (2011). Validity and reliability of optojump photoelectric cells for estimating vertical jump height. *The Journal of Strength & Conditioning Research, 25*(2), 556–560.

Haff, G.G., Ruben, R.P., Lider, J., Twine, C., & Cormie, P. (2015). A comparison of methods for determining the rate of force development during isometric midthigh clean pulls. *The Journal of Strength & Conditioning Research, 29*(2), 386–395.

Hara, M., Shibayama, A., Takeshita, D., & Fukashiro, S. (2006). The effect of arm swing on lower extremities in vertical jumping. *Journal of Biomechanics, 39*(13), 2503–2511.

Hara, M., Shibayama, A., Takeshita, D., Hay, D.C., & Fukashiro, S. (2008). A comparison of the mechanical effect of arm swing and countermovement on the lower extremities in vertical jumping. *Human Movement Science, 27*(4), 636–648.

Haugen, T.A., Tønnessen, E., & Seiler, S. (2015). Correction factors for photocell sprint timing with flying start. *International Journal of Sports Physiology and Performance, 10*(8), 1055–1057.

Haugen, T.A., Tønnessen, E., Svendsen, I.S., & Seiler, S. (2014). Sprint time differences between single- and dual-beam timing systems. *The Journal of Strength & Conditioning Research, 28*(8), 2376–2379.

Hayes, L.D., Bickerstaff, G.F., & Baker, J.S. (2010). Interactions of cortisol, testosterone, and resistance training: Influence of circadian rhythms. *Chronobiology International, 27*(4), 675–705.

Johnson, T.M., Brown, L.E., Coburn, J.W., Judelson, D.A., Khamoui, A.V., Tran, T.T., & Uribe, B.P. (2010). Effect of four different starting stances on sprint time in collegiate volleyball players. *The Journal of Strength & Conditioning Research, 24*(10), 2641–2646.

Kenny, I.C., Caireallàin, A.Ó., & Comyns, T.M. (2012). Validation of an electronic jump mat to assess stretch-shortening cycle function. *The Journal of Strength & Conditioning Research, 26*(6), 1601–1608.

Kibele, A. (1998). Possibilities and limitations in the biomechanical analysis of countermovement jumps: A methodological study. *Journal of Applied Biomechanics, 14*(1), 105–117.

Kirby, T., McBride, J., Haines, T., & Dayne, A. (2011). Relative net vertical impulse determines jumping performance. *International Journal of Sports Physiology and Performance, 27*(3), 207–214.

Krustrup, P., Mohr, M., Amstrup, T., Rysgaard, T., Johansen, J., Steensberg, A., Pedersen, P.K., & Bangsbo, J. (2003). The yo-yo intermittent recovery test: Physiological response, reliability, and validity. *Medicine and science in sports and exercise, 35*(4), 697–705.

Markovic, G., Dizdar, D., Jukic, I., & Cardinale, M. (2004). Reliability and factorial validity of squat and countermovement jump tests. *The Journal of Strength & Conditioning Research, 18*(3), 551–555.

Matuszak, M.E., Fry, A.C., Weiss, L.W., Ireland, T.R., & McKnight, M.M. (2003). Effect of rest interval length on repeated 1 repetition maximum back squats. *The Journal of Strength & Conditioning Research, 17*(4), 634–637.

McBride, J., Kirby, T., Haines, T., & Skinner, J. (2010). Relationship between relative net vertical impulse and jump height in jump squats performed to various squat depths and with various loads. *International Journal of Sports Physiology and Performance, 5*(4), 484–496.

McMahon, J.J., Jones, P.A., & Comfort, P. (2016). A correction equation for jump height measured using the just jump system. *International Journal of Sports Physiology and Performance, 11*(4), 555–557.

McMahon, J.J., Jones, P.A., & Comfort, P. (2017a). Comment on: "Anthropometric and physical qualities of elite male youth rugby league players". *Sports Medicine, 47*(12), 2667–2668.

McMahon, J.J., Kyriakidou, I., Murphy, S., Rej, S.J., Young, A.L., & Comfort, P. (2017b). Reliability of five-, ten- and twenty-metre sprint times in both sexes assessed using single-photocell electronic timing gates. *Professional Strength and Conditioning, 44*, 17–21.

McMahon, J.J., Suchomel, T.J., Lake, J.P., & Comfort, P. (2018). Understanding the key phases of the countermovement jump force-time curve. *Strength and Conditioning Journal, 40*(4), 96–106.

Moir, G.L. (2008). Three different methods of calculating vertical jump height from force platform data in men and women. *Measurement in Physical Education and Exercise Science, 12*(4), 207–218.

Nuzzo, J.L., Anning, J.H., & Scharfenberg, J.M. (2011). The reliability of three devices used for measuring vertical jump height. *The Journal of Strength & Conditioning Research, 25*(9), 2580–2590.

Onambele-Pearson, N.L., & Pearson, S.J. (2007). Time-of-day effect on patella tendon stiffness alters vastus lateralis fascicle length but not the quadriceps force-angle relationship. *Journal of Biomechanics, 40*(5), 1031–1037.

Owen, N.J., Watkins, J., Kilduff, L.P., Bevan, H.R., & Bennett, M.A. (2014). Development of a criterion method to determine peak mechanical power output in a countermovement jump. *The Journal of Strength & Conditioning Research, 28*(6), 1552–1558.

Pearson, S.J., & Onambele, G.N.L. (2006). Influence of time of day on tendon compliance and estimations of voluntary activation levels. *Muscle and Nerve, 33*(6), 792–800.

Ramsbottom, R., Brewer, J., & Williams, C. (1988). A progressive shuttle run test to estimate maximal oxygen uptake. *British Journal of Sports Medicine, 22*(4), 141–144.

Souissi, N., Bessot, N., Chamari, K., Gauthier, A., Sesboüé, B., & Davenne, D. (2007). Effect of time of day on aerobic contribution to the 30-s wingate test performance. *Chronobiology International, 24*(4), 739–748.

Street, G., McMillan, S., Board, W., Rasmussen, M., & Heneghan, J.M. (2001). Technical note sources of error in determining countermovement jump height with the impulse method. *Journal of Applied Biomechanics, 17*(1), 43–54.

Walsh, M., Arampatzis, A., Schade, F., & Bruggemann, G.P. (2004). The effect of drop jump starting height and contact time on power, work performed, and moment of force. *Journal of Strength and Conditioning Research, 18*(3), 561–566.

Walsh, M.S., Böhm, H., Butterfield, M.M., & Santhosam, J. (2007). Gender bias in the effects of arms and countermovement on jumping performance. *The Journal of Strength & Conditioning Research, 21*(2), 362–366.

Whitmer, T.D., Fry, A.C., Forsythe, C.M., Andre, M.J., Lane, M.T., Hudy, A., & Honnold, D.E. (2015). Accuracy of a vertical jump contact mat for determining jump height and flight time. *The Journal of Strength & Conditioning Research, 29*(4), 877–881.

Wretenberg, P., Feng, Y., & Arborelius, U.P. (1996). High- and low-bar squatting techniques during weight-training. *Medicine and Science in Sports and Exercise, 28*(2), 218–224.

Yeadon, M.R., Kato, T., & Kerwin, D.G. (1999). Measuring running speed using photocells. *Journal of Sports Sciences, 17*(3), 249–257.

5 Structured testing vs. continual monitoring

Paul Comfort, Paul. A. Jones and W. Guy Hornsby

Introduction

This chapter provides a discussion regarding the use of structured performance testing sessions versus the continual monitoring of athlete performance, finally discussing a combined approach. Monitoring of endocrine function and mood are not discussed in any detail as they are not "performance" measures, and while potentially useful tend not to reflect changes in performance (Kraemer et al., 2004; Balsalobre-Fernandez et al., 2014; Crewther et al., 2016).

In terms of structured testing we refer to the use of testing sessions that take place, usually at the beginning and end of pre-season and again at specified time points, with mid- and end of season commonly used within team sports. This approach usually requires an entire day to be dedicated to a specific battery of tests to screen for injury risk factors and determine the athletes' performance levels in each of the athletic characteristics (e.g. force, power, aerobic capacity) which are determinants of performance in their specific sport. In contrast, continual monitoring refers to more regular (daily/weekly/monthly) assessments of performance which take place, usually at the start of each training day, to monitor "fatigue" or "readiness" or to determine the effects of previous training or competition and can be used to determine subsequent amendments to training volume or intensity. Monitoring processes can rotate across days and training phases in line with the aims of each mesocycle, with the frequency of such testing determined by the duration in which changes are likely to be observed based on the sensitivity of the testing metrics. The information presented in this chapter, therefore, provides practitioners with guidance regarding which approach may be most appropriate within their sport and organisation.

Structured testing

This approach is common within team sports, whereby one or two days during the first week of pre-season testing may be dedicated to determining the squad and individual performance levels across a variety of specific physical characteristics (Figure 5.1). This usually commences with anthropometric characteristics (Chapter 13), assessment of injury risk/neuromuscular control (Chapter 6), jump (Chapter 7), short sprint (Chapter 8), change of direction performance (Chapter 9), strength and/or power (Chapters 10 and 11) and aerobic capacity or lactate threshold testing (Chapter 12). In such instances the least fatiguing assessments are usually performed first to minimise any effect on the subsequent tests. The results of such testing can then be used to develop/adapt individual training programmes to ensure optimal development of each physical characteristic, as required by the sport or

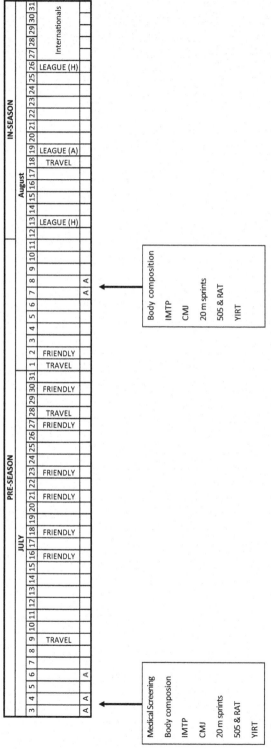

Figure 5.1 An example of structured testing for a Premier League soccer team. Two days (A) are allocated at the start and end of pre-season (prior to the first league game) for medical screening and performance assessments. Ideally (A), baseline physical performance tests are repeated >48 hours in order to establish between-session reliability. Assessments should then be repeated mid-season (December) and end of the season (May) to allow an effective evaluation of the team's seasonal programming.

position in question. It is essential that the interaction between such assessment methods is considered and that they are not used in isolation. For example if sprint and jump performances are substandard, along with strength and power, while anthropometrics and aerobic capacity are good, it is likely that relative strength is the key area to address, as force production underpins sprint and jump performance and power development (Seitz et al., 2014; Suchomel et al., 2016) (this is discussed in more detail in Chapter 14).

Continual monitoring

Continual monitoring to evaluate individual athletes' responses to stressors is regularly employed within high-performance sports; such methods include the use of (Figure 5.2):

- questionnaires to determine the extent of job/study- and family-related stressors
- self-report questionnaires regarding muscle soreness, feelings of frustration and cheer-fulness using Likert scales
- global positioning systems (GPS) and accelerometry to measure field- and court-based workloads
- volume load (sets × reps × load) and training intensity (average load) performed in the weight room
- training-related tissue damage and inflammation measurements with biochemical markers such as creatine kinase and C-reactive protein
- performance tests to determine changes in neuromuscular function

The countermovement jump (CMJ) is commonly used to identify changes in neuromuscular function, in response to the stress of both training and competition. However, gross measures of CMJ performance, such as jump height and peak power, do not appear to be sensitive enough to identify changes in neuromuscular function; however, more detailed temporal phase analyses of the resultant force-time data do appear to be sensitive enough to identify subtle changes in neuromuscular performance (Gathercole et al., 2015). This is potentially attributable to the fact that athletes alter their jump strategy by modulating lower-limb stiffness to achieve maximal jump height through different means (McMahon et al., 2017a, 2017b) (this is briefly discussed in Chapter 7). If monitoring of temporal phase characteristics is too time-consuming a simpler deconstruction of jump strategy, such as reactive strength index (RSI) (Flanagan et al., 2008) or RSI modified (RSImod) (Ebben and Petushek, 2010; Suchomel et al., 2015a, 2015b), may be more insightful than jump height alone (see Chapter 11). RSI and RSImod provide information regarding movement duration and jump height. An increase in movement time but a constant jump height is indicative of a more compliant strategy, which may be associated with neuromuscular fatigue, while a consistent jump height achieved in a reduced movement time indicates an improved neuromuscular capability.

Regular monitoring of strength, during key exercises, such as the squat and clean, provides the opportunity to determine changes in training load in the subsequent mesocycle. Such assessments can include the performance of a repetition maximum (RM) test, appropriate to the current mesocycle (as illustrated in Table 5.1), or repetitions to failure at a given training load. Where during the final (de-load) week of the mesocycle, assistance work is removed, and volume is reduced, to minimise fatigue, but key performance exercises are assessed.

From these resultant 3- and 5-RM performances, or repetitions to failure at a set load, it is possible to predict the individual's 1-RM (Hoeger et al., 1987; Brzycki, 1993; Brechue

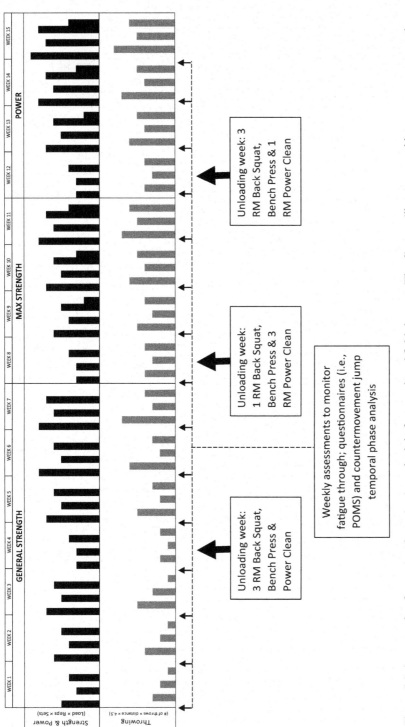

Figure 5.2 An example of a continual monitoring schedule for a track and field thrower. The diagram illustrates weekly assessments to monitor the athlete's level of fatigue during this heavy preparation phase. During unloading weeks repetition maximum testing takes place to aid in exercise prescription for the subsequent block of training. Volume load (load × reps × sets) and intensity (mean relative load) of strength/ power training and throwing (number of throws × distance (m) × 4.5 [constant]) are also monitored.

Table 5.1 Suggested repetition maximum testing at the end of selected mesocycles.

Mesocycle	Strength	Max strength	Power
Sets/rep's/intensity	3/5/85–90%	5/3/90–95%	5/3/70–85
Squat	5- or 3-RM	3- or 1-RM	3-RM
Power clean	3-RM	3-RM	1-RM

& Mayhew 2012). Additionally, if a 3- or 5-RM has been assessed training loads can simply be set for the next mesocycle based on these loads; for example if the 5-RM is established at the end of the strength phase, this load can be used for the first week of the maximum strength phase, which should permit five sets of three repetitions, as the 5-RM equates to ~90% of the 1-RM.

Prediction of 1-RM performance may also be enhanced with the assessment of barbell velocity during submaximal efforts, based on the load-velocity relationship (Gonzalez-Badillo & Sanchez-Medina, 2010; Bazuelo-Ruiz et al., 2015; Picerno et al., 2016; Banyard et al., 2017; Loturco et al., 2017) (see Chapter 10). It has recently become popular to monitor barbell velocity during warm-up sets during training to determine levels of fatigue/recovery and provide slight adjustments to the daily training load. If the individual demonstrates a decrease in velocity (usually >10% of the previous or established velocity at a given load/ intensity), during a specific exercise, which may signify residual fatigue, the coach/athlete may then adapt the intensity or volume of the session to ensure that the appropriate stimulus is achieved (Gonzalez-Badillo et al., 2015). Conversely, if the athlete demonstrates noticeable increases in velocity during the warm-up sets, compared to their "normal" velocities, the intensity (absolute load) can be increased to ensure an appropriate level of overload is achieved.

It is important to note that not adequately pursuing specific training goals and objectives of the various phases of the periodisation/programming plan while collecting data can often lead to coaches becoming "lost in the data". This lack of foresight often creates a situation in which the data become the driver of the prescription vs. an important tool that supports and aids coaching decisions as well as helping detect potential problems ahead of time. Sands and Stone (2005) explain that periodic monitoring of the training process of an athlete is crucial in understanding how an athlete is responding to the training programme and whether alterations or changes need to be made to the training plan. Ideally, this should be done through an evidenced-based phase potentiation (periodised) training protocol, and more often than not the monitoring programme will demonstrate that the athletes are responding as expected.

Sport science and strength and conditioning are applied sciences and as such sometimes things do not go as planned. Injury or non-training stress, specifically outside stressors such as sleep, diet, psychosocial aspects, etc., can contribute both positively and negatively to recovery or adaptation. Additionally, in higher levels of sport (elite, sub-elite), athletes are more often training at higher volumes and intensities due to being closer to their genetic ceilings and thus their intensity thresholds for adaptation are elevated. For example, Häkkinen et al. (1987) demonstrated that advanced Finnish weightlifters typically perform ≥80% of 1-RM for their given target weight room sets. This increases the level of preciseness demanded by coaches, and makes managing all aspects of training more important. For advanced athletes who are much closer to their genetic ceiling, mistakes are more expensive and monitoring can potentially allow small problems to be detected early on and addressed before becoming catastrophic problems (e.g. major injury).

In addition to identifying small problems before they become too disruptive, monitoring provides better insight into and understanding of how an athlete is responding to the training prescription. A thought-provoking paper on predicting athlete performance by Sands and McNeal (2000) presented the idea that while quantitatively predicting future adaptations and performances in complete detail is impossible, we can at least postdict. In other words, while we can predict the general direction of the adaptation process, we are much less effective at accurately predicting the magnitude of adaptation and specific performance outcomes (Sands & McNeal, 2000). This is well illustrated in that if the same training stimulus is repeated it will not produce exactly the same result the second time around (Smith 2003). Athletes tend to respond to training stress in an individual yet characteristic manner (Sands & McNeal, 2000; Sands & Stone, 2005). For example, athletes who undergo a phase of high-volume, strength endurance training (e.g. three sets of ten) will become fatigued; however, the degree to which each individual athlete is fatigued and the magnitude of the subsequent strength-endurance adaptations (and perhaps hypertrophic response) will be individual (idiosyncratic).

Training is a long-term process of causes and effects that cascade down a complicated path thus making exact quantitative predictions impossible (Sands & McNeal, 2000). Once the past is postdicted, we may be able to better understand and direct the present in the desired direction (Sands & McNeal, 2000). Additionally, alterations as a result of the training programme typically involve a lag time or "delayed training effect" (DTE) (DeWeese et al., 2015a, 2015b). The mechanistic underpinnings of the DTE are varied but include re-education of better-trained motor units and dissipation of fatigue (Bobbert & Van Soest, 1994; Plisk & Stone, 2003; DeWeese et al., 2015a, 2015b), however, the length of this delay is often impossible to predict. Again, the DTE makes monitoring of variables a necessity to help ensure the desired adaptations do in fact occur and aids with understanding time lines of adaptation.

Combined approaches

While a combined approach may be ideal, this also depends on the time, equipment and staff available to effectively conduct testing, appropriately analyse data and make subsequent adjustments to the athletes' training schedule, if appropriate. Such an approach uses structured testing at specific time points (e.g. start and end of pre-season, and mid-, end of season) for key performance characteristics, along with continual monitoring of specific performances (e.g. strength testing and jump performance) as a means of monitoring neuromuscular fatigue. Additionally, collection of external load (e.g. weight-room volume load, GPS) and internal load (e.g. heart rate, biochemical) data can allow the coach insight into what facilitated the neuromuscular alterations. Potentially, this process can aid the prescription of training loads in the subsequent mesocycle. However, with recent developments in force plate technology and more sophisticated and automated software packages, detailed analysis and inspection of force-time characteristics during jump testing are now almost instantaneous, and also more affordable.

Ideally, there is very close interplay between the planning process and its subsequent execution (Olbrecht 2000). In practice this is not always the case and seemingly for "measured" sports (track and field, weightlifting, swimming, etc.) the prescription and subsequent implementation tend to be more similar than for game-based sports (football, basketball, baseball, etc.). This is probably due to the nature of the sport: for example, for measured sports the majority of what the athletes do in training is quantified ahead of time in more detail and is carried out in a more controlled manner (e.g. sprint times and distances, volume load in the weight room, etc.). Olbrecht (2000) proposes that this interaction should result in an uninterrupted loop of (1) planning, (2) executing, (3) measuring the training effects and (4) revisiting the training plan to verify whether or not the predetermined training stimuli should be adjusted for upcoming mesocycles. Olbrecht (2000) refers to this as "training steering" and suggests that each feedback loop provides insight into an athlete's individual training responses, thus creating greater training efficiency and a greater "return" from the training programme. Important aspects of this process include (1) planning the prescription in numerical form, (2) recording and quantifying the prescription while it is being carried out (Mujika & Padilla 2000, 2003), (3) measuring external responses (e.g. indicators of fatigue) and (4) assessing adaptations of key performance variables. Lastly, underlying the entire strategy that allows Olbrecht's (2000) important fourth step (revisiting the plan) to occur is that during the construction of the training plan expectations are made (adaptation objectives) for given phases of training. The expected adaptations are based not simply on coach experience, but as much as possible on objective scientific evidence. Predetermined expectations (1) allow for purposeful assessment of the training plan as well as (2) aiding the actual planning process. For this second contention, identifying what adaptations to focus on and when allows for a well-thought-out sequencing of specific training phases and once an adaptation(s) objective is targeted, a coach can then shift attention to appropriate programming (sets, reps, exercises).

A worthwhile question to ask is, "does the training response match the predetermined training goal/adaptation focus(i)?" For example, periods of higher stress are necessary to facilitate certain adaptations and if a coach were to simply "back off" because athletes demonstrate signs of fatigue, in this specific situation, they may sacrifice long-term development. Indeed, at certain periods, such as the competition phase or periods of fixture congestion in team sports, managing fatigue may become a priority. In such situations, continual monitoring, using appropriate, quick, non-fatiguing measures, is essential.

No matter which approach is adopted it is very important to familiarise the athletes with all testing procedures, to minimise any learning effect and to determine the measurement error and what level of change in a given test score is likely to be meaningful: this is discussed in detail in Chapters 3 and 4.

References

Balsalobre-Fernandez, C., Tejero-Gonzalez, C.M., et al. (2014). Relationships between training load, salivary cortisol responses and performance during season training in middle and long distance runners. *PLoS One, 9*(8), e106066.

Banyard, H.G., Nosaka, K., et al. (2017). Reliability and validity of the load-velocity relationship to predict the 1RM back squat. *The Journal of Strength & Conditioning Research, 31*(7), 1897–1904.

Bazuelo-Ruiz, B., Padial, P., et al. (2015). Predicting maximal dynamic strength from the load-velocity relationship in squat exercise. *The Journal of Strength & Conditioning Research, 29*(7), 1999–2005.

Bobbert, M.F., & Van Soest, A.J. (1994). Effects of muscle strengthening on vertical jump height: a simulation study. *Medicine & Science in Sports & Exercise, 26*(8), 1012–1020.

Brechue, W.F., & Mayhew, J.L. (2012). Lower-body work capacity and one-repetition maximum squat prediction in college football players. *The Journal of Strength & Conditioning Research, 26*(2), 364–372.

Brzycki, M. (1993). Strength testing – predicting a one-rep max from reps to failure. *Journal of Physical Education, Recreation & Dance, 64*, 88–90.

Crewther, B.T., Carruthers, J., et al. (2016). Temporal associations between individual changes in hormones, training motivation and physical performance in elite and non-elite trained men., *Biology of Sport, 33*(3), 215–221.

DeWeese, B.H., Hornsby, G., et al. (2015a). The training process: Planning for strength and power training in track and field. Part 1: Theoretical aspects. *Journal of Sport and Health Science 4*(4), 308–317.

DeWeese, B.H., Hornsby, G. et al. (2015b). The training process: Planning for strength and power training in track and field. Part 2: Practical and applied aspects. *Journal of Sport and Health Science, 4*(4), 318–324.

Ebben, W.P., & Petushek, E.J. (2010). Using the reactive strength index modified to evaluate plyometric performance. *The Journal of Strength & Conditioning Research 24*(8), 1983–1987.

Flanagan, E.P., Ebben, W.P., et al. (2008). Reliability of the reactive strength index and time to stabilization during depth jumps. *The Journal of Strength & Conditioning Research, 22*(5), 1677–1682.

Gathercole, R., Sporer, B., et al. (2015). Alternative countermovement-jump analysis to quantify acute neuromuscular fatigue. *International Journal of Sports Physiology and Performance, 10*(1), 84–92.

Gonzalez-Badillo, J.J., Pareja-Blanco, F., et al. (2015). Effects of velocity-based resistance training on young soccer players of different ages. *The Journal of Strength & Conditioning Research, 29*(5), 1329–1338.

Gonzalez-Badillo, J.J., & Sanchez-Medina, L. (2010). Movement velocity as a measure of loading intensity in resistance training. *International Journal of Sports Medicine, 31*(5), 347–352.

Hakkinen, K., Komi, P.V., et al. (1987). EMG, muscle fibre and force production characteristics during a 1 year training period in elite weight-lifters. *European Journal of Applied Physiology and Occupational Physiology, 56*(4), 419–427.

Hoeger, W.W.K., Barette, S.L., et al. (1987). Relationship between repetitions and selected percentages of one repetition maximum. *The Journal of Strength & Conditioning Research, 1*(1), 11–13.

Kraemer, W.J., French, D.N., et al. (2004). Changes in exercise performance and hormonal concentrations over a big ten soccer season in starters and nonstarters. *The Journal of Strength & Conditioning Research, 18*(1), 121–128.

Loturco, I., Kobal, R., et al. (2017). Predicting the maximum dynamic strength in bench press: The high precision of the bar velocity approach. *The Journal of Strength & Conditioning Research, 31*(4), 1127–1131.

McMahon, J.J., Murphy, S., et al. (2017a). Countermovement-jump-phase characteristics of senior and academy rugby league players. *International Journal of Sports Physiology and Performance, 12*(6), 803–811.

McMahon, J.J., Rej, S.J., et al. (2017b). Sex differences in countermovement jump phase characteristics. *Sports, 5*(1), 8.

Mujika, I., & Padilla, S. (2000). Detraining: loss of training-induced physiological and performance adaptations. Part I: short term insufficient training stimulus. *Sports Medicine, 30*(2), 79–87.

Mujika, I., & Padilla, S. (2003). Scientific bases for precompetition tapering strategies. *Medicine & Science in Sports & Exercise, 35*(7), 1182–1187.

Olbrecht, J. (2000). *The science of winning*. Bedfordshire, UK: Swimshop.

Picerno, P., Iannetta, D., et al. (2016). 1RM prediction: a novel methodology based on the force-velocity and load-velocity relationships. *European Journal of Applied Physiology, 116*(10), 2035–2043.

Plisk, S., & Stone, M.H. (2003). Periodization strategies. *Strength & Conditioning Journal, 25*, 19–37.

Sands, W.A., & McNeal, J.R. (2000). Predicting athlete preparation and performance: A theoretical perspective. *Journal of Sport Behavior, 23*, 289–310.

Sands, W.A., & Stone, M.H. (2005). Are you progressing and how would you know? *Olympic Coach, 17*, 4–10.

Seitz, L.B., Reyes, A., et al. (2014). Increases in lower-body strength transfer positively to sprint performance: A systematic review with meta-analysis. *Sports Medicine, 44* (12), 1693–1702.

Smith, D.J. (2003). A framework for understanding the training process leading to elite performance. *Sports Medicine, 33*(15), 1103–1126.

Suchomel, T.J., Bailey, C.A., et al. (2015a). Using reactive strength index-modified as an explosive performance measurement tool in Division I athletes. *The Journal of Strength & Conditioning Research, 29*(4), 899–904.

Suchomel, T.J., Nimphius, S., et al. (2016). The importance of muscular strength in athletic performance. *Sports Medicine, 46*(10), 1419–1449.

Suchomel, T.J., Sole, C.J., et al. (2015b). A comparison of reactive strength index-modified between six U.S. collegiate athletic teams. *The Journal of Strength & Conditioning Research, 29*(5), 1310–1316.

Part II
Assessment methods

6 Assessment of factors associated with injury risk

Lee C. Herrington, Allan G. Munro and Paul A. Jones

6.1 Introduction

Can you predict risk of injury from the performance of a single or a number of tests? The simple answer to this question is no, there are just too many factors involved in the development of injury (Figure 6.1). A considerable number of factors exist which have meaningful individual roles in the risk of injury occurrence or can interact with other factors to increase the risk. It is likely that certain factors will have a more critical role in increasing the threat of injury. The most important factor is likely to be the athlete's global and local tissue chronic loading capacity (strength) (Abernethy & Bleakley, 2007; Lauersen et al., 2014). Considerable work on the role of chronic capacity and its role in injury occurrence has been undertaken by Gabbett and colleagues (Windt et al., 2017; Windt & Gabbett, 2017).

The occurrence of injury would appear to be related to the application of loads in excess of what the tissue is capable of withstanding. This indicates that there would have to be an increase in load from the tissue's current chronic or established loading levels, which then results in a change in the acute-chronic load ratio. The acute-chronic ratio relates to the amount of training the athlete has completed over a prolonged period, compared with the amount undertaken recently. This ratio is calculated by comparing the acute load (i.e. training performed during the current week) with the chronic load (i.e. the training performed over the last four weeks). Training load could be calculated from either external workload, such as kilometres ran or amount of weight lifted and/or internal load such as minutes exercised multiplied by a perceived exertion rating. Once calculated, an acute-chronic workload of 0.5 would indicate that an athlete had undertaken only half as much workload in the most recent week as in the previous four weeks, whereas a value of 2.0 would indicate that the athlete was undertaking twice as much work in the current week compared to the previous four weeks. As it has been previously reported that workloads of greater than 1.5 appear to elevate the risk of injury (Blanch & Gabbett, 2016) the athlete in the latter case has an elevated threat of injury. Many factors could impact on acute activity levels and so potentially decrease the ratio, which might reduce risk at that point (you are less likely to get injured when you are not training), but if the situation persists and then there is a rapid return to "full training" the ratio is likely to become excessive and increase threat (Figure 6.1). A typical example of how this increased threat could occur is when an athlete has not been able to train fully because of illness, work or life commitments, a break or holiday, and then goes back into full training.

Another factor which could magnify the impact of these acute changes in loading stress on the tissues is the way the athlete moves and their ability to dissipate the load throughout the whole body rather than allowing the stress to become localised. This factor has been

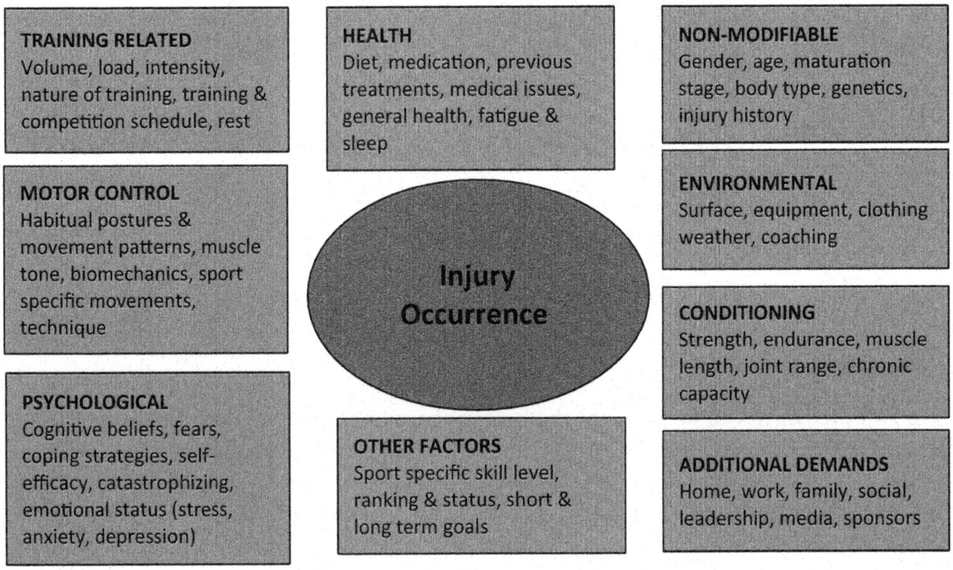

TRAINING RELATED
Volume, load, intensity, nature of training, training & competition schedule, rest

HEALTH
Diet, medication, previous treatments, medical issues, general health, fatigue & sleep

NON-MODIFIABLE
Gender, age, maturation stage, body type, genetics, injury history

MOTOR CONTROL
Habitual postures & movement patterns, muscle tone, biomechanics, sport specific movements, technique

ENVIRONMENTAL
Surface, equipment, clothing weather, coaching

Injury Occurrence

CONDITIONING
Strength, endurance, muscle length, joint range, chronic capacity

PSYCHOLOGICAL
Cognitive beliefs, fears, coping strategies, self-efficacy, catastrophizing, emotional status (stress, anxiety, depression)

OTHER FACTORS
Sport specific skill level, ranking & status, short & long term goals

ADDITIONAL DEMANDS
Home, work, family, social, leadership, media, sponsors

Figure 6.1 Factors associated with injury occurrence.

globally called neuromuscular control of movement and again, like injury threat itself, a number of factors can impact on it (Figure 6.2). Neuromuscular control is fundamentally the ability to deliver a movement in "optimal" manner which minimises loading stresses or maximises the distribution of the loading stresses on the tissues. Tests of neuromuscular control are usually carried out as a closed-chain multi-segment movement in a prescribed closed skill manner (e.g. single-leg squat or single-leg landing).

6.2 The philosophy behind screening tests

The nature of the test movement undertaken, other than being a closed-chain multi-segmental "functional" movement, is rarely considered within the literature, with a variety of different movement tasks being utilised. For task selection to be more sensitive though a number of factors need to be considered, which include the nature of the activities undertaken in the sport, the nature of the major injuries in the sport (and if they can be linked to specific movements or activities) and the individual athlete's injury history (and if this can be linked to specific movements or activities).

Certain movements are likely to be common to the majority of sports: squatting, landing on one or two legs, balancing on the limb and rapidly generating and absorbing force and these movements are likely to form the core of any screening tasks, as will be presented later in this chapter. The outcome from testing is often dichotomised into a pass or fail, but again what a pass or a fail means is rarely discussed and even less so what to do about a negative result in particular. The approach taken within this chapter is to distinguish tests into primary or secondary tests. The primary tests are those described above, that is, the closed-chain multi-segmental "functional" movements. A secondary test is a test looking to assess and understand why the athlete has failed the primary test. Within this screening

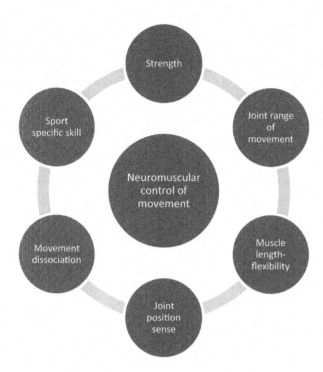

Figure 6.2 Factors associated with poor neuromuscular control of movement.

philosophy there is therefore no need to undertake secondary tests unless the primary test has been failed and is still failed after the athlete has been coached on how to undertake and perform the test movement appropriately.

If the athlete fails the primary test initially and is still failing it despite appropriate coaching of the movement then secondary testing can be undertaken to gain a deeper understanding of why the athlete might still be failing the test. Figure 6.2 presents a number of factors which can have a significant impact on the ability to perform the test appropriately. The athlete could be failing the test because they have insufficient strength or range of movement to either control or allow the movement to occur. They could equally have poor proprioception, which affects the ability to deliver the appropriate movement, in terms of either understanding where their limbs are in space (joint position sense) or their ability to move limbs in isolation of each other (limb dissociation). But the biggest reason they will fail the primary test will always be their lack of understanding of how to perform the movement appropriately (combination of all the factors: Figure 6.2), hence coaching of the movement first should always be tried.

Coaching feedback can be provided in the form of both internal and external feedback. Internal feedback is often described as the knowledge of performance, and relates to developing an internal awareness of the task's performance: the athlete might be asked to consider the joint range or amount of muscle tension (Wulf et al., 2010). External (or augmented) feedback involves the use of external targets or cues to enhance performance. External feedback can come from a variety of sources, for example, visual demonstration or using a mirror, video or verbal instruction. External feedback can enhance the ability

Table 6.1 Guidance for providing feedback.

Provide feedback only when the magnitude of the error is very large
Use a reducing feedback schedule as training progresses
Allow the individual athlete to have control over the areas receiving feedback
Use summary feedback after a number of attempts rather than after individual attempts

---

to learn a skill, but it is still important to consider content, timing and frequency of the feedback to optimise its impact (Wulf et al., 2010). When using verbal feedback, the aim is to provide supplementary information relating to the knowledge of performance and the results of movement, both of which are critical to skill learning. Knowledge of performance is related to the execution of the movement, typically the quality of the movement. Knowledge of results pertains to the actual outcome of the movement, whether the goal was achieved or not. Table 6.1 provides guidance for providing feedback.

6.3 Understanding the use of screening tests

6.3.1 Reliability and validity in the context of injury screening

Knowledge of the reliability and validity of measurement tools is imperative for their use within the field of research and applied practice. A brief commentary and summary of key terms (Table 6.2) is only provided here, as a more detailed discussion on reliability and validity is provided in Chapter 3.

Generally speaking within strength and conditioning (S&C), concurrent validity (Table 6.2) is the most important type of validity to explore. However, when assessing injury risk factors, practitioners and researchers may be interested in the ability of the test to discriminate between groups (construct validity).

With regard to reliability (Table 6.2), considering that screening tests may be conducted in the field by either a single or multiple examiners and across different time points, knowledge of inter-, intra- and between-session reliability is required. To quantify reliability in each case both relative and absolute reliability should be expressed (Table 6.2). Relative reliability is often assessed using intra-class correlation coefficients (ICCs) (see Chapter 3). However, the drawback of ICCs is the lack of information regarding the actual difference between measures and its sensitivity to sample heterogeneity (Atkinson & Nevill, 1998; Rankin & Stokes, 1998), although this is improved if confidence intervals are also provided. Therefore, absolute reliability measures should be determined such as standard error of measurement (SEM) and co-efficient of variation (CV) (Rankin & Stokes, 1998; Atkinson & Nevill, 1998), which are covered in Chapter 3. Ideally, a high ICC (≥0.80) with low SEM and CV (<10%) would indicate good reliability of a measure.

When assessing the change in an individual's score on a test, it cannot be assumed that the difference observed is a true change. The scores observed will include some variability, due to either random or systematic error (Atkinson & Nevill, 1998). Therefore, for a true change in performance to be observed, the difference in scores must be greater than the measurement error associated with the test: hence, the importance of assessing absolute reliability (measurement error) in order to allow S&C coaches to evaluate an intervention. A limitation of SEM and CV measures to evaluate this is that only 68% of all test scores

Table 6.2 Definition of key terms related to validity and reliability of measurement tools.

Validity	The extent to which the observed value agrees with the actual value of a measure (Hopkins, 2000). Three types of validity are important with regard to assessing factors associated with injury risk:
1. Logical validity	Whether the test involves the performance that is being measured (Thomas et al., 2005).
2. Criterion validity	How the scores on a test relate to a recognised standard or criterion. This also includes concurrent and predictive validity (Thomas et al., 2005).
3. Construct validity	How a test measures or relates to a hypothetical construct (Thomas et al., 2005).
Reliability	The extent to which scores for a subject sample can be reproduced in the same participants in subsequent tests (Batterham & George, 2003).
Random error	The "noise" in a measurement, typically seen as within-subject variation, inconsistencies in the measurement protocol or the examiner's measurements (Atkinson & Nevill, 1998; Hopkins, 2000).
Systematic noise	The trend for measures to be different due to learning effects or fatigue (Atkinson & Nevill, 1998; Batterham & George, 2003).
Intra-tester reliability	The consistency of measures with repeated trials assessed by the same examiner.
Inter-tester reliability	The consistency with which different testers achieve the same score on the same participants.
Between-session or test-retest reliability	The reproducibility of the observed value when the test is repeated (Hopkins, 2000).
Relative reliability	The degree to which individuals maintain their position in a sample of repeated measures (Atkinson and Nevill, 1998).
Absolute reliability	The degree to which repeated measurements vary for individuals (Atkinson & Nevill, 1998).

fall within one SEM or CV of the true score, rather than the 95% criterion commonly used (Atkinson & Nevill, 1998; Thomas et al., 2005). As a result, the smallest detectable difference (SDD) (see Chapter 3) should be determined, which is the minimum value that should be exceeded to distinguish between random measurement error and a real (statistically significant) change (Atkinson & Nevill, 1998; Eliasziw et al., 1994). For a practically meaningful difference between two measures, the difference should be greater than the SDD. This gives S&C coaches greater knowledge with which to evaluate changes made during rehabilitation or training.

6.3.2 Diagnostic accuracy

Diagnostic accuracy is the ability to discriminate between individuals with and without a specific disorder. When assessing the accuracy of a clinical test and providing a correct diagnosis the following test properties of diagnostic accuracy need to be established: sensitivity (does the test capture all those who get injured?), specificity (does it capture only those who get injured?), positive prediction value (how many with a positive test score get injured?) and negative prediction value (how many with a negative test score get injured?) (Bahr,

2016). Furthermore, likelihood ratios (Whiteley, 2016) (Box 6.1) or receiver operating characteristic curve analyses (Pepe et al., 2004) should be determined to identify the predictive ability of the test (i.e. using the accuracy of a test and translating this into the probability that the athlete will get injured or not). A method to determine diagnostic accuracy and likelihood ratios is outlined in Box 6.1.

One challenge presented with regard to injury risk screening is that screening tests such as eccentric strength for hamstring injury are often measured on a continuous range, whereas

---

Box 6.1 Determining diagnostic accuracy

1. Develop a 2 × 2 contingency table (Table 1.1) to describe the nature of the results (i.e. false, true, negative, positive).
2. Once the contingency table is formed, using the information contained and the formulas outlined in Table 1.2, various features of the diagnostic test can be established.
3. Once the likelihood ratios have been established then Table 1.3 can be used to interpret the information.

Table 1.1 An example 2 × 2 contingency table.

	Reference standard positive	*Reference standard negative*
Diagnostic test positive	True positive results A	False positive results B
Diagnostic test negative	C False negative results	D True negative results

Table 1.2 Formulas to determine key characteristics of the diagnostic test.

Statistic	*Formula*	*Description*
Overall accuracy	(A+D)/(A+B+C+D)	The percentage of individuals who are correctly diagnosed
Sensitivity	A/(A+C)	The proportion of patients with the conditions who have a positive test result
Specificity	D/(B+D)	The proportion of patients without the condition who have a negative test result
Positive predictive value	A/(A+B)	The proportion of individuals with a positive test result who have the condition
Negative predictive value	D(C+D)	The proportion of individuals with a negative test result who do not have the condition
Positive likelihood ratio	Sensitivity/(1 – specificity)	If the test is positive, the increase in odds favouring the condition
Negative likelihood ratio	(1 – sensitivity)/specificity	If the test is negative, the decrease in odds favouring the condition

Table 1.3 Interpretation of likelihood ratios.

Positive likelihood ratio	Negative likelihood ratio	Interpretation
>10	<0.1	Generate large and often conclusive shifts in probability
5–10	0.1–0.2	Generate moderate shifts in probability
2–5	0.2–0.5	Generate small but sometimes important shifts in probability
1–2	0.5–1	Alter probability to a small and rarely important degree

screening tests for disease are designed to have "yes" or "no" outcomes, thus considerable overlap often exists between injured and uninjured individuals (Bahr, 2016). Establishing a "cut-off" value for a particular test to distinguish between high and low injury risk groups is required, but presents difficulties in achieving adequate levels of sensitivity and specificity (for a more detailed discussion see Bahr, 2016). Sensitivity and specificity are inversely related; thus, if you want a test to capture all injured players/athletes (sensitivity) then specificity will decline, leading to more uninjured athletes being established as "high risk". This may present a potential problem to the S&C professional, who may have difficulty in getting athletes and coaches to "buy in" to the testing battery and interventions proposed. It might be further problematic if more sophisticated and costly methods are adopted and thus clinical utility (practicality of the test) maybe a further consideration for the design of a test battery.

6.4 Common screening tests

6.4.1 Lower quadrant

Movement screening

Screening of lower-limb tasks such as the single-leg squat (SLS), single-leg landing (SLL) and drop jump (DJ) in the literature is often undertaken using three-dimensional motion analysis. Whilst this is appropriate for research, it may not be appropriate for use in clinical practice due to financial, spatial and temporal costs, which has led to the development of two-dimensional (2D) motion analysis techniques. Qualitative and quantitative 2D techniques have been developed to assess lower-limb biomechanics (Noyes et al., 2005; Willson and Davis, 2008; Onate et al., 2010; Herrington & Munro, 2014).

Frontal plane projection angle (FPPA) is an example of quantitative 2D analysis that has been used to measure frontal plane knee motion in athletic, general and injured populations (Munro et al., 2012a, 2012b; Willson & Davis, 2008; Herrington & Munro, 2010). FPPA uses markers at the mid-points of the ankle malleoli and femoral condyles and on the thigh along a line from the knee marker to the anterior superior iliac spine (ASIS), with the practitioner drawing an angle indicating frontal plane motion of the knee (Figure 6.3). Normative data on football, basketball and volleyball players and recreational athletes are shown in Table 6.3.

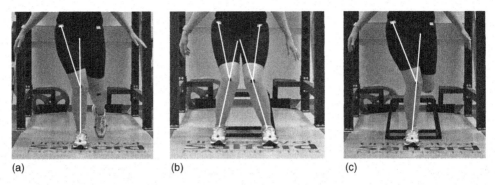

(a)   (b)   (c)

Figure 6.3 Frontal plane projection angle (FPPA) conventions for single-leg squat (a), drop jump landing (b) and single-leg landing (c).

Table 6.3 Normative data for FPPA.

Authors	Population	Single-leg squat	Single-leg land	Drop jump
Herrington & Munro (2010)	Recreational women		5–12°	7–13°
	Recreational men		1–9°	3–8°
Munro et al. (2012a)	Recreational women	11°	7.3°	8.2°
	Recreational men	8.6°	4.7°	0°
Munro et al. (2012b)	Female basketball		9.8°	0°
	Female soccer		6°	1.4°
Willson and Davis (2008)	PFPS women	7°		
Willson et al. (2006)	Multi-sport women			4°
	Multi-sport men			0°

Performance during the SLS task can be assessed using the QASLS (Table 6.4), a qualitative assessment tool developed specifically for lower-limb loading tasks (Herrington & Munro, 2014). A pilot study has also shown that the QASLS tool can predict injury risk in soccer and hockey players (Horobin & Thawley, 2015). No specific cut-off score for increased injury risk is currently available. However, increasing experiential evidence would suggest scores less than 3 indicate decreased predisposition.

Single-leg squat test

The single-leg squat (SLS) task is a closed kinetic chain task that requires strength, proprioception, neuromuscular control and adequate range of motion at the hip, knee and ankle joints (Box 6.2). The SLS predicts kinematics demonstrated during running, cutting and landing (Whatman et al., 2011; Munro et al., 2017; Alenezi et al., 2014; Atkin et al., 2014) and distinguishes between participants with and without patellofemoral joint pain (Willson and Davis, 2008).

Table 6.4 A qualitative screening tool for single-leg loading tasks.

Qualitative analysis of single leg loading Date : Condition: Left	Patient : Right Bilateral		
QASLS	Task: Single leg squat Single leg step down Single leg hop for dist	Left	Right
Arm strategy	Excessive arm movement to balance		
Trunk alignment	Leaning in any direction		
Pelvic plane	Loss of horizontal plane		
	Excessive tilt or rotation		
Thigh motion	WB thigh moves into hip adduction		
	NWB thigh not held in neutral		
Knee position	Patella pointing towards 2nd toe (noticeable valgus)		
	Patella pointing past inside of foot (significant valgus)		
Steady stance	Touches down with NWB foot		
	Stance leg wobbles noticeably		
	Total		

WB = Weight bearing; NWB = Non-weight bearing

Box 6.2 Single-leg squat task procedure

1. Participants take a single-leg stance on the leg to be tested.
2. Participants squat to at least 45° knee flexion and no greater than 60°, over a period of 5 seconds.
3. Participants are typically allowed two or three practice trials to ensure they are comfortable and familiar with the test.
4. Trials are only accepted if the participant squats within the desired degrees of knee flexion and maintains balance throughout.

Single-leg landing test

The single-leg landing (SLL) task (Box 6.3) is relevant for assessment as unilateral landings are a more common ACL injury mechanism than bilateral landings (Faude et al., 2005). Research has also shown that individuals demonstrate increased hip adduction and knee valgus during unilateral tasks compared to bilateral tasks (Pappas et al., 2007; Myklebust et al., 1998).

Box 6.3 Single-leg landing task procedure

1. Participants take a unilateral stance on the non-test limb, on a 28 cm step.
2. Participants drop from the step, leaning forward and dropping as vertically as possible to a pre-defined mark on the floor.
3. Participants land on the test limb and maintain balance for at least 2 seconds.
4. Participants are typically allowed two or three practice trials to ensure they are comfortable and familiar with the test.

The increased demand to decelerate landing forces during the SLL task compared to a bilateral task, such as the drop jump (DJ) landing task, may mean this screening task is more sensitive in identifying those who display dynamic knee valgus. Indeed, Harty et al. (2011) showed that ground reaction forces during the SLL was 3.4 body weight in comparison to 1.8 body weight in the DJ task, despite landing from a lower height. Munro et al. (2017) found that the female football and basketball players demonstrated greater dynamic knee valgus during an SLL task than a DJ task. Jones et al. (2014) have also shown that knee valgus angles and moments during the SLL task significantly correlate with those demonstrated during cutting and pivoting tasks.

The SLL task is relatively under-studied in the current literature in comparison with the SLS and DJ tasks, but shows potential for screening lower-limb injury risk. The QASLS tool (TABLE 6.4) can also be utilised with the SLL task to assess movement strategies.

Drop jump test

The drop jump, or drop vertical jump landing test, is a task widely used in the literature and screening (Box 6.4). Research studies have shown that high knee valgus moments during the DJ task are related to increased risk of primary and secondary ACL injury and PFPS (Hewett et al., 2005; Myer et al., 2010; Paterno et al., 2010). However, the bilateral nature of the drop jump task may limit its sensitivity for identifying those at risk of injury during unilateral landing or cutting maneouvres. For example, Kristianlund and Krosshaug (2013) have shown that knee valgus moments during the DJ task do not relate to those during a cutting task.

The Landing Error Scoring System (LESS) (Figure 6.4) has been developed to qualitatively assess the DJ task (Onate et al., 2010). The LESS has been shown to identify individuals with poor technique during a DJ (Padua et al., 2009), although its ability to predict injury and a cut-off score for increased injury risk have yet to be established (Smith et al., 2012; Padua et al., 2015).

Box 6.4 Drop jump task procedure

1. Participants take a shoulder width stance on a 28 cm step.
2. Participants drop from the step, leaning forward and dropping as vertically as possible to land bilaterally on a pre-defined mark on the floor.
3. Uplon landing, partcipants immediately perform a maximal vertical jump, finally landing back on the landing target.
4. Arm movement is allowed, with no set instructions given, other than to jump and land naturally.
5. Participants are typically allowed two or three practice trials to ensure they are comfortable and familiar with the test.

Frontal-Plane Motion	Sagittal-Plane Motion
1. Stance width	**6. Initial landing of feet**
☐ Normal (0)	☐ Toe to heel (0)
☐ Wide (1)	☐ Heel to toe (1)
☐ Narrow (1)	☐ Flat (1)
2. Maximum foot-rotation position	**7. Amount of knee-flexion displacement**
☐ Normal (0)	☐ Large (0)
☐ Externally rotated (1)	☐ Average (1)
☐ Internally rotated (1)	☐ Small (2)
3. Initial foot contact	**8. Amount of trunk-flexion displacement**
☐ Symmetric (0)	☐ Large (0)
☐ Not symmetric (1)	☐ Average (1)
	☐ Small (2)
	9. Total joint displacement in the sagittal plane
4. Maximum knee-valgus angle	
☐ None (0)	☐ Soft (0)
☐ Small (1)	☐ Average (1)
☐ Large (2)	☐ Stiff (2)
5. Amount of lateral trunk flexion	**10. Overall impression**
☐ None (0)	☐ Excellent (0)
☐ Small to moderate (1)	☐ Average (1)
	☐ Poor (2)

Figure 6.4 The Landing Error Scoring System (LESS) developed by Padua et al. (2009).

Tuck jump test

The tuck jump test (TJT) involves assessing the athlete's ability to undertake multiple repetitive jumps (Box 6.5), so it not only assesses landing ability but also provides an indication of reactive strength capabilities and some inherent perturbation, more accurately reflecting the movement demands and high-risk mechanics involved in competition. Based on the

---

Box 6.5 Marking criteria

If the participant fails to meet the criteria below then they score 1, if they meet the criteria they score 0 for the respective category.

Knee and thigh motion

1. Knee valgus on landing (hip, knee and foot aligned, no collapse of the knee inwards).
2. Thighs not reaching parallel (peak of jump).
3. Thighs not equal side to side (during flight).

Foot position during landing

4. Foot placement not shoulder width apart.
5. Foot placement not parallel (front to back).
6. Foot contact timing not equal (asymmetrical landing).
7. Does not land in same footprint (inconsistent point of landing).
8. Excessive landing contact noise.

Plyometric technique

9. Pause between jumps.
10. Technique declines prior to 10 seconds.

Scoring sheet:

Name :	*Score*
Knee and thigh motion	
1. Knee valgus on landing	
2. Thighs not reaching parallel (peak of jump)	
3. Thighs not equal side to side (during flight)	
Foot position during landing	
4. Foot placement not shoulder width apart	
5. Foot placement not parallel (front to back)	
6. Foot contact timing not equal	
7. Does not land in same footprint	
8. Excessive landing contact noise	
Plyometric technique	
9. Pause between jumps	
10. Technique declines prior to 10 seconds	
Total score	

marking criteria (Box 6.5), the athlete scores a point if they generate any of the errors listed during the ten repetitions of the test, so the maximum score would be 10, with 0 indicating no errors in performance (Box 6.5).

The TJT has been shown to have excellent intra-tester and inter-tester reliability (Fort-Vanmeerhaeghe et al., 2017; Herrington et al., 2013; Read et al., 2016), though Dudley et al. (2013) found practitioner experience may impact on reliability of scoring. The measure was also sensitive to a positive change with training (verbal-visual feedback) (Stroube et al., 2013). The test distinguished performance between those in high- and low-risk sports for ACL injury (Hogg et al., 2016) and between novice and experienced skaters (Slater et al., 2016), highlighting some reasonable discriminatory abilities.

Functional movement screen

There are several performance and/or movement competency-based tests: one of the most frequently reported and used is the Functional Movement Screen (FMS). The FMS test is a battery of seven movement tasks and three additional clearing tests assessed by visual observation using standardised criteria for scoring. The FMS test has been shown to have excellent intra- and inter-tester reliability. Despite the findings related to reliability, other measurement properties of the test are less well established or lack any support at all. A recent review casts doubt on the test's ability to predict injury at all (Moran et al., 2017).

Performance of the FMS test was not associated with sprint or agility test performance (Hartigan et al., 2014; Lockie et al., 2015), or the 3D kinematics occurring during the tests (Whiteside et al., 2016). It did relate to occupational performance in firefighters and the police, identifying that older and more obese individuals perform worse (Cornell et al., 2016; Orr et al., 2016). The FMS score failed to differentiate between athletic and non-athletic students (Engquist et al., 2015) or show any change following exercise programmes (Wright et al., 2015). It also failed to differentiate between individuals who had been cleared to return to sport following ACL reconstruction surgery and those who had not (Mayer et al., 2015). FMS might be useful in identifying the level of athleticism of an individual (Perry et al., 2013), though typical scores reported across multiple sports tend to show a lack of sensitivity. Physically active individuals show an average range of scores between 13.1 and 15.7, runners between 13.1 and 14.3, military personnel 16.2–16.7 and American football players 16.9. Scores of less than 17 (Letafatkar et al., 2014) and 14 (Kiesel et al., 2007, 2014) have both been associated with increased injury risk, but, as can been seen from the normative data above, whole groups of athletes in a multitude of sports fail to meet this criteria cut-off, with Fuller et al. (2017) finding over 60% of elite Australian Rules players had a score of less than 14. So the test would appear to lack the sensitivity and specificity to identify injury, which is shown in the relatively low specificity and sensitivity (less than 75% at best) findings across a number of papers (Kiesel et al., 2014).

Star excursion balance test

The star excursion balance test (SEBT) is a test for dynamic balance and dissociation of movement (Box 6.6). Within the literature two forms of the test are generally reported: the full test (SEBT), which involves measuring reach distances in eight directions, and a truncated version of the test, the Y balance test, which involves measuring reach distances performed in only three directions (anterior, posteromedial and posterolateral), as these form part of the full SEBT test: for clarity the full test is described in Box 6.6.

Box 6.6 The star excursion balance test (SEBT)

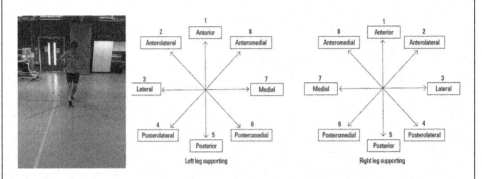

The SEBT is performed with the subject standing in the middle of a grid, illustrated in the figure above, on the leg to be tested. The foot is aligned with the first metatarsal phalangeal joint in the centre of the grid. The subject is instructed to reach as far as possible along the spoke arm, only putting the limb down with minimal weight at the point they can reach no further. Then they are instructed to reach down the next direction. Individuals' distances along the eight lines are measured and then normalised against the subject's leg length (the distance between the anterior superior iliac spine and the tip of the medial malleolus), values being expressed as a percentage of leg length. When undertaking the test there appears to be a significant learning effect, with Munro and Herrington (2010) establishing that SEBT scores are reliably consistent after the fourth trial. So the athlete should undertake three practice reaches, with the fourth score being the one measured.

Typical reach distance (normalised to leg length) for SEBT

Typical values for all reach distances are presented in the table below. When interpreting the test results, it is important to assess symmetry between both limbs (different between limbs) and also the individual's reach distance to see if they are below what would be typical.

Direction	*Reach distance (% leg length)*	
	Male	*Female*
Anterior	80–92	73–92
Anteromedial	82–91	82–91
Medial	87–91	87–91
Posteromedial	87–107	87–99
Posterior	85–88	85–88
Posterolateral	81–106	81–93
Lateral	71–76	71–79
Antero-lateral	73–78	73–78

The SEBT and Y balance test have been used to assess global lower-limb injury risk, with differences in anterior reach distance between limbs of greater than 4 cm increasing risk by 2.2–2.7 times (Plisky et al., 2006) with a sensitivity of 59% and specificity of 72% (Smith et al., 2012), though Stiffler et al. (2017) reported a difference of greater than 2 cm in anterior reach had even greater sensitivity (78–89%) but slightly less specificity (67%) in predicting lower-limb injuries, though certainly the latter results should be viewed with caution as the SDD was reported by van Lieshout et al. (2016) as 4.4% of leg length for anterior reach and 6.9% in the Munro and Herrington (2010) study. With regard to specific injuries, lateral ankle ligament sprains are three times more likely to occur if anterior reach is less than 67% of leg length (Gribble et al., 2016), 48% increased risk if posterolateral reach distance is less than 80% of leg length (de Noronha et al., 2013) and if posteromedial risk distance is less than 77% of leg length then there is a four-fold increased risk (Attenborough et al., 2017).

Hop for distance tests

Hop for distance tests, where the subject hops as far as possible, are commonly used during rehabilitation from injury (Fitzgerald et al., 2000; Clark, 2001; Adams et al., 2012). The hop tests include the single, triple and crossover hop for distance and the 6-metre timed hop. Hop tests can indicate the willingness of the individual to land on the injured limb, whilst the uninjured limb can also be used as a control for comparison purposes. A number of studies have shown that hop tests are able to distinguish deficits between injured and uninjured limbs (Petschnig et al., 1998; Barber et al., 1990; Goh & Boyle, 1997; Noyes et al., 1991; Eastlack et al., 1999; Rudolph et al., 2000; Caffrey et al., 2009). This can aid assessment of progress throughout rehabilitation and help inform when an athlete is ready to return to competition (Lephart & Henry, 1995; Barber et al., 1990; Noyes et al., 1991). In addition, hop test measures undertaken at 6 months post injury or post ACL-reconstruction surgery have been shown to predict function 1-year post injury or surgery (Grindem et al., 2011; Logerstedt et al., 2012). To date, there is no evidence pertaining to whether hop tests can predict future injury risk.

Limb symmetry index (LSI) is a measure commonly used to determine function of limbs (Table 6.8). For screening purposes in healthy populations, the LSI simply indicates the function of one limb versus the other, usually the dominant vs. non-dominant (Table 6.8). When used with injured participants, LSI is calculated by dividing the distance hopped on the injured limb versus the non-injured limb to give a percentage value. This value indicates the function of the injured limb versus the uninjured limb, although there is some contention as to the threshold to determine limb asymmetry (see Section 6.3.3).

Hop tests have also been used as a performance indicator. The single and triple hop tests have been shown to correlate with an athlete's strength and power (Hamilton et al., 2008; Petschnig et al., 1998; Noyes et al., 1991; Nyberg et al., 2006; Greenberger & Paterno, 1995; Negrete & Brophy, 2000). These studies suggest that hop tests can provide an overview of an athlete's functional ability, which includes their strength, power and balance (Barber et al., 1990; Noyes et al., 1991; Lephart et al., 1992) although they may not be sensitive to specific limitations or injury risk. Normative data can be found in Table 6.5. Only papers that have included separate values for men and women have been included; despite evidence of significant differences between sexes in hop test performance, limited literature is available in which sex has been separated.

Box 6.7 Hop protocols

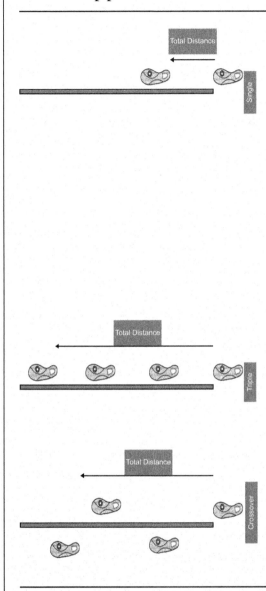

Single hop for distance test procedure

1. Participants stand on the test leg at the start line.
2. Participants hop as far forwards as possible along the line of the tape measure and land on the same limb.
3. Distance hopped is measured to the rear of the foot upon landing.
4. Participants are required to maintain the final landing for a minimum of 2 seconds.

Unsuccessful hops are classified as a loss of balance, an extra hop on landing or the touching down of either the contralateral lower extremity or the upper extremity.

5. Conduct three practice trials and three measured trials.
6. A 30-second rest period is allowed between trials.

Triple hop for distance test procedure

1. Participants stand on the test leg at the start line.
2. Participants perform three consecutive maximal hops along the line of the tape measure and land on the same limb.
3. Repeat steps 3–6 above.

Crossover hop for distance test procedure

1. Participants stand on the test leg at the start line.
2. Participants perform three consecutive maximal hops alternately crossing the 15-cm-wide line and land on the same limb.
3. Repeat steps 3–6 above.

Hop for distance test procedures are outlined in Box 6.7. Considerations for the number of practice trials required are also important. The consensus from several papers appears to be that three practice trials is adequate (Munro & Herrington, 2011; Bolgla & Keskula, 1997; Ross et al., 2002). Additionally, the reliability of the timed 6-metre hop test has consistently been shown to be poor, therefore it is not recommended for screening purposes (Munro & Herrington, 2011).

Table 6.5 Normative data for horizontal hop tests.

Author	Population	Distance (m) Male	Female
Single hop for distance			
Barber et al. (1990)	Elite soccer	2.03	
Barber et al. (1990)	Recreational athletes	1.50	1.15
Barber et al. (1990)	Competitive athletes	1.88	1.22
Munro & Herrington (2011)	Recreational athletes	1.89	1.57
Myers et al. (2014)	Collegiate soccer and basketball	1.92	1.49
O'Donnell et al. (2006)	ACL-deficient	1.58	
O'Donnell et al. (2006)	Healthy controls	1.75–1.78	
Petschnig et al. (1998)	ACLR (13 weeks post-op)	1.37	
Petschnig et al. (1998)	ACLR (54 weeks post-op)	1.73	
Petschnig et al. (1998)	Healthy controls	1.9–1.95	
Triple hop for distance			
Munro & Herrington (2011)	Recreational athletes	5.84	5.05
Myers et al. (2014)	Collegiate soccer and basketball	6.32	4.70
Petschnig et al. (1998)	ACLR (13 weeks post-op)	4.02	
Petschnig et al. (1998)	ACLR (54 weeks post-op)	5.25	
Petschnig et al. (1998)	Healthy controls	5.7–5.79	
Crossover hop for distance			
Munro & Herrington (2011)	Recreational athletes	5.55	4.71
Myers et al. (2014)	Collegiate soccer and basketball	5.70	4.06

6.4.2 Upper quadrant

Shoulder tests

GLENOHUMERAL INTERNAL ROTATION DEFICIT (GIRD) TEST

Increased or decreased mobility is often noted in the sporting population. A resultant decrease in shoulder internal rotation of 20° or more on the dominant side when compared with the opposite side has been noted in athletes. This loss of internal rotation is referred to as GIRD (glenohumeral internal rotation deficit) (Box 6.8). Less than a 20° side difference for internal rotation and <10% side difference for total range of movement have been considered as acceptable values which are unlikely to contribute to pathology. Predictive findings for injury have been proposed as loss of >25° in internal rotation, and a loss of 20° internal rotation combined with a loss of 5% in total range of movement doubles the risk of injury in professional baseball pitchers. Reliability is reported to be good to excellent for internal and external rotation range of motion (ICC, 0.85–0.99). The minimal detectable change statistic derived varies between 4.44° and 8.03° depending on the specific test and equipment used (Cools et al., 2014).

Closed-chain upper-limb test

The Closed Kinetic Chain Upper-Extremity Stability Test (CKCUEST) is an option for examining upper-limb stability (Box 6.9). The CKCUEST is a multi-joint movement

---

Box 6.8 Glenohumeral internal rotation deficit (GIRD) test procedure

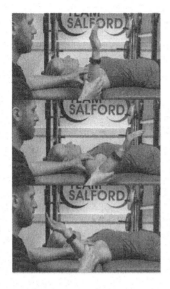

- The arm on the side being tested is abducted to 90° and positioned with the humerus in line with the acromion.
- The elbow is flexed to 90° and the examiner passively moves and measures the joint range of rotation.
- For measures of external shoulder range, the examiner moves the shoulder passively to end of range, while noting that no compensatory movement occurs at the shoulder girdle.
- For internal range of shoulder motion, the examiner palpates the anterior aspect of the acromion with one hand and moves the shoulder into passive internal rotation.
- End of range is considered to be the last point in range before the acromion starts to move.
- Both goniometers and inclinometers can be used for the assessment of shoulder range of motion.

---

assessment which induces instability in the subject and performance can depend on muscular strength levels, balance, coordination and, consequently, the physical ability of the individual.

The reliability for the test has been reported as moderate to good (ICC 0.68–0.86) with minimal detectable change values of four to six touches. The test has been shown to be able to discriminate between those with and those without subacromial impingement syndrome (Tucci et al., 2014) and was predictive of injury to either arm with a 0.79 sensitivity and 0.83 specificity, when undertaken as a pre-season test (Pontillo et al., 2014).

6.5 Muscle strength assessment

Muscular strength is a prominent factor associated with injury occurrence with regard to muscle strain injury (Figure 6.1) and poor neuromuscular control (Figure 6.2) during athletic tasks. Thus, assessment of muscle strength of relevant muscle groups is an obvious consideration for developing an injury risk profile for an athlete. Poor hip muscle strength (external rotation/ abduction) is implicated in poor neuromuscular control of squatting and landing tasks (Padua et al., 2005; Claibourne et al., 2006; Jacobs et al., 2007; Lawrence et al., 2008) and will be discussed here along with the assessment of hamstring and hip adduction strength as muscle groups commonly injured in sport.

6.5.1 Hip strength assessment

From the screening tests for dynamic valgus mentioned above, once an athlete with instruction still "fails" for poor neuromuscular control, then secondary factors need to

Box 6.9 Closed-chain upper-limb test

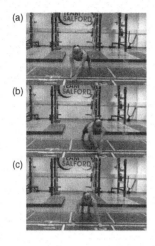

- Two pieces of tape are placed on the floor parallel to each other 36 inches apart.
- The subject begins in an elevated position similar to a standard push-up with one hand on each piece of tape, the body straight and parallel to the floor, and feet no greater than shoulder width apart (a).
- When the test begins, the subject removes one hand from the floor, touches the opposing hand on the opposite line and then replaces the hand on the original line (b).
- The subject then removes the other hand from the floor, touching the opposite line and returning it to the original line (c).
- A single test consists of alternating touches for 15 seconds.
- Subjects are instructed to attempt as many touches as possible during the 15 seconds while maintaining proper push-up form.
- Subjects perform two maximal-effort trials each lasting 15 seconds with 45 seconds of rest in between the trials.
- In the event a subject does not return the hand to the tape or does not touch the opposing hand during a repetition, the repetition is not recorded.
- The average number of touches between the two trials is calculated and recorded.

---

be considered. Poor hip abduction and external rotation strength may provide less resistance to hip adduction and internal rotation indicative of dynamic valgus during squatting, landing, running and cutting activities (Padua et al., 2005). Previous studies have found hip adduction and hip internal rotation as significant predictors of knee valgus at initial contact and peak valgus during landing (Padua et al., 2005). Moreover, Imwalle et al. (2009) have found hip adduction to be the single biggest predictor (25%) of knee abduction (valgus) angle during 45 and 90° cuts in female footballers. Thus, proximal control of the thigh is paramount to prevent excessive knee valgus during athletic tasks.

Previous research has identified that isometric hip external rotator and abductor strength can differentiate between females with and without patellofemoral pain (Lloyd-Ireland et al., 2003) and males and females (Leetun et al., 2004; Jacobs et al., 2007) and to be a significant predictor of general injury status (Leetun et al., 2004). With regard to the association of hip strength and movement control, Claiborne et al. (2006) found concentric hip abduction strength to be related to frontal plane knee motion during a single leg squat, whereas Jacobs et al. (2007) found females displayed lower hip abduction strength than males and larger knee valgus during a landing task, which was found to be moderately correlated to hip abduction strength. Padua et al. (2005) found significant relationships between knee valgus at initial contact and peak knee valgus during a 30 cm jump landing task and strength of the gluteus maximus, hip external rotators and gluteus medius muscles in 63 males and 54 females, with gluteus medius strength a significant but low predictor of knee valgus at initial contact and peak knee valgus. Finally, Lawrence et al. (2008) found that isometric hip external rotation strength was significantly correlated with vertical GRF (ρ = −0.468), net anterior shear force (ρ = −0.448) and external knee valgus moments (ρ = −0.471) during a single-leg landing task in 32 females. Conversely, Hollman et al. (2009) found no relationship between hip external rotation strength and knee valgus during a single-limb step-down task. Norcross et al. (2009) also found no association between hip abduction and external rotation strength and frontal plane knee motion during a lateral step-down task.

The conflicting results and low predictive ability for the association of hip strength and poor movement mechanics may be due to the specificity of the tests involved in terms of velocity of movement and mode of contraction. For instance, the majority of studies (Lloyd-Ireland et al., 2003; Leetun et al., 2004; Jacobs et al., 2007; Lawrence et al., 2008) use isometric contractions with hand-held dynamometers (HHD). Although reliable, it is debatable whether a measure of isometric strength provides a valid evaluation of an ability to resist hip adduction and internal rotation during the weight-acceptance phase of these athletic tasks. A measure of eccentric hip external rotation and abduction strength may provide a more valid measure of the ability to "resist" these undesired motions and thus could provide stronger relationships between hip motion and knee valgus moments during landing and cutting. Claiborne et al. (2006) explored the relationships between concentric and eccentric hip strength and knee valgus motion during single-leg squats, but found only concentric abduction to be significantly related. Conversely, Marche Baldon et al. (2012) found eccentric abduction and external rotation strength to be the best predictors of single-leg triple long jump distance and 6 m single-leg hop times, relating this to improved neuro-muscular control of landing. However, they did not directly evaluate knee valgus motion during these tasks.

Specific evaluation of concentric and eccentric hip strength requires the use of isokinetic dynamometry (discussed later) and has resource and time implications. The use of HHD (isometric methods) offers an inexpensive method that could be easily administered by practitioners in the clinical setting. HHD is considered a reliable technique for assessing hip abduction and external rotation strength (Bohannon et al., 2008; Thorborg et al., 2010; Kawaguchi & Babcock, 2010). However, it is often highlighted that when subjects can overpower the testers either through the type of movement or strength of the subject, the reliability of this technique could be compromised (Kelln et al., 2008; Kollock et al., 2008). The use of restraints (Box 6.10) as opposed to relying on examiner resistance in the use of HHD has previously been advocated (Lloyd-Ireland et al., 2003; Leetun et al., 2004) and should be adopted to improve reliability. The testing position and the lever arm used for testing also seem to influence the reliability of the procedure and should be standardised. A recommended method for assessment of isometric hip abduction and external rotation strength is outlined in Box 6.10.

6.5.2 Hip adductor strength assessment

Groin injuries are common in multi-directional field-based sports such as soccer (Werner et al., 2009; Ekstrand et al., 2011b; Walden et al., 2015), Australian Rules (Orchard et al., 1998), Gaelic football (Murphy & O'Malley, 2012), rugby union (Brooks et al., 2005a, 2005b) and ice hockey (Emery et al., 1999), with the assessment of hip muscle strength playing an important role in the clinical assessment of groin and hip problems. HHD again

Box 6.10 Hand-held dynamometry methods

The **hip abduction isometric strength test** should be performed with the subjects lying on their side on a plinth. Pillows are placed between the subject's legs, so that the hip to be tested is horizontal (photo a). A strap is placed around the pelvis and secured firmly around the underside of the plinth to stabilise the trunk. An HHD is then placed directly over a mark located 5 cm proximal to the lateral knee joint line and held in place by a strap which is secured firmly around the underside of the table. The subject is required to abduct (push the leg up) against the strap's resistance with maximal effort for 3 seconds (photo a). The force value displayed is recorded and the device re-zeroed before the next trial.

(a)

Hip external rotation isometric strength testing is performed with subjects positioned on a plinth with the hips and knees flexed to 90°. To prevent substitution by the hip adductors, a strap is used to stabilise the thigh of the tested leg and a piece of dense foam is placed so that the centre of the force pad is directly over a mark that is 5 cm proximal to the medial malleolus. The dynamometer is held in place by a strap which is then fastened to an immovable object (photo b). The subject is required to push against the strap's resistance with maximal effort for 3 seconds (photo b). The force value displayed on the dynamometer is recorded and the device re-zeroed before the next trial. One practice trial and three experimental trials should be performed for each test with 1 minute rest between trials.

Data analysis: the peak value from each trial of each test is recorded and averaged for data analysis. To express as maximal moment (Nm), the force recorded is multiplied by the moment arm. The moment arm is the distance from the axis of rotation to the application centre of the load cell of the dynamometer. Moment should then be normalised by bodyweight (Nm/kg bodyweight); thus, the influence of differences in body mass and limb lengths is controlled.

(b)

is a widely used measure in the assessment of adductor strength in relation to groin and hip pain with an isometric "make" (Thorborg et al., 2011a, 2014) and eccentric "break" (Tyler et al., 2001; Thorborg et al., 2011a, 2014) tests used in the literature.

In a prospective study in professional ice hockey players, Tyler et al. (2001) measured hip abduction and adduction strength in a side-lying position wherein the players had to resist a manually applied force by the examiner ("break" test). The authors found players who suffered adductor injury ($n = 8$) had 18% lower adduction strength than uninjured players and adduction strength was 78% of mean abduction strength in the injured limb players compared to 95% in uninjured players, which was more pronounced in the injured limb. Discriminant analysis revealed that players with hip adduction strength less than 80% of abduction strength were 17.1 times more likely to suffer adductor strains, but no specificity or sensitivity statistics were reported. Furthermore, the authors did not take into account limb length or mass in strength measurements. Thorborg et al. (2014), using a similar approach to Tyler et al. (2001), but also incorporating isometric assessments ("make" test) in male soccer players found that only eccentric hip adduction strength was lower in soccer players with adductor-related groin pain (>4 weeks) in the dominant leg (n = 21) compared with asymptomatic controls (n = 16) [2.47 ± 0.49 vs. 3.12 ± 0.43 Nm/kg]. Alternatively, Thorborg et al. (2011a) used a method to assess isometric hip adduction and abduction strength involving lying supine and found that the isometric hip adduction/ abduction ratio was significantly lower in soccer players with groin pain (n = 10) during hip adduction testing compared with players with a pain-free (n = 76) test (0.80 ± 0.14 vs. dominant limbs 1.04 ± 0.18 Nm/kg, and non-dominant limbs 1.06 ± 0.17 Nm/kg). These studies highlight the importance of adductor strength assessments in creating an athlete profile for potential muscle strain injuries; however, the above-mentioned manual muscle testing methods can only be effectively used with an experienced examiner due to the reliability issues mentioned earlier. Thus, practitioners may require simpler methods to examine strength in this muscle group.

The adductor "squeeze test" may be one such option and is quantified by using the cuff of a sphygmomanometer, which is placed between the knees of an athlete, and the athlete is then instructed to squeeze the cuff as hard as they can using both legs whilst lying supine on a plinth (Figure 6.5). The highest pressure displayed on the sphygmomanometer dial (to the nearest 5 mmHg) during the test is then recorded. The test is effectively a bilateral test with the output determined by the weaker limb.

The test can be performed in positions of 0°, 45° and 90° hip flexion. Delahunt et al. (2011a) found that 45° hip flexion was the optimum position for assessment as this elicited greatest adductor longus EMG activation and pressure scores (0°: 202.50 ± 57.28 mmHg; 45°: 236.76 ±47.29 mmHg; 90°: 186.11 ± 44.01 mmHg; P < 0.05). Furthermore, Delahunt et al. (2011b) found that the 45° hip flexion produced the greatest reliability (Table 6.6). Malliaras et al. (2009) also reported good test-re-test reliability (Table 6.6) in football players and were able to discriminate between players with and without groin pain. The "squeeze test" at 45° hip flexion has also been shown to identify Gaelic football players with long-standing groin problems (Nevin & Delahunt, 2014).

The "squeeze test" can also be performed using HHD, with Fulcher et al. (2010) reporting good to excellent intra- and inter-rater reliability in 30 semi-professional soccer players. Crow et al. (2009) found that decreased hip adductor strength measured via the adductor squeeze test had decreased strength preceding and at the onset of groin pain in elite youth Australian Rules footballers, indicating the usefulness of such an assessment to track players at increased risk of adductor strain injury. This suggestion is supported by a meta-analysis (Mosler et al., 2015) that found strong evidence that reduced strength on the adductor squeeze test discriminated between athletes with and without groin pain.

Limitations of the adductor squeeze test are that often, particularly when a sphygmomanometer is used, the data are not normalised by lever length or mass of the subjects, which may impact on comparisons with normative data. Furthermore, as the test is a bilateral test, isolated unilateral measures of either limb cannot be gathered in order to compare between limbs or provide hip adduction/abduction ratios.

Figure 6.5 The adductor squeeze test.

Table 6.6 Reported reliability for the adductor squeeze test.

Method	Authors	Subjects	Values
Sphygmomanometer method	Delahunt et al. (2011b)	18 male Gaelic football players	Intra-rater: 0° hip flexion; ICC = 0.89; 45° hip flexion ICC = 0.92; 90° hip flexion ICC = 0.90.
	Malliaras et al. (2009)	29 male soccer and Australian football players	Intra-rater: [ICC = 0.81; SEM = 20 mmHg (0° hip flexion); ICC = 0.91; SEM = 20 mmHg (30° hip flexion); ICC = 0.94; SEM = 15 mmHg (45° hip flexion)]. Inter-rater: [ICC = 0.80; SEM = 20 mmHg (0° hip flexion); ICC = 0.82; SEM = 20 mmHg (30° hip flexion); ICC = 0.83; SEM = 20 mmHg (45° hip flexion)].
Hand-held dynamometry method	Fulcher et al (2010)	30 male semi-professional soccer players	Intra-rater ICCs of 0.76 (0° hip flexion); 0.86 (45° hip flexion) 0.89 (90° hip flexion) Inter-rater ICCs of 0.85 (0° hip flexion); 0.77 (45° hip flexion); and 0.87 (90° hip flexion).

6.5.3 Hamstring strength assessment

Hamstring strain injuries (HSI) are common in a number of sprint-related sports such as athletics (Lysholm & Wiklander, 1987; Alonso et al., 2009, 2010, 2012), soccer (Hawkins et al., 2001; Ekstrand et al., 2011b, 2013), rugby union (Brooks et al., 2005a, 2005b), Australian Rules football (Orchard et al., 2013) and Gaelic football (Roe et al., 2016). A wide range of extrinsic (e.g. fixture congestion; sharp increases in volume of high speed running) and intrinsic risk factors (e.g. muscle architecture) are associated with HSI (Bengtsson et al., 2013; Duhig et al., 2016; Timmins et al., 2015). High-speed running results in high-velocity eccentric loading (Schache et al., 2012), as during the late swing phase of the gait cycle the hamstrings work eccentrically to decelerate both the thigh and lower leg in preparation for ground contact and HSIs have been linked to this phase (Heiderscheit et al., 2005; Thelen et al. 2005; Schache et al., 2012).Thus, hamstring muscle strength characteristics, particularly low eccentric strength (Jonhagen et al., 1994; Opar et al., 2015), as well as angle of peak moment (Brockett et al., 2004) and muscle imbalance (Yamamoto, 1993; Orchard et al., 1997; Cameron et al., 2003; Fousekis et al., 2010; Bourne et al., 2015), have also been associated with HSI. However, there are a variety of methods to assess hamstring muscle strength qualities, with little agreement and considerable debate on the optimum methods to do so.

Isokinetic dynamometry

Sprinters with a history of hamstring injury have been shown to differ from uninjured ones by weaker eccentric strength at all isokinetic speeds (at 30, 180 and 230°/s) and in concentric contractions at low velocities (at 30°/s) (Jonhagen et al., 1994). However, contrary to previous research, a meta-analysis by Freckleton and Pizzari (2013) suggested increased quadriceps peak moment, not hamstring peak moment, as an HSI risk factor. Furthermore, Van Dyk et al. (2016) found low eccentric hamstring and quadriceps strength (at 60°/s) as "weak" predictors of HSI in professional soccer players in the Qatar league over four seasons, questioning the use of isokinetics. Although this probably highlights what was raised at the start of this chapter with regard to "screening", any one single factor will not predict injury occurrence due to the multi-faceted aetiology of injury, thus practitioners may still gather information regarding isokinetic strength to help create an athlete profile that allows practitioners to address potential problems through exercise prescription.

It is beyond the scope of this chapter to discuss the use of isokinetics at length; key considerations are summarised in Table 6.7 and can apply to assessment of other muscle groups (e.g. hip strength assessments). The authors recommend reading the chapter by Baltzopoulos (2008) for a more detailed review.

The joint angular position at which peak moment occurs is important to report, as it provides information about the mechanical properties of the activated muscle groups (Baltzopoulos, 2008). The knee flexor angle of peak moment has gained attention as a potential injury risk factor for HSI (Brockett et al., 2004). However, there is no clear evidence to provide support for this measure to predict HSI occurrence. It is believed that the angle of peak moment provides an indication of fascicle length and in-series sarcomere strain (Morgan, 1990) and it is hypothesised that eccentrically induced muscle damage is influenced by the proportion of range of motion (ROM) of a muscle on the descending limb of the force-length relationship, with this proportion of ROM thought to involve greater sarcomere instability, which predisposes to increases in muscle damage. However, the angle

Table 6.7 Summary of the key considerations for conducting isokinetic assessment.

Key variables	Strength during isokinetic assessment is quantified by the maximum moment and should be achieved within three to six repetitions (Baltzopoulos, 2008). An average moment (peak) from a number of trials should not be reported, as an average may be taken from different joint positions and thus does not provide information about the joint–moment position relationship (Baltzopoulos, 2008).
Angular velocity	Aside from the muscle group and mode of assessment (i.e. concentric vs. eccentric), practitioners need to decide on an appropriate angular velocity at which to assess. To assess strength, angular velocities $<60°·s^{-1}$ should be considered. Many practitioners may consider assessing at faster speeds $>180°·s^{-1}$, to provide an assessment at more functional sports-specific speeds. However, the measurement limits of many dynamometers (e.g. Biodex system 4 concentrically 500°/s; eccentrically 300°/s; Cybex Humac Norm 500°/s) fail to reach typical angular velocities achieved during many sports-specific movements (knee angular velocity during maximal instep kick in soccer: 1134±257 [Lees &Nolan, 2002]; maximum velocity sprinting –460 ± 86 to 601 ± 143°/s [Besodis et al., 2008]).
Joint alignment	Practitioners should ensure that the dynamometer axis is aligned to the best approximation of the joint axis, as any errors here could lead to (a) incorrect lever arm length of the limb in determining joint moment and (b) the force vector from the limb to the dynamometer not applied perpendicular to the lever. Practitioners should thoroughly ensure that the joint aligns to the dynamometer around the expected position of the angle of peak moment and ensure that compression of the subject's soft tissues and cushion of the dynamometer seat do not affect the alignment of the joint axis (Baltzopoulos, 2008).
Inspection of "isokinetic range"	Measurement at greater angular velocities reduces the available "isokinetic range" as greater ranges of movement are required to reach and decelerate from greater velocities. Thus, careful examination of the moment–angular velocity profiles is essential to ensure that peak moment at these greater velocities is achieved within isokinetic range and reliability of such measures may also be compromised.
Gravity correction	Data should be gravity-corrected to ensure that the peak moments of muscle groups working against gravity are not underestimated and those working with gravity are not overestimated. Most dynamometers include a function to assess the weight of the limb at a set position and this is then gravity-corrected throughout the full range of motion to ensure the gravity correction takes into account the changes in the gravitational lever arm throughout the full range of motion. It is recommended in the case of knee extensor and flexor strength assessment that the weight of the limb is measured at 30° of flexion (0° full extension of the knee) to ensure that tension from the hamstring muscle-tendon complex does not add to the weight of the limb if this was measured nearer to full knee extension (Baltzopoulos, 2008).

of peak moment in this regard has a number of limitations, as highlighted by Timmins et al. (2015), including: (1) the lack of muscle specificity with isokinetic assessment involving a group of muscles around the knee joint and their moment arm changes with a given knee angle, (2) the use of slow concentric muscle actions in the literature when high-speed eccentric muscle actions are of greater interest, (3) the low reliability of the measure and (4) the involvement of various neural contributions to the measure (e.g. RFD). Along with the lack of available evidence to support this measure to predict HSI, it cannot be recommended as a marker for HSI.

The use of isokinetics is considered by many to lack "functionality" due to the seated position adopted in, for example, assessment of knee extensor and flexor strength. However, such views maybe considered dismissive given that in trying to gather information to develop an injury profile, practitioners simply require a measure of the strength of a muscle group, rather than being concerned whether the test is "sports-specific", although the test position should attempt to assess at typical joint angles and ROM of competition actions performed by the athlete. Another limitation is the cost and availability of isokinetic dynamometers to practitioners.

NordBord™

Other measures of eccentric hamstring strength include the NordBord™. The NordBord™ is based on the Nordic hamstring lower (NHL) exercise, which has been widely used in hamstring-injury prevention programmes to develop eccentric hamstring strength (Mjolnes et al., 2004) and shown a great deal of efficacy in preventing HSI (Gabbe et al., 2006; Brooks et al., 2006; Arnason et al., 2008; Petersen et al., 2011; Van der Horst et al., 2015). During an NHL the athlete begins in a kneeling position and with support around the ankles slowly falls forward, attempting to resist the increasing gravitational moment by activation of the hamstrings. Once the athlete reaches a point where they can no longer resist the increasing gravitational moment they fall to the floor into a press-up position. A NordBord™ device measures the forces acting through both limbs where the athlete is supported through strain gauges. Opar et al. (2013) have reported the NordBord™ to be highly reliable (ICC = 0.83–0.90; CV = 5.8–8.5%) and able to detect residual weakness in previously injured elite athletes (Opar et al., 2013; Timmins et al. 2015). In a prospective study of HSI in Australian Rules football, Opar et al (2015) found that NordBord™ values <256 N at the start of pre-season and <279 N at the end of pre-season increased the chance of HSI by 2.7 and 4.3 times, respectively. Subsequently, Timmins et al. (2015) found NordBord™ values <337 N increased HSI in elite soccer players; in contrast, Bourne et al. (2015) found no association between low eccentric strength assessed through the NordBord™ and HSI in rugby union players of various levels during one season.

A limitation of the NordBord™ is the associated cost, limiting its widespread availability to a range of practitioners. However, a field-based option that would be more readily available is the Nordic Breakpoint Angle (NBPA) test, which basically involves the NHL videoed in the sagittal plane. Using video analysis techniques, the NBPA is determined (Figure 6.6) when the athlete can no longer resist the increasing gravitational moment. Sconce et al. (2015) found the NBPA to be strongly correlated to eccentric isokinetic knee flexor peak moment (average of both limbs) ($R = -0.808$; $r^2 = 65\%$) in 16 male and female soccer players. Thus, the NBPA could act as field-based assessment of eccentric knee flexor strength. However, obvious limitations include the inability to assess individual limbs, and allowing comparisons between subjects' variations in upper-body mass needs to be considered. Furthermore, although Sconce et al. (2015) reported good reliability (ICC = 0.969; CV = 4.85%; SEM = 1.47°), the authors used a subjective measure of NBPA. To overcome some of these limitations, an estimate of gravitational moment at breakpoint and monitoring the change in centre of mass (CM) velocity during the NHL could be used to identify the sudden increase in CM velocity when the athletes stop resisting during the NHL.

Figure 6.6 A Nordic Hamstring Lower with Nordic breakpoint angle illustrated. Breakpoint is the frame of video at which the athlete can no longer resist the increasing gravitational moment.

Reciprocal knee joint muscle strength imbalance

Reciprocal knee joint muscle strength imbalance has traditionally been assessed by the isokinetic concentric flexor (hamstrings) to concentric extensor (quadriceps) peak moment ratio (CON:H/Q) and several studies have found low CON:H/Q to be associated with HSI amongst athletes (Yamamoto, 1993; Orchard et al., 1997; Cameron et al., 2003; Yeung et al., 2009). In contrast, others have not found any relationship between muscle balance ratios and HSI (Bennell et al., 1998). A limitation of the CON:H/Q is that it is not specific to the mechanism of HSI. As the quadriceps contract concentrically the hamstrings lengthen passively before contracting eccentrically to decelerate the lower limb and stabilise the knee joint. This lack of specificity could be the reason behind the inconclusive evidence that the CON:H/Q predicts HSI (Bennell et al., 1998).

To overcome this limitation a "dynamic control ratio" (eccentric hamstrings/ concentric quadriceps) (DCR) was proposed (Aagaard et al., 1998), which takes into account the functional role of the hamstrings about the knee joint (during late swing phase). Previous research has not found either the CON:H/Q or DCR to be able to predict HSI in Australian Rules footballers (Bennell et al., 1998). Similarly, Henderson et al. (2010) found no evidence that hamstring strength or ratios show an increased chance of HSI, whilst a meta-analysis (Freckleton & Pizzari, 2013) questioned the use of both ratios as HSI risk factors, as often studies have insufficient sample size and lack consistency with the choice of measurement velocities.

One criticism of the DCR is that it only takes into account the peak moment values, which can occur at different angular positions in the overall ROM and are not joint-angle-specific. This has been acknowledged previously (Aagaard et al., 1998) by representing the DCRs at angles of 30°, 40° and 50° of knee flexion and angle-specific ratios have been reported in soccer players (Evangelidis et al., 2015). However, due to inter-subject variability in moment-angle plots, such an approach is difficult to interpret, as a decision has to be made regarding which ratio is more meaningful.

Coombs and Garbutt (2002) suggested representing the DCR throughout the whole ROM and finding a "point of equality" (DCR equilibrium point) where the DCR equals one, whereas Graham-Smith et al. (2013) proposed a "dynamic control profile" (DCP), which involves representing the net joint moment (eccentric flexor – concentric extensor) over the entire ROM (Figure 6.7) and identifies the ROM whereby the knee flexors (hamstrings) eccentrically are stronger than the knee extensors (quadriceps) concentrically (angle of cross-over [AOC]). The rationale is that the greater this range is (i.e. the AOC is closer to 90° of flexion), then the greater is the range in which the hamstrings can control the moment generated by the quadriceps and possibly a reduced risk of injury. Graham-Smith et al. (2013) reported excellent between-session reliability for the angle of cross-over (ICC = 0.934; SEM = 1.94°; CV = 5.88%) in 23 male team sport athletes at $60°·s^{-1}$, better than traditional (ICC = 0.875; SEM = 0.03, CV = 6.08%) and DCR (ICC = 0.85; SEM = 0.04, CV = 6.32%) and angle-specific ratios (DCR 50°; ICC = 0.935; SEM = 0.04, CV = 6.41%; DCR 40°; ICC = 0.923; SEM = 0.08, CV = 6.41%; DCR 30°; ICC = 0.939; SEM = 0.08, CV = 7.23%). Alt et al. (2016) examined the reliability of the DCR equilibrium (DCRe) angle and moment in 33 males by examining the isokinetic strength of the knee flexors and extensors in prone and supine positions, respectively. The authors reported systematic bias for DCRe moment at $30°·s^{-1}$ only in this variable over three test occasions and that relative and absolute reliability improved with increasing angular velocity (DCRe angle; $30°·s^{-1}$; ICC = 0.699; SEM = 11.2%; $90°·s^{-1}$; ICC = 0.804; SEM = 7.2%; $150°·s^{-1}$ = 0.833; SEM = 6.4%; DCRe moment; $30°·s^{-1}$; ICC = 0.619; SEM = 11.4%; $90°·s^{-1}$; ICC = 0.820; SEM = 6.6%; $150°·s^{-1}$ = 0.906; SEM = 4.9%) and that it was equivalent to traditional and DCR methods. Despite the good reliability reported there is a lack of studies that have examined the efficacy of using angle-specific methods to find "at-risk" athletes. However, recent research (Van Dyk et al., 2017) examining the clinical value of a range of isokinetic and NordBord™ hamstring strength and muscle balance characteristics in 413 professional soccer players in the Qatar league found no association with the occurrence of HSI. This again highlights the multifactorial nature of such injuries.

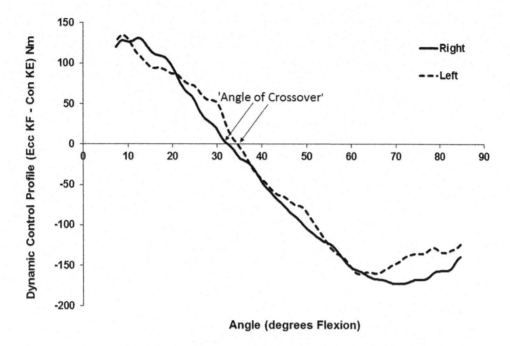

Figure 6.7 The Dynamic Control Profile represents the net joint moment (eccentric knee flexors (KF) – concentric knee extensors (KE)) throughout the full range of motion (0° [full knee extension] to 90° of flexion). The point that the net joint moment crosses zero on the *x*-axis is the angle of cross-over, whereby the moment generated by the knee extensors concentrically supersedes the knee flexors eccentrically (Graham-Smith et al., 2013).

Bilateral strength imbalance

Muscle imbalance describes substantial deviation from normative data or muscle performance difference between limbs (Impellizzeri et al., 2007; Schlumberger, et al., 2008). Handedness, previous injury or specific sport demands are possible reasons that could lead to bilateral muscle imbalances or muscle strength asymmetry (MSA) in athletes (Newton et al., 2006; Jones & Bampouras, 2010).

Previous research has found an association between bilateral hamstring imbalance determined through isokinetics and HSI (Orchard et al., 1997; Crosier et al., 2002; Fousekis et al., 2010), whilst some have suggested that bilateral imbalance is associated with non-contact ACL injury (Hewett et al., 1996; Myer et al., 2004). Using the NordBord™, Bourne et al. (2015) found that bilateral strength imbalance was associated with HSI, with >15% and >20% (uninjured limb/injured limb ratio converted to a percentage) leading to 2.4- and 3.6-fold increases in HSI, respectively. Conversely, Opar et al. (2015) and Timmins et al. (2015) did not find strength asymmetry >10% to increase the risk of HSI.

Currently there are several methodological issues regarding determination of MSA: firstly, the variety of formulas available to determine MSA. In a review Bishop et al. (2016), identified nine different formulas to determine MSA (Table 6.8); the variety of formulas used was due to asymmetries being reported based on right vs. left, dominant vs. non-dominant

Table 6.8 Variation of methods to assess reciprocal and bilateral muscle strength imbalance.

Measure	Method	Reference
Reciprocal		
Traditional ratio	Peak CON KF moment/peak CON KE moment.	Yammamoto et al. (1993); Cameron et al. (2003); Orchard et al. (1997)
Dynamic control ratio (DCR)	Peak ECC KF moment/peak CON KE moment.	Aagaard et al. (1998)
Angle-specific ratios	Establish traditional and DCR ratios at specified angles with 10-degree increments.	Aagaard et al. (1998); Coombs & Garbutt (2002)
DCRe angle	Angle of flexion from anatomical zero (straight limb) whereby peak moment profiles for ECC KF moment and CON KE moment cross.	Coombs & Garbutt (2002); Alt et al. (2016)
Angle of crossover	The dynamic control profile represents the net joint moment (ECC KF – CON KE) throughout the full ROM (0° [full knee extension] to 90° of flexion). The angle at which the net joint moment decreases below zero is the angle of crossover.	Graham-Smith et al. (2013)
Bilateral		
Limb symmetry index 1	(NDL/DL) × 100	Munro & Herrington (2011)
Limb symmetry index 2	(1 – NDL/DL) × 100	Schilitz et al. (2009)
Limb symmetry index 3	(Right – left)/0.5 (right – left) × 100	Bell et al. (2014)
Bilateral strength asymmetry	(Strong limb – weak limb)/strong limb × 100	Impellizzeri *et al.* (2007)
Bilateral asymmetry index 1	(DL – NDL)/(DL + NDL) × 100	Kobayashi et al. (2013)
Bilateral asymmetry index 2	[2 × (DL – NDL)/(DL + NDL)] × 100	Sugiyama et al. (2014)
Asymmetry index	(DL – NDL)/(DL + NDL/2) × 100	Robinson et al. (1987)
Symmetry index	(High/low)/total × 100	Sato & Heise (2012)
Absolute asymmetry	(Right – left)/(max: right or left) × 100	Aldukhail et al. (2013)
Asymmetry angle (ASA)	45° – ARCTAN (left/right)/90° × 100	Zifchock et al. (2008)

CON KF = concentric knee flexor; CON KE = concentric knee extensor; ECC KF = eccentric knee flexor; ROM = range of motion; DL = dominant leg; NDL = non-dominant leg.

and strong vs. weak, preferred and non-preferred limb comparisons. Furthermore variety exists in which limb (strong, weak, right/left, maximum of both or average of both) acts as the reference (denominator) value. Bampouras and Dewhurst (2017) compared asymmetry values in timed 6 m hop and three-hop tests when using absolute difference as the numerator and varied denominator values (strong, weak, right, left and average of the two). The authors found no practical significant difference between values when using different denominator values, but a sex × calculation method interaction suggested that for gender comparisons the right leg should be used as the denominator. Moreover, Bishop et al. (2016) using example data suggested similar asymmetry values are observed between many

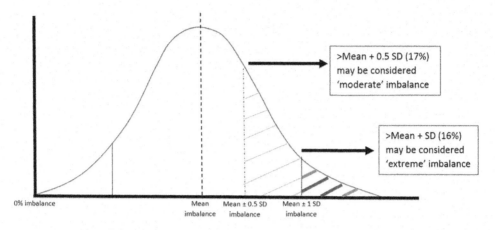

Figure 6.8 Hypothetical model for determining a cut-off threshold to identify bilateral muscle strength imbalances for a given muscle strength quality in a specific population.

of the different asymmetry formulas. However, the authors recommended that strong and weak comparisons should not be used if looking to track asymmetry in athletes, as due to injury numerator and denominator values could change due to detraining of the injured leg and thus different values are being compared. Furthermore, Bishop et al. (2016) argued that the asymmetry angle (Table 6.8) developed by Zifchock et al. (2008) avoids much of the confusion of which limb should act as the denominator. However, currently there is a lack of sports performance and injury research utilising the asymmetry angle.

A second issue with regard to asymmetry is what values (e.g. cut-off percentage) would be considered as detrimental for injury risk. Previous suggestions for detecting MSA have suggested >10–15% between limbs (Kannus, 1994). Specifically, with hop test an LSI of greater than 85% (15% imbalance) (Barber et al., 1990) indicates that "normal" limb symmetry exists, whereas others proposed an LSI of 90% (10% imbalance) as normal (Munro and Herrington, 2011). However, the level of MSA is dependent on the mode of assessment and muscle strength quality under investigation (Jones & Bampouras, 2010). Aldukhail et al. (2013) and Graham-Smith et al. (2015) have suggested the use of mean + standard deviation absolute asymmetry of a given population in order to determine cut-off criteria for detecting MSA and revealed differences in cut-off percentages for isokinetics, hop and vertical jump tests (Aldukhail et al., 2013). This may be considered a conservative estimate to find athletes with "high" imbalance which would represent 16% of a given population of athletes based on typical normal distribution (Figure 6.8) and may be considered a realistic approximation given the lack of evidence associating MSA with performance decrement and injury risk. Less conservative estimates such as using the absolute mean ± 0.2 SD (43.2% considered imbalanced) have been utilised in sports performance literature in an attempt to identify a cut-off in MSA that could lead to performance decrement (Lockie et al., 2014; Dos'Santos et al., 2017). Whilst attempts have been made to examine whether MSA influences performance, no literature has examined different cut-off criteria and the influence on injury risk. More research is required to examine potential cut-off criteria for diagnosing MSA and whether this can be used to examine potential injury risk, in particular, establishing population norms using standardised assessment methods to be able to identify potential cut-offs.

6.7 Summary

The primary function of any screening activity is to identify those individuals at elevated risk of injury. Having read through this chapter it should become plain that this is not a simple task and it is unlikely that a single test will be able to fulfil this function. The best which can be achieved is to identify those individuals who have an increased predisposition to injury because of the deficits demonstrated whilst undertaking the tasks. It would appear that they are more likely to become injured if the loads they are exposed to are increased rapidly in a non-progressive manner. This is an important statement as failing the test does not guarantee you will get injured; equally passing does not guarantee an injury-free future! What screening achieves is the identification of the degree of vulnerability which could be exposed if subjected to rapid changes in loading stress.

If screening tests are going to identify the vulnerable predisposed individuals, they need to show both reliability and validity, in order to be robust enough to identify meaningful differences in performance. When conducting any screening tests it is critical then to minimise any random and systematic errors, so all testing needs to be carefully planned and all tests practised in advance. Failure to do so is likely to create so much measurement noise that any meaningful differences in scores or performance will be lost.

When an athlete has been identified as predisposed to injury through the screening test(s), the reasons why they have failed need to be identified so a management plan can be put in place to reduce their vulnerability. To maximise the success of these interventions, they need to be tailored to the individual and the unique reasons why they have failed the screening tasks and so became vulnerable.

References

Aagard, P., Simonsen, E.B., Magnusson, S.P., Larsson, B., & Dyhre-Poulsen, P. (1998). A new concept for isokinetic hamstring: quadriceps muscle strength ratio. *American Journal of Sports Medicine, 26*(2), 231–237

Abernethy, L., & Bleakley, C. (2007) Strategies to prevent injury in adolescent sport: a systematic review. *British Journal of Sports Medicine. 41*, 627–638.

Adams, D., Logerstedt, D.S., Hunter-Giordano, A., Axe, M.J., & Snyder-Mackler, L. (2012). Current concepts for anterior cruciate ligament reconstruction: a criterion-based rehabilitation progression. *Journal of Orthopaedic and Sports Physical Therapy, 42*, 601–614.

Aldukhail, A., Jones, P.A., Gilliard, H., & Graham-Smith, P. (2013). Clinical diagnosis of muscle strength asymmetry. In: *The 19th Congress of the European Society of Biomechanics*, 25–28 August 2013, Patras, Greece.

Alenezi, F., Herrington, L., Jones, P., & Jones, R. (2014). Relationships between lower limb biomechanics during single leg squat with running and cutting tasks: a preliminary investigation. *British Journal of Sports Medicine, 48*, 560–561.

Alonso, J.-M., Junge, A., Renstrom, P., Engebretsen, L., Mountjoy, M., & Dvorak, J. (2009). Sports Injuries surveillance during the 2007 IAAF World Athletics Championships. *Clinical Journal of Sports Medicine, 19*(1); 26–32.

Alonso, J.-M., Tscholl, P.M., Engebretsen, L., Mountjoy, M., Dvorak, J.. & Junge, A. (2010). Occurrence of injuries and illnesses during the 2009 IAAF World Athletics Championships. *British Journal of Sports Medicine. 44*, 1100–1105.

Alonso, J.-M., Edouard, P., Fischetto, G., Adams, B., Depiesse, F., & Mountjoy, M. (2012). Determination of future prevention strategies in elite track and field: analysis of Daegu 2011 IAAF Championships injuries and illnesses surveillance. *British Journal of Sports Medicine, 46*, 505–514.

Alt, T., Knicker, A.J., & Strüder, H.K. (2016).The dynamic control ratio at the equilibrium point (DCRe): introducing relative and absolute reliability scores. *Journal of Sports Sciences.* doi: 10.1080/02640414.2016.1184298.

Arnason, A., Anderson, T.E., Holme, I., Engebretsen, L., & Bahr, R. (2008). Prevention of hamstring strains in elite soccer: an intervention study. *Scandinavian Journal of Medicine & Science in Sports, 18,* 40–48.

Atkin, K., Herrington, L., Alenzi, F., Jones, P.A., & Jones, R. (2014). The relationship between 2D knee valgus angle during single leg squat, single leg landing and forward running. *British Journal of Sports Medicine, 48,* 563.

Atkinson, G., & Nevill, A.M. (1998). Statistical methods for assessing measurement error (reliability) in variables relevant to sports medicine. *Sports Medicine, 26*(4); 217–238

Attenborough, A., Sinclair, P., Sharp, T., Greene, A., Stuelcken, M., Smith, R., & Hiller, C. (2017). The identification of risk factors for ankle sprains sustained during netball participation. *Physical Therapy in Sport, 23,* 31–36.

Bahr, R. (2016). Why screening tests to predict injury do not work—and probably never will…: a critical review. *British Journal of Sports Medicine, 50,* 776–780.

Bampouras, T.M., & Dewhurst, S. (2018). A comparison of bilateral muscular imbalance ratio calculations using functional tests. *Journal of Strength & Conditioning Research, 32*(8), 2216–2220.

Baltzopoulos, V. (2008) Isokinetic dynamometry. In C. Payton & R. Bartlett (Eds.), *Biomechanical evaluation of movement in sport and exercise. The British Association of Sport and Exercise Sciences Guidelines* (2nd ed., pp 103–128). London: Routledge.

Barber, S.D., Noyes, F.R., Mangine, R.E., McCloskey, J.W., & Hartman, W. (1990). Quantitative assessment of functional limitations in normal and anterior cruciate ligament-deficient knees. *Clinical Orthopaedics and Related Research, 255,* 204–214.

Batterham, A.M., & George, K. (2003). Reliability in evidence-based clinical practice: A primer for allied health professionals. *Physical Therapy in Sport, 4*(3), 122–128.

Bengtsson, H., Ekstrand, J., & Hägglund, M. (2013). Muscle injury rates in professional football increase with fixture congestion: an 11-year follow-up of the UEFA Champions League injury study. *British Journal of Sports Medicine, 47,* 743–747.

Bell, D.R., Sanfilippo, J.L., Binkley, N., & Heiderscheit, B.C. (2014). Lean mass asymmetry influences force and power asymmetry during jumping in collegiate athletes. *The Journal of Strength & Conditioning Research, 28,* 884–891.

Bennell, K., Wajswelner, H., Lew, P., Schall-Riaucour, A., Leslie, S., Plant, D., & Cirone, J. (1998). Isokinetic strength testing does not predict hamstring injury in Australian rules footballers. *British Journal of Sports Medicine, 32,* 309–314.

Besodis, I.N., Kerwin, D.G., & Salo, A. (2008). Lower-limb mechanics during the support phase of maximum-velocity sprint running. *Medicine and Science in Sports and Exercise, 40*(4), 707–715.

Bishop, C., Read, P., Chavda, S., & Turner, A. (2016). Asymmetries of the lower limb: The calculation conundrum in strength training and conditioning. *Strength and Conditioning Journal, 38,* 27–32.

Blanch, P., & Gabbett, T. (2016). Has the athlete trained enough to return to play safely? The acute-chronic workload permits clinicians to quantify a players risk. *British Journal of Sports Medicine, 50*(8), 471–475.

Bohannon, R.W., Vigneault, J., & Rizzon, J. (2008). Hip external and internal rotation strength: Consistency over time and between sides. *Isokinetics and Exercise Science, 16* (2), 107–111.

Bolgla, L.A., & Keskula, D.R. (1997). Reliability of lower extremity functional performance tests. *Journal of Orthopaedic and Sports Physical Therapy, 26,* 138–142.

Bourne, M.N., Opar, D.A, Williams, M.D., & Shield, A.J. (2015). Eccentric knee flexor strength and risk of hamstring injuries in rugby union: a prospective study. *American Journal of Sports Medicine, 43* (11), 2663–2670.

Brockett, C.L., Morgan, D.L., & Proske, U. (2004). Predicting hamstring strain injury in elite athletes. *Medicine and Science in Sports and Exercise, 36*, 379–387.

Brooks, J.H.M., Fuller, C.W., Kemp, S.P.T., & Reddin, D.B. (2005a). Epidemiology of injuries in English professional rugby union: part1 match injuries. *British Journal of Sports Medicine, 39*(10), 757–766.

Brooks, J.H.M., Fuller, C.W., Kemp, S.P.T., & Reddin, D.B. (2005b). Epidemiology of injuries in English professional rugby union: part 2 training injuries. *British Journal of Sports Medicine, 39*(10), 767–775.

Brooks, J.H.M, Fuller, C.W., Kemp, S.P.T., & Reddin, D.B. (2006). Incidence, risk and prevention of hamstring muscle injuries in professional rugby union. *American Journal of Sports Medicine, 34*, 1297–1306.

Caffrey, E., Docherty, C.L., Schrader, J., & Klossner, J. (2009). The Ability of 4 single-limb hopping tests to detect functional performance deficits in individuals with functional ankle instability. *Journal of Orthopaedic & Sports Physical Therapy, 39*, 799–806.

Cameron, M., Adams, R., & Maher, C. (2003). Motor control and strength as predictors of hamstring injury in elite players of Australian football. *Physical Therapy in Sport, 4*, 159–166.

Claiborne, T.L., Armstrong, C.W., Gandhi, V., & Pincivero, D.M. (2006). Relationship between hip and knee strength and knee valgus during a single leg squat, *Journal of Applied Biomechanics, 22*(1), 41–50.

Clark, N.C. (2001). Functional performance testing following knee ligament injury. *Physical Therapy In Sport, 2*, 91–105.

Cools, A., Wilde, L.D., van Tongel, A., & Cambier, D. (2014). Measuring shoulder external and internal rotation strength with a hand-held dynamometer, and range of motion using a goniometer and a digital inclinometer: Comprehensive intra- and inter rater reliability study of several testing protocols. *British Journal of Sports Medicine, 48*, 580–581. doi:10.1136/bjsports-2014-093494.56.

Coombs, R., & Garbutt, G. (2002). Developments in the use of the hamstring/quadriceps ratio for the assessment of muscle balance. *Journal of Sports Science and Medicine, 1*(3), 56–62.

Cornell, D., Gnacinski, S., Zamzow, A., Mims J., & Ebersole, K. (2016). Influence of body mass index on movement efficiency among firefighter recruits *Work, 54*(3), 679–687.

Croisier, J.L., Forthomme, B., Namurois, M.H., Vanderthommen, M., & Crielaard, J.M. (2002). Hamstring muscle strain recurrence and strength performance disorders. *American Journal of Sports Medicine, 30*, 199–203.

Crow, J.F., Pearce, A.J., Veale, J.P., Vander-Westhuizen, D., Coburn, P.T., & Pizzari, T. (2009). Hip adductor muscle strength is reduced preceding and during the onset of groin pain in elite junior Australian football players. *Journal of Science and Medicine in Sport, 13*, 202–204.

Delahunt, E., McEntee, B.L., Kennelly, C., Coughlan, G.F., & Green, B.S. (2011a). The thigh adductor squeeze test: 45° of hip flexion as the optimal test position for eliciting adductor muscle activity and maximum pressure values. *Manual Therapy, 16*, 476–480.

Delahunt, E., McEntee, B.L., Kennelly, C., Green, B.S., & Coughlan, G.F. (2011b). Intrarater reliability of the adductor squeeze test in Gaelic Games athletes. *Journal of Athletic Training, 46*(3), 241–245.

Denegar, C.R., & Ball, D.W. (1993). Assessing reliability and precision of measurement: an introduction to intraclass correlation and standard error of measurement. *Journal of Sports Rehabilitation, 2*(1), 35–42.

De Noronha, M., Franca, L., Haupenthal, A., & Nunes, G. (2013). Intrinsic predictive factors for ankle sprain in active university students. *Scandinavian Journal of Medicine & Science in Sports, 23*(5), 541–547.

Dos'Santos, T., Thomas, C., Jones, P.A., & Comfort, P. (2017). Asymmetries in single and triple hop are not detrimental to change of direction speed. *Journal of Trainology, 6*(2), 35–41.

Dudley, L., Smith, C., Olson, B., Chimera, N., Schmitz, B., & Warren, M. 2013 Interrater and intrarater reliability of the tuck jump assessment by health professionals of varied educational backgrounds. *Journal of Sports Medicine.* doi: 10.1155/2013/483503.

Duhig, S., Shield, A.J., Opar, D., Gabbett, T.J., Ferguson, C., & Williams, M. (2016). Effect of high-speed running on hamstring strain injury risk. *British Journal of Sports Medicine, 50,* 1536–1540.

Eastlack, M., Axe, M., & Snyder-Mackler, L. (1999). Laxity, instability, and functional outcome after ACL injury: copers versus non-copers. *Medicine and Science in Sports and Exercise, 31,* 210–215.

Eliasziw, M., Young, S.L., Woodbury, M.G., & Fryday-Field, K. (1994). Statistical methodology for the concurrent assessment of interrater and intrarater reliability: using goniometric measurements as an example. *Physical Therapy, 74*(8), 777–778.

Ekstrand, J., Hägglund, M., & Waldén, M. (2011a). Epidemiology of muscle injuries in professional football (soccer). *American Journal of Sports Medicine, 39,* 1226–1232.

Ekstrand, J., Hägglund, M., & Waldén, M. (2011b). Injury incidence and injury patterns in professional football: the UEFA injury study. *British Journal of Sports Medicine, 45,* 553–558.

Ekstrand, J., Hägglund, M., Kristenson, K., Magnusson, H., & Waldén, M. (2013). Fewer ligament injuries but no preventive effect on muscle injuries and severe injuries: an 11-year follow-up of the UEFA Champions League injury study. *British Journal of Sports Medicine, 47,* 732–737.

Emery, C.A., Meeuwisse, W.H., & Powell, J.W. (1999). Groin and abdominal strain injuries in the National Hockey League. *Clinical Journal of Sport Medicine, 9,* 151–156.

Enquist, K., Smith, C., Chimera, N., & Warren, M. (2015). Performance comparison of student athletes and general college students on the FMS and the Y balance tests. *The Journal of Strength & Conditioning Research, 29*(8), 2296–2303.

Evangelidis, P.E., Pain, M.T.G., & Folland, J. (2015). Angle-specific hamstring-to-quadriceps ratio: A comparison of football players and recreationally active males. *Journal of Sports Sciences, 33*(3), 309–319.

Faude, O., Junge, A., Kindermann, W., & Dvorak, J. (2005). Injuries in female soccer players – A prospective study in the German national league. *American Journal of Sports Medicine, 33,* 1694–1700.

Fitzgerald, G.K., Axe, M.J., & Snyder-Mackler, L. (2000). Proposed practice guidelines for nonoperative anterior cruciate ligament rehabilitation of physically active individuals. *Journal of Orthopaedic and Sports Physical Therapy, 30,* 194–203.

Fousekis, K., Tsepis, E., & Vagenas, G. (2010). Lower limb strength in professional soccer players: Profile, asymmetry, and training age. *Journal of Sports Science and Medicine, 9,* 364–373.

Fort-Vanmeerhaeghe, A., Montalvo, A., Lloyd, R., Read, P., & Myer, G. (2017). Intra and inter rater reliability of the modified tuck jump test. *Journal of Sports Science and Medicine, 16*(1), 117–124.

Freckleton, G., & Pizzari, T. (2013). Risk factors for hamstring muscle strain injury in sport: A systematic review and meta-analysis. *British Journal of Sports Medicine, 47*(6), 351–358.

Fulcher, M.L., Hanna, C.M., & Raina-Elley, C. (2010). Reliability of handheld dynamometry in assessment of hip strength in adult male football players. *Journal of Science and Medicine in Sport, 13,* 80–84.

Fuller, J., Chalmers, S., Debendictis, T., Townsley, S., Lynagh, M., Gleeson, C., Zacharia, A., Thomson, S., & Margarey, M. (2017). High prevalence of dysfunctional, asymmetrical and painful movement in junior Australian football players assessed using the FMS. *Journal of Science and Medicine in Sport, 20*(2), 134–138

Gabbe, B.J, Branson, R., & Bennell, K.L. (2006). A pilot randomised controlled trial of eccentric exercise to prevent hamstring injuries in community-level Australian football. *Journal of Science and Medicine in Sport, 9,* 103–109.

Goh, S., & Boyle, J. (1997). Self evaluation and functional testing two to four years post ACL reconstruction. *Australian Journal of Physiotherapy, 43*, 255–262.

Graham-Smith, P., Jones, P.A., Comfort, P., & Munro, A.G. (2013). The reliability of a new method to assess knee joint muscle strength imbalance. *International Journal of Athletic Therapy & Training,18*(5), 1–5.

Graham-Smith, P., Aldukhail, A., & Jones, P.A. (2015). Agreement between attributes associated with bilateral jump asymmetry. *Poster presented at the International Society of Biomechanics in Sport conference*, 29 June – 3 July 2015, Poitiers, France.

Greenberger, H.B., & Paterno, M.V. (1995). Relationship of knee extensor strength and hopping test performance in the assessment of lower extremity function. *Journal of Orthopaedic & Sports Physical Therapy, 22*, 202–206.

Gribble, P., Terada, M., Beard, M., Kosik, K., Lepley, A., McCann, R., Pietrosimone, B., & Thomas, A. (2016). Prediction of lateral ankle sprains in football players based on clinical tests and body mass. *American Journal of Sports Medicine, 44*(2), 460–467.

Grindem, H., Logerstedt, D., Eitzen, I., Moksnes, H., Axe, M.J., Snyder-Mackler, L., Engebretsen, L., & Risberg, M.A. (2011). Single-legged hop tests as predictors of self-reported knee function in nonoperatively treated individuals with anterior cruciate ligament injury. *American Journal of Sports Medicine, 39*, 2347–2354.

Hamilton, R.T., Shultz, S.J., Schmitz, R.J., & Perrin, D.H. (2008). Triple-hop distance as a valid predictor of lower limb strength and power. *Journal of Athletic Training, 43*, 144–151.

Hartigan, E., Lawrence, M., Bisson, B., Torgerson, E., & Knight, R. (2014). Relationship of the FMS screen in line lunge to power, speed and balance measures. *Sports Health, 6*(3), 197–202.

Harty, C.M., Dupont, C.E., Chmielewski, T.L., & Mizner, R.L. (2011). Intertask comparison of frontal plane knee position and moment in female athletes during three distinct movement tasks. *Scandinavian Journal Of Medicine & Science In Sports, 21*, 98–105.

Hawkins, R.D., Hulse, M.A., Wilkinson, C., Hodson, A., & Gibson, M. (2001). The association football medical research programme: an audit of injuries in professional football. *British Journal of Sports Medicine, 35*, 43–47.

Heiderscheit, B.C., Hoerth, D.M., Chumanov, E.S., Swanson, S.C., Thelen, B.J., & Thelen, D.G. (2005). Identifying the time of occurrence of a hamstring strain injury during treadmill running: A case study. *Clinical Biomechanics, 20*, 1072–1078.

Henderson, G., Barnes, C.A., & Portas, M.D. (2010). Factors associated with increased propensity for hamstring injury in English Premier League soccer players. *Journal of Science and Medicine in Sport, 13*, 397–402

Herrington, L., & Munro, A. (2010). Drop jump landing knee valgus angle; normative data in a physically active population. *Physical Therapy in Sport, 11*, 56–59.

Herrington, L., Myer, G., & Munro, A. (2013). Intra and intertester reliability of the tuck jump assessment. *Physical Therapy in Sport, 14*(3), 152–155.

Herrington, L., & Munro, A. (2014). A Preliminary investigation to establish the criterion validity of a qualitative scoring system of limb alignment during single leg squat and landing. *Journal of Exercise, Sports & Orthopedics, 1*, 1–6.

Hewett, T.E., Myer, G.D., Ford, K.R., Heidt, R.S., Jr., Colosimo, A.J., Mclean, S.G., Paterno, M.V., & Succop, P. (2005). Biomechanical measures of neuromuscular control and valgus loading of the knee predict anterior cruciate ligament injury risk in female athletes: a prospective study. *American Journal of Sports Medicine, 33*, 492–501.

Hewett, T.E., Stroupe, A.L., Nance, T.A., & Noyes, F.R. (1996). Plyometric training in female athletes. Decreased impact forces and increased hamstring torques. *American Journal of Sports Medicine, 24*(6), 765–773.

Hogg, P., Warren, M., Smith, C., & Chimera, N. 2016 Functional hop tests and tuck jump assessment scores between female division 1 collegiate athletes participating in high vs. low ACL injury risk sports. ATPA combined sections Meeting.

Hollman, J.H., Ginos, B.E., Kozuchowski, J., Vaughn, A.S., Krause, D.A., & Youdas, J.W. (2009). Relationships between knee valgus, hip-muscle strength, and hip-muscle recruitment during a single-limb step-down. *Journal of Sports Rehabilitation, 18*(1), 104–117.

Hopkins, W.G. (2000). Measures of reliability in sports medicine and science. *Sports Medicine, 30*(1), 1–15.

Horobin, P., & Thawley, P. (2015). Prospective use of a neuromuscular screening tool to determine risk of athletic injury. *British Journal of Sports Medicine, 49,* 1416.

Imwalle, L.E., Myer, G.D., Ford, K.R., & Hewett, T.E. (2009). Relationships between hip and knee kinematics in athletic women during cutting maneuvers: A possible link to noncontact anterior cruciate ligament injury and prevention. *Journal of Strength & Conditioning Research, 23*(8), 2223–2230.

Impellizzeri, F.M., Rampinini, E., Maffiuletti, N., & Marcora SM. (2007). A vertical jump force test for assessing bilateral strength asymmetry in athletes. *Medicine & Science in Sports & Exercise, 39*(11), 2044–2050.

Jacobs, C.A., Uhl, T.L., Mattacola, C.G., Shapiro, R., & Rayens, W.S. (2007). Hip abductor function and lower extremity landing kinematics: Sex differences. *Journal of Athletic Training, 42*(1), 76–83.

Jones, P.A., & Bampouras, T.M. (2010). A comparison of isokinetic and functional methods of assessing bilateral strength imbalance. *Journal of Strength & Conditioning Research, 24*(6), 1553–1558.

Jones, P.A., Herrington, L.C., Munro, A.G., & Graham-Smith, P. (2014). Is there a relationship between landing, cutting, and pivoting tasks in terms of the characteristics of dynamic valgus? *American Journal of Sports Medicine, 42,* 2095–2102.

Jonhagen, S., Nemeth, G., & Eriksson, E. (1994). Hamstring injuries in sprinters. The role of concentric and eccentric hamstring muscle strength and flexibility. *American Journal of Sports Medicine, 22,* 262–266.

Kannus, P. (1994) Isokinetic evaluation of muscular performance: implications for muscle testing and rehabilitation. *International Journal of Sports Medicine, 15,* S11–S18.

Kawaguchi, J.K., & Babcock, G. (2010). Validity and reliability of handheld dynametric strength assessment of hip extensor and abductor muscles. *Athletic Training and Sports Health Care, 2*(1), 11–17.

Kelln, B.M., Mckeon, P.O., Gontkof, L.M., & Hertel, J. (2008). Hand-held dynamometry: Reliability of lower extremity muscle testing in healthy, physically active, young adults. *Journal of Sport Rehabilitation, 17*(2), 160–170.

Kiesel, K., Plisky, P., & Voight M. (2007). Can serious injury in professional football be predicted by a preseason FMS? *North American Journal of Sports Physical Therapy, 2*(3), 147–158.

Kiesel, K., Butler, R., & Plisky, P. (2014). Prediction of injury by limited and asymmetrical functional movement patterns in American football players. *Journal of Sports Rehabilitation, 23*(2), 88–94.

Kobayashi, Y., Kubo, J., Matsubayashi, T., Matsuo, A., Kobayashi, K., & Ishii, N. (2013). Relationship between bilateral differences in single-leg jumps and asymmetry in isokinetic knee strength. *Journal of Applied Biomechanics, 9,* 61–67.

Kollock, R.O., Onate, J.A., & Van Lunen, B.L. (2008). Clinical evaluation and testing: assessing muscular strength at the hip joint. *Athletic Therapy Today, 13*(2), 18–24.

Kristianlund, E., & Krosshaug, T. (2013). Comparison of drop jumps and sportspecific sidestep cutting. *American Journal of Sports Medicine, 41,* 684–688.

Lauersen, J.B., Bertelsen, D.M., & Andersen, L.B. (2014). The effectiveness of exercise interventions to prevent sports injuries: a systematic review and meta-analysis of randomised controlled trials. *British Journal of Sports Medicine, 48,* 871–877.

Lawrence, R.K., Kernozek, T.W., Miller, E.J., Torry, M.R., & Reuteman, P. (2008). Influences of hip external rotation strength on knee mechanics during single-leg landings in females. *Clinical Biomechanics, 23*(6), 806–813.

Lees, A., & Nolan, L. (2002). In W. Spinks, T. Reilly & A. Murphy (Eds.), *Three-dimensional kinematic analysis of the instep kick under speed and accuracy conditions: Science and football IV* (pp. 16–21). London: Routledge.

Leetun, D.T., Lloyd-Ireland, M., Willson, J.D., Ballantyne, B.T., & McClay-Davis, I. (2004). Core stability measures as risk factors for lower extremity injury in athletes. *Medicine and Science in Sports and Exercise, 36*(6), 926–934.

Lephart, S., Perrin, D., Fu, F., Gieck, J., McCue, F., & Irrgang, J. (1992). Relationship between selected physical characteristics and functional capacity in the anterior cruciate ligament insufficient athlete. *Journal of Orthopaedic and Sports Physical Therapy, 16*, 174–181.

Lephart, S.M. & Henry, T.J. (1995). Functional rehabilitation for the upper and lower-extremity. *Orthopedic Clinics of North America, 26*, 579–592.

Lloyd-Ireland, M., Willson, J.D., Ballantyne, B.T., & Mcclay Davis, I. (2003) Hip strength in females with and without patellofemoral pain. *Journal of Orthopaedic and Sports Physical Therapy, 33*(11), 671–676.

Letafatkar, A., Hadadnezhad, M., Shojaedin, S., & Mohamadi, E. (2014). Relationship of FMS score and history of injury. *International Journal of Sports Physical Therapy, 9*(1), 21–27.

Lockie, R.G., Callaghan, S.J., Berry, S.P., Cooke, E.R., Jordan, C.A., Luczo T.M., & Jeffriess, M.D. (2014). Relationship between unilateral jumping ability and asymmetry on multidirectional speed in team-sport athletes. *Journal of Strength & Conditioning Research, 28*(12), 3557–3566.

Lockie, R., Schultz, A., Jordan, C., Callaghan, S., Jeffriess, M., & Luczo, T. (2015). Can selected FMS assessments be used to identify movement deficiencies that could affect multidirectional speed and jump performance? *The Journal of Strength & Conditioning Research, 29*(1), 195–205.

Logerstedt, D., Grindem, H., Lynch, A., Eitzen, I., Engebretsen, L., Risberg, M.A., Axe, M.J., & Snyder-Mackler, L. (2012). Single-legged hop tests as predictors of self-reported knee function after anterior cruciate ligament reconstruction: the Delaware-Oslo ACL cohort study. *American Journal of Sports Medicine, 40*, 2348–2356.

Lysholm, J., & Wiklander, J. (1987). Injuries in runners. *American Journal of Sports Medicine, 15*, 168–171.

Malliaras, P., Hogan, A., Nawrocki, A., Crossley, K., & Schache, A. (2009) Hip flexibility and strength measures: reliability and association with athletic groin pain. *British Journal of Sports Medicine, 43*, 739–744.

Marche Baldon, R., Lobato, D.F.M., Carvalho, L.P., Wun, P.Y.M., Presotti, C.V., & Serrao, F.V. (2012). Relationships between eccentric hip isokinetic torque and functional performance. *Journal of Sports Rehabilitation, 21*(1), 26–33.

Mayer, S., Queen, R., Taylor, D., Moorman, C., Toth, A., Garrett, W., & Butler, R. (2015). Functional testing differences in ACL reconstruction patients released vs. not released to return to sport. *American Journal of Sports Medicine, 43*(7), 1648–1655.

Mjølsnes, R., Arnason, A., Osthagen, T., Raastad, T., & Bahr, R. (2004). A 10-week randomised trial comparing eccentric vs concentric hamstring strength training in well-trained soccer players. *Scandinavian Journal of Medicine and Science in Sport, 14*, 311–317.

Morgan, D.L. (1990). New insights into the behavior of muscle during active lengthening. *Biophysical Journal, 57*(2), 209–221.

Moran, R., Schneiders, A., Mason, J., & Sullivan, S. (2017). Do FMS composite scores predict subsequent injury? A systematic review with meta-analysis. *British Journal of Sports Medicine*. doi: 10.1136/bjsports-2016-096938.

Mosler, A.B., Agricola, R., Weir, A., Hölmich, P., & Crossley, K.M. (2015). Which factors differentiate athletes with hip/groin pain from those without? A systematic review with meta-analysis. *British Journal of Sports Medicine, 49*, 810–822.

Myer, G.D., Ford, K.R., & Hewett, T.E. (2004). Rationale and clinical techniques for anterior cruciate ligament injury prevention among female athletes. *Journal of Athletic Training, 39*(4), 352–364.

Munro, A., Herrington, L., & Carolan, M. (2012a). Reliability of two-dimensional video assessment of frontal plane knee valgus during common athletic screening task. *Journal of Sport Rehabilitation, 21,* 7–11.

Munro, A., Herrington, L., & Comfort, P. (2012b). Comparison of landing knee valgus angle between female basketball and football athletes: possible implications for anterior cruciate ligament and patellofemoral joint injury rates. *Physical Therapy in Sport, 13,* 259–264.

Munro, A., Herrington, L., & Comfort, P. (2017). The relationship between 2-dimensional knee-valgus angles during single-leg squat, single-leg-land, and drop-jump screening tests. *Journal of Sport Rehabilitation, 26,* 72–77.

Munro, A., & Herrington, L. (2010). Between session reliability of the star excursion balance test. *Physical Therapy in Sport, 11,* 128–132.

Munro, A.G., & Herrington, L.C. (2011). Between-session reliability of four hop tests and the agility T-test. *The Journal of Strength & Conditioning Research, 25,* 1470–1477.

Murphy, J.C., O'Malley, E., Gissane, C., & Blake, C. (2012). Incidence of injury in Gaelic Football. *American Journal of Sports Medicine, 40*(9), 2113–2120.

Myer, G.D., Ford, K.R., Foss, K.D.B., Goodman, A., Ceasar, A., Rauh, M.J., Divine, J.G., & Hewett, T.E. (2010). The incidence and potential pathomechanics of patellofemoral pain in female athletes. *Clinical Biomechanics, 25,* 700–707.

Myers, B.A., Jenkins, W.L., Killian, C., & Rundquist, P. (2014). Normative data for hop tests in high school and collegiate basketball and soccer players. *International Journal of Sports Physical Therapy, 9,* 596–603.

Myklebust, G., Maehlum, S., Holm, I., & Bahr, R. (1998). A prospective cohort study of anterior cruciate ligament injuries in elite Norwegian team handball. *Scandinavian Journal of Medicine & Science in Sports, 8,* 149–153.

Negrete, R., & Brophy, J. (2000). The relationship between isokinetic open and closed chain lower extremity strength and functional performance. *Journal of Sport Rehabilitation, 9,* 46–61.

Newton, R.U., Gerber, A., Nimphius, S., Shim, J.K., Doan, B.K., Robertson, M., Pearson, D.R., Graig, B.W., Hakkinen, K., & Kraemer, WJ. (2006). Determination of functional strength imbalance of the lower extremities. *Journal of Strength & Conditioning Research, 20*(4), 971–977.

Nevin, F., & Delahunt, E. (2014) Adductor squeeze test values and hip joint range of motion in Gaelic football athletes with longstanding groin pain. *Journal of Science and Medicine in Sport, 17,* 155–159.

Norcross, M.F., Halverson, S.D., Hawkey, T.J., Blackburn, J.T., & Padua, D.A. (2009). Evaluation of the lateral step-down test as a clinical assessment of hip musculature strength. *Athletic Training & Sports Health Care, 1*(6), 272–278

Noyes, F.R., Barber-Westin, S.D., Fleckenstein, C., Walsh, C., & West, J. (2005). The drop-jump screening test: difference in lower limb control by gender and effect of neuromuscular training in female athletes. *American Journal of Sports Medicine, 33,* 197–207.

Noyes, F.R., Barber, S.D., & Mangine, R.E. (1991). Abnormal lower limb symmetry determined by function hop tests after anterior cruciate ligament rupture. *American Journal of Sports Medicine, 19,* 513–518.

Nyberg, B., Granhed, H., Peterson, K., Piros, C., & Svantesson, U. (2006). Muscle strength and jumping distance during 10 years post ACL reconstruction. *Isokinetics and Exercise Science, 14,* 363–370.

O'Donnell, S., Thomas, S.G., & Marks, P. (2006). Improving the sensitivity of the hop index in patients with an ACL deficient knee by transforming the hop distance scores. *BMC Musculoskeletal Disorders, 7,* 9.

Onate, E., Cortes, N., Welch, C., & Van Lunen, B. (2010). Expert versus novice interrater reliability and criterion validity of the landing error scoring system. *Journal of Sport Rehabilitation, 19*, 41–56.

Opar, D., Piatkowski, T., Williams, M.D., & Shield, A.J. (2013). A novel device using the Nordic hamstring exercise to assess eccentric knee flexor strength: a reliability and retrospective injury study. *Journal of Orthopaedic & Sports Physical Therapy, 43*(9), 636–640.

Opar, D.A., Williams, M.D., Timmins, R.G., Hickey, J., Duhig, S.J., & Shield, A.J. (2015). Eccentric hamstring strength and hamstring injury risk in Australian footballers. *Medicine & Science in Sports & Exercise, 47*(4), 857–865.

Orchard, J., Marsden, J., Lord, S., & Garlick, D. (1997). Preseason hamstring muscle weakness associated with hamstring injury in Australian footballers. *American Journal of Sports Medicine, 25*, 81–85.

Orchard, J., Wood, T., Seward, T., & Broad A. (1998). Comparison of injuries in elite senior and junior Australian football. *Journal of Science and Medicine in Sport, 1*(2), 82–88.

Orchard, J.W., Seward, H., & Orchard, J.J. (2013). Results of 2 decades of injury surveillance and public release of data in the Australian football league. *American Journal of Sports Medicine, 41*(4), 734–741.

Orr, R., Pope, R., Stierli, M., & Hinton, B. (2016). A FMS profile of an Australian state police force: a retrospective cohort study. *BMC Musculoskeletal Disorders, 17*, 296–305.

Padua, D.A., Distefano, L.J., Beutler, A.I., De La Motte, S.J., Distefano, M.J., & Marshall, S.W. (2015). The landing error scoring system as a screening tool for an anterior cruciate ligament injury-prevention program in elite-youth soccer athletes. *Journal of Athletic Training, 50*, 589–595.

Padua, D.A., Marshall, S.W., Boling, M.C., Thigpen, C.A., Garrett, W.E., & Beutler, A.I. (2009). The Landing Error Scoring System (LESS) is a valid and reliable clinical assessment tool of jump-landing biomechanics the JUMP-ACL study. *American Journal of Sports Medicine, 37*, 1996–2002.

Padua, D.A., Marshall, S.W., Beutler, A.I., Demaio, M., Boden, B.P., Yu, B., & Garrett, W.E. (2005) Predictors of knee valgus angle during a jump-landing task. *Medicine and Science in Sports and Exercise, 37*(5), S398.

Pappas, E., Hagins, M., Sheikhzadeh, A., Nordin, M., & Rose, D. (2007). Biomechanical differences between unilateral and bilateral landings from a jump: gender differences. *Clinical Journal of Sport Medicine, 17*, 263–268.

Paterno, M.V., Schmitt, L.C., Ford, K.R., Rauh, M.J., Myer, G.D., Huang, B., & Hewett, T.E. (2010). Biomechanical measures during landing and postural stability predict second anterior cruciate ligament injury after anterior cruciate ligament reconstruction and return to sport. *American Journal of Sports Medicine, 38*, 1968–1978.

Pepe, M.S., Janes, H., Longton, G., Leisenring, W., & Newcomb, P. (2004). Limitations of the odds ratio in gauging the Performance of a diagnostic, prognostic, or screening marker. *American Journal of Epidemiology, 159*, 882–890.

Perry, F., & Koehle, M. (2013). Normative data for the FMS in middle age. *The Journal of Strength & Conditioning Research, 27*(2), 458–462.

Petersen, J., Thorborg, K., Bachmann-Nielsen, M., Budtz-Jørgensen, E., & Holmich, P. (2011). Preventive effect of eccentric training on acute hamstring injuries in men's soccer a cluster-randomized controlled trial. *American Journal of Sports Medicine, 39*(11), 2296–2303.

Petschnig, R., Baron, R., & Albrecht, M. (1998). The relationship between isokinetic quadriceps strength test and hop tests for distance and one-legged vertical jump test following anterior cruciate ligament reconstruction. *Journal of Orthopaedic and Sports Physical Therapy, 28*, 23–31.

Plisky, P., Rauh, M., Kaminski, T., & Underwood, F. (2006). Star excursion balance test as a predictor of lower extremity injury in high school basketball players. *Journal of Orthopaedic & Sports Physical Therapy, 36*(12), 911–919.

Pontillo, M., Spinelli, B., & Sennett, B. (2014). Prediction of in-season shoulder injury from preseason testing in division 1 collegiate football players. Sports Health, *6*(6), 497–503.

Rankin, G., & Stokes, M. (1998). Reliability of assessment tools in rehabilitation: an illustration of appropriate statistical analyses. *Clinical Rehabilitation, 12*(3), 187–199.

Read, P., Oliver, J., De Ste Croix, M., Myer, G., & Lloyd, R. (2016). Reliability of the tuck jump test screening assessment in elite male youth soccer players. *The Journal of Strength & Conditioning Research, 30*(6), 1510–1516.

Robinson, R.O., Herzog, W., & Nigg, BM. (1987). Use of force platform variables to quantify the effects of chiropractic manipulation on gait symmetry. *Journal of Manipulative & Physiological Therapeutics, 10*, 172–176.

Roe, M., Murphy, J.C., Gissane, C., & Blake, C. (2016). Hamstring injuries in elite Gaelic football: an 8-year investigation to identify injury rates, time-loss patterns and players at increased risk. *British Journal of Sports Medicine.* doi:10.1136/bjsports-2016–096401.

Ross, M.D., Langford, B., & Whelan, P.J. (2002). Test-retest reliability of 4 single-leg horizontal hop tests. *Journal of Strength and Conditioning Research, 16*, 617–622.

Rudolph, K.S., Axe, M.J. & Snyder-Mackler, L. (2000). Dynamic stability after ACL injury: who can hop? *Knee Surgery, Sports Traumatology, Arthroscopy, 8*, 262–269.

Sato, K., & Heise, G.D. (2012). Influence of weight distribution asymmetry on the biomechanics of a barbell squat. *The Journal of Strength & Conditioning Research, 26*, 342–349.

Schache, A.G., Dorn, T.W., Blanch, P.D., Brown, N.A.T., & Pandy, M.G. (2012). Mechanics of the human hamstring muscles during sprinting. *Medicine and Science in Sports and Exercise, 44*(4), 647–658.

Schiltz, M., Lehance, C., Maquet, D., Bury, T., Crielaard, J.M., & Croisier, J.L. (2009). Explosive strength imbalances in professional Basketball players. *Journal of Athletic Training, 44*, 39–47.

Schlumberger, A., Laube, W., Bruhn, S., Herbeck, B., Dahlinger, M., Fenkart, G., Schmidtbleicher, D., & Mayer, F. (2006). Muscle imbalances—fact or fiction? *Isokinetics and Exercise Science, 14*, 3–11.

Sconce, E., Jones, P., Turner, E., Comfort, P., & Graham-Smith, P. (2015). The validity of the Nordic hamstring lower as a field-based assessment of eccentric hamstring strength. *Journal of Sports Rehabilitation, 24*(1), 13–20.

Shrout, P.E. & Fleiss, J.L. (1979). Intraclass correlations: Uses in assessing rater reliability. *Psychological Bulletin, 86*(2), 420–428.

Slater, L., Vriner, M., Zapalo, P., Arbour, K., & Hart, JM. (2016). Difference in agility, strength, and flexibility in competitive figure skaters based on level of expertise and skating discipline. *The Journal of Strength & Conditioning Research, 30*(12), 3321–3328.

Smith, H.C., Johnson, R.J., Shultz, S.J., Tourville, T., Holterman, L.A., Slauterbeck, J., Vacek, P.M., & Beynnon, B.D. (2012). A prospective evaluation of the Landing Error Scoring System (LESS) as a screening tool for anterior cruciate ligament injury risk. *American Journal of Sports Medicine, 40*, 521–526.

Stiffler, M., Bell, D., Sanfilippo, J., Hertel, J., Pickett, K., & Heiderscheit, B. (2017). Star excursion balance test anterior asymmetry is associated with injury status in division one athletes. *Journal of Orthopaedic & Sports Physical Therapy, 47*(5), 339–346.

Stroube, B., Myer, G., Brent, J., Ford, K., Heidt, R., & Hewett, T. (2013). Effects of task specific augmented feedback on deficit modification during performance of the tuck jump exercise. *Journal of Sport Rehabilitation, 22*(1), 7–18.

Sugiyama, T., Kameda, M., Kageyama, M., Kiba, K., Kanehisa, H., & Maeda, A. (2014). Asymmetry between the dominant and non-dominant legs in the kinematics of the lower extremities during a running single leg jump in collegiate basketball players. *Journal of Sports Science and Medicine, 13*, 951–957.

Thomas, J., Nelson, J., & Silverman, S. (2005). *Research methods in physical activity* (5th edn.). Champaign, IL: Human Kinetics.

Thelen, D.G., Chumanov, E.S., Best, T.M., Swanson, S.C., & Heiderscheit, B.C. (2005). Simulation of biceps femoris musculo-tendon mechanics during the swing phase of sprinting. *Medicine & Science in Sports & Exercise, 37*, 1931–1938.

Thorborg, K., Petersen, J., Magnusson, S.P., & Holmich, P. (2010). Clinical assessment of hip strength using a hand-held dynamometer is reliable. *Scandinavian Journal of Medicine and Science in Sports, 20*(3), 493–501.

Thorborg, K., Couppé, C., Petersen, J., Magnusson, S.P., & Hölmich, P. (2011a). Eccentric hip adduction and abduction strength in elite soccer players and matched controls: a cross-sectional study. *British Journal of Sports Medicine, 45*, 10–13.

Thorborg, K., Serner, A., Petersen, J., Moller-Madsen, T., Magnussen, P., & Hölmich, P. (2011b). Hip adduction and abduction strength profiles in elite soccer players. *American Journal of Sports Medicine, 39*(1), 121–125.

Thorborg, K., Branci, S., Nielsen, M.P., Tang, L., Bachmann, M., & Homich, P. (2014). Eccentric and isometric hip adduction strength in male soccer players with and without adductor-related groin pain. *Orthopaedic Journal of Sports Medicine, 2*(2), 1–7.

Timmins, R.G., Shield, A.J., Williams, M.D., & Opar, D.A. (2015) Is there evidence to support the use of the angle of peak torque as a marker of hamstring injury and re-injury risk? *Sports Medicine*. doi:10.1007/s40279-015-0378-8.

Timmins, R.G., Bourne, M.N., Shield, A.J., Williams, M.D., Lorenzen, C., & Opar, D.A. (2015). A short biceps femoris long head fascicle length and eccentric knee flexor weakness increase risk of hamstring injury: A prospective cohort study in 152 elite professional football players. *British Journal of Sports Medicine*. doi:10.1136/bjsports-2015-095362.

Tucci, H., Martins, J., Sposito, C., Camarini, P., & Oliveira, A. (2014). Closed kinetic chain extremity stability test: A reliability study in persons with and without shoulder impingement syndrome. *BMC Musculoskeletal Disorders, 15*. doi:10.1186/1471-2474-15-1.

Tyler, T.F., Nicholas, S.J., Campbell, R.J., & McHugh M.P. (2001). The association of hip strength and flexibility with the incidence of adductor muscle strains in professional ice hockey players. *American Journal of Sports Medicine, 29*(2), 124–128.

Van Der Horst, N., Smits, D.-W., Petersen, J., Goedhart, E.A., & Backx, F.J.G. (2015). The preventive effect of the Nordic hamstring exercise on hamstring injuries in amateur soccer players. *American Journal of Sports Medicine, 43*(6), 1316–1323.

Van Dyk, N., Bahr, R., Whiteley, R., Tol, J.L., Kumar, B.D., Hamilton, B., & Witvrouw, E. (2016). Hamstring and quadriceps isokinetic strength deficits are weak risk factors for hamstring strain injuries. *American Journal of Sports Medicine*. doi: 10.1177/0363546516632526.

Van Dyk, N., Bahr, R., Burnett, R.F., Whiteley, R., Bakken, A., Mosler, A., Farooq, A., & Witvrouw, E. (2017). A comprehensive strength testing protocol offers non-clinical value in predicting risk of hamstring injury: A prospective cohort study of 413 professional football players. *British Journal of Sports Medicine*. doi:10.1136/bjsports-2017-097754.

Van Lieshout, R., Reijneveld, E., Van Den Berg, S., Haerkens, G., Koenders, N., De Leeuw, A., Van Oorsouw, R., Scheffer, E., Weterings, S., & Stukstette, M. (2016). Reproducibility of the modified Star Excursion Balance test composite score and specific reach direction scores. *International Journal of Sports Physical Therapy, 11*(3), 356–365.

Waldén, M., Hägglund, M., & Ekstrand, J. (2015). The epidemiology of groin injury in senior football: a systematic review of prospective studies. *British Journal of Sports Medicine, 49*, 792–797.

Werner, J., Hagglund, M., Walden, M., & Ekstrand, J. (2009). UEFA injury study: A prospective study of hip and groin injuries in professional football over seven consecutive seasons. *British Journal of Sports Medicine, 43*, 1036–1040.

Whatman, C., Hing, W., & Hume, P. (2011). Kinematics during lower extremity functional screening tests Are they reliable and related to jogging? *Physical Therapy In Sport, 12*, 22–29.

Whiteley, R. (2016). Screening and likelihood ratio infographic. *British Journal of Sports Medicine, 50*, 837–838.

Whiteside, D., Deneweth, J., Pohorence, M., Sandoval, B., Russell, J., Mclean, S., Zernicke, R., & Goulet, G. (2016). Grading the FMS: A comparison of manual (real time) and objective methods. *The Journal of Strength & Conditioning Research, 30*(4), 924–933.

Willson, J.D., & Davis, I.S. (2008). Utility of the frontal plane projection angle in females with patellofemoral pain. *Journal of Orthopaedic & Sports Physical Therapy, 38*, 606–615.

Willson, J.D., Ireland, M.L., & Davis, I. (2006). Core strength and lower extremity alignment during single leg squats. *Medicine & Science in Sports & Exercise, 38*, 945–952.

Windt, J., Zumbo, B., Sporer, B., Macdonald, K., & Gabbett, T. (2017). Why do workload spikes cause injuries and which athletes are at higher risk? Mediators and moderators. *British Journal of Sports Medicine, 51*(13), 993–994.

Windt J., & Gabbett, T. (2017) How do training and competition workloads relate to injury? The workload-injury aetiology model. *British Journal of Sports Medicine, 51*(5), 428–435.

Wright, M., Portas, M., Evans, V., & Weston, M. (2015). The effectiveness of 4 weeks of fundamental movement training on FMS and physiological performance in physically active children. *The Journal of Strength & Conditioning Research, 29*(1), 254–261.

Wulf, G., Shea, C., & Lewthwaite, R. (2010). Motor skill learning and performance: a review of influential factors. *Medical Education, 44*, 75–84.

Yamamoto, T. (1993). Relationship between hamstring strains and leg muscle strength. *Journal of Sports Medicine and Physical Fitness, 33*, 194–199.

Yeung, S.S., Suen, A.M., & Yeung, E.W. (2009). A prospective cohort study of hamstring injuries in competitive sprinters: Preseason muscle imbalance as a possible risk factor. *British Journal of Sports Medicine, 43*, 589–594.

Zifchock, R.A., Davis, I., Higginson, J., & Royer, T. (2008). The symmetry angle: A novel, robust method for quantifying asymmetry. *Gait & Posture, 27*, 622–627.

7 Vertical jump testing

John J. McMahon, Jason P. Lake and Timothy J. Suchomel

7.1 Introduction

A critical component of directing the physical preparation of athletes is the assessment of their neuromuscular capacity. One of the most frequent methods used for ascertaining this information is vertical jumping; of this, the unloaded (i.e. no external load such as a barbell) countermovement vertical jump (CMJ) appears to be the most popular in the literature (Cormie et al., 2008, 2009; Gathercole et al., 2015; McMahon et al., 2017b, 2017c). Therefore, throughout this chapter, the reader can assume that reference to vertical jumping will mean the CMJ unless otherwise stated. The use of this test is typically rationalised by the fact that it is a relatively easy assessment to control, athletes require minimal familiarisation to be able to complete it and because it can provide a glut of information about neuromuscular and stretch-shortening cycle (SSC) function (Cormie et al., 2008, 2009; Gathercole et al., 2015; McMahon et al., 2017b, 2017c). At this point it should be noted that this jump assessment may not be suitable for all athletes. Or, more specifically, there may be more appropriate jump tests for certain athletes/sports. However, discussion of its relevance is beyond the scope of this chapter. Instead, we will focus on the many different factors that practitioners should consider to obtain valid and reliable results that can be used to profile their athletes when using the CMJ test. This will be achieved by providing guidelines for conducting the CMJ test, including the different equipment that can be used to assess the CMJ, the protocols that should be employed when using this different equipment, how data should be analysed, and how the practitioner can effectively use these data to inform their athletes' training regimens.

7.2 Equipment

The equipment that practitioners use to obtain CMJ data will depend on three main factors: (1) what data they are interested in, (2) what equipment and software they have access to and (3) how quickly they require the information. That said, it is generally accepted that the "gold standard" method to obtain CMJ data is the force platform. Affordable and valid commercial force platforms have been recently developed (Lake et al., 2016b, 2017; Peterson Silveira et al., 2016), meaning that practitioners are likely to utilise them more frequently when conducting CMJ testing. Therefore, this part of the chapter will outline the use of force platforms for conducting CMJ assessments and will then compare the numerous other alternative (field-based) methods that are commercially available to practitioners. This will then flow into the next section where we discuss the protocols that practitioners should use to ensure that they are able to confidently acquire the information they are interested in from their force-time records and, indeed, from alternative equipment. The reader is also referred to Chapter 11 for specific information regarding the different methods of assessing power (which includes force in its calculation) and the impact on the resultant variables.

7.2.1 Force platform

Force platforms generally include strain gauges or piezoelectric sensors that measure force applied to the platform (based on Newton's Law of Reaction) which, for CMJ assessments performed on the ground, is referred to as the ground reaction force (GRF, Figure 7.1). For specific details on how different force platforms work, the reader is referred to a recent article on this topic by Beckham et al. (2014). Force platforms can be permanently imbedded into the ground (or into weightlifting platforms, as is becoming increasingly popular) or used portably. More expensive in-ground force platforms will quantify GRF in three directions (vertical, anterior-posterior and medio-lateral) while most cheaper portable alternatives provide either a combination of vertical and anterior-posterior GRF data (2D) or vertical GRF data (1D) alone. When assessing CMJ performance using any force platform, however, it is only the vertical GRF that is typically of interest. Additionally, as mentioned earlier, some cheaper 2D and 1D portable strain gauge force platforms have been validated against gold

Figure 7.1 A basic illustration of the vertical force applied by an athlete (grey arrow) to the force platform (grey rectangle) and the equal (in magnitude) and opposite (in direction) vertical ground reaction force applied by the force platform to the athlete (black arrow).

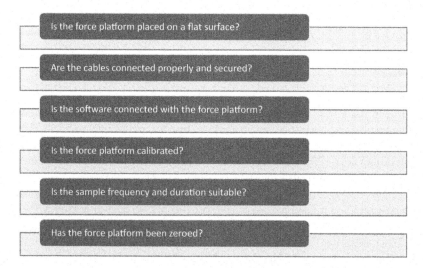

Is the force platform placed on a flat surface?

Are the cables connected properly and secured?

Is the software connected with the force platform?

Is the force platform calibrated?

Is the sample frequency and duration suitable?

Has the force platform been zeroed?

Figure 7.2 Common considerations given to the set-up of force platforms prior to collecting vertical jump force-time data.

standard in-ground piezoelectric sensor force platforms in relation to CMJ performance assessment (Lake et al., 2016b, 2017; Peterson Silveira et al., 2016), thus promoting their use by strength and conditioning practitioners. It should be noted, however, that portable force platforms tend be smaller than in-ground force platforms and so two of the former (one positioned under each foot) are recommended for CMJ assessments.

Regardless of the of type of force platform used to assess CMJ performance, there are common considerations which must be given to their set-up to increase the validity and reliability of resultant force-time data (Figure 7.2). Of the common considerations summarised in Figure 7.2, sample frequency tends to differ widely across CMJ studies, sometimes due simply to the type of force platform used (for example, the 400-series strain gauge force platform [Fitness Technology, Adelaide, Australia] has a maximum sample frequency of 600 Hz). The influence of sample frequency on a representative CMJ force-time record is shown in Figure 7.3. One study suggested that a minimum sample frequency of 200 Hz could be used to collect CMJ force-time data (Hori et al., 2009). The suggestion made by Hori et al. (2009) was based on (1) the attainment of high reliability for selected kinetic variables and (2) a low percentage difference in the mean of these kinetic variables when sampled at 200 Hz versus 500 Hz (the highest sample frequency included). However, an earlier study recommended a minimum sample frequency of 1000 Hz for CMJ force-time assessments (Street et al., 2001) and this was more recently endorsed as the criterion sample frequency for such assessments (Owen et al., 2014). We, therefore, recommend a minimum force-platform sample frequency of 1000 Hz (if the force platform used has this capability) when conducting CMJ testing.

7.2.2 *Field-based equipment*

Alternative equipment to the force platform is available to practitioners who wish to assess the CMJ performances of their athletes but who do not have access to a force platform.

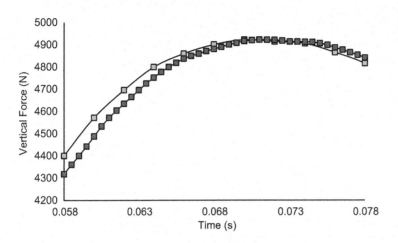

Figure 7.3 An example of the influence of force-platform sampling frequency (500 Hz [light grey squares] versus 2000 Hz [dark grey squares]) on the countermovement jump force-time record just before and after the attainment of peak force.

In the "field" (pun intended) of strength and conditioning, alternative equipment to the industry gold standard (in this case, the force platform) is often referred to as field-based equipment. In relation to assessing CMJ performances, field-based equipment can be categorised based on the method(s) it uses to quantify CMJ performance (namely jump height). It is important, however, that the strength and conditioning practitioner is aware of the limitations of quantifying CMJ performances via field-based equipment, and indeed by using jump height alone, before interpreting resultant data (McMahon et al., 2017a). An overview of the main field-based equipment used to assess CMJ performance, including their benefits and limitations, and a comparison with the force platform (where applicable) is provided in Table 7.1.

7.3 Protocols

Optimising CMJ assessment protocols when a force platform is used to obtain data has been of interest to biomechanists for several years and several studies have set out to identify appropriate protocols (Hatze, 1998; Kibele, 1998; Linthorne, 2001; Street et al., 2001; Vanrenterghem et al., 2001). This is important because the protocol that the practitioner uses will influence what data are collected, and consequently the quality of CMJ performance data. Research shows that the key factors that practitioners must control are whether arm swing is permitted or not, body position immediately before the word of command to perform the CMJ is given, the verbal instructions that the practitioner gives the athlete (mainly in relation to speed and range of movement and aiming for maximal jump height) and landing position (applies particularly to flight time estimates of jump height). Again, the crux of this section relates to protocols that are best suited to force-platform-derived CMJ assessments, as accurate force-time assessment is extremely dependent on many of these protocols, but the consequences of not standardising protocols on CMJ data derived from field-based equipment will also be discussed where applicable. Finally, the precise number of CMJ trials to be assessed will

Table 7.1 An overview of common field-based equipment used to quantify vertical jump performance, including their main benefits and limitations.

Equipment	Main variables	Main benefits	Main limitations
Jump mats (e.g. Just Jump System)	• Jump height* • Contact time • Flight time • Reactive strength index	• Reliable • Portable • Instantaneous results	• Tends to overestimate flight time and thus jump height and reactive strength index
Optoelectronic devices (e.g. Optojump)	• Jump height* • Contact time • Flight time • Reactive strength index	• Reliable • Valid • Portable • Instantaneous results	• Underestimates jump height slightly (around 1 cm)
Video cameras (e.g. smart phone with app, such as MyJump)	• Jump height* • Reactive strength index • Force-velocity profile	• Very accessible • Very cheap • Reliable • Valid	• Time consuming due to post-test processing requirement (compared to some other equipment) • Large video files take up limited space on phone
Accelerometers (e.g. Myotest)	• Jump height • Peak and mean velocity • Peak and mean power • Reactive strength index	• Reliable • Portable • Instantaneous results	• Overestimates jump height (particularly when using the TOV method)
Linear position transducers (e.g. GymAware)	• Jump height • Peak power • Peak force • Peak velocity	• Reliable • Portable • Instantaneous results	• Deviates from vertical-only displacement • Bar (usual attachment point) and COM movement do not always coincide • Overestimates jump height
Jump and reach devices (e.g. Vertec)	• Jump height	• Reliable • Portable • Instantaneous results	• Values influenced by shoulder range of motion • Requires that contact with the vanes coincides with peak COM displacement • Overestimates jump height due to its calculation (difference between height reached whilst standing and height during the jump) • Only provides insight into jump height

* = jump height estimated from flight time only; COM = centre of mass; TOV = take-off velocity.

not be advised in this section, but it is prudent to assess more than one trial to reduce random errors (Henry, 1967). Performing multiple trials also reduces the typical error of measurement of associated test variables, which would desirably increase their sensitivity for detecting changes in athlete performance, providing a more complete athlete profile (Haugen & Buchheit, 2016).

7.3.1 Arm swing

When deciding on which protocols to adhere to when conducting CMJ testing, the inclusion or exclusion of arm swing is likely to be considered. Before deciding, the influence that arm swing may have on the validity and reliability of force-time variables, including jump height, should be considered. If conducting a jump and reach assessment then arm swing is, of course, a requirement, but understanding how arm swing influences CMJ performance data is still useful from a test standardisation and interpretation perspective.

Beginning with reliability, a study by Slinde et al. (2008) reported that inter-session reliability of CMJ height, when measured using a contact mat, was similar when arm swing was permitted and not permitted (intraclass correlation coefficient values equalled 0.93 for combined male and female jump height data recorded using both technique variations). When CMJs were performed with and without arm swing on a force platform, reliability for a range of force, velocity, displacement and power variables was excellent and very similar for both technique variations (Harman et al., 1990). In terms of absolute intra-session reliability comparisons, the coefficient of variation in jump height for CMJs performed on a force platform with (2.68 ± 0.45%) and without (2.28 ± 0.41%) arm swing has been shown to be similar (Hara et al., 2008). The results of these three studies suggest that arm swing has minimal effect on CMJ variable reliability. However, arm swing technique differences can result in small alterations to centre of mass (COM) velocity and height at take-off (Gutiérrez-Dávila et al., 2014), which will be different to what is achieved at touchdown (due to differences in arm position at touchdown compared to take-off). This can lead to (even greater) inaccuracies in jump height estimations using the flight time method (Linthorne, 2001). It should also be noted that arm swing technique may differ between individuals and/or testing sessions and this would be likely to have a negative influence on data accuracy and reliability.

Each of the three studies discussed above reported that CMJ height was always higher when arm swing was permitted (Hara et al., 2008; Harman et al., 1990; Slinde et al., 2008). The additional CMJ height gained when including arm swing is attributed to increased lower extremity work which, in turn, is attributed to greater propulsive torque produced at the hip (Hara et al., 2008). One should remember that the analysis of CMJ force-time data, and additional variables that are derived via the integration of said data, provides insight into linear COM kinetics and kinematics only and does not inform us of limb or joint contributions. Therefore, unless there is a specific rationale for including arm swing in vertical jump testing batteries (e.g. for volleyball athletes), it would be prudent to avoid doing so to improve data reliability and enable more accurate comparisons of CMJ performance between testing sessions.

7.3.2 Starting position

Before commencing the CMJ, the athlete should stand upright (lower body in a neutral anatomical position), with their arms akimbo or holding a wooden dowel (or an alternative near-massless bar) across their upper back (unless arm swing will be permitted) and their feet hip-shoulder width apart. Once they have adopted this starting position, it is imperative that they remain as still as possible for at least 1 second before jumping if force-time data are being collected (Owen et al., 2014). The reason for this will be discussed in section 7.4.1. The starting position described above should also be adopted if using field-based equipment to measure CMJ performance unless a linear position transducer (LPT) is being used, although there is no requirement to hold the starting position for any set duration before the jump. When using an LPT, whether it be attached to a wooden dowel held across the upper back or a waist harness, it is necessary to "zero" COM take-off height. This is done whilst athletes are standing in a fully plantar flexed position (Thomasson & Comfort, 2012), before they adopt their starting position in line with the earlier discussion points.

7.3.3 Countermovement technique

The countermovement (combined flexion of hips and knees, including some dorsiflexion, resulting in COM lowering [encompassing the unweighting and braking phases of the CMJ – as discussed in section 7.4.3]) is the first movement that occurs in the CMJ. The two main considerations regarding countermovement technique relate to movement speed and depth (i.e. countermovement displacement). Compared with the athlete's natural or preferred countermovement technique, a shallower and quicker countermovement will be likely to result in disproportionately larger forces and shorter phase times resulting in a reduced impulse and thus velocity, whereas the opposite will be likely to occur if a deeper and faster countermovement is performed (Jidovtseff et al., 2014; McMahon et al., 2016). Encouraging the athlete to adopt their preferred countermovement depth appears to be best practice from a reliability perspective (Petronijevic et al., Publish ahead of print) and will provide the strength and conditioning practitioner with an opportunity to quantify the athlete's natural jump strategy (and possible changes to said strategy thereafter). Additionally, a recent study highlighted the difficulties in standardising countermovement depth (by approximating joint angles, e.g. 90-degree knee flexion angle), to enable fairer comparisons to squat jump performance (Sánchez-Sixto et al., Publish ahead of print). Irrespective of the athlete's preferred countermovement depth, they should always be encouraged to perform the countermovement as quickly as possible to initiate the SSC.

7.3.4 Jump technique

Regardless of the instructions given to the athlete in relation to countermovement technique, the jump phase of the CMJ (i.e. combined extension of the hips, knees and ankles [i.e. plantar flexion] that raises the COM [encompassing the propulsion and flight phases of the CMJ]) should always be instructed to be performed as fast as possible, with the aim of attaining maximal jump height. Indeed, the faster the COM leaves the ground (termed "take-off"), the higher the jump will be. The reasons for this will be explained in section 7.4.5.2.

7.3.5 Landing position

If the flight time method of estimating jump height must be used (i.e. when using certain field-based equipment), then it is important to ensure athletes avoid flexing their hips, knees and ankles (dorsiflexion) during the flight phase and at the instant of touchdown. The reasons for this will be explained in section 7.4.5.1. Irrespective of the equipment used to assess CMJ performance, there is usually little need for athletes to decelerate quickly during the landing phase of a CMJ test. Consequently, athletes are often instructed to "absorb" the landing by flexing at the hips, knees and ankles after impacting the force platform (or other device/floor if not using a force platform), thereby applying a net impulse characterised by a smaller force being applied over a longer duration. Athletes who are not given, or do not adhere to, this instruction will produce larger peak landing forces which is unnecessary (e.g. this may be injurious).

7.4 Data analysis

This section will consider the way data should be analysed to obtain the variables we recommend for CMJ analysis. As with previous sections, it will begin by considering the analysis of force-time data in a logical sequence and this will form the foundation to discuss the appropriate analysis of data obtained using other methods. That said, it should be noted that many of the points which apply to CMJ force-time data analysis cannot be applied to data obtained using other methods. This will become clearer as this section progresses.

Commercial force-platform software packages can automate the processing of most CMJ force-time data calculations that are likely to be of interest to the strength and conditioning practitioner, but it is worth noting that this can also be done using Microsoft Excel if the former is inaccessible (Chavda et al., 2018). Another noteworthy discussion point is that some commercial force-platform software packages may include automatic filtering of the CMJ force-time data. It has been recommended, however, that unfiltered CMJ force-time data should be analysed due to various filters (and their varying cut-off frequencies) leading to underestimations of CMJ height (Street et al., 2001).

7.4.1 Determining bodyweight (weighing phase)

An extremely important, but perhaps often overlooked, component of analysing CMJ force-time data is accurately determining the athlete's bodyweight. As mentioned in the starting position section of this chapter, it is imperative that the athlete remains as still as possible for at least 1 second before commencing the jump. Bodyweight is then usually calculated as the average (mean) vertical force reading over this 1 second weighing phase (McMahon et al., 2017b, 2017c; Owen et al., 2014). Some studies have subtracted the peak residual force (recorded during the flight phase, when the force platform is unloaded) from the bodyweight reading to account for signal noise (Kibele, 1998; Vanrenterghem et al., 2001). While this approach will provide information about the signal noise in general, it cannot provide information about "human noise" during the weighing phase. The most important consideration here, however, is that a consistent approach to bodyweight determination is applied to enable accurate data comparisons between trials, sessions and athletes.

Accurate calculation of bodyweight is essential for two reasons: firstly, it is used to identify a threshold to determine the onset of movement (to be discussed in section 7.4.3.1) and secondly, it (and/or the body mass derived from it) is included in forward dynamics procedures (to be discussed in section 7.4.2). The suggested minimum weighing duration of 1 second is largely a consequence of a study which reported that weighing durations of ≤ 1 second lead to a ≥ 1% overestimation of CMJ height (calculated based on the impulse-momentum relationship) (Street et al., 2001). A ≥ 1% overestimation of CMJ height is considered unacceptable (Owen et al., 2014; Street et al., 2001), hence our recommendation of including at least a 1 second weighing duration in CMJ force-time data analyses. It is worth noting that numerical double integration of the CMJ force-time record (to yield COM displacement, as discussed later) is very sensitive to accurate body mass determination. For example, Vanrenterghem et al. (2001) reported a 1.7% variability in body mass across CMJ trials which resulted in a 4.5 cm deviation in total height (contact height [the difference between standing and take-off COM height] plus flight height [i.e. jump height], as calculated from COM displacement data). It has been recommended, therefore, that a single body mass value should never be applied to all of a given athlete's CMJ force-time data recorded during the same testing session (Vanrenterghem et al., 2001).

7.4.2 Forward dynamics

When jumping vertically, the athlete must overcome bodyweight, and so the resultant force (commonly referred to as the net force) acting on the athlete's COM is of interest when exploring the influence of applied force on COM motion (Linthorne, 2001). The net force acting on the athlete's COM is calculated by subtracting the athlete's bodyweight from the vertical GRF record. Net impulse is then derived by calculating the area underneath the net force-time record. Based on known associations between mechanical variables, as governed by Newton's Laws of motion, it is then possible to obtain other kinetic and kinematic variables from the original (or filtered) CMJ net force-time record, a process often referred to as forward dynamics. For example, it is possible to numerically integrate acceleration derived from the CMJ net force-time record (net force ÷ body mass) to determine COM velocity and displacement, as these variables are often used to identify the different phases of the jump (to be discussed in section 7.4.3). Velocity and displacement can also feed into other calculations of interest, such as work and power. The process of calculating each of these variables will be discussed later in this section.

Before the above-mentioned calculations are explained, we should briefly discuss the different types of numerical integration that are typically used in CMJ force-time data analysis procedures. The trapezoid rule of numerical integration is most commonly used for this purpose. Higher-order methods of numerical integration (i.e. the application of Simpson's rule) are thought to not significantly improve the accuracy of CMJ performance variables (Kibele, 1998). The trapezoid method of numerical integration can lead to a ≤ 0.3% under-estimation of CMJ height, which is considered to be quite a small error (Street et al., 2001), and this method is easier to implement in software-based calculations, which may explain its frequent use. We, therefore, recommend the trapezoid method of numerical integration for the analyses of CMJ force-time records, but further consideration must be given to when numerical integration commences and at what frequency.

7.4.2.1 Integration start point and frequency

As mentioned earlier, small errors in body mass determination (even as low as 0.5% error) during the weighing phase can induce errors in CMJ height (Vanrenterghem et al., 2001), but this error was suggested to diminish when integrating force-time data over a sufficient duration and frequency (Vanrenterghem et al., 2001). However, contrary to what Owen et al. (2014) recommended, Street et al. (2001) showed that, when subjects stood still, integrating the force-time data (i.e. commencing forward dynamics procedures) anywhere from 0 to 1.5 seconds (the time range tested) before the onset of movement had no meaningful effect on CMJ height. It would seem fine, therefore, for force-time data integration to commence from the start of the weighing phase or, indeed, just before the jump commences. It seems then that numerical integration frequency is a more important consideration from an error-reduction perspective. For example, numerical integration frequencies of 50, 100, 200, 500 and 1000 Hz have been compared in relation to their effect on contact height and jump height (Vanrenterghem et al., 2001). Errors were largest overall at 50 Hz and larger at 100 Hz when compared with 200–1000 Hz, suggesting that at least a 200 Hz integration frequency should be adopted. If the original CMJ force-time data were sampled at 1000 Hz then we recommend adopting a 1000 Hz numerical integration frequency (as this is just as easy to employ as any of the aforementioned alternative numerical integration frequencies and simply means that integration is performed on a sample-by-sample basis).

7.4.2.2 Velocity

For the velocity-time record to be obtained, the acceleration-time record must first be calculated. This is achieved by dividing the net force-time record by the athlete's body mass. The acceleration-time record that this yields is then numerically integrated with respect to time using the trapezoid rule to give the velocity-time record. Incidentally, velocity can also be obtained by successively summing the result of dividing impulse by mass on a sample-by-sample basis, reinforcing the relationship between impulse and velocity.

7.4.2.3 Displacement

The displacement-time record is obtained by numerically integrating the velocity-time record, again using the trapezoid rule. This is often referred to as numerical double integration of the CMJ force-time record. As mentioned earlier, numerical double integration is very sensitive to accurate body mass determination (Vanrenterghem et al., 2001). The displacement-time curve is thus more prone to error accumulation than the velocity-time curve, although much of this can be avoided if correct procedures are followed.

7.4.2.4 Work

Once the displacement-time record has been calculated, the work done on the athlete's COM can be calculated by multiplying force by displacement on a sample-by-sample basis. It is important to remember that the accuracy of the work calculation will be negatively affected by the error synonymous with the derivation of displacement (see previous section). Work can also be calculated by averaging power (discussed below) over the phase(s) of interest and then multiplying it by the corresponding phase time(s).

7.4.2.5 Power

Power will be discussed in detail in Chapter 11, but it warrants a brief discussion in this section given that it is often included in force-platform-derived CMJ test outputs. Power can be defined as the rate at which mechanical work is performed, so given that work can be calculated as described above, all that is required to obtain power is to divide work by time on a sample-by-sample basis. Multiplying the vertical GRF by velocity also yields power and it is this method of calculating power that can then be used to calculate average power and then work, as described in the above section.

7.4.3 Phase identification

Recent studies have shown that a comprehensive insight into athletes' neuromuscular function can be gained through detailed analyses of CMJ force-time curves throughout specific phases (Ebben et al., 2007; Laffaye et al., 2014; Rice et al., 2017; Riggs & Sheppard, 2009; Sole et al., 2018) or the entire jump (Cormie et al., 2008, 2009; Gathercole et al.,

2015; McMahon et al., 2017b, 2017c), when compared to measuring the output of the jump alone (i.e. jump height). Therefore, it is important that practitioners who wish to use force-platform-based CMJ assessments can recognise the constituent parts of the CMJ force-time curve (McMahon et al., 2018b), and understand their relative contribution to CMJ performance and how they can be manipulated through coaching and strength and conditioning. To achieve this, the different CMJ phases must be identified using robust methodologies; this has not always been the case in the research literature (Rice et al., 2017; Riggs & Sheppard, 2009) and so warrants discussion with a view to its practical application.

7.4.3.1 Onset of movement threshold

The onset of movement in the CMJ is usually identified as the instant at which bodyweight is reduced below a set force threshold. This force threshold has varied across studies (Eagles et al., 2015), but the most recent "criterion" method was suggested by Owen et al. (2014). This method identifies a force threshold equal to 5 times the standard deviation of bodyweight (calculated in the weighing phase), hence the importance of standing still during the weighing phase (i.e. to minimise the standard deviation of bodyweight and thus increase the sensitivity of the onset of movement force threshold). The 5 standard deviation approach is used because it identifies a meaningful change in force (i.e. there is a 1 in 3.5 million chance that the change in force occurs by chance or as a consequence of signal noise). Owen et al. (2014) recommended going back 30 milliseconds from the instant at which the force threshold is passed, however, because they identified that movement would have already started by this instant and thus the associated COM velocity would not equal zero. Thus, the onset of movement is deemed to have occurred 30 milliseconds before the first instant in the CMJ force-time record that vertical force is less than the value equal to bodyweight minus the force threshold.

A 5–10 millisecond (equal to 5–10 samples if force-time data were sampled at 1000 Hz) error in identifying the onset of movement has little effect ($\leq 0.1\%$) on the derived COM velocity and displacement calculations, however, due to a lesser rate of change in force at this stage when compared to take-off and landing (see later sections) (Kibele, 1998). Although misidentifying the onset of movement may have little effect on numerically integrated data, it would be likely to have a more profound effect on time-related variables (e.g. time to take-off, time to peak force etc.) and thus associated metrics such as rate of force development (Eagles et al., 2015) and reactive strength index modified (McMahon et al., 2018a). It would be prudent, therefore, to at least adopt a consistent onset of movement threshold across trials, sessions and athletes for comparative purposes.

7.4.3.2 Unweighting phase

The unweighting phase occurs after the weighing phase, whereby the athlete commences a countermovement by first relaxing the agonist muscles (Linthorne, 2001), resulting in combined flexion of hips and knees, and ankles. The unweighting phase begins, therefore, at the onset of movement and continues as force decreases further below body weight before increasing back to bodyweight (Hatze, 1998; Kibele, 1998; Linthorne, 2001; McMahon et al., 2017b, 2017c; Mizuguchi et al., 2015; Sole et al., 2018), on the ascending aspect of the force-time curve (Figure 7.4). Therefore, the unweighting phase, as the name implies,

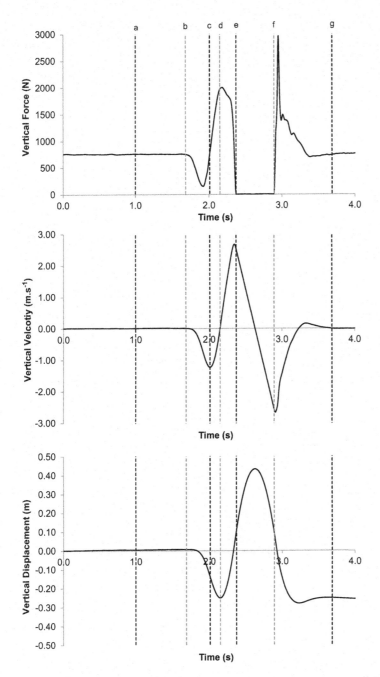

Figure 7.4 A typical countermovement jump vertical force-time (top), velocity-time (middle) and displacement-time (bottom) curve, where a = end of the weighing phase, b = onset of movement (which also represents the start of the unweighting phase), c = onset of the braking phase (which also represents the end of the unweighting phase), d = onset of the propulsion phase (which also represents the end of the braking phase), e = instant of take-off (which also represents the end of the propulsion phase), f = instant of touchdown (which also represents the start of the landing phase) and g = end of landing phase.

comprises the entire area of the force-time curve (before take-off) that is below bodyweight (Figure 7.4). The instant at which force returns to bodyweight coincides with the instant at which peak negative COM velocity (before take-off) is achieved (Figure 7.4). Plotting the velocity-time curve alongside the force-time curve is visually useful, therefore, in revealing the exact point at which different phases, including the unweighting phase, occur (Figure 7.4).

7.4.3.3 Braking phase

The third CMJ phase is the braking phase, whereby the athlete decelerates (i.e. "brakes") their COM. Hence the braking phase commences one sample after the instant of peak negative COM velocity (attained at the end of the unweighting phase) and continues through to zero COM velocity (i.e. when the athlete stops, momentarily in a squat position) (Hatze, 1998; Kibele, 1998; Linthorne, 2001; McMahon et al., 2017b, 2017c). The end of the braking phase coincides, therefore, with the lowest countermovement COM displacement (deepest part of the squat) (Hatze, 1998; Kibele, 1998; McMahon et al., 2017b, 2017c), as shown in Figure 7.4.

7.4.3.4 Propulsion phase

The fourth CMJ phase is the propulsion phase (Hatze, 1998; Mizuguchi et al., 2015; Sole et al., 2018), whereby athletes forcefully extend their hips, knees and ankles to propel their COM vertically. This phase technically begins when a positive COM velocity is achieved (Hatze, 1998; Kibele, 1998; Linthorne, 2001) but a velocity threshold of 0.01 m·s^{-1} (which usually represents one sample after zero velocity when collecting force data at 1000 Hz) has been recently used with success to identify the onset of the propulsion phase for large (full squad) data sets (McMahon et al., 2017b, 2017c, 2018a). The propulsion phase continues until take-off (the thresholds used to determine this are discussed in the next section).

Plotting the displacement-time curve alongside the force-time curve in this phase is visually useful as it shows how it is composed of a vertical COM displacement that becomes positive when it exceeds the zero COM displacement that was set when the athlete was standing upright and still during the weighing phase (Figure 7.4). It can be assumed, therefore, that the peak positive COM displacement gained in the propulsion phase reflects the COM displacement achieved through plantarflexing the ankles (Figure 7.4), as the athlete should adopt a neutral ankle angle (90°) during the weighing phase when standing upright. This is sometimes referred to as contact height and informs one of how much extra COM displacement an athlete generates via a forceful plantarflexion, which may be a limiting factor for some (Kibele, 1998).

It is also interesting to note that peak COM velocity is attained before rather than at take-off, which coincides with the instant at which bodyweight is reached again on the descending aspect of the force-time curve and when zero COM displacement is achieved (Figure 7.4). At this point the COM begins to decelerate (Hatze, 1998; Mizuguchi et al., 2015; Sole et al., 2018), probably due to the shank and foot segments adding to the effective mass being accelerated at this point, although positive COM displacement continues through to the next phase.

7.4.3.5 Flight phase

The fifth CMJ phase is the flight phase, where the athlete leaves the ground with the intention of attaining maximal jump height (peak positive COM displacement). As alluded to above, the flight phase commences at take-off (when force falls below a set threshold), which will be discussed in the next section. From the point where peak positive COM displacement is achieved (Figure 7.4), which coincides with a momentary COM velocity of zero, the athlete descends back towards the ground and touchdown occurs when the selected force threshold is exceeded, thus denoting the end of the flight phase.

7.4.3.5.1 TAKE-OFF AND TOUCHDOWN THRESHOLD

As with the determination of the onset of movement, many force thresholds have been used to identify take-off and touchdown in the literature. A force threshold equal to 5 times the standard deviation of flight force (when the force platform is unloaded), taken over a 300-millisecond portion of the flight phase, has been successfully used to identify take-off and touchdown in recent work (McMahon et al., 2017b, 2017c, 2018a). This method is only valid when the flight phase duration exceeds 300 milliseconds, so including the force data points pertaining to the mid-portion of the flight phase only (as discussed by Chavda et al., 2018) could be an alternative option for calculating take-off and touchdown thresholds for loaded CMJ assessments (or when assessing athletes who cannot jump with a flight time greater than this value). Incorrectly identifying the instant of take-off by as little as 2–3 milliseconds can lead to approximately a 2% variation in velocity and CMJ height (Kibele, 1998), with a 3 millisecond misplacement reportedly leading to a 0.9 cm absolute error in CMJ height estimates using the take-off velocity method (Vanrenterghem et al., 2001). In relative error terms, force thresholds of 6 N and 10 N above true zero (when signal noise was accounted for) led to 1% and 1.5% overestimations in CMJ height, respectively (Street et al., 2001). These errors, although considered small, can be reduced further by collecting force-time data at a sufficiently high sampling and integration frequency (Vanrenterghem et al., 2001), in line with earlier discussions. Therefore, one should consider these sources of error wisely when collecting and analysing the CMJ force-time data and, again, apply a consistent take-off and touchdown threshold across trials, sessions and athletes.

7.4.3.6 Landing phase

The sixth and final CMJ phase is the landing phase, whereby the athlete applies a net impulse that will match the propulsion impulse to decelerate and then stop the COM from the velocity attained at touchdown. The landing phase is considered to have ended, therefore, when COM velocity reaches zero (Figure 7.4), which coincides with the peak negative COM displacement achieved during this phase (lowest landing squat position, Figure 7.4). The landing phase can also be split into two sub-phases (impact [between touchdown and peak force] and stabilising [between peak force and peak negative COM displacement]) for additional information about landing strategy/ability (Lake et al., 2016a), which may be of interest to some researchers and practitioners. The time between the instant of touchdown and the end of landing phase is often considered to represent the time to stabilisation.

7.4.4 Calculating mean, peak and sum variables

Once numerical integration and phase identification of CMJ force-time records has been completed, it is possible to calculate mean, peak and sum variables for each phase of interest quite easily. As mentioned earlier, commercial force platform software packages can automatically make most calculations, but this can also be done using Microsoft Excel if the former is inaccessible (Chavda et al., 2018). If using Microsoft Excel, mean, peak and summed variables can be calculated by using the =AVERAGE, =MAX (or =MIN for peak negative values) and =SUM formulas, respectively. These can then be applied to the specific CMJ phases of interest in Microsoft Excel (Chavda et al., 2018), mostly by applying a combination of INDEX and MATCH functions that relate to the thresholds discussed in the previous section. A summary of mean, peak and summed variables that may be of interest to the strength and conditioning practitioner can be found in Table 7.2.

7.4.5 Calculating jump height

Jump height is a primary variable of interest for almost all practitioners who have administered the CMJ test with their athletes, irrespective of the equipment used. The two main methods of calculating jump height are the flight time method and the take-off velocity method (Linthorne, 2001). Both methods estimate jump height from our understanding of the law of conservation of mechanical energy and the impulse-momentum relationship (Linthorne, 2001; Moir, 2008). Most field-based devices calculate jump height from flight time, as summarised in Table 7.1, but it is probably the most common method applied to CMJ force-time assessments too, despite the errors associated with it (Kibele, 1998). Nevertheless, we explain each of the aforementioned methods of calculating jump height and briefly discuss their relative merits and limitations.

7.4.5.1 Flight time method

Estimating jump height from flight time is based on the application of kinematic equations for one-dimensional motion under constant (gravitational) acceleration (Linthorne, 2001). One expression of the equation for estimating jump height from flight time is as follows:

$$JH = \frac{FT^2 \times 9.81}{8}$$

where JH = jump height and FT = flight time.

Using flight phase duration (i.e. flight time) to estimate jump height relies on the assumption that the apex of the jump (peak positive COM displacement) occurs at the instant of half of the duration of the flight phase. This only holds true, however, if COM height is the same at take-off and touchdown (Kibele, 1998). Consequently, any alterations in joint geometry (e.g. hip, knee or ankle flexion before touchdown) will affect this calculation. Consequently, this method can yield errors of around 0.5–2 cm in jump height estimates (Kibele, 1998). If the flight time method must be used, then it is important to instruct athletes to avoid flexing hips, knees and ankles during the flight phase and at touchdown.

Table 7.2 Overview of common mean, peak and summed variables derived from vertical jump tests performed on a force platform.

Variable type	Variable	Unit	Variable description
Mean	Braking force	N	The average force produced in the braking phase
	Propulsion force	N	The average force produced in the propulsion phase
	Braking power	W	The average power produced in the braking phase
	Propulsion power	W	The average power produced in the propulsion phase
	Braking velocity	$m\cdot s^{-1}$	The average velocity produced in the braking phase
	Propulsion velocity	$m\cdot s^{-1}$	The average velocity produced in the propulsion phase
	Braking rate of force development	$N\cdot s^{-1}$	The average rate of force development produced in the braking phase
	Landing force	N	The average force produced in the landing phase
Peak	Braking force	N	The maximum force produced in the braking phase
	Propulsion force	N	The maximum force produced in the propulsion phase
	Braking power	W	The minimum (i.e. peak negative) power produced in the braking phase
	Propulsion power	W	The maximum power produced in the propulsion phase
	Braking velocity	$m\cdot s^{-1}$	The minimum (i.e. peak negative) velocity produced in the braking phase
	Propulsion velocity	$m\cdot s^{-1}$	The maximum velocity produced in the propulsion phase
	Braking rate of force development	$N\cdot s^{-1}$	The maximum rate of force development produced in the braking phase
	Countermovement displacement	m	The minimum (i.e. peak negative) displacement achieved between the onset of movement and then end of the braking phase
	Propulsion displacement	m	The maximum displacement produced in the propulsion phase
	Landing force	N	The maximum force produced in the landing phase
Summed	Net braking impulse	Ns	The total area underneath the net force-time curve in the braking phase
	Net propulsion impulse	Ns	The total area underneath the net force-time curve in the propulsion phase
	Net landing impulse	Ns	The total area underneath the net force-time curve in the landing phase
	Area under the force-velocity curve	W	The total area underneath the entire force-velocity curve
	Braking work	J	The total area underneath the net force-displacement curve in the braking phase
	Propulsion work	J	The total area underneath the net force-displacement curve in the propulsion phase

7.4.5.2 Take-off velocity method

Estimating jump height using the take-off velocity method is based on the law of conservation of mechanical energy, whereby the kinetic energy (half mass × velocity²) at take-off is equal to the potential energy (mass × gravitational acceleration × height) at the apex the jump. A greater COM velocity at take-off is attained by applying larger propulsion net impulse (net force × time) and work (force × displacement). This is due to the impulse-momentum and work-energy theorems, respectively. The impulse-momentum theorem states that a change in a body's momentum (in this case, the athlete's mass × its velocity) is equal to the net impulse applied to it. The work-energy theorem states that the work done on an object equals the change in the kinetic energy of the object. The equation for estimating jump height from take-off velocity is as follows:

$$JH = \frac{v^2}{2 \times 9.81}$$

where JH = jump height and v = vertical take-off velocity.

Due to the issues surrounding the flight time-based estimation of jump height (Kibele, 1998), practitioners and researchers should instead consider using the take-off velocity method of estimating jump height (Moir, 2008). However, this method is not without its flaws. For example, if an accurate measure of the athlete's bodyweight cannot be obtained (for example, if they did not remain still during the weighing phase) then the velocity derived from the CMJ force-time curve will be inaccurate. In such instances, the flight time method may actually provide a more accurate estimation of jump height. This reinforces the need to implement robust data collection protocols in line with earlier discussions.

7.5 Data interpretation

This section will briefly consider how data should be interpreted. In keeping with previous sections, it will mainly consider the interpretation of CMJ force-time data as most field-based equipment provide jump height only. If jump height increases, then velocity at take-off must have increased through the application of a larger propulsion net impulse and work. Without sampling force data (or displacement [e.g. via LPT technology] or velocity [e.g. via accelerometer technology] data and subsequently applying inverse dynamics) throughout the CMJ, however, one is unable to ascertain whether propulsion net impulse and work increased due to increased propulsion force, or due to increased propulsion time (net impulse) and displacement (work), or both. Thankfully, inspecting the force-time data sampled throughout each previously defined phase of the CMJ enables a more detailed interpretation of the performance changes which led to an increased jump height. Assuming an athlete's body mass remains relatively constant between testing occasions, the following phase-by-phase alterations in CMJ force-time characteristics prior to take-off can be interpreted as positive performance adaptations that led to increased jump height:

Unweighting phase: a greater unweighting net impulse means that a greater peak negative COM velocity was achieved. In other words, the athlete performed a more rapid unweighting phase. This means that the athlete must apply an equally large net impulse in the braking phase to reduce momentum to zero (to momentarily stop in the lowest squat position) (Kibele, 1998; Mizuguchi et al., 2015). The unweighting phase is important, therefore, as it influences the rate and magnitude of force that must be produced during the braking phase which, in turn, will be likely to influence SSC function (Kibele, 1998).

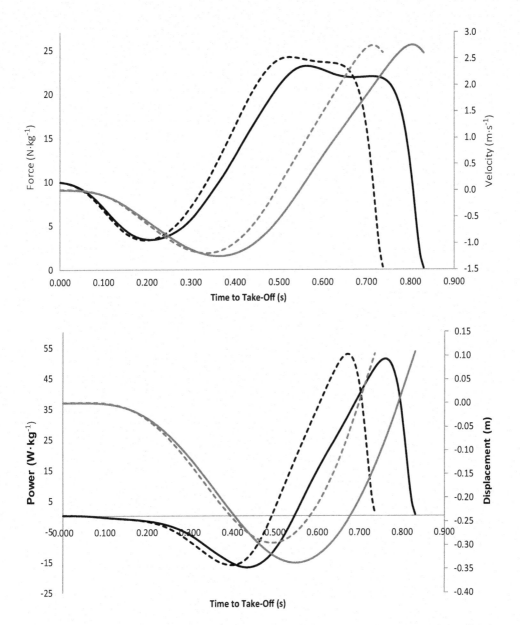

Figure 7.5 Countermovement jump force-time (black lines) and velocity-time (grey lines) curves (top) and power-time (black lines) and displacement-time (grey lines) curves (bottom) for athletes who attained a high (dashed lines) versus a low (solid lines) reactive strength index modified.

Braking phase: if braking phase time remains the same or shortens, this means the athlete will have applied a more force-dominant braking net impulse (i.e. braking net impulse must have increased to match the increased unweighting net impulse and if braking phase time reduced or remained constant, then braking force must have increased to achieve this, assuming the athlete's countermovement depth is consistent). Such a strategy will, therefore, be characterised by a taller (large force) and thinner (short time) active net impulse and a higher rate of force development in the braking phase (McMahon et al., 2017b, 2017c, 2018a; Mizuguchi et al., 2015; Sole et al., 2018).

Propulsion phase: the force at the onset of the propulsion phase is determined by the force at the end of the braking phase and the peak forces attained for each of these phases usually occur within a very short time of one another (usually towards the very end of the braking phase and the very start of the propulsion phase, assuming the athlete minimises the amortisation phase). The shape of the propulsion force-time curve (certainly during the early part of this phase) is, therefore, influenced by the braking peak force, with a larger braking peak force requiring a larger propulsion force to be applied quickly to minimise time spent transitioning between phases and to re-accelerate body mass sooner. If the athlete achieves a quick transition between braking and propulsion phases, one will probably be unable to distinguish between the peak force attained in each phase. If the increase in propulsion net force outweighs a reduction in propulsion phase time (or, indeed, if propulsion phase time remains unchanged), propulsion net impulse will have increased, thus leading to the increased jump height recorded.

The phase-by-phase performance changes described above are in line with a recent cross-sectional study which revealed that athletes who naturally jumped higher in CMJ but with a shorter time to take-off (reflective of a higher reactive strength index modified, a metric which is discussed in detail in Chapter 14) achieved a shallower and quicker countermovement (McMahon et al., 2018a). We therefore advocate that such characteristics (Figure 7.5) should be viewed as a positive adaptation to CMJ performance given that athletes are usually required to produce high forces in short time periods as part of their respective sports. The opposite characteristics (i.e. reduced force and longer time to take-off, even if jump height is maintained or increases) should be viewed as a negative adaptation, if the aim is to improve the athlete's rapid force-producing capability. Methods of determining meaningful changes in performance tests results, including jump test variables, are discussed in Chapter 16.

7.6 References

Beckham, G., Suchomel, T., & Miziguchi, S. (2014). Force plate use in performance monitoring and sports science testing. *New Studies in Athletics, 3*, 25–37.

Chavda, S., Bromley, T., Jarvis, P., Williams, S., Bishop, C., Turner, A.N., Lake, J.P., & Mundy, P.D. (2018). Force-time characteristics of the countermovement jump: Analyzing the curve in Excel. *Strength & Conditioning Journal, 40*(2), 67–77.

Cormie, P., McBride, J.M., & McCaulley, G.O. (2008). Power-time, force-time, and velocity-time curve analysis during the jump squat: impact of load. *Journal of Applied Biomechanics, 24*(2), 112–120.

Cormie, P., McBride, J.M., & McCaulley, G.O. (2009). Power-time, force-time, and velocity-time curve analysis of the countermovement jump: Impact of training. *The Journal of Strength & Conditioning Research, 23*(1), 177–186.

Eagles, A.N., Sayers, M.G.L., Bousson, M., & Lovell, D.I. (2015). Current methodologies and implications of phase identification of the vertical jump: A systematic review and meta-analysis. *Sports Medicine, 45*(9), 1311–1323.

Ebben, W., Flanagan, E., & Jensen, R. (2007). Gender similarities in rate of force development and time to takeoff during the countermovement jump. *Journal of Exercise Physiology Online, 10*, 10–17.

Gathercole, R., Sporer, B., Stellingwerff, T., & Sleivert, G. (2015). Alternative countermovement-jump analysis to quantify acute neuromuscular fatigue. *International Journal of Sports Physiology and Performance, 10*(1), 84–92.

Gutiérrez-Dávila, M., Amaro, F.J., Garrido, J.M., & Rojas, F.J. (2014). An analysis of two styles of arm action in the vertical countermovement jump. *Sports Biomechanics, 13*(2), 135–143.

Hara, M., Shibayama, A., Takeshita, D., Hay, D.C., & Fukashiro, S. (2008). A comparison of the mechanical effect of arm swing and countermovement on the lower extremities in vertical jumping. *Human Movement Science, 27*(4), 636–648.

Harman, E.A., Rosenstein, M.T., Frykman, P.N., & Rosenstein, R.M. (1990). The effects of arms and countermovement on vertical jumping. *Medicine and Science in Sports and Exercise, 22*(6), 825–833.

Hatze, H. (1998). Validity and reliability of methods for testing vertical jumping performance. *Journal of Applied Biomechanics, 14*(2), 127–140.

Haugen, T., & Buchheit, M. (2016). Sprint Running Performance Monitoring: Methodological and Practical Considerations. *Sports Medicine, 46*(5), 641–656.

Henry, F.M. (1967). "Best" versus "Average" Individual Scores. *Research Quarterly, 38*(2), 317–320.

Hori, N., Newton, R.U., Kawamori, N., McGuigan, M.R., Kraemer, W.J., & Nosaka, K. (2009). Reliability of performance measurements derived from ground reaction force data during countermovement jump and the influence of sampling frequency. *The Journal of Strength & Conditioning Research, 23*(3), 874–882.

Jidovtseff, B., Quievre, J., Nigel, H., & Cronin, J. (2014). Influence of jumping strategy on kinetic and kinematic variables. *Journal of Sports Medicine and Physical Fitness, 54*(2), 129–138.

Kibele, A. (1998). Possibilities and limitations in the biomechanical analysis of countermovement jumps: A methodological study. *Journal of Applied Biomechanics, 14*(1), 105–117.

Laffaye, G., et al. (2014). Countermovement jump height: Gender and sport-specific differences in the force-time variables. *The Journal of Strength & Conditioning Research, 28*(4): 1096–1105.

Lake, J., Mundy, P., & Carden, P. (2016a). The effect of barbell load on vertical jump landing force-time characteristics. *The Journal of Strength & Conditioning Research, 30*(S1), S147–S148.

Lake, J.P., Mundy, P.D., Comfort, P., McMahon, J.J., Suchomel, T.J., & Carden, P. (2017). The validity of portable force plate countermovement vertical jump reactive strength and force-time characteristics. *40th Annual National Conference and Exhibition of the National Strength and Conditioning Association*. Las Vegas, NV.

Lake, J.P., Murrell, J., Mundy, P.D., Carden, P., Comfort, P., McMahon, J.J., & Suchomel, T.J. (2016b). Validity and reliability of inexpensive portable force plate jump height. *39th Annual National Conference and Exhibition of the National Strength and Conditioning Association*. New Orleans, LA.

Linthorne, N.P. (2001). Analysis of standing vertical jumps using a force platform. *American Journal of Physics, 69*(11), 1198–1204.

McMahon, J.J., Jones, P.A., & Comfort, P. (2017a). Comment on: "Anthropometric and physical qualities of elite male youth rugby league players". *Sports Medicine, 47*(12), 2667–2668.

McMahon, J.J., Jones, P.A., Suchomel, T.J., Lake, J., & Comfort, P. (2018a). Influence of reactive strength index modified on force- and power-time curves. *International Journal of Sports Physiology and Performance, 13*(2), 220–227.

McMahon, J.J., Murphy, S., Rej, S.J., & Comfort, P. (2017b). Countermovement-jump-phase characteristics of senior and academy rugby league players. *International Journal of Sports Physiology and Performance, 12*(6), 803–811.

McMahon, J.J., Rej, S.J., & Comfort, P. (2017c). Sex differences in countermovement jump phase characteristics. *Sports, 5*(1), 8.

McMahon, J.J., Ripley, N.J., & Rej, S.J. (2016). Effect of modulating eccentric leg stiffness on concentric force-velocity characteristics demonstrated in the countermovement jump. *Journal of Sports Sciences, 34*(S1), S19.

McMahon, J.J., Suchomel, T.J., Lake, J.P., & Comfort, P. (2018b). Understanding the key phases of the countermovement jump force-time curve. *Strength and Conditioning Journal, 40*(4), 96–106.

Mizuguchi, S., Sands, W.A., Wassinger, C.A., Lamont, H.S., & Stone, M.H. (2015). A new approach to determining net impulse and identification of its characteristics in countermovement jumping: reliability and validity. *Sports Biomechanics, 14*(2), 258–272.

Moir, G.L. (2008). Three Different methods of calculating vertical jump height from force platform data in men and women. *Measurement in Physical Education and Exercise Science, 12*(4), 207–218.

Owen, N.J., Watkins, J., Kilduff, L.P., Bevan, H.R., & Bennett, M.A. (2014). Development of a criterion method to determine peak mechanical power output in a countermovement jump. *The Journal of Strength & Conditioning Research, 28*(6), 1552–1558.

Peterson Silveira, R., Stergiou, P., Carpes, F.P., Castro, F.A.D.S., Katz, L., & Stefanyshyn, D.J. (2016). Validity of a portable force platform for assessing biomechanical parameters in three different tasks. *Sports Biomechanics, 16*(2), 177–186.

Petronijevic, M.S., Garcia-Ramos, A., Mirkov, D.M., Jaric, S., Valdevit, Z., & Knezevic, O.M. (Publish ahead of print). Self-preferred initial position could be a viable alternative to the standard squat jump testing procedure. *The Journal of Strength & Conditioning Research.*

Rice, P.E., Goodman, C.L., Capps, C.R., Triplett, N.T., Erickson, T.M., & McBride J.M. (2017). Force- and power-time curve comparison during jumping between strength-matched male and female basketball players. *European Journal of Sport Science, 17,* 286–293.

Riggs, M.P., & Sheppard, J.M. (2009). The relative importance of strength and power qualities to vertical jump height of elite beach volleyball players during the counter-movement and squat jump. *Journal of Human Sport and Exercise, 4,* 221–236.

Sánchez-Sixto, A., Harrison, A., & Floría, P. (Publish ahead of print). La importancia de la profundidad del contramovimiento en el ciclo estiramiento-acortamiento/Importance of countermovement depth in stretching and shortening cycle analysis. *Revista Internacional de Medicina y Ciencias de la Actividad Física y el Deporte.*

Slinde, F., Suber, C., Suber, L., Edwén, C.E., & Svantesson, U. (2008). Test-retest reliability of three different countermovement jumping tests. *The Journal of Strength & Conditioning Research, 22*(2), 640–644.

Sole, C.J., Mizuguchi, S., Sato, K., Moir, G.L., & Stone, M.H. (2018). Phase characteristics of the countermovement jump force-time curve: A comparison of athletes by jumping ability. *The Journal of Strength & Conditioning Research, 32*(4), 1155–1165.

Street, G., McMillan, S., Board, W., Rasmussen, M., & Heneghan, J.M. (2001). Sources of error in determining countermovement jump height with the impulse method. *Journal of Applied Biomechanics, 17*(1), 43–54.

Thomasson, M.L., & Comfort, P. (2012). Occurrence of fatigue during sets of static squat jumps performed at a variety of loads. *The Journal of Strength & Conditioning Research, 26*(3), 677–683.

Vanrenterghem, J., De Clercq, D., & Cleven, P.V. (2001). Necessary precautions in measuring correct vertical jumping height by means of force plate measurements. *Ergonomics, 44*(8), 814–818.

8 Sprint testing

Robert Lockie

8.1 Introduction to linear speed

Linear speed is an essential quality for many athletes and, accordingly, is a recommended characteristic to assess (McGuigan, 2015; Triplett, 2012). There are several different components to a maximal sprint, and the importance of these will vary amongst different athletic populations. A velocity or speed curve produced from a 100-metre (m) sprint, which tracks the speed at which an individual is running relative to the distance covered, highlights the different components of a sprint. Debaere et al. (2013) described four phases: a start action, an acceleration phase, a phase of maximum speed, followed by deceleration to the end. These phases are noted on the curve shown in Figure 8.1, which was reproduced from Usain Bolt's 100-m sprint at the London Olympic Games final in 2012 (Krzysztof and Mero, 2013). As noted by Lockie (2016), the shape of this curve will essentially be the same for anyone starting a maximal sprint from a stationary position; only the magnitudes of the values will change.

In many sports, the ability to reach a high sprinting speed is important, as a faster athlete can cover a greater distance in a shorter time period. Olympic-level sprinters can achieve a speed in excess of 12 metres per second ($m \cdot s^{-1}$) (Krzysztof and Mero, 2013), and tend to reach this peak within the 40–60 m range of a 100-m sprint (Slawinski et al., 2010). However, acceleration distances in excess of 40 m or more are generally not practical for field or court sport athletes. The nature of these sports often does not allow participants to cover the distance required to attain maximum speed, due to confounding factors such as opponents, pursuit of a ball and the boundaries inherent to each sport (Young et al., 1995). As an example, in Australian football (Dawson et al., 2004), rugby union (Deutsch et al., 2007) and soccer (Krustrup et al., 2005; Mohr et al., 2003), the mean duration of a linear sprint during a match is approximately 2 seconds. A 2-second sprint equates to an approximate distance of 10 m for many males and females (Dawes et al., 2015; Duthie et al., 2006a; Lockie et al., 2011, 2013b, in press b; Magal et al., 2009). Sprints of this short distance and duration will not allow for the attainment of peak speed, particularly if starting from a stationary position. To make full use of their speed, most athletes should try and accelerate as quickly as possible (Lockie et al., 2011; Spinks et al., 2007), and team sport athletes can attain their peak speed after approximately 30 m of a maximal sprint (Duthie et al., 2006a; Vescovi, 2012). These distances are important to consider, as they can set the boundaries for the sprint tests adopted by a practitioner.

Determining whether an athlete is performing at their optimal speed level requires knowledge of the history of the athlete's speed profiles, and any external factors that might affect this (Cheng et al., 2010). A range of equipment is available which the practitioner can use to

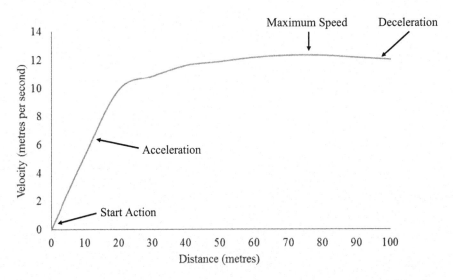

Figure 8.1 A 100-m sprint velocity or speed curve highlighting the start action, acceleration, maximum speed and deceleration phases.

Table 8.1 Different sprint testing equipment, the company that produces the equipment, the company or example sale websites and the approximate costs of this equipment in US dollars. These prices do not include sales taxes or shipping.

Equipment	Company	Website	Approximate cost in US dollars
Stopwatches	Varied	www.amazon.com	~$2–$200
Radar gun	Applied Concepts, Inc.	www.stalkerradar.com	~$500–$2000
Timing gates	Brower Timing Systems	http://browertiming.com/	Start timer: ~$1000
		www.power-systems.com/	Single gate: ~$500
	Swift Performance	http://swiftperformance.com/	Two gate: ~$6000
		http://performbetter.co.uk	Four gate: ~$12,500
			Single gate: ~$580
	Fusion Sport	www.fusionsport.com	One gate: ~$800
			Two gates: ~$10,000
			Four gates: ~$14,000
			Six gates: ~$18,000
			Eight gates: ~$22,000
Optojump	Microgate	www.optojump.com/	~$2000–$22,000
		http://performbetter.co.uk	(1 metre up to 10 metres)

assess sprint performance. Most teams and sporting institutes will be constrained by financial considerations, which will ultimately result in practitioners deciding on a cost-benefit rationale to determine how they will measure the sprint performance of their athletes (Earp and Newton, 2012). Table 8.1 displays the approximate costs of several different types of commercially available timing systems. Additionally, practitioners should understand the strengths and limitations of the available equipment, as this will inform how sprint data can be recorded and interpreted.

8.2 Sprint testing equipment

8.2.1 Introduction

The gold standard for sprint timing is a fully automated system, incorporating pressure-sensitive starting blocks and high-resolution photo-finish cameras (Haugen and Buchheit, 2016). However, a system such as this is not feasible for most practitioners, due to excessive cost and impracticalities for use in the field. This chapter will focus on equipment that has the most practical value, from both a cost and ease of use perspective. Two primary statistical measures will be discussed; intra-class correlation coefficients (ICCs) and coefficient of variation (CV). ICCs measure the trial-to-trial reliability of data (i.e. how similar multiple trials are for an individual), with ICCs equal to or above 0.70 generally considered acceptable (Baumgartner and Chung, 2001). CV is measured as a percentage and provides an indication of the spread of data relative to the mean; values of 5% or less are typically considered acceptable for a measurement device (Hopkins, 2000a). A summary of the reliability and measurement error data for different timing systems, as well as potential sources of error, can be viewed in Table 8.2. These will be discussed in this chapter.

8.2.2 Hand-held timing devices

Hand-held timing devices such as stopwatches are the simplest method to measure sprint performance. Experienced timers are able to record reliable sprint time data via the use of hand-held devices (Hetzler et al., 2008; Mann et al., 2015; Mayhew et al., 2010). However, stopwatches (or timing applications available on mobile or cell phones and tablets) are limited by an individual's reaction time, and thus tend to feature larger measurement errors compared to other timing methods (Haugen and Buchheit, 2016). Several studies have demonstrated that the times recorded by hand-held stopwatches versus that of electronic timing devices are significantly different, with times over 36.6 m being faster when recorded manually (Ebben et al., 2009; Mann et al., 2015; Mayhew et al., 2010). Historically, correction factors of –0.20 s have been applied to stopwatch times in an attempt to make them comparable to electronically recorded times (Fry and Kraemer, 1991). Hetzler et al. (2008), however, demonstrated several issues with applying a standard correction factor by comparing hand-held stopwatch times with a Brower electronic timing gate system measuring the 200-m running performance of trained runners and cyclists. Times were recorded for every 25-m interval, and Hetzler et al. (2008) found that there were no significant differences in stopwatch times and the electronic timing system. Furthermore, the stopwatch times were not consistently faster or slower than the electronic times. This would eliminate the use of a correction factor, as this would actually increase the error associated with hand-held sprint times.

If practitioners are limited to the use of hand-held timing devices, explicit instructions regarding hand placement, standing position relative to the start and finish of the sprint, stopwatch operation, and the start/stop protocol should be provided (Hetzler et al., 2008). This should ensure consistency with timing procedures, and limit the errors associated with the data. From a practical perspective, the use of hand-held timing devices during sprint training sessions could be useful as a means of providing immediate feedback to the athlete.

Table 8.2 Reliability (intra-class correlation coefficients [ICC]) and measurement error (coefficient of variation [CV]) for popular sprint timing systems over different sprint intervals, and the common sources of error for each system.

Equipment	Study	Participants	Sprint distances	ICCs	CVs	Primary sources of error
Stopwatches	Hetzler et al. (2008)	Recreational runners	25-m intervals over 200 m	Single timer = 0.917; multiple timers = 0.982	–	• Reaction time of the timer • Position of the timer relative to the start and finish of the sprint • Inappropriate application of correction factor
	Mayhew et al. (2010)	Division II collegiate American football players	0.36.6 m	0.987	–	
	Mann et al. (2015)	Division I collegiate American football players	0.36.6 m	0.984	1.7%	
LAVEG laser gun	Bullock et al. (2008)	Elite skeleton athletes	5–10 m and 0–30 m	0.99 and 0.98	–	• Device has to be manually aimed at the sprinter • Start position used • Movement variability during acceleration • Spurious reflections from anything other than the intended target
	Poulos et al. (2010)	Adolescent track and field athletes	0–10 m and 0–50 m	–	3.1% and 1.9%	
Brower timing gates	Comfort et al. (2011)	Elite rugby league players	0–5 m, 0–10 m and 0–20 m	0.97, 0.98 and 0.97	–	• Variability between single beam vs. dual beam vs. single beam with data post-processing systems • False signals caused by limbs breaking light beams before the torso • Variations in gate height • Variations in start distance • Start position used • Movement variability during acceleration
	Winchester et al. (2008)	Collegiate track and field athletes	0–20 m, 20–40 m and 0–40 m	0.922–0.987, 0.944–0.983 and 0.944–0.999	–	
	Shalfawi et al. (2012)	Physical education students	0–10 m, 0–20 m and 0–30 m	0.91, 0.91 and 0.99	2.3%, 2.9% and 0.9%	
	Carr et al. (2015)	First-class county cricketers	0–5 m, 0–10 m and 0–20 m	0.948, 0.964 and 0.964	–	
	Mann et al. (2015)	Division I collegiate American football players	0–36.6 m	0.988	1.5%	

Device	Study	Population	Distances	Reliability (ICC)	CV (%)
	Darrall-Jones et al. (2016)	Adolescent rugby league and rugby union players	0–10 m, 0–20 m, 0–30 m and 0–40 m	–	3.05%, 1.82%, 1.95% and 1.33%
Swift Speedlight timing gates	Glaister et al. (2007)	Physically active university students	0–10 m, 0–20 m and 0–30 m	Best = 0.79, 0.87 and 0.91 Mean = 0.88, 0.92 and 0.94	Best = 2.24%, 1.74% and 1.51% Mean = 1.58%, 1.45% and 1.34%
	Cronin and Templeton (2008)	Physically active university students	0–10 m and 0–20 m	–	1.1–1.2% and 0.69–0.83%
	Galbett et al. (2008)	Experienced rugby league players	0–5 m, 0–10 m and 0–20 m	0.84, 0.87 and 0.96	3.2%, 1.9% and 1.3%
	Lim and Kong (2013)	Trained sprinters	0–10 m, 0–20 m and 0–30 m	0.754, 0.918 and 0.942	–
	Scanlan et al. (2015)	Regional- or state-level basketballers	0–6 m	0.99	1.7%
Fusion Sport timing gates	Oliver and Meyers (2009)	Recreational athletes	0–10 m	–	2.5%
	Green et al. (2010)	Experienced rugby union players	0–10 m and 0–30 m	0.88 and 0.97	–
	Lockie et al. (2013a)	Amateur cricketers	0–5 m, 0–10 m and 0–30 m 0–5 m and 0–17.68 m	0.80, 0.87, and 0.97 0.87 and 0.96	–
	Lockie et al. (2013b)	Amateur Australian football players	0–5 m, 0–10 m and 0–20 m	0.76, 0.85 and 0.96	5.1%, 3.5% and 1.9%
	Callaghan et al. (2014)	Amateur cricketers	0–5 m and 0–17.68 m	0.93 and 0.95	–

As this information is not necessarily being recorded for historical use, the influence of error on the times is less impactful. Nevertheless, due to the relatively large absolute errors associated with the hand-held timing devices, electronic timing is preferable for sprint testing (Haugen and Buchheit, 2016).

8.2.3 Radar guns and laser devices

Radar guns or laser devices are examples of electronic timing devices used to assess sprint performance. An advantage of these devices is that performance can be tracked for the entirety of a sprint. This allows for measurement of where maximum speed occurs during a sprint, which can only be estimated if sprint times are measured in intervals such as for hand-held timing devices or timing gates. Radar guns use the Doppler effect, as the gun transmits an electromagnetic signal that interacts with the sprinter, before returning to the device at a different frequency (Chen et al., 2006). Any changes in the properties of the returned signal are detected by the radar gun, and these data are converted into a speed measurement. Laser devices measure time delays of reflected pulsed infrared light. Moreover, as a laser device emits a narrow cone of light, it can be less sensitive to spurious reflections from other objects extraneous to the target (Harrison et al., 2005). To record a sprint, these devices are typically positioned on a tripod approximately 2 m behind the sprinter at a height of 1 m, where the practitioner can manually aim the device (Chelly and Denis, 2001; Harrison et al., 2005). An example set-up is shown in Figure 8.2.

Figure 8.2 An example set-up for the measurement of a sprint using a radar gun.

The Stalker Radar System (Applied Concepts Inc., Richardson, USA) equipment has been used to track a 20-m sprint in male rugby union players (Macadam et al., 2017), 40-m sprint performance in elite sprinters (Chelly and Denis, 2001) and 100-m performance in physical education students (Morin et al., 2006). Chelly and Denis (2001) defined the reliability of this system by measuring subjects moving at 1–7 m·s^{-1} and rolling balls moving between 8 and 22 m·s^{-1}, and comparing the data to a photocell system. The resulting correlations were very high (correlation coefficient [r] = 0.999), indicating reliable data.

The LAVEG laser system (Jenoptik, Jena, Germany) has measured the 20-m sprint performance of elite rugby league players (Comfort et al., 2011), 30-m sprint performance of skeleton athletes (Bullock et al., 2008) and the 50-m sprint performance of adolescent track and field athletes (Poulos et al., 2010) and adult sprinters (Bezodis et al., 2012). Poulos et al. (2010) documented CV data of 3.1% and 1.9% for 0–10 m and 0–50 m time recorded by the LAVEG system, respectively. However, the distance at which maximum speed was reached was more variable, with a CV of 18.2%. In skeleton athletes, Bullock et al. (2008) found the 5–10 m time and 0–30 m times had ICCs of 0.99 and 0.98, respectively. Comfort et al. (2011) found that for elite rugby league players, the 0–5 m, 0–10 m and 0–20 m sprint times also demonstrated high reliability, with ICCs of 0.97, 0.98 and 0.97, respectively. These studies collectively show that radar and laser devices can record reliable sprint time and speed data.

There are limitations associated with radar or laser devices. The practitioner must ensure a consistent target location of the radar or laser on the athlete as they sprint away from the device. Radar or laser devices must be operated manually, and the target must be adjusted as the sprinter initiates their sprint (Cheng et al., 2010). Laser devices produce relatively high levels of random errors in the first 5 m of a maximal sprint, due to changes in the position of the upper body during acceleration (Bezodis et al., 2012; Bullock et al., 2008). Therefore, if acceleration is the focus of a sprint assessment, other data collection methods (e.g. timing gates) may be preferred over a radar or laser device. If a practitioner wishes to measure maximum speed, or when an athlete reaches their maximum speed, then a radar or laser device would be useful.

8.2.4 Photocell systems – timing gates

Photocell or timing gate systems are very popular for the assessment of sprint performance (Haugen and Buchheit, 2016). A timing gate consists of a light source or transmitter, and an optical pick-up or reflector (Cronin and Templeton, 2008). The transmitter and reflector are positioned opposite each other, forming a gate that can be run through, and the light beam from the transmitter hits the reflector and is bounced back to the transmitter where it is detected. When sets of transmitter and reflector gates are arranged at separations along a runway, a series of beams are produced that can be successively interrupted by an individual sprinting through them. If the voltage output from each beam is logged, a pulse wave will be produced, which rises on beam interruption and falls upon reinstatement of the beam (Yeadon et al., 1999). It is through this process that time between each gate can be recorded, and data are typically recorded on a hand-held personal computer or tablet. The practitioner should be positioned close to the first gate to ensure the hand-held personal computer or tablet is in range of the gates, and to monitor the start of the athlete (Figure 8.3).

Figure 8.3 The position of the test administrator with the hand-held recording device for sprint testing with a timing light system. The athlete has been positioned 0.5 m behind the first timing gate.

Timing gate systems can be single- or dual-beam, and can also incorporate algorithms that post-process the recorded data. The use of a dual-beam gate, or post-processing of signal data, can reduce any timing errors associated with the recorded time. This is because the major source of error from a timing gate system is a false signal, which occurs when the light beam is broken by an outstretched arm or leg, rather than the torso of the sprinter (Cronin and Templeton, 2008; Earp and Newton, 2012; Yeadon et al., 1999). The height of the timing gate can influence which body part breaks the light beam. Yeadon et al. (1999) found that when a timing gate was placed at a height 1.25 m (torso height for their subjects), the light beam was broken twice, separately by the arm and torso, in a majority of cases. A low height for timing gates (0.60 m) can also be problematic, as the legs are more likely to break the beam than the torso (Cronin and Templeton, 2008). Depending on the system, hip height usually serves as a suitable guide for setting up the gates (Winchester et al., 2008; Yeadon et al., 1999). Cronin and Templeton (2008) further recommend that practitioners standardise their testing procedures and be consistent with their gate heights

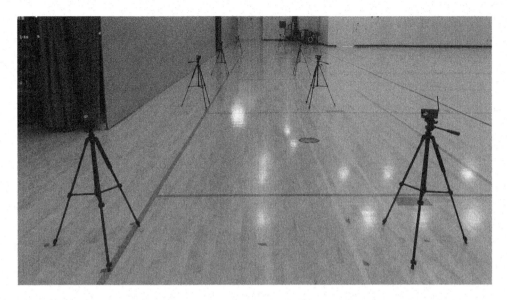

Figure 8.4 The Brower timing system set up to record a 20 m sprint.

to allow for longitudinal comparisons. This is because data recorded from gates positioned at different heights will generally produce times that are not interchangeable (Altmann et al., 2017; Cronin and Templeton, 2008).

There are a number of different timing gate systems available to the practitioner; this chapter will highlight three. Firstly, Brower Timing Systems (Knoxville, USA) use a single beam between the gates (Darrall-Jones et al., 2016; Haugen et al., 2012; Winchester et al., 2008). An example set-up for a 20-m sprint can be viewed in Figure 8.4. Single-beam systems are most susceptible to recording false signals when a limb breaks the infrared light between the gates rather than the torso (Darrall-Jones et al., 2016; Earp and Newton, 2012). This places a great emphasis on gate height positioning to limit the potential for a swinging arm to interrupt the light beam. In addition to this, any variations between timing gate systems tend be negligible as distance increases (Altmann et al., 2017; Darrall-Jones et al., 2016; Earp and Newton, 2012; Shalfawi et al., 2012), which provides applicability for a single-beam system. Winchester et al. (2008) measured the 0–20 m, 20–40 m and 0–40 m intervals in a 40-m sprint completed by collegiate track and field athletes, and the ICCs ranged from 0.922 to 0.999. When measuring the 20-m sprint performance of first-class county cricketers, Carr et al. (2015) documented ICCs of 0.948, 0.964 and 0.964, for the 0–5 m, 0–10 m and 0–20 m intervals, respectively. In a 36.6-m sprint performed by Division I American football players, an ICC of 0.988 and CV of 1.5% were recorded by Mann et al. (2015). Darrall-Jones et al. (2016) found CVs of 3.05%, 1.82%, 1.95% and 1.33% for the 0–10 m, 0–20 m, 0–30 m and 0–40 m intervals, respectively, of a 40-m sprint when performed by junior rugby players. Shalfawi et al. (2012) measured both reliability and measurement error for a 30-m sprint performed by male and female physical education students. ICCs and CVs for the 0–10 m, 0–20 m and 0–30 m intervals were 0.91 and 2.3%, 0.91 and 2.9% and 0.99 and 0.9%, respectively. Taken together, these studies highlight that even with a single-beam system, reliable sprint data can be recorded over a range of distances.

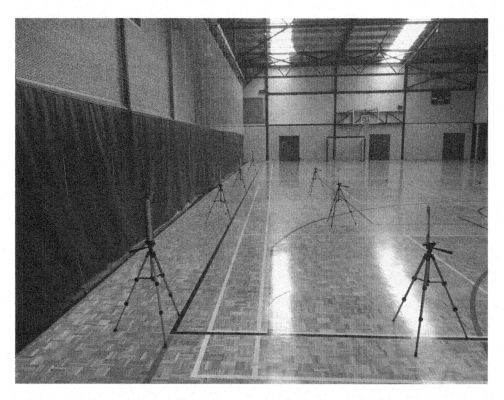

Figure 8.5 The Swift Speedlight timing system set up to record a 20 m sprint.

Swift Speedlight (Swift Performance, Lismore, Australia) is a modulated dual-beam system with polarising filters (Cronin and Templeton, 2008; Glaister et al., 2007). A dual-beam system means that light beams are positioned at two heights (Figure 8.5). This should limit the effects of an arm breaking a single beam, as time is only recorded when both beams are broken. Glaister et al. (2007) measured 0–10 m, 0–20 m and 0–30 m sprint times in male university students in a 12 × 35 m repeated-sprint test, and found the best (ICC = 0.79–0.91; CV = 1.51–2.24%) and mean (ICC = 0.88–0.94; CV = 1.34–1.58%) times were all reliable. In a maximal 30-m sprint completed by track sprinters, Lim and Kong (2013) also found times recorded over the 0–10 m, 0–20 m and 0–30 m intervals were reliable, with ICCs ranging from 0.754 to 0.942. Experienced rugby league players attained ICCs and CVs ranging from 0.84 to 0.96 and 1.3 to 2.9%, respectively, for the 0–5 m, 0–10 m and 0–20 m interval times in a 20-m sprint (Gabbett et al., 2008). Cronin and Templeton (2008) investigated 0–10 m and 0–20 m sprint times completed by university students, and CVs ranged from 1.1 to 1.2% and 0.69 to 0.83%, respectively. Within a basketball-specific fitness test, Scanlan et al. (2015) found an ICC of 0.99 and CV of 1.7% for a 6-m sprint. Thus, in addition to single-beam systems, dual-beam timing gates can also record reliable sprint data across different intervals.

The SmartSpeed system (Fusion Sport, Sumner Park, Australia), shown in Figure 8.6, is single-beam but utilises error detection and post-processing of the signal data (Stanton et al., 2016). Stanton et al. (2016) stated that in the event of multiple triggers (e.g. an

Figure 8.6 The Fusion Sport timing system set up to record a 20 m sprint.

arm and a torso), the algorithm in the system interprets the longest trigger as the true time. This helps to improve the reliability of the recorded data. In support of this, Oliver and Meyers (2009) found a CV of 2.5% for a 10-m sprint performed by male recreational athletes, while Green et al. (2010) documented ICCs of 0.88 and 0.97 for the 0–10 m and 0–30 m intervals of a 30-m sprint performed by male rugby union players. Lockie et al. (2013b) found ICCs of 0.76, 0.85 and 0.96, respectively, for the 0–5 m, 0–10 m and 0–20 m intervals of a 20-m sprint when completed by amateur Australian footballers. The CVs for time over these intervals were 5.1%, 3.5% and 1.9%, respectively. The lower ICC and higher CV for the 0–5 m interval could have been influenced by the standing start that was used for the sprint, as there is greater variability in the body position during acceleration (Cronin and Templeton, 2008). When testing male cricketers, Lockie et al. (2013a) found ICCs of 0.80, 0.87 and 0.97 for the 0–5 m, 0–10 m and 0–30 m intervals of a 30-m sprint. Furthermore, when utilising a cricket-specific sprint test over a distance of 17.68 m (the length of a cricket pitch), Lockie et al. (2013a) found ICCs of 0.87 and 0.96 for the 0–5 m and 0–17.68 m intervals. Callaghan et al. (2014) also assessed male cricketers over the 0–5 m and 0–17.68 m sprint intervals, and found high ICCs of 0.93 and 0.95, respectively. Earp and Newton (2012) asserted that timing systems with false-signal processing represent the best technique in relation to recording sprint times and should be considered the gold standard.

There are limitations common across timing gate systems. Multiple gates are required if the practitioner wishes to measure more intervals within a test distance, and this can increase cost. Furthermore, timing gates will only provide split times and average speeds, as opposed to instantaneous speeds during a sprint (Cheng et al., 2010). While this information is clearly useful, practitioners will need to use other methods (e.g. radar or laser devices) if they wish to measure instantaneous speed during a sprint. Nevertheless, within the context of these limitations, and the specific procedures required for setting up timing gates (i.e. ensuring a gate height and using a system that limits the recording of false signals), the practitioner can be confident that the systems described in this chapter can be used to record reliable data.

8.2.5 The Optojump system

Another analysis system that utilises infrared light beams is the Optojump (Microgate, Bolzano, Italy). This a modular optical acquisition system which consists of photoelectric cells built within two parallel 1-m-length bars: one emits infrared light, while the other receives the light beams. The photoelectric cells that emit the infrared beams are positioned 0.03 m above ground level at 0.03 m intervals, and the bars are connected to a personal computer (Ammann et al., 2016; Glatthorn et al., 2011; Kratky and Muller, 2013). The Optojump system can measure technique components of sprinting, including step length and frequency, and contact and flight time. Dolenec and Čoh (2009) noted that although centre of mass speed cannot be measured, the average speed of an athlete can be represented by a body part. For the Optojump system, this is the athlete's foot, as this segment will break the infrared beams. To ensure accurate measurement, the subject's step technique should be consistent (Dolenec and Čoh, 2009). This essentially means that only the maximum speed phase of a sprint can be measured with relative accuracy, as step length and frequency are relatively stable during this period (Krzysztof and Mero, 2013; Luhtanen and Komi, 1978).

Dolenec and Čoh (2009) investigated the times recorded by Brower timing gates and the Optojump system during a 20-m sprint interval that followed a flying start in male and female sprinters. The timing gates were set up to measure time for each 5-m interval within the 20-m sprint zone, so that speed could be calculated. However, it was not possible to determine the beginning and end of specific distances within the Optojump bars to compare to the timing gates, so Dolenec and Čoh (2009) had to estimate distances by the foot contact that was closest to the start and finish within each 5-m section. This decreased the accuracy of the distance measurements, and the speeds recorded from the timing gates and Optojump were not comparable. Furthermore, Ammann et al. (2016) found that the maximal speed contact times of middle-distance runners measured by the Optojump system were underestimated when compared to a gold-standard measurement of a high-speed video camera. Ammann et al. (2016) did note that contact time data were reliable, so could be used to monitor changes in this variable with time, but could not be compared to other systems.

There are other limitations to the Optojump system. In order to measure multiple steps, multiple parallel bars need to be placed in succession, which will increase costs. For example, Debaere et al. (2013) utilised 40 m of Optojump equipment (i.e. 40 1-m paired bars) to measure step kinematics over this distance in track sprinters. Acceleration technique cannot be accurately measured due to the change in step kinematics that occurs during this phase. Furthermore, even when running at higher speeds, individuals may not display symmetrical steps (Belli et al., 1995), which could reduce the accuracy of kinematic measurements by the Optojump system. Nonetheless, this system can provide real-time measurement of step kinematics during maximum-speed sprinting, and could be used to track technique adaptations. Other testing methods, however, should be used to measure changes in sprint times over distances specific to an athlete.

8.3 Sprint testing methodological considerations

8.3.1 Starting position

The most common starts used for sprint testing are either a standing start with a two-point standing, split-stance (Figure 8.7A) or a three-point stance where both feet and one hand

Figure 8.7 The two-point, the three-point start (a) and standing split-stance start (b).

are in contact with the ground (Figure 8.7B) (Duthie et al., 2006b). The use of starting blocks is specific to track sprinters, and should be limited to this population. The standing split-stance start will be appropriate for most athletes, as this body position is more commonly adopted during match-play (i.e. a maximal sprint is initiated from a standing position). Duthie et al. (2006b) also questioned the viability of using the three-point start in populations where familiarisation is required. However, certain testing protocols may make a particular starting position mandatory. For example, the three-point start is a requirement for the 36.6-m sprint at the National Football League American football combine (Kuzmits and Adams, 2008; Robbins, 2010). Athletes should be aware of the requirements for the sprint test they must undertake, especially if it could influence their draft status and future employment (Kuzmits and Adams, 2008; Robbins, 2010). This could result in a need to familiarise and practise prior to the testing day (Duthie et al., 2006b), so that the athlete displays the relevant competency. Nonetheless, most athletes should use a two-point standing, split-stance for the start of a sprint test.

In addition to this, the times recorded for sprints with different types of starts are not interchangeable (Duthie et al., 2006b), so practitioners must ensure there is consistency with the body position, technique and instructions provided to athletes. To ensure consistency, practitioners could adapt the instructions provided by Winkelman et al. (2017) for setting up an athlete in a two-point stance:

- Stand at the start line with your feet hip-width apart.
- Get into your typical two-point stance by placing one foot behind the start line and placing your other foot back at a comfortable distance.

- Set your arms so that they are positioned opposite from your legs.
- Load into your legs and shift forward so that you feel tension and a readiness to sprint forward with no delay.

8.3.2 Distance behind the start line

One particular method for the start is to position the athlete a particular distance behind the start line (Figure 8.3). This distance typically ranges between 0.3 and 1 m (Altmann et al., 2015), and is for the most part essential when using timing gates (Haugen et al., 2015). However, start distances of 0.3 m (Poulos et al., 2010), 0.5 m (Comfort et al., 2011) and 1 m (Bullock et al., 2008) have also been used in laser timing protocols. There can be the argument that because the starting position is behind the zero line, the true distance covered will be greater than the intended distance. In addition to this, the degree of momentum gained prior to breaking the first light beam is the primary source of variation when considering different start techniques for sprint testing (Duthie et al., 2006b). Nevertheless, start distances have featured in many sprint testing studies, and that led Altmann et al. (2015) to compare three different start distances (0.3 m, 0.5 m and 1 m) for a 0–5 m sprint in male college students. The 0–5 m times for the 1 m start distance were significantly faster than the 0.3 m and 0.5 m distances, but there were no significant differences in 0–5 m time between the 0.3 m and 0.5 m start distances. From these results, Altmann et al. (2015) recommended using the 0.3 m start distance.

A limitation of using a start distance of 0.3 m is that it may artificially reduce the forward lean of taller athletes during the start. If a taller subject leans too far forward, they may unintentionally break the light beam of the first gate (Figure 8.8). To avoid this, the 0.5 m start distance can be adopted (Figure 8.3), as this should ensure that a split stance can be safely used without the first gate being broken prior to the sprint, regardless of the size of the athlete. Different populations have been assessed using this start distance, including male first-class county cricketers (Carr et al., 2015), male (Buchheit et al., 2012; Lockie et al., 2016a; Mendez-Villanueva et al., 2011) and female (Lockie et al., 2016c, in press a, in press b) soccer players and high-school (Lockie et al., 2017) and junior-college (Lockie et al., 2016b) American football players. In addition to this, Haugen et al. (2015) suggested that correction factors can be applied to linear sprints that utilise different start distances to allow for comparisons across different protocols. Nevertheless, the main consideration is that when assessing the same population of athletes over extended periods of time, the practitioner should use the same start distance consistently across test sessions.

To eliminate the need to start a certain distance behind the start line, start pads have been incorporated within sprint testing with timing gates. These operate by the athlete exerting pressure on the pad, usually with the hand or foot. Upon take-off, the release of pressure will initiate timing (Duthie et al., 2006b; Winchester et al., 2008). Duthie et al. (2006b) suggested that the benefits of a start pad is a possible decrease in the conscious or unconscious control of body movements that an athlete might undertake for fear of initiating a timing system prior to start take-off. As the hands will leave the ground before the feet during a sprint start (Gutierrez-Davilla et al., 2006), it is arguably best to position the plant hand on the start pad if the practitioner wishes to measure sprint performance from the initiation of movement. However, this will also require the athlete to be familiar with a three-point start. If athletes are not familiar with this start position, the practitioner should use a standing, split-stance that is 0.3–0.5 m behind the start line when using timing gates.

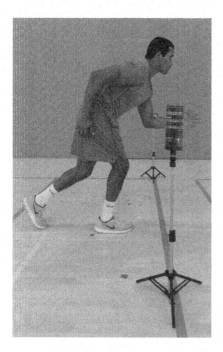

Figure 8.8 A subject falsely breaking the first light beam due to a start line too close to the first gate.

8.3.3 Number of trials

Sprint testing will often feature a number of trials to ensure either consistent or the best performance by an athlete, which may not be achieved if only one trial is performed. Moir et al. (2004) recommended three trials to achieve a reliable best time for a 20-m sprint. However, the number of trials may be limited by the time available for testing, particularly if there is a large volume of athletes that need to be assessed. For example, American football combine testing typically features two trials of a 36.6-m sprint (Iguchi et al., 2011; Lockie et al., 2016b). Cronin and Templeton (2008) intimated that due to the reliability of a good timing-light system, practitioners may only need to record one or two trials to gather reliable information. Furthermore, when conducting sprint testing on track and field athletes, Haugen et al. (2012) found that approximately 80% of their subjects attained their fastest 40-m sprint performance within two trials. Practitioners should attempt to complete two or three sprint trials for their athletes during testing sessions, although two trials may be sufficient if time is limited.

8.3.4 Sprint distances, intervals and flying times

Numerous studies have documented that acceleration and maximum speed are different sprint qualities (Debaere et al., 2013; Little and Williams, 2005; Vescovi and McGuigan, 2008; Young et al., 1995). This means that both must be assessed, as just because an athlete has a high sprint acceleration it does not always mean they will attain a high maximum

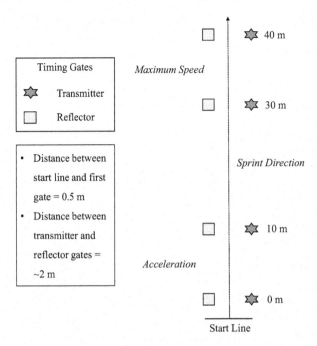

Figure 8.9 An example 40 m sprint test set up for a four-gate timing system where acceleration (0–10 m interval) and maximum speed (30–40 m interval) can be recorded.

speed, and vice versa. In order to ensure testing efficiency, it is important that a practitioner selects a sprint distance and uses equipment that allows for the concurrent measurement of acceleration and maximum speed specific to their athletes.

Young et al. (2008) analysed sprint data from two Australian football teams that utilised timing gate systems. Both teams measured 0–10 m and 0–20 m times, as well as flying times; one team used the 20–30 m interval, while the other measured the 30–40 m interval. When correlating the sprint times, Young et al. (2008) found near-perfect relationships ($r = 0.94$) between 0–10 m and 0–20 m sprint times, which suggested both provided a measure of acceleration. The relationship strength decreased when considering relationships between the 0–10 m and 0–20 m times and the flying sprint times ($r = 0.50$–0.77). The practical implications were that sprint intervals up to 20 m from a stationary start will indicate acceleration. Sprints over 30–40 m distances should afford a measure of maximum speed for most athletes (Young et al., 2008), although track sprinters may require distances up to 50–60 m (Bezodis et al., 2008; Young et al., 1995). Flying times (i.e. the last 10-m interval in the sprint) should be used to provide the metric for maximum speed. An example set-up with timing gates, where both acceleration and maximum speed could be measured in a 40-m sprint, is shown in Figure 8.9.

8.3.5 Other extraneous factors

As circadian rhythms can influence athletic performance (Atkinson and Reilly, 1996), practitioners should attempt to conduct sprint testing at the same time of day across multiple sessions (see Chapter 4). Guy et al. (2015) found that faster 100-m and 200-m sprint events in athletics world championships occurred in temperatures above 25° Celsius (or 77° Fahrenheit). However, warmer conditions can result in a faster rate of fatigue across multiple sprint efforts (Girard et al., 2015), so this could become an issue if a practitioner utilises a high number of sprint trials during testing. Wind can be a confounding factor for sprint testing if conducted outdoors; wind speeds above 2 m·s^{-1} can provide an approximate 0.10–0.12 s advantage in 100-m sprint times for male and female sprinters (Linthorne, 1994). Conducting sprint testing indoors can reduce the influence of factors such as heat, wind and rain. This could also allow for the use of a consistent testing surface, which is another factor to consider.

Sprint testing for many athletes is often conducted on training surfaces (i.e. grass or turf pitches) which are equivalent to the surfaces used for competition. Although this may not always be ideal (i.e. field testing can be susceptible to adverse weather conditions), this may be the only environment available to the practitioner. Interestingly, Gains et al. (2010) found that there were no significant differences between 36.6-m sprint times recorded by Brower timing gates whether performed on a natural grass or field turf surface by collegiate American football players. In contrast, Brechue et al. (2005) illustrated that performing a 36.6-m sprint on a natural grass surface led to 3% slower times than for sprints completed on an athletics track in collegiate American football players when hand-timed by coaches using stopwatches. The surface used for sprint testing could also lead to different footwear worn by the athletes. For example, in the study conducted by Brechue et al. (2005), the American football players wore their game cleats (or boots) when sprint testing on grass, and rubber-soled athletic shoes for the track sprints. Shoe stiffness can influence sprint performance, although athletes may select shoes that are optimal for their own physiological and force-velocity characteristics when sprinting (Stefanyshyn and Fusco, 2004). As a result, practitioners should note the surface used for testing, in addition to the footwear worn by athletes. This could provide some context if there is any variation between testing occasions, and in attempts to be consistent across sessions.

8.3.6 Interpretation of results

Once the data have been recorded, the practitioner must decide the best way to interpret this information. Firstly, the decision must be made whether to analyse the best or average times for a group of sprint trials. The best time indicates the fastest an athlete can sprint over a given distance, which is generally the objective of sprint testing. Average times can indicate the consistency of performance, and these data can exhibit better reliability (Glaister et al., 2007) and lower error (Haugen and Buchheit, 2016). Bond et al. (2017) suggested that in order to gauge whether an athlete's sprint performance had changed over time, the practitioner should consider the mean time and the standard deviation between sprint trials. The standard deviation would indicate whether the athlete's mean time had changed from the previous testing session, as these data takes into account the variability of the system used to time the athlete. Nevertheless, where possible practitioners should consider the best and average sprint times for an athlete over a given distance.

In order to investigate whether there has been a change in athletic performance, practitioners can use magnitude-based inferences. This requires the consideration of the change in performance, typical error of measurement (TEM) for the test and smallest worthwhile change (SWC) (Haugen and Buchheit, 2016). SWC for a sprint test can be estimated via two methods (Haugen and Buchheit, 2016; Hopkins et al., 2009). The first method is based on observations of direct performance benefits, where changes in sprint performance via training can be expressed during match-play. As an example, Haugen et al. (2014) stated that a 0.30–0.50 m distance, which equated to a sprint time of ~0.04–0.06 s over a 20-m sprint, would be enough to gain a decisive advantage over an opponent. As a result, a change in sprint performance of this magnitude would be considered meaningful.

The second method for estimating SWC is via statistical calculations, whereby the between-athlete standard deviation is multiplied by 0.2–0.3 (a small-to-moderate effect) to derive the SWC (Haugen and Buchheit, 2016; Hopkins et al., 2009). If the SWC exceeds the TEM for the sprint test, the practitioner can assume an actual change in performance has occurred. There are Excel spreadsheets available to aid in calculating these variables (Hopkins, 2000b). Furthermore, Haugen and Buchheit (2016) stated that the SWC for the 0–5 m interval was ~1.5%, while for intervals above 10 m it was ~1.0%. Haugen and Buchheit (2016) did acknowledge that group homogeneity will influence these calculations, and thus recommended practitioners consider how changes in sprint time translate to an actual distance. This will provide a practical application of changes in sprint test performance that would be transferrable to competition. Statistical approaches to reliability and measurement error are explored in detail in Chapter 3.

8.4 Conclusion

Practitioners must be able to measure the sprint performance of their athletes with accuracy and reliability. A number of different systems are available, and practitioners should consider the cost, benefits and limitations of this equipment specific to their situation. Reliable data can be recorded by different systems, including radar and laser systems and timing gates. What will assist with the collection of reliable data is the consistent use of specific start positions and protocols for testing. The practitioner must also place the data into context with the prevailing weather and surface used for testing. Lastly, magnitude-based inferences can be used to interpret test data to document whether their athletes have experienced meaningful changes in sprint performance.

8.5 References

Altmann, S., Hoffmann, M., Kurz, G., Neumann, R., Woll, A., & Haertel, S. (2015). Different starting distances affect 5-m sprint times. *Journal of Strength and Conditioning Research, 29*, 2361–2366.

Altmann, S., Spielmann, M., Engel, F.A., Neumann, R., Ringhof, S., Oriwol, D., & Haertel, S. (2017). Validity of single-beam timing lights at different heights. *Journal of Strength and Conditioning Research, 31*, 1994–1999.

Ammann, R., Taube, W., & Wyss, T. (2016). Accuracy of PARTwear inertial sensor and Optojump optical measurement system for measuring ground contact time during running. *Journal of Strength and Conditioning Research, 30*, 2057–2063.

Atkinson, G., & Reilly, T. (1996). Circadian variation in sports performance. *Sports Medicine, 21*, 292–312.

Baumgartner, T.A., & Chung, H. (2001). Confidence limits for intraclass reliability coefficients. *Measurement in Physical Education and Exercise Science, 5*, 179–188.

Belli, A., Lacour, J.R., Komi, P.V., Candau, R., & Denis, C. (1995). Mechanical step variability during treadmill running. *European Journal of Applied Physiology and Occupational Physiology, 70*, 510–517.

Bezodis, I.N., Kerwin, D.G., & Salo, A.I. (2008). Lower-limb mechanics during the support phase of maximum-velocity sprint running. *Medicine and Science in Sports and Exercise, 40,* 707–715.

Bezodis, N.E., Salo, A.I., & Trewartha, G. (2012). Measurement error in estimates of sprint velocity from a laser displacement measurement device. *International Journal of Sports Medicine, 33,* 439–444.

Bond, C.W., Willaert, E.M., & Noonan, B.C. (2017). Comparison of three timing systems: Reliability and best practice recommendations in timing short-duration sprints. *Journal of Strength and Conditioning Research, 31,* 1062–1071.

Brechue, W.F., Mayhew, J.L., & Piper, F.C. (2005). Equipment and running surface alter sprint performance of college football players. *Journal of Strength and Conditioning Research, 19,* 821–825.

Buchheit, M., Simpson, B.M., Peltola, E., & Mendez-Villanueva, A. (2012). Assessing maximal sprinting speed in highly trained young soccer players. *International Journal of Sports Physiology & Performance, 7,* 76–78.

Bullock, N., Martin, D.T., Ross, A., Rosemond, C.D., Jordan, M.J., & Marino, F.E. (2008). Acute effect of whole-body vibration on sprint and jumping performance in elite skeleton athletes. *Journal of Strength and Conditioning Research, 22,* 1371–1374.

Callaghan, S.J., Lockie, R.G., & Jeffriess, M.D. (2014). The acceleration kinematics of cricket-specific starts when completing a quick single. *Sports Technology, 7,* 39–51.

Carr, C., McMahon, J.J., & Comfort, P. (2015). Relationships between jump and sprint performance in first-class county cricketers. *Journal of Trainology, 4,* 1–5.

Chelly, S.M., & Denis, C. (2001). Leg power and hopping stiffness: relationship with sprint running performance. *Medicine and Science in Sports and Exercise, 33,* 326–333.

Chen, V.C., Li, F., Ho, S.S., & Wechsler, H. (2006). Micro-Doppler effect in radar: phenomenon, model, and simulation study. *IEEE Transactions on Aerospace and Electronic Systems, 42,* 2–21.

Cheng, L., Tan, H., Kuntze, G., Bezodis, I.N., Hailes, S., Kerwin, D.G., & Wilson, A. (2010). A low-cost accurate speed-tracking system for supporting sprint coaching. *Proceedings of the Institution of Mechanical Engineers, Part P: Journal of Sports Engineering and Technology, 224,* 167–179.

Comfort, P., Graham-Smith, P., Matthews, M.J., & Bamber, C. (2011). Strength and power characteristics in English elite rugby league players. *Journal of Strength and Conditioning Research, 25,* 1374–1384.

Cronin, J.B., & Templeton, R.L. (2008). Timing light height affects sprint times. *Journal of Strength and Conditioning Research, 22,* 318–320.

Darrall-Jones, J.D., Jones, B., Roe, G., & Till, K. (2016). Reliability and usefulness of linear sprint testing in adolescent rugby union and league players. *Journal of Strength and Conditioning Research, 30,* 1359–1364.

Dawes, J.J., Orr, R.M., Elder, C.L., Krall, K., Stierli, M., & Schilling, B. (2015). Relationship between selected measures of power and strength and linear running speed amongst Special Weapons and Tactics police officers. *Journal of Australian Strength and Conditioning, 23,* 23–28.

Dawson, B., Hopkinson, R., Appleby, B., Stewart, G., & Roberts, C. (2004). Player movement patterns and game activities in the Australian Football League. *Journal of Science and Medicine in Sport, 7,* 278–291.

Debaere, S., Jonkers, I., & Delecluse, C. (2013). The contribution of step characteristics to sprint running performance in high-level male and female athletes. *Journal of Strength and Conditioning Research, 27,* 116–124.

Deutsch, M.U., Kearney, G.A., & Rehrer, N.J. (2007). Time-motion analysis of professional rugby union players during match-play. *Journal of Sports Sciences, 25,* 461–472.

Dolenec, A., & Čoh, M. (2009). Comparison of photocell and optojump measurements of maximum running velocity. *Kinesiologia Slovenica, 15*, 16–24.

Duthie, G.M., Pyne, D.B., Marsh, D.J., & Hooper, S.L. (2006a). Sprint patterns in rugby union players during competition. *Journal of Strength and Conditioning Research, 20*, 208–214.

Duthie, G.M., Pyne, D.B., Ross, A.A., Livingstone, S.G., & Hooper, S.L. (2006b). The reliability of ten-meter sprint time using different starting techniques. *Journal of Strength and Conditioning Research, 20*, 246–251.

Earp, J.E., & Newton, R.U. (2012). Advances in electronic timing systems: Considerations for selecting an appropriate timing system. *Journal of Strength and Conditioning Research, 26*, 1245–1248.

Ebben, W., Petushek, E., & Clewien, R. (2009). A comparison of manual and electronic timing during 20 and 40 Yards sprints. *Journal of Exercise Physiologyonline, 12*, 34–38.

Fry, A.C., & Kraemer, W.J. (1991). Physical performance characteristics of American collegiate football players. *Journal of Applied Sport Science Research, 5*, 126–138.

Gabbett, T.J., Kelly, J.N., & Sheppard, J.M. (2008). Speed, change of direction speed, and reactive agility of rugby league players. *Journal of Strength and Conditioning Research, 22*, 174–181.

Gains, G.L., Swedenhjelm, A.N., Mayhew, J.L., Bird, H.M., & Houser, J.J. (2010). Comparison of speed and agility performance of college football players on field turf and natural grass. *Journal of Strength and Conditioning Research, 24*, 2613–2617.

Girard, O., Brocherie, F., & Bishop, D.J. (2015). Sprint performance under heat stress: A review. *Scandinavian Journal of Medicine and Science in Sports, 25*, 79–89.

Glaister, M., Howatson, G., Lockey, R.A., Abraham, C.S., Goodwin, J.E., & Mcinnes, G. (2007). Familiarization and reliability of multiple sprint running performance indices. *Journal of Strength and Conditioning Research, 21*, 857–859.

Glatthorn, J.F., Gouge, S., Nussbaumer, S., Stauffacher, S., Impellizzeri, F.M., & Maffiuletti, N.A. (2011). Validity and reliability of Optojump photoelectric cells for estimating vertical jump height. *Journal of Strength and Conditioning Research, 25*, 556–560.

Green, B.S., Blake, C., & Caulfield, B.M. (2010). A valid field test protocol of linear speed and agility in rugby union. *Journal of Strength and Conditioning Research, 25*, 1256–1262.

Gutierrez-Davilla, M., Dapena, J., & Campos, J. (2006). The effect of muscular pre-tensing on the sprint start. *Journal of Applied Biomechanics, 22*, 194–201.

Guy, J.H., Deakin, G.B., Edwards, A.M., Miller, C.M., & Pyne, D.B. (2015). Adaptation to hot environmental conditions: An exploration of the performance basis, procedures and future directions to optimise opportunities for elite athletes. *Sports Medicine, 45*, 303–311.

Harrison, A.J., Jensen, R.L., & Donoghue, O. (2005). A comparison of laser and video techniques for determining displacement and velocity during running. *Measurement in Physical Education and Exercise Science, 9*, 219–231.

Haugen, T., & Buchheit, M. (2016). Sprint running performance monitoring: Methodological and practical considerations. *Sports Medicine, 46*, 641–656.

Haugen, T., Tonnessen, E., Hisdal, J., & Seiler, S. (2014). The role and development of sprinting speed in soccer. *International Journal of Sports Physiology and Performance, 9*, 432–441.

Haugen, T., Tonnessen, E., & Seiler, S. (2015). Correction factors for photocell sprint timing with flying start. *International Journal of Sports Physiology and Performance, 10*, 1055–1057.

Haugen, T.A., Tonnessen, E., & Seiler, S.K. (2012). The difference is in the start: Impact of timing and start procedure on sprint running performance. *Journal of Strength and Conditioning Research, 26*, 473–479.

Hetzler, R.K., Stickley, C.D., Lundquist, K.M., & Kimura, I.F. (2008). Reliability and accuracy of handheld stopwatches compared with electronic timing in measuring sprint performance. *Journal of Strength and Conditioning Research, 22*, 1969–1976.

Hopkins, W.G. (2000a). Measures of reliability in sports medicine and science. *Sports Medicine, 30*, 1–15.

Hopkins, W.G. (2000b). Precision of the estimate of a subject's true value (Excel spreadsheet). *A new view of statistics*. Available at: http://sportsci.org/resource/stats/xprecisionsubject. xls. Accessed 28 April 2017.

Hopkins, W.G., Marshall, S.W., Batterham, A.M., & Hanin, J. (2009). Progressive statistics for studies in sports medicine and exercise science. *Medicine and Science in Sports and Exercise, 41*, 3–13.

Iguchi, J., Yamada, Y., Ando, S., Fujisawa, Y., Hojo, T., Nishimura, K., Kuzuhara, K., Yuasa, Y., & Ichihashi, N. (2011). Physical and performance characteristics of Japanese Division 1 collegiate football players. *Journal of Strength and Conditioning Research, 25*, 3368–3377.

Kratky, S., & Muller, E. (2013). Sprint running with a body-weight supporting kite reduces ground contact time in well-trained sprinters. *Journal of Strength and Conditioning Research, 27*, 1215–1222.

Krustrup, P., Mohr, M., Ellingsgaard, H., & Bangsbo, J. (2005). Physical demands during an elite female soccer game: importance of training status. *Medicine and Science in Sports and Exercise, 37*, 1242–1248.

Krzysztof, M., & Mero, A. (2013). A kinematics analysis of three best 100 m performances ever. *Journal of Human Kinetics, 36*, 149–160.

Kuzmits, F.E., & Adams, A.J. (2008). The NFL combine: does it predict performance in the National Football League? *Journal of Strength and Conditioning Research, 22*, 1721–1727.

Lim, J.J., & Kong, P.W. (2013). Effects of isometric and dynamic postactivation potentiation protocols on maximal sprint performance. *Journal of Strength and Conditioning Research, 27*, 2730–2736.

Linthorne, N.P. (1994). The effect of wind on 100-m sprint times. *Journal of Applied Biomechanics, 10*, 110–131.

Little, T., & Williams, A.G. (2005). Specificity of acceleration, maximum speed, and agility in professional soccer players. *Journal of Strength and Conditioning Research, 19*, 76–78.

Lockie, R.G. (2016). The effects of linear and change-of-direction speed training on the sprint performance of young adults. In F. Eminivić & M. Dopsaj (Eds.), *Physical activity effects on the anthropological status of children, youth and adults*. Hauppauge, NY: Nova Science Publishers.

Lockie, R.G., Callaghan, S.J., & Jeffriess, M.D. (2013a). Analysis of specific speed testing for cricketers. *Journal of Strength and Conditioning Research, 27*, 2981–2988.

Lockie, R.G., Davis, D.L., Birmingham-Babauta, S.A., Beiley, M.D., Hurley, J.M., Stage, A.A., Stokes, J.J., Tomita, T.M., Torne, I.A., & Lazar, A. (2016a). Physiological characteristics of incoming freshmen field players in a men's Division I collegiate soccer team. *Sports, 4*. doi:10.3390/sports4020034.

Lockie, R.G., Farzad, J., Orjalo, A.J., Giuliano, D.V., Moreno, M.R., & Wright, G.A. (2017). A methodological report: Adapting the 505 change-of-direction speed test specific to American football. *Journal of Strength and Conditioning Research, 31*, 539–547.

Lockie, R.G., Jalilvand, F., Moreno, M.R., Orjalo, A.J., Risso, F.G., & Nimphius, S. (in press a). Yo-Yo Intermittent Recovery Test Level 2 and its relationship to other typical soccer field tests in female collegiate soccer players. *Journal of Strength and Conditioning Research*. doi:10.1519/JSC.0000000000001734.

Lockie, R.G., Lazar, A., Orjalo, A.J., Davis, D.L., Moreno, M.R., Risso, F.G., Hank, M.E., Stone, R.C., & Mosich, N.W. (2016b). Profiling of junior college football players and differences between position groups. *Sports, 4*. doi:10.3390/sports4030041.

Lockie, R.G., Moreno, M.R., Lazar, A., Orjalo, A.J., Giuliano, D.V., Risso, F.G., Davis, D.L., Crelling, J.B., Lockwood, J.R., & Jalilvand, F. (in press b). The physical and athletic performance characteristics of Division I collegiate female soccer players by position. *Journal of Strength and Conditioning Research*, Publish ahead of print. doi:10.1519/JSC.0000000000001561.

Lockie, R.G., Murphy, A.J., Knight, T.J., & Janse De Jonge, X.A.K. (2011). Factors that differentiate acceleration ability in field sport athletes. *Journal of Strength and Conditioning Research, 25*, 2704–2714.

Lockie, R.G., Schultz, A.B., Callaghan, S.J., Jeffriess, M.D., & Berry, S.P. (2013b). Reliability and validity of a new test of change-of-direction speed for field-based sports: the Change-of-Direction and Acceleration Test (CODAT). *Journal of Sports Science and Medicine, 12*, 88–96.

Lockie, R.G., Stecyk, S.D., Mock, S.A., Crelling, J.B., Lockwood, J.R., & Jalilvand, F. (2016c). A cross-sectional analysis of the characteristics of Division I collegiate female soccer field players across year of eligibility. *Journal of Australian Strength and Conditioning, 24*, 6–15.

Luhtanen, P., & Komi, P.V. (1978). Mechanical factors influencing running speed. In E. Asmussen & K. Jorgensen (Eds.), *Biomechanics VI-B*. Baltimore, MD: University Park Press.

Macadam, P., Simperingham, K.D., & Cronin, J.B. (2017). Acute kinematic and kinetic adaptations to wearable resistance during sprint acceleration. *Journal of Strength and Conditioning Research, 31*, 1297–1304.

Magal, M., Smith, R.T., Dyer, J.J., & Hoffman, J.R. (2009). Seasonal variation in physical performance-related variables in male NCAA Division III soccer players. *Journal of Strength and Conditioning Research, 23*, 2555–2559.

Mann, J.B., Ivey, P.J., Brechue, W.F., & Mayhew, J.L. (2015). Validity and reliability of hand and electronic timing for 40-yd sprint in college football players. *Journal of Strength and Conditioning Research, 29*, 1509–1514.

Mayhew, J.L., Houser, J.J., Briney, B.B., Williams, T.B., Piper, F.C., & Brechue, W.F. (2010). Comparison between hand and electronic timing of 40-yd dash performance in college football players. *Journal of Strength and Conditioning Research, 24*, 447–451.

McGuigan, M.R. (2015). Principles of test selection and administration. In G.G. Haff & N.T. Triplett (Eds.), *Essentials of strength training and conditioning* (4th edn.). Champaign, IL: Human Kinetics.

Mendez-Villanueva, A., Buchheit, M., Kuitunen, S., Douglas, A., Peltola, E., & Bourdon, P. (2011). Age-related differences in acceleration, maximum running speed, and repeated-sprint performance in young soccer players. *Journal of Sports Sciences, 29*, 477–484.

Mohr, M., Krustrup, P., & Bangsbo, J. (2003). Match performance of high-standard soccer players with special reference to development of fatigue. *Journal of Sports Sciences, 21*, 519–528.

Moir, G., Button, C., Glaister, M., & Stone, M.H. (2004). Influence of familiarization on the reliability of vertical jump and acceleration sprinting performance in physically active men. *Journal of Strength and Conditioning Research, 18*, 276–280.

Morin, J.B., Jeannin, T., Chevallier, B., & Belli, A. (2006). Spring-mass model characteristics during sprint running: correlation with performance and fatigue-induced changes. *International Journal of Sports Medicine, 27*, 158–165.

Oliver, J.L., & Meyers, R.W. (2009). Reliability and generality of measures of acceleration, planned agility, and reactive agility. *International Journal of Sports Physiology and Performance, 4*, 345–354.

Poulos, N., Kuitunen, S., & Buchheit, M. (2010). Effect of preload squatting on sprint performance in adolescent athletes. *New Studies in Athletics, 25*, 95–103.

Robbins, D.W. (2010). The National Football League (NFL) combine: does normalized data better predict performance in the NFL draft? *Journal of Strength and Conditioning Research, 24*, 2888–2899.

Scanlan, A.T., Dascombe, B.J., & Reaburn, P.R. (2015). Development of the Basketball Exercise Simulation Test: A match-specific basketball fitness test. *Journal of Human Sport and Exercise, 9*, 700–712.

Shalfawi, S.A. I., Enoksen, E., Tønnessen, E., & Ingebrigtsen, J. (2012). Assessing test-retest reliability of the portable Brower Speed Trap II testing system. *Kinesiology, 44*, 24–30.

Slawinski, J., Bonnefoy, A., Leveque, J.M., Ontanon, G., Riquet, A., Dumas, R., & Cheze, L. (2010). Kinematic and kinetic comparisons of elite and well-trained sprinters during sprint start. *Journal of Strength and Conditioning Research, 24,* 896–905.

Spinks, C.D., Murphy, A.J., Spinks, W.L., & Lockie, R.G. (2007). Effects of resisted sprint training on acceleration performance and kinematics in soccer, rugby union and Australian football players *Journal of Strength and Conditioning Research, 21,* 77–85.

Stanton, R., Hayman, M., Humphris, N., Borgelt, H., Fox, J., Del Vecchio, L., & Humphries, B. (2016). Validity of a smartphone-based application for determining sprinting performance. *Journal of Sports Medicine.* doi:10.1155/2016/7476820.

Stefanyshyn, D., & Fusco, C. (2004). Increased shoe bending stiffness increases sprint performance. *Sports Biomechanics, 3,* 55–66.

Triplett, N.T. (2012). Speed and agility. In T. Miller (Ed.), *NSCA's guide to tests and assessments.* Champaign, IL: Human Kinetics.

Vescovi, J.D. (2012). Sprint speed characteristics of high-level American female soccer players: Female Athletes in Motion (FAiM) study. *Journal of Science and Medicine in Sport, 15,* 474–478.

Vescovi, J.D., & McGuigan, M.R. (2008). Relationships between sprinting, agility, and jump ability in female athletes. *Journal of Sports Sciences, 26,* 97–107.

Winchester, J.B., Nelson, A.G., Landin, D., Young, M.A., & Schexnayder, I.C. (2008). Static stretching impairs sprint performance in collegiate track and field athletes. *Journal of Strength and Conditioning Research, 22,* 13–19.

Winkelman, N.C., Clark, K.P., & Ryan, L.J. (2017). Experience level influences the effect of attentional focus on sprint performance. *Human Movement Science, 52,* 84–95.

Yeadon, M.R., Kato, T., & Kerwin, D.G. (1999). Measuring running speed using photocells. *Journal of Sports Sciences, 17,* 249–257.

Young, W., Mclean, B., & Ardagna, J. (1995). Relationship between strength qualities and sprinting performance. *Journal of Sports Medicine and Physical Fitness, 35,* 13–19.

Young, W., Russell, A., Burge, P., Clarke, A., Cormack, S., & Stewart, G. (2008). The use of sprint tests for assessment of speed qualities of elite Australian rules footballers. *International Journal of Sports Physiology and Performance, 3,* 199–206.

9 Change of direction and agility

Paul A. Jones and Sophia Nimphius

Speed is a vital component in many sports. Whilst in some sports such as track sprinting this may be the sole determinant of performance, in field- and court-based sports the use and presentation of speed are expressed in different ways and decide critical match events. For instance, in soccer, sprinting is the most common action associated with goal-scoring situations (Faude et al., 2012); however, the average sprint distance of 20 m in soccer indicates that many of the sprints are too short for maximal velocity to occur (Burgess et al., 2006; Vigne et al., 2010). The short distances of sprinting are interspersed by numerous changes in movement patterns (Bloomfield et al., 2007). As such, field- and court-based sports are characterised by frequent changes in activity patterns. Professional netballers have been reported to execute a change in activity pattern on average every 6 seconds (Davidson et al., 2008; Chandler et al., 2014). Similarly, soccer players change movement pattern every 4–6 seconds (Stolen et al., 2005), whilst in field hockey a directional change of movement is recorded every 5.5 seconds (Spencer et al., 2002), further reducing the likelihood of maximum sprint velocity being achieved in such sports. Therefore, the ability to change movement pattern, perhaps to evade a defender, or react to an attacker, often referred to as "agility", can become as critically important as maximal speed.

In field- and court-based sports, a variety of movement patterns are also performed. In an analysis of English Premier League soccer (Bloomfield et al., 2007), percentages of time spent standing, walking, jogging, running and sprinting by all players (regardless of position) were 4.6 ± 3.2, 14.2 ± 4.3, 28.1 ± 9.6, 11.1 ± 6.8 and 4.8 ± 3.2, respectively, whilst 9.9 ± 4.7 and 9.3 ± 2.6 were spent performing the locomotion activities of skipping and shuffling, respectively. In addition, on average 727 ± 203 turns and swerves were performed, with 609 ± 193 being 0–90° to the left or right (Bloomfield et al., 2007). These data highlight the variety of movements and the importance and prevalence of change of direction ability for match play. Overall, it is no surprise why agility or the ability to change direction is an important quality to assess and develop in athletes from field- and court-based sports.

Early definitions of agility suggested that it was "the ability to *explosively* brake, change direction, and accelerate again" (Plisk, 2000). However, when observing a number of field- and court-based sports such a definition fails to reflect the number of movement patterns or the perceptual elements involved during "on-field" agility. Agility has most comprehensively been defined as "a rapid and accurate whole-body movement, with change of velocity or direction, in response to a stimulus" (Sheppard and Young, 2006), although the definition perhaps does not reflect the wide range of movement patterns and actions involved in field- and court-based sports. Jeffreys (2006) defined agility as "a serial skill composed of a series of discrete movement patterns", without acknowledging the perceptual and decision-making factors involved within expressions of agility in field- and court-based sports.

Collectively, agility could be defined as a rapid and accurate whole-body movement with change of velocity, direction or movement pattern in response to a stimulus. Nevertheless, what is clear is that agility is dependent on two sub-components: (a) perceptual-cognitive or decision-making factors and (b) physical factors related to the change of direction or change of movement patterns (i.e. muscle strength qualities and technique). The latter component, often referred to as change of direction (COD) ability or COD speed, is most often associated with "the ability to decelerate, reverse or change movement direction and accelerate again" (Jones et al., 2009). However, the ability to maintain velocity during a COD, often performed without a clear "plant" step (i.e. a curvilinear path of movement or "turning") or the ability to perform or change mode of travel to and from "transitional" movements (i.e. side shuffle or back pedal), termed manoeuvrability (DeWeese & Nimphius, 2016), is also a form of COD ability that has been more recently defined and discussed. Until recently, given the lack of understanding of agility, many of the traditional tests of "agility", such as the 505, T-test, Illinois, pro-agility and L-run, have been mistakenly referred to as tests of agility and are now considered as tests of COD speed, manoeuvrability or both. Consequently, a valid assessment of agility must involve some reaction to a stimulus in addition to execution of a COD to ensure the assessment examines the perceptual-motor capacity of the athlete, or both the perceptual-cognitive and physical factors described previously.

Assessment of change of direction speed

Development of COD speed provides the physical and technical foundation to develop agility (Nimphius et al., 2016a). Due to this foundational skill requirement to build future agility performance, strength and conditioning coaches need to select appropriate tests to evaluate COD speed. There are a variety of common tests available to strength and conditioning coaches to evaluate athletes' COD speed. Examples include the 505 (Draper and Lancaster, 1985; Jones et al. 2009; Barber et al., 2016), pro-agility (Sierer et al., 2008), L-run or three-cone drill (Sierer et al., 2008; Gabbett et al 2008), T-test (Munro & Herrington, 2011) and the Illinois test (Vescovi & McGuigan, 2008). Many of the tests mentioned in this chapter use timing cells to record test completion times. It is beyond the scope of this chapter to discuss the application of timing cells. A brief summary of important considerations is provided in Box 9.8. Please refer to Chapter 8 for a more in-depth coverage of timing systems. An example summary of different COD speed tests is presented in Table 9.1 with classifications previously described in the chapter to assist in determining the sub-qualities of COD examined by the test. For an extensive overview of a range of COD speed tests the interested reader should refer to a recent review by Nimphius et al. (2018).

The 505 test was originally developed by Draper and Lancaster (1985). The 505 test involves a 5 m approach and return separated by a single 180° turn and can be performed from a 15 m (traditional) or 5 m approach (modified) (Gabbett et al 2008; Barber et al., 2016) (Box 9.1). The 505 can also be used to assess the COD ability on either limb (Nimphius et al., 2016a) and has been used in a wide range of sports including soccer (Turner et al., 2016), rugby league (Gabbett et al., 2008), netball (Barber et al., 2016; Thomas et al., 2016a), cricket (Foden et al., 2015; Thomas et al., 2016b; Nimphius et al., 2016a) and softball (Nimphius et al., 2010). Both versions of the test have been reported to be reliable (Gabbett et al., 2008; Nimphius et al., 2010; Sayers, 2015; Stewart et al., 2014; Thomas et al. 2016; Barber et al. 2016). Barber et al. (2016) examined the

Table 9.1 Example classification of existing change of direction speed and agility tests.

	COD with a "cutting" movement	Manoeuvrability		Perceptual-cognitive (test requires response to a stimulus)	Metabolic requirement (time to complete test)	Total distance
		To maintain velocity or curvilinear	Change in mode			
Traditional 505	180°	✘	✘	✘	~ 3 s	10 m
T-test	90°	✘	✓	✘	~ 7.5–13 s	36. 56 m
L-run	180°	✓	✘	✘	~ 7 s	~ 27 m
Illinois agility test	180°	✓	✘	✘	~ 13–19 s	~ 60 m
Common Y-agility tests	~ 45°	Depends on tactic	✘	✓	~ 1.5–2.5 s	~ 8–11 m

Data originally reported in Nimphius et al. (2018) and table modified from Nimphius (2017). COD with a cutting movement is a "traditional COD" whereas those with a curvilinear movement pattern with no true "plant" step are differentiated into manoeuvrability. Change in mode is a test that includes movement pattern change (e.g. sprint to side shuffle).

within- and between-session reliability of the traditional and modified 505 test in netball players. The authors reported excellent within (traditional; intraclass correlation coefficient [ICC] = 0.90–0.97; modified; ICC = 0.96–0.97) and between (traditional; ICC = 0.951; standard error of measurement [SEM] = 0.04 s; smallest detectible difference [SDD] = 0.1 s [3.97%]; modified ICC = 0.968; SEM = 0.04 s; SDD = 0.11 s [3.91%]) session reliability and found that performance stabilised after 2 weeks for the modified 505 test and 3 weeks for the traditional 505 test, suggesting that one and two familiarisation sessions are required for each test, respectively.

The T-test is another widely used test of COD speed and manoeuvrability and incorporates forward running, side-shuffling and back-pedalling around a T-shaped course (Box 9.2). The test has the advantage of incorporating the common game-related movement patterns of side-shuffling and back-pedalling and has been found (Sporis et al., 2010) to be appropriate for defenders in soccer based on observed positional differences. Within- and between-session reliability for the T-test has generally been reported to be excellent (Pauole et al., 2000; Sporis et al., 2010; Munro & Herrington, 2011; Stewart et al., 2014). Munro and Herrington (2011) reported that one familiarisation trial is required to stabilise performance during the T-test.

The pro-agility and L-run (or three-cone drill) are tests used in the NFL combine (Sierer et al., 2008). The pro-agility test has been shown to be able to discriminate between drafted and non-drafted players (Sierer et al., 2008), whereas the "L run" has been shown to have the greatest association with draft pick ranking in American football players selected for professional teams (Sierer et al., 2008). The pro-agility involves two 180° turns separated by a 10-yard sprint, preceded and followed by two 5-yard sprints (Box 9.3). The L-run involves three initial 5-yard shuttles followed by a 90° turn, 5-yard sprint, 180° turn, 5-yard sprint, 90° turn and a final 5-yard sprint (Box 9.4). Therefore, one should note that the pattern of movement that separates these two tests is the inclusion of a curvilinear movement that will

Box 9.1 COD speed tests: traditional and modified 505 tests

- The athlete starts at the 15 m line (Figure 9.1) and sprints towards the turn line.
- The athlete then negotiates a 180° turn and sprints back towards the start line.
- The time from when the subject crosses the 5 m line (Figure 9.1) to when they cross the 5 m line again on the return run is recorded using timing cells set up at the 5 m line (Figure 9.1).
- Trials are disqualified if the athlete fails to touch or cross the turn line.
- A modified version of the test involves starting just before the start-stop timing position and removes the initial 10 m approach (Modified 505 test).
- The change of direction deficit (traditional 505 time – 10 m maximal linear sprint time) should be determined to evaluate the athlete's isolated change of direction ability (Nimphius et al., 2016a).

For the traditional 505 test, the addition of a set of timing cells at the start of the test could be incorporated to evaluate the 10 m approach time, to determine whether the athlete is adopting a "pacing strategy" which can be quantified (10 m run-up – 10 m maximal linear sprint time) (Nimphius et al., 2018)).

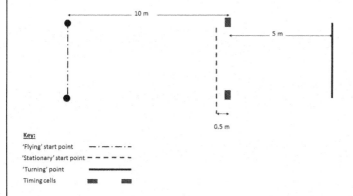

Key:

'Flying' start point	— · — · — · —
'Stationary' start point	— — — — —
'Turning' point	▬▬▬▬▬
Timing cells	▬ ▬

Figure 9.1 Test set-up for the traditional and modified 505 tests.

be performed in the L-run in an effort to maintain velocity, whereas both tests include the common COD movement of decelerate, reverse and re-accelerate (Table 9.1). In addition to American football, the pro-agility test has also been used in soccer (Vescovi & McGuigan, 2008; Lockie et al., 2016) and lacrosse (Vescovi & McGuigan, 2008), whereas the L-run has been used in rugby league (Gabbett et al., 2008). Gabbett et al. (2008) reported the L-run to be highly reliable (between-session ICC = 0.95; typical error = 2.8%) in male rugby league players, while Stewart et al. (2014) also reported both the L-run and pro-agility to have excellent within-session reliability (L-run; ICC = 0.80–0.88; SEM = 0.18–0.16 s; coefficient of variation [CV] = 2.2–1.6%; pro-agility ICC = 0.67–0.82; SEM = 0.13–0.11 s; CV = 2.5–1.8%) in physical education students.

Box 9.2 COD speed and manoeuvrability: T-test

- Three cones are arranged as depicted in Figure 9.2.
- The time to complete the course is recorded with timing cells placed at point A.
- The subject starts at point A and sprints through the timing cells to point B, touching the base of the cone with the right hand.
- Then, while facing forward and not crossing the feet, the athlete shuffles to the left 4.6 m and touches the base of the cone at point C with the left hand.
- The subject then shuffles to the right 9.1 m and touches the base of the cone at point D with the right hand.
- Finally, the athlete shuffles to the left 4.6 m touching the base of the cone at point B with the left hand, and then backpedals through the timing cells at point A.
- Trials are disqualified if the subject fails to touch each cone, crosses the feet during the shuffling or fails to face forward throughout the test.
- The test can be re-oriented so the athletes starts with a shuffle to the right as well.

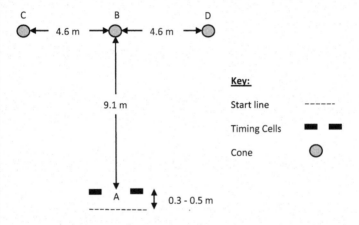

Figure 9.2 Test set-up for the T-test.

A variation of the L-run for soccer is the 4 × 5 m sprint test developed by Sporis et al. (2010). The test is similar to the L-run, but removes the initial shuttles between cones A and B (Box 9.4), the 4.6 m distances are increased to 5 m and at the third cone (C) the athlete turns 90° to the left and sprints 5 m to a fourth cone, where a 180° turn is performed and a final 5 m sprint through the timing cells set near cone C in Figure 9.4. The advantage of the L-run and 4 × 5 m sprint test is that they combine 90° cuts from both limbs with 180° turns, which are actions often involved in sports such as soccer (Bloomfield et al., 2007). Another test involving multiple 180° turns is the 9, 3, 6, 3, 9 test (Sporis et al., 2010), which basically involves sprinting 9, 3, 6, 3 and 9 metres sequentially separated by a 180° turn. The test can be adapted to include backward running (back-pedalling) with forward running (Sporis et al., 2010). Sporis et al. (2010) found that the test was appropriate for midfielders in soccer, whereas the 4 × 5 m sprint test was most appropriate for attackers in soccer based

Box 9.3 COD speed tests: pro-agility

- The athlete should straddle the start line using a three-point stance (point A in Figure 9.3).*
- From the start position, the athlete turns 90° to the right and sprints 4.6 m (black arrow in Figure 9.3) to the first turning point (B), touching the base of the cone with the right hand, turns 180° and sprints 9.1 m (grey arrow in Figure 9.3) to the second turning point (C), touching the base of the cone with the left hand. The athlete again turns 180° and sprints 4.6 m (dashed arrow in Figure 9.3) back through the timing cells at the centre line (A).
- Trials are disqualified if the athlete fails to touch the base of the cones at turning points B and C.

* Typically the pro-agility is hand-timed from starting on the centre line, but to enhance reliability timing cells are recommended. One option is to place timing cells at the centre line (point A, Figure 9.3) and the athlete begins 0.5 m before the timing cells, similar to previous research by Vescovi and McGuigan (2008), who purposely used a "flying start" to accommodate timing cells. Alternative options include using a hand/finger release trigger or have the athlete straddle either side of the timing cells, with the cells triggered when the rear foot "sweeps" past the timing cells (Stewart et al., 2014). Alternatively, some timing cells can be set for the start to begin on "exit" of the timing cell, starting the athlete with their trunk situated between the two timing cells and the time starting when exiting the start location. However, it is important to ensure any comparative data intended to be used are collected with the same timing and positioning as this test has multiple timing start variations.

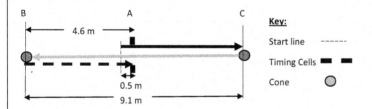

Figure 9.3 The test set-up for the pro-agility test. The athlete should begin from the start line, sprint 4.6 m to the left (black arrow), turn 180° and sprint 9.1 m (grey arrow) to the second turning point and turn 180° and sprint 4.6 m (dashed arrow) back to the centre starting point.

on examining positional differences in test performance. However, potential disadvantages of the tests lasting longer than ~6 s is the adding of another physiological quality (anaerobic capacity) to the requirement of the test which should be considered, particularly when evaluating changes in performance over time (e.g. whether the improvement was an improvement of COD performance or greater anaerobic capacity) (Nimphius, 2014, 2018).

Box 9.4 Manoeuvrability test: L-run or three-cone drill

- Figure 9.4 shows the L-run test set-up with three cones placed in an L-shape 4.6 m apart.
- The athlete sprints 4.6 m from the first cone (A) through the timing cells at the start to cone B and returns to the first (A) after touching the line with the right hand.
- The athlete then sprints to cone B again and turns 90° to the right.
- The athlete then sprints 4.6 m to cone C, where the athlete turns 180° counter-clockwise around the cone and sprints 4.6 m back to cone B.
- Finally, the athlete turns 90° to the left and sprints the final 4.6 m back through the timing cells at cone A.

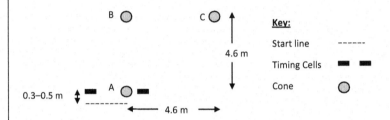

Figure 9.4 The "L-run" test set-up.

Finally, the Illinois test is a long-standing test of COD speed developed by Cureton (1951). The test (Box 9.5) involves the athlete beginning from a press-up position and on "Go" sprinting up and back along a 9.14 m track and then circling and running in and out of four cones spaced along the same 9.14 m distance. The test is completed by performing two more sprints (up and back) along the 9.14 m course. The Illinois agility test has been widely used in basketball (Hoffman et al., 1996), soccer and lacrosse (Vescovi & McGuigan, 2008). Furthermore, excellent within-session reliability (ICC = 0.89; SEM = 0.39 s; CV = 1.95%) in 44 physical education students (Stewart et al., 2014) and between-session reliability (ICC = 0.96; SEM = 0.19 s; SDD = 0.52 s) in 105 University team sport athletes (Hachana et al., 2013) have been reported. Although widely used and involving some actions associated with sports (short sprints and 180° turns), the stage of running in and out of cones lacks any meaningful association with sport movement demands but may be considered an assessment of manoeuvrability (Table 9.1). Further, the length of time required to complete the test (distance) and the amount of linear sprinting in the test may confound results with the metabolic capacity and linear sprint ability of the athlete (Nimphius, 2014, 2018), making it difficult to isolate the COD or manoeuvrability ability of the athlete.

The selection of an appropriate COD speed test for a given sport is largely dependent on the common movement patterns involved within that sport. However, tests may also be selected for the physical demand the test elicits on an athlete for return-to-play evaluation or general athletic quality assessment (Nimphius, 2017). For instance, the 505 test, which involves a forward sprint, 180° turn and re-acceleration toward the original starting

Box 9.5 Manoeuvrability: the Illinois test

- A rectangle measuring 9.14 × 3.65 m must be clearly marked and divided in half along its length by four cones positioned at equidistant intervals. The centres of the first and fourth cones must be positioned directly over the midpoint of the 3.65 m sides (Figure 9.5).
- The subject starts in a front lying position with the vertex of the head on the starting line, forearms flexed at the elbows and hands just outside the shoulders.
- On "Go" the subject rises from this position, runs as quickly as possible to the end line, turns and sprints back to the starting line.
- After turning again, the subject then weaves in and out of the centre cones towards the end line and then back to the start line.
- At this point the subject turns and again sprints to the end line and then back to the start line.
- The time to complete this course can be measured using stopwatches.

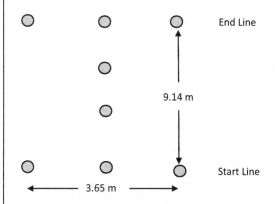

Figure 9.5 The test set-up for the Illinois test

point: from a sport perspective, the test mimics running and turning between wickets in cricket and thus the test has a strong association with the movement patterns associated with that sport. Indeed, 505 test performance has been found to have a strong association with Run 2 and Run 3 tests in cricket (Foden et al., 2015). Further, this movement pattern (without the ground touch) is often observed in backdoor cuts in basketball and has been classified to be the second most frequent turn or swerve in soccer (90–180°) (Bloomfield et al., 2007). However, given the planned structure involved with many of the above-mentioned tests, the ecological validity with regard to game performance in a given sport is often questioned. For instance, the pro-agility (Box 9.2) used in the NFL combine (Sierer et al., 2008) hardly matches the changing patterns of play for all positions on the field in American football. Realistically the above-mentioned tests or any other designed to mimic movement patterns in a sport will not achieve an exact replication due to the constantly changing patterns of play on the field. However, test selection should be based on the actions involved in the test matching the common or critical (e.g. movements that precede significant events such as a goal or creation of open space) actions involved in the sport. For instance, if 180° turns are common or critical (e.g. backdoor cut) in the sport then 505 or pro-agility tests could be used. If the sport involves frequent side-shuffling and back-pedalling, then maybe the T-test would be more appropriate. Further, the test choice must be determined with respect to the purpose of the assessment (e.g. is it to replicate common patterns, assess a specific aspect of athleticism or to evaluate confidence and physical capacity prior to return to play or transition to more open and demanding drills, tests or scenarios?).

As briefly mentioned previously, another limitation of many traditional COD speed tests is often the test duration. A test of COD speed should be of short duration, as the longer the test, the less emphasis there is on assessing COD speed, but more on anaerobic capacity and sprint ability since more time is spent running between COD actions (Nimphius et al., 2016a). For instance, typical test durations for the T-test, Illinois, L-run and pro-agility are 8–12 seconds (Sporis et al., 2010; Munro & Herrington, 2011), 14–18 seconds (Vescovi & McGuigan, 2008), 6–8 seconds (Gabbett et al., 2008; Sierer et al., 2008) and 4–5 seconds (Sierer et al., 2008; Nimphius et al., 2013), respectively. In addition, the duration of the 4 × 5 m sprint test was found to be 5.5 to 6.5 seconds (Sporis et al., 2010), whereas the 9, 3, 6, 3, 9 test was found to last 7–8 seconds. Therefore, performance on all of these tests may be influenced by metabolic limitations (Vescovi & McGuigan, 2008) and sprint ability (Nimphius et al., 2016a) and less by COD ability. Furthermore, many of the above-mentioned tests due to the involvement of transitional movements (e.g. T-test) or a curvilinear path of running (e.g. L-run and Illinois) are suggested to be more appropriate assessments of manoeuvrability rather than an isolated measure of COD ability (Nimphius, 2014; DeWeese & Nimphius, 2016; Nimphius et al., 2018).

The 505 test avoids the limitation of test duration as the typical completion times last 2–3 seconds (Gabbett et al., 2008; Jones et al., 2009, Nimphius et al., 2016a). The 505 removes much of the task complexity of other tests because it only has one turn with a particular emphasis during the "traditional" 505 on deceleration ability prior to a COD. However, the total completion time of a 505 test may not necessarily provide a measure of COD ability. For instance, Nimphius et al. (2013) found that only 31% of the time during a 505 test is spent turning, with the remainder of the time decelerating and accelerating. This is further supported by biomechanical studies with final contact time representing approximately 19.5–20% of completion times of 180° pivot tasks from various approaches (Jones et al., 2016; Graham-Smith et al., 2009). Therefore, linear sprinting ability may also influence 505 completion times and is perhaps more pronounced during traditional compared to modified 505 tests due to the greater entry velocity developed during the initial 10 m sprint. This notion is supported by several studies that have found a relationship between linear sprinting speed and 505 test performance (Graham-Smith and Pearson, 2005; Gabbett et al., 2008; Jones et al., 2009) despite the recognition that they are different physical qualities (Young et al., 2001). Furthermore, Sayers (2015) used 3D motion analysis to examine COD performance times over distances of 0.3, 0.5 and 1 m before and after the turn, measured as the time for the centre of mass to cover each distance before and after the turn. Results revealed strong relationships between 505 time and 5, 10 and 20 m sprint performance; however, the strength of these correlations was reduced when COD ability was measured 0.5 m and 0.3 m before and after the turn, thus highlighting that 505 performance time is biased by linear sprinting ability. The approach by Sayers (2015) to measure COD ability over shorter distances (i.e. less than 1 m before and after the turn) might be considered a more appropriate method to assess COD ability, with the authors recommending a 1-0-1 test. However, test-retest reliability of these measures did decline as distances of measurement decreased (505 ICC = 0.97, typical error of measurement [TEM] = 0.032 s, CV = 1.3% vs. 1 m ICC = 0.82, TEM = 0.024 s, CV = 2.4%; 0.5 m ICC = 0.72, TEM = 0.024 s, CV = 3.5%, 0.3 m ICC = 0.65, TEM = 0.024; CV = 4.5%). Furthermore, applying such an approach with timing cells may be problematic with false triggering of the timing cells likely.

A novel approach to overcome the limitation of linear sprinting speed influencing 505 test performance is to calculate the COD deficit (Nimphius et al., 2013, 2016a), whereby a 10 m sprint time is subtracted from the 505 time. The lower the value the greater is the COD ability. This concept was initially proposed and investigated in 66 collegiate American football players by Nimphius et al. (2013). Each player performed 40-yard sprints with a 10-yard split and pro-agility trials with a split time for the first 10 yards of the test (a single 180° turn). To determine COD deficit, the 10-yard sprint split time was subtracted from the 10-yard split time from the pro-agility test. Hence, the resultant time provides an indication of the time taken to negotiate a 180° turn. Significant ($p < 0.001$) correlations were observed between pro-agility scores (total and split time) and 10-yard sprint performance. However, a low non-significant correlation was observed between COD deficit and 10-yard sprint time ($r = 0.19$), but significant moderate correlations were observed to pro-agility ($r = 0.54$) and pro-agility split times ($r = 0.61$). These data suggest that the COD deficit offers a measure of COD speed independent of linear sprinting speed. More recently, Nimphius et al. (2016a) investigated the application of the COD deficit within the 505 test in 17 cricketers. The authors found that COD deficit correlated with 505 ($r = 0.74$–0.81) but not 10 m sprint time ($r = -0.11$–0.10), whilst 505 time correlated with sprint time ($r = 0.52$–0.70). Furthermore, when Z scores were examined five of the 17 subjects were classified differently in terms of COD ability when using 505 or COD deficit. The results provided further support for the use of COD deficit to isolate and quantify an individual's COD ability, independent of their linear sprinting speed. The concept of calculating a COD deficit has been further explored at various cutting angles (Cuthbert et al., 2018; Nimphius et al., 2016b) and transitioning between modes of travel (e.g. sprint to shuffle) (Nimphius et al., 2016b). Furthermore, the COD deficit has also been shown to be more adept at detecting asymmetries in COD ability when using the 505 test (Dos'Santos et al., 2018).

It is clear that assessment of time to completion of any COD task may provide an oversimplification of an athlete's COD ability. With available resources such as 3D motion analysis, force platforms and high-speed cameras additional information on approach (deceleration), contact times and re-acceleration phases can be provided. This would allow an evaluation of an athlete's deceleration and re-acceleration abilities. However, the associated costs and practicality (i.e. lab-based) would preclude application of such analyses. High-speed (> 100 Hz) cameras are now more readily available and can be incorporated in the field; however, 2D analysis to derive centre-of-mass velocities to determine approach and exit velocities maybe too time-consuming for a strength and conditioning coach and delay feedback to athletes. A novel approach has been developed (Hader et al., 2015) that has used two LAVEG speed guns to measure approach (10 m) speed toward and exiting (10 m) from 45° and 90° cuts (one would be required for a 180° turn as used by Graham-Smith and Pearson (2005)). The timing system has been shown to provide acceptable levels of validity and reliability to assess a range of movement characteristics (e.g. peak and minimum speed, distance at peak speed) during such tasks (Hader et al., 2015) and thus may be an option for practitioners with available resources. In addition to changes in measurement equipment, Nimphius et al. (2018) suggest ensuring the "why" of the testing is considered and therefore making informed decisions as to which of the following is most beneficial: consideration of isolating the COD being assessed by shortening the length of the test (as can also be accomplished with calculation of COD deficit), considering the calculation of a COD momentum (COM velocity × body mass) for contact sports, qualitative analysis of the movement to determine efficiency or particularly upon return-to-play scenarios, and considering whether the test is intended to measure change in mode of travel, ability to maintain velocity (termed manoeuvrability) versus intending to assess COD as defined by Jones et al. (2009).

In summary, assessment of COD speed is essential to establish the fundamental technical and physical foundation to develop agility. Several reliable tests of COD speed and/ or manoeuvrability exist in the literature. The selection of the most appropriate test for a given sport is dependent on the movement actions involved within that sport or the intended technical or physical demand that one seeks to place upon the athlete during the chosen test. Careful consideration of the design of the test is required to ensure that the test provides a valid assessment of COD speed, ensuring that the test duration is not too long, leading to a larger influence of metabolic conditioning and sprint ability on test performance. Steps should be taken to account for the impact of running speed on test performance, with the COD deficit offering a simple solution to account for this within 505 tests. Further, the specificity of different forms of COD speed should not be considered globally transferable (e.g. ability to change mode, decelerate rapidly versus maintain velocity during a COD) and may have to be examined separately (Table 9.1).

Assessment of agility

In order to assess agility, COD tests must involve athletes responding to stimuli. In essence, previously mentioned COD speed tests discriminate between those who are "fast movers" and "slow movers" (Gabbett et al., 2008). A true test of agility needs to assess the athlete's "perceptual-cognitive" ability along with their ability to move quickly (perceptual-motor ability), hence the test needs to discriminate between those who are "fast movers and fast thinkers" and those who are "slow movers and slow thinkers", with athletes who are "fast movers and slow thinkers" and "slow movers and fast thinkers" in between (Gabbett et al., 2008). As mentioned above, due to the lack of understanding of agility until recently, true assessments of agility are less well established than COD speed assessments and it is only over the last 15 years that more ecologically valid measures of agility have been developed through the use of light- and video-based systems. For an extensive review on the different measures of agility one can refer to a review by Paul et al. (2016) or a recent review that includes an overview of both COD speed tests and agility tests by Nimphius et al. (2018).

The earliest advance for improving the ecological validity of COD speed tests into what are now termed "agility" tests came from light systems, which have often been used in biomechanical studies (Besier et al., 2001) in order to compare between planned and unanticipated cutting and pivoting tasks. Furthermore, commercially available systems with light stimuli or triggers have been available for some time. Oliver and Meyers (2009) found such systems to be reliable measures of agility; however, light systems do not allow assessment of the "anticipatory (perceptual-cognitive) skills" such as visual scanning, pattern recognition and knowledge of situations (Sheppard & Young, 2006). Further, the use of a light-based system has been shown to result in different postural adjustments and knee moments compared to the more ecologically valid video-based systems (Lee et al., 2013) that will be discussed later in the chapter.

Research has shown that expert soccer (Helsen and Pauwels, 1993; Williams et al., 1994; Williams and Davids, 1998) players display anticipatory skills superior to those of less-skilled players. Moreover, expert soccer players are better able to recognise and recall typical patterns of play from memory (Williams et al., 1993) and have more effective visual search strategies than non-experts (Helsen and Pauwels, 1993; Williams et al., 1994; Williams and Davids, 1998), leading to an improved ability to anticipate situations. It has been established that expert performers have a superior ability to identify useful anticipatory information from early in their opponent's movement patterns, referred to as "advanced cue utilisation" (Williams et al., 1994; Williams, 2000; Vaeyens et al., 2007a). Furthermore, skilled performers use their superior knowledge to control eye movement patterns (i.e. number of fixations, duration of fixations, reliance on peripheral vision) in order to find and retrieve important sources of information (Williams, 2000), which may be influenced by the task, such as offensive and defensive situations (Helsen and Pauwels, 1993; Williams et al., 1998), field of view (e.g. 11 vs. 11 compared to one vs. one and three vs. three situations) (Williams et al., 1994, 1998) and different offensive situations (e.g. four vs. three, five vs. three) (Vaeyens et al., 2007a, 2007b). Hence why increasing the number of defenders or the type of stimulus presented (arrow versus single defender versus two defenders) results in significant changes in knee moments and posture in athletes (Lee et al., 2013a). Therefore, given the differences that exist between expert and non-expert sports performers, an effective agility test needs to be able to discriminate between sport ability levels, as higher-level players should have better "perceptual-cognitive" abilities than lower-level players. In order to assess this quality, athletes need to respond to actions of an opponent or passages of play within an agility test, which can be achieved by responding to (a) video images (Farrow et al., 2005) or (b) human stimulus (Sheppard & Young, 2006). Such tests have been termed "reactive agility tests" (RAT) (Sheppard & Young, 2006), although the term "reactive" is redundant given the definition of agility mentioned earlier.

From a performance perspective, two studies have illustrated the effectiveness of such tests compared to light or other signals to indicate a direction change. Young et al. (2011) compared two types of reactive agility test: one involving video images and another using arrows (arrow-RAT) to indicate the direction change. The video-based test revealed significant differences between different ability levels of Australian Rules football players, whereas the arrow-RAT revealed only trivial differences between ability levels, illustrating that in order to assess "perceptual-cognitive" elements within an agility test and discriminate between ability levels, a stimulus involving actual movements of an opponent is required as the response stimulus. In further support of this, Henry et al. (2011) compared video- and light-based tests in high- and low-performance Australian Rules footballers and a group of non-footballers. The authors found a certain degree of commonality between light- and video-based tests ($r = 0.75$), but the faster (shorter) decision times associated with the light-based system suggested that a light-based stimulus does not allow enough "cognitive" demand and thus is a less valid measure of (reactive) agility than tests involving a stimulus from actual movement of an opponent.

Video-based systems

Video-based systems offer a solution to assess an athlete's "perceptual-cognitive" ability in relation to agility performance. Farrow et al. (2005) first developed a video-based system to evaluate this in netball. The authors examined the performance of three groups of netball players (high [$n = 12$], moderate [$n = 12$] and low-skilled [$n = 8$] players) during a planned and unanticipated test. The planned test involved players side-shuffling through a start gate (gate 1) 4 m, then back 2 m, before sprinting forward 1 m through a second timing gate (gate 2); they then sprinted 4.1 m to a third timing gate in either a left or right direction (gate 3). The unanticipated trials involved the same set-up, but gate 2 was linked to a laptop which triggered the playing of a netball-specific video clip which was projected on a screen in front of the athlete (approximately >5 m away). The players had to respond to the visual stimulus and run through gate 3 in either a left or right direction depending on the visual cues from the video stimulus. For the unanticipated tests, five measures were recorded: shuffle time (gate 1 to gate 2), sprint time (gate 2 to gate 3), total time (gate 1 to gate 3), decision time from 50 Hz video (time of display occlusion to first definitive foot contact initiating the direction change) and response accuracy. Significant differences in sprint time, total time and decision time (effectively perception-response time) were observed between high- and low-skilled players for unanticipated trials. Moderately skilled players had significantly faster sprint times than low-skilled in the unanticipated trials. No differences were observed between groups in planned trials, suggesting that the unanticipated protocol was able to discriminate between high- and low-skilled players, whereas COD ability (planned trials) did not discriminate between player ability levels. Pearson's correlation between unanticipated and planned sprint times was 0.7, suggesting that both tests shared approximately 50% common variance and thus could be considered assessments of independent qualities. One limitation of the study was that video data were collected at only 50 Hz to measure decision time, which may impact on the precision in determining the time difference between video occlusion and the athlete's definitive foot contact prior to initiating the direction change and may have impacted on the ability to discriminate between groups for decision time in this study.

Research has been undertaken using similar approaches in rugby league (Serpell et al. 2010), Australian Rules football (Young et al., 2011; Henry et al., 2011) and basketball (Spiteri et al., 2014). Serpell et al. (2010), using 15 NRL and 15 National youth rugby league players, involved a similar approach to Farrow with the removal of the initial side-shuffling component and slightly longer sprint distances (10 m approx.). Each player performed eight trials with eight videos randomly selected from 12 available, whilst planned trials were performed removing the video stimulus. No correlation was found between COD (planned trials) and unanticipated trials ($p = 0.08$). Furthermore, significant differences were observed between unanticipated sprint and response times between NRL and youth players, suggesting the video-based protocol could discriminate between ability levels and that unanticipated and planned versions of the test assessed different qualities. Henry et al. (2011) used a similar approach in Australian Rules football players, but an initial 7 m approach included an "abort gate" at 3 m to ensure the players approached at the correct velocity and received the video stimulus at the exact moment of the direction change. The results again revealed that high-level players produced significantly faster agility and movement (time from response initiation to triggering the finish gate) times than non-players, and a moderate correlation ($r = 0.68$) was found between agility time on the video-based and planned tests.

One of the possible drawbacks of such an approach is perhaps the time-consuming preparation required to develop and update a video library in order to carry out regular assessment and monitoring of agility performance. Moreover, the development of video clips requires careful consideration to develop true "match like" scenarios to present to the athlete. Other factors to consider are the cost of additional hardware and software and expertise to develop the protocol. Furthermore, although the stimulus in each study was displayed as a life-sized image on a screen, the 2D presentation of the image may limit the amount and specificity of the cues which the athlete has to react to (Farrow et al., 2005), which may not affect the reaction time but does change the visual search strategy used to complete the task in comparison to a 3D stimulus (Lee et al., 2013b).

Another potential limitation of video-based systems is that due to the large potential response variability associated with different scenarios presented to athletes often mixed reliability of the protocols is reported. For instance, Farrow et al. (2005) reported an ICC of 0.83 for completion time in their video-based protocol in netball players, whilst Young et al. (2011) reported poor reliability for their video-based test (ICC = 0.33; CV = 2.7%; typical error [TE] = 0.07 s) in 50 junior Australian Rules football players, although the authors did report that the reliability was better than the arrow-based test (ICC = 0.1; CV = 3.4%; TE = 0.09 s) used in that study. Serpell et al. (2010) reported good reliability for completion times (ICC = 0.82; SEM = 0.01), but poor reliability for perception-response time (ICC = 0.31; SEM = 0.01), perhaps due to the low sampling rate of the video (50 Hz) that is often used to evaluate perception-response times in these studies. High-speed video (>100 Hz) is recommended to accurately determine perception-response time. Spiteri et al. (2014) reported good reliability (ICC = 0.81; CV= 3.3%), despite using a more complex protocol that involved two CODs in response to two different video stimuli.

To conclude, video-based tests offer a valid approach that improves the ecological validity of COD speed tests by including assessment of an athlete's "perceptual-cognitive" ability. Specifically differentiating the perception-response time from total movement time would provide further information to evaluate the athlete's perceptual-cognitive ability. Careful consideration of edited video clips, movement tasks and measurement of perception-response time is needed in the design of a reliable protocol. One limitation of the approach is the extensive preparation time to develop a video library to carry out regular assessment and monitoring of agility performance. An example video-based test can be seen in Box 9.6. Further research evaluating more ecologically valid projections of scenarios (e.g. 3D stereoscopic with one- and two-defender scenarios) has been used to evaluate changes in kinematics and kinetics (Lee et al., 2013a); however, this type of "video-based" assessment is still very novel and has yet to be evaluated in a performance perspective, but will have the same limitations as even current 2D video assessments.

Human stimulus

Alternative approaches to video use movements of a tester as the stimulus. Sheppard and Young (2006) developed a reactive agility test (RAT) whereby the tester begins on a timing mat and the athlete begins on a start line (5 m apart) with timing cells 5 m either side of the athlete and the tester 2 m in front of the athlete. Once the tester leaves the timing mat, and runs to one side, the athlete needs to respond to the direction of the tester and sprint through the timing cells to the side the tester turned to (i.e. mimicking a defensive situation) (Box 9.7). The athlete responds to one of four scenarios: (1) step forward with right foot and change direction to the left; (2) step forward with the left foot and change direction to the right; (3) step forward with the right foot, then left, and change direction to the right; or (4) step forward with the left foot, then right, and change direction to the left. Sheppard and Young (2006) found that elite athletes recorded faster agility times than sub-elite athletes (d = 1.23), which was not the case for the sprint and planned COD tests. Furthermore, the correlations between sprint and RAT and planned COD and RAT were r = 0.333 and r = 0.331, respectively, illustrating that the RAT could discriminate between

Box 9.6 Agility: video-based reactive agility test (Y-agility tests)

There are many variations of video-based systems to assess agility. A simple version is explained below and shown in Figure 9.6.

- The test involves the athlete sprinting 4 m through a set of timing cells to a change of direction point.
- The timing cells need to be linked to a laptop synchronised with a video projection system.
- The video image is then played on the screen directly in front of the athlete.
- The duration of video needs to be matched to the time required by the athlete to reach the 4 m change of direction point.
- The video image should display a sports-specific scenario, in which the athlete needs to react to and cut 45° to either the left or right and sprint a further 4 m to the final timing gates. The video should be occluded at the point of defining stimulus to indicate the direction change.
- The final agility time is recorded.
- The average of multple trials (e.g. 12) is taken due to high variability between different responses and may include an equal number of trials to the left or right and type of scenario.
- **Peception-response time**
- A high-speed video camera (>100 Hz) is placed behind the athlete and is used to quantify the time (1/sample rate of the video × number of frames) between the defining stimulus from the video replay (i.e. intitial footfall of an approaching athlete or video occlusion) to the initial foot plant to initiate the direction change of the athlete.
- The accuracy of the athlete's responses should be recorded.

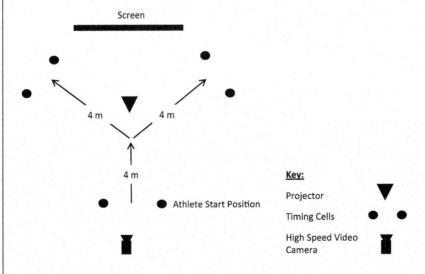

Figure 9.6 Test set-up for a video-based agility test.

athletes of different performance levels and has a low association with planned COD; thus, the RAT was assessing an independent quality.

With available equipment, the protocol requires less preparation time and is easier to administer than video-based systems. Human-stimulus protocols have been widely used in rugby league (Gabbett et al., 2008, 2011a, 2011b; Gabbett & Benton, 2009), basketball (Scanlan et al., 2014a, 2014b) and Australian Rules football (Veale et al., 2010). The latter used a slightly modified version that involved an initial 2 m, unanticipated stimulus, cutting 45°, 5 m to the left or right and then another planned cut 45° in the opposite direction for another 5 m. This protocol overcomes one of the limitations of Sheppard and Young's (2006) method, in that the athletes are having to react when already moving at a higher speed, whereas previous protocols involve athletes responding under low-velocity of movement conditions (Sheppard & Young, 2006; Gabbett et al., 2008; Gabbett & Benton, 2009).

A limitation of Sheppard's original protocol is that the test did not evaluate an athlete's ability to "anticipate" or did not consider the tester time as part of the overall agility time. This has been subsequently evaluated with the addition of a high-speed camera to evaluate the athlete's response time between definitive footfalls prior to initiating the COD between the tester and athlete (Gabbett et al., 2008; Young & Willey, 2010). Young and Willey (2010) measured the following variables during the RAT from high-speed video in semi-professional Australian Rules footballers: tester time (first forward movement [trigger timer] of tester to their definitive foot plant to initiate COD), response time of the athlete (time from tester definitive foot plant to initiate COD to athlete definitive foot plant to initiate COD) and response-movement time (athlete definitive foot plant to initiate COD to crossing the gates [stop timer]). A large correlation ($r = 0.77$) was observed between total time and response time and total time and movement time ($r = 0.59$) and although tester time showed a low co-efficient of variation (5.1%), total time and tester time showed a significant low association ($r = 0.37$). Similarly, Scanlan et al. (2014a) reported large associations of response ($r = 0.76$) and decision time ($r = 0.58$) with agility time in 12 male basketball players, with response time the sole predictor ($r^2 = 0.58$) of agility time, although it should be noted that inappropriate statistics were performed for the latter finding given the low sample size. As with the video-based tests mentioned above, the perception-response time is an important component of the RAT and should be evaluated, whilst tester time needs to be controlled by using high-speed video recordings to isolate its influence.

As with video-based tests, the RAT has repeatedly been shown to be able to discriminate between athlete performance standards (e.g. elite versus sub-elite). Gabbett et al. (2008) found significant differences between grade 1 and grade 2 rugby league athletes in terms of the RAT, but not for L-run, traditional or modified 505 COD tests or decision (perception-response) time. The association between the RAT and COD test was found to explain 16–34% of performance, again suggesting that the RAT and traditional COD tests assess separate qualities. Gabbett and Benton (2009) also compared elite and sub-elite rugby league players and found significant differences between groups in total time to complete the test, decision time and response accuracy ($d = 1.39, 0.62, 0.58$, respectively). Finally, Veale et al. (2010) found that their modified version of the RAT was able to discriminate between different ability levels of U18 Australian Rules football players. Gabbett et al (2011b) also found that reactive agility ($r = 0.29$) was one factor associated with the number of line break assists (an offensive match statistic) in professional rugby league match play. One limitation of the RAT is that such approaches may not truly assess the athlete's ability to respond in game-like scenarios. However, scenarios could be developed within such a test to evoke offensive and defensive situations. For instance, the tester and athlete could mimic marking in the penalty area for a corner in soccer or other one-on-one situations in sport.

Box 9.7 Agility tests: reactive agility test

- The reactive agility test (RAT) involves the athlete beginning on a start line, with timing cells set 2 metres forward and 5 metres to the left and right of the athlete (Figure 9.7).
- The tester is positioned directly in front of the athlete, 5 metres away.
- The tester begins the test by stepping forward 0.5 metres through a pair of timing cells to trigger the start of the test.*
- Once the tester initiates a movement forward the tester performs one of the following four manoeuvres:

  1. Step forward with right foot and change direction to the left.
  2. Step forward with the left foot and change direction to the right.
  3. Step forward with the right foot, then left, and change direction to the right.
  4. Step forward with the left foot, then right, and change direction to the left.

- The athlete is required to react to the tester's movement and sprint through the correct timing gate depending on which direction the tester moves toward (e.g. if the tester moves to the left, the athlete has to move to the tester's left).**
- Typically, an average of 12 trials, randomly allocating four different cues, is reported due to the high variability between different responses.

*Please note a timing mat could be used, whereby the tester steps off the mat to trigger the timer.

** This approach would reflect defensive situations, whereas if an S&C coach preferred to evaluate offensive situations then the athlete would need to move in the opposite direction to the testers movements (e.g. if the tester moves to the left, the athlete moves to the tester's right).

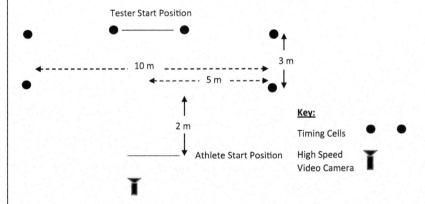

Figure 9.7 Test set-up for a reactive agility test (Sheppard & Young, 2006).

Perception-response time

- A high-speed video camera (>100 Hz) should be placed behind the athlete.
- From the video, the time between the initial foot strike of the tester to initiate the direction change to the initial foot strike of the athlete with the foot eliciting the change of direction is determined by the formula: 1/sampling rate of the video × number of frames between the two instances.[#]

[#] Please note this timing can record a negative time, if the athlete is able to correctly anticipate the direction change by the tester.

Box 9.8 Use of timing cells for change of direction and agility tests

The use of timing cells is covered in Chapter 8. However, a brief overview is provided here. Timing cells should be set around hip height to ensure only one body part breaks the beam (Yeadon et al., 1999). Dual-beam timing cells are preferred to single-beam to improve accuracy (Haugen et al., 2014). Furthermore, the distance between timing cells along the runway should be measured on both sides of the running lane to ensure consistent placement of the timing cells. For reliable data collection, when administering any test with timing cells a standardised starting technique should be used and there should be no prior movements by the athlete. Finally, the athlete should start between 0.3 and 0.5 m behind the timing cell at the start; allowing the athlete to start further than this recommended distance from the starting cell will influence performance as each athlete would gain a "flying" start (Haugen et al., 2015). The exact selection of the standardised start distance will be based on the most appropriate distance to avoid an early triggering of the timing cell.

Despite the large potential response variability associated with different scenarios presented to athletes during the RAT, research has shown the RAT to be reliable and perhaps more so than the video-based systems reported earlier. Sheppard and Young (2006) reported an ICC of 0.87 in a low-performance group of Australian Rules football players, whereas Gabbett et al. (2008) in grade 1 and 2 rugby league players reported ICCs and typical errors (TE) for total time, decision accuracy and decision time of 0.92, 2.1%, 0.93, 3.9% and 0.95, 7.8%, respectively. Scanlan et al. (2014b) reported good (ICC = 0.89–0.99; CV = 1.9–2%) reliability for all outcome measures, albeit in a small sample (n = 5) of male basketball players, and excellent intra-tester reliability of outcome measures derived from video data from 60 trials (ICC = 1.00; CV = 0.69%). Furthermore, the reliability of tester and athlete movements has been investigated (Spiteri et al., 2012), during a similar RAT that involved an athlete moving forward to a 3 m line where they responded to movements of a tester situated 6 metres in front of the athlete and then moving 2 m to the left or right. Spiteri et al. (2012) reported good reliability for movements performed by the human stimulus

(ICC = 0.71–0.99; CV = 1.11–4.77%) and athlete running times (offensive: ICC = 0.91; CV = 3.30%; TE = 0.06; defensive: ICC = 0.90; CV = 3.60%; TE = 0.05). These findings support the implementation of a human stimulus to evoke athlete responses during agility, providing the tester is experienced with such protocols, which may require adequate training and familiarisation prior to administration.

Practical implications

Once a profile is developed of the athlete that evaluates their physical (COD speed), perceptual-cognitive (part of agility assessment) and perceptual-motor (agility) abilities (see Table 9.2 for a comprehensive description of uniquely different COD evaluations one may undertake), then a periodised developmental programme can be designed that considers a holistic approach. It is beyond the scope of this chapter to cover the development of agility: only a brief summary is provided here. For more information see Nimphius (2014), DeWeese and Nimphius (2016) and Nimphius (2017). Development of relative strength and a range of speed-strength qualities across the force-velocity spectrum (Nimphius, 2014) are important for the physical demands of performance of various COD tasks. Particular attention should be paid to the development of eccentric strength of the athlete to tolerate the large braking forces experienced during COD, as previous research has shown an association between eccentric strength and COD performance (Jones et al., 2009, 2017; Spiteri et al., 2013), whilst De Hoyo et al. (2016) have shown positive benefits of 10 weeks' eccentric training on force-time characteristics during side-step and cross-cutting in under-19 professional male soccer players.

Planned COD drills should gradually progress in terms of intensity and complexity (increasing amounts of contextual interference) to develop the physical capacity and movement solution diversification associated with successful COD performance (Nimphius, 2017). Although improvements in COD speed through physical and technical aspects may be developed in a few months, perceptual-cognitive ability may take several years of sports practice in order to develop the task-specific knowledge base to improve anticipation (Williams, 2000). However, improvements in "reactive" agility and "perception-response" time have been seen in as little as 3 weeks (Serpell et al., 2011) through perception-action guided discovery drills using video images as the response stimulus. Development of perceptual-cognitive abilities may be beyond the scope of practice of a strength and conditioning coach, but the design of agility programmes may facilitate the athlete's perceptual-cognitive development. From a progressive loading perspective, the progression of drills from planned low-velocity movements to higher-velocity cutting, followed by combining movements (e.g. side-shuffle to sprint) and varying the tasks and constraints of these drills will allow for the development of technical ability. Once a sound technical basis is developed, unanticipated stimulus can be added, again from a loading perspective, understanding that reducing the time or space available for a decision will increase the joint loading and interestingly that generic stimuli (e.g. arrow or light) actually elicit greater joint moments about the knee (Lee et al., 2013). However, such progression and integration from planned to unanticipated drills should assist with injury prevention, so that athletes can make postural adjustments prior to the direction change when ground reaction forces and hazardous knee joint loads maybe elevated (Besier et al., 2001; Lee et al., 2013a; Jones et al., 2016).

Skill-based conditioning games may also be used as part of the agility developmental programme to further enhance an athlete's perceptual-cognitive abilities (DeWeese &

Table 9.2 Summary of the different purposes of COD that may be assessed with underpinning purpose, examples, benefits and limitations.

COD Focus	Purpose	Example test	Benefits	Limitations
COD with high-velocity braking	Examine physical capacity (and often "confidence") in braking strategy as well as "in and out" COD ability	Traditional 505 or first half of a T-test	Demanding on the braking prior to actual COD; examines physical capacity for braking	Planned assessment so positioning may not be the same movement with stimulus
COD with "aggressive" cutting angle (60° – 90°)	Examine body position when there is a more demanding cut angle (physical capacity only)	First half of T-test modified with running exit or altered exit angle (e.g. 60° – 75°)	Opportunity to examine body position prior to placing athlete in agility scenario with aggressive cut	Planned assessment so positioning may not be the same movement with stimulus
Maintenance of velocity (manoeuvrability)	Examine ability to minimise braking (hold curvilinear running) or "learning to turn"	Slalom COD tests or Illinois agility	Examines unique COD capacity often not considered but common in sport	Depending on chosen assessment, often uncommon to do multiples of such manoeuvres; can replace with single-bend turn or "shallow" cut (< 45°)
Change in mode of travel (manoeuvrability)	Examine ability to transition between multiple modes of travel	T-test	Complex movements that may be common in sports, particularly in defensive movement patterns; evaluate generic physical capacity	Planned assessment so positioning may not be the same movement with stimulus

(*continued*)

Table 9.2 (Cont.)

COD Focus	Purpose	Example test	Benefits	Limitations
One-vs.-one agility	Examine perceptual-motor ability (split into physical capacity or motor capacity and perceptual-cognitive ability)	Y-agility tests (with various stimuli)	Allows for assessment of both physical and perceptual-cognitive ability (mixed perceptual-motor assessment)	Only a one-vs.-one scenario, which delimits generalisability; does not examine perceptual-cognitive factors of visual scanning, knowledge of situation and pattern recognition
One-vs.-two agility	Examine perceptual-motor ability (split into physical capacity or motor capacity and perceptual-cognitive ability)	Two-defender 3D stereoscopic agility task (see Lee et al., 2013a)	As above with additional ecological validity of more complex scenario	Equipment availability and as with all current agility tests, the movement pattern following the decisions has mostly been delimited to "shallow" cutting patterns

Nimphius, 2016; Sheppard et al., 2014; Paul et al., 2016). Young and Rodgers (2014) found that small-sided games moderately improved total (reactive) agility time (using the protocol of Young et al., 2011) due to large changes in perception-response time in U18 Australian Rules footballers, whilst Chaouachi et al. (2014) found that small-sided games improved agility test (Sheppard & Young, 2006 protocol) performance (with ball) in young soccer players compared to training with planned COD drills. Thus, skill-based conditioning games when designed to encourage evasion skills (Young & Rodgers, 2014) should be used to enhance agility performance, with improvements in decision-making speed likely to be enhanced over movement speed due to the small confinements of small-sided games (Paul et al., 2016). However, one must also remember that programmed exposures to COD loading should accompany skill-based conditioning drills since the mechanical demands in these games can vary vastly from athlete to athlete (Gaudino et al., 2014).

Summary

Agility is an important quality in field- and court-based sports and is dependent on perceptual-cognitive factors and factors related to the mechanics of COD or other related movement patterns combining together to provide the best perceptual-motor response possible. The physical (or motor) factors are often referred to as COD ability and are evaluated by COD speed tests. Evaluating agility for sport requires a multi-factorial approach whereby the physical, technical (COD speed tests) and perceptual-cognitive elements are evaluated. Numerous reliable tests of COD speed and/or manoeuvrability are available, including the 505 (traditional and modified), pro-agility, T-test, L-run and Illinois tests. When deciding on the most appropriate COD test to use in a test battery, the movement patterns (e.g. cutting, pivoting, back-pedalling, side-shuffling) of the sport and/or the physical demand one is seeking to examine (e.g. high-velocity braking or low-velocity acceleration and deceleration) need to be considered. A limitation of many traditional COD speed tests is the test duration, as a test of COD speed should be of short duration to eliminate the influence of anaerobic capacity and sprint ability on test performance. The 505 test avoids the limitation of test duration as the typical completion times last 2–3 seconds; however, performance is often influenced by sprint ability. Therefore, the impact of running speed on test performance should be accounted for through the use of the COD deficit or through other more specific descriptors of the COD performance (e.g. entry and exit velocity or qualitative assessment of the COD performance).

An effective test of agility needs to assess the athlete's perceptual-cognitive ability along with their ability to change direction in response to a stimulus (e.g. perceptual-motor ability). Video-based systems offer an avenue to do this but may become complex in their design and time-consuming in preparation, whereas human stimulus approaches whereby a tester evokes the anticipatory stimulus provide a reliable and cost-effective method to assess agility. Perception-response times need to be assessed with these tests to evaluate the athlete's perceptual-cognitive ability and require high-speed (>100 Hz) videoing of the test where both the stimulus and athlete are in view to capture the stimulus (i.e. video occlusion or definitive foot plant of the tester) and definitive foot plant to initiate direction change of the athlete. Despite the advances in agility tests, it should be acknowledged that a majority of the tests currently performed and described in this chapter delimit the perceptual-cognitive measure to a one vs. one scenario, which still requires anticipation and reaction time components of perceptual-cognitive ability but reduces or excludes the measurement of other components that would contribute to game performance or decision-making (e.g. visual scanning, knowledge of situation and pattern recognition). Therefore, the appropriate selection of either a physical focused examination of performance using a COD speed test, or a measure of agility will always have limitations (Table 2). However, it is the careful planning and understanding of the information that is most relevant with an understanding of the inherent limitations of all assessments that will allow one to make the best decisions and use the data in the most informative way to determine the physical and perceptual-cognitive needs of the athlete when assessing agility.

References

Barber, O.R., Thomas, C., Jones, P.A., McMahon, J.J., & Comfort, P. (2016). Reliability of the 505 change-of-direction test in netball players. *International Journal of Sports Physiology and Performance, 11*, 377–380.

Besier, T.F., Lloyd, D.G., Ackland, T.R., & Cochrane, J.L. (2001) Anticipatory effects on knee joint loading during running and cutting maneuvers. *Medicine & Science in Sports & Exercise, 33*, 1176–1181.

Bloomfield, J., Polman, R., & O'Donoghue, P. (2007). Physical demands of different positions in FA Premier League soccer. *Journal of Sports Science and Medicine, 6*(1), 63.

Burgess, D.J., Naughton, G., & Norton, K.I. (2006) Profile of movement demands of national football players in Australia. *Journal of Science and Medicine in Sport, 9*(4), 334–341.

Chandler, P.T., Pinder, S.J., Curran, J.D., & Gabbett, T.J. (2014). Physical demands of training and competition in collegiate netball players. *The Journal of Strength & Conditioning Research, 28*(10), 2732–2737.

Chaouachi, A., Chtara, M., Hammami, R., Chtara, H., Turki, O., & Castagna, C. (2014). Multidirectional sprints and small-sided games training effects on agility and change of direction abilities in youth soccer. *The Journal of Strength & Conditioning Research, 28*(11), 3121–3127.

Cureton, T. (1951). *Physical fitness of champions.* Urbana: University of Illinois Press.

Cuthbert, M., Thomas, C., Dos'Santos, T., & Jones, P.A. (2018). The application of change of direction deficit to evaluate cutting ability. *The Journal of Strength & Conditioning Research* (E-Pub ahead of print).

Davidson, A., & Trewartha, G. (2008). Understanding the physiological demands of netball: A time-motion investigation. *International Journal of Performance Analysis in Sport, 8*(3), 1–17.

De Hoyo, M., Sanudo, B., Carrasco, L., Mateo-Cortes, J., Dominguez-Cobo, S., Fernandes, O., Del Ojo, J.J., & Gonsalo-Skok, O. (2016). Effects of 10-week eccentric overload training on kinetic parameters during change of direction in football players. *Journal of Sports Science, 34*, 1380–1387.

Deweese, B.H., & Nimphius, S. (2016). Program design and technique for speed and agility training. In G.G. Haff & N.T. Triplett (Eds.), *Essentials of strength training and conditioning* (4th edn., pp. 521–557). Champaign, IL: Human Kinetics.

Dos'Santos, T., Thomas, C., Comfort, P., & Jones, P.A. (2018). Assessing asymmetries in change of direction speed performance; application of change of direction deficit. *The Journal of Strength & Conditioning Research* (E-Pub ahead of print).

Draper, J.A., & Lancaster, M.G. (1985). The 505 test: A test for agility in the horizontal plane. *Australian Journal of Science and Medicine in Sport, 17*(1), 15–18.

Farrow, D., Young, W., & Bruce, L. (2005). The development of a test of reactive agility for netball: a new methodology. *Journal of Science and Medicine in Sport, 8*(1), 52–60.

Faude, O., Koch, T., & Meyer, T. (2012).Straight sprinting is the most frequent action in goal situations in professional football. *Journal of Sports Science, 30*(7), 625–631.

Foden, M., Astley, S., Mcmahon, J.J., Comfort, P., Matthews, M.J., & Jones, P.A. (2015). Relationships between speed, change of direction and jump performance with cricket specific speed tests in male academy cricketers. *Journal of Trainology, 4*(2), 37–42.

Gabbett, T., & Benton, D. (2009). Reactive agility of rugby league players. *Journal of Science and Medicine in Sport, 12*, 212–214.

Gabbett, T.J., Jenkins, D.G., & Abernethy, B. (2011a). Relative importance of physiological, anthropometric and skill qualities to team selection in professional rugby league. *Journal of Sports Science, 29*(13), 1453–1461.

Gabbett, T.J., Jenkins, D.G., & Abernethy, B. (2011b). Relationships between physiological, anthropometric and skill qualities and playing performance in professional rugby league players. *Journal of Sports Science, 29*(15), 1655–1664.

Gabbett, T.J., Kelly, J.N., & Sheppard, J.M. (2008). Speed, change of direction speed, and reactive agility of rugby league players. *The Journal of Strength & Conditioning Research, 22*(1), 174–181.

Graham-Smith, P., Atkinson, L. Barlow, R., & Jones, P. (2009). Braking characteristics and load distribution in 180° turns. Proceedings of the 5th Annual UK Strength and Conditioning Association Conference, Wyboston Lakes, Bedfordshire, 5–7 June. pp. 6–7.

Graham-Smith, P., & Pearson, S.J. (2005). An investigation into the determinants of agility performance. *Proceedings of the 3rd International Biomechanics of the Lower Limb in Health, Disease and Rehabilitation*; Manchester, UK, September 5–7.

Gaudino, P., Alberti, G., & Iaia, F.M. (2014). Estimated metabolic and mechanical demands during different small-sided games in elite soccer players. *Human Movement Science, 36*, 123–133.

Hachana, Y., Chaabène, Nabli, M.A., Attia, A., Moualhi, J., Farhat, N., & Elloumi, M. (2013). Test-retest reliability, criterion-related validity, and minimal detectable change of the Illinois agility test in male team sports athletes. *The Journal of Strength & Conditioning Research, 27*(10), 2752–2759.

Hader, K., Palazzi, D., & Buchheit, M. (2015). Change of direction speed in soccer: How much braking is enough? *Kinesiology, 47*(1), 67–74.

Haugen, T., Svendsen, I.S., & Seiler, S. (2014). Sprint time differences between single and dual beamed timing systems. *The Journal of Strength & Conditioning Research, 28*(8), 2376–2379.

Haugen, T., Tønnessen, E., & Seiler, S. (2015). Correction factor for photocell sprint timing with flying start. *International Journal of Sports Physiology and Performance, 10*(8), 1055–1057.

Helsen, W.F., & Pauwels, J.M. (1993). The relationship between expertise and visual information processing in sport. In J.L. Starkes and F. Allard (Eds.), *Cognitive issues in motor expertise* (pp. 109–134). Amsterdam: Elsevier.

Henry, G., Dawson, B., Lay, B., & Young, W. (2011). Validity of a reactive agility test for Australian football. *International Journal of Sports Physiology and Performance, 6*(4), 534–545.

Hoffman, J., Tenenbaum, G., Maresh, C., & Kraemer, W. (1996). Relationship between athletic performance tests and playing time elite college basketball players. *The Journal of Strength & Conditioning Research, 10*, 67–71.

Jeffreys, I. (2006). Motor learning – applications for agility, Part 1. *Strength & Conditioning Journal, 28*(5), 72–78.

Jones, P., Bampouras, T., & Marrin, K. (2009). An investigation into the physical determinants of change of direction speed. *Journal of Sports Medicine and Physical Fitness, 49*(1), 97–104.

Jones, P.A., Herrington, L.C., & Graham-Smith, P. (2016). Braking characteristics during cutting and pivoting in female soccer players. *Journal of Electromyography and Kinesiology, 30*, 46–54.

Jones, P.A., Thomas, C., Dos'Santos, T., Mcmahon, J.J., & Graham-Smith, P. (2017). The role of eccentric strength in 180° turns in female soccer players. *Sports, 5*(2), 42.

Lee, M.J., Lloyd, D.G., Lay, B.S., Bourke, P.D., & Alderson, J.A. (2013a). Effects of different visual stimuli on postures and knee moments during sidestepping. *Medicine & Science in Sports & Exercise, 45*(9), 1740–1748.

Lee, M.J., Tidman, S.J., Lay, B.S., Bourke, P.D., Lloyd, D.G., & Alderson, J.A. (2013b). Visual search differs but not reaction time when intercepting a 3D versus 2D videoed opponent. *Journal of Motor Behavior, 45*(2), 107–115.

Lockie, R.G., Stecyk, S.D., Mock, S.A., Crelling, B., Lockwood, J.R., & Jalilvand, F. (2016). A cross-sectional analysis of the characteristics of division I collegiate female soccer field players across year of eligibility. *Journal of Australian Strength and Conditioning, 24*(4), 6–15.

Munro, A.G., & Herrington, L.C. (2011). Between session reliability of four hop tests and the agility t-test. *The Journal of Strength & Conditioning Research, 25*(5), 1470–1477.

Nimphius, S. (2014). Increasing agility. In D. Joyce & D. Lewindon (Eds.), *High-performance training for sports* (pp. 185–198). Champaign, IL: Human Kinetics.

Nimphius, S., Callaghan, S.J., & Lockie, R. (2016a). Change of direction deficit: A more isolated measure of change of direction performance than total 505 time. *The Journal of Strength & Conditioning Research, 30*, 3024–3032.

Nimphius, S., Callaghan, S.J., & Hawser, A. (2016b). Comparison of simplified change of direction tests. *The Journal of Strength & Conditioning Research, 30*(Supplement 2), S155–S156.

Nimphius, S., Geib, G., Spiteri, T., & Carlisle, D. (2013). "Change of direction" deficit measurement in division I American football players. *Journal of Australian Strength and Conditioning, 21*, 115–117.

Nimphius, S., McGuigan, M.R., & Newton, R.U. (2010). Relationships between strength, power, speed and change of direction performance of female softball players. *The Journal of Strength & Conditioning Research, 24*(4), 885–895.

Nimphius, S. (2017). Training change of direction and agility. In A. Turner & P. Comfort (Eds.), *Advanced strength and conditioning: An evidence-based approach* (pp. 291–309) Abingdon, Oxon: Routledge.

Nimphius, S., Callaghan, S.J., Bezodis, N.E., & Lockie, R.G. (2018). Change of direction and agility tests: Challenging our current measures of performance. *Strength & Conditioning Journal, 40*(1), 26–38.

Oliver, J.L., & Meyers, R.W. (2009). Reliability and generality of measures of acceleration, planned agility and reactive agility. *International Journal of Sports Physiology and Performance, 4*, 345–354.

Paul, D.J., Gabbett, T.J., & Nassis, G.P. (2016). Agility in team sports: Testing, training, and factors affecting performance. *Sports Medicine, 46*, 421–442.

Pauole, K., Madole, K., Garhammer, J., Lacourse, M., & Rozenek, R. (2000). Reliability and validity of the T-test as a measure of agility, leg power and leg speed in college-aged men and women. *The Journal of Strength & Conditioning Research, 14*(4), 443–450.

Plisk, S.S. (2000). Speed, agility, and speed endurance development. In T.R. Baechle & R.W. Earle (Eds.), *Essentials of strength training and conditioning* (2nd edn., pp. 471–491). Champaign, IL: Human Kinetics.

Sayers, M.G.L. (2015). Influence of test distance on change of direction speed test results. *The Journal of Strength & Conditioning Research, 29*(9), 2412–2416.

Scanlan, A., Humphries, B., Tucker, P.S., & Dalbo, V. (2014a). The influence of physical and cognitive factors on reactive agility performance in men basketball players. *Journal of Sports Science, 32*(4), 367–374.

Scanlan, A., Tucker, P.S., & Dalbo, (2014b). A comparison of linear speed, closed-skill agility, and open-skill agility qualities between backcourt and front court adult semi-professional male basketball players. *The Journal of Strength & Conditioning Research, 28*(5), 1319–1327.

Serpell, B.G., Ford, M., & Young, W.B. (2010).The development of a new test of agility for rugby league. *The Journal of Strength & Conditioning Research, 24*(12), 3270–3277.

Serpell, B.G., Young, W.B., & Ford, M. (2011). Are the perceptual and decision making components of agility trainable? A preliminary investigation. *The Journal of Strength & Conditioning Research, 25*(5), 1240–1248.

Sheppard, J.M., Dawes, J.J., Jeffreys, I., Spiteri, T., & Nimphius, S. (2014). Broadening the view of agility: A scientific review of the literature. *Journal of Australian Strength and Conditioning, 22*(3), 6–29.

Sheppard, J.M., & Young, W.B. (2006). Agility literature review: Classifications, training and testing. *Journal of Sports Science, 24*(9), 919–932.

Sierer, S.P., Battaglini, C.L., Mihalik, J.P., Shields, E.W., & Tomasini, N.T. (2008). The National Football League combine: Performance differences between drafted and non-drafted players entering the 2004–2005 drafts. *The Journal of Strength & Conditioning Research, 22*(1), 6–12.

Spencer, M., Lawrence, S., Rechichi, C., Bishop, D., Dawson, B., & Goodman, C. (2002). Time-motion analysis of elite field hockey. *Journal of Science and Medicine in Sport, 5*(4), 102.

Spiteri, T., Cochrane, J.L., & Nimphius, S. (2012). Human stimulus reliability during an offensive and defensive agility protocol. *Journal of Australian Strength and Conditioning, 20*, 14–21.

Spiteri, T., Nimphius, S., Hart, N.H., Specos, C., Sheppard, J.M., & Newton, R.U. (2014). Contribution of strength characteristics to change of direction and agility performance in female basketball players. *The Journal of Strength & Conditioning Research, 28*(9), 2415–2423.

Sporis, G., Jukic, I., Milanovic, L., & Vucetic, V. (2010). Reliability and factorial validity of agility tests for soccer players. *The Journal of Strength & Conditioning Research, 24*(3), 679–686.

Stewart, P.F., Turner, A.N., & Miller S.C. (2014). Reliability, factorial validity and interrelationships of five commonly used change of direction speed tests. *Scandinavian Journal of Medicine & Science in Sports, 24*, 500–506.

Stolen, T., Chamari, K., Castagna, C. & Wisloff, U. (2005). Physiology of soccer: an update. *Sports Medicine, 35*(6), 501–36.

Thomas, C., Comfort, P., Dos'Santos, T., & Jones, P.A. (2016). Relationship between Isometric strength, sprint, and change of direction speed in male academy cricketers. *Journal of Trainology, 5*(2), 18–23.

Thomas, C., Ismail, K.T., Comfort, P., Jones, P.A., & Dos'Santos, T. (2016). Physical profiles of regional academy Netball players. *Journal of Trainology, 5*(2), 30–37.

Turner, E. (2016). *Physical and match performance of female soccer players.* PhD Thesis. University of Salford.

Vaeyens, R., Lenoir, M., Williams, A.M., Mazyn, L., & Philippaerts, R.M. (2007a). The effects of task constraints on visual search behavior and decision-making skill in youth soccer players. *Journal of Sport & Exercise Psychology, 29*, 147–169.

Vaeyens, R., Lenoir, M., Williams, A.M., & Philippaerts, R.M. (2007b). Mechanisms underpinning successful decision marking in skilled youth soccer players: An analysis of visual search behaviours. *Journal of Motor Behaviour, 39*(5), 395–408.

Veale, J.P., Pearce, A.J., & Carlson, J.S. (2010). Reliability and validity of a reactive agility tests for Australian football. *International Journal of Sports Physiology and Performance, 5*, 239–248.

Vescovi, J.D., & McGuigan, M.R. (2008). Relationships between sprinting, agility, and jump ability in female athletes. *Journal of Sports Science, 26*(1), 97–107.

Vigne, G., Gaudino, C., Rogowski, I., Alloatti, G., & Hautier, C. (2010). Activity profile in elite Italian soccer team. *International Journal of Sports Medicine, 31*(5), 304–310.

Williams, M. (2000). Perceptual skill in soccer: Implications for talent identification and development. *Journal of Sports Sciences, 18*(9), 737–750.

Williams, M., & Davids, K. (1998). Visual search strategy, selective attention, and expertise in soccer. *Research Quarterly for Exercise and Sport, 69*, 111–128.

Williams, A.M., Davids, K., Burwitz, L., & Williams, J.G. (1994). Visual search strategies of experienced and inexperienced soccer players. *Research Quarterly for Exercise and Sport, 65*, 127–135.

Williams, A.M., Davids, K., Burwitz, L., & Williams, J.G. (1993). Cognitive knowledge and soccer performance. *Perceptual and Motor Skills, 76*, 579–593.

Yeadon, M.R., Kato, T., & Kerwin, D.G. (1999). Measuring running speed using photocells. *Journal of Sports Sciences, 17*, 249–257.

Young, W., Farrow, D., Pyne, D., McGregor, W., & Handke, T. (2011). Validity and reliability of agility tests in junior Australian football players. *The Journal of Strength & Conditioning Research, 25*(12), 3399–3403.

Young, W.B., McDowell, M.H., & Scarlett, B.J. (2001). Specificity of sprint and agility training methods. *The Journal of Strength & Conditioning Research, 15*, 315–319.

Young, W., & Rodgers, N. (2014). Effects of small-sided game and change of direction training on reactive agility and change of direction speed. *Journal of Sports Sciences, 32*(4), 307–314.

Young, W.B., & Willey, B. (2010). Analysis of a reactive agility field test. *Journal of Science & Medicine in Sport, 13*, 376–378.

10 Strength – isometric and dynamic testing

G. Gregory Haff

Introduction

Muscular strength is considered to be a cornerstone underpinning many sporting activities such as jumping, sprinting and changing direction (Haff and Stone, 2015; Stone et al., 2002). In addition, higher levels of muscular strength exert a protective effect against fatigue-induced decrements in sports performance (Gabbett, 2016). These protective effects are particularly important in contact sports such as American football and rugby where physical collisions play a large role in determining performance outcomes (Gabbett and Ryan, 2009; Austin et al., 2011). Highlighting the importance of muscular strength, Gabbett (2016) has reported that lower-body strength exerts a protective effect against fatigue-induced reductions in tackling performance. With muscular strength contributing to overall tackling ability (Gabbett, 2016; Speranza et al., 2015, 2016), it is easy to see that specific strategies designed to maximise muscular strength are needed in these types of sports.

Fundamentally, muscular strength can be defined as the ability to exert force (Stone et al., 2002) against an external object or resistance (Suchomel et al., 2016). This ability can be placed upon a theoretical continuum ranging from a strength deficit (i.e. not enough strength) to what is often referred to as a strength reserve (Buchner et al., 1992; Suchomel et al., 2016). Based upon the work of Buchner et al. (1992), a theoretical relationship between strength, performance (Suchomel et al., 2016), fatigue resistance and injury can be constructed (Figure 10.1).

In addition to reduction in performance capacity and fatigue resistance a higher risk of injury is generally associated with lower levels of muscular strength. When an individual's strength levels increase from an area of deficit and cross the first threshold there is an increase in association between strength gains and sports performance enhancement (Gabbett, 2016), as well as a reduction in injury risk and increased fatigue resistance (Suchomel et al., 2016, Gabbett, 2016). If the athlete is able to dramatically improve their ability to produce force they will eventually pass through the second threshold and begin to establish a strength reserve. It is likely that an athlete may continue to gain strength in this phase but the association with performance is not substantial (Suchomel et al., 2016). That being said, increasing the strength reserve may actually add to injury prevention and fatigue resistance, giving the athlete more reserves to draw upon during critical times of need. Ultimately the model presented suggests that when appropriate resistance training methods are employed an individual's strength levels can be increased to a level at which sports performance capabilities are increased or even maximised (Suchomel et al., 2016), resistance to fatigue is increased and injury risk is reduced.

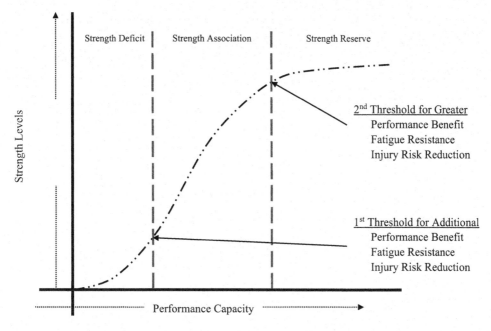

Figure 10.1 Theoretical relationship between strength and performance.
Source: Adapted from Suchomel et al. (2016) and Buchner et al. (1992).

Central to the ability to maximise training adaptations, overall strength level must be quantified in some manner (Haff and Haff, 2012). The most common method for evaluating maximal strength is to establish the one-repetition maximum (1-RM) (Buckner et al., 2017). However, other methods such as isometric (Maffiuletti et al., 2016) and isokinetic (Rouis et al., 2015) tests have also been used. It is likely that to establish a true understanding of an athlete's muscular strength levels multiple measurements of strength need to be considered (Buckner et al., 2017).

Therefore, in order to assist the strength and conditioning professional in establishing methods of assessing muscular strength, the primary purpose of this chapter is to (1) examine the basic methods that can be used to assess muscular strength and (2) propose standardised methods for assessing muscular strength.

Strength testing – review of the literature

Muscular strength is a well-established attribute that is an important contributor to sports performance, fatigue resistance and injury prevention. As such the development of muscular strength is considered to be one of the more important physical training targets when working with athletes (Haff and Nimphius, 2012; Bompa and Haff, 2009; Stone et al., 2002). Based upon its overall importance muscular strength should be evaluated as part of a comprehensive athlete-monitoring plan. The most common method of monitoring an athlete's muscular strength is the assessment of the 1-RM (Buckner et al., 2017). While the

Table 10.1 Common force variables quantified from the analysis of an isometric force-time curve.

Variable		Abbreviation	Unit	Calculation method
Peak force	Absolute peak force	PF	N	PF produced – body mass
	Relative peak force	PF_{Rel}	$N \cdot kg^{-1}$	PF ÷ body mass (kg)
	Allometrically scaled peak force	PF_{Allo}	$N \cdot kg^{-0.67}$	PF ÷ body mass $(kg)^{0.67}$
Force	Force at 50 ms	F_{50}	N	F at 50 ms – body mass
	Relative force at 50 ms	F_{Rel50}	$N \cdot kg^{-1}$	F_{50} ÷ body mass (kg)
	Allometrically scaled force at 50 ms	F_{Allo50}	$N \cdot kg^{-0.67}$	F_{50} ÷ body mass $(kg)^{0.67}$
	Force at 100 ms	F_{100}	N	F at 100 ms – body mass
	Relative force at 100 ms	F_{Rel100}	$N \cdot kg^{-1}$	F_{100} ÷ body mass (kg)
	Allometrically scaled force at 100 ms	$F_{Allo100}$	$N \cdot kg^{-0.67}$	F_{100} ÷ body mass $(kg)^{0.67}$
	Force at 150 ms	F_{150}	N	F at 150 ms – body mass
	Relative force at 150 ms	F_{Rel150}	$N \cdot kg^{-1}$	F_{150} ÷ body mass (kg)
	Allometrically scaled force at 150 ms	$F_{Allo150}$	$N \cdot kg^{-0.67}$	F_{150} ÷ body mass $(kg)^{0.67}$
	Force at 200 ms	F_{200}	N	F at 200 ms – body mass
	Relative force at 200 ms	F_{Rel200}	$N \cdot kg^{-1}$	F_{200} ÷ body mass (kg)
	Allometrically scaled force at 200 ms	$F_{Allo200}$	$N \cdot kg^{-0.67}$	F_{200} ÷ body mass $(kg)^{0.67}$
	Force at 250 ms	F_{250}	N	F at 250 ms – body mass
	Relative force at 250 ms	F_{Rel250}	$N \cdot kg^{-1}$	F_{250} ÷ body mass (kg)
	Allometrically scaled force at 250 ms	$F_{Allo250}$	$N \cdot kg^{-0.67}$	F_{250} ÷ body mass $(kg)^{0.67}$

1-RM is a very useful diagnostic tool that can aid in the construction of resistance training programmes it does not give detailed information about how the athlete makes force. In order to provide this information, the ability to create a force-time curve during either isometric or dynamic movements can provide a more diagnostic representation of the athlete's force generating capacity.

Isometric testing: isometric testing methods are generally used to generate force-time curves that can be analysed to determine an athlete's maximal and explosive strength levels (Zatsiorsky and Kraemer, 2006). Typically, isometric assessments are undertaken with the use of a force plate (Haff et al., 2015), isokinetic dynamometer (Tillin et al., 2012) or a load cell (Folland et al., 2014; James et al., 2017) which allows for the generation of a force-time curve (Haff et al., 2015). The force-time curve can be analysed to determine various force (Table 10.1) (Haff et al., 2015), RFD (Table 10.2) (Maffiuletti et al., 2016) and impulse measurements (Folland et al., 2014).

The most common force measurements taken include peak force (PF) and forces at pre-determined time periods (Tillin et al., 2010; Beckham et al., 2013) as well as the RFD (Figure 10.2a) (Maffiuletti et al., 2016). Additionally, the RFD can be quantified during overlapping time periods starting from 0, e.g. from 0–200 ms from onset (Aagaard et al., 2002; Haff et al., 2015), or consecutive periods, e.g. 100–200 ms (Penailillo et al., 2015), relative to force onset (Figure 10.2b). Additionally, it is now becoming commonplace to

Table 10.2 Common rate of force development variables quantified from the analysis of an isometric force-time curve.

Variable	Abbreviation	Unit	Calculation method
Rate of force development	RFD	$N \cdot s^{-1}$	$\Delta Force \div \Delta Time$
Average rate of force development	RFD_{AVG}	$N \cdot s^{-1}$	PF ÷ time to PF from force on-set
Peak rate of force development	pRFD	$N \cdot s^{-1}$	PF ÷ sampling window
Rate of force development 0–50 ms	RFD_{0-50}	$N \cdot s^{-1}$	F at 50 ms ÷ 50 ms
Rate of force development 0–100 ms	RFD_{0-100}	$N \cdot s^{-1}$	F at 100 ms ÷ 100 ms
Rate of force development 0–150 ms	RFD_{0-150}	$N \cdot s^{-1}$	F at 150 ms ÷ 150 ms
Rate of force development 0–200 ms	RFD_{0-200}	$N \cdot s^{-1}$	F at 200 ms ÷ 200 ms
Rate of force development 0–250 ms	RFD_{0-250}	$N \cdot s^{-1}$	F at 250 ms ÷ 250 ms
Rate of force development 50–100 ms	RFD_{50-100}	$N \cdot s^{-1}$	(F at 100 ms – 50 ms) ÷ 50 ms
Rate of force development 100–200 ms	$RFD_{100-200}$	$N \cdot s^{-1}$	(F at 200 ms – 100 ms) ÷ 100 ms
Rate of force development 200–250 ms	$RFD_{200-250}$	$N \cdot s^{-1}$	(F at 250 ms – 200 ms) ÷ 50 ms

quantify the impulse in these same pre-determined time periods (Figure 10.2b). Impulse is the integral beneath the force time recording (Folland et al., 2014) and provides information about the time history of the contraction including the overall influence of all of the examined RFD measurements (Aagaard et al., 2002). Ultimately, the ability to dissect the force-time curve allows for various aspects of strength to be quantified and monitored.

Central to effective analysis of the force-time curve for ground-based activities is the quantification of the onset or commencement of the isometric muscle action (Dos'Santos et al., 2017a). A variety of methods for quantifying the force onset have been suggested in the scientific literature (Comfort et al., 2015; Dos'Santos et al., 2017a; West et al., 2011) with a threshold of 5 SD of mean force determined during a 1 second quiet standing period prior to force application most effectively accounting for signal noise (Dos'Santos et al., 2016). The use of a standardised method for defining the onset of the isometric muscle action is important because it will increase the certainty that the measured force changes are meaningful.

Another popular force-time curve measurement is the peak RFD (PRFD), i.e. the steepest part of the force-time curve over a specific epoch. A variety of epochs ranging from 2 to 50 ms have been reported in the scientific literature (Haff et al., 2015, 2005, 1997; Beckham et al., 2013; Kawamori et al., 2006; Leary et al., 2012). Maffiuletti et al. (2016) suggest that smaller epochs are more sensitive to unsystematic variance and are less reliable when quantifying the PRFD. Therefore, it is recommended that before selecting an epoch for quantifying the PRFD careful thought should be given to the purpose of the measure being undertaken (Maffiuletti et al., 2016).

The most common methods for collecting isometric force-time curves in the applied sport setting involve the use of the isometric mid-thigh pull (IMTP) and the isometric

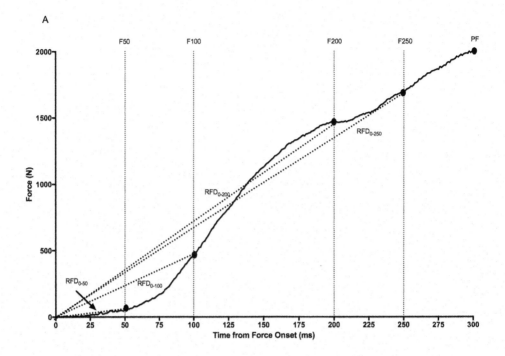

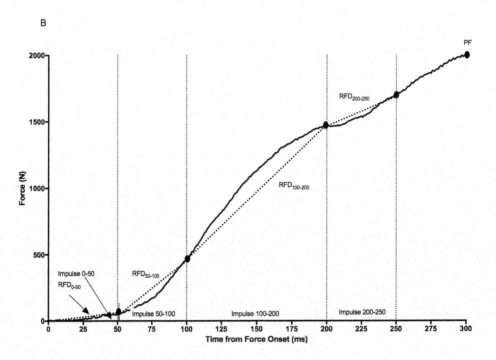

Figure 10.2 Common force-time curve measures.

squat (ISQT). More recently, the isometric leg press (ILP) has emerged as another method for quantifying the force-time characteristics of the lower body (Zaras et al., 2016). These multi-joint lower-body tests appear to offer a greater transferability to dynamic sport-specific movements which engage the lower body (Stone et al., 2004). The most common upper-body isometric test is the isometric bench press (IBP) (Young et al., 2014).

Isometric mid-thigh pull testing: the IMTP was first presented by Haff et al. (1997) as a testing method for examining the force-time curve characteristics of weightlifters. This novel isometric test was designed to replicate the body position at the beginning of the second pull during the snatch or clean (Haff et al., 1997) where the highest forces are generated during the pulling motion (Garhammer, 1993). In this body position the trunk is upright (Haff et al., 1997, 2015; Beckham et al., 2018), the knee angle ranges between 130 and 145° (Haff et al., 2015; Beckham et al., 2013) and the hip angle is between 124 and 175° (Beckham et al., 2013, Ahead of print; Kawamori et al., 2006). Comfort et al. (2015) have questioned the impact of the body position during the IMTP, reporting that body position has no meaningful impact on the PF or RFD achieved during the test. Conversely, more recent research suggests that the body position does in fact exert a significant and meaningful impact on the force-time curve results achieved during the IMTP (Beckham et al., 2012, 2018). The important caveat is that the person being tested should be in their optimal second pull position and not arbitrarily placed into a set knee or hip angles based upon those that have been published in the literature. The second pull position is highly individualised and is impacted by an individual's anthropometrics, thus the knee and hip angles presented in the literature generally represent the average angles for the group being tested.

In order to perform the IMTP a customised testing system, which allows for step-wise adjustments of the isometric position, coupled with a force platform is required (Haff et al., 1997, 2015) (Figure 10.3).

Haff et al. (1997) developed a specialised testing system designed specifically for performing the IMTP and the ISQT. This system allows for the positioning of a fixed

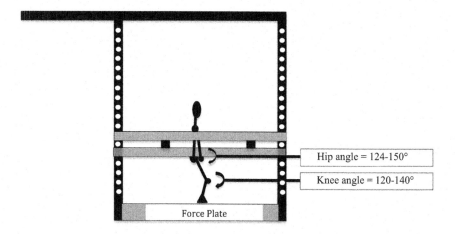

Hip angle = 124-150°

Knee angle = 120-140°

Force Plate

Figure 10.3 Isometric mid-thigh pull apparatus.

bar, made from cold rolled steel, to be adjusted to any position with the use of pins and hydraulic jacks. By employing this system, the exact second pull position achieved in the snatch or clean can be achieved when performing the IMTP (Haff et al., 2005). In addition, this original system utilised a single force plate. More recently multiple force plates have been used when performing the IMTP in order to examine force production asymmetries (Bailey et al., 2015). The ability to examine force production asymmetries during the IMTP test may yield valuable information that can be related to sports performance (Bailey et al., 2015) or more importantly injury prevention or rehabilitation (Jordan et al., 2015).

Ultimately, to be a useful diagnostic tool the IMTP needs to be performed with standardised methods and a systematic approach to both the collection and analysis of the force-time curves. If appropriate controls are used the PF and forces at predetermined time points are highly reliable (Haff et al., 2015; Comfort et al., 2015). For example, Thomas et al. (2015) report that the IMTP results in a highly reliable PF based upon the intra-class correlation (ICC= 0.96, 90% confidence interval [90% CI] = 0.91–0.99), coefficient of variation % (CV% = 4.3, 90% CI = 3.3–6.5), typical error (TE = 113.7 N) and % change in mean (−1.0%). Similarly, Haff et al. (2015) have reported that the forces achieved at specific time bands are highly reliable with CV% that are <5% and ICCs that are >0.90. Overall it is well accepted that the IMTP is a very reliable method for quantifying maximal force-generating capacity.

While the PF and time-band-specific forces have exhibited very good reliability, the reliability of the RFD has not been consistently reported (Haff et al., 2015). Specifically, Haff et al. (2015) have reported that the sampling epoch used when determining the peak RFD can significantly impact the reliability of the measure. Based upon this work a sampling window of 20 ms is typically recommended as it produces the best reliability (ICC = 0.90, CI = 0.73–0.97; CV% = 12.9%, CI = 0.5–20.7). Based upon the current literature it has been suggested that using pre-determined RFD time bands, such as the onset to 200 ms, produces a much more reliable RFD measure (Haff et al., 2015; Dos'Santos et al., 2016). Dos'Santos et al. (2016) report that the RFD from onset to 200 ms is highly reliable based upon the CV% (CV% = 7.5, CI = 6.2–9.6) and ICC (ICC = 0.90, CI = 0.82–0.95). Similarly, Haff et al. (2015) report that time band RFD measures are highly reliable. As such it is now common to examine RFD measures in specific time bands (Table 10.2).

Based upon the origins of the IMTP test and the key position that it tests it is not unexpected that the PF determined during the test is highly correlated with the maximal weight lifted in the competitive weightlifting movements (i.e. snatch and clean & jerk) and their derivatives (i.e. power clean and power snatch) (Stone et al., 2003; Nuzzo et al., 2008) (Figure 10.4). It has also been reported that the IMTP PF is highly related to 1-RM in the back squat (Wang et al., 2016) and bench press (McGuigan et al., 2010) (Figure 10.4).

The PF determined during the IMTP has also been related to change of direction ability (Thomas et al., 2015), 5–20 m sprint time (Thomas et al., 2015), 25–333 m sprint cycling time (Stone et al., 2004), throwing distances in the shot put and weight bag throw (Stone et al., 2003) and vertical jump performances (Kawamori et al., 2006).

When looking at sports performance it is often necessary to produce high amounts of forces in short periods of time. For example, Nagahara et al. (2017) report that the average ground contact time during acceleration sprint performance ranges from 98 ms to 170 ms. Therefore, it is not surprising that the amount of force generated in 100 ms on the IMTP test is significantly ($p \leq 0.05$) related to 5 m ($r = -0.71$), 10 m ($r = -0.54$) and 20 m ($r = -0.75$) sprint performance (West et al., 2011; Thomas et al., 2015).

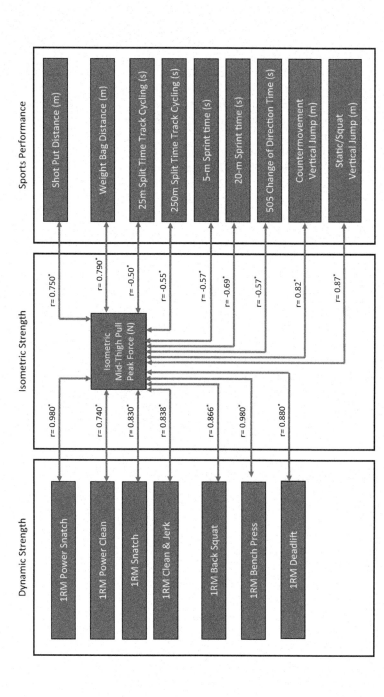

Figure 10.4 Relationships between performance and strength measures.

Source: Data collected from Wang et al. (2016), Beckham et al. (2013), Nuzzo et al. (2008), Stone et al. (2003), McGuigan et al. (2010), Stone et al. (2004), Thomas et al. (2015), Kawamori et al. (2006), De Witt et al. (2018).
* = p ≤ 0.05.

While force-generating capacities are often significantly related to markers of perform-ance, the RFD has not consistently mirrored these relationships (Khamoui et al., 2011; McGuigan et al., 2010). However, significant ($p \leq 0.05$) correlations have been reported between the peak RFD and 5 m ($r = -0.58$), 10 m ($r = -0.66$), 20 m ($r = -0.71$) and COD ($r = -0.57$) times (Thomas et al., 2015; West et al., 2011). Additionally, when examining the relationship between the RFD for a 0–250 ms time period there are significant ($p \leq 0.05$) correlations with the snatch ($r = 0.781$), clean & jerk (0.722) and total achieved in weightlifting ($r = 0.751$) (Beckham et al., 2013). Overall the contemporary methodolo-gies suggest that predetermined time-band RFDs are more reliable and more "diagnostic". However, more research is needed to understand how to use these measures in a prescrip-tive manner or as a monitoring tool.

Isometric squat testing: the ISQT is another commonly used test in which force-time curves can be created to evaluate lower-body force-generating capacities (Young et al., 2014; Bazyler et al., 2015; Blazevich et al., 2002). As with the IMTP the ISQT should be conducted at the joint angle at which the highest forces are produced (Bazyler et al., 2015; Kulig et al., 1984). When looking at the back squat a knee angle of ~120–140° is often considered to be where the highest forces are generated (Bazyler et al., 2015; Nuzzo et al., 2008). An argument can also be made for testing the ISQT at a knee angle of 90° because this has often been associated with the "sticking region" in the dynamic lift (Blazevich et al., 2002). As such knee angles of 90° (Demura et al., 2010; Newton et al., 2002; Bazyler et al., 2015; Blazevich et al., 2002; Pekünlü & Özsu, 2014), 120° (Young, 1995; Young et al., 1999; Bazyler et al., 2015) and 140° (Nuzzo et al., 2008) are commonly tested in the scientific literature. To date only one study has reported the hip angle (i.e. 110°) used during the ISQT (Newton et al., 2002). While more research is needed looking at various combinations of knee and hip angles the most common knee angles tested are 90° and 120°.

Central to the ability to conduct an ISQT test is a system which couples the ability to perform step-wise positional adjustments of the isometric position with a force platform which is used to quantify ground reaction forces (Figure 10.5) (Nuzzo et al., 2008; Bazyler

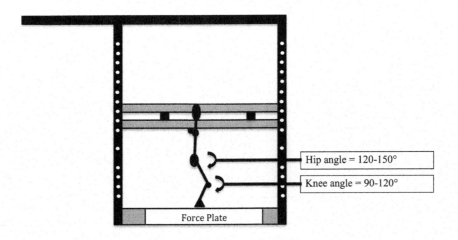

Figure 10.5 Isometric squat apparatus.

et al., 2015). The isometric testing system first proposed by Haff et al. (1997) has the capacity to be adapted to the performance of the ISQT test. More recently, Bazyler et al. (2015) have utilised dual force platforms in order to evaluate force asymmetries, which may yield valuable information about injury risk or progress during rehabilitation from injury (Jordan et al., 2015), whilst providing insight into sports performance capacity.

Similar to the IMTP there is a need for the ISQT to be performed with a standardised methodology and a systematic approach to both the collection and analysis of the ground reaction forces determined with the test. When this occurs the quantification of the PF during the test is considered to be highly reliable for both the 90° and 120° knee angles (Bazyler et al., 2015). For example, Bazyler et al. (2015) report very high ICCs and low relative technical error of the measurement (TEM) for the PF at 90° (ICC = 0.97; TEM = 2.29%) and 120° (ICC = 0.99; TEM = 2.79%). Similarly, Pekünlü and Özsu (2014) report high ICCs (ICC = 0.93; 95% CI = 0.86–0.96) and low CVs (CV% = 3.4%, 95% CI = 2.9–4.5%) for PF achieved during an ISQT test. Based upon the contemporary scientific literature the quantification of maximal force-generating capacity is very reliable when assessed with the ISQT.

When looking at the quantification of the RFD with the ISQT the data are less reliable (Bazyler et al., 2015). While there are limited data exploring the RFD during the ISQT it appears that the overall reliability achieved is very similar to that seen in the IMTP. For example, Bazyler et al. (2015) report good reliability when the RFD is quantified during the ISQT when it is performed with 90° (ICC = 0.90) and 120° (ICC = 0.90) knee angles. However, they also report the TEM is somewhat high for RFD measures at 90° (TEM = 8.12%) and 120° (TEM = 9.44%) knee angles. Overall much more research is needed exploring the reliability of the force-time curve measurements taken during the ISQT.

Due to its relationship to the back squat it is not unexpected that the PFs achieved during the ISQT are significantly correlated with 1-RM full and partial back squat (Bazyler et al., 2015). For example, Blazevich et al. (2002) reported a significant relationship between the PF achieved in an ISQT performed at 90° and the 1-RM back squat. Similarly, Bazyler et al. (2015) found significant correlations ($p \leq 0.05$) between the PF and 1-RM full squat (90°: $r = 0.864$; 120°: $r = 0.597$) and 1-RM partial squat (90°: $r = 0.705$; 120°: $r = 0.789$). The ISQT has generally been found to be significantly ($p \leq 0.05$) correlated with the IMTP ($r = 0.758$) (Nuzzo et al., 2008). Overall it would be suspected that the ISQT would be related to the 1-RM of some of the weightlifting derivatives, but this has yet to be verified in the scientific literature.

When attempting to relate the results of the ISQT to other sporting movements there are limited data in the scientific literature. Recently, Loturco et al. (2016a) reported that maximal force achieved in the ISQT was significantly related to fixed jab ($r = 0.68$, 0.28–0.92), fixed cross ($r = 0.83$, 0.49–0.93), self-selected jab ($r = 0.69$, 0.32–0.94) and self-selected cross ($r = 0.73$, 0.45–0.95) in boxing. Based upon the inter-relationship between the IMTP and the ISQT it is likely that PF achieved in the ISQT can be related to other performance measures, but this has yet to be explored in the scientific literature.

While the ISQT appears to be a reliable test that has some relationship to markers of sports performance there are some concerns about this test's safety. Specifically, due to the positional demands of the test, pilot data from our laboratory suggest that there is an increased risk of injury to the lower back; therefore the IMTP may be a safer alternative.

Isometric leg press (ILP): while ISQT testing has been commonly used to assess lower-body force-time curves there may be an increased risk of lower-back injuries, especially with

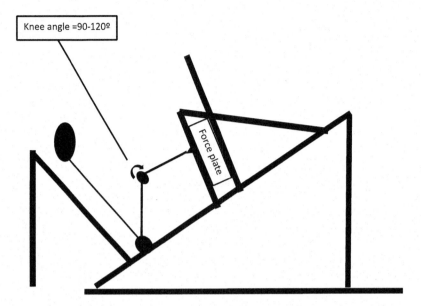

Knee angle =90-120º

Force plate

Figure 10.6 Isometric leg press apparatus.

athletes who have a history of back problems (Kumar, 1994). As an alternative, lower-body force-time curves have been collected with the use of an ILP (Marcora & Miller, 2000; Zaras et al., 2016). In order to quantify force-time curve characteristics with the ILP a standard leg press must be modified in order to allow it to be fixed, so that specific knee and hip angles can be tested, and coupled with at least one force plate (Figure 10.6) (Bogdanis et al., Ahead of print; Zaras et al., 2016) or load cell (Ioakimidis et al., 2004; Marcora & Miller, 2000). The ability to adjust the ILPs' positions allows for the joint angles assessed during the isometric test to be better related to the dynamic movement.

Similar to the ISQT, the ILP is typically conducted with a knee angle between 90° and 120° (Bogdanis et al., Ahead of print; Ioakimidis et al., 2004; Kubo et al., 2005; Marcora and Miller, 2000; Zaras et al., 2016). For example, Marcora and Miller (2000) noted that the PF achieved at 120° is significantly greater than the PF at 90°, which is in line with data collected during the ISQT. While there are some data on PF and RFD values collected with the ILP there are limited data on the actual reliability of this method of evaluating lower-body strength (Baur et al., 2016). Baur et al. (2016) report that using an ILP device can result in highly reliable PF (ICC = 0.87, test-rest variability = 5.3 ± 11.0 N, system-atic bias = 5–6%) and RFD (ICC = 0.93, test-rest variability = 6.9 ± 20.2 N/s, systematic bias = 1–4%) data. Overall much more research is needed examining the reliability of the ILP as a tool for assessing lower-body force-time curves.

Currently there are limited data which relate the force-time curve variables achieved in an ILP to dynamic strength or markers of athletic performance (Marcora and Miller, 2000; Zaras et al., 2016). In one of the few studies published looking at the force-time curve characteristics of the ILP and their relationship to strength and performance, Zaras et al. (2016) report significant ($p \le 0.05$) correlations between the RFD_{0-250} and the hang power clean (r = 0.636–0.710), back squat (r = 0.592–0.687) and leg press $(r$ = 0.760–0.843).

Additionally, the RFD_{0-250} was also significantly ($p \leq 0.05$) correlated to the shot-put front throw ($r = 0.749-0.846$) and shot-put throw from the power position ($r = 0.599-0.698$). The PF and the RFD ($r = 0.71$, $p \leq 0.05$) achieved during the ILP performed at 120° have also been correlated to squat jump performance (PF: $r = 0.53$, $p = 0.053$; RFD: $r = 0.71$, $p \leq 0.05$). While these data suggest that force-time curve data collected during an ILP have some relationship to markers of performance, much more research is warranted exploring the use of this type of testing.

Isometric bench press (IBP): when examining upper-body strength qualities, the use of an IBP test can give insight into the force-generating capacities of the upper body (Young et al., 2014). Murphy et al. (1995) first presented a methodology for conducting an IBP, which required the use of a plyometric power system which allowed the bar to be fixed while the athlete applied forces while lying supine on a bench press that was positioned on top of a force plate. More recently, Young et al. (2014, 2015) have used a non-counter-balanced Smith machine to fix a bar at 2-cm intervals in conjunction with a bench that is fixed atop a force platform (Figure 10.7).

Regardless of how data are collected during the performance of the IBP one of the key things to consider is the elbow position selected during the test. Typically, the IBP is tested with the elbows at 90° and 120° (Murphy and Wilson, 1996; Murphy et al., 1995). When looking at various elbow angles Young et al. (2014) reported that PF was the greatest with an elbow angle of 150° and the lowest when the elbow was at 60°. Additionally, the PF values achieved were highly reliable at 60° (ICC = 0.93, 90% CI = 0.87–0.97; CV% = 1.2, 90% CI = 0.97–1.59, TE = 39.9 N), 90° (ICC = 0.89, 90% CI = 0.79–0.94; CV% = 1.6, 90% CI = 1.29–2.10, TE = 58.4 N), 120° (ICC = 0.94, 90% CI = 0.88–0.97; CV% = 1.5, 90% CI = 1.21–1.99, TE = 60.6 N) and 150° (ICC = 0.97, 90% CI = 0.93–0.98; CV% = 1.6, 90% CI = 1.29–2.12, TE = 52.9 N). Conversely, none of the RFD measures met acceptable reliability cut-offs (i.e. CV%, ICC and TE). While these data suggest that the IBP test produces reliable PF data further research is warranted examining the forces and RFDs achieved during specific epochs.

When examining the relationship between the PF values achieved in the IBP and dynamic performances there are limited data in the scientific literature (Murphy et al., 1995). Murphy

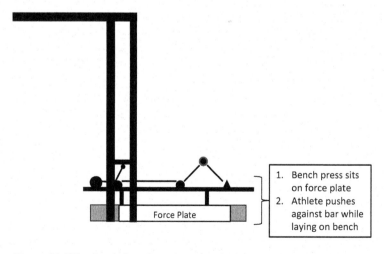

Figure 10.7 Isometric bench press apparatus.

et al. (1995) report significant ($p \leq 0.05$) correlations between the PF generated during the IBP with the elbow at 90° and 1-RM bench press ($r = 0.78$), bench press throw (BPT) with 15% of 1-RM ($r = 0.61$), BPT with 30% of 1-RM ($r = 0.69$) and BPT with 60% ($r = 0.67$). Based upon these relationships Young et al. (2015) created a dynamic strength index score by dividing the BPT PF by the IBP PF (see Chapter 14 for additional detail). This ratio was then used to guide training practices by prescribing specific training interventions to target either explosive strength or maximal force-generating capacity. Overall there is limited research looking at the use of the IBP as a performance test or monitoring tool.

Maximal dynamic testing

The most common method for evaluating muscular strength is determining the maximum weight that can be lifted for a prescribed number of repetitions (Newton et al., 2011). When attempting to evaluate strength either the 1-RM or three repetition maximum (3-RM) tests are employed (McGuigan et al., 2013). If strength endurance is being evaluated the maximum weight that can be lifted for 8–12 RM tests may be evaluated (Haff and Dumke, 2012).

Recently, Buckner et al. (2017) have argued that maximal testing is a specific skill and that a variety of tests should be used when assessing muscular strength. It has also been suggested that athletes who incorporate the exercises tested in training will produce more reliable testing results. While this argument is compelling it is well documented that novice or untrained people can perform maximal testing, such as the 1-RM, after as little as two or three familiarisation sessions and produce reliable strength data (Amarante do Nascimento et al., 2013). Regardless of the methodology used to test dynamic strength the athletes tested should have stable technique in order to reduce potential injury risk and maximise the diagnostic capacity of the test. Overall the testing of the 1-RM is considered to be very safe for both clinical and athletic populations and is considered the gold standard of muscular strength testing (Haff and Haff, 2012).

The most common exercises tested in the strength and conditioning environment are the bench press, back squat and power clean (McMaster et al., 2014). If we look at this type of strength testing it is important to consider that the use of a machine can give different results when compared to free weights (McMaster et al., 2014). For example, when a free-weight bench press is compared to a fixed lifting apparatus such as a Smith machine or chest press device there are generally differences in the 1-RM (M_{diff} = 8–13%; ES 0.35–0.70) achieved (Langford et al., 2007; Cotterman et al., 2005). Similarly, when looking at free-weight squatting there is generally a difference in the 1-RM achieved (M_{diff} = 2%; ES 0.9) (Cotterman et al., 2005). Overall, when looking at dynamic testing it is important that the strength and conditioning professional consider the method used to perform the exercise and how it relates to the training that the athlete will undergo as differences in maximal results between machines and free weights can result in programmatic errors when cross-referenced.

Overall dynamic strength testing is highly reliable (ICC > 0.90; CV < 4.5%) if standardised procedures are utilised when conducting the test (McMaster et al., 2014). For example, a machine-based bench press is very reliable (ICC = 0.997–1.00; CV = 0.23–0.48%) when a bar-to-chest depth is used when performing the test (Seo et al., 2012). Similarly, Banyard et al. (2017) determined that the 1-RM back squat is highly reliable (ICC = 0.99, CV% = 2.1%, standard error of the measurement = 2.9kg) when conducted with standardised methods. In fact, the 1-RM back squat has a smallest detectable difference of 5.5%, or 7.3 kg (Comfort and McMahon, 2015). The 1-RM power clean is also considered to be very reliable in a multitude of populations (Comfort and McMahon, 2015; Faigenbaum et al., 2012) and has a smallest detectable difference of 5.2%, or 3.8 kg (Comfort and McMahon, 2015). When conducting these types of test, it is important to consider the movement pattern, contraction type (i.e. eccentric-concentric, concentric only, eccentric only) and the warm-up strategy employed to prepare the athlete to give a maximal effort as these may impact the reliability of the test.

Another strategy for testing strength is to predict the 1-RM by performing repetition maximum testing with sub-maximal loads (Mayhew et al., 2008). In order to maximise the accuracy of these prediction equations one can use loads that allow for lower-repetition schemes to be determined, typically <10 repetitions (Haff and Haff, 2012). Depending upon the prediction equation used there can be a constant error of −7.1 to 7.2 and a percentage error of −24.0 to 22.9% between the actual and predicted 1-RM (Mayhew et al., 2008). There are numerous prediction equations that have been presented in the literature with varying degrees of reliability. Table 10.3 contains prediction equations that tend to be the most reliable.

Recently there has been great interest in predicting maximal strength based upon the force-velocity relationship (Banyard et al., 2017; Gonzalez-Badillo and Sanchez-Medina, 2010; Picerno et al., 2016; Rontu et al., 2010). This method of estimating the 1-RM appears to be reliable for the Smith machine bench press (CV% = 1.12) and free-weight bench press (CV% = 1.15) (Loturco et al., 2017). Similar to these data the use of velocity to predict 1-RM for the half back squat has also been found to be reliable when performed in a Smith machine (CV% = 0.30–0.75%) (Loturco et al., 2016b). However, it is important to note that the majority of studies that have reported high reliability for predicting the 1-RM from velocity measures have used a momentary pause of ~1.5 s between the eccentric and concentric phases of the lift (Sanchez-Medina et al., 2010). When no pause is performed during the free-weight back squat velocity prediction methods have largely been found to be unreliable (ICC 0.72–0.90; CV% 5.7–12.2%; SEM = 8.6–16.8kg) (Banyard et al., 2017). Based upon these data it appears that the most reliable and accurate method to determine the 1-RM is to actually perform it in the exercise of interest (Banyard et al., 2017; Garcia-Ramos et al., 2018).

Strength testing – practical applications – testing protocols

When selecting a strength testing protocol, it is important to select a combination of isometric and dynamic tests in order to gain a wider perspective on the athlete's strength profile which can be used to inform training practices. In order to facilitate the collection of these data the follow protocols are recommended.

Isometric testing: in order to perform isometric testing a specialised racking system (Haff et al., 2015, 1997), portable isometric rack (James et al., 2017; Secomb et al., 2015), modified Smith machine (Young et al., 2015) or customised leg press (Zaras et al., 2016) that is coupled with a force plate or load cell is required. However, recent research suggests that dynamometers (i.e. load cells etc.) tend to underestimate force measurements when compared to force plate methods (Dobbin et al., 2018).

Regardless of the isometric testing method used it is important that standardised procedures are implemented. Specifically, prior to testing it is important to consider (1) the

Table 10.3 Maximal strength prediction equations.

Source		Equation	Constant error (kg)			Error (%)			ICC
			Mean	±	SD	Mean	±	SD	
Adams	(Adams, 1998)	1RM (kg) = RepWt/(1−0.02 × RTF)	0.7	±	4.2	2.9	±	16.1	0.90
Brown	(Brown, 1992)	1RM (kg) = (Reps × 0.0338+0.9849) × RepWt	0.9	±	2.9	3.7	±	10.8	0.95
Kemmler et al.	(Kemmler et al., 2006)	1RM (kg) = RepWt (0.988+(0.0104 × RTF)+(0.0019xRTF^2)−(0.0000584 × RTF^3))	−1.5	±	2.6	−4.7	±	9.1	0.96
Mayhew et al.	(Mayhew et al., 1992)	1RM (kg) = RepWt/(0.522 = 0.419 e$^{-0.055RTF}$)	0.2	±	2.6	1.2	±	9.0	0.96
O'Conner et al.	(O'Conner et al., 1989)	1RM (kg) = 0.025 (RepWt × RTF) + RepWt	−0.8	±	2.6	−2.1	±	9.0	0.96
Reynolds et al.	(Reynolds et al., 2006)	1RM (kg) = RepWt/(0.5551 e$^{-0.0723RTF+0.4847}$)	0.8	±	2.8	3.4	±	10.4	0.96
Wathen	(Wathen, 1994)	1RM (kg) = RepWt/(0.488 + 0.538 e$^{-0.075RTF}$)	1.3	±	2.9	4.9	±	10.5	0.96

note: 1RM = one repetition maximum; Constant error = predicted 1RM – actual 1RM; RepWT = repetition weight, a load used to perform repetitions; RTF = repetitions to fatigue.

Note: adapted from Mayhew et al. (2008).

use of familiarisation sessions, (2) the warm-up protocol used, (3) the instructions given prior to the test, (4) the sampling frequency used to generate the force-time curve, (4) what filtering is used to process samples, (5) the length of contraction tested, (6) the number of trials performed, (7) the rest interval between trials and (8) the filtering method used to process the file. A basic description of how to standardise these factors is presented in Table 10.4.

Once the force-time curve data have been collected they can then be analysed for selected force (Table 10.1) and RFD (Table 10.2) variables. Based upon the current body of scientific knowledge standardised procedures for the various isometric tests can be recommended, as presented in Table 10.5.

Isometric mid-thigh pull testing: when performing the IMTP test it is important that the testing rack is set to a height that allows the athlete to mirror the second pull position in weightlifting. The athlete should be positioned so that they have an upright trunk position (Haff et al., 1997, 2015) and a slight bend of the knee (Beckham et al., 2018). This position has been suggested to correspond to a knee angle of ~120–140° (Haff et al., 2008) and a hip angle of ~124–175° (Beckham et al., 2013) depending upon the individual athlete's anthropometrics. However it is likely that a hip angle should be in the range ~124–150° as an angle of 175° would result in the athlete leaning backwards and applying significant pre-tension to the bar (Dos'Santos et al., 2017b; Comfort et al., 2015; Beckham et al., 2013). Knee and hip angles are verified with a hand-held goniometer (Haff et al., 1997) or with the use of electronic goniometers which collect for the duration of the test.

If the test is to be used as part of a regular testing battery it is critical that accurate measures of the grip and stance width are recorded and then used for all testing sessions in order to ensure repeatability. Additionally, to ensure the test is standardised the distance from the floor to the fixed bar should also be recorded as this facilitates the ability to replicate positions over time. To grip the bar the athlete should use standard lifting straps (Dos'Santos et al., 2016) or a combination of lifting straps and athletic tape (Haff et al., 2015) in order to ensure grip is maintained throughout the test. The athlete should be in the prescribed position and lightly grip the bar and only pull on the bar and apply force to the ground after the standardised countdown is complete and the command to initiate the test is given. If the athlete pushes downward on the bar and the visual force-time curve tracing reveals a downward deflection (i.e. unloading) prior to the application of vertical force the trial should be repeated.

Isometric squat testing: to implement the ISQT test a specialised racking system, such as the one proposed by Haff et al. (1997), needs to be used in order to allow the athlete to achieve a knee angle of 90° or 120° (Bazyler et al., 2015). As with the IMTP it is important to quantify the height of the isometric bar from the floor and measure the knee and hip angles used during the test. To achieve the appropriate squatting position the barbell below the seventh cervical vertebra on the trapezius pars descendens (Hartmann et al., 2013). Once this position is achieved the knee and hip angles, as well as the foot stance position (Tufano et al., 2016), should be recorded. This is of particular importance if this test is to be used as part of a regular testing battery. Prior to the initiation of the test the athlete should apply "constant tension against the bar" (Bazyler et al., 2015). While the test is conducted a visual inspection of the force-time curve should be made in order to determine if the trial is performed correctly. Things to consider when evaluating the trial include early application of force to the bar or a rapid unloading prior to the application of force. If these occur then additional trials should be conducted.

Table 10.4 Basic considerations for performing isometric tests.

Item	Recommendation
Familiarisation	A minimum of one familiarisation session is recommended when using isometric testing methods (Maffiuletti et al., 2016). Generally, trained athletes are more reliable at giving maximal isometric efforts especially if the isometric muscle action is related to the dynamic lifts they perform (Beckham et al., 2018). As such it is recommended that between one and three familiarisation sessions are performed in order to maximise the reliability of the test.
Warm-up	Prior to initiating an isometric testing session, it is important that a standardised warm-up is used. Typically, this warm-up entails a general warm-up consisting of dynamic activity such as 3 minutes of cycling (Halperin et al., 2016), followed by 5 minutes of dynamic stretches. After the general warm-up a series of dynamic lifting exercises, such as mid-thigh pulls or squats, can be performed with light loads (Dos'Santos et al., 2016). A series of progressively harder isometric actions are then performed at perceived intensities of 50%, 70% and 90% of maximum (Dos'Santos et al., 2016; Kraska et al., 2009).
Instructions	Recent work from Halperin et al. (2016) suggests using an external focus results in significantly greater force production when compared to internally focused controlled instructions. As such, based upon this work instructions should be related to the mode of being tested. For example, in the IMTP or ISQT instructions such as "push the ground as hard and as fast as you possible can" should be used. The test is then initiated with the use of an auditory countdown of "3, 2, 1, go". The word go is often substituted with "push" or "pull" depending upon the movement being tested.
Sampling frequency	When performing isometric assessments, it is generally recommended that sampling frequencies that are ≥1kHz are used in order to ensure accuracy, especially in time-dependent variables such as the RFD and Impulse (Maffiuletti et al., 2016; McMaster et al., 2014). Specifically, Maffiuletti et al. (2016) have suggested that it is important to sample at a high frequency (i.e. ≥ 1 kHz; ≥1 data point per millisecond) in order to accurately measure RFD, identify contraction onset (Tillin et al., 2012), synchronise with EMG (Konrad, 2005) and accurately measure motor unit response times (Tillin et al., 2010).
Contraction length	The isometric effort is generally performed for between 3 and 6 seconds in duration (McMaster et al., 2014).
Number of trials	It is generally recommended that at least three to five trials are collected (Maffiuletti et al., 2016) with no more than 250 N between each PF measure (Kraska et al., 2009).
Rest Interval	Generally, a rest interval of 45 s to 1 minute between maximal isometric trials has been reported in the literature (Kraska et al., 2009; Dos'Santos et al., 2016). The most common recommendation is to use a 1 minute rest interval.
Filtering	Once data acquisition is completed a minimal amount of filtering or smoothing should be undertaken in order to minimise error rates. If filtering must be applied then a zero-lag, low-pass filter, such as a fourth-order Butterworth filter with the highest possible cut-off frequency, should be used to minimise the potential for time shifts (Maffiuletti et al., 2016).

Table 10.5 Basic isometric assessment protocols.

Factor		Isometric mid-thigh pull	Isometric squat	Isometric leg press	Isometric bench press
Instructions		"Push the ground as hard and as fast as you possibly can"	"Push the ground as hard and as fast as you possibly can"	"Push up as hard and as fast as you possibly can"	"Push up as hard and as fast as you possibly can"
		"Pull on the bar as hard and as fast as you possibly can"	"Push on the bar as hard and as fast as you possibly can"	"Push with both legs as hard and as fast as you possibly can"	"Push with both arms as hard and as fast as you possibly can"
Sampling frequency		≥ 1 kHz	≥ 1 kHz	≥ 1 kHz	≥ 1 kHz
Contraction duration		3–5 s	3–5 s	3–5 s	3–5 s
Number of trials		3–5	3–5	3–5	3–5
Rest between trials		1–3 min	1–3 min	1–3 min	1–3 min
Filtering		If needed use a zero-lag, low-pass filter, such as a fourth-order Butterworth filter with the highest possible cut-off frequency			
Measurements	Peak force	PF	PF	PF	PF
		PF_{Rel}	PF_{Rel}	PF_{Rel}	PF_{Rel}
		PF_{Allo}	PF_{Allo}	PF_{Allo}	PF_{Allo}
	Force	F_{100}	F_{100}	F_{100}	F_{100}
		F_{Rel100}	F_{Rel100}	F_{Rel100}	F_{Rel100}
		$F_{Allo100}$	$F_{Allo100}$	$F_{Allo100}$	$F_{Allo100}$
		F_{200}	F_{200}	F_{200}	F_{200}
		F_{Rel200}	F_{Rel200}	F_{Rel200}	F_{Rel200}
		$F_{Allo200}$	$F_{Allo200}$	$F_{Allo200}$	$F_{Allo200}$
	Rate of force development	RFD_{0-100}	RFD_{0-100}	RFD_{0-100}	RFD_{0-100}
		RFD_{0-200}	RFD_{0-200}	RFD_{0-200}	RFD_{0-200}
		RFD_{0-250}	RFD_{0-250}	RFD_{0-250}	RFD_{0-250}

Isometric leg press: when performing the ILP a leg press that is coupled with one or two force plates and can be locked into a static position is required. As noted previously, a knee angle of 90° or 120° is typically assessed with this test (Bogdanis et al., Ahead of print; Zaras et al., 2016). As with other isometric tests it is important to standardise and record the knee position and the foot placement in order to allow the test to be replicated and used as a monitoring tool. With the ILP, when the athlete is in the appropriate position and the desired knee angle is achieved the athlete will maintain contact with the force plate whilst applying a minimal amount of force. Upon the command, they will push against the force plate(s) in an attempt to produce as much force as fast as possible. As with other isometric tests it is important to perform a visual inspection of the data to ensure that the force-time curves are generated correctly.

Isometric bench press: the performance of the IBP requires the coupling of a specialised testing rack (i.e. Smith machine or other system) that is combined with a force plate (Young et al., 2014) or load cell (Ignjatović et al., 2009) that allows for the acquisition of force-time curves. As with the IMTP it is important that positioning is standardised during this test and consistently used when using the test as part of a regular testing battery. The most common elbow angles used when performing the IBP are 90° and 120° (Murphy and Wilson, 1996; Murphy et al., 1995; Young et al., 2014). With this test, it is probably best to use the 90° elbow angle because it exhibits a greater relationship to dynamic movements and the 120° because it results in the highest forces. With the IBP test, it is important that the grip width is standardised and recorded for each athlete (Young et al., 2014). Young et al. (2014) also recommend allowing the athlete to self-select their "strongest" shoulder position and maintain this position for all tests. Similar to other isometric tests a visual monitoring of the force-time curve should be performed during the test to ensure that the force-time curve is correct. Finally, as with dynamic bench press tests it is critical that five points of contact are maintained throughout the duration of the test.

Maximal dynamic testing

The use of isoinertial strength testing is probably the most common method for assessing maximal strength (Newton et al., 2011). Generally, strength and conditioning professionals tend to assess a 1-RM or some number of repetitions to volitional failure (i.e. 3–10-RM) in order to evaluate an athlete's strength levels and guide programming decisions (Table 10.6).

1-RM testing: the gold standard of dynamic strength testing is the 1-RM, which is typically performed with large mass exercises such as the back squat, bench press and power clean (Table 10.7) (Brown et al., 2013; Haff and Haff, 2012).

One of the central factors that impact the ability to accurately assess a 1-RM is the technical proficiency of the athlete. If the athlete is not technically proficient then other methods of assessing strength are probably warranted. With athletes who have resistance training experience, it is easier to perform a 1-RM test as they are better able to estimate their 1-RM (Newton et al., 2011). Additionally, these athletes tend to be familiar with the exercises being tested and the processes that are involved with performing a 1-RM. As with all tests familiarisation can exert a strong impact on the accurate determination of an accurate 1-RM (Newton et al., 2011). Therefore, at least two familiarisation sessions should be performed prior to determination of the 1-RM. When performing a 1-RM test a total of no more than six sets should be used with 3–5 minutes of rest between sets

Table 10.6 Protocols for measuring dynamic muscular strength.

Step	One-repetition maximum	Three-repetition maximum	Five-repetition maximum	Ten-repetition maximum
Warm-up	10 repetitions at 50% of estimated 1-RM	10 repetitions at 50% of estimated 3-RM	10 repetitions at 50% of estimated 5-RM	10 repetitions at 50% of estimated 10-RM
Set 1	5 repetitions at 70% of estimated 1-RM	5 repetitions at 70% of estimated 3-RM	5 repetitions at 70% of estimated 5-RM	10 repetitions at 70% of estimated 10-RM
Set 2	3 repetitions at 80% of estimated 1-RM	3 repetitions at 80% of estimated 3-RM	5 repetitions at 80% of estimated 5-RM	10 repetitions at 80% of estimated 10-RM
Set 3	1 repetition at 90% of estimated 1-RM	3 repetitions at 90% of estimated 3-RM	5 repetitions at 90% of estimated 5-RM	10 repetitions at 90% of estimated 10-RM
Set 4	1-RM attempt	3-RM attempt	5-RM attempt	10-RM attempt
Set 5	1-RM attempt	3-RM attempt	5-RM attempt	10-RM attempt
Set 6	1-RM attempt	3-RM attempt	5-RM attempt	10-RM attempt
Rest between sets	3–5 minutes			

Note: adapted from Brown et al. (2013), Newton et al. (2011), Haff and Haff (2012).

(Table 10.5). If the athlete being tested does not know their approximate 1-RM, it can be estimated from a submaximal test to volitional failure or a percentage of body weight (Haff and Haff, 2012).

Repetition maximum testing: multiple-repetition strength testing requires the completion of a pre-determined number of repetitions, typically ≤10, with the heaviest possible load. As noted previously RM testing can be used to estimate the 1-RM, with the highest accuracy coming from repetition ranges <6 (Haff and Haff, 2012). The most commonly used RM test for maximal strength is the 3-RM test, which is generally reliable and can be used to accurately estimate the actual 1-RM. The second most common RM test for maximal strength is the 5-RM test. The 10-RM test is often used for testing strength endurance (Haff and Haff, 2012). Regardless of which RM is being tested a standardised progressive protocol should be used (Table 10.6).

Conclusions

Maximal strength is an important factor which underpins sports performance and exerts a significant impact on overall health and wellness. One of the key roles of a strength and conditioning professional is to develop the maximal strength levels of the athletes they train and design programme structures which translate that strength into sports performance. Central to the ability to accomplish these goals is the ability to test maximal strength in several domains. To truly understand an athlete's strength capacities a mix of isometric and dynamic strength tests should be used.

Table 10.7 Guidelines for testing common dynamic lifts.

Exercise	Basic guidelines	Technique	Technique violation
Back squat	A high-bar back squat should be performed Athlete should lower to a position where the top of the thigh is below parallel to the floor (i.e. crease of hip is below the level of the top of the knee)	A valid RM occurs if the weight is lowered to the appropriate depth and then the legs are extended to a full extension with the trunk as upright as possible	Losing controlled spinal position Lifting heels from floor Not lowering to required depth Raising hips before shoulder elevation Resting more than 3 s between repetitions for multiple-repetition tests
Bench press	Athlete must maintain five points of contact (i.e. head, shoulders, buttocks, right foot and left foot) Bar is lowered in a controlled manner until it makes contact with the highest point of the chest	A valid RM occurs if the weight is lowered to the highest point of the chest in a controlled manner prior to executing a full elbow extension	Not maintaining five points of contact Failing to make contact with the chest Excessively bouncing the bar off the chest Resting more than 3 s between repetitions for multiple-repetition tests
Power clean	The power clean is performed on a designated area, preferably a lifting platform with a barbell that rotates and with bumper plates The bar is lifted from the floor to the shoulders in one motion	A valid RM occurs if the barbell is lifted from the floor to shoulders in one fluid motion, the feet are shuffled into a squat stance and the legs are slightly bent on reception	Bar is received in a full squat position (i.e. clean) instead of on slightly bent legs Reception stance is excessively wide The bar does not rest on the shoulders upon reception

References

Aagaard, P., Simonsen, E.B., Andersen, J.L., Magnusson, P., & Dyhre-Poulsen, P. (2002). Increased rate of force development and neural drive of human skeletal muscle following resistance training. *Journal of Applied Physiology, 93*, 1318–1326.

Amarante Do Nascimento, M., Januario, R.S., Gerage, A.M., Mayhew, J.L., Cheche Pina, F.L., & Cyrino, E.S. (2013). Familiarization and reliability of one repetition maximum strength testing in older women. *The Journal of Strength & Conditioning Research, 27*, 1636–1342.

Austin, D., Gabbett, T., & Jenkins, D. (2011). Tackling in a professional rugby league. *The Journal of Strength & Conditioning Research, 25*, 1659–1663.

Bailey, C.A., Sato, K., Burnett, A., & Stone, M.H. (2015). Force Production asymmetry in male and female athletes of differing strength. *International Journal of Sports Physiology and Performance, 10*, 504–508.

Banyard, H.G., Nosaka, K., & Haff, G.G. (2017). Reliability and validity of the load-velocity relationship to predict the 1RM back squat. *The Journal of Strength & Conditioning Research, 31*, 1897–1904.

Baur, H., Groppa, A.S., Limacher, R., & Radlinger, L. (2016). Low-budget instrumentation of a conventional leg press to measure reliable isometric-strength capacity. *Journal of Sport Rehabilitation*, Technical Notes *18*, 2014–2041.

Bazyler, C.D., Beckham, G.K., & Sato, K. (2015). The use of the isometric squat as a measure of strength and explosiveness. *The Journal of Strength & Conditioning Research, 29*, 1386–1392.

Beckham, G., Mizuguchi, S., Carter, C., Sato, K., Ramsey, M., Lamont, H., Hornsby, G., Haff, G., & Stone, M. (2013). Relationships of isometric mid-thigh pull variables to weightlifting performance. *Journal of Sports Medicine and Physical Fitness, 53*, 573–581.

Beckham, G.K., Lamont, H.S., Sato, K., Ramsey, M.W., Haff, G.G., & Stone, M.H. (2012). Isometric strength of powerlifters in key positions of the conventional deadlift. *Journal of Trainology, 1*, 32–35.

Beckham, G. K., Sato, K., Mizuguchi, S., Haff, G. G., & Stone, M. H. (2018). Effect of Body Position on Force Production During the Isometric Mid-Thigh Pull. *The Journal of Strength & Conditioning Research, 32*(1), 48–56.

Blazevich, A.J., Gill, N., & Newton, R.U. (2002). Reliability and validity of two isometric squat tests. *The Journal of Strength & Conditioning Research, 16*, 298–304.

Bogdanis, G.C., Tsoukos, A., Kaloheri, O., Terzis, G., Veligekas, P., & Brown, L.E. (Ahead of print). Comparison between unilateral and bilateral plyometric training on single and double leg jumping performance and strength. *The Journal of Strength & Conditioning Research.*

Bompa, T.O., & Haff, G.G. (2009). *Periodization: Theory and methodology of training.* Champaign, IL: Human Kinetics.

Brown, L.E., Khamoui, A.V., & Jo, E. (2013). Test administration and interpretation. In T.J. Chandler & L.E. Brown (Eds.), *Conditioning for strength and human performance.* Philadelphia, PA: Lippincott Williams & Wilkins.

Buchner, D.M., Beresford, S.A., Larson, E.B., Lacroix, A.Z., & Wagner, E.H. (1992). Effects of physical activity on health status in older adults. II. Intervention studies. *Annual Review of Public Health, 13*, 469–488.

Buckner, S.L., Jessee, M.B., Mattocks, K.T., Mouser, J.G., Counts, B.R., Dankel, S.J., & Loenneke, J.P. (2017). Determining Strength: A Case for Multiple Methods of Measurement. *Sports Med, 47*, 193–195.

Comfort, P., Jones, P.A., Mcmahon, J.J., & Newton, R. (2015). Effect of knee and trunk angle on kinetic variables during the isometric midthigh pull: Test–retest reliability. *International Journal of Sports Physiology & Performance, 10*, 58–63.

Comfort, P., & McMahon, J.J. (2015). Reliability of maximal back squat and power clean performances in inexperienced athletes. *The Journal of Strength & Conditioning Research, 29*, 3089–3096.

Cotterman, M.L., Darby, L.A., & Skelly, W.A. (2005). Comparison of muscle force production using the Smith machine and free weights for bench press and squat exercises. *The Journal of Strength & Conditioning Research, 19*, 169–176.

Demura, S., Miyaguchi, K., Shin, S., & Uchida, Y. (2010). Effectiveness of the 1RM estimation method based on isometric squat using a back-dynamometer. *The Journal of Strength & Conditioning Research, 24*, 2742–2748.

De Witt, J.K., English, K.L., Crowell, J.B., Kalogera, K.L., Guilliams, M.E., Nieschwitz, B.E., Hanson, A.M., & Ploutz-Snyder, L.L. (2018). Isometric mid-thigh pull reliability and relationship to deadlift 1RM. *The Journal of Strength & Conditioning Research, 32*(2):525–533.

Dobbin, N., Hunwicks, R., Jones, B., Till, K., Highton, J., & Twist, C. (2018). Criterion and construct validity of an isometric mid-thigh pull dynamometer for assessing whole body strength in professional rugby league players. *International Journal of Sports Physiology and Performance, 13*(2):235–239.

Dos'Santos, T., Jones, P.A., Kelly, J., Mcmahon, J.J., Comfort, P., & Thomas, C. (2016). Effect of sampling frequency on isometric midthigh-pull kinetics. *International Journal of Sports Physiology and Performance, 11*, 255–260.

Dos'Santos, T., Jones, P. A., Comfort, P., & Thomas, C. (2017a). Effect of Different Onset Thresholds on Isometric Mid-Thigh Pull Force-Time Variables. *The Journal of Strength & Conditioning Research, 31*(12), 3463–3473.

Dos'Santos, T., Thomas, C., Jones, P.A., McMahon, J.J., & Comfort, P. (2017b). The Effect Of Hip Joint Angle On Isometric Mid-Thigh Pull Kinetics. *The Journal of Strength & Conditioning Research, 31*(10), 2748–2757.

Faigenbaum, A.D., McFarland, J.E., Herman, R.E., Naclerio, F., Ratamess, N.A., Kang, J., & Myer, G.D. (2012). Reliability of the one-repetition-maximum power clean test in adolescent athletes. *Journal of Strength and Conditioning Research/National Strength & Conditioning Association, 26*, 432–437.

Folland, J.P., Buckthorpe, M.W., & Hannah, R. (2014). Human capacity for explosive force production: Neural and contractile determinants. *Scandinavian Journal of Medicine & Science in Sports, 24*, 894–906.

Gabbett, T., & Ryan, P. (2009). Tackling technique, injury risk, and playing performance in high-performance collision sport athletes. *International Journal of Sports Science & Coaching, 4*, 521–533.

Gabbett, T.J. (2016). Influence of fatigue on tackling ability in rugby league players: Role of muscular strength, endurance, and aerobic qualities. *PLoS One, 11*, e0163161.

Garcia-Ramos, A., Pestana-Melero, F.L., Perez-Castilla, A., Rojas, F.J., & Haff, G.G. (2018). Differences in the load-velocity profile between four bench press variants. *International Journal of Sports Physiology and Performance, 13*(3):326–331.

Garhammer, J. (1993). A review of power output studies of Olympic and powerlifting: methodology, performance prediction, and evaluation tests. *The Journal of Strength & Conditioning Research, 7*, 76–78.

Gonzalez-Badillo, J.J., & Sanchez-Medina, L. (2010). Movement velocity as a measure of loading intensity in resistance training. *International Journal of Sports Medicine, 31*, 347–352.

Haff, G.G., Carlock, J.M., Hartman, M.J., Kilgore, J.L., Kawamori, N., Jackson, J.R., Morris, R.T., Sands, W.A., & Stone, M.H. (2005). Force-time curve characteristics of dynamic and isometric muscle actions of elite women Olympic weightlifters. *The Journal of Strength & Conditioning Research, 19*, 741–748.

Haff, G.G., & Dumke, C. (2012). *Laboratory manual for exercise physiology.* Champaign, IL: Human Kinetics.

Haff, G.G., & Haff, E.E. (2012). Resistance training program design. In M.H. Malek & J.W. Coburn (Eds.), *Essentials of periodization* (2nd edn.). Champaign, IL: Human Kinetics.

Haff, G.G., Jackson, J.R., Kawamori, N., Carlock, J.M., Hartman, M.J., Kilgore, J.L., Morris, R.T., Ramsey, M.W., Sands, W.A., & Stone, M.H. (2008). Force-time curve characteristics and hormonal alterations during an eleven-week training period in elite women weightlifters. *The Journal of Strength & Conditioning Research, 22*, 433–446.

Haff, G.G., & Nimphius, S. (2012). Training principles for power. *Strength & Conditioning Journal, 34*, 2–12.

Haff, G.G., Ruben, R.P., Lider, J., Twine, C., & Cormie, P. (2015). A comparison of methods for determining the rate of force development during isometric midthigh clean pulls. *The Journal of Strength & Conditioning Research, 29*, 386–395.

Haff, G.G., & Stone, M.H. (2015). Methods of developing power with special reference to football players. *Strength & Conditioning Journal, 37*, 2–16.

Haff, G.G., Stone, M.H., O'Bryant, H.S., Harman, E., Dinan, C.N., Johnson, R., & Han, K.H. (1997). Force-time dependent characteristics of dynamic and isometric muscle actions. *The Journal of Strength & Conditioning Research, 11*, 269–272.

Halperin, I., Williams, K.J., Martin, D.T., & Chapman, D.W. (2016). The effects of attentional focusing instructions on force production during the isometric midthigh pull. *The Journal of Strength & Conditioning Research, 30*(4): 919–923.

Hartmann, H., Wirth, K., & Klusemann, M. (2013). Analysis of the load on the knee joint and vertebral column with changes in squatting depth and weight load. *Sports Medicine, 43,* 993–1008.

Ignjatović, A., Stanković, R., Herodek, K., & Radovanović, D. (2009). Investigation of the relationship between different muscle strength assessments in bench press action. *Facta universitatis-series: Physical Education and Sport, 7,* 17–25.

Ioakimidis, P., Gerodimos, V., Kellis, E., Alexandris, N., & Kellis, S. (2004). Combined effects of age and maturation on maximum isometric leg press strength in young basketball players. *Journal of Sports Medicine and Physical Fitness, 44,* 389–397.

James, L.P., Roberts, L.A., Haff, G.G., Kelly, V.G., & Beckman, E.M. (2017). Validity and reliability of a portable isometric mid-thigh clean pull. *The Journal of Strength & Conditioning Research, 31,* 1378–1386.

Jordan, M.J., Aagaard, P., & Herzog, W. (2015). Lower limb asymmetry in mechanical muscle function: A comparison between ski racers with and without ACL reconstruction. *Scandinavian Journal of Medicine & Science in Sports, 25,* e301–e309.

Kawamori, N., Rossi, S.J., Justice, B.D., Haff, E.E., Pistilli, E.E., O'Bryant, H.S., Stone, M.H., & Haff, G.G. (2006). Peak force and rate of force development during isometric and dynamic mid-thigh clean pulls performed at various intensities. *The Journal of Strength & Conditioning Research, 20,* 483–491.

Khamoui, A.V., Brown, L.E., Nguyen, D., Uribe, B.P., Coburn, J.W., Noffal, G.J., & Tran, T. (2011). Relationship between force-time and velocity-time characteristics of dynamic and isometric muscle actions. *The Journal of Strength & Conditioning Research, 25,* 205–210.

Kraska, J.M., Ramsey, M.W., Haff, G.G., Fethke, N., Sands, W.A., Stone, M.E., & Stone, M.H. (2009). Relationship between strength characteristics and unweighted and weighted vertical jump height. *International Journal of Sports Physiology and Performance, 4*(4), 461–473.

Konrad, P. (2006). The ABC of EMG: A practical introduction to kinesiological electromyography. Scottsdale, AZ: Noraxon USA Inc.

Kubo, K., Kanehisa, H., & Fukunaga, T. (2005). Influences of repetitive drop jump and isometric leg press exercises on tendon properties in knee extensors. *The Journal of Strength & Conditioning Research, 19,* 864–870.

Kulig, K., Andrews, J.G., & Hay, J.G. (1984). Human strength curves. *Exercise and Sport Sciences Reviews, 12,* 417–466.

Kumar, S. (1994). Lumbosacral compression in maximal lifting efforts in sagittal plane with varying mechanical disadvantage in isometric and isokinetic modes. *Ergonomics, 37,* 1975–1983.

Langford, G.A., McCurdy, K.W., Ernest, J.M., Doscher, M.W., & Walters, S.D. (2007). Specificity of machine, barbell, and water-filled log bench press resistance training on measures of strength. *The Journal of Strength & Conditioning Research, 21,* 1061–1066.

Leary, B.K., Statler, J., Hopkins, B., Fitzwater, R., Kesling, T., Lyon, J., Phillips, B., Bryner, R.W., Cormie, P., & Haff, G.G. (2012). The relationship between isometric force-time curve characteristics and club head speed in recreational golfers. *The Journal of Strength & Conditioning Research, 26,* 2685–2697.

Loturco, I., Kobal, R., Moraes, J.E., Kitamura, K., Cal Abad, C.C., Pereira, L.A., & Nakamura, F.Y. (2017). Predicting the maximum dynamic strength in bench press: The high precision of the bar velocity approach. *The Journal of Strength & Conditioning Research, 31,* 1127–1131.

Loturco, I., Nakamura, F.Y., Artioli, G.G., Kobal, R., Kitamura, K., Cal Abad, C.C., Cruz, I.F., Romano, F., Pereira, L.A., & Franchini, E. (2016a). Strength and power qualities are highly associated with punching impact in elite amateur boxers. *The Journal of Strength & Conditioning Research, 30,* 109–116.

Loturco, I., Pereira, L.A., Cal Abad, C.C., Gil, S., Kitamura, K., Kobal, R., & Nakamura, F.Y. (2016b). Using bar velocity to predict the maximum dynamic strength in the half-squat exercise. *International Journal of Sports Physiology and Performance, 11,* 697–700.

Maffiuletti, N.A., Aagaard, P., Blazevich, A.J., Folland, J., Tillin, N., & Duchateau, J. (2016). Rate of force development: physiological and methodological considerations. *European Journal of Applied Physiology, 116*, 1091–1116.

Marcora, S., & Miller, M.K. (2000). The effect of knee angle on the external validity of isometric measures of lower body neuromuscular function. *Journal of Sports Science, 18*, 313–319.

Mayhew, J.L., Johnson, B.D., Lamonte, M.J., Lauber, D., & Kemmler, W. (2008). Accuracy of prediction equations for determining one repetition maximum bench press in women before and after resistance training. *The Journal of Strength & Conditioning Research, 22*, 1570–1577.

McGuigan, M.R., Newton, M.J., Winchester, J.B., & Nelson, A.G. (2010). Relationship between isometric and dynamic strength in recreationally trained men. *The Journal of Strength & Conditioning Research, 24*, 2570–2573.

McGuigan, M.R., Sheppard, J.M., Cormack, S.J., & Taylor, K.L. (2013). Strength and power assessment protocols. In R.K. Tanner & C.J. Gore (Eds.), *Physiological Testing of Elite Athletes* (2nd edn.). Champaign, IL: Human Kinetics.

McMaster, D., Gill, N., Cronin, J., & McGuigan, M. (2014). A brief review of strength and ballistic assessment methodologies in sport. *Sports Medicine, 44*, 603–623.

Murphy, A.J., & Wilson, G.J. (1996). Poor correlations between isometric tests and dynamic performance: relationship to muscle activation. *European Journal of Applied Physiology, 73*, 353–357.

Murphy, A.J., Wilson, G.J., Pryor, J.F., & Newton, R.U. (1995). Isometric assessment of muscular function: the effect of joint angle. *Journal of Applied Biomechanics, 11*, 205–215.

Nagahara, R., Mizutani, M., Matsuo, A., Kanehisa, H., & Fukunaga, T. (2017). Association of step width with accelerated sprinting performance and ground reaction force. *International Journal of Sports Medicine, 38*(7):534–540.

Newton, R.U., Cormie, P., & Cardinale, M. (2011). Principles of athlete testing. In M. Cardinale, R.U. Newton, & K. Nosaka (Eds.) *Strength and conditioning: Biological and practical applications*. Chichester: Wiley-Blackwell.

Newton, R.U., Hakkinen, K., Hakkinen, A., McCormick, M., Volek, J., & Kraemer, W.J. (2002). Mixed-methods resistance training increases power and strength of young and older men. *Medicine & Science in Sports & Exercise, 34*, 1367–1375.

Nuzzo, J.L., McBride, J.M., Cormie, P., & McCaulley, G.O. (2008). Relationship between countermovement jump performance and multijoint isometric and dynamic tests of strength. *The Journal of Strength & Conditioning Research, 22*, 699–707.

Pekünlü, E., & Özsu, İ. (2014). Avoiding systematic errors in isometric squat-related studies without pre-familiarization by using sufficient numbers of trials. *Journal of Human Kinetics, 42*, 201–213.

Penailillo, L., Blazevich, A., Numazawa, H., & Nosaka, K. (2015). Rate of force development as a measure of muscle damage. *Scandinavian Journal of Medicine & Science in Sports, 25*, 417–427.

Picerno, P., Iannetta, D., Comotto, S., Donati, M., Pecoraro, F., Zok, M., Tollis, G., Figura, M., Varalda, C., Di Muzio, D., Patrizio, F., & Piacentini, M.F. (2016). 1RM prediction: A novel methodology based on the force-velocity and load-velocity relationships. *European Journal of Applied Physiology, 116*, 2035–2043.

Rontu, J.P., Hannula, M.I., Leskinen, S., Linnamo, V., & Salmi, J.A. (2010). One-repetition maximum bench press performance estimated with a new accelerometer method. *The Journal of Strength & Conditioning Research, 24*, 2018–2025.

Rouis, M., Coudrat, L., Jaafar, H., Filliard, J.R., Vandewalle, H., Barthelemy, Y., & Driss, T. (2015). Assessment of isokinetic knee strength in elite young female basketball players: correlation with vertical jump. *Journal of Sports Medicine and Physical Fitness, 55*, 1502–1508.

Sanchez-Medina, L., Perez, C.E., & Gonzalez-Badillo, J.J. (2010). Importance of the propulsive phase in strength assessment. *International Journal of Sports Medicine, 31*, 123–129.

Secomb, J.L., Nimphius, S., Farley, O.R., Lundgren, L.E., Tran, T.T., & Sheppard, J.M. (2015). Relationships between lower-body muscle structure and, lower-body strength, explosiveness and eccentric leg stiffness in adolescent athletes. *Journal of Sports Science and Medicine, 14*, 691–697.

Seo, D.I., Kim, E., Fahs, C.A., Rossow, L., Young, K., Ferguson, S.L., Thiebaud, R., Sherk, V.D., Loenneke, J.P., Kim, D., Lee, M.K., Choi, K.H., Bemben, D.A., Bemben, M.G., & So, W.Y. (2012). Reliability of the one-repetition maximum test based on muscle group and gender. *Journal of Sports Science and Medicine, 11*, 221–225.

Speranza, M.J., Gabbett, T.J., Johnston, R.D., & Sheppard, J.M. (2015). Muscular strength and power correlates of tackling ability in semiprofessional rugby league players. *The Journal of Strength & Conditioning Research, 29*, 2071–2078.

Speranza, M.J., Gabbett, T.J., Johnston, R.D., & Sheppard, J.M. (2016). Effect of strength and power training on tackling ability in semiprofessional rugby league players. *The Journal of Strength & Conditioning Research, 30*, 336–343.

Stone, M.H., Moir, G., Glaister, M., & Sanders, R. (2002). How much strength is necessary? *Physical Therapy in Sport, 3*, 88–96.

Stone, M.H., Sanborn, K., O'Bryant, H.S., Hartman, M., Stone, M.E., Proulx, C., Ward, B., & Hruby, J. (2003). Maximum strength-power-performance relationships in collegiate throwers. *The Journal of Strength & Conditioning Research, 17*, 739–745.

Stone, M.H., Sands, W.A., Carlock, J., Callan, S., Dickie, D., Daigle, K., Cotton, J., Smith, S.L., & Hartman, M. (2004). The importance of isometric maximum strength and peak rate-of-force development in sprint cycling. *The Journal of Strength & Conditioning Research, 18*, 878–884.

Suchomel, T.J., Nimphius, S., & Stone, M.H. (2016). The Importance of muscular strength in athletic performance. *Sports Medicine, 46*, 1419–1449.

Thomas, C., Comfort, P., Chiang, C., & Jones, P.A. (2015). Relationship between isometric mid-thigh pull variables and sprint and change of direction performance in collegiate athletes. *Journal of Trainology, 4*, 6–10.

Tillin, N.A., Jimenez-Reyes, P., Pain, M.T., & Folland, J.P. (2010). Neuromuscular performance of explosive power athletes versus untrained individuals. *Medicine and Science in Sports and Exercise, 42*, 781–790.

Tillin, N.A., Pain, M.T., & Folland, J.P. (2012). Contraction type influences the human ability to use the available torque capacity of skeletal muscle during explosive efforts. *Proceedings. Biological sciences Royal Society, 279*, 2106–2115.

Tufano, J.J., Conlon, J.A., Nimphius, S., Brown, L.E., Seitz, L.B., Williamson, B.D., & Haff, G.G. (2016). Maintenance of velocity and power with cluster sets during high-volume back squats. *International Journal of Sports Physiology and Performance, 11*, 885–892.

Wang, R., Hoffman, J.R., Tanigawa, S., Miramonti, A.A., La Monica, M.B., Beyer, K.S., Church, D.D., Fukuda, D.H., & Stout, J.R. (2016). Isometric mid-thigh pull correlates with strength, sprint, and agility performance in collegiate rugby union players. *The Journal of Strength & Conditioning Research, 30*, 3051–3056.

West, D.J., Owen, N.J., Jones, M.R., Bracken, R.M., Cook, C.J., Cunningham, D.J., Shearer, D.A., Finn, C.V., Newton, R.U., Crewther, B.T., & Kilduff, L.P. (2011). Relationships between force-time characteristics of the isometric midthigh pull and dynamic performance in professional rugby league players. *The Journal of Strength & Conditioning Research, 25*, 3070–3075.

Young, K.P., Haff, G.G., Newton, R.U., Gabbett, T.J., & Sheppard, J.M. (2015). Assessment and monitoring of ballistic and maximal upper body strength qualities in athletes. *International Journal of Sports Physiology and Performance, 10*, 232–247.

Young, K.P., Haff, G.G., Newton, R.U., & Sheppard, J.M. (2014). Reliability of a novel testing protocol to assess upper body strength qualities in elite athletes. *International Journal of Sports Physiology and Performance, 9,* 871–875.

Young, W. (1995). Laboratory strength assessment of athletes. *New Studies in Athletics, 10,* 89–96.

Young, W., Wilson, G., & Byrne, C. (1999). Relationship between strength qualities and performance in standing and run-up vertical jumps. *Journal of Sports Medicine and Physical Fitness, 39,* 285–293.

Zaras, N.D., Stasinaki, A.N., Methenitis, S.K., Krase, A.A., Karampatsos, G.P., Georgiadis, G.V., Spengos, K.M., & Terzis, G.D. (2016). Rate of force development, muscle architecture, and performance in young competitive track and field throwers. *The Journal of Strength & Conditioning Research, 30,* 81–92.

Zatsiorsky, V.M., & Kraemer, W.J. (2006). *Science and practice of strength training.* Champaign, IL: Human Kinetics.

11 Assessment of power

Jason P. Lake and Peter Mundy

1. Introduction

The development of power is a critical component of athlete preparation (Baker, 2001; Kaneko et al., 1983; Kawamori et al., 2005; Stone et al., 2003). However, a degree of uncertainty remains about what power actually is, how power should be calculated and the most effective way to develop power. Researchers have shown that power can be improved with resistance exercise by increasing the strength of skeletal muscle (the force component) or the speed at which strength can be expressed (the velocity component) (Stone et al., 2003). However, it is worth noting that as one becomes stronger and is able to apply more force to the same mass, the impulse should increase, increasing subsequent movement velocity. Therefore, this chapter will focus on what power actually is in addition to the different methods that can be used to obtain it. The chapter will focus primarily on studies that have investigated countermovement vertical jumping, which is the movement for which power appears to be most often applied, but will also consider some common resistance exercises. Studies investigating concentric-only jumping (commonly referred to as the squat jump, although this has also been used to describe the countermovement jump) are also considered in this chapter due to the similar body configuration at the start of the push-off phase, as well as the similar coordination during the push-off phase (Bobbert et al., 1996). Therefore, unless otherwise distinguished, jumping will refer to both countermovement jumping and concentric-only jumping. For the sake of brevity, other topics are included only when a relevant feature has been highlighted particularly well via another aspect of human analysis.

2. Jumping power

External mechanical work must be performed to accelerate and raise the centre of mass (CM) of the body during dynamic athletic tasks (Cavagna, 1975, Equation 1). Hence, the rate of external mechanical work, defined as the external mechanical power output (referred to simply as power hereafter, Equation 2), is commonly hypothesised to be one of the main performance-determining factors in a multitude of time-constrained dynamic athletic tasks, particularly those requiring one movement sequence to produce a high-velocity at take-off or impact (Cormie et al., 2011a, 2011b; Kawamori & Haff, 2004; Newton & Kraemer, 1994).

Mechanical work quantifies the displacement of a mass:

$$\text{Work} = \text{Force} \times \text{Displacement} \qquad \text{(Equation 1)}$$

(Dugan et al., 2004; Hori et al., 2007; Li et al., 2008)

As mentioned above, power is the rate at which mechanical work is performed and can be calculated by either dividing work by time or, as is more common in the strength and conditioning literature, by multiplying the force exerted during movement by its velocity:

$$Power = Force \times Velocity \hspace{4cm} (Equation\ 2)$$

(Dugan et al., 2004; Hori et al., 2007; Li et al., 2008)

Previously, it has been suggested that athletes who produce greater power during unloaded (no positive or negative external loading applied) and externally loaded jumping perform better in dynamic athletic tasks such as jumping, sprinting and weightlifting (Baker & Nance, 1999; Cronin & Hansen, 2005; Cunningham et al., 2013; Dowling & Vamos, 1993; Gonzalez-Badillo & Marques, 2010; Hansen et al., 2011b; Hori et al., 2008; Kawamori et al., 2005; Nimphius et al., 2010; Sheppard et al., 2008; Young et al., 2005). Consequently, jumping power appears to discriminate between individual activity profiles (Caia et al., 2013; Driss et al., 2001; McBride et al., 1999; Nibali et al., 2013; Nuzzo et al., 2010; Pazin et al., 2012; Stone et al., 2003; Vuk et al., 2012), as well as levels of competitive playing ability (Argus et al., 2012; Baker, 2002; Hansen et al., 2011b; Sheppard et al., 2008, 2012; Young et al., 2005). Therefore, to optimise periodic testing and training prescription, a great deal of research has focused on the relationship between external loading and jumping power.

With regard to loaded jumping, it is commonly argued that the influence of external loading on jumping power is underpinned by the inverse association between external loading and the velocity of the system CM (Cormie et al., 2007b, 2008; Dayne et al., 2011; Leontijevic et al., 2012; Markovic & Jaric, 2007; McBride et al., 2011; Nibali et al., 2013; Pazin et al., 2012; Suzovic et al., 2013; Turner et al., 2012; Vuk et al., 2012). As external loading dictates the force-generating capacity of the lower extremities, this association is often ascribed to the hyperbolic relationship between force and velocity demonstrated in isolated muscles (Hill, 1938, 1953): as force-generating capacity increases, a concomitant decrease in contraction and movement velocity occurs, and vice versa. As such, it is argued that power is maximised under the external loading condition which facilitates an optimal compromise between submaximal force and submaximal velocity (Cormie et al., 2011b); this is often referred to as the optimal load. However, readers should be aware that the importance of the intrinsic force-velocity-power relationship is argued to only play a small part of the effects of external loading reported within the literature, with musculoskeletal modelling data demonstrating that it is more likely to be associated with optimised control (or a lack thereof) (Bobbert, 2014).

When interpreting the literature, practitioners must consider the type of jump performed (countermovement jump vs. squat jump [concentric only]), the type and position of the external loading applied (barbell, hexagonal barbell, Smith machine, dumbbells, weighted vest, elastic resistance), the subsequent external loading spectrum constraints (negative vs. positive external loading), the external loading parameters (single external load, incremental absolute external loads, incremental relative external loads [% of one-repetition maximum (1-RM) vs. % of body mass]) and the population investigated (for example, trained vs. untrained, male vs. female). Interpretation of the literature is also confounded by the specific qualifiers (average power vs. peak power, absolute vs. normalisation [allometric vs. ratio]) and measurement (instruments, calculations) details related to power which are required to meaningfully explore load-power data (Knudson, 2009) that are not currently standardised. Therefore, it is important to discuss the limitations associated with the use of power as a performance-determining factor.

3. Power as a performance-determining factor

The importance of power is commonly established using the statistical relationship between power and the outcome of dynamic athletic tasks (e.g. correlations, regressions). However, this statistical relationship is not the same as a mechanistic relationship between increased power and the outcome of dynamic athletic tasks. The statistical relationship between power and the outcome of dynamic athletic tasks may exist for numerous reasons; however, not all of them indicate the mechanistic role of greater power.

In the context of jumping, there is theoretically a direct cause-and-effect relationship between the work performed on the system CM and the height jumped (work-energy theorem) (see Chapter 7 also). Similarly, there is theoretically a direct cause and effect relationship between the impulse applied to the system CM and the height jumped (impulse-momentum theorem). The work-energy theorem and the impulse-momentum theorem are both re-expressions of Newton's Second Law in an integral form (see Chapter 7 also). That is, the work-energy theorem and the impulse-momentum theorem simply describe motion in different dimensions – one spatial (work-energy) and one temporal (impulse-momentum). In brief, changes in the body or system CM's momentum are due to the impulse applied to the body or system CM, which depends primarily on the time over which a net force is applied (Figure 11.1). Conversely, kinetic energy of the body or system CM changes when work is performed on the body or system CM, which depends on the displacement over which the net force is applied. It is worth noting that if displacement increases it is likely that the time over which the net force is applied will increase too, therefore increasing the impulse (see Figure 11.2 also).

For example, the first description of Figure 11.1 provides a traditional, and correct, summary of impulse. However, the second and third examples could be applied to progressively heavier back squats. As load increases a larger impulse must be applied to displace the heavier load, and different strategies may be used: more force can be applied over the same amount of time, or less or the same amount of force may be applied for longer. When considering the mechanistic role of the work performed and the impulse applied, the statistical relationship between power and the outcome of dynamic athletic tasks can be brought into question (Knudson, 2009; Winter, 2009; Winter et al., 2016; Winter & Knudson, 2011). For example, an increase in the work performed and the impulse applied would result in an increase in the height jumped. An increase in work and impulse may also increase power, which may create a statistical relationship between power and the jump height even in the absence of a mechanistic relationship. This may explain

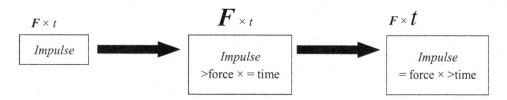

Figure 11.1 Constituent components of impulse and their possible interactions.

why power is sometimes poorly correlated with the outcome of dynamic athletic tasks, although such information is often not acknowledged (Cronin & Sleivert, 2005; Knudson, 2009). However, it is important to reiterate that correlation does not equal causation, and that these associations have commonly been confounded by the method used to calculate power, the jumper's body mass and their countermovement depth (Aragón-Vargas & Gross, 1997; Markovic et al., 2014).

At first, the importance of power may not be readily apparent from either the work-energy theorem or the impulse-momentum theorem. During the push-off (propulsion) phase of jumping, the system CM gains kinetic energy when work (the product of force and displacement) is performed on the system CM (work-energy theorem) (see Chapter 7). The kinetic energy gained is proportional to the square of the vertical velocity of the system CM, and therefore determines the peak vertical displacement of the system CM during the flight phase (jump height – see Chapter 7 also). However, during the braking (eccentric) phase of countermovement jumping, the lowering of the system CM is constrained by human anatomy. As such, greater work performed on the system CM results in a shorter push-off phase duration, as the push-off phase is performed at a greater average velocity (displacement divided by time). Therefore, although work is not by definition constrained by time, the greater the work performed on the CM during the push-off phase of jumping, the less time there is available to perform the work due to increased acceleration and therefore velocity. As average power is the rate at which work is performed over a phase of interest (for example, the push-off phase), the greater the peak vertical displacement of the system CM during the flight phase (jump height), the greater the average power required. Hence, it may be postulated that average propulsive power, rather than peak propulsive power, is a performance-limiting factor.

To avoid premature take-off and therewith a premature termination of work production, power must continue to increase during the push-off phase (Bobbert, 2014). Therefore, peak power may also be an important factor for performance (Bobbert, 2014). However, it should be stressed that the development of a high peak power does not necessarily mean a parallel development of average power (Bosco et al., 1983), despite the correlations previously presented (Hori et al., 2007). As such, if practitioners are interested in the power capacity of their athletes, it is prudent to understand and consider both peak and average power.

4. Measuring power: methodological issues

The two most commonly used methods for investigating the effects of external loading on jumping power, the force-platform method and the combined method, have been described extensively in the literature (Cormie et al., 2007a, 2007b; Crewther et al., 2011; Dugan et al., 2004; Hansen et al., 2011b; Hori et al., 2007; Lake et al., 2012; Li et al., 2008). However, it should be noted that five different methods have generally been used in the literature in recent years (Table 11.1). In brief, both of the two main methods calculate power as the product of the force applied to and the velocity of the system CM (represented by the barbell in the combined method). However, neither method is ubiquitously accepted as the criterion ("gold standard") method, with contradictory recommendations commonly reported within previous method comparison studies (Figures 11.2 and 11.3) (Cormie et al., 2007a, 2007b; Crewther et al., 2011; Hansen et al., 2011b; Hori et al., 2007; Lake et al., 2012; Li et al., 2008). Therefore, within this part of the chapter, the force-platform method and the combined method are described for theoretical clarity, and associated contradictions discussed. Further, due to issues associated with the practicality of the aforementioned methods, commonly

Table 11.1 The most common different methods used to calculate back-squat mechanical power output.

Method 1	**Vertical bar force** (bar mass × *g*) × **vertical bar velocity**	Coelho et al. (2003), Jandacka & Vaverka (2008), Jennings et al. (2005). Similar approach used by Baker (2001), Izquierdo et al. (2002), Wilson et al. (1993)
Method 2	**Vertical bar force** (bar mass × *g*) + (bar mass × bar acceleration) × **vertical bar velocity**	Bosco et al. (1995), Cronin et al. (2000), Dugan et al. (2004), Hori et al. (2007), Li et al. (2008), Mastropaolo (1992), Sleivert & Taingahue (2004), Stone et al. (2003)
Method 3	**Vertical ground reaction force** × **vertical centre of mass velocity** $(\int_0^t a\,dt = (\frac{1}{m}\int_0^t (GRF - BW)dt)$	Driss et al. (2001), Haff et al. (1997), Kawamori et al. (2005), Kilduff et al. (2007), Li et al. (2008), McBride et al. (1999), Moir et al. (2005), Patterson et al. (2009), Rahmani et al. (2001)
Method 4	**Vertical ground reaction force** × **vertical bar velocity**	Burnett et al. (2004), Cormie et al. (2007b,c), McBride et al. (2002), Winchester et al. (2005)
Method 5	**Vertical system force** (system mass × *g*) + (system mass × bar acceleration) × **vertical bar velocity**	Harris et al. (2007), Hori et al. (2007), Newell et al. (2005)

used pragmatic alternatives are also discussed. This methodological discussion is of particular importance to the chapter, as without considering the way in which power is calculated, methodological integrity may be compromised, rendering the discussion and comparison of both previous and future results inappropriate (Knudson, 2009; Winter et al., 2016).

4.1 Force-platform method

Historically, power has been measured during unloaded jumping using a force platform (Cavagna, 1975). Mathematically, there are several ways in which power can be calculated using a force platform; however, formally, this method calculates the rate of change of the effective energy of the system CM (Bobbert, 2014). Within the literature, power is commonly obtained as the product of the vertical ground reaction force and the vertical velocity of the system CM. Within this method, vertical ground reaction force is used to represent the force applied to the system CM (Newton's Third Law). The vertical velocity of the system CM is then obtained by time integration of acceleration data; that is, vertical ground reaction force minus body (or system, if a loaded jump) weight divided by body or system mass (Cavagna, 1975 – see Chapter 7 also). For each time point, power is then calculated as the scalar product of the vertical ground reaction force and the vertical velocity of the system CM. Alternatively, vertical ground reaction force can be integrated with respect to

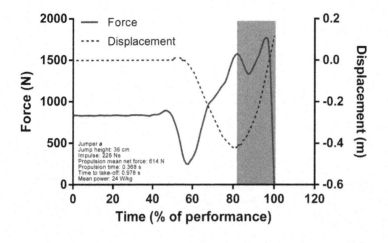

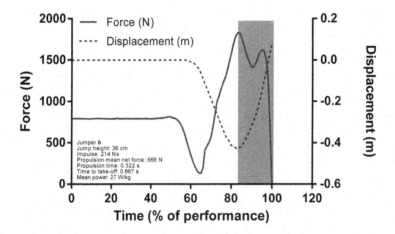

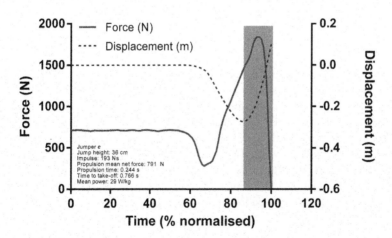

Figure 11.2 Example of different jump strategies and the effect on biomechanical variables.

(a)

Push Press Force

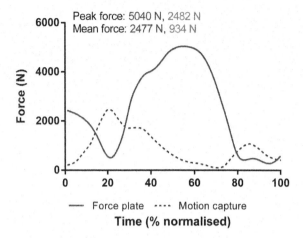

(b)

Push Press Velocity

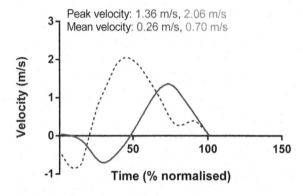

(c)

Push Press Power

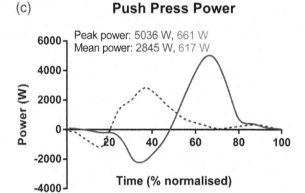

Figure 11.3 A comparison of (a) force-time, (b) velocity-time and (c) power-time curves and values, calculated using force-time and displacement-time data, during the push press.

time, which is then divided by body (or system) mass to calculate the vertical velocity of the system CM, and then combined with the vertical ground reaction force data to calculate power, or vertical ground reaction force can be integrated with respect to displacement to calculate mechanical work, and then divided by push-off time to calculate power. It is important to note that only the vertical component of the ground reaction force is commonly considered, as approximately 97% of the total power during the push-off phase of unloaded countermovement jumping is used for vertical propulsion (Hatze, 1998).

Theoretically, the force-platform method is derived from Newton's Second Law, whereby the motion of the CM is fully determined by the system's mass, the forces applied to this mass and the initial velocity of the system CM (Cavagna, 1975). Assuming a valid quiet standing or squatting period prior to the initiation of movement to ensure an initial velocity of zero, the possible sources of error originate from the force-platform electronics, the analog-to-digital conversion and the data-processing methods (Kibele, 1998) (See Chapter 7). Recently, Owen et al. (2014) presented excellent guidelines for calculating peak power during unloaded countermovement jumping, which produced errors of less than 1%. Further, the possible sources of error when integrating vertical ground reaction force data have been extensively documented, and necessary precautions for minimising error within vertical ground reaction force and velocity data presented (Kibele, 1998; Street et al., 2001; Vanrenterghem et al., 2001). With adherence to the aforementioned methodological rigour, the force-platform method can accurately determine both the force applied to and the vertical velocity of the CM during jumping. Therefore, in the authors' opinion, the force-platform method is the theoretical criterion method ("gold standard") for calculating jump power.

The most common criticisms of the force-platform method are the cost and practicality (Chiu et al., 2004; Crewther et al., 2011; Cronin et al., 2004). However, it should therefore be noted that excellent guidelines for constructing single-axis force platforms have previously been published (Major et al., 1998), with some commercially available single-axis force platforms being cheaper than the commonly proposed commercially available single-point field alternatives (e.g. linear position transducers). However, more recently, the use of the force-platform method as the criterion method has been criticised within the strength and conditioning literature (Cormie et al., 2007b; Dugan et al., 2004), with an alternative criterion method proposed: the combined method.

4.2 Combined method

Within the strength and conditioning literature, the combined method appears to be the most commonly used method for investigating the effects of external loading on jumping power. Similar to the force-platform method, vertical ground reaction force data are used to represent the force applied to the system CM (Newton's Third Law). However, in contrast to the force-platform method, the vertical velocity of the system CM is calculated by the differentiation of displacement-time data (typically obtained from an Olympic barbell or an aluminium, plastic or wooden bar alternative during unloaded jumping), which are collected using various motion-capture equipment: e.g. a high-speed digital camera system (Li et al., 2008), a linear position transducer (Cormie et al., 2007a, 2007b), two linear position transducers (Cormie et al., 2007a, 2007b) or an optoelectronic motion-capture system (Moir et al., 2012).

It has been suggested that the combined method uses accurate force-platform vertical ground reaction force values to represent the force applied to the system CM, but ostensibly requires less "data manipulation" than the force-platform method to calculate the velocity of the system CM, thus decreasing the risk of accumulating error (Dugan et al., 2004). However, both the force-platform method and the combined method require only a single "data manipulation" to obtain the velocity of the system CM, whereby data are either integrated (force-platform method) or differentiated (combined method) once, respectively. Upon comparison, the two types of "data manipulation" yield a different outcome with regard to signal noise: integration suppresses noise in the velocity signal, whereas differentiation amplifies noise in the velocity signal. As such, the combined method often requires filtering, which introduces potential error due to over-smoothing or under-smoothing of the true signal (Winter, 2009).

Interestingly, there also appears to be little consideration for the potential error introduced by the different motion-capture equipment used in the literature (Cormie et al., 2007a, 2007b), the sampling frequency used (McMaster et al., 2014), the method of differentiation used, or the error associated with asymmetric lifting technique (Chiu et al., 2008). Therefore, paradoxically, not only does the extra equipment make the combined method less accessible to practitioners, it also does not logically improve the measurement of power. This is further evidenced by little, if any, difference in the between-session reliability of peak velocity and peak power between the force-platform method and the combined method (Hansen et al., 2011b).

Perhaps a more important concern regarding the combined method pertains to the fundamental underpinning biomechanical premise (Hansen et al., 2011b; Hori et al., 2007; Lake et al., 2012; Li et al., 2008). The combined method acquires displacement-time data from some sort of "barbell", assuming synchronous movement with the system CM (Cormie et al., 2007b; Dugan et al., 2004). When compared to the force-platform method, both peak power (Hansen et al., 2011b; Hori et al., 2007) and average power (Hori et al., 2007) values generated by the combined method (force platform and one linear position transducer) were significantly greater during an externally loaded (40 kg) countermovement jump. Further, a non-systematic overestimation of average power but not peak power was observed when the combined method (force platform and one linear position transducer) and a combined method corrected for horizontal barbell motion (force platform and two linear position transducers) were compared to the force-platform method across an external loading spectrum of 0 to 85% of a back squat 1-RM (Cormie et al., 2007b).

As the vertical ground reaction force data used in the force-platform method and the combined method are often identical, this systematic overestimation is logically a product of the "barbell" moving at a significantly greater velocity than that of the CM (Lake et al., 2012; Li et al., 2008) (Figure 11.4). However, statistical tests designed to test for significant differences (*t*-tests, ANOVA models, effect size) may not be appropriate for determining whether two measurement methods are in agreement (McLaughlin, 2013). In context, agreement refers to how much the combined method is likely to differ from the force-platform method: if this difference does not cause problems in clinical interpretation, then the two methods can be used interchangeably (Altman & Bland, 1983; Bland & Altman, 1986, 1999). Little is known about the agreement between jumping power obtained using the force platform and combined methods or the influence that the magnitude of external load may have on agreement. Recent work by Mundy et al. (2016) shows that although differences between jumping power obtained using both of these methods decrease as jumping load increases, even the smallest differences between the two methods proved unacceptable. Therefore, previous studies investigating the effects of

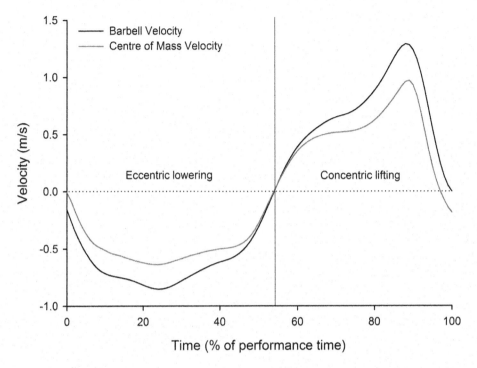

Differences between Back Squat Barbell and Centre of Mass Velocity

Figure 11.4 A comparison of velocity calculated based on barbell and system centre of mass velocity, during the back squat.

external loading on jumping power may be confounded by fundamental methodological issues.

4.3 Single-point methods

In the absence of a force platform, a video camera or linear position transducer (e.g. potentiometer or encoder) can be utilised to estimate both the force applied to and the velocity of the system CM. Within these methods, a single point upon the jumper is chosen to represent jumper CM. Velocity of the CM is estimated by differentiating the displacement of this single point with respect to time, which in turn is differentiated with respect to time to calculate the acceleration of the CM. The force applied to the CM is then estimated as the product of mass and the summation of the acceleration of the CM and the acceleration due to gravity (Newton's Second Law). For each time point, power is then calculated as the product of the estimated force applied to and the velocity of the CM.

Unlike the force-platform method or the combined method, concerns regarding the "data manipulation" required by single-point methods are commonly expressed. The differentiation process amplifies noise in both the velocity and acceleration records (Winter, 2009; Wood, 1982), compromising the validity of the calculated force and power values

(Cormie et al., 2007b; Dugan et al., 2004). Therefore, single-point methods may depend largely on the equipment (Cormie et al., 2007a, 2007b), the sampling frequency (McMaster et al., 2014), the method of differentiation, and the data smoothing procedures used to remove this amplified noise (Harris, Cronin, Taylor, Boris, & Sheppard, 2010), demanding an adequate description of the underlying process (Winter, 2009; Wood, 1982).

As with the combined method, perhaps the most important issue is related to the fundamental biomechanical premise. To correctly apply Newton's Second law, the calculation of force should use compatible mass and acceleration (Li et al., 2008). Thus, if the point does not represent that of the CM, an inappropriate acceleration value will be combined with jumper mass, producing a force value that does not represent the force applied to the CM, resulting in a miscalculation of power (Li et al., 2008). Therefore, it is imperative that the single point represents the mass of interest regardless of whether that is the CM of the body, the barbell, or the system (Lake et al., 2012) (Figures 11.3 and 11.4).

As with the combined method, when investigating the effects of external loading on jumping, using the "barbell" as the single point (Chiu et al., 2004; Cormie et al., 2007a; Crewther et al., 2011; Hansen et al., 2011b; Hori et al., 2007) appears to be the preferred method to represent the CM. However, as alluded to in the "combined method" section, this method assumes that the external load moves in parallel with the CM, including when external load increases (Cormie et al., 2007a., 2007b; Dugan et al., 2004). Upon investigating countermovement jumping and squat jumping with external loads of 30%, 50% and 70% of a back squat 1-RM, Chiu et al. (2004) reported no differences between the peak force obtained from a linear position transducer and force platform. This may suggest that the displacement of the barbell represents that of the CM as they both appear to move in a vertical and linear path, and that the single point is arbitrary (Chiu et al., 2004). However, Chiu et al. (2004) did not report or compare velocity or power values between the two methods. Further, Chiu et al. (2004) stringently controlled the jumping range of motion to 10% of the participant's height, and although this improved the representation of peak force, it perhaps did so by reducing ecological validity (Argus et al., 2011), as athletes are likely to have optimised control under the given conditions (Bobbert, 2014).

Conversely, there is a growing body of evidence to suggest that this assumption of synchronous movement is erroneous (Hori et al., 2007; Lake et al., 2012; Mundy et al., 2016) and is a misapplication of mechanical principles (Li et al., 2008). During externally loaded (40 kg) countermovement jumping, both Hori et al. (2007) and Hansen et al. (2011b) demonstrated that peak velocity of the barbell obtained from a single linear position transducer was significantly greater than that of the CM, indicating percentage differences of 12.1% and 42.8%, respectively. Further support has been presented across various external loads using two linear position transducers (Cormie et al., 2007a), video systems (Lake et al., 2012), and on-line motion-capture systems (McBride et al., 2011). Most notably, McBride et al. (2011) demonstrated a linear increase in percentage difference from 20.8% to 70.2% in peak velocity across an external loading spectrum of 0 to 90% back squat 1-RM, in 10% increments. Therefore, regardless of the equipment used, it appears that when a "barbell" is chosen to represent the CM, it will overestimate its velocity because of a poor estimation of the CM motion. However, due to the statistical methods commonly used, little is known about the agreement between the methods (Altman & Bland, 1983; Bland & Altman, 1986, 1999; McLaughlin, 2013).

It is important to note that if only barbell mass is used instead of system mass, the power applied to the barbell can be calculated this way (Hori et al., 2007; McBride et al., 2011).

Biomechanically, this is a fundamentally sound estimation of power; however, this may not reflect the power produced by the lower-body, specifically during conditions of lighter external loading (Hori et al., 2007). By excluding body mass, the load-power relationship appears to be reversed, with the force component of the power calculation greatly reduced during lighter external loads (Dugan et al., 2004). This is of particular concern during unloaded jumping, whereby if the mass component is zero, then the force component is zero. As power is the product of force and velocity, it too will be zero, providing little, if any, information to practitioners. Conversely, at higher external loads, the exclusion of body mass is a smaller relative reduction in the system load, thus power is affected less (Dugan et al., 2004; Smilios et al., 2013). Therefore, the point used to represent the object of interest and the mass values used are important considerations when using single-point field methods (Hori et al., 2007).

An alternative, yet still practical single-point method is to use a point approximating the pelvis (Chiu & Salem, 2010; Cronin et al., 2004; Gard et al., 2004; Gullstrand et al., 2009; Ranavolo et al., 2008). For example, when investigating both countermovement jumping and squat jumping, Cronin et al. (2004) reported no differences in peak and average force between a linear position transducer attached to a waist harness and the force-platform method. However, as with the majority of the studies discussed so far, comprehensive statistics for assessing the agreement were not reported (Altman & Bland, 1983; Bland & Altman, 1986, 1999; McLaughlin, 2013), nor was the influence of external loading investigated. Therefore, as the system CM position changes with external loading, uncertainty arises regarding the extrapolation of these findings to conditions of external loading, which limits the use of this method for the practitioner.

4.4 Body segmental analysis methods

Due to the issues associated with single-point methods, it is important to note that the displacement of the system CM may also be calculated using the body segmental analysis method (Gard et al., 2004; Gullstrand et al., 2009; Kibele, 1998; Ranavolo et al., 2008), which is based on marker position data acquired via either videography systems or on-line systems. The body segmental analysis method calculates the total body or system CM position as the weighted average of the individual segments' CM (Gard et al., 2004; Gullstrand et al., 2009; Ranavolo et al., 2008; Winter, 2009). After calculating the displacement of the body or system CM, power may be calculated using the methods described above (Lake et al., 2012). However, hardware and software for on-line systems are often expensive and require a skilled and knowledgeable operator, with hardware set-up, data collection and data-processing time-consuming. As such, further discussion is outside the scope of the present chapter. Conversely, although less accurate, videography systems, including digitisation software, are readily available to practitioners (Garhammer & Newton, 2013). However, due to its limited use within research, this method will not be discussed further, with readers referred to Garhammer (1993) for common methodological issues, and Garhammer and Newton (2013) for videography setup considerations.

4.5 Computation method

A simple, alternative method proposed for measuring force, velocity and power during jumping is the computation method (Samozino et al., 2008). The computation method relies solely on body mass, jump height and push-off distance. In concept, jump height can be measured using videography or a jump mat, assuming adequate control over landing position is enforced. Upon comparison to the gold-standard force-platform method, Samozino et al. (2008) reported a mean bias of 11 N, 0.017 m/s and 2 W for mean force, mean velocity and mean power, respectively. Although the 95% limits of agreement were not reported numerically, the methods appear interchangeable within practice based on

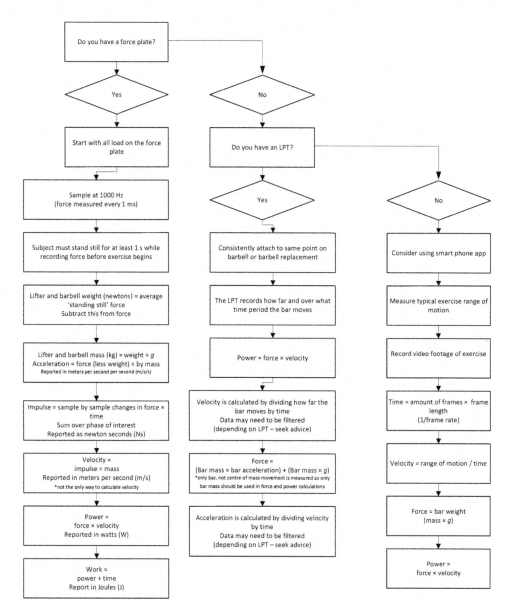

g = acceleration of gravity, which is 9.81 m/s/s in the UK

Figure 11.5 Example of the appropriate processes for assessing power, depending on the equipment available.

the plots presented. However, although promising, the sample size was probably too small to establish validity ($n = 11$), as the 95% confidence intervals around the limits would have been unacceptably large ($\pm$ root (3 standard deviation^2/sample size)). Further, the trials were pooled without controlling for multiple observations (Bland & Altman, 1999). Perhaps more importantly, use of the computation method requires the push-off distance (countermovement depth) to be either constrained or calculated alternatively. As alluded to earlier, constraining the push-off distance decreases ecological validity (Argus et al., 2011) as athletes are likely to have optimised control under the given external loading conditions (Bobbert, 2014), whereas calculating countermovement depth alternatively potentially decreases the practicality of the computation method.

5. Conclusion

This chapter identified that "power" is often expressed as a "clearly defined, generic neuro-muscular or athlete performance characteristic" rather than as an application of the actual mechanical definition (Winter et al., 2016). It appears that this misapplication has led to considerable inaccuracy and confusion, primarily because it often fails to represent the performance being assessed (Winter et al., 2016). Therefore, the appropriate use of the actual mechanical definition was discussed in the context of jumping performance. This discussion was central to the development of a theoretically valid framework.

This chapter also exposed the presence of two perceived criterion ("gold standard") methods currently used to measure power during externally loaded jumping: the force-platform method and the combined method (Figure 11.3 and 11.4). Therefore, the force-platform method and the combined method were described for theoretical clarity, and associated contradictions discussed. Further, due to issues associated with the practicality of the aforementioned methods, commonly used pragmatic alternatives were also discussed. This methodological discussion was of particular importance to this chapter, because without considering the way in which power is calculated, methodological integrity can be compromised, rendering the discussion and comparison of results inappropriate (Knudson, 2009) (Figure 11.5).

References

Altman, D.G., & Bland, J.M. (1983). Measurement in medicine: The analysis of method comparison studies. *The Statistician, 32,* 307–317.

Aragón-Vargas, L.F., & Gross, M.M. (1997). Kinesiological factors in vertical jump performance: Differences among individuals. *Journal of Applied Biomechanics, 13*(1), 24–44.

Argus, C.K., Gill, N.D., & Keogh, J.W. (2012). Characterization of the differences in strength and power between different levels of competition in rugby union athletes. *Journal of Strength and Conditioning Research, 26*(10), 2698–2704.

Baker, D. (2001). Acute and long-term power responses to power training: Observations on the training of an elite power athlete. *Strength & Conditioning Journal, 23*(1), 47–56.

Baker, D. (2002). Differences in strength and power among junior-high, senior-high, college-aged, and elite professional rugby league players. *Journal of Strength and Conditioning Research, 16*(4), 581–585.

Baker, D., & Nance, S. (1999). The relation between running speed and measures of strength and power in professional rugby league players. *Journal of Strength and Conditioning Research, 13*(3), 230–235.

Bland, J.M., & Altman, D.G. (1986). Statistical methods for assessing agreement between two methods of clinical measurement. *Lancet, 1*(8476), 307–310.

Bland, J.M., & Altman, D.G. (1999). Measuring agreement in method comparison studies. *Statistical Methods in Medical Research, 8*(2), 135–160.

Bobbert, M.F. (2014). Effect of unloading and loading on power in simulated countermovement and squat jumps. *Medicine & Science in Sports & Exercise, 46*(6), 1176–1184.

Bobbert, M.F., Gerritsen, K.G., Litjens, M.C., & Van Soest, A.J. (1996). Why is countermovement jump height greater than squat jump height? *Medicine & Science in Sports & Exercise, 28*(11), 1402–1412.

Bosco, C., Belli, A., Astrua, M., Tihanyi, J., Pozzo, R., Kellis, S., Tsarpela, O., Foti, C., Manno, R., & Tranquilli, C. (1995). A dynamometer for evaluation of dynamic muscle work. *European Journal of Applied Physiology and Occupational Physiology, 70*(5), 379–386.

Bosco, C., Luhtanen, P., & Komi, P.V. (1983). A simple method for measurement of mechanical power in jumping. *European Journal of Applied Physiology and Occupational Physiology, 50*(2), 273–282.

Burnett, A., Beard, A., Newton, R., & Netto, K. (2008). A comparison of methods to calculate the optimal load for maximal power output in the power clean. Paper presented at the International Society of Biomechanics in Sport, Ottawa, Canada.

Caia, J., Doyle, T.L., & Benson, A.C. (2013). A cross-sectional lower-body power profile of elite and subelite Australian football players. *Journal of Strength and Conditioning Research, 27*(10), 2836–2841.

Cavagna, G.A. (1975). Force platforms as ergometers. *Journal of Applied Physiology, 39*(1), 174–179.

Chiu, L., Schilling, B., Fry, A., & Weiss, L. (2004). Measurement of resistance exercise force expression. *Journal of Applied Biomechanics, 20* (2), 204–212.

Chiu, L.Z., & Salem, G.J. (2010). Pelvic kinematic method for determining vertical jump height. *Journal of Applied Biomechanics, 26*(4), 508–511.

Chiu, L.Z., Schilling, B.K., Fry, A.C., & Salem, G.J. (2008). The influence of deformation on barbell mechanics during the clean pull. *Sports Biomechanics, 7*(2), 260–273.

Cormie, P., Deane, R., & McBride, J.M. (2007a). Methodological concerns for determining power output in the jump squat. *Journal of Strength and Conditioning Research, 21*(2), 424–430.

Cormie, P., McBride, J.M., & McCaulley, G.O. (2007b). Validation of power measurement techniques in dynamic lower body resistance exercises. *Journal of Applied Biomechanics, 23*(2), 103–118.

Cormie, P., McCaulley, G.O., Triplett, N.T., & McBride, J.M. (2007c). Optimal loading for maximal power output during lower-body resistance exercises. *Medicine and Science in Sports and Exercise, 39*(2), 340–349.

Cormie, P., McBride, J.M., & McCaulley, G.O. (2008). Power-time, force-time, and velocity-time curve analysis during the jump squat: Impact of load. *Journal of Applied Biomechanics, 24*(2), 112–120.

Cormie, P., McGuigan, M.R., & Newton, R.U. (2011a). Developing maximal neuromuscular power: Part 1- biological basis of maximal power production. *Sports Medicine, 41*(1), 17–38.

Cormie, P., McGuigan, M.R., & Newton, R.U. (2011b). Developing maximal neuromuscular power: Part 2 - training considerations for improving maximal power production. *Sports Medicine, 41*(2), 125–146.

Crewther, B.T., Kilduff, L.P., Cunningham, D.J., Cook, C., Owen, N., & Yang, G.Z. (2011). Validating two systems for estimating force and power. *International Journal of Sports Medicine, 32*(4), 254–258.

Cronin, J.B., & Hansen, K.T. (2005). Strength and power predictors of sports speed. *Journal of Strength and Conditioning Research, 19*(2), 349–357.

Cronin, J., & Sleivert, G. (2005). Challenges in understanding the influence of maximal power training on improving athletic performance. *Sports Medicine, 35*(3), 213–234.

Cronin, J.B., Hing, R.D., & McNair, P.J. (2004). Reliability and validity of a linear position transducer for measuring jump performance. *Journal of Strength and Conditioning Research, 18*(3), 590–593.

Cronin, J.B., McNair, P.J., & Marshall, R.N. (2000). The role of maximal strength and load on initial power production. *Medicine and Science in Sports and Exercise, 32*(10), 1763–1769.

Cunningham, D.J., West, D.J., Owen, N.J., Shearer, D.A., Finn, C.V., Bracken, R.M., . . . Kilduff, L.P. (2013). Strength and power predictors of sprinting performance in professional rugby players. *The Journal of Sports Medicine and Physical Fitness, 53*(2), 105–111.

Dayne, A.M., McBride, J.M., Nuzzo, J.L., Triplett, N.T., Skinner, J., & Burr, A. (2011). Power output in the jump squat in adolescent male athletes. *Journal of Strength and Conditioning Research, 25*(3), 585–589.

Dowling, J., & Vamos, L. (1993). Identification of kinetic and temporal factors related to vertical jump performance. *Journal of Applied Biomechanics, 9,* 95–110.

Driss, T., Vandewalle, H., Quievre, J., Miller, C., & Monod, H. (2001). Effects of external loading on power output in a squat jump on a force platform: A comparison between strength and power athletes and sedentary individuals. *Journal of Sports Sciences, 19*(2), 99–105.

Dugan, E.L., Doyle, T.L., Humphries, B., Hasson, C.J., & Newton, R.U. (2004). Determining the optimal load for jump squats: A review of methods and calculations. *Journal of Strength and Conditioning Research, 18*(3), 668–674.

Gard, S.A., Miff, S.C., & Kuo, A.D. (2004). Comparison of kinematic and kinetic methods for computing the vertical motion of the body center of mass during walking. *Human Movement Science, 22*(6), 597–610.

Garhammer, J. (1993). A review of power output studies of Olympic and power-lifting: Methodology, performance prediction, and evaluation tests. *The Journal of Strength & Conditioning Research, 7*(2), 76–89.

Garhammer, J., & Newton, H. (2013). Applied video analysis for coaches: weightlifting examples. *International Journal of Sports Science & Coaching, 8*(3), 581–594.

Gonzalez-Badillo, J.J., & Marques, M.C. (2010). Relationship between kinematic factors and countermovement jump height in trained track and field athletes. *Journal of Strength and Conditioning Research, 24*(12), 3443–3447.

Gullstrand, L., Halvorsen, K., Tinmark, F., Eriksson, M., & Nilsson, J. (2009). Measurements of vertical displacement in running, a methodological comparison. *Gait Posture, 30*(1), 71–75.

Hansen, K.T., Cronin, J.B., Pickering, S.L., & Douglas, L. (2011). Do force-time and power-time measures in a loaded jump squat differentiate between speed performance and playing level in elite and elite junior rugby union players? *Journal of Strength and Conditioning Research, 25*(9), 2382–2391.

Haff, G.G., Stone, M., O'Bryant, H.S., Harman, E., Dinan, C., Johnson, R., & Han, K.-H. (1997). Force-time dependent characteristics of dynamic and isometric muscle actions. *The Journal of Strength & Conditioning Research, 11*(4), 269–272.

Harris, N.K., Cronin, J.B., & Hopkins, W.G. (2007). Power outputs of a machine squat-jump across a spectrum of loads. *Journal of Strength and Conditioning Research, 21*(4), 1260.

Harris, N., Cronin, J., Taylor, K., Boris, J., & Sheppard, J. (2010). Understanding Position Transducer Technology for Strength and Conditioning Practitioners. *Strength & Conditioning Journal, 32*(4), 66–79.

Hatze, H. (1998). Validity and reliability of methods for testing vertical jumping performance. *Journal of Applied Biomechanics, 14*(2), 127–140.

Hill, A.V. (1938). The heat of shortening and the dynamic constants of muscle. *Proceedings of the Royal Society of London. Series B, Containing papers of a Biological character. Royal Society, 126,* 136–195.

Hill, A.V. (1953). The mechanics of active muscle. *Proceedings of the Royal Society of London. Series B, Containing papers of a Biological character. Royal Society, 141*(902), 104–117.

Hori, N., Newton, R.U., Andrews, W.A., Kawamori, N., McGuigan, M.R., & Nosaka, K. (2007). Comparison of four different methods to measure power output during the hang power clean and the weighted jump squat. *Journal of Strength and Conditioning Research, 21*(2), 314–320.

Hori, N., Newton, R.U., Andrews, W.A., Kawamori, N., McGuigan, M.R., & Nosaka, K. (2008). Does performance of hang power clean differentiate performance of jumping, sprinting, and changing of direction? *Journal of Strength and Conditioning Research, 22*(2), 412–418.

Izquierdo, M., Håkkinen, K., Gonzalez-Badillo, J.J., Ibanez, J., & Gorostiaga, E.M. (2002). Effects of long-term training specificity on maximal strength and power of the upper and lower extremities in athletes from different sports. *European Journal of Applied Physiology, 87*(3), 264–271.

Jandacka, D., & Vaverka, F. (2008). A regression model to determine load for maximum power output. *Sports Biomechanics, 7*(3), 361–371.

Jennings, C.L., Viljoen, W., Durandt, J., & Lambert, M.I. (2005). The reliability of the FitroDyne as a measure of muscle power. *Journal of Strength and Conditioning Research, 19*(4), 859.

Kaneko, M., Fuchimoto, T., Toji, H., & Suei, K. (1983). Training effect of different loads on the force–velocity relationship and mechanical power output in human muscle. *Scandinavian Journal of Medicine and Science in Sports, 5*, 50–55.

Kawamori, N., & Haff, G.G. (2004). The optimal training load for the development of muscular power. *Journal of Strength and Conditioning Research, 18*(3), 675–684.

Kawamori, N., Crum, A.J., Blumert, P.A., Kulik, J.R., Childers, J.T., Wood, J.A., Stone, M.H., & Haff, G.G. (2005). Influence of different relative intensities on power output during the hang power clean: Identification of the optimal load. *Journal of Strength and Conditioning Research, 19*(3), 698–708.

Kibele, A. (1998). Possibilities and limitations in the biomechanical analysis of countermovement jumps: A methodological study. *Journal of Applied Biomechanics, 14*(1), 105–117.

Kilduff, L.P., Bevan, H., Owen, N., Kingsley, M., Bunce, P., Bennett, M., & Cunningham, D. (2007). Optimal loading for peak power output during the hang power clean in professional rugby players. *International Journal of Sports Physiology and Performance, 2*(3), 260–269.

Knudson, D.V. (2009). Correcting the use of the term "power" in the strength and conditioning literature. *Journal of Strength and Conditioning Research, 23*(6), 1902–1908.

Lake, J.P., Lauder, M.A., & Smith, N.A. (2012). Barbell kinematics should not be used to estimate power output applied to the Barbell-and-body system center of mass during lower-body resistance exercise. *Journal of Strength and Conditioning Research, 26*(5), 1302–1307.

Leontijevic, B., Pazin, N., Bozic, P.R., Kukolj, M., Ugarkovic, D., & Jaric, S. (2012). Effects of loading on maximum vertical jumps: Selective effects of weight and inertia. *Journal of Electromyography and Kinesiology, 22*(2), 286–293.

Li, L., Olson, M.W., & Winchester, J.B. (2008). A proposed method for determining peak power in the jump squat exercise. *Journal of Strength and Conditioning Research, 22*(2), 326–331.

Major, J.A., Sands, W.A., McNeal, J.R., Paine, D.D., & Kipp, R. (1998). Design, construction, and validation of a portable one-dimensional force platform. *The Journal of Strength & Conditioning Research, 12*(1), 37–41.

Markovic, G., & Jaric, S. (2007). Positive and negative loading and mechanical output in maximum vertical jumping. *Medicine and Science in Sports and Exercise, 39*(10), 1757–1764.

Markovic, S., Mirkov, D.M., Nedeljkovic, A., & Jaric, S. (2014). Body size and countermovement depth confound relationship between muscle power output and jumping performance. *Human Movement Science, 33*, 203–210.

Mastropaolo, J.A. (1992). A test of the maximum-power stimulus theory for strength. *European Journal of Applied Physiology and Occupational Physiology, 65*(5), 415–420.

McBride, J.M., Triplett-McBride, T., Davie, A., & Newton, R.U. (1999). A comparison of strength and power characteristics between power lifters, olympic lifters, and sprinters. *Journal of Strength and Conditioning Research, 13*(1), 58–66.

McBride, J.M., Triplett-McBride, T., Davie, A., & Newton, R.U. (2002). The effect of heavy- vs. light-load jump squats on the development of strength, power, and speed. *The Journal of Strength & Conditioning Research, 16*(1), 75–82.

McBride, J.M., Haines, T.L., & Kirby, T.J. (2011). Effect of loading on peak power of the bar, body, and system during power cleans, squats, and jump squats. *Journal of Sports Sciences, 29*(11), 1215–1221.

McLaughlin, P. (2013). Testing agreement between a new method and the gold standard-how do we test? *Journal of Biomechanics, 46*(16), 2757–2760.

McMaster, D.T., Gill, N., Cronin, J., & McGuigan, M. (2014). A brief review of strength and ballistic assessment methodologies in sport. *Sports Medicine, 44*(5), 603–623.

Moir, G., Sanders, R., Button, C., & Glaister, M. (2005). The influence of familiarization on the reliability of force variables measured during unloaded and loaded vertical jumps. *Journal of Strength and Conditioning Research, 19*(1), 140.

Moir, G.L., Gollie, J.M., Davis, S.E., Guers, J.J., & Witmer, C.A. (2012). The effects of load on system and lower-body joint kinetics during jump squats. *Sports Biomechanics, 11*(4), 492–506.

Mundy, P.D., Lake, J.P., Carden, P.J.C., Smith, N.A., & Lauder, M.A. (2016). Agreement between the force platform method and the combined method measurements of power output during the loaded countermovement jump. *Sports Biomechanics, 15*(1), 23–35.

Newell, P.B., Dugan, E.L., & Kruger, S.E. (2005). Linear position transducer/force platform method for determining power output during free-standing jump squats. *Medicine & Science in Sports & Exercise, 37*(5), S410.

Newton, R.U., & Kraemer, W.J. (1994). Developing explosive muscular power: Implications for a mixed methods training strategy. *Strength and Conditioning Journal, 16*(5), 20–31.

Nibali, M.L., Chapman, D.W., Roberts, R.A., & Drinkwater, E.J. (2013). A rationale for assessing the lower-body power profile in team sport athletes. *Journal of Strength and Conditioning Research, 27*(2), 388–397.

Nimphius, S., McGuigan, M.R., & Newton, R.U. (2010). Relationship between strength, power, speed, and change of direction performance of female softball players. *Journal of Strength and Conditioning Research, 24*(4), 885–895.

Nuzzo, J.L., McBride, J.M., Dayne, A.M., Israetel, M.A., Dumke, C.L., & Triplett, N.T. (2010). Testing of the maximal dynamic output hypothesis in trained and untrained subjects. *Journal of Strength and Conditioning Research, 24*(5), 1269–1276.

Owen, N.J., Watkins, J., Kilduff, L.P., Bevan, H.R., & Bennett, M.A. (2014). Development of a criterion method to determine peak mechanical power output in a countermovement jump. *Journal of Strength and Conditioning Research, 28*(6), 1552–1558.

Pazin, N., Berjan, B., Nedeljkovic, A., Markovic, G., & Jaric, S. (2012). Power output in vertical jumps: Does optimum loading depend on activity profiles? *European Journal of Applied Physiology, 113*(3), 577–589.

Patterson, C., Raschner, C., & Platzer, H.-P. (2009). Power variables and bilateral force differences during unloaded and loaded squat jumps in high performance alpine ski racers. *The Journal of Strength and Conditioning Research, 23*(3), 779–787.

Ranavolo, A., Don, R., Cacchio, A., Serrao, M., Paoloni, M., Mangone, M., & Santilli, V. (2008). Comparison between kinematic and kinetic methods for computing the vertical displacement of the center of mass during human hopping at different frequencies. *Journal of Applied Biomechanics, 24*(3), 271–279.

Rahmani, A., Viale, F., Dalleau, G., & Lacour, J.-R. (2001). Force/velocity and power/velocity relationships in squat exercise. *European Journal of Applied Physiology, 84*(3), 227–232.

Sleivert, G., & Taingahue, M. (2004). The relationship between maximal jump-squat power and sprint acceleration in athletes. *European Journal of Applied Physiology, 91*(1), 46–52.

Samozino, P., Morin, J.B., Hintzy, F., & Belli, A. (2008). A simple method for measuring force, velocity and power output during squat jump. *Journal of Biomechanics, 41*(14), 2940–2945.

Sheppard, J.M., Cormack, S., Taylor, K.L., McGuigan, M.R., & Newton, R.U. (2008). Assessing the force-velocity characteristics of the leg extensors in well-trained athletes: The incremental load power profile. *Journal of Strength and Conditioning Research, 22*(4), 1320–1326.

Sheppard, J.M., Nolan, E., & Newton, R.U. (2012). Changes in strength and power qualities over two years in volleyball players transitioning from junior to senior national team. *Journal of Strength and Conditioning Research, 26*(1), 152–157.

Smilios, I., Sotiropoulos, K., Christou, M., Douda, H., Spaias, A., & Tokmakidis, S.P. (2013). Maximum power training load determination and its effects on load-power relationship, maximum strength, and vertical jump performance. *Journal of Strength and Conditioning Research, 27*(5), 1223–1233.

Street, G., McMillan, S., Board, W., Rasmussen, M., & Heneghan, M.J. (2001). Sources of Error in Determining Countermovement Jump Height With the Impulse Method. *Journal of Applied Biomechanics, 17*(1), 43–54.

Stone, M.H., O'Bryant, H.S., McCoy, L., Coglianese, R., Lehmkuhl, M., & Schilling, B. (2003). Power and maximum strength relationships during performance of dynamic and static weighted jumps. *Journal of Strength and Conditioning Research, 17*(1), 140–147.

Suzovic, D., Markovic, G., Pasic, M., & Jaric, S. (2013). Optimum load in various vertical jumps support the maximum dynamic output hypothesis. *International Journal of Sports Medicine, 34*(11), 1007–1014.

Turner, A.P., Unholz, C.N., Potts, N., & Coleman, S.G. (2012). Peak power, force, and velocity during jump squats in professional rugby players. *Journal of Strength and Conditioning Research, 26*(6), 1594–1600.

Vanrenterghem, J., De Clercq, D., & Van Cleven, P. (2001). Necessary precautions in measuring correct vertical jumping height by means of force plate measurements. *Ergonomics, 44*(8), 814–818.

Vuk, S., Markovic, G., & Jaric, S. (2012). External loading and maximum dynamic output in vertical jumping: The role of training history. *Human Movement Science, 31*(1), 139–151.

Wilson, G.J., Newton, R.U., Murphy, A.J., & Humphries, B.J. (1993). The optimal training load for the development of dynamic athletic performance. *Medicine and Science in Sports and Exercise, 25*(11), 1279–1286.

Winchester, J.B., McBride, J.M., Maher, M.A., Mikat, R.P., Allen, B.K., Kline, D.E., & McGuigan, M.R. (2008). Eight weeks of ballistic exercise improves power independently of changes in strength and muscle fiber type expression. *The Journal of Strength & Conditioning Research, 22*(6), 1728–1734.

Winter, D.A. (2009). *Biomechanics and Motor Control of Human Movement* (4th ed.). Hoboken, NJ: John Wiley.

Winter, E.M., & Knudson, D.V. (2011). Terms and nomenclature. *Journal of Sports Sciences, 29*(10), 999–1000.

Winter, E.M., Abt, G., Brookes, F.B., Challis, J.H., Fowler, N.E., Knudson, D.V., … Yeadon, M.R. (2016). Misuse of "power" and other mechanical terms in sport and exercise science research. *Journal of Strength and Conditioning Research, 30*(1), 292–300.

Wood, G.A. (1982). Data smoothing and differentiation procedures in biomechanics. *Exercise and Sport Sciences Reviews, 10*, 308–362.

Young, W.B., Newton, R.U., Doyle, T.L., Chapman, D., Cormack, S., Stewart, G., & Dawson, B. (2005). Physiological and anthropometric characteristics of starters and non-starters and playing positions in elite Australian Rules football: A case study. *Journal of Science and Medicine in Sport, 8*(3), 333–345.

12 Aerobic performance assessment

Fred J. DiMenna and Andrew M. Jones

Part 1

Introduction

While all world-class athletes are incredible performance machines, the Olympic decathlete is, perhaps, the most remarkable when physiological traits responsible for athletic success are considered. Indeed, the ten track-and-field events that constitute the decathlete's docket run the gamut from brief-burst activities like shot-put and javelin to a running event that requires over 4 minutes to complete. Consequently, this athlete must demonstrate prowess during activities with a wide range of energetic requirements. While all body energy needs are satisfied by the same energy-transferring molecule (adenosine triphosphate; ATP), the method by which ATP is made available during such diverse events is different. The human body does not store large amounts of ATP nor does it use much of that which it stores. Hence, the rate of ATP production during competition must essentially match the athlete's ATP turnover rate. ATP is made available by both aerobic and anaerobic means with proportional involvement dependent upon how rapidly it is required.

Aerobic energy production

When a decathlete throws a javelin or puts a shot, the rate of ATP hydrolysis and immediacy with which it is required conspire to make anaerobic ATP production the "exclusive" provider of energy. Specifically, for any burst activity (i.e. an all-out ballistic effort lasting less than 1 second), the phosphocreatine (PCr) store in muscle provides for the required ATP. Moreover, when such all-out effort is sustained for a brief period, rapid glycolysis and a contribution from the adenylate-kinase reaction augment the PCr contribution to allow a high level of performance to be maintained with minimal aerobic involvement. However, once all-out effort is extended for longer than ~10 seconds, contributions from these easily-accessed forms of substrate-level phosphorylation wane, while oxidative phosphorylation assumes a greater role. For example, when sprint distance is increased to 400 m (i.e. ~50 s of all-out effort), a crossover to predominantly aerobic ATP production occurs after ~25 s of exercise so that aerobic metabolism provides for ~43% of total energy transfer over the course of the race (Spencer & Gastin 2001). Finally, when the decathlete runs the 1500 m, ~84% of the required energy is provided via aerobic energy transfer (Spencer & Gastin 2001).

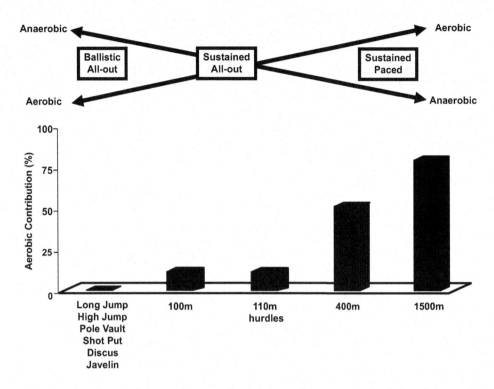

Figure 12.1 Estimates of the aerobic contribution to total energy transfer during the ten events of the decathlon.

Aerobic capacity

Four of the events that a decathlete performs involve a significant contribution from aerobic energy transfer (Figure 12.1); hence, a robust aerobic capacity is important for success in this and other sports where effort is sustained. Moreover, all anaerobic energy transfer during exercise is ultimately compensated for with ATP generated aerobically. For example, following a 400m sprint, post-exercise aerobic metabolism remains high to rebuild depleted PCr stores and remove accumulated lactate. Consequently, aerobic capacity is also important for athletes who perform events that are predominantly anaerobic in nature, particularly when the efforts must be repeated (repeat-sprint ability). Moreover, when such repeated bouts of high-intensity exercise are performed with insufficient opportunity for complete recovery, there is a decreased ability to derive energy from substrate-level phosphorylation on successive bouts with a concomitant shift to ATP produced aerobically (Parolin et al., 1999). Collectively, this means that well-developed aerobic capacity is important for every athlete with the possible exception of those who perform the most fleeting singular efforts.

Assessing aerobic capacity

Given its relative importance, it stands to reason that athlete assessment should include tests that measure aerobic capacity. Specifically, parameters that reflect aerobic capacity are used to establish an appropriate pace during competition and also to prescribe and monitor training regimes to enhance performance. However, there are myriad measurements used for this purpose and each has strengths and weaknesses with respect to validity and ease and reproducibility of measurement. Since the seminal work of A.V. Hill in the early twentieth century (Hill et al., 1924; Hill & Lupton, 1923), the criterion measure of aerobic "functional" capacity has been the maximal rate at which oxygen can be consumed (VO_{2max}). However, in recent years, there is growing appreciation for parameters which reflect the fraction of maximal capacity that an athlete can use while performing prolonged exercise. Consequently, a comprehensive protocol to test aerobic capacity should also include assessment of parameters indicative of this ability; for example, critical power/velocity (CP/CV), which is a direct measurement of the ability to perform mechanical work. From a practical standpoint, CP/CV represents the highest rate of energy turnover that can be maintained without drawing on the finite energetic reserve (W') that limits the ability to sustain high-intensity work (Jones et al., 2010). This means that CP/CV could be considered the true indicator of aerobic functional capacity. Moreover, there are other physiological variables that can be measured in response to exercise that imply functional capacity including the lactate threshold (LT) (Farrell et al., 1979; Tanaka et al., 1983), lactate turnpoint (LTP) (Ribiero et al., 1986) and maximal lactate steady state (MLSS) (Billat et al., 2003). Finally, assessing the aerobic cost of mechanical work (exercise economy) provides practical information that is useful for athlete training and performance (Conley & Krahenbuhl, 1980).

Maximal rate of oxygen consumption

The important difference between substrate-level and oxidative phosphorylation is that the former results in phosphorylation of ADP via direct transfer of a phosphate group while the latter depends on oxidation of reducing equivalents in the electron-transport chain of muscle mitochondria. This means that atmospheric oxygen (O_2) must be available as an oxidising agent when the latter form of energy transfer is in effect. This is why aerobic capacity is typically assessed by determining the maximal rate at which O_2 can be consumed. Indeed, VO_{2max} has traditionally been considered the gold-standard measurement of aerobic capacity and VO_{2max} testing is routinely employed for athlete assessment. However, despite the strong theoretical basis for VO_{2max} as a correlate of endurance exercise performance, research to confirm its ability to predict performance in various endurance events has returned equivocal findings. For example, Kenney and Hodgson studied eight 5000 m runners and five 3000 m steeplechase athletes (VO_{2max} = 72.4 ± 1.2 ml·min^{-1}·kg^{-1}) and found no association between performance time and VO_{2max} for either group (Kenney & Hodgson, 1985). Similarly, Legaz Arrese et al. calculated mean velocity during the best performance of the season for 27 elite male middle-distance runners (VO_{2max} = 71.3 ± 4.5 ml·min^{-1}·kg^{-1}) during 800, 1500, 3000 and 5000 m races and found a significant association with VO_{2max} only for the 3000 m event (Legaz Arrese et al., 2007). However, mean velocity was highly correlated with the fraction of VO_{2max} utilised during the 1500, 3000 and 5000 m races. Conversely, Fay et al. found significant correlations between VO_{2max} and race pace for 13 female runners for 5, 10 and 16.09 km races (Fay et al., 1989). Importantly, the subjects in this study were more diverse with respect to conditioning (e.g., a VO_{2max} range of 51.7–68.4 ml·min^{-1}·kg^{-1}), which lends credence to the contention that in a more heterogeneously conditioned group VO_{2max} does, indeed, predict endurance performance while in more homogeneous groups other factors (e.g. biomechanical and/or anthropometric influences) provide separation.

Exercise economy

For athletes possessing similar VO_{2max} values, the absolute work rate that can be performed at a given VO_2 (exercise economy) is an important factor. For example, Conley and Krahenbuhl assessed 12 experienced distance runners with similarly high VO_{2max} values (71.7 ± 2.8 ml·min^{-1}·kg^{-1}) and found that running economy accounted for ~65% of the variation in 10 km performance while VO_{2max} exerted no effect (Conley & Krahenbuhl, 1980). The authors concluded that a high VO_{2max} was important because it helped subjects gain membership to an elite performance cluster within which economy discriminated further proficiency. This is in line with findings from longitudinal analyses, which suggest that economy and performance can be improved after long-term training in elite athletes despite an unchanged VO_{2max} (Jones, 1998; Legaz Arrese et al., 2005).

Measuring VO_{2max} and exercise economy

Exercise economy and VO_{2max} can be assessed using a series of discrete constant-work-rate exercise bouts (CWRE) or a continuous bout during which work rate is increased in stages (step incremental exercise) until limit of tolerance (T_{lim}). During these tests, the "steady-state" increase in VO_2 above baseline is used to quantify exercise economy while the attainment of the same VO_2 despite increasing work rate (a "VO_2 plateau") represents VO_{2max}. Incremental exercise where work rate is applied continuously in a linear manner until exhaustion has also been shown to provide a reproducible VO_{2peak} (Whipp et al., 1981) that is not different compared to the VO_{2max} measured during a step incremental test with similar work-rate increments (Zhang et al., 1991). Moreover, even though such a "smooth-ramp" incremental test occurs entirely in the non-steady state, exercise economy can be inferred by calculating the slope of a regression line fit to the VO_2/work-rate data (Whipp et al., 1981). Finally, data from incremental exercise can also provide a composite measure of exercise economy and VO_{2max} by solving for the VO_{2max} value in the regression equation describing the VO_2/work-rate relationship. Interestingly, the "velocity at VO_{2max}" (V-VO_{2max}) so derived has been shown to have the highest correlation with performance during a 16 km running time trial compared to often-used parameters including VO_{2max} and running economy per se (McLaughlin et al., 2010).

Verifying VO_{2max}

It is intuitive that the highest VO_2 measured during an exercise bout during which work rate is increased incrementally in stages or as a continuous ramp until exhaustion (VO_{2peak}) is the "true" VO_{2max} if no increase is observed despite increasing work rate during latter stages of the test. Indeed, this concept emerged when A.V. Hill and colleagues had subjects perform CWRE running at a variety of speeds on different days and found that there was a specific VO_2 beyond which no further increase could occur regardless of how much speed was increased (Hill et al., 1924; Hill & Lupton 1923) (Figure 12.2). However, some subjects did not demonstrate this plateau and once singular bouts became the accepted way to measure VO_{2max}, it also became apparent that a VO_2 plateau is not an obligatory feature of incremental tests to exhaustion (Day et al., 2003) even for elite athletes who would be likely to apply maximum effort (Doherty et al., 2003). This means that the VO_{2peak} measured during such a test should be verified before it is accepted as the VO_{2max}. However, questions have arisen regarding the best way to do so. Traditionally, a cluster of "secondary criteria"

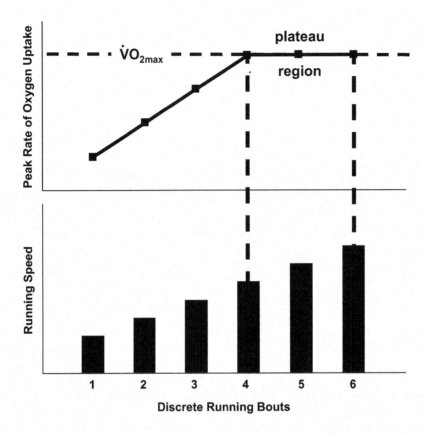

Figure 12.2 The concept of a maximal rate of O_2 uptake was first recognised in the early twentieth century when Hill and colleagues graphed the peak rate of O_2 uptake during discrete running bouts and found that at the highest speeds encountered, there was a specific rate beyond which no further increase could occur (i.e. a "VO_2 plateau").

(e.g. a criterion level for RER, blood lactate concentration and/or heart rate) have been used, but it is now apparent that inter-subject variability renders these general guidelines inadequate for this purpose (Poole et al., 2008). Indeed, research shows that using these criteria can allow for acceptance of a VO_{2max} that is 30–40% below the true value and/or invalid rejection (Midgley et al., 2006; Poole et al., 2008). Recent research suggests that a better strategy is to take advantage of the fact that there is a range of constant work rates that will result in attainment of VO_{2max} prior to exhaustion; i.e. work rates within the "severe-intensity domain" (Poole & Jones, 2012). This means that the VO_2 response to any work rate in the severe domain that is above the highest achieved on the incremental test can be used to test for the presence of a VO_2 plateau (Poole & Jones, 2017).

Expressing exercise economy

Exercise economy is typically determined as the oxidative cost of a given rate of work. For example, the standard way to assess running economy is to measure VO_2 while a subject runs on a treadmill at a constant speed at which a VO_2 steady state can be achieved (i.e. a speed at which aerobic metabolism supplies all of the energetic requirements once the transition to the work rate has taken place). Comparisons between individuals can then be made by using the modelled VO_2/velocity relationship to estimate the VO_2 cost of a standard velocity; for example, 12 to 21 km·h^{-1} with 16 km·h^{-1} (~268 m·min^{-1}) being most common (Barnes & Kilding, 2015). Once the oxidative cost is calculated, it can be expressed relative to body mass either as a rate (ml·kg^{-1}·min^{-1}) or an absolute amount for coverage of a specific distance (ml·kg^{-1}·km^{-1}). However, it is important to note that using VO_2 as a proxy for energy expenditure does not account for inter-subject variability in substrate use at a given running speed. For example, Fletcher et al. (2009) assessed highly trained middle- and long-distance runners and found that caloric cost per kilometre increased significantly as running speed was increased from 75% to 95% of the speed at LT while the VO_2 cost per kilometre remained unchanged. Accordingly, the authors recommend expressing running economy as a caloric- instead of oxidative-unit cost (e.g. kcal·kg^{-1}·km^{-1}). The one drawback with this approach, however, is that unlike the oxidative cost of exercise, caloric cost does not allow for determination of the fraction of VO_{2max} that will be required to perform the task. Fletcher et al. (2009) also stress that subjects should run at similar intensities relative to LT as opposed to a common absolute speed, which might present a disparate relative challenge for different runners.

Lactate threshold/gas exchange threshold

The blood-lactate response to exercise provides a window into muscle metabolism that can be measured with relative ease. At rest, the concentration of lactate ions in the blood ([La$^-$]) remains fixed at ~1 mM because the activity of lactate-producing and lactate-consuming tissue is balanced. During moderate-intensity CWRE, this dynamic equilibrium is maintained and [La$^-$] does not increase; however, when higher work rates are encountered, systemic production exceeds consumption and [La$^-$] accumulates. The first sustained increase of [La$^-$] in venous blood during incremental exercise was originally termed the "anaerobic threshold" based on the belief that the accumulation signalled an O_2-availability limitation and resultant shift to anaerobic energy metabolism (Davis et al., 1983). However, due to the elegant work of Brooks and colleagues (1985), we now have better insight and, specifically, an understanding that this breakpoint does not reflect a significant change in anaerobiosis. Instead, it simply indicates that cellular redox and phosphorylation potentials have been altered. Importantly, much like moderate CWRE, there is a range of work rates above LT that can be sustained "indefinitely" with minimal metabolic perturbation despite elevation of [La$^-$] above resting levels. This range comprises the heavy-intensity domain within which elevated, but stable [La$^-$] values are observed (Poole & Jones, 2012). The VO_2 response also reaches an elevated steady state in the heavy-intensity domain; however, attainment of a stable VO_2 is delayed due to the presence of the VO_2 slow component, which complements the primary response thereby elevating the metabolic cost of work (e.g. >8–10 ml·min^{-1}·W^{-1}, which is the VO_2 cost for moderate-intensity leg-cycle ergometry) (Whipp, 1971; Whipp & Wasserman, 1972). The LT is typically determined during a laboratory-based incremental test comprising stages of 3–5 minutes. Upon completion of each stage, a blood sample is obtained and tested for [La$^-$] and these values are plotted against work rate to identify the final stage during which lactate equilibrium is maintained (Figure 12.3). In addition to work rate, the metabolic rate at LT can also be determined by calculating the average VO_2 once steady state is achieved during the stage.

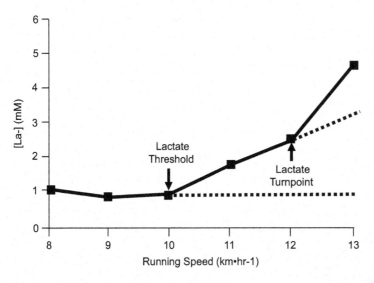

Figure 12.3 A plot of [La⁻] upon completion of 3-minute stages during treadmill running at increasing speed.

The LT has proven to be a strong predictor of endurance exercise performance (Farrell et al., 1979; Tanaka et al., 1983) that increases as a chronic adaptation to endurance training (Poole et al., 1990). Consequently, LT assessment comprises an important component of athlete testing. However, the invasive nature of the measurement might preclude its use in some settings. Moreover, the incremental nature of the typical step protocol does not provide sufficient discriminatory power to precisely identify the work rate aligned with LT. For example, for the response profile depicted in Figure 12.3, lactate equilibrium might have been lost anywhere between 10 and 11 km·h⁻¹. Each of these limitations can be circumvented by using the aforementioned ramp protocol where work rate is increased continuously as a linear function of time. Specifically, this test allows for estimation of LT at a precise metabolic (and, by extension, work) rate noninvasively because once LT is passed, the rates of carbon dioxide production (VCO_2) and expiratory ventilation (V_E) increase disproportionately compared to VO_2 due to the presence of "non-metabolic" CO_2 consequent to bicarbonate buffering of hydrogen ions ([H⁺]) that accompany [La⁻] (Beaver et al., 1986; Whipp et al., 1981). Therefore, a "gas exchange threshold" (GET) that approximates LT can be determined by inspecting gas-exchange and ventilatory data collected at the mouth during the test.

Lactate turnpoint/respiratory compensation point

Following LT, a second change in the slope of the lactate response to an incremental increase in work rate occurs at higher work rates when La⁻ accumulation accelerates. This second threshold, which typically occurs at a [La⁻] of ~2.5–4.0 mM, is called the lactate turnpoint (LTP) (Figure 12.3). Compared to LT, for trained athletes, LTP is likely to represent a better index of endurance capacity because it approximates the highest metabolic rate that can be sustained at a steady state during CWRE (CP/CV or the maximal lactate steady state; MLSS) (Ribiero et al., 1986). Knowledge of the LTP is, therefore, important for determining pacing strategies for extended endurance events.

Like LT, it has been suggested that LTP can be determined non-invasively by investigating pulmonary gas-exchange and ventilatory data. Specifically, LTP should be aligned with the point at which ventilatory compensation is required because bicarbonate buffering can no longer maintain homeostatic pH (respiratory compensation point; RCP). However, confirmation of this contention is lacking (Simon et al., 1983) and the very notion of a specific work rate that precipitates ventilatory compensation across different incremental protocols appears flawed (Leo et al., 2017). For example, with slower incrementation, RCP occurs at a lower work rate and, indeed, when lengthy stages are employed and the incremental rate is sufficiently slow, the "isocapnic" buffering region that separates GET from RCP (Whipp et al., 1989) is eliminated completely so that only one ventilatory breakpoint is present (Cross & Sabapathy, 2012). In concert with the use of myriad monikers to describe the aforementioned four breakpoints (Binder et al., 2008), this lack of differentiation is likely to be responsible for the confusion that still exists in the literature regarding specific point(s) being referenced. There is, however, evidence to suggest that RCP is associated with a specific metabolic rate, which might prove useful for differentiating "sustainable" from non-sustainable work (Keir et al., 2015).

Incremental exercise testing

As previously mentioned, incremental exercise tests have become the gold standard for assessing aerobic capacity via measurement of VO_{2max}. Furthermore, the blood-lactate and/or gas-exchange response during incremental exercise can be analysed to determine LT and/or GET and LTP and/or RCP. However, the search for the best standardised protocol to use for these purposes remains elusive (Beltz et al., 2016). With respect to the mode of an incremental test, leg-cycle ergometry is popular for general-fitness testing because of its ease of administration and applicability for individuals with coordination and/or orthopaedic limitations. However, in 1969, Hermansen and Saltin found that 47 of 55 subjects achieved a higher VO_{2peak} during inclined treadmill running compared to leg cycling (Hermansen & Saltin, 1969), which is consistent with the notion that most individuals achieve a higher VO_{2peak} during treadmill exercise when a large percentage of total muscle mass is involved. However, there are conflicting findings regarding whether inclined running allows for a higher (Freund et al., 1986; Hermansen & Saltin, 1969; Mayhew & Gross, 1975, Pokan et al., 1995; Taylor et al., 1955) or similar (Freund et al., 1986; Kasch et al., 1976) VO_{2peak} compared to horizontal running, which might reflect the trained status of the subjects (Allen et al., 1986; Freund et al., 1986). Furthermore, treadmill running per se might not elicit higher VO_{2peak} values for athletes who are trained for other forms of endurance exercise. For example, Ricci and Léger (1983) observed a higher VO_{2peak} for trained cyclists during cycling on an ergometer compared to treadmill running. Strømme et al. (1977) also found that cyclists achieve a higher VO_{2peak} during cycling compared to uphill running and confirmed similar mode specificity for cross-country skiers and rowers. The authors concluded that athletes should be tested during sport-specific performance.

In contrast to the constant-work-rate bouts that researchers used to determine VO_{2max} in the first half of the twentieth century, incremental bouts are advantageous because testing can be completed in one session. Consequently, when research confirmed that such bouts yield a similar VO_{2peak} compared to the discrete-bout protocol (Maksud & Coutts, 1971; McArdle et al., 1973), they became the common mode of testing. However, single-session incremental tests can also be performed discontinuously (i.e. with recovery intervals interspersed between stages), which might provide greater test specificity for intermittent-sport athletes. For example, Alexander and Mier (2011) had college soccer players perform the same incremental treadmill protocol (constant speed, increasing grade) both with and without 60-second active-recovery intervals between stages and found that the athletes achieved a higher work rate and corresponding VO_{2peak} with the intermittent protocol. Conversely, Riboli et al. report that for physically active subjects, similar VO_{2peak} values were attained for continuous and discontinuous treadmill running even though a higher peak velocity was achieved when the recovery intervals were interspersed (Riboli et al., 2016). The latter finding is consistent with the traditional interpretation of VO_{2max}, which posits a value that cannot be exceeded regardless of the work rate attained during maximal exercise (Hill et al., 1924; Hill & Lupton, 1923). It has also been suggested that laboratory-based incremental tests that are typically used to determine the VO_{2max} of athletes in individual endurance sports where competition demands can be closely approximated (e.g. runners, cyclists, rowers and cross-country skiers) might not be specific for intermittent- and/or team-sport athletes. Consequently, "field-based" tests have been developed for determining the VO_{2max} of athletes in sports like tennis (Fernandez-Fernandez et al., 2014) and soccer (Aziz et al., 2005). These tests include the multi-stage 20 m shuttle run test (MSRT) (Aziz et al., 2005; Léger & Lambert, 1982, Léger et al., 1988), which is a continuous test, and intermittent protocols like the yo-yo intermittent endurance test (YIET) (Bangsbo, 1994), the yo-yo intermittent recovery test (YIRT) (Bangsbo et al., 2008) and the 30–15 intermittent fitness test (30–15 IFT) (Buchheit, 2008). It stands to reason that these tests improve both ease of administration and ecological validity by testing athletes during challenges that mimic the physical demands of their specific competition. However, this gain in sport specificity is offset by a loss of the high degree of reliability that laboratory-based measurements offer (Reilly et al., 2009). Moreover, other parameters revealed by field-based tests (e.g. distance covered during the YIET) might be more appropriate for assessing sport-specific endurance performance in intermittent sports compared to VO_{2max} per se (Aziz et al., 2005).

It is important to note a number of other challenges that have been made to the concept of an immutable mode-specific VO_{2max} across different types of incremental testing protocols. For example, some research suggests that the duration of an incremental test can influence the measured VO_{2peak}. For example, Buchfuhrer et al. found that VO_{2peak} was higher on incremental tests involving work-rate increments resulting in a T_{lim} that did not exceed 8–17 minutes (Buchfuhrer et al., 1983). Similarly, Astorino et al. report a lower VO_{2peak} for tests that required 14 compared to 6 or 10 minutes to complete (Astorino et al., 2004), while Yoon et al. found a higher value for 8-minute tests compared to three other durations (5, 12 and 16 minutes) although this was the case for male subjects only (Yoon et al., 2007). Collectively, these findings suggest that a work-rate increment that allows for completion of 8–10 minutes of incremental exercise until exhaustion is appropriate. The reason for the inability of longer tests to reveal the "true" VO_{2max} is unclear, but might have to do with a tightening of the already-existent central circulatory limitation (e.g. venous return and stroke volume reductions secondary to increasing body temperature) (Astorino et al., 2004; Gonzalez-Alonso & Calbet, 2003). Subject motivation and/or the location of fatigue (e.g. central vs. peripheral; Burnley & Jones, 2018) might also be altered when test length exceeds the optimal duration.

In addition to test length, with respect to work-rate increments, some recent research suggests that protocols that allow subjects to "self-regulate" increases according to perceived exertion to achieve test termination at a known end point ("closed-loop" tests) allow for attainment of a higher VO_{2peak} and, therefore, the "true" VO_{2max} (Astorino et al., 2015;

Mauger & Sculthorpe, 2012). However, while speculation abounds, a definitive explanation as to how a psychological factor like autonomy might influence physiological constraints to VO_{2max} is lacking (Poole, 2014) and in subsequent research, a similar (Chidnok et al., 2013a; Faulkner et al., 2015; Hanson et al., 2016; Hogg et al., 2015; Sperlich et al., 2015; Straub et al., 2014) or lower (Scheadler & Devor, 2015) VO_{2peak} was observed with the self-regulated protocol even when peak work rate was higher (Scheadler & Devor, 2015). Consequently, the preponderance of evidence suggests that incremental protocols that rely on subject self-regulation can be used to determine the same VO_{2max} revealed by traditional open-loop tests where a tester is in control of work-rate implementation.

Fractional utilisation of VO_{2max}

The time for which VO_{2max} can be sustained once it is reached is short (e.g. ~1–3 minutes) (Midgley et al., 2006). Consequently, most athletes either do not reach VO_{2max} during competition or do so for only short periods before intensity of effort must be reduced or exercise ceased. This means that for most athletes, the majority of their competition time involves work at a submaximal VO_2. However, it is important to note that the VO_2 response to an increase in work rate is not linear and the non-linearity is not constant across individuals (DiMenna & Jones, 2009). Consequently, the ability to sustain work at a given percentage of VO_{2max} can be markedly different for athletes even if they possess the same VO_{2max} value. Accordingly, in addition to VO_{2max} and exercise economy, aerobic assessment should include measurements that test the ability to sustain a high VO_2 relative to VO_{2max} for an extended period.

Critical power/velocity

As previously mentioned, the severe-intensity domain encompasses a range of constant work rates characterised by attainment of VO_{2max} with exhaustion imminent not long thereafter (Poole & Jones, 2012; Poole et al., 1988). When these work rates (x axis) are plotted against T_{lim} (y axis), the plots can be fitted with a hyperbolic model to reveal an asymptote that represents the highest sustainable rate of work (i.e. the critical power or velocity depending on mode of exercise; CP/CV) (Figure 12.4) (Monod & Scherrer, 1965; Poole et al., 1988). Moreover, when exercise above CP/CV is performed, the curvature constant of the modelled fit (W') reflects a finite energetic reserve that dictates the time for

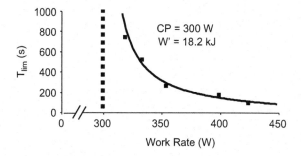

Figure 12.4 A plot of the time for which cycling can be sustained against a variety of high-intensity work rates.

which exercise above CP/CV can be sustained (Monod & Scherrer, 1965). Indeed, this value, which might reflect a fixed substrate-level energetic reserve (e.g. phosphocreatine, muscle glycogen) and/or accumulation of fatigue-related metabolites (e.g. [H$^+$], inorganic phosphate and extracellular potassium) can be determined and expressed in kilojoules to help predict T$_{lim}$ for discrete high-intensity work rates for an athlete (Jones et al., 2010). Collectively, this means that a parameter that reflects the maximal rate at which aerobic energy transfer occurs "exclusively" (and, therefore, the maximum sustainable pace during continuous training) and a parameter that can be used to determine the time for which high-intensity work intervals above CP can be maintained during high-intensity interval training (Chidnok et al., 2013b) can each be determined from the same testing battery. However, the traditional CP paradigm requires four to six laboratory visits during which CWRE bouts at different high-intensity work rates are performed to determine the associated T$_{lim}$. Consequently, despite the time-honoured recognition of the usefulness of this paradigm (Monod & Scherrer, 1965) heretofore, this type of testing has not become a routine component of athlete assessment. However, it has recently been shown that a single 3-minute all-out test can be used to exhaust W′ thereby revealing CP as the work rate that can be sustained toward the end of the test (Vanhatalo et al., 2007). Interestingly, this type of all-out exercise (i.e. maximal effort from start to finish with no evidence of pacing) also allows for determination of VO$_{2max}$, which is achieved and maintained after the first ~90 seconds of cycling (Jones et al., 2010). Consequently, the traditional measure of "functional capacity" and one that better reflects the limit of aerobic functionality for an athlete can both be determined from the same 3-minute bout.

Maximal lactate steady state

Much like CP, a testing paradigm comprising multiple CWRE bouts at discrete work rates on separate days can be used to determine MLSS, which is the highest power output or velocity that can be maintained without a progressive increase in [La$^-$] over time (Figure 12.5). It stands to reason that MLSS would represent the power/velocity above which anaerobic energy metabolism begins to play an important role, which means that in theory, MLSS should be aligned with CP/CV (Poole et al., 1988, 1990). However, the preponderance of evidence from studies that have directly measured both parameters in the same subjects suggests that MLSS occurs at a lower work rate regardless of whether CP/CV is determined using the multi-bout (Dekerle et al., 2003; Denadai et al., 2005; Pringle & Jones 2002) or all-out (Mattioni Maturana et al., 2016) format. Indeed, compared to MLSS, exercise at CP was shown to be associated with continued increases in [La$^-$] and VO$_2$ over time (Pringle & Jones 2002). One caveat when interpreting this finding is that "exercise at CP" is a somewhat misguided concept because of the margin of error associated with measuring the parameter. Hence, when assessing physiological responses relative to CP/CV, it is more insightful to do so during exercise performed outside a range situated about CP/CV (e.g. a work rate 10% below and 10% above; Jones et al., 2008). Regardless of this distinction, however, it has been suggested that for endurance events that require >30 minutes to complete, MLSS might be the more relevant parameter for determining an appropriate race pace (Billat et al., 2003).

With respect to a "steady state" in the [La$^-$] response, an exact definition of what constitutes "no change" is lacking, but an increase of ≤1 mM between minutes 10 and 30 of a 30-minute bout is often used as the criterion (Londeree, 1986). Consequently, to "precisely" titrate MLSS, a subject might be required to complete as many as five 30-minute

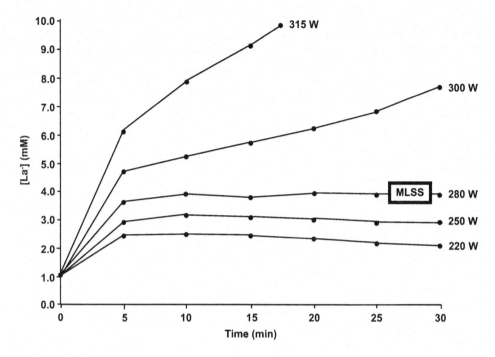

Figure 12.5 A plot of [La⁻] every 5 minutes during cycling exercise at a variety of constant work rates.

exercise bouts at different high-intensity work rates on separate days (Figure 12.5). Moreover, every 5 minutes during these bouts, [La⁻] is assessed; hence, a large number of blood draws are required. Collectively, these factors make inclusion of MLSS testing impractical for typical athlete assessment. Fortunately, as previously mentioned, LTP, which can be determined during incremental exercise with sufficient sensitivity (e.g. small work-rate increments and long enough stages to allow the measured [La⁻] to reflect accumulation associated with the work rate), appears to provide a reasonable estimate of MLSS (Aunola & Rusko, 1992; Kilding & Jones, 2005; Smith & Jones, 2001).

Part 2

Step incremental treadmill test

Test implementation

This laboratory test is used to determine VO_{2max}, $V-VO_{2max}$, LT, LTP and economy during running. The test described below is a discontinuous protocol involving two discrete parts that are separated by ~15 minutes of active recovery; however, the same results can be obtained with one continuous protocol with grade constant and speed increased throughout. Regardless of this distinction, prior to beginning the test, a finger-tip blood sample is taken to determine resting [La⁻]. Similar measurements are taken following each stage during the test and pulmonary gas-exchange and heart-rate data should also be collected throughout.

The first part of the protocol begins with 10–15 minutes of warm-up jogging at a self-selected pace. The treadmill grade is set at 1% to simulate the energetic cost of outdoor running (Jones & Doust, 1996). Following the warm-up, the speed for the first stage is set at 11–15 km·h^{-1} (depending upon the fitness level of the athlete) with incrementation of 1 km·h^{-1} following each 3-minute stage. The goal is for the athlete to complete five to nine stages with test termination when he/she is within one stage of T_{lim} (e.g. heart rate within 5–10 b·min^{-1} of maximum, [La$^-$] > 4 mM). The speed during this final stage (V_{final}) should be noted. Upon completion of each stage during this part of the test, the runner should support their weight on the guardrail and lift their feet to straddle the belt while the blood sample is taken. Running should resume immediately when the blood draw is complete (~15–30 s) with timing of the next stage beginning once the subject is running unsupported. Following completion of the requisite stages, the subject engages in an active form of recovery (e.g. walking/light jogging on treadmill) for ~15 minutes after which he/she runs at a 1% grade at a speed set at 2 km·h^{-1} below V_{final}. From this point, speed is progressed and once V_{final} is reached (e.g. after 1–2 minutes), timing of this part begins and treadmill grade is increased by 1% per minute until T_{lim} (typically 5–10 minutes). Once again, pulmonary-gas-exchange and heart-rate measurements should be done during this test and [La$^-$] should be assessed at T_{lim} and during recovery (e.g. at minutes 1, 3, 5, 7 and 10 post exercise).

Data interpretation

Data from the first part of the step incremental treadmill test are used to determine running economy, LT and LTP. For example, running economy can be expressed relative to body mass for each stage as the VO_2 cost (e.g. average during the final 60 seconds of the stage) of running either that particular speed or a given distance (see Table 12.1 for general classifications) while LT and LTP are identified by plotting [La$^-$] values (*y* axis) against speed (*x* axis) (Figure 12.3).

The athlete's VO_{2max} and V-VO_{2max} are determined from the second part of the step incremental treadmill test. With respect to the measurement of VO_2 per se, it is important to note that there is often considerable breath-to-breath variability and "noise" in VO_2 data so that the value associated with a single breath should not be used to define VO_{2max}. Instead, a reasonable strategy is to use the highest 30 s value, which can be determined by applying a three-point rolling average to data exported in 10-second bins. Once the highest value (which might not be the final 30 s one) is determined, it can be expressed in both absolute and relative (to body mass) terms and compared to established norms for athletes (Table 12.2). The V-VO_{2max} can then be determined by multiplying the measured VO_{2max} (in ml·kg^{-1}·min^{-1}) by 60 and dividing the product by the running economy (in ml·kg^{-1}·km^{-1}) determined during the first part of the test.

Ramp incremental cycling test + verification bout

Test implementation

This laboratory test is used to determine VO_{2max}, exercise economy, GET and RCP. It requires the use of an ergometer that allows for gradual continuous increases in work rate; hence, this test was originally developed and has traditionally been done using leg cycling on an electronically braked ergometer (Whipp et al., 1981). However, a protocol that

Table 12.1 General classifications of running economy expressed as the VO_2 cost of running a specific speed and the O_2 cost of running a specific distance.

Classification	VO_2 at 16 km·h⁻¹ $(ml·kg^{-1}·min^{-1})$	O_2 cost of running $(ml·kg^{-1}·km^{-1})$
Excellent	44–47	170–180
Very good	47–50	180–190
Average	50–54	190–210
Poor	55–58	210–220

Table 12.2 General classifications of VO_{2max} relative to body mass ($ml·kg^{-1}·min^{-1}$) at a variety of levels of performance for athletes in the United Kingdom.

Classification	Male	Female
World class	80–90	70–80
International	70–80	60–70
National	65–75	55–65
National junior	60–70	50–60

utilises a linear increase in speed coupled with a curvilinear increase in grade to apply a linear increase in work rate during treadmill exercise has more recently been developed (Porszasz et al., 2003). For leg cycling, the test begins with the subject pedalling at a predetermined cadence with work rate set at 40–50 W to account for the elevated internal O_2 cost and potential ergometer nonlinearity at lower work rates (Boone & Bourgois, 2012). Pulmonary gas-exchange and heart-rate data are collected throughout and blood is drawn toward the end of the baseline period to determine [La⁻]. The ramp increase in work rate is commenced with cadence held constant once 5 minutes of baseline cycling has been completed. The ramp slope should be chosen to allow for ~10 minutes of exercise prior to exhaustion. A criterion for T_{lim} based on a drop in cadence (e.g. ≥10 rev·min⁻¹) despite maximum subject effort and strong verbal encouragement from the tester should be established a priori. Once T_{lim} is reached, the athlete should rest for 5–10 minutes after which he/she resumes cycling at the same cadence at a constant work rate that is above that which was achieved on the incremental test, but still sufficiently low to allow for the completion of ~3–6 minutes of cycling.

Data interpretation

As was the case with the step incremental treadmill test, VO_2 data collected during the ramp incremental cycling test and verification bout should be bin- and rolling-averaged so that a VO_{2peak} from both bouts can be determined. To test for the presence of a VO_2 plateau across the two bouts, the VO_2/work-rate data from the latter portion of the incremental test (e.g. the 4 minutes immediately preceding the final 2 minutes) are fitted with a linear function and the resulting regression equation is used to predict the VO_2 requirement of the final stage of the incremental bout and the "supramaximal" work rate of the verification bout. If the actual VO_{2peak} measured for the incremental bout falls below the predicted value by

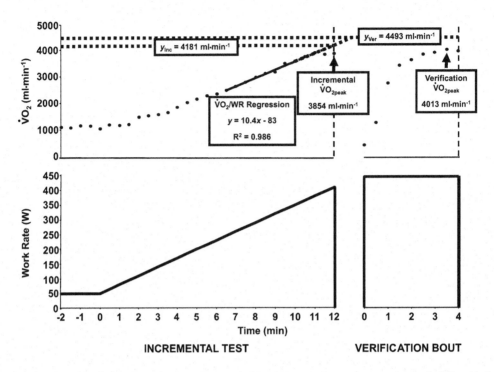

Figure 12.6 A plot of 30-s average VO₂ values (top panels) during ramp incremental cycling (left panel) and a subsequent constant-work-rate verification bout each performed to the limit of tolerance (dashed vertical lines).

>50% of the increment that should be present for the increase in work rate, a VO_2 plateau during the incremental bout is confirmed and the actual and predicted VO_2 from the verification bout are compared in a similar manner for verification (Figure 12.6, Boxes 12.1 and 12.2; Midgley et al., 2009).

To infer exercise economy from data collected during the ramp incremental cycling test, the VO_2/work-rate slope from the entire response can be calculated although there is evidence to suggest that this slope changes once GET is surpassed (Barstow et al., 2000; Hansen et al., 1988; Zoladz et al., 1995). Consequently, slopes for the sub- and supra-GET region are often determined. Regardless of this distinction, however, it is important to note that finite VO_2 kinetics and the transit delay from site of respiration (the muscle cell) to site of measurement (the mouth) conspire to create a lag in the VO_2 response following initiation of work (Figures 12.6 and 12.7). Consequently, this delay, which is termed the "mean response time" (MRT), must be determined (Box 12.3) or estimated (e.g. 40 s; Whipp et al., 1981) so that data collected during this period can be excluded from the fit. All data collected following achievement of a VO_2 plateau (see above) are also not reflective of the response and should be excluded from the model (Figure 12.7). Once the response data are isolated in this manner, the data in the two regions are fitted as a function of time with a linear model ($y = ax + b$) where VO_2 and time are the dependent and independent variables, respectively. The slope revealed by these equations is used to infer exercise economy below and above GET (Figure 12.7).

Box 12.1 Testing for the presence of a VO_2 plateau during ramp incremental cycling

(1) Thirty-second average VO_2 data in response to the ramp incremental increase in cycling work rate were fitted with a linear function with fitting window constrained to the 4-minute period ending 2 minutes prior to T_{lim} (6–10 minutes) to reveal a VO_2/work-rate regression equation of $y = 10.4x - 83$.

(2) The regression equation derived in Step 1 was used to estimate the VO_2 cost of the peak work rate achieved on the incremental ramp test (410 W):

$$y_{Inc} = [(10.4 \text{ ml·min}^{-1}\text{·W}^{-1})(410 \text{ W})] - 83 \text{ ml·min}^{-1}$$
$$y_{Inc} = 4181 \text{ ml·min}^{-1}$$

(3) The difference between the actual VO_{2peak} measured on the incremental ramp test (highest 30-s value; 3854 ml·min^{-1}) and the estimated VO_2 from Step 2 was calculated:

$$4181 \text{ ml·min}^{-1} - 3854 \text{ ·min}^{-1} = 327 \text{ ml·min}^{-1}$$

(4) A plateau was deemed present if the difference calculated in Step 3 was greater than 50% of the change that was predicted by the regression slope determined in Step 1 for the final 2 minutes of work-rate incrementation:

$$(10.4 \text{ ml·min}^{-1}\text{·W}^{-1})(60 \text{ W}) = 624 \text{ ml·min}^{-1}$$
$$327 \text{ ml·min}^{-1} / 624 \text{ ml·min}^{-1} = 52\%$$

Box 12.2 Testing for verification of VO_{2max} during ramp incremental cycling

(1) Thirty-second average VO_2 data in response to the ramp incremental increase in cycling work rate were fit with a linear function with fitting window constrained to the four-minute period ending two minutes prior to T_{lim} (6–10 minutes) to reveal a VO_2/work-rate regression equation of $y = 10.4x - 83$.

(2) The regression equation derived in Step 1 was used to estimate the VO_2 cost of the work rate maintained during a constant-work-rate verification bout performed 10 minutes after cessation of the ramp test at a work rate that was 30 W greater than the peak work rate attained on the ramp test (440 W):

$$y_{Ver} = [(10.4 \text{ ml·min}^{-1}\text{·W}^{-1})(410 \text{ W})] - 83 \text{ ml·min}^{-1}$$
$$y_{Ver} = 4493 \text{ ml·min}^{-1}$$

(3) The difference between the actual VO_{2peak} measured during the verification bout (highest 30-s value; 4013 ml·min^{-1}) and the estimated VO_2 from Step 2 was calculated:

$$4493 \text{ ml·min}^{-1}-4013 \text{ ml·min}^{-1} = 480 \text{ ml·min}^{-1}$$

(4) Verification of VO_{2max} was confirmed if the difference calculated in Step 3 was greater than 50% of the change that was predicted by the regression slope determined in Step 1 for the 90-W increase in work rate that was present for the verification bout compared to the final value of the fitting region:

$$(10.4 \text{ ml·min}^{-1}\text{·W}^{-1})(90 \text{ W}) = 936 \text{ ml·min}^{-1}$$
$$480 \text{ ml·min}^{-1}/936 \text{ ml·min}^{-1} = 51\%$$

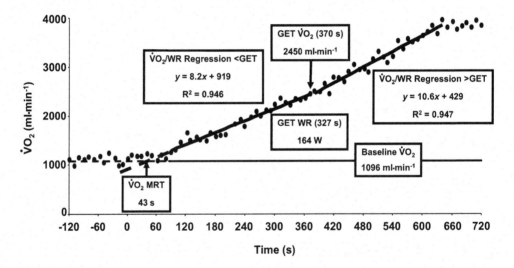

Figure 12.7 A plot of 10-s average VO_2 values during ramp incremental cycling.

As previously mentioned, the metabolic rate at GET (GET_{met}) is determined by examining the relationship between the VO_2 and VCO_2 responses (i.e. the V-slope method) (Beaver et al., 1986; Whipp et al., 1981) (Figure 12.8). Furthermore, once GET is surpassed, the rate of expiratory ventilation (V_E) remains linked to VCO_2; hence, GET_{met} is confirmed by identifying the point at which V_E increases disproportionately in relation to VO_2 (i.e. V_E/VO_2 increases) with O_2 tension increasing in expired air (Figure 12.9). Alternatively, identifying the metabolic rate at RCP (RCP_{met}) requires examination of the relationship between the VCO_2 and V_E responses to determine the point at which they become unlinked (i.e. the point at which V_E/VCO_2 increases while CO_2 tension decreases in expired air) (Figure 12.9). Finally, to align GET_{met} with a specific work rate (GET_{work}), the work-rate increment that occurred during the initial "VO_2 lag" (Figures 12.6 and 12.7) should be subtracted from the work rate that was being maintained when GET_{met} was identified (Box 12.3, Figure 12.7).

Box 12.3 Calculating the VO_2/work-rate slopes below and above GET and the mean response time for ramp incremental cycling exercise

(1) The GET_{met} was determined (see text and Figures 12.6 and 12.7) as 2450 ml·min^{-1}.

(2) The baseline VO_2 (the average VO_2 during the pre-ramp period of 50-W cycling excluding the first 120 s and final 30 s) was calculated as 1096 ml·min^{-1} (see horizontal dashed line).

(3) Ten-second average VO_2 data in response to the ramp incremental increase in cycling work rate were fitted with a linear function with the fitting window constrained temporally from the VO_2 value that began the sustained and progressive increase above VO_{2base} (determined by visual inspection) to GET_{met} to reveal a sub-GET VO_2/work-rate regression equation of $y = 8.2x + 919$. The slope of this equation (8.2 ml·min^{-1}·W^{-1}) represents an index of exercise economy. The regression equation for the supra-GET region (all data from GET_{met} to the point at which a VO_2 plateau was extant) was determined in a similar manner to reveal a supra-LT slope of 10.6 ml·min^{-1}·W^{-1}.

(4) The sub-GET regression equation derived in Step 3 was used to estimate the work rate (x) at which $y = VO_{2base}$ (i.e. the work rate immediately preceding the initial increase in VO_2, which signalled that the "VO_2 lag" in comparison to work rate had reached fruition:

1096 ml·min^{-1} = 8.2x + 919 ml·min^{-1}
x = 21.6 W

(5) The work rate derived in Step 4 was converted to a time by dividing by the ramp rate:

MRT = (21.6 W)/(30 W·min^{-1})
MRT = 0.72 min (43 s)

(6) The time derived in step 5 was subtracted from the time at which GET_{met} was identified (370 s) to determine the time (327 s) and, by extension, work rate (164 W) at which GET occurred.

Twenty-metre multi-stage shuttle run test

Test implementation

This field test is used to either directly measure or indirectly estimate VO_{2max} and V-VO_{2max} for intermittent-sport athletes (Léger & Lambert, 1982; Léger et al., 1988; Paradisis et al., 2014). If a direct measurement of VO_{2max} is desired, pulmonary gas-exchange data are collected throughout the test using a portable unit. Alternatively, if such a measurement is not feasible and/or an indirect estimate will suffice, a prediction can be made using the maximal velocity that the subject achieves on the test. Advantages of the latter approach

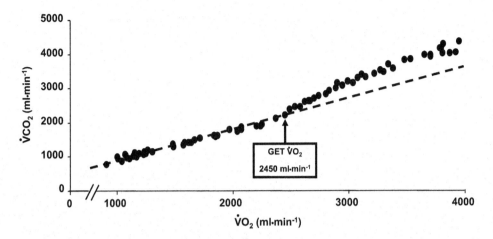

Figure 12.8 A plot of the rate of CO_2 production against the rate of O_2 consumption during ramp incremental cycling with a work-rate increment of 1 W every 2 s.

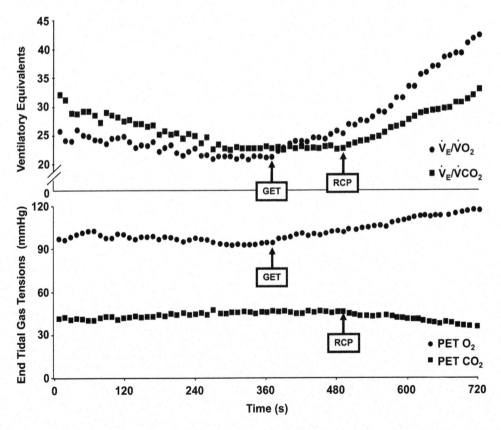

Figure 12.9 Identification of the metabolic rate at the GET via the V-slope method (Figure 12.8) can be confirmed by studying the responses of minute ventilation and end-tidal gas tensions during the incremental test.

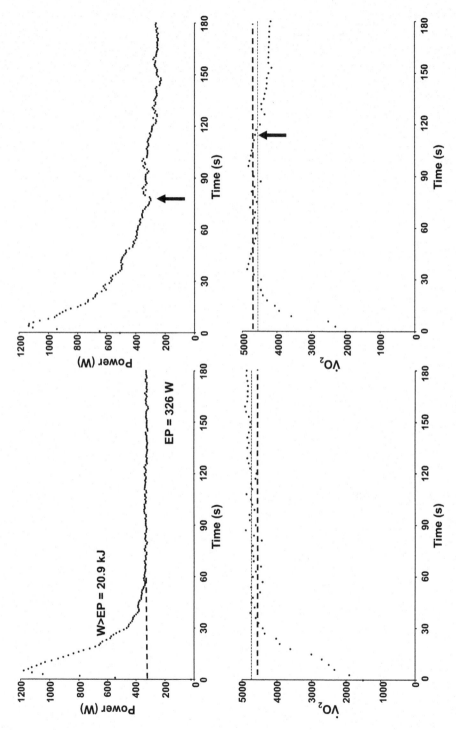

Figure 12.10 A plot of instantaneous power output (top panels) and the rate of O₂ consumption (bottom panels) for two subjects performing a 3-minute all-out cycling test.

include its practicality (e.g. no expensive equipment required) and time efficiency (i.e. multiple subjects can be tested at once). Importantly, the criterion-related validity for estimation of VO_{2max} in this manner is moderate-to-high (Mayorga-Vega et al., 2015) although there is some evidence that the estimate will be an under-prediction compared to treadmill-derived VO_{2max} in some types of athletes (St Clair Gibson et al., 1998, Grant et al., 1995).

The MSRT involves running back and forth on a course defined by lines or cones placed 20 m apart. It is, therefore, practical because it can be performed either indoors or outdoors in a relatively small space. The pace is established by signals emitted by an audio tape at a specific frequency. The initial velocity is set at 8.0 $km \cdot h^{-1}$ with increases of 0.5 $km \cdot hr^{-1}$ per 60 s stage (Léger & Gadoury, 1989). Subjects are instructed to complete as many stages as possible, with the test terminated when pace cannot be maintained (e.g. when the subject is ≥3 m from the 20 m line at the time of the signal) (Léger & Lambert, 1982).

Data interpretation

For direct determination of VO_{2max} from data derived during the 20-m multistage shuttle test, breath-by-breath values should be bin- and rolling-averaged as previously described. For indirect determination, the maximal speed attained on the test (x value) should be entered into the following regression equation (Flouris et al., 2005) to estimate VO_{2max} (y value):

$$y = 6.65x - 35.80$$

Using a modified version of the test with initial velocity set at 8.5 $km \cdot h^{-1}$, performance on the MSRT has also been used to estimate $V\text{-}VO_{2max}$ (y value) by entering the number of shuttles completed (x value) into the following regression equation (Paradisis et al., 2014):

$$y = 0.0937x + 6.890$$

Yo-yo intermittent recovery test level 1 and level 2

Test implementation

These field tests are used to assess an athlete's capacity to perform intermittent exercise requiring maximal activation of the aerobic system (level 1) or the ability to recover from repeat exercise with a high contribution from anaerobic energy turnover (level 2) (Bangsbo et al., 2008). They also provide a valid estimate of VO_{2max} for intermittent-sport athletes (Bangsbo et al., 2008; Thomas et al., 2006). The test involves running back and forth on a course defined by start/finish and turn lines or cones placed 20 m apart. It is, therefore, practical because it can be performed either indoors or outdoors in a relatively small space. An additional line or cone is placed 5 m behind the start/finish one. Each 40-m turn/return bout comprises a sprint to and back from the turn line/cone followed by a 10-s active-recovery period during which the subject jogs back and forth one time on the course defined by the additional line/cone. The pace is established by signals emitted by an audio tape at a specific frequency. Following warm-up, the signal dictates a pace that requires four running bouts at 10.0–13.0 $km \cdot h^{-1}$ followed by seven running bouts at 13.5–14.0 $km \cdot h^{-1}$ (Krustrup et al., 2003). Thereafter, it continues with stepwise increases of 0.5 $km \cdot h^{-1}$ after every eight bouts until test termination, which occurs when the subject fails to reach the finish line two times. Total distance covered prior to test termination is recorded as the test result.

Data interpretation

Total distance covered during the yo-yo intermittent recovery test is a reliable measurement that can be used to examine changes in performance potential over time (Bangsbo et al., 2008). Furthermore, the total distance covered on the test (x value) can be entered into the following regression equations (Bangsbo et al., 2008) to estimate VO_{2max} (y value):

$y = 0.0084x + 36.4$ (level 1)
$y = 0.0136x + 45.3$ (level 2)

Five × 6-second cycle test

Test implementation

This test is used in the physiological testing of team-sport athletes to assess repeat-sprint ability; however, to increase sport-specific validity, it should be modified to correspond to the common sprint distances involved in the given sport (Bishop et al., 2001). For the standard version of the test, subjects begin by completing a 5-minute warm-up on the cycle ergometer after which they perform a 10-s all-out sprint. The total work performed during the initial 6 seconds of this sprint is used as a criterion score against which performance during the five 6-second bouts that constitute the testing protocol will be assessed. The testing sequence, which is initiated 5 minutes following the criterion bout, involves 6 seconds of all-out cycling performed every 30 seconds for five repeats. Five seconds before starting each sprint, subjects should assume a "ready position" to await a countdown and during the sprint, subjects can maintain a standing position if so desired. During the 24-s rest period between sprints, subjects are allowed to turn the pedals at a self-selected pace or rest completely. The total work completed during the five sprints is cumulated once the sequence has been completed.

Data interpretation

The total work performed during the criterion bout is calculated and multiplied by five to establish the "ideal work" corresponding to the five-sprint sequence. This number is divided into the actual total work completed across the five sprints and the quotient is then multiplied by 100 to derive a %-decrement score that reflects "repeat-sprint ability" at least for the work/rest duration and repetition combinations of the protocol that was employed (Bishop et al., 2001).

Three-minute all-out test

Test implementation

This laboratory test is used to estimate CP and W′ and measure VO_{2max}. Testing is typically done on a leg-cycle ergometer; however, some researchers have recently experimented with a track-running all-out protocol with instantaneous speed assessed by accelerometry (Broxterman et al., 2013). For the cycling all-out test, two testing sessions are required because a ramp incremental cycling test is needed during a preliminary testing session to establish VO_{2max}, GET_{work} (see above) and the peak work rate. The work rate that lies midway between GET_{work} and peak (50%Δ) is used to determine the load against which the subject performs the all-out cycling ≥48 hours after the first visit. For subjects who are inexperienced with all-out exercise, a familiarisation trial should also be included during a preliminary session prior to actual testing.

For the 3-minute all-out test, subjects begin by performing a warm-up of moderate-intensity cycling followed by 5 minutes of rest. Gas-exchange and ventilatory data are collected throughout the test and second-by-second work-rate values are recorded either with purpose-built software or by video recording of the ergometer's power meter. The actual test begins with 3 minutes of baseline cycling against no load at the subject's preferred cadence followed immediately by 3 minutes of all-out effort. Subjects should increase their cadence to ~110 rpm during the final 5 seconds of the baseline period prior to application of the load. The resistance on the pedals during the all-out cycling is set using the linear mode of the ergometer so that the subject will attain the work rate at 50%Δ upon reaching their preferred cadence (linear factor = power/cadence squared). Importantly, absolutely no pacing should be employed during the test so subjects should be instructed to maintain their cadence as high as possible at all times. Strong verbal encouragement should be provided throughout; however, to discourage pacing, subjects should not be informed as to elapsed time or time remaining.

Data interpretation

Breath-by-breath VO_2 data from the 3-minute all-out test should be bin- and rolling-averaged as previously described to determine the VO_{2peak} for the all-out test. Importantly, to verify all-out effort throughout, the value for the test should be similar to the VO_{2max} from the incremental bout. To estimate CP, the power output maintained toward the end of the all-out bout (e.g. the average power output for the final 30 s) is calculated (Figure 12.10) (Vanhatalo et al., 2007). The power-time integral above this "end-test power" (EP) represents the work that was performed above EP (WEP), which approximates the W′ revealed by conventional CP testing (Vanhatalo et al., 2007).

References

Alexander, R.P., & Mier, C.M. (2011). Intermittent vs continuous graded exercise test for VO2max in college soccer athletes. *International Journal of Exercise Science, 4*(3), 185–191.

Allen, D., Freund, B.J., & Wilmore, J.H. (1986). Interaction of test protocol and horizontal run training on maximal oxygen uptake. *Medicine & Science in Sports & Exercise, 18*(5), 581–587.

Astorino, T.A., McMillan, D.W., Edmunds, R.M., & Sanchez, E. (2015). Increased cardiac output elicits higher VO2max in response to self-paced exercise. *Applied Physiology, Nutrition, and Metabolism, 40*, 223–229.

Astorino, T.A., Rietschel, J.C., Tam, P.A., Taylor, K., Johnson, S.M., Freedman, T.P., & Sakarya, C.E. (2004). Reinvestigation of optimal duration of VO2max testing. *Journal of Exercise Physiologyonline, 7*, 1–8.

Aunola, S., & Rusko, H. (1992). Does anaerobic threshold correlate with maximal lactate steady-state? *Journal of Sports Sciences, 10*(4), 309–323.

Aziz, A.R., Tan, F.H., & The, K.C. (2005). A pilot study comparing two field tests with the treadmill run test in soccer players. *Journal of Sports Science and Medicine, 4*(2), 105–112.

Bangsbo J. (1994). *Fitness training in football: A scientific approach* (pp. 1–336). Bagsværd: HO Storm.

Bangsbo, J., Iaia, F.M., & Krustrup, P. (2008). The Yo-Yo intermittent recovery test: a useful tool for evaluation of physical performance in intermittent sports. *Sports Medicine, 38*(1), 37–51.

Barnes, K.R., & Kilding, A.E. (2015). Running economy: measurement, norms, and determining factors. *Sports Medicine - Open, 1*, 8.

Barstow, T.J., Jones, A.M., Nguyen, P.H., & Casaburi, R. (2000). Influence of muscle fibre type and fitness on the oxygen uptake/power output slope during incremental exercise in humans. *Experimental Physiology, 85*(1), 109–116.

Beaver, W.L., Wasserman, K., & Whipp, B.J. (1986). A new method for detecting anaerobic threshold by gas exchange. *Journal of Applied Physiology, 60*(6), 2020–2027.

Beltz, N.M., Gibson, A.L., Janot, J.M., Kravitz, L. Mermier, C.M., & Dalleck, L.C. (2016). Graded exercise testing protocols for the determination of VO_2max: Historical perspectives, progress, and future considerations. *Journal of Sports Medicine*, Article ID 3968393.

Billat, V.L., Sirvent, P., Py, G., Koralsztein, J.P., & Mercier, J. (2003). The concept of maximal lactate steady state: A bridge between biochemistry, physiology and sport science. *Sports Medicine, 33*(6), 407–426.

Binder, R.K., Wonisch, M., Corra, U., Cohen-Solal, A., Vanhees, L, Saner, H., & Schmid J.P. (2008). Methodological approach to the first and second lactate threshold in incremental cardiopulmonary exercise testing. *European Journal of Cardiovascular Prevention & Rehabilitation, 15*(6), 726–734.

Bishop, D., Spencer, M., Duffield, R., & Lawrence, S. (2001). The validity of a repeat sprint ability test. *Journal of Science and Medicine in Sport, 4*(1), 19–29.

Boone, J., & Bourgois, J. (2012). The oxygen uptake response to incremental ramp exercise: methodological and physiological issues. *Sports Medicine, 42*(6), 511–526.

Brooks G.A. (1985). Anaerobic threshold: review of the concept and directions for future research. *Medicine & Science in Sports & Exercise, 17*(1), 22–34.

Broxterman, R.M., Ade, C.J., Poole, D.C., Harms, C.A., & Barstow, T.J. (2013). A single test for the determination of parameters of the speed-time relationship for running. *Respiratory Physiology & Neurobiology, 185*(2), 380–385.

Buchfuhrer, M.J., Hansen, J.E., Robinson, T.E., Sue, D.Y, Wasserman K., & Whipp, B.J. (1983). Optimizing the exercise protocol for cardiopulmonary assessment. *Journal of Applied Physiology: Respiratory, Environmental and Exercise Physiology, 55*(5), 1558–1564.

Buchheit, M. (2008). The 30–15 intermittent fitness test: accuracy for individualizing interval training of young intermittent sport players. *The Journal of Strength & Conditioning Research, 22*(2), 365–374.

Burnley, M., & Jones, A.M. (2018). Power-duration relationship: Physiology, fatigue, and the limits of human performance. *European Journal of Sports Science, 18*(1), 1–12.

Chidnok, W., Dimenna, F.J., Bailey, S.J., Burnley, M., Wilkerson, D.P., Vanhatalo, A., & Jones, A.M. (2013a). VO2max is not altered by self-pacing during incremental exercise. *European Journal of Applied Physiology, 113*(2), 529–539.

Chidnok, W., DiMenna, F.J., Fulford, J., Bailey, S.J., Skiba, P.F., Vanhatalo, A., & Jones, A.M. (2013b). Muscle metabolic responses during high-intensity intermittent exercise measured by (31)P-MRS: relationship to the critical power concept. *American Journal of Physiology. Regulatory, Integrative and Comparative Physiology, 305*(9), R1085–1092.

Conley, D.L., & Krahenbuhl, G.S. (1980). Running economy and distance running performance of highly trained athletes. *Medicine & Science in Sports & Exercise, 12*(5), 357–360.

Cross T.J., & Sabapathy, S. (2012). The respiratory compensation "point" as a determinant of O2 uptake kinetics? *International Journal of Sports Medicine, 33*(10), 854.

Davis, H.A., Bassett, J., Hughes, P., & Gass, G.C. (1983). Anaerobic threshold and lactate turnpoint. *European Journal of Applied Physiology and Occupational Physiology, 50*(3), 383–392.

Day, J.R., Rossiter, H.B., Coats, E.M., Skasick, A., & Whipp, B.J. (2003). The maximally attainable VO2 during exercise in humans: the peak vs. maximum issue. *Journal of Applied Physiology, 95*(5), 1901–1907.

Dekerle, J., Baron, B., Dupont, L., Vanvelcenaher, J., & Pelayo, P. (2003). Maximal lactate steady state, respiratory compensation threshold and critical power. *European Journal of Applied Physiology, 89*(3–4), 281–288.

Denadai, B.S., Gomide, E.B., & Greco, C.C. (2005). The relationship between onset of blood lactate accumulation, critical velocity, and maximal lactate steady state in soccer players. *The Journal of Strength & Conditioning Research, 19*(2), 364–368.

DiMenna, F.J. and Jones, A.M. (2009). "Linear" versus "Nonlinear" O2 responses to exercise: Reshaping traditional beliefs. *Journal of Exercise Science & Fitness, 7,* 67–84.

Doherty, M., Nobbs, L., & Noakes, T.D. (2003). Low frequency of the "plateau phenomenon" during maximal exercise in elite British athletes. *European Journal of Applied Physiology, 89,* 619–623.

Farrell, P.A., Wilmore, J.H., Coyle, E.F., Billing, J.E., & Costill, D.L. (1979). Plasma lactate accumulation and distance running performance. *Medicine & Science in Sports, 11*(4), 338–344.

Faulkner, J., Mauger, A.R., Woolley, B., & Lambrick, D. (2015). The efficacy of a self-paced VO2max test during motorized treadmill exercise. *International Journal of Sports Physiology and Performance, 10*(1), 99–105.

Fay, L., Londeree, B.R., LaFontaine, T.P., & Volek, M.R. (1989). Physiological parameters related to distance running performance in female athletes. *Medicine & Science in Sports & Exercise, 21*(3), 319–324.

Fernandez-Fernandez, J., Ulbricht, A., & Ferrauti, A. (2014). Fitness testing of tennis players: How valuable is it? *British Journal of Sports Medicine, 48,* i22–31.

Fletcher, J.R., Esau, S.P., & Macintosh, B.R. (2009). Economy of running: beyond the measurement of oxygen uptake. *Journal of Applied Physiology, 107*(6) 1918–1922.

Flouris, A.D., Metsios, G.S., & Koutedakis, Y. (2005). Enhancing the efficacy of the 20 m multistage shuttle run test. *British Journal of Sports Medicine., 39*(3), 166–170.

Freund, B.J., Allen, D., & Wilmore, J.H. (1986). Interaction of test protocol and inclined run training on maximal oxygen uptake. *Medicine & Science in Sports & Exercise, 18*(5), 588–592.

Gonzalez-Alonso, J., & Calbet, J.A.L. (2003). Reductions in systemic and skeletal muscle blood flow and oxygen delivery limit maximal aerobic capacity in humans. *Circulation, 28,* 824–830.

Grant, S., Corbett, K., Amjad, A.M, Wilson, J., & Aitchison, T. (1995). A comparison of methods of predicting maximum oxygen uptake. *British Journal of Sports Medicine, 29*(3), 147–152.

Hansen, J.E., Casaburi, R., Cooper, D.M., & Wasserman, K. (1988). Oxygen uptake as related to work rate increment during cycle ergometer exercise. *European Journal of Applied Physiology and Occupational Physiology, 57*(2), 140–145.

Hanson, N.J., Scheadler, C.M., Lee, T.L., Neuenfeldt, N.C., Michael, T.J., & Miller, M.G. (2016). Modality determines VO2max achieved in self-paced exercise tests: validation with the Bruce protocol. *European Journal of Applied Physiology, 116*(7), 1313–1319.

Hermansen, L., & Saltin, B. (1969). Oxygen uptake during maximal treadmill and bicycle exercise. *Journal of Applied Physiology, 26*(1), 31–37.

Hill, A.V., Long, C.N.H., & Lupton, H. (1924). Muscular exercise, lactic acid and the supply and utilization of oxygen. *Proceedings of the Royal Society B: Biological Sciences, 96,* 438–475.

Hill, A.V., & Lupton, H. (1923). Muscular exercise, lactic acid and the supply and utilization of oxygen. *Quarterly Journal of Medicine, 16,* 135–171.

Hogg, J.S., Hopker, J.G., & Mauger, A.R. (2015). The self-paced VO2max test to assess maximal oxygen uptake in highly trained runners. *International Journal of Sports Physiology and Performance, 10*(2), 172–177.

Jones, A.M. (1998). A five year physiological case study of an Olympic runner. *British Journal of Sports Medicine, 32*(1), 39–43.

Jones, A.M., & Doust, J.H. (1996). A 1% treadmill grade most accurately reflects the energetic cost of outdoor running. *Journal of Sports Science, 14*(4), 321–327.

Jones, A.M., Vanhatalo, A., Burnley, M., Morton, R.H., & Poole, D.C. (2010). Critical power: implications for determination of VO2max and exercise tolerance. *Medicine & Science in Sports & Exercise, 42*(10), 1876–1890.

Jones, A.M., Wilkerson, D.P., A., DiMenna, F., Fulford, J., & Poole, D.C. (2008). Muscle metabolic responses to exercise above and below the "critical power" assessed using 31P-MRS. *American Journal of Physiology. Regulatory, Integrative and Comparative Physiology, 294*(2), R585–593.

Kasch F.W., Wallace J.P., Huhn R.R, Krogh L.A., & Hurl P.M. (1976). VO2max during horizontal and inclined treadmill running. *Journal of Applied Physiology, 40*(6), 982–983.

Keir, D.A., Fontana, F.Y., Robertson, T.C., Murias, J.M., Paterson, D.H., Kowalchuk, J.M., & Pogliaghi, S. (2015). Exercise Intensity Thresholds: Identifying the Boundaries of Sustainable Performance. *Medicine & Science in Sports & Exercise, 47*(9), 1932–1940.

Kenney, W.L., & Hodgson, J.L. (1985). Variables predictive of performance in elite middle-distance runners. *British Journal of Sports Medicine, 19*(4), 207–209.

Kilding, A.E., & Jones, A.M. Validity of a single-visit protocol to estimate the maximum lactate steady state. *Medicine & Science in Sports & Exercise, 37*(10), 1734–1740.

Legaz-Arrese, A., Munguía-Izquierdoa, D., Nuviala Nuvialaa, A., Serveto-Galindob, O., Moliner Urdialesa, D., & Reverter Masíaa, J. (2007). Average VO2max as a function of running performances on different distances. *Science & Sports, 22*(1), 43–49.

Legaz Arrese, A., Serrano Ostáriz, E., Jcasajús Mallén, J.A., & Munguía Izquierdo, D. (2005). The changes in running performance and maximal oxygen uptake after long-term training in elite athletes. *Journal of Sports Medicine and Physical Fitness., 45*(4), 435–440.

Léger, L., & Gadoury, C. (1989). Validity of the 20 m shuttle run test with 1 min stages to predict VO2 max in adults. *Canadian Journal of Sports Science, 14*(1), 21–26.

Léger, L.A., & Lambert, J. (1982). A maximal multistage 20-m shuttle run test to predict VO2 max. *European Journal of Applied Physiology and Occupational Physiology, 49*(1), 1–12.

Léger, L.A., Mercier, D., Gadoury, C., & Lambert, J. (1988). The multistage 20 metre shuttle run test for aerobic fitness. *Journal of Sports Science, 6*(2), 93–101.

Leo, J.A., Sabapathy, S., Simmonds, M.J., & Cross, T.J. (2017). The respiratory compensation point is not a valid surrogate for critical power. *Medicine & Science in Sports & Exercise.* Epub ahead of print. doi:10.1249/MSS.0000000000001226.

Londeree, B.R. (1986). The use of laboratory test results with long distance runners. *Sports Medicine, 3*(3), 201–213.

Maksud, M.G., & Coutts, K.D. (1971). Comparison of a continuous and discontinuous graded treadmill test for maximal oxygen uptake. *Medicine & Science in Sports, 3*, 63–65.

Mattioni Maturana, F., Keir, D.A., McLay, K.M., & Murias, J.M. (2016). Can measures of critical power precisely estimate the maximal metabolic steady-state? *Applied Physiology, Nutrition, and Metabolism, 41*(11), 1197–1203.

Mauger, A.R., & Sculthorpe N. (2012). A new VO2max protocol allowing self-pacing in maximal incremental exercise. *British Journal of Sports Medicine, 46*(1), 59–63.

Mayhew, J.L., & Gross, P.M. (1975). Comparison of grade-incremented versus speed-incremented maximal exercise tests in trained men. *British Journal of Sports Medicine, 9*(4), 191–195.

Mayorga-Vega, D., Aguilar-Soto, P., & Viciana, J. (2015). Criterion-related validity of the 20-m shuttle run test for estimating cardiorespiratory fitness: A meta-analysis. *Journal of Sports Science and Medicine, 14*(3), 536–547.

McArdle, W.D., Katch, F.I., & Pechar, G.S. (1973). Comparison of continuous and discontinuous treadmill and bicycle tests for max VO2. *Medicine & Science in Sports & Exercise, 5*, 156–160.

McLaughlin, J.E., Howley, E.T., Bassett, D.R. Jr, Thompson, D.L., & Fitzhugh, E.C. (2010). Test of the classic model for predicting endurance running performance. *Medicine & Science in Sports & Exercise, 42*(5), 991–997.

Midgley, A.W., Carroll, S., Marchant, D., McNaughton, L.R., & Siegler, J. Evaluation of true maximal oxygen uptake based on a novel set of standardized criteria. *Applied Physiology, Nutrition, and Metabolism, 34*(2), 115–123.

Midgley, A.W., McNaughton, L.R., & Wilkinson, M. (2006). The relationship between the lactate turnpoint and the time at VO2max during a constant velocity run to exhaustion. *International Journal of Sports Medicine, 27*(4), 278–282.

Monod, H., & Scherrer, J. (1965). The work capacity of a synergic muscular group. *Ergonomics, 8,* 329–338.

Paradisis, G.P., Zacharogiannis, E., Mandila, D., Smirtiotou, A., Argeitaki, P., & Cooke, C.B. Multi-stage 20-m shuttle run fitness test, maximal oxygen uptake and velocity at maximal oxygen uptake. *Journal of Human Kinetics, 41,* 81–87.

Parolin, M.L., Chesley, A., Matsos, M.P., Spriet, L.L., Jones, N.L., & Heigenhauser, G.J. (1999). Regulation of skeletal muscle glycogen phosphorylase and PDH during maximal intermittent exercise. *American Journal of Physiology, 277*(5 Pt 1), E890–900.

Pokan, R., Schwaberger, G., Hofmann, P., Eber, B., Toplak, H., Gasser, R., Fruhwald, F.M., Pessenhofer, H., & Klein, W. (1995). Effects of treadmill exercise protocol with constant and ascending grade on leveling-off of O2 uptake and VO2max. *International Journal of Sports Medicine, 16*(4), 238–242.

Poole, D.C. (2014). Discussion: 'the efficacy of the self-paced VO2max test to measure maximal oxygen uptake in treadmill running'. *Applied Physiology, Nutrition, and Metabolism, 39*(5), 581–582.

Poole, D.C., & Jones, A.M. (2012). Oxygen uptake kinetics. *Comprehensive Physiology, 2*(2), 933–996.

Poole, D.C., & Jones, A.M. (2017). Measurement of the maximum oxygen uptake VO2max: VO2peak is no longer acceptable. *Journal of Applied Physiology, 122*(4), 997–1002.

Poole, D.C., Ward, S.A., Gardner, G.W., & Whipp, B.J. (1988). Metabolic and respiratory profile of the upper limit for prolonged exercise in man. *Ergonomics, 31*(9), 1265–1279.

Poole, D.C., Ward, S.A., & Whipp, B.J. (1990). The effects of training on the metabolic and respiratory profile of high-intensity cycle ergometer exercise. (1990). *European Journal of Applied Physiology, 59,* 421–429.

Poole, D.C., Wilkerson, D.P., & Jones, A.M. (2008). Validity of criteria for establishing maximal O2 uptake during ramp exercise tests. *European Journal of Applied Physiology, 102*(4), 403–410.

Porszasz, J., Casaburi, R., Somfay, A., Woodhouse, L.J., & Whipp, B.J. (2003). A treadmill ramp protocol using simultaneous changes in speed and grade. *Medicine & Science in Sports & Exercise, 35*(9), 1596–1603.

Pringle, J.S., & Jones, A.M. (2002). Maximal lactate steady state, critical power and EMG during cycling. *European Journal of Applied Physiology, 88*(3), 214–226.

Reilly, T., Morris, T., & Whyte, G. (2009). The specificity of training prescription and physiological assessment: a review. *Journal of Sports Science, 27*(6), 575–589.

Riboli, A., Emiliano, C., Rampichini, S., Venturelli, M., Alberti, G., Limonta, E., Veicsteinas, A., & Esposito F. (2016). Comparison between continuous and discontinuous incremental treadmill test to assess the velocity at VO2max. *Journal of Sports Medicine and Physical Fitness.* April 13 [Epub ahead of print].

Ricci, J., & Léger, L.A. (1983). VO2max of cyclists from treadmill, bicycle ergometer and velodrome tests. (1983). *European Journal of Applied Physiology and Occupational Physiology, 50*(2), 283–289.

Scheadler, C.M., & Devor, S.T. (2015). VO2max measured with a self-selected work rate protocol on an automated treadmill. *Medicine & Science in Sports & Exercise, 47*(10), 2158–2165.

Simon, J., Young, J.L., Gutin, B., Blood, D.K., & Case, R.B. (1983). Lactate accumulation relative to the anaerobic and respiratory compensation thresholds. *Journal of Applied Physiology: Respiratory, Environmental and Exercise Physiology, 54*(1), 13–17.

Smith, C.G., & Jones, A.M. (2001). The relationship between critical velocity, maximal lactate steady-state velocity and lactate turnpoint velocity in runners. *European Journal of Applied Physiology, 85*(1–2), 19–26.

Spencer, M.R., & Gastin, P.B. (2001). Energy system contribution during 200- to 1500-m running in highly trained athletes. *Medicine & Science in Sports & Exercise, 33*(1), 157–162.

Sperlich, P.F., Holmberg, H.C., Reed, J.L., Zinner, C., Mester, J., & Sperlich B. (2015). Individual versus standardized running protocols in the determination of VO2max. *Journal of Sports Science and Medicine, 14*(2), 386–393.

St Clair Gibson, A., Broomhead, S., Lambert, M.I., & Hawley, J.A. (1998). Prediction of maximal oxygen uptake from a 20-m shuttle run as measured directly in runners and squash players. *Journal of Sports Science, 16*(4), 331–335.

Straub, A.M., Midgley, A.W., Zavorsky, G.S., & Hillman, A.R. (2014). Ramp-incremented and RPE-clamped test protocols elicit similar VO2max values in trained cyclists. *European Journal of Applied Physiology, 114*(8), 1581–1590.

Stromme, S.B., Ingjer, F., & Meen, H.D. (1977). Assessment of maximal aerobic power in specifically trained athletes. *Journal of Applied Physiology: Respiratory, Environmental and Exercise Physiology, 42*(6), 833–837.

Tanaka, K., Matsuura, Y., Kumagai, S., Matsuzaka, A., Hirakoba, K., & Asano, K. (1983). Relationships of anaerobic threshold and onset of blood lactate accumulation with endurance performance. *European Journal of Applied Physiology and Occupational Physiology, 52*(1), 51–56.

Taylor, H.L., Buskirk, E., & Henschel, A. (1955). Maximal oxygen intake as an objective measure of cardio-respiratory performance. *Journal of Applied Physiology, 8*, 73–80.

Thomas, A., Dawson, B., & Goodman, C. (2006). The yo-yo test: reliability and association with a 20-m shuttle run and VO(2max). *International Journal of Sports Physiology and Performance, 1*(2),137–49.

Vanhatalo, A., Doust, J.H., & Burnley, M. (2007). Determination of critical power using a 3-min all-out cycling test. *Medicine & Science in Sports & Exercise, 39*(3), 548–555.

Whipp, B.J. (1971). Rate constant for the kinetics of oxygen uptake during light exercise. *Journal of Applied Physiology, 30*, 261–263.

Whipp, B.J., Davis, J.A., Torres, F., & Wasserman, K. (1981). A test to determine parameters of aerobic function during exercise. *Journal of Applied Physiology: Respiratory, Environmental and Exercise Physiology, 50*, 217–221.

Whipp, B.J., Davis, J.A., & Wasserman K. (1989). Ventilatory control of the 'isocapnic buffering' region in rapidly-incremental exercise. *Respiration Physiology, 76*, 357–367.

Whipp, B.J., & Wasserman, K. (1972). Oxygen uptake kinetics for various intensities of constant-load work. *Journal of Applied Physiology, 33*, 351–356.

Yoon, B.K., Kravitz, L., & Roberggs, R. (2007). VO2max, protocol duration, and the VO2 plateau. *Medicine & Science in Sports & Exercise, 39*(7), 1186–1192.

Zhang, Y.Y., Johnson, M.C. 2nd, Chow, N., & Wasserman K. (1991). Effect of exercise testing protocol on parameters of aerobic function. *Medicine & Science in Sports & Exercise, 23*(5), 625–630.

Zoladz, J.A., Rademaker, A.C., & Sargeant, A.J. (1995). Non-linear relationship between O2 uptake and power output at high intensities of exercise in humans. *Journal of Physiology, 488*(Pt 1), 211–217.

13 Body composition assessment

*Carl Langan-Evans, James P. Morton
and Graeme L. Close*

Part 1

Introduction

Anthropometry (from Greek *anthropos* "human" and *metron* "measure") refers to the scientific discipline concerned with multifactorial measurement of the human organism. A sub-discipline of anthropometry known as *kinanthropometry* is concerned with the measurement of morphological factors including proportion, composition, shape and maturation. *Body composition*, therefore, refers to the specific structures of the human body and namely the individual tissues these structures are composed of. To examine either differences or changes in these tissues, Wang and colleagues (1992) proposed a five-tier approach to body composition analysis sectioned into the atomic, molecular, cellular, tissue/system and whole body sections (see Table 13.1). Whilst an in-depth review of each of these sections is beyond the scope of this chapter, it is important for practitioners to examine and understand how these sections may be modulated via differing training and/or nutritional interventions. For the further practical examination of anthropometric body composition, the remainder of this chapter will concentrate on methods focused on the cellular, tissue/system and whole-body sections.

Exploration of the changes that occur at these differing sections are often *compartmentalised* dependent on the measurement method used (a whole-body measurement could be assessed in a single compartment, e.g. stature). At the whole-body section, changes in anthropometric factors such as stature, body mass (BM) and regional girths can be examined relatively simply via singular compartmental measurements. Examination of body composition changes at both the tissue/system and cellular sections can be further subdivided into methods which employ either anatomical or chemical measures of assessment (Ackland et al., 2012). These measures of assessment are generally divided into either two (fat mass [FM]; fat-free mass [FFM]) or three (FM; lean mass [LM]; bone mineral content [BMC]) compartmental models and it is also possible to multi-compartmentalise assessment using a combination of measurement techniques (e.g. FM; LBM; BMC; total body water [TBW]) (see Table 13.1).

To examine body composition sections and compartments effectively, practitioners also need to be aware of the many measurement tools available and their respective validity. Body composition measurement can be sectioned into three levels of validation hierarchy (Eston & Reilly, 2009) (see Table 13.1).

- **Level one** methods are classified as any direct measurement (e.g. stature, BM), whereas individual tissues can only be assessed through cadaveric dissection.

Table 13.1 Sections, compartments and validities of body composition measurement at differing levels. A section may be assessed by a range of measurement methods which have differing compartments and/or validities.

Sections	Compartmental model	Validity
1. Atomic Oxygen/carbon/hydrogen/other	**1. Singular** Body mass/stature/girths	**1. Direct**
2. Molecular Water/lipid/protein/other	**2. Two** Fat mass/fat free mass	**2. Indirect**
3. Cellular Cell mass/extracellular fluids/ extracellular solids	**3. Three** Fat mass/lean mass/bone mineral content	
4. Tissue/system Skeletal muscle/adipose tissue/ bone/blood/other	**4. Four** Fat mass/lean mass/bone mineral content/total body water	**3. Doubly indirect**
5. Whole body Human organism		

- **Level two** are indirect methods of body composition assessment, where via a specific measurement apparatus a subsequent estimation of body composition allows a calculation of tissues to be established.
- **Level three** are doubly indirect methods conducted utilising a level two measurement, were an estimation of body density is established and then often converted to an FM% using a prediction equation.

Level two methods are heavily reliant on the standardisation of their protocols to enhance accuracy of measurement, whereas level three methods also assume these factors with an additional confounding variable often based on highly sample-specific equations, e.g. sex, ethnicity, training status etc. Therefore practitioners should not only be aware of *what* they are measuring, but also *how* they are measuring body composition to ensure the most favourable levels of accuracy. Needless to say, however, the valid, reliable and accurate measurement of body composition can still be regarded as one of the most challenging fields of kinanthropometry.

Body composition tissues

Practitioners need to assess and examine changes in body composition over time in response to training and dietary manipulation and see how this relates to sporting performance. Three particular tissues that have associations with sporting performance are fat mass, lean mass and bone mineral content.

Fat mass

Fat mass (FM) can be subdivided into either essential or non-essential tissues. Essential FM tissues are stored in the organs (brain, heart, liver, kidneys, spleen, lungs and intestines) and bone marrow and entwine the central nervous system. Non-essential FM tissues can also be subdivided into both visceral (around the abdominal organs) and subcutaneous (contained under the skin surface) types. It is important to note that both of these FM tissues vary in quantity between individuals of differing age, sex and ethnicity, whilst also being mediated by nutritional intake and training status. Essential FM in females is higher than in males given the sex specific differences in endocrine related functioning for sexual reproduction. Typically females store up to 7% more essential FM, independent of the aforementioned areas including the breasts, pelvis and upper leg regions (Katch et al., 1980). On this basis essential FM levels are regarded as around 6% and 13% for males and females respectively. From a practical point of view, consider a scenario where a coach has set an acceptable level of FM across a male team squad at 10%. If we examined two players from the squad, where player 1 has a body mass of 70 kg and player 2 100 kg, then the allowance of total FM in kilograms would be 7 kg and 10 kg for each player, respectively. Given that essential FM is regarded as 6% in males, player 1 has 2.8 kg of additional FM whereas player 2 has 4 kg. It is on this basis that practitioners should understand the differences between both *absolute* and *relative* FM changes. In both males and females, essential FM tissues are ultimately required for fundamental physiological function and any reduction of these tissue masses will ultimately lead to the impairment of both health and performance (Keys et al., 1950).

Lean mass

Lean mass (LM) is of great interest to practitioners given that, fundamentally, increases in this tissue can potentially lead to performance enhancement via improved skeletal muscle contraction in strength-, power- and speed-based activities. LM is generally an individualised tissue given that is dependent on a number of factors (in the same manner as FM) including age, sex, somatotype and ethnicity as well as being modulated by nutrition and training-based activities that will either increase or decrease muscle volume content. Typically, when examined using three or four compartmental indirect measurement tools, LM estimations do not differentiate between differing protein-composed tissues, i.e. smooth, cardiac and skeletal muscle. It is also important to consider the chemical composition of these tissues as in the case of skeletal muscle, which is composed of only 20% protein structures (myosin, actin, tropomyosin, troponin, myoglobin), 5% salts, phosphates, ions, glycogen, intramuscular triglycerides and up to 75% water (McArdle et al., 2013). Given the implications of changes to these chemical compositions it is highly important to standardise body composition protocols prior to assessment, as discussed later in this chapter.

Bone mineral content

Bone mineral content (BMC) and also bone mineral density (BMD) are of interest to practitioners given that bone structure can be modulated via osteogenic stimulation as in the case of mechanical loading during various training interventions (Dalén & Olsson, 1974). BMC tissue is composed of 60% inorganic matter (mainly calcium and phosphorus) and 40% organic matter (mostly collagen). As with both FM and LM, BMC is also an individualised tissue dependent upon genetic, environmental, nutritional and training factors. In practice during body composition assessments, BMC and BMD can be established from multi-compartmental indirect methods such as dual X-ray absorptiometry (DXA), magnetic resonance imaging (MRI) or quantitative computerised tomography (pQCT) scans. Despite the aforementioned individualised nature of this tissue, some of these methods are able to generate Z and T scores for whole body and regional measurements, which are compared to large-scale generalised databases. However, there is debate about the effectiveness of these methods to assess both "true" BMC and BMD given their limitations. As DXA only measures in a 2D image and bases both BMC and BMD on bone size rather than volume, the method can only account for around 60% of the actual changes in bone tissues over repeated timescales (Seeman, 1998).

Body composition and sporting performance

Whilst methods to assess body composition have been continually developed, the importance of both anatomical and chemical body composition to sporting performance is consistently debated. The concept of "morphological optimisation" (Norton & Olds, 2001) highlights that an *ideal* body composition for sporting performance needs to be considered on an individualised basis. Given that only direct singular measurements of kinanthropometry, such as stature, BM and body mass index (BMI), have been found to statistically predict success in certain sporting events, it can be difficult to define what an ideal body composition may actually be for athletes of differing anthropometrical characteristics (Olds, 2009; Sinning, 1985). As certain morphological factors in athletes are constant at a given maturation status and cannot be manipulated in the same way BM can, the concept of an *optimum* composition of whole body tissues and their respective masses in differing sporting events can be controversial. In context, increases or decreases in BM can be modulated in a number of ways independent of changes to the aforementioned body composition tissues. For example in "weight" mediated sports, a low BM can be advantageous for sporting performance as in the case of gravitational sports, where mass hinders propulsion, also in weight-categorised sports, where a prescribed mass is required to compete, and aesthetic sports, where higher scores can be obtained based on lean body physique (Ackland et al., 2012). However, consistent loss of BM can lead to negative behaviours associated with disordered eating, low energy availability and acute/chronic dehydration which ultimately may lead to relative energy deficiency in sports (RED-S) syndromes (Mountjoy et al., 2014). Conversely sports that require a higher BM (such as rugby) may need athletes to increase mass independent of LM, i.e. via FM tissues, which is beneficial for greater momentum and collisions but negatively associated with performance-based acceleration relative power output (Olds, 2009) and relative aerobic capacity. There has been a plethora of research studies that have characterised the ideal body composition of a number of differing sporting events and whilst these can prove useful as a point of reference, practitioners must never lose site of the concept of morphological optimisation. When examining body composition, practitioners should take a global view of all the anthropometric factors which may lead to either improved or diminished sporting performance variables, as characterised in Table 13.2.

Measurement methodology – whole-body level

Body mass, stature and girth measurements are direct and singular compartmental methods that give simple data outputs, which are sensitive to longitudinal anthropometric change. These methods can also be combined to generate other outcome measures such as BMI.

Body mass

Body mass (synonymously described as weight) can be measured via weighing scales to generate values measured in kilograms (kg) and grams (g), pounds (lbs) or stones (st). Weighing

Table 13.2 Benefits of lower or higher values in anthropometrical variables for sporting performance.

Stature	Limb length	Body mass	Lean mass	Fat mass
Lower				
Rapid movement of the body for angular acceleration and gyration	Transferring load through high velocity and short distances	Acceleration and propulsion against gravity, heat dissipation or aesthetics/ weight categorisation	Propulsion against gravity for extended periods, heat dissipation or aesthetics/ weight categorisation	Greater power-to-mass ratio for acceleration and propulsion, heat dissipation or aesthetics/ weight categorisation
Higher				
Maximum distance or position for a pulled, thrown, stricken or caught object	High linear velocity requirement at the end of a limb during a pulling, throwing, striking or catching movement	High inertia/ momentum for movements and collisions or aesthetics/ weight categorisation	Greater power-to-mass ratio for acceleration and propulsion including moving external loads or aesthetics/ weight categorisation	Higher inertia/ momentum and collisions independent of increases in LM, sports which require buoyancy and/or heat insulation

scales operate by giving values that are indicative of the body's mass against gravitational acceleration (9.81 m•s^{-2}). Whilst generally accepted as a standardised piece of equipment there are factors that practitioners must consider when measuring BM with this apparatus. First is the type of weighing scale being utilised as there are multiple variations, including electronic (walk on/hanging) and spring (beam bar/dial/tubular) versions, measurement values of which cannot always be used interchangeably (see Figure 13.6) (Burns & Rohde, 1988). Generally electronic versions are best as these measure mass via a load cell sensor, which can be calibrated against known values to within 50 g (0.05 kg). Additional considerations include the geographical location and placement of a weighing scale as gravitational acceleration can differ up to 0.5% across the globe and any uneven grounding of the scale will result in measurement error (which is why many modern scales are now manufactured with integrated spirit levels).

Stature

Stature (synonymously described as height) can be measured via a stadiometer to generate values measured in metres (m), centimetres (cm) and millimetres (mm) or feet (ft) and inches (in). Stadiometers are composed of a ruler and sliding horizontal arm, which is positioned on top of the head (see Figure 13.7). Again, this apparatus is accepted as a standard piece of equipment, but practitioners must also take into account a number of considerations including both standing and sitting stature measurements. Positioning of the individual prior to measurement is also important, given foot placement, slouching and even breathing can all alter the measurement unless standardised (Stewart & Marfell-Jones, 2011).

Girths

Girth (also described as size) can be measured via anthropometric tape to generate values measured in cm, mm or in. Anthropometric tape measures are 7 mm in width with a 3 cm unmarked area prior to the zero-measurement line (see Figure 13.8). Again, whilst both a simple and standardised measurement tool there are also considerations that must be taken into account by practitioners prior to use. Anthropometric tape measures should be made of steel to limit extensibility yet flexible enough to allow movement around body segments, limbs and landmarks. Anthropometric tape measure types made of other materials should be calibrated to assess any potential levels of excessive extensibility, which may lead to measurement error. The practitioner must also consider the placement of the individual being measured including how standing/sitting positions and also muscle contractions can alter repeated measurements (Stewart & Marfell-Jones, 2011).

A study of the validity, reliability and technical error of repeated BM, stature and waist girth measurements (Geeta et al., 2009) highlighted that both intra- and inter-examiner applications were all within an acceptable 5% coefficient of variation. When taking into the consideration the aforementioned factors, trained practitioners can implement measurement of BM, stature and girths relatively easily and effectively.

Measurement methodology – cellular and tissue level

Densitometry

Densitometry is a two-compartmental indirect measurement method, which calculates the density of a given mass by either water volume or air displacement. Hydrodensitometry (hydrostatic or underwater weighing) calculates body density (BD) via the Archimedes principle where a mass will displace its own given volume within water. This method is particularly time-consuming and requires specialist equipment, often only found in scientific laboratories and not available to practitioners in the field. Air displacement plethysmography (ADP) is another method that utilises a similar principle of body volume (BV) calculation, which has now been commercialised in the form of the BODPOD (COSMED, Rome, Italy) (see Figure 13.26). A review by Fields and colleagues (2002) highlights that to initially calculate BD, ADP technology utilises the inverse pressure relationship via Poisson's Law in two separately enclosed chambers. For Poisson's Law to be applied, volumetric calculation must occur under adiabatic conditions (without the transfer of heat), which is why during measurement the use of a swim cap and lycra clothing is required to reduce isothermal air volumes near the skin and body hair (see Figure 13.27). Isothermal air generated by the lungs is then measured using the BODPOD inbuilt pulmonary plethysmography system or calculated using a prediction equation. Finally, once corrected BV has been established this is divided by BM to calculate BD, which generates body composition values of FM and FFM using a number of generalised predictive equations.

Skinfold assessment

Surface anthropometry via skinfold measurement is a two-compartmental indirect (if measured in sum of skinfolds) and doubly indirect (if a percentage of FM% is calculated) method, which is applied with the use of a calliper to a double fold of gripped skin (see

Figures 13.16 and 13.25) (Martin et al., 1985). In the initial stage, this method has a number of reliability issues including an assumption of constant skin thickness in the double fold between differing sites (both intra- and inter-individually) and constant skinfold compressibility. These factors are affected not only by age, sex, measurement site, skin temperature and hydration status but also by the grip of the anthropometrist and the pressure applied by the calliper (Martin et al., 1992).

To that end the International Society for the Advancement of Kinanthropometry (ISAK) was formed and an educational and certification platform established in an attempt to standardise a surface anthropometry skinfold protocol among practitioners (Stewart & Marfell-Jones, 2011). After initial measurement, an individual's body density is then estimated by an equation, which is often based on hydrodensitometry although recently more equations are being generated from DXA- and ADP-derived regressions (Eston & Reilly, 2009). In the third and final stage of measurement, FM is calculated from yet another predictive equation, which is often based on general populations with limited equations for athletic demographics (Reilly et al., 2009). Given the inaccuracies manifested in FM measurement generated from predictive skinfold equations, there has been a call for practitioners to focus solely on the use of the sum of skinfolds (often eight sites) as this can be a far more reliable and sensitive indicator of body compositional change over time (Johnston, 1982; Reilly et al., 2009). Table 13.3 highlights the lower, middle and upper values of a range of sports provided by high-performance practitioners working in the field.

Dual-energy X-ray absorptiometry

Dual-energy X-ray absorptiometry (DXA) is a three-compartmental indirect method and an in-depth review of the technical aspects of its use has been published by Bazzochi and colleagues (2016). DXA operates by initially passing both high- and low-energy X-ray

Table 13.3 Sum of skinfold measurements for lower, middle and upper values across a range of differing sports using the ISAK eight-site methodology including bicep, tricep, subscapular, abdomen, suprailiac, iliac crest, mid thigh and medial calf.

	Males			Females		
	Lower	*Middle*	*Upper*	*Lower*	*Middle*	*Upper*
Rugby						
Backs	40–45	45–60	60–75	55–60	60–70	70–80
Forwards	40–55	55–70	70–90	65–70	70–80	80–95
7s	45–50	50–65	65–75	-	-	-
Football	40–45	45–55	55–65	60–65	65–75	75–85
Road cycling	30–35	35–40	40–50	-	-	-
Distance running	30–40	40–45	45–55	40–55	55–70	70–85
Cricket						
Bowlers	55–60	60–70	70–80	75–80	80–100	100–120
Batsmen	70–80	80–100	100–120	90–100	100–120	120–140
Combat athletes	35–40	40–55	55–65	45–50	50–65	65–75
Tennis	40–45	45–55	55–65	50–55	55–65	65–75
Field hockey	35–45	45–60	60–70	55–65	65–80	80–90
Swimming	40–45	45–55	55–65	55–70	70–80	80–95

photons through the body via a pencil or fan beam (see Figure 13.30). The energy of these beams is attenuated by both the density and volume of differing body tissues, i.e. soft tissues (FM and LM) allow a greater passage of photons and harder tissues (BMC) allow less. At the secondary level, software is then utilised to calculate the coefficient of the two differing high- and low-energy peaks in order to generate an R-value, which is constant for BMC in all participants. Body composition of the differing compartment tissues is estimated via pixilation of the generated image 40–45% of which contains BMC and the remaining pixels are then utilised to calculate both FM and LM (see Figures 13.33 & 13.34). Recently, there have been a number of standardisation issues which highlight reduced reliability in DXA measurement including pre-scan nutritional (Bone et al., 2016), hydration (Toomey et al., 2017) and exercise (Nana et al., 2012) statuses and as such this has led to the development of a best-practice protocol (Nana et al., 2016, 2015). The dose of radiation delivered during measurement amounts to around 2–10 µSv dependent on the make, model and type of scan being utilised and, in comparison with other X-ray-based assessments which can vary from 50 to 10,000 µSv, this can be considered quite low. In context this is equal to only one day of annual natural background radiation experienced in normal living or is the equivalent to eating 100 g of Brazil nuts or five bananas. However, despite this, practitioners should be aware of both legal and ethical constraints which must be considered prior to use of DXA and this may differ in differing geographical locations.

Bioelectrical impedance analysis

Bioelectrical impedance analysis (BIA) is a multi-compartmental doubly indirect method, grounded on the principle that an electrical current can pass at varying rates throughout the body and as such can establish the composition of differing tissues based on their conductivity (see Figures 13.28 and 13.29) (Dehghan & Merchant, 2008).

As LM contains both intra- and extracellular water, the electrical current flow is able to pass freely whereas in non-conducting tissues, e.g. FM, conductivity is reduced. In the initial stage BIA operates on the assumption that the body has a consistent composition with a fixed cross-sectional area and identical density distribution (Dehghan & Merchant, 2008). Secondly, as BIA calculation of body composition is based on the flow of electrical current through total body fluid, the connected limb, i.e. arms and/or legs, contributes a large proportion of the whole-body impedance (approximately 50%) despite their limited overall contribution to total BM. Conversely the trunk, which has the greatest contribution to total BM, only provides a small proportion of the whole body impedance (approximately 12%) (Coppini et al., 2005). Finally (and similarly to anthropometric skinfold assessment) BIA then calculates body composition via equations, which are again population-specific and cannot be applied to generalised demographics (Ward et al., 2000). There have been a number of studies showing that the accuracy and reliability of BIA are reduced further when nutritional (Slinde & Rossander-Hulthen, 2001) and hydration status (Lukaski et al., 1986), exercise (Caton et al., 1988) and body temperature (Gudivaka et al., 1996) are not standardised prior to assessment.

Comparing results from differing methods

There has been a large body of research examining the relationships between all the aforementioned cellular and tissue body composition methods given they can all generate values of FM. In the majority of these studies either hydrodensitometry or DXA are referred to as the criterion method against which other measures are compared. Given the many assumptions that both of these methods are based upon (as highlighted earlier) practitioners must approach the results of these studies with caution. When both hydrodensitometry and DXA have been assessed against a true criterion method, i.e. cadaveric dissection, neither can accurately assess FM values (Elowsson et al., 1998) or LM and BMC in the case of DXA (Scafoglieri et al., 2011). Practitioners must also be aware that results using the same method but with differing makes and models of assessment tool are also not able to be easily compared. For example there are three differing models of DXA scanning machines, values of which cannot be compared interchangeably (Genton et al., 2002; Tothill et al., 1994) and even intra-generated values from the same model of scanner have been shown to differ (Lantz et al., 1999; Paton et al., 1995).

Practitioners must pragmatically consider that as each method is based on differing compartmental models, with either indirect or doubly indirect validities and differing standardisation procedures, the comparison of these methods is fraught with complication. Therefore, measurements of the same tissue with differing methods cannot be used interchangeably with any degree of accuracy.

Case study example from practice

Taken from an interventional case study conducted at our laboratory, a male combat sport athlete (age 19 years; stature 166.3 cm; BM 72.5 kg; competing in a 68 kg weight category) wanted to assess the possibility of competing in a 63 kg category over an 8-week time period, in order to gain competitive advantages in limb length given his limited stature. To make an initial judgement about the feasibility of this, BM losses would need to be informed by at least a tissue/system and multi-compartmental apparatus with the highest possible level of validity. In this instance the measurement was provided by DXA. The athlete's DXA results (subtotal minus the head) showed that the athlete had 2.2 kg of BMC, 54.5 kg of LM and 11.3 kg of FM. To determine the possibility that the athlete could make the weight category both safely and effectively an estimative calculation of essential FM at the target BM was required as follows:

63 kg BM/100 × 6% essential FM = 3.8 kg

If this value is rounded to 4 kg then it was possible for the athlete to lose around 7 kg of FM and by subtracting this value from the current BM (72.5 kg) achieve a target BM of 65.5 kg without any disruption to both health and performance. The 2.5 kg of additional mass could be further reduced using acute BM manipulation techniques, i.e. reducing gut content, sodium intake, limited acute dehydration (Reale et al., 2017). As DXA could not be used too frequently due to the associated ethical and legislative constraints, measurements of sum of skinfolds (Σ8SKf) taken at the eight standard ISAK sites were assessed weekly to examine change at more regular intervals (see Figure 13.2). DXA measurements were sequentially repeated at 4 weeks and 7 weeks and also the day prior and the day of weigh-in. At 4 weeks, the athlete had reduced BM by 5.1 kg (see Figure 13.1) with a 17.3 mm reduction in Σ8SKf thickness which occurred at a weekly range of 5.3–6.3 mm in tandem with associated weekly BM losses. FM was reduced by 2.6 kg (see Figures 13.4 and 13.5) whilst LM (see Figure 13.3) and BMC remained stable at 55.0 kg and 2.2 kg respectively. As highlighted, the associated loss of BM cannot be explained by losses in FM alone (this could potentially be attributed to differences in gut content), which adds to the previous issues emphasised earlier on in the chapter with the measurement of BC utilising DXA technology.

At 7 weeks (1 week prior to weigh-in) the athlete further reduced BM by another 1.4 kg and Σ8SKf thickness by 6.5 mm. Again, there was a 1.8 kg reduction in FM whilst LM (54.6 kg) and BMC (2.3 kg) remained stable. As both BM and FM values reduced by lesser values than the previous time course the associated Σ8SKf thickness reduction was also less (ranging from 1.4 to 3.0 mm per week), demonstrating the sensitivity of skinfold measurement at repeated time points. Whilst not as informative as DXA, in terms of highlighting the losses of mass in associated tissues, it is clear that the athlete was reducing body composition and was now approaching the lower limit of skinfold thickness, as highlighted in Table 13.3.

The athlete achieved the target weight category, weighing in at 62.7 kg, manipulating gut content and sodium balance in the final 7-day period with a further 1.8 kg loss of BM achieved by inducing acute dehydration. Concomitantly, Σ8SKf was still sensitive enough to highlight these losses with a further 4.7 mm reduction. DXA values measured at the day before and day of weigh-in highlight the reductions of differing associated tissues at the various stages of BM manipulation. BMC remained stable throughout at 2.3 kg, whereas FM was only reduced by a further 0.5 kg and LM now reduced by 1.6 kg in the 7 days and furthermore by 2.1 kg in the final 24 hours prior to weigh-in. This emphasises the fact that DXA does indeed measure more than just skeletal muscle contractile proteins given that reductions in LM values are more likely attributed to reductions in gut/muscle glycogen content and TBW.

Overall the athlete lost 9.8 kg of BM of which 4.9 kg in FM and 3.7 in LM as measured via DXA. As stressed earlier this demonstrates the difficulty in assessing body compositional change accurately and at best (even with well standardised procedures) the estimative nature of generated values. However, it must be highlighted that utilising these tools still allows a practitioner to make informed decisions when it comes to training and nutritional modulation.

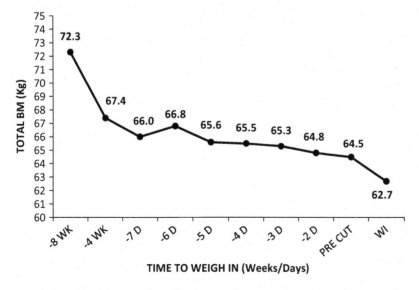

Figure 13.1 Time course of total body mass losses in a male combat sport athlete over an 8 week period prior to weigh-in.

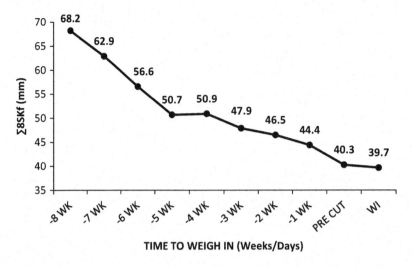

Figure 13.2 Time course of Σ8SKf in a male combat sport athlete over an 8 week period prior to weigh-in.

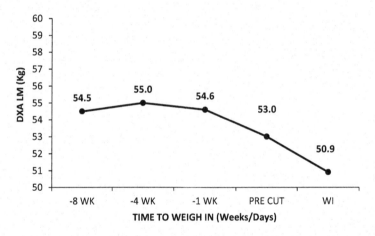

Figure 13.3 Time course of LM changes measured by DXA in a male combat sport athlete over an 8 week period prior to weigh-in.

Conclusion

If a complete view of body composition is required, then the use of multi-compartmental methods such as DXA to measure changes over defined time points can be valuable. However, it is clear that these measurement methods are both expensive and can require a high degree of standardisation to be accurate, which may be beyond the scope of practice. It can be perfectly acceptable for practitioners to employ simple direct and indirect measures, i.e. BM, stature, girths and sum of skinfolds, to examine changes across more frequent assessments of body composition. However, as with multi-compartmental methods, these still required

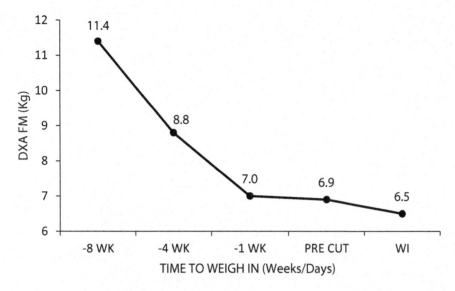

Figure 13.4 Time course of FM changes measured by DXA in a male combat sport athlete over an 8 week period prior to weigh-in.

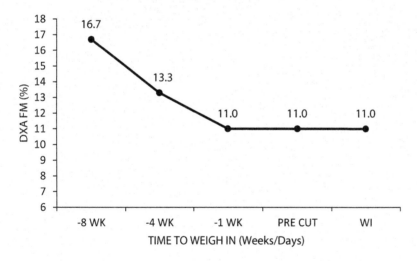

Figure 13.5 Time course of FM% changes measured by DXA in a male combat sport athlete over an 8 week period prior to weigh-in.

to be standardised and can only give a limited view of changes that occur to body composition in the differing tissues. Whatever the context and whichever measurement tools may be available, it is key to gather as much information as possible to decipher body compositional adjustments that have changed or will change as a result of differing training and/or nutritional interventions. Finally, the importance of morphological optimisation and which anthropometric factors are holistically required for sporting performance of athletes of differing gender, ethnicity, maturation status and sporting events should always be considered.

Part 2

Whole body anthropometry (body mass)

Equipment

- ideally an electronic or spring scale

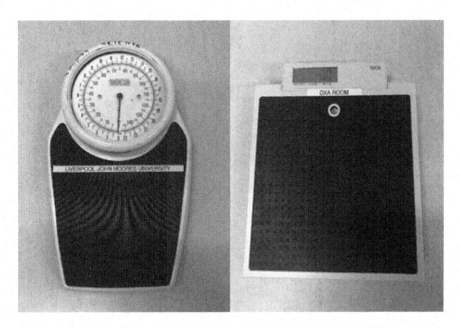

Figure 13.6 Walk-on spring dial (left image) and electronic (right image) BM weighing scales.

Participant standardisation procedure

BM should be measured at the same time of day during each test (ideally in the morning). The participant should be euhydrated and have evacuated the bowel and bladder. All jewellery and footwear should be removed. Clothing can be removed or the same attire worn each time.

Testing procedure

Stage 1: Ensure scale is calibrated according to manufacturer's guidelines and positioned on a level surface.

Stage 2: Direct participant to stand on the scale and remain still during measurement.

Stage 3: Record stable measurement and repeat procedure for second measurement if a high level of accuracy is required.

Whole body anthropometry (stature)

Equipment

- stadiometer

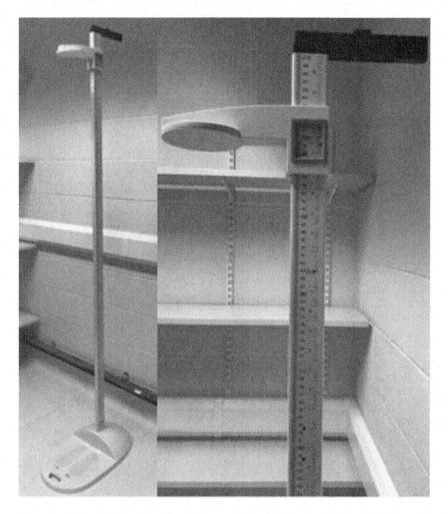

Figure 13.7 Standing stadiometer (left image) and sliding arm (right image).

Participant standardisation procedure

Stature should be measured at the same time of day during each test (ideally in the morning). Participants' footwear should be removed.

Testing procedure

Stage 1: Ensure the stadiometer is positioned on a level surface.

Stage 2: Direct participant to stand on the stadiometer plate with feet together and have the posterior segments (heels, gluteals and upper back) touching the measuring ruler. Ensure the participant head position is neutral, looking directly forward, and instruct them to inhale and then exhale prior to moving the sliding arm to the top of the head.

Stage 3: Record stable measurement and repeat procedure for second measurement if a high level of accuracy is required. Stature in conjunction with BM values can be used to generate BMI utilising the following calculation of BM in kg divided by stature in metres squared (kg/m^2).

Surface anthropometry (girths)

Equipment

- anthropometric tape measure

Figure 13.8 Anthropometric tape measure.

Participant standardisation procedure

Girth measurements should be conducted at the same time of day during each test. The participant should be euhydrated and clothing can be repositioned and/or removed as required for each measurement site.

Testing procedure

Stage 1: Neck – with the participant's head in neutral position the neck girth measurement is taken at the superior point of the Adam's apple with care taken not to pull the tape too tight and compress the skin.

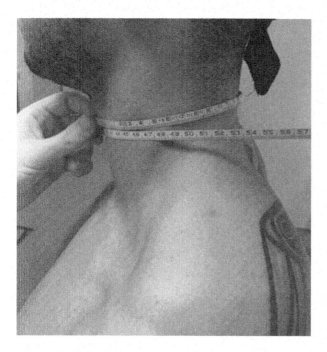

Figure 13.9 The neck girth position.

Stage 2: Relaxed arm – with the participant's arm positioned at the side of the body the relaxed arm measurement is taken at the midpoint between the acromion process and the radial head.

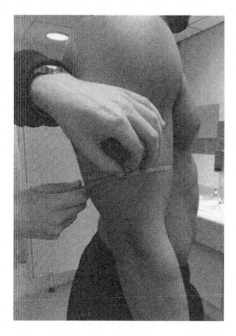

Figure 13.10 The relaxed arm girth position.

Stage 3: Flexed/tensed arm – with the arm in a flexed position and parallel to the ground, the participant is requested to forcibly tense the bicep muscle and the flexed/tensed arm girth measurement is taken at the peak girth site or alternatively at the same site as the relaxed arm girth measurement.

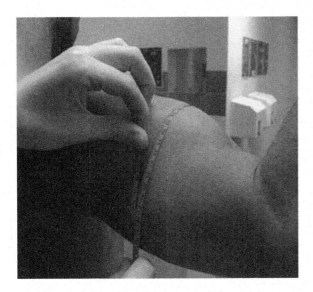

Figure 13.11 The flexed/tensed arm girth position.

Stage 4: Waist – with the participant's arms folded at the chest, the waist girth measurement is taken between the lowest (tenth) rib border and the iliac crest. The participant should breathe normally and the measurement is taken at the end of an exhalation with the tape in neutral position.

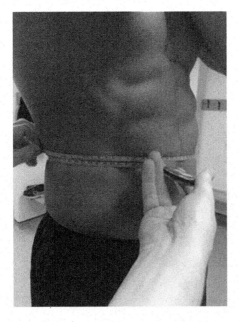

Figure 13.12 The waist girth position.

Stage 5: Hips – with the participant's arms folded at the chest, the hip girth measurement is taken at the widest point of the gluteals with the tape in a neutral position.

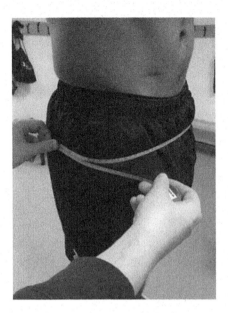

Figure 13.13 The hip girth position.

Stage 6: Thigh (mid position) – with the participant's arms folded at the chest, the thigh girth measurement is taken at the midpoint between the greater trochanter and the lateral condyle of the tibia.

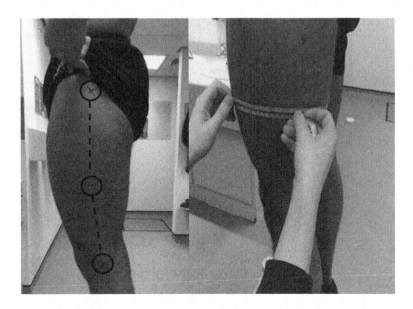

Figure 13.14 The midpoint position between the greater trochanter and the lateral condyle of the tibia and the mid-thigh girth position.

Stage 7: Calf – with the participant's arms folded at the chest and the leg placed at a 90°
flexed standing position, the calf girth measurement is taken at the peak girth position
with the tape in neutral position.

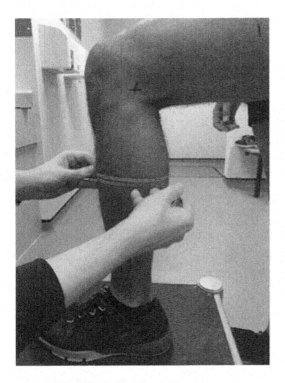

Figure 13.15 The calf girth position.

See ISAK International Standards for Anthropometric Assessment by Stewart and Marfell-
Jones (2011) for a more in-depth review of girth positions and measurements.

Surface anthropometry (skinfolds)

Equipment

- skinfold callipers (ISAK recommend Harpenden metal callipers and these should be calibrated to at least 40 mm in 0.2 mm divisions)
- anthropometric tape measure
- marking pen

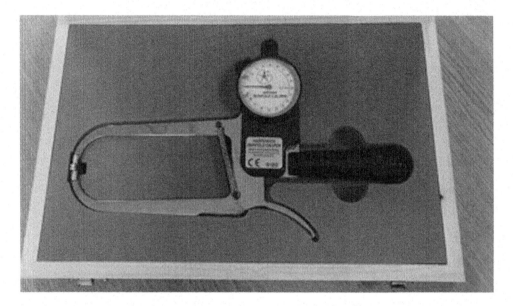

Figure 13.16 Skinfold measurement equipment (Harpenden callipers).

Participant standardisation procedure

Skinfolds should be measured at the same time of day during each test (ideally in the morning). The participant should be euhydrated and clothing can be repositioned and/or removed as required for each measurement site.

Testing procedure

Stage 1: Triceps – with the participant's arm relaxed by the side of the body a measurement is taken at the midpoint between the acromion process and the radial head. The triceps skinfold site is positioned at the posterior part of the arm from the midpoint site.

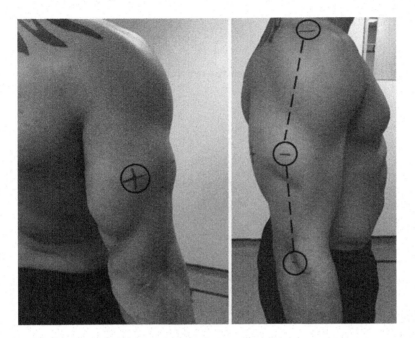

Figure 13.17 The midpoint position between the acromion process and the radial head and the triceps skinfold site.

Stage 2: Biceps – with the participant's arm abducted and at the same measurement position between the acromion process and the radial head, the biceps skinfold site is positioned at the anterior part of the arm from the midpoint site.

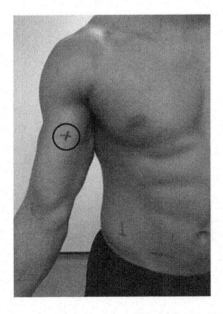

Figure 13.18 The biceps skinfold site.

Stage 3: Subscapular – with the participant's arm relaxed by the side of the body, palpate the inferior point of the scapular and draw a lateral 2 cm line at a 45°. The subscapular skinfold site is positioned at the midpoint of the line.

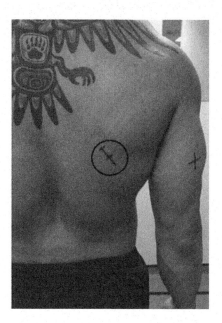

Figure 13.19 The subscapular skinfold site.

Stage 4: Iliac crest – with the participant's arms folded at the chest, palpate the border of the ilium and locate/mark the most superior point (the iliac crest). The iliac crest skinfold site is located at the superior point above this marking at the natural fold of the skin.

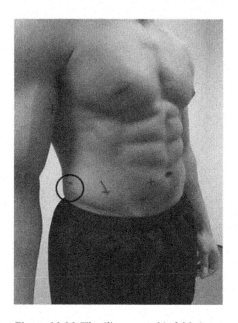

Figure 13.20 The iliac crest skinfold site.

Stage 5: Suprailiac (also referred to by ISAK as the supraspinale) – with the participant's arms folded at the chest, palpate the border of the ilium and locate/mark the most inferior point. The suprailiac skinfold site is located above this marking at the natural fold of the skin in line with the iliac crest skinfold site and diagonal to the axilla (armpit).

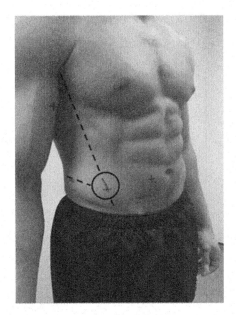

Figure 13.21 The suprailiac skinfold site.

Stage 6: Abdomen – with the participant's arm relaxed by the side of the body, mark a position 5 cm to the right-hand side of the centre point of the navel.

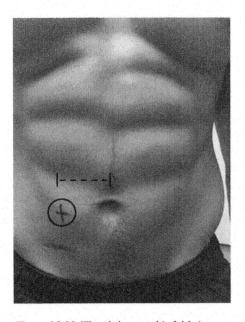

Figure 13.22 The abdomen skinfold site.

Stage 7: Thigh (anterior position) – with the participant seated and the knee bent at 90°, a measurement is taken at the midpoint between the inguinal fold and the superior border of the patella. The thigh skinfold site is positioned at the anterior part of the leg from the midpoint site.

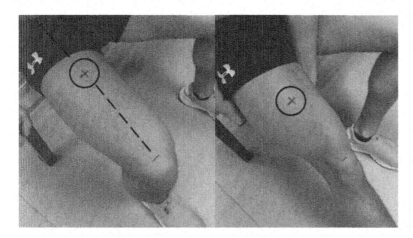

Figure 13.23 The anterior thigh skinfold site with knee flexed at 90° (left image) or extended and supported for participants with reduced skinfold thickness (right image).

Stage 8: Calf (medial position) – with the participant's arms folded at the chest and the leg placed at a 90° flexed standing position, the calf skinfold measurement is taken at the medial position of the peak calf girth measurement position (see Figure 13.14).

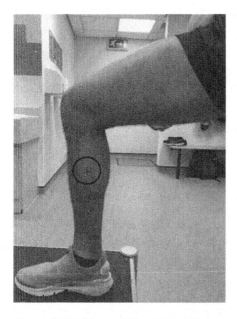

Figure 13.24 The medial calf skinfold site.

Pinch procedure: skinfold measurements are taken at the marked line of each respective site. The area should be pinched and raised so that a double fold of skin plus the underlying subcutaneous FM tissue (with attention taken not to pinch LM tissue) is held between the thumb and index finger of the non-dominant hand (see Figure 13.25).

Measurement procedure: the nearest edge of the skinfold calliper jaws is applied 1 cm away from the edge of the pinch site. If the calliper is placed too deep or too shallow incorrect values may be recorded so practice is necessary to ensure the same pinch size and location for repeated measures (see Figure 13.25). Measurement is recorded 2 seconds after the full pressure of the calliper is applied and all sites should be measured twice (in the same order as listed) to examine technical error of measurement (TEM) values. If the initial two values have a greater TEM than 5% then a third round of measurements should be conducted.

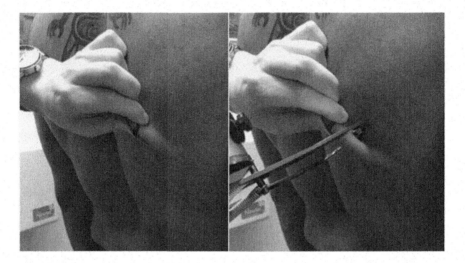

Figure 13.25 The skinfold pinch (left image) and measurement (right image) procedures.

Once the measurements have been recorded these should be collated together to generate the Σ8SKf, which can be compared to respective sports in Table 13.3. Subsequent estimations of FM% can be generated utilising BD via the equations of either Siri (495/BD) – 450 or Brozek (457/BD) – 414.2.

See ISAK International Standards for Anthropometric Assessment by Stewart and Marfell-Jones (2011) for a more in-depth review of skinfold sites and measurements.

Air displacement plethysmography (ADP)

Equipment

- ADP unit, i.e. the BODPOD (positioned in an area with a thermoneutral environment)
- computer, monitor, software
- calibration cylinder
- electronic scale
- stadiometer
- nose clip

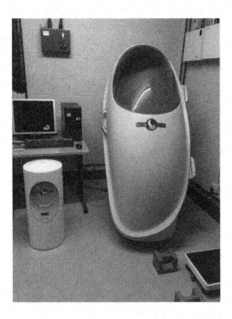

Figure 13.26 BODPOD ADP unit, calibration cylinder and measuring equipment.

Participant standardisation procedure

The participant should be euhydrated, have evacuated the bowel and bladder and not conducted any exercise prior to the testing procedure. All jewellery and clothing should be removed and the participant should wear a tight-fitting swimsuit or compression clothing as well as a swim cap to compress head hair. For male participants, any facial hair should be removed or compressed in a similar manner to head hair.

Figure 13.27 Participant attire for ADP assessment.

Testing procedure

Stage 1: Participant's information is entered into the software system including names, date of birth, gender, stature and ethnicity. An ID can be assigned to the participant and all information retrieved for future measurement.

Stage 2: An appropriate density model and thoracic gas volume (either measured, retrieved from a previous test, predicted or manually entered) are selected.

Stage 3: An initial volume calibration is conducted with the testing chamber empty. If measured thoracic volume has been selected, then a disposable filter and breathing tube should also be entered into the chamber at this stage.

Stage 4: A second volume calibration is conducted with the calibration cylinder being placed in the chamber.

Stage 5: The software will then prompt for the participant to have their BM measured on the electronic scale.

Stage 6: The participant then enters the chamber for two 50 second measurements. In between each measurement the door to the chamber is opened and closed. If the measurements are within 150 ml then the average of the two measurements is used. If they are outside this range a third measurement it conducted. If the third measurement is unsuccessful go back to Stage 3 and repeat initial calibration. Participant movement, heavy breathing patterns and/or coughing/sneezing can induce measurement error.

Stage 7: If the measured thoracic gas volume has been selected then the participant remains in the chamber, they attach the nose clip and put the breathing tube into their mouth. They follow the same breathing pattern as prompted by the software system.

Stage 8: Once measurement has concluded, the software system will automatically generate the body composition data and these can be printed or exported to an external package such as Microsoft Excel for further analysis.

See www.youtube.com/watch?v=FoGHJAj32W4 for instructional video.

Bioelectrical impedance analysis (BIA)

Equipment

- BIA unit
- computer, monitor, software
- cable leads
- electrodes
- alcohol wipes
- electronic scale
- stadiometer

Figure 13.28 Eight-site tetra-polar standing BIA system.

Participant standardisation procedure

The participant should be fasted and have not conducted any exercise for 8 hours prior to the testing procedure. The participant should be euhydrated and have evacuated the bowel and bladder. All jewellery should be removed. For lead and electrode-based bi-polar (hand to hand or foot to foot) and tetra-polar (hand to foot) systems, the participant should lie in a supine position on a non-metallic surface with arms and legs separated from the trunk for 10 minutes prior to assessment.

Testing procedure

Stage 1: Dependent on which system is used, commence calibration according to the manufacturer's guidelines.

Stage 2: Measure the participant's BM on the electronic scale and stature on the stadiometer.

Stage 3: Participant's information is entered into the unit directly or the unit software system including names, date of birth, gender, stature and BM (and in some systems ethnicity).

Stage 4: Clean conductor sites with alcohol swipes, i.e. hands, bottom of feet or for lead-based systems all sites where the electrodes will be placed.

Stage 5: Stand on electrodes and/or hold hand grip electrodes (see Figure 13.28). For lead-based systems see Figure 13.29 for tetra-polar electrode placement.

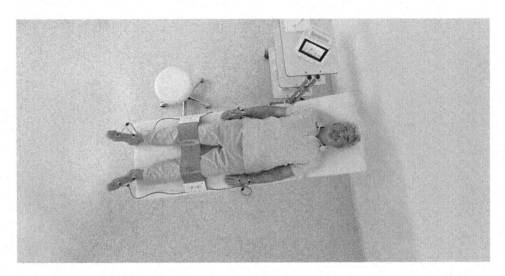

Figure 13.29 Four-site tetra-polar lead-based BIA system.

Stage 6: Commence measurement according to manufacturer's guidelines.

Stage 7: Body composition and impedance data can be assessed directly from the unit or the software system according to manufacturer's guidelines.

Dual X-ray absorptiometry (DXA)

Equipment

- DXA unit
- computer, monitor, software
- spine phantom block
- electronic scale
- stadiometer
- foam padding

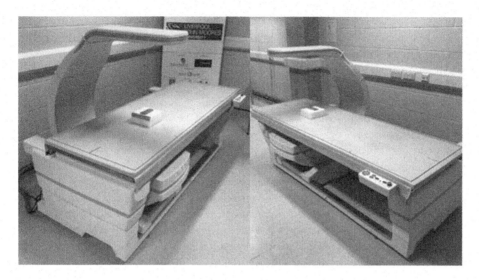

Figure 13.30 Hologic Horizon DXA system and spine phantom.

Participant standardisation procedure

The participant should be fasted and have not conducted any exercise for 8 hours prior to the testing procedure. The participant should be euhydrated and have evacuated the bowel and bladder. All jewellery should be removed. Given the low dosage of radiation delivered during scans all female participants must be asked about the possibility of pregnancy.

Testing procedure

Stage 1: Dependent on which system is used, commence calibration according to the manufacturer's guidelines including relevant spine phantom, step phantom and radiographic uniformity tests (see Figure 13.31).

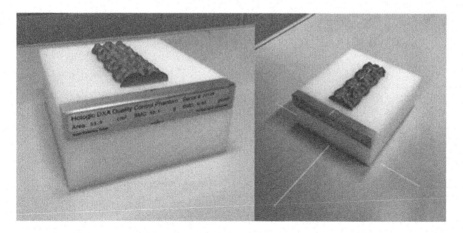

Figure 13.31 Hologic Horizon DXA system spine phantom and placement for calibration.

Stage 2: Measure the participant's BM on the electronic scale and stature on the stadiometer.

Stage 3: Participant's information is entered into the software system including names, date of birth, gender, ethnicity, stature and BM. An ID can be assigned to the participant and all information retrieved for future measurement.

Stage 4: The participant is directed to lie supine in a central position on the DXA bed (see Figure 13.32). Traction of the participant's neck and legs should be conducted to improve spinal alignment and foam padding can be used to separate the arms in an abducted position. Legs should be positioned with a gap between the feet in a supinated position (tape can be used if the participant is uncomfortable holding this position). For individuals of high stature the participant should be positioned so the lower portion of the body is included in the scan and the head is outside the scanning area. For individuals of large BM and/or surface area the scan can be conducted on one half of the body segment and then repeated on the opposite side. Some DXA software systems will automatically generate a whole scan based on one half body segment but this is just a symmetrical image of the initial scan and may not be an accurate reflection of BM in the opposing segment.

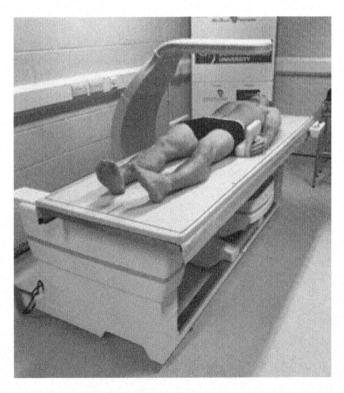

Figure 13.32 Hologic Horizon DXA system with participant placement.

Stage 5: Measurement should be commenced according to manufacturer's guidelines and the participant directed not to move during the scan and remain as still as possible.

Stage 6: Analysis should be conducted by segmenting the participant's scan into respective regions, i.e. arms, trunk and legs. Dependent on the system used and where directed analysis of the android/gynoid regions/ratios should be conducted (see Figure 13.33).

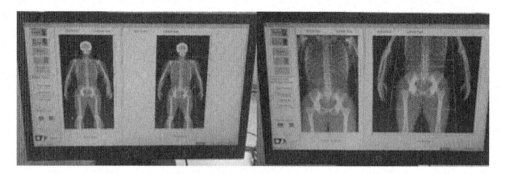

Figure 13.33 Hologic Horizon DXA system software scan with regional analysis (left image) and android/gynoid ratio analysis (right image).

Stage 7: Results are then generated by the system software which highlight both regional BMC/BMD and BC (Figure 13.34). These results can be saved for further re-analysis and also printed (Figure 13.35) as required. Results should be interpreted minus the head segment value (where the system allows).

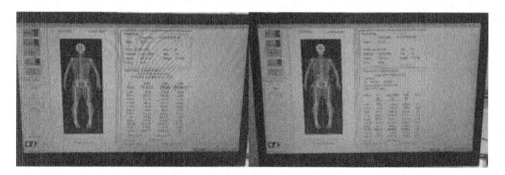

Figure 13.34 Hologic Horizon DXA system software scan results for BMC and BMD (left image) and regional BC analysis (right image).

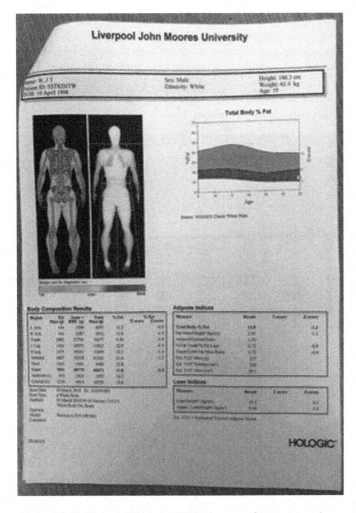

Figure 13.35 Hologic Horizon DXA system software printed scan results for regional BC analysis including adipose/lean indices and z-scores.

See paper by Nana et al. 2014 for DXA Best Practice Protocol: https://journals.
humankinetics.com/doi/pdf/10.1123/ijsnem.2013-0228.

References

Ackland, T.R., Lohman, T.G., Sundgot-Borgen, J., Maughan, R.J., Meyer, N.L., Stewart,
A.D., & Muller, W. (2012). Current status of body composition assessment in sport: review
and position statement on behalf of the ad hoc research working group on body composition health and performance, under the auspices of the I.O.C. Medical Commission. *Sports
Medicine, 42*(3), 227–249. doi:10.2165/11597140-000000000-00000.
Bazzocchi, A., Ponti, F., Albisinni, U., Battista, G., & Guglielmi, G. (2016). DXA: Technical
aspects and application. *European Journal of Radiology, 85*(8), 1481–1492. doi:10.1016/
j.ejrad.2016.04.004

Bone, J.L., Ross, M.L., Tomcik, K.A., Jeacocke, N.A., Hopkins, W.G., & Burke, L.M. (2016). Manipulation of Muscle Creatine and Glycogen Changes DXA Estimates of Body Composition. *Medicine & Science in Sports & Exercise*. doi:10.1249/mss.0000000000001174

Burns, J.O., & Rohde, J.E. (1988). Weighing scales: design and choices. *Indian Journal of Pediatrics, 55*(1 Suppl.), S31–37.

Caton, J.R., Mole, P.A., Adams, W.C., & Heustis, D.S. (1988). Body composition analysis by bioelectrical impedance: effect of skin temperature. *Medicine & Science in Sports & Exercise, 20*(5), 489–491.

Coppini, L.Z., Waitzberg, D.L., & Campos, A.C. (2005). Limitations and validation of bioelectrical impedance analysis in morbidly obese patients. *Current Opinion in Clinical Nutrition & Metabolic Care, 8*(3), 329–332.

Dalén, N., & Olsson, K.E. (1974). Bone Mineral Content and Physical Activity. *Acta Orthopaedica Scandinavica, 45*(1–4), 170–174. doi:10.3109/17453677408989136.

Dehghan, M., & Merchant, A.T. (2008). Is bioelectrical impedance accurate for use in large epidemiological studies? *Nutrition Journal, 7*, 26–26. doi:10.1186/1475-2891-7-26.

Elowsson, P., Forslund, A.H., Mallmin, H., Feuk, U., Hansson, I., & Carlsten, J. (1998). An evaluation of dual-energy X-Ray absorptiometry and underwater weighing to estimate body composition by means of carcass analysis in piglets. *Journal of Nutrition, 128*(9), 1543–1549.

Eston, R.G., & Reilly, T. (2009). *Kinanthropometry and exercise physiology laboratory manual: Tests, procedures and data.* Abingdon, Oxon: Routledge.

Fields, D.A., Goran, M.I., & McCrory, M.A. (2002). Body-composition assessment via air-displacement plethysmography in adults and children: a review. *American Journal of Clinical Nutrition, 75*(3), 453–467.

Geeta, A., Jamaiyah, H., Safiza, M.N., Khor, G.L., Kee, C.C., Ahmad, A.Z., ... Faudzi, A. (2009). Reliability, technical error of measurements and validity of instruments for nutritional status assessment of adults in Malaysia. *Singapore Medical Journal, 50*(10), 1013–1018.

Genton, L., Hans, D., Kyle, U.G., & Pichard, C. (2002). Dual-energy X-ray absorptiometry and body composition: differences between devices and comparison with reference methods. *Nutrition, 18*(1), 66–70.

Gudivaka, R., Schoeller, D., & Kushner, R.F. (1996). Effect of skin temperature on multifrequency bioelectrical impedance analysis. *Journal of Applied Physiology, 81*(2), 838–845.

Johnston, F.E. (1982). Relationships between body composition and anthropometry. *Human Biology, 54*(2), 221–245.

Katch, V.L., Campaigne, B., Freedson, P., Sady, S., Katch, F.I., & Behnke, A.R. (1980). Contribution of breast volume and weight to body fat distribution in females. *American Journal of Physical Anthropology, 53*(1), 93–100. doi:10.1002/ajpa.1330530113.

Keys, A., Brozek, J., Henschel, A., Michelsen, O., Taylor, H.L., Simonson, E., ... Wells, S.M. (1950). *The biology of human starvation.* Vols. 1 and 2: Minneapolis.: University of Minnesota Press.

Lantz, H., Samuelson, G., Bratteby, L.E., Mallmin, H., & Sjostrom, L. (1999). Differences in whole body measurements by DXA-scanning using two Lunar DPX-L machines. *International Journal of Obesity and Related Metabolic Disorders, 23*(7), 764–770.

Lukaski, H.C., Bolonchuk, W.W., Hall, C.B., & Siders, W.A. (1986). Validation of tetrapolar bioelectrical impedance method to assess human body composition. *Journal of Applied Physiology, 60*(4), 1327–1332.

Martin, A.D., Drinkwater, D.T., Clarys, J.P., Daniel, M., & Ross, W.D. (1992). Effects of skin thickness and skinfold compressibility on skinfold thickness measurement. *American Journal of Human Biology, 4*(4), 453–460. doi:10.1002/ajhb.1310040404.

Martin, A.D., Ross, W.D., Drinkwater, D.T., & Clarys, J.P. (1985). Prediction of body fat by skinfold caliper: assumptions and cadaver evidence. *International Journal of Obesity, 9*(Suppl. 1), 31–39.

McArdle, W.D., Katch, F.I., & Katch, V.L. (2013). *Sports and exercise nutrition.* Philadelphia: Wolters Kluwer/Lippincott Williams & Wilkins.

Mountjoy, M., Sundgot-Borgen, J., Burke, L., Carter, S., Constantini, N., Lebrun, C., ... Ljungqvist, A. (2014). The IOC consensus statement: Beyond the female athlete triad–relative energy deficiency in sport (RED-S). *British Journal of Sports Medicine, 48*(7), 491–497. doi:10.1136/bjsports-2014–093502.

Nana, A., Slater, G.J., Hopkins, W.G., & Burke, L.M. (2012). Effects of daily activities on dual-energy X-ray absorptiometry measurements of body composition in active people. *Medicine & Science in Sports & Exercise, 44*(1), 180–189. doi:10.1249/MSS.0b013e318228b60e.

Nana, A., Slater, G.J., Hopkins, W.G., Halson, S.L., Martin, D.T., West, N.P., & Burke, L.M. (2016). Importance of standardized DXA protocol for assessing physique changes in athletes. *International Journal of Sport Nutrition and Exercise Metabolism, 26*(3), 259–267. doi:10.1123/ijsnem.2013-0111

Nana, A., Slater, G.J., Stewart, A.D., & Burke, L.M. (2015). Methodology review: using dual-energy X-ray absorptiometry (DXA) for the assessment of body composition in athletes and active people. *International Journal of Sport Nutrition and Exercise Metabolism, 25*(2), 198–215. doi:10.1123/ijsnem.2013-0228

Norton, K., & Olds, T. (2001). Morphological evolution of athletes over the 20th century: causes and consequences. *Sports Medicine, 31*(11), 763–783.

Olds, T. (2009). Body composition and sports performance. In R.J. Maughan (Ed.), *Olympic textbook of science in sport*. Chichester: Wiley-Blackwell.

Paton, N.I., Macallan, D.C., Jebb, S.A., Pazianas, M., & Griffin, G.E. (1995). Dual-energy X-ray absorptiometry results differ between machines. *Lancet, 346*(8979), 899–900.

Reale, R., Slater, G., & Burke, L.M. (2017). Acute-weight-loss strategies for combat sports and applications to Olympic success. *International Journal of Sports Physiology and Performance, 12*(2), 142–151. doi:10.1123/ijspp.2016-0211.

Reilly, T., George, K., Marfell-Jones, M., Scott, M., Sutton, L., & Wallace, J.A. (2009). How well do skinfold equations predict percent body fat in elite soccer players? *International Journal of Sports Medicine, 30*(8), 607–613. doi:10.1055/s-0029-1202353.

Scafoglieri, A., Provyn, S., Wallace, J., Louis, O., Tresignie, J., Bautmans, I., ... Pieter Clarys, J. (2011). Whole body composition by hologic QDR 4500/A DXA: System reliability versus user accuracy and precision. Intechopen. doi:10.5772/15613.

Seeman, E. (1998). Growth in bone mass and size—are racial and gender differences in bone mineral density more apparent than real? *The Journal of Clinical Endocrinology & Metabolism, 83*(5), 1414–1419. doi:10.1210/jcem.83.5.4844.

Sinning, W.E. (1985). Body composition and athletic performance. *Limits of human performance. The academy papers, 18,* 45–56.

Slinde, F., & Rossander-Hulthen, L. (2001). Bioelectrical impedance: Effect of 3 identical meals on diurnal impedance variation and calculation of body composition. *American Journal of Clinical Nutrition, 74*(4), 474–478.

Stewart, A., & Marfell-Jones, M. (2011). *International standards for anthropometric assessment.* Lower Hutt, New Zealand: International Society for the Advancement of Kinanthropometry.

Toomey, C.M., McCormack, W.G., & Jakeman, P. (2017). The effect of hydration status on the measurement of lean tissue mass by dual-energy X-ray absorptiometry. *European Journal of Applied Physiology, 117*(3), 567–574. doi:10.1007/s00421-017-3552-x.

Tothill, P., Avenell, A., Love, J., & Reid, D.M. (1994). Comparisons between Hologic, Lunar and Norland dual-energy X-ray absorptiometers and other techniques used for whole-body soft tissue measurements. *European Journal of Clinical Nutrition, 48*(11), 781–794.

Wang, Z.M., Pierson, R.N., Jr., & Heymsfield, S.B. (1992). The five-level model: a new approach to organizing body-composition research. *American Journal of Clinical Nutrition, 56*(1), 19–28.

Ward, L.C., Heitmann, B.L., Craig, P., Stroud, D., Azinge, E.C., Jebb, S., ... Leonard, D. (2000). Association between ethnicity, body mass index, and bioelectrical impedance. Implications for the population specificity of prediction equations. *Annals of the New York Academy of Sciences, 904,* 199–202.

14 Combined assessment methods

Timothy J. Suchomel, John J. McMahon and Jason P. Lake

Part 1 – Review of literature

14.1 Introduction

This chapter will begin by exploring why combined assessment methods (CAMs) are useful in identifying specific deficits in an athlete's performance and therefore areas to prioritise development. Differences between methods (e.g. reactive strength index [RSI] and reactive strength index-modified [RSImod]) will be discussed, along with how/whether the resultant values can be compared. The first part of this chapter will conclude with a brief discussion on the validity, reliability and measurement error of combined assessment methods. The second part of the chapter will provide specific protocols which should be adopted in both research and applied settings when using these assessments, along with a summary of what the results may indicate.

14.2 Combined assessment methods

While a variety of methods are used to assess an athlete's performance, many methods are limited to assessing a single variable used from a single test. Combined assessment methods are unique in that they use either multiple variables from a single test (e.g. RSI: ground contact time and jump height from a drop jump) or single variables from multiple tests (e.g. dynamic strength deficit [DSD]: peak force from both a countermovement jump and isometric mid-thigh pull [IMTP]). Commonly used CAMs and the variables used to calculate them are displayed in Table 14.1. The following will provide an overview of the literature that has examined each of the listed CAMs.

Dynamic strength deficit / index

A CAM that has recently received a lot of attention is the dynamic strength deficit (DSD). Previous literature has indicated that the DSD is a reliable measurement and can be evaluated during both lower- (Comfort et al., 2017; Thomas et al., 2017, 2015; McMahon et al., 2017a; Sheppard et al., 2011) and upper-body (Young et al., 2014) exercises in athletes. As displayed in Table 14.1, DSD provides a ratio between ballistic force production and maximal isometric force production. Thus, DSD may be used in an attempt to identify what an athlete's training emphasis (ballistic or maximal force development) should be. With considerations for the lower body, Sheppard et al. (2011) suggested that a DSD of ≤ 0.60 indicates that ballistic training is necessary as only 60% of an athlete's maximal

Table 14.1 Combined assessment methods commonly used to assess athlete performance.

Combined assessment method	Equation
Dynamic strength deficit/index	CMJ peak force · IMTP peak force^{-1}
	SJ peak force · IMTP peak force^{-1}
	CMJ peak force · IS peak force^{-1}
	SJ peak force · IS peak force^{-1}
	BP throw peak force · IBP peak force^{-1}
Eccentric utilisation ratio	CMJ variable · SJ variable^{-1}
Force-velocity profile	SJ relative peak force · SJ peak velocity*
	Sprint horizontal force · sprint velocity**
Pre-stretch augmentation percentage	(CMJ variable – SJ variable) · (SJ variable) $^{-1}$ · 100
Reactive strength index	DJ height · DJ ground contact time^{-1}
	Repeated hop height · ground contact time^{-1}
Reactive strength index-modified	CMJ height · CMJ time to take-off^{-1}

Notes: CMJ = countermovement jump; IMTP = isometric mid-thigh pull; SJ = static squat jump; IS = isometric squat; BP = bench press; IBP = isometric bench press; DJ = drop jump; * = jumps must be performed at different loads to create a profile; ** = various sprint distances must be completed to create a profile.

isometric force is being used during a jump, while a DSD of ≥ 0.80 indicates that a focus on maximal strength within training is necessary as the athlete is producing at least 80% of their maximal isometric force capacity during a jump. In contrast, no recommendations for the upper body currently exist, although a similar scale may be applied to a similar population. It should be noted, however, that athletes who are relatively weak (i.e. low relative isometric strength) may produce lower DSD values and thus maximal strength instead of ballistic (or concurrent) training may be preferable to provide the necessary strength foundation (Cormie et al., 2010b). Although no standards of relative isometric strength have been established, much literature supports the notion that athletes who are able to squat ≥ 2× their body mass may be able to jump higher, sprint faster and change direction more effectively (Suchomel et al., 2016a).

Beyond providing an indication of where an athlete's training emphasis should be, previous research has displayed differences in DSD between different collegiate athletic teams (Thomas et al., 2017) as well as those that possess unique temporal phase characteristics during CMJs (McMahon et al., 2017a). Interestingly, correlations between DSD and ballistic and isometric performance variables show weak relationships (Secomb et al., 2015). Unpublished data from 50 male Division I collegiate athletes (baseball, soccer and tennis) show similar trends, with a negative moderate relationship between DSD and IMTP rate of force development (r = −0.43) and trivial to small relationships with RSImod (r = 0.21), CMJ height (r = 0.03) and relative peak power (r = 0.10). Furthermore, similar trends were shown in 21 female Division I collegiate athletes (volleyball, soccer and tennis), with DSD showing a negative moderate relationship with IMTP rate of force development (r = −0.35) and trivial to small relationships with RSImod (r = 0.08), CMJ height (r = 0.00) and relative peak power (r = −0.16) (unpublished data). Provided the extant literature, practitioners should note that while DSD may be used to suggest which emphasis (ballistic or maximal isometric force production) an athlete should focus on, a higher, or lower, DSD value may not be indicative of a highly explosive performance. This is not surprising given the various demands of sporting events as well as the interplay between muscular strength and ballistic performance (Suchomel & Stone, 2017; Suchomel et al., 2016a; Minetti, 2002;

Zamparo et al., 2002; Stone et al., 1981). Thus, further research, especially longitudinal training studies, is needed to determine the effectiveness of DSD when it comes to providing information about what training stimulus is necessary to enhance performance in a given individual.

Eccentric utilisation ratio and pre-stretch augmentation percentage

Previous literature indicated that a perfect relationship (i.e. $r = 1.00$) existed between eccentric utilisation ratio (EUR) and pre-stretch augmentation percentage (PSAP) (Suchomel et al., 2016b) and thus both variables will be discussed together from this point. EUR is calculated as a ratio of CMJ performance compared to SJ performance using the same variable (McGuigan et al., 2006). PSAP uses the difference between CMJ and SJ performances, divides it by the SJ performance to create a comparison score and multiplies the result by 100 to get a percentage (Walshe et al., 1996). Both EUR and PSAP are used to determine how much an individual can benefit from using the stretch-shortening cycle during a CMJ compared to the concentric-only movement of SJ. It should be noted that because these variables essentially provide the same information, the decision to use EUR or PSAP should be chosen based on how comfortable the sport scientist and/or sport coaches are with interpreting ratios or percentages.

By determining the difference in performance between the CMJ and SJ, sport scientists may be able to understand how much an athlete may benefit from using a stretch-shortening cycle over the course of the training year as well as determine what an individual's training focus should be (McGuigan et al., 2013). The most common variables to use when monitoring EUR and PSAP are CMJ and SJ height and peak power. However, it is important to note that while jump height can be incredibly useful, it may be pertinent to consider jump strategy (see Chapter 7 – Vertical jump testing). For example, jump height tends to increase if the propulsion displacement increases (i.e. the propulsion phase commences from a lower centre of mass position, via a deeper squat) due to its effects on propulsion net impulse (reduction in propulsion force is outweighed by increase in propulsion time) and work. Thus, if the propulsion displacement differs between the CMJ and the SJ, then any superior performances noted for the CMJ cannot be attributed to the stretch-shortening cycle alone. Furthermore, previous research has indicated that EUR may vary based on the sport as well as the training phase athletes are currently in (McGuigan et al., 2006). Additional research tracked EUR in Australian Rules football players over the course of several years and noted that although there were no statistical differences, moderate practical changes occurred during both unloaded and loaded conditions (McGuigan et al., 2009), indicating that EUR may be sensitive to various training stimuli over the course of each training year. This agrees with the findings presented by Doyle (2005), but contrasts with Hawkins et al. (2009), although the latter study examined a non-athletic population.

Force-velocity profiles

Many resistance training programmes are designed with the end goal of developing muscular power. This is not surprising considering that previous literature has noted that muscular power may differentiate the performance of athletes from different sports and standards (Baker, 2001; Hawley et al., 1992; Wisløff et al., 2004; Nimphius et al., 2010). The power produced during a movement is equal to the product of force and velocity (i.e. Power = Force · Velocity). However, it should be noted that depending on the exercise, load, an athlete's strength, neuromuscular fatigue and work capacity, maximal power output can be achieved using different strategies, including a force emphasis (Power = FORCE · velocity) and a velocity emphasis (Power = Force · VELOCITY). Furthermore, this could also be achieved by increasing both force and velocity proportionately. For example, the force-velocity profile of athletes may be trained using weight-lifting derivatives as discussed by Suchomel et al. (2017). In this example, FORCE · velocity may be trained using mid-thigh pulls at 120–140% of one repetition maximum (1RM) (Comfort et al., 2015, 2012b), while force · VELOCITY may be trained using jump shrugs at 30–45% 1RM (Suchomel et al., 2014b, 2013a), and Force · Velocity may be trained using hang power cleans at 65–80% 1RM (Suchomel et al., 2014a; Kawamori et al., 2005).

Original force-velocity profiling was discussed within the scientific literature as a method used to identify the external load that produces the greatest power output during various exercises (i.e. the optimal load). This method has been termed load-power profiling or load-velocity profiling. Previous literature has examined both upper- (Soriano et al., 2017; Thomas et al., 2007; Muñoz-López et al., 2017; Balsalobre-Fernández et al., 2017; Bevan et al., 2010; Baker et al., 2001a) and lower-body resistance training exercises (Thomas et al., 2007; Soriano et al., 2015; Dayne et al., 2011; McBride et al., 2011, 1999; Baker et al., 2001b; Cormie et al., 2007c, 2007a, 2007b), with an abundance of research examining the loading profiles of weightlifting movements and their derivatives (Cormie et al., 2007c, 2007b; Comfort et al., 2012a; Kilduff et al., 2007; Kawamori et al., 2005; Suchomel & Sole, 2017; Kipp et al., 2016; Suchomel et al., 2015b, 2014b, 2014a, 2013a; Thomas et al., 2007; McBride et al., 2011). As previously mentioned, much of the above literature sought to identify the load that produces the greatest power output. It is believed that using these loads or load ranges will produce the greatest power adaptations. Recent literature indicated that load-velocity profiles can serve as reliable variables that may be used to monitor an individual's training adaptations (Banyard et al., 2017; Lake et al., 2017).

More recently, force-velocity profiling has been used as a monitoring tool to determine where an individual's potential weaknesses are when it comes to jumping and sprinting. Previous studies have indicated that force-velocity profiles can be constructed for athletes during both jumping and sprinting (Jiménez-Reyes et al., 2017b; Samozino et al., 2016, 2014, 2012, 2008). Furthermore, the optimal force-velocity profile can be constructed based on the athlete's testing results. In a recent review, Morin and Samozino (2016) discussed the construction and interpretation of vertical jumping and sprinting force-velocity profiles. The authors concluded that force-velocity profiling can be used to identify an athlete's weakness when it comes to improving their jump or sprint performance as well as providing practitioners with direction when it comes to training to improve the athlete's weakness. A recent study displayed the effectiveness of using force-velocity profiling to develop individualised training programmes to improve jump performance (Jiménez-Reyes et al., 2017a). The results of the previous study indicated that training programmes that were designed to improve those at a force-deficit, velocity-deficit, or those who were well-balanced, improved the jumping performance of the individuals more efficiently than those who simply trained using a classic programme that was not designed based on a force-velocity imbalance. While the authors promoted their methods of training within the study, it has been acknowledged by previous literature that while force-velocity profiling may provide information regarding what muscle characteristics need to be developed, it does not determine how these characteristics should be developed (Samozino et al., 2016, 2008).

As shown in Table 14.1, force-velocity profiling typically involves performing the same exercise with multiple loads or sprinting a given distance with multiple split times. However, it should be noted that a CAMs approach can be used to create force-velocity profiles used for monitoring training adaptations as well. Two previous studies combined jump squats performed at various loads and isometric squats to create force-velocity profiles (James et al., 2017; Cormie et al., 2010a). Using this approach during 10 week training studies, the authors of each study were able to monitor force-velocity profile changes and compare the training adaptations between strong and weak individuals (James et al., 2017) and differences between strength-based or power-based resistance training (Cormie et al., 2010a). While the above studies used jump squats (i.e. countermovement jumps) and the isometric squat, sport scientists may also consider using a squat jump performed at various loads and the IMTP. However, practitioners should be aware that using different exercises to create a force-velocity profile may alter the profile's information. For example, Jiménez-Reyes et al. (2014) indicated that a countermovement jump profile may be unique compared to a squat jump profile by shifting the force-velocity profile to the right and achieving higher maximal power outputs and velocities. While it may be obvious that different exercises create different profiles, it is important to consider what is already being used as part of the athlete's monitoring protocol as well as what equipment is available for monitoring purposes.

Reactive strength index

The reactive strength index, as indicated above, provides a ratio between an athlete's drop jump (DJ) height and their ground contact time (i.e. time from initial foot contact to leaving the ground during a DJ) or repeated hop test jump height and ground contact time (Lloyd et al., 2012). The literature indicates that RSI may be used to assess an athlete's reactive strength characteristics (Flanagan et al., 2008), their performance in training (McClymont, 2003) lower-body stiffness (Kipp et al., 2017), and may provide insight into an athlete's level of neuromuscular fatigue (Hamilton, 2009).

While RSI is a versatile metric that may be used to monitor an athlete's performance in multiple aspects, it is not without its limitations. The DJ may not be as common within an athlete-monitoring protocol compared to a CMJ or SJ. This may be due to a number of factors. The first and most obvious is the fact that sport scientists and practitioners would have to use an additional apparatus (e.g. plyometric box) from which the athletes must drop off before landing on the ground and jumping. Although not overly burdensome, additional equipment adds another aspect athlete-monitoring that must be taken into consideration, especially when travelling with a team. Second, the instructions used during a DJ may alter how the jump is performed. Young et al. (1995) indicated that individuals may perform DJs differently if they are cued to jump for maximum height, minimise ground contact time, or a combination of both. Sport scientists should be mindful of these findings when testing and monitoring athletes. Third, some athletes may be able to use a rapid stretch-shortening cycle action better than others and may thus benefit from a higher box. In fact, previous literature has indicated that the optimal drop height for each individual may vary based on an individual's strength (Matic et al., 2015; Griggs, 2016).

In addition to the above, there tends to be a discrepancy between the box height from which the athlete attempts to drop off and the actual height that they drop from. In other words, despite consistent task instructions to drop off the box, athletes tend to lower themselves by stepping down slightly before dropping towards the ground. The difference between box height and actual drop height has been reported to be in the range of 26% lower to 33% higher in scientific studies (Costley et al., 2017; Baca, 1999). There are proposed methods of correcting for this discrepancy when using one or two force platforms to assess DJ performance (Baca, 1999) but, of course, these cannot be applied to field-based methods of assessing DJ performance and they have rarely been applied to DJ force-time assessments in the published literature. Therefore, actual drop height is likely to be different from box height whenever the DJ is performed, and the exact difference may change between testing sessions. This means that any within- and between-athlete differences in DJ RSI values may be partly attributed to differences in actual drop height.

Reactive strength index – modified

Similar to RSI, RSImod provides a ratio between an athlete's jump height and time taken to jump; however, RSImod substitutes the CMJ in place of the DJ while time to take-off is substituted in place of ground contact time. Despite substituting different variables, previous research has displayed strong relationships between traditional RSI and RSImod (McMahon et al., 2018), indicating that similar trends in performance exist within individuals. It should be noted that although a large relationship was noted between the two RSI variants, it equated to just 22% shared variance (McMahon et al., 2018). These results suggest that the two RSI variants do not explain each other very well, indicating that they do not assess entirely the same reactive strength qualities and thus should not be used interchangeably. Nevertheless, RSImod has been shown to be a reliable variable (Suchomel et al., 2015a; Ebben & Petushek, 2010) and has been examined in many capacities. Previous research has indicated that differences in RSImod exist between collegiate athletic teams (Suchomel et al., 2015c) as well as between male and female athletes (Suchomel et al., 2015a), but RSImod also provides an indication of an athlete's ability to use the stretch-shortening cycle during jumping (Suchomel et al., 2016b) and their explosiveness based on their rapid force production characteristics (i.e. rate of force development) (Kipp et al., 2015, McMahon et al., 2017b), and may influence the shape of an individual's force- and power-time characteristics (McMahon et al., 2017b) (see Chapter 7 on jumps). Furthermore, unpublished data indicate that, like RSI, RSImod may be used to provide insight into an athlete's neuromuscular fatigue (see Figures 14.2 and 14.3 in Part 2 below). Given its versatility as a performance variable, sport scientists and practitioners may consider including RSImod within their athlete-monitoring metrics. However, practitioners should also exercise caution if using RSImod as the lone performance variable and should instead consider monitoring RSImod concurrently with other variables to provide a greater overall picture of athlete development.

While there are a number of advantages to using RSImod athlete-monitoring protocols, there are also disadvantages that should also be recognised. First, in order to calculate RSImod, a force platform is needed. In contrast to the traditional RSI measure, using RSImod requires athletes to begin standing on a force platform and perform a CMJ, instead of dropping onto a switch mat that will calculate an athlete's time spent on the ground during a jump. A second limitation using RSImod are the instructions and cues given to the athlete. Previous literature indicated that verbal instructions improved RSImod with several different plyometric exercises (Suchomel et al., 2013b). Sport scientists and practitioners should be aware of this effect and ensure that the instructions given to each athlete before testing are consistent.

Part 2 – Practical applications of combined assessment methods

The following sections will provide practical examples of how to use the CAMs discussed above to monitor and adjust training. It is important to note that many of these assessment methods are typically used as part of an overall athlete-monitoring protocol and should be used to provide practitioners with a piece of information as to how to modify an athlete's training to achieve the desired adaptations rather than be used as stand-alone assessments.

Monitoring application of dynamic strength deficit/index

As mentioned above, the DSD/DSI provides a ratio between the peak force produced during a dynamic task (e.g. CMJ or SJ) and the peak force produced during an isometric task (e.g. isometric squat or isometric mid-thigh pull). This ratio, in theory, should be able to provide practitioners with some insight into what the athlete should focus on within their training. Sheppard et al. (2011) indicated that athletes with a DSD of ≤ 0.60 may benefit from emphasising ballistic training, while athletes with a DSD of ≥ 0.80 may benefit from emphasising maximal strength training. Table 14.2 displays example training recommendations based on athlete DSD data. As noted in the final example in Table 14.2, it is important to consider other variables, such as jump height and maximal strength, when making training recommendations based on DSD data. For example, as Athlete C has a DSD ratio of 0.60, but can only jump 30 cm during a SJ and back squat 1.2 times their bodyweight, the emphasis in their training should be maximal strength training, rather than ballistic training. While many methods of training can be implemented to improve this athlete's maximal strength (Suchomel et al., 2018), it is important to consider what methods are going to benefit individual athletes based on their ability levels as well as the benefits of specific types of training (e.g. improved rate of force development [RFD], power output, etc.). In fact, previous research has indicated that increasing maximal strength leads to increases in RFD and rapid force production (Andersen & Aagaard, 2006; Aagaard et al., 2002), especially in weaker athletes.

Monitoring application of eccentric utilisation ratio

Similar to DSD, EUR provides a ratio that may guide training decisions for athletes. However, like DSD, it is important to consider other monitoring data surrounding the achieved ratio. For example, McGuigan and colleagues (2006) indicated that EUR (jump height or peak power ratio) increased during the preseason phase of training for rugby union and field hockey athletes (moderate-large effects). It is likely that the previous study found these differences due to the prescription of more specific training methods leading

Table 14.2 Example athlete dynamic strength deficits and training recommendations.

	Dynamic strength deficit ratio	*Squat jump height (cm)*	*Relative squat strength (kg·kg⁻¹)*	*Recommended training focus*
Athlete A	0.50	50	1.80	Ballistic training
Athlete B	0.85	40	1.50	Maximal strength
Athlete C	0.60	30	1.20	Maximal strength

Table 14.3 Example athlete peak power eccentric utilisation ratios and training recommendations.

	Eccentric utilisation ratio	Relative maximal squat strength (kg·kg⁻¹)	CMJ relative peak power (W·kg⁻¹)	SJ relative peak power (W·kg⁻¹)	Recommended training focus
Athlete A	1.10	1.24	51.2	46.4	Maximal strength
Athlete B	1.00	2.24	75.3	75.2	Ballistic exercise
Athlete C	0.97	1.62	56.2	57.9	Maximal strength

Notes: SJ = squat jump; CMJ = countermovement jump.

into the competitive season. For example, while high-intensity exercises may be prescribed during both the pre-season and in-season training phases, exercises with higher velocities may be prescribed to enhance RFD and peak power (Suchomel et al., 2018). Moreover, the latter prescription of exercises typically coincides with faster SSC muscle actions, which in turn allows the athlete to improve their SSC capabilities. Table 14.3 displays example EUR data and training recommendations based on the ratios. Like the other CAMs discussed within this chapter, it is important that practitioners do not "chase" specific EUR values with the hopes of achieving peak athletic performance. If practitioners elect to monitor EUR, it is suggested that other metrics (see Chapters 7–13) should be monitored concurrently to provide a greater overall picture of an athlete's development.

Monitoring application of force-velocity profiles

Monitoring an athlete's jumping or sprinting performance has become more common within a long-term athlete-development training approach. Sport scientists have started looking beyond the traditional measures of jump height and peak power. One method that sport scientists are using is performing jumps with multiple loads to establish a force-velocity profile. Using this method, practitioners may monitor changes in how athletes produce power under different loads, but may also determine whether the athlete has a force or velocity deficit that may need to be trained. Figure 14.1 displays force-velocity profiles of four athletes who performed SJs under six different loading conditions. Using the interpretation methods discussed by Morin et al. (2016), Athlete D may have what is considered as a force deficit based on the steep drop-off in force production as load increases. Thus, a general training recommendation for Athlete D would be to emphasise training methods that promote increases in maximal strength rather than ballistic methods. In contrast, Athletes A, B and C may need to focus on both maximal strength and ballistic methods of training based on a more linear decrease in velocity and increase in relative force production while load increases. This method of combined training has been discussed by Haff and Nimphius (2012).

Monitoring application of reactive strength index

The ability to use a rapid SSC action appears to be important in sport movements that require a limited time between eccentric and concentric muscle actions to be successful (e.g. sprinting, cutting, etc.). A DJ has been classified as a rapid SSC action (<250 ms) (Young,

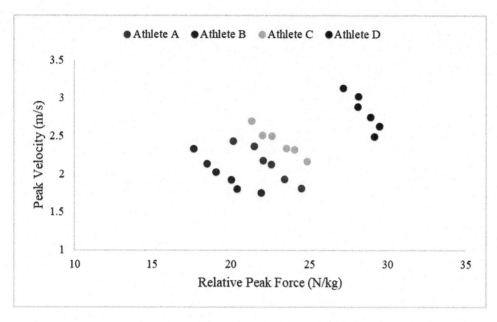

Figure 14.1 Athlete force-velocity profiles performing squat jumps with loads at bodyweight, bodyweight + 10%, bodyweight + 20%, bodyweight + 30%, bodyweight + 40% and bodyweight + 50%.

1995), assuming the proper instructions are given (Young et al., 1995). Thus, it would appear that using a variable, such an RSI would be valuable because it compares the height of the DJ and the time it takes to achieve that jump height (i.e. ground contact time) after an athlete's feet touch the ground after dropping from a raised surface. Previous literature has indicated that RSI may be used to monitor neuromuscular fatigue in elite youth soccer players (Hamilton, 2009). Monitoring RSI like the previous study can be relatively simple depending on the type of equipment and software used. For example, practitioners may use a switch mat and any stable raised surface that athletes can step off and drop onto the measuring device. However, it is important that practitioners note the height of the raised surface. Although stronger athletes can typically handle, and benefit their jump height from, more rapid SSC actions that tend to result from a greater drop height, weaker athletes may not. This is supported by literature that has discussed using optimal DJ heights for athletes of different abilities (Matic et al., 2015; Griggs, 2016).

Monitoring application of reactive strength index-modified

Gathercole et al. (2015) indicated that CMJ variables other than jump height should be used to monitor neuromuscular fatigue characteristics, specifically those that reflect the neuromuscular strategy used during the jump. As mentioned above, RSImod has been described as a variable that relates to an athlete's explosive strength characteristics (Kipp et al., 2015), but may also be used to effectively assess SSC utilisation due to its timing component (e.g. time to take-off) (Suchomel et al., 2016b). The ability to produce force rapidly

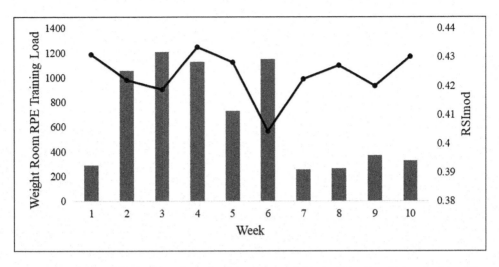

Figure 14.2 Longitudinal monitoring of weight-room training load (rating of perceived exertion × session duration) (bars) and RSImod (line) in a Division I collegiate volleyball team during the competitive season.

(i.e. RFD) is typically inversely related to resistance training volume-load (Walker et al., 2012; Tran et al., 2006), unless the athletes in question are novice athletes with limited resistance training experience. However, given the relationships of RSImod and RFD, it is possible that RSImod would show similar inverse relationships with resistance training volume-load. Figure 14.2 displays in-season monitoring of weight-room rating of perceived exertion training and RSImod within a Division I women's volleyball team. As the figure indicates, an obvious inverse trend shows that if training load increased the previous week, RSImod decreased the following week and vice versa. From a practical standpoint, it appears that RSImod may be used as an indicator of fatigue within a team; however, practitioners should keep in mind that variables, including RSImod, should be tracked in both a team and individual manner to determine whether a meaningful change took place. Moreover, because RSImod is a ratio between jump height and time to take-off, it is important to look at not just the ratio, but its component parts as well. Figure 14.3 shows the same in-season monitoring of weight-room rating of perceived exertion training graphed with time to take-off.

Summary

There are a number of CAMs that may be used to monitor athletes of different abilities. The DSI, EUR, force-velocity profile, RSI and RSImod of athletes can be used to both assess performance as well as provide information about what training emphasis should be prescribed to improve an athlete's performance. However, it is important to note that each method has its limitations and should be calculated concurrently with other monitoring variables to provide a greater overall picture regarding the development of athletes. Finally, it should be noted that practitioners should not focus on attaining specific testing values, but should consider the overall development of the athlete when prescribing training methods to improve performance.

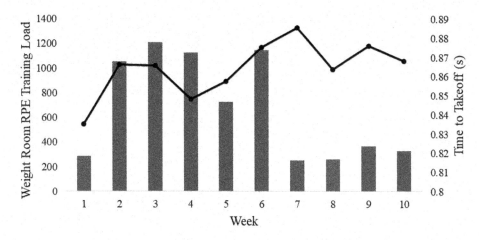

Figure 14.3 Longitudinal monitoring of weight-room training load (rating of perceived exertion × session duration) (bars) and time to take-off (line) in a Division I collegiate volleyball team during the competitive season.

References

Aagaard, P., Simonsen, E.B., Andersen, J.L., Magnusson, P., & Dyhre-Poulsen, P. (2002). Increased rate of force development and neural drive of human skeletal muscle following resistance training. *Journal of Applied Physiology, 93*, 1318–1326.

Andersen, L.L., & Aagaard, P. (2006). Influence of maximal muscle strength and intrinsic muscle contractile properties on contractile rate of force development. *European Journal of Applied Physiology, 96*, 46–52.

Baca, A. (1999). A comparison of methods for analyzing drop jump performance. *Medicine & Science in Sports & Exercise, 31*, 437–442.

Baker, D. (2001). A series of studies on the training of high-intensity muscle power in rugby league football players. *The Journal of Strength & Conditioning Research, 15*, 198–209.

Baker, D., Nance, S., & Moore, M. (2001a). The load that maximizes the average mechanical power output during explosive bench press throws in highly trained athletes. *The Journal of Strength & Conditioning Research, 15*, 20–24.

Baker, D., Nance, S., & Moore, M. (2001b). The load that maximizes the average mechanical power output during jump squats in power-trained athletes. *The Journal of Strength & Conditioning Research, 15*, 92–97.

Balsalobre-Fernández, C., García-Ramos, A., & Jiménez-Reyes, P. (2017). Load–velocity profiling in the military press exercise: Effects of gender and training. *International Journal of Sports Science & Coaching.* Epub ahead of print, 1747954117738243.

Banyard, H.G., Nosaka, K., Vernon, A.D., & Haff, G.G. (2017). The reliability of individualized load-velocity profiles. *International Journal of Sports Physiology and Performance.* Epub ahead of print.

Bevan, H.R., Bunce, P.J., Owen, N.J., Bennett, M.A., Cook, C.J., Cunningham, D.J., Newton, R.U., & Kilduff, L.P. (2010). Optimal loading for the development of peak power output in professional rugby players. *The Journal of Strength & Conditioning Research, 24*, 43–47.

Comfort, P., Fletcher, C., & McMahon, J.J. (2012a). Determination of optimal loading during the power clean, in collegiate athletes. *The Journal of Strength & Conditioning Research, 26*, 2970–2974.

Comfort, P., Jones, P.A., & Udall, R. (2015). The effect of load and sex on kinematic and kinetic variables during the mid-thigh clean pull. *Sports Biomechanics, 14*, 139–156.

Comfort, P., Thomas, C., Dos'Santos, T., Jones, P.A., Suchomel, T.J., & Mcmahon, J.J. (2017). Comparison of dynamic strength index calculated using the squat jump and countermovement jump. *International Journal of Sports Physiology and Performance*. Epub ahead of print.

Comfort, P., Udall, R., & Jones, P.A. (2012b). The effect of loading on kinematic and kinetic variables during the midthigh clean pull. *The Journal of Strength & Conditioning Research, 26*, 1208–1214.

Cormie, P., McBride, J.M., & Mc, G.O. (2007a). The influence of body mass on calculation of power during lower-body resistance exercises. *The Journal of Strength & Conditioning Research, 21*, 1042–1049.

Cormie, P., McBride, J.M., & McCaulley, G.O. (2007b). Validation of power measurement techniques in dynamic lower body resistance exercises. *Journal of Applied Biomechanics, 23*, 103–118.

Cormie, P., McCaulley, G.O., Triplett, N.T., & McBride, J.M. (2007c). Optimal loading for maximal power output during lower-body resistance exercises. *Medicine & Science in Sports & Exercise, 39*, 340–349.

Cormie, P., Mcguigan, M.R., & Newton, R.U. (2010a). Adaptations in athletic performance after ballistic power versus strength training. *Medicine & Science in Sports & Exercise, 42*, 1582–1598.

Cormie, P., McGuigan, M.R., & Newton, R.U. (2010b). Influence of strength on magnitude and mechanisms of adaptation to power training. *Medicine & Science in Sports & Exercise, 42*, 1566–1581.

Costley, L., Wallace, E., Johnston, M., & Kennedy, R. (2017). Reliability of bounce drop jump parameters within elite male rugby players. *Journal of Sports Medicine and Physical Fitness*. Epub ahead of print.

Dayne, A.M., McBride, J.M., Nuzzo, J.L., Triplett, N.T., Skinner, J., & Burr, A. (2011). Power output in the jump squat in adolescent male athletes. *The Journal of Strength & Conditioning Research, 25*, 585–589.

Doyle, T.L.A. (2005). How effectively is the stretch-shortening cycle being used by athletes? *Strength and Conditioning Coach, 13*, 7–12.

Ebben, W.P., & Petushek, E.J. (2010). Using the reactive strength index modified to evaluate plyometric performance. *The Journal of Strength & Conditioning Research, 24*, 1983–1987.

Flanagan, E.P., Ebben, W.P., & Jensen, R.L. (2008). Reliability of the reactive strength index and time to stabilization during depth jumps. *The Journal of Strength & Conditioning Research, 22*, 1677–1682.

Gathercole, R., Sporer, B., Stellingwerff, T., & Sleivert, G. (2015). Alternative countermovement-jump analysis to quantify acute neuromuscular fatigue. *International Journal of Sports Physiology and Performance, 10*, 84–92.

Griggs, C.V. (2016). Relationship between lower body strength, countermovement jump height, and optimal drop jump height. Master of Arts Master's Thesis, East Tennessee State University.

Haff, G.G., & Nimphius, S. (2012). Training principles for power. *Strength & Conditioning Journal, 34*, 2–12.

Hamilton, D. (2009). Drop jumps as an indicator of neuromuscular fatigue and recovery in elite youth soccer athletes following tournament match play. *Journal of Australian Strength and Conditioning, 17*, 3–8.

Hawkins, S.B., Doyle, T.L. A., & McGuigan, M.R. (2009). The effect of different training programs on eccentric energy utilization in college-aged males. *The Journal of Strength & Conditioning Research, 23*, 1996–2002.

Hawley, J.A., Williams, M.M., Vickovic, M.M., & Handcock, P.J. (1992). Muscle power predicts freestyle swimming performance. *British Journal of Sports Medicine, 26*, 151–155.

James, L.P., Haff, G.G., Kelly, V.G., Connick, M., Hoffman, B., & Beckman, E.M. (2017). The impact of strength level on adaptations to combined weightlifting, plyometric and ballistic training. *Scandinavian Journal of Medicine & Science in Sports*. Epub ahead of print.

Jiménez-Reyes, P., Samozino, P., Brughelli, M., & Morin, J.-B. (2017a). Effectiveness of an individualized training based on force-velocity profiling during jumping. *Frontiers in Physiology, 7*, 677.

Jiménez-Reyes, P., Samozino, P., Cuadrado-Peñafiel, V., Conceição, F., González-Badillo, J.J., & Morin, J.-B. (2014). Effect of countermovement on power–force–velocity profile. *European Journal of Applied Physiology, 114*, 2281–2288.

Jiménez-Reyes, P., Samozino, P., Pareja-Blanco, F., Conceição, F., Cuadrado-Peñafiel, V., González-Badillo, J.J., & Morin, J.-B. (2017b). Validity of a simple method for measuring force-velocity-power profile in countermovement jump. *International Journal of Sports Physiology and Performance, 12*, 36–43.

Kawamori, N., Crum, A.J., Blumert, P.A., Kulik, J.R., Childers, J.T., Wood, J.A., Stone, M.H., & Haff, G.G. (2005). Influence of different relative intensities on power output during the hang power clean: Identification of the optimal load. *The Journal of Strength & Conditioning Research, 19*, 698–708.

Kilduff, L.P., Bevan, H., Owen, N., Kingsley, M.I., Bunce, P., Bennett, M., & Cunningham, D. (2007). Optimal loading for peak power output during the hang power clean in professional rugby players. *International Journal of Sports Physiology and Performance, 2*, 260–269.

Kipp, K., Kiely, M.T. & Geiser, C.F. (2015). The reactive strength index modified is a valid measure of explosiveness in collegiate female volleyball players. *The Journal of Strength & Conditioning Research*. Epub ahead of print.

Kipp, K., Kiely, M.T., Giordanelli, M.D., Malloy, P.J., & Geiser, C.F. (2017). The reactive strength index reflects vertical stiffness during drop jumps. *International Journal of Sports Physiology and Performance*. Epub ahead of print.

Kipp, K., Malloy, P.J., Smith, J., Giordanelli, M.D., Kiely, M.T., Geiser, C.F., & Suchomel, T.J. (2016). Mechanical demands of the hang power clean and jump shrug: A joint-level perspective. *The Journal of Strength & Conditioning Research*. Epub ahead of print.

Lake, J.P., Naworynsky, D., Duncan, F., & Jackson, M. (2017). Comparison of different minimal velocity thresholds to establish deadlift one repetition maximum. *Sports, 5*, 70.

Lloyd, R.S., Oliver, J.L., Hughes, M.G., & Williams, C.A. (2012). Age-related differences in the neural regulation of stretch-shortening cycle activities in male youths during maximal and sub-maximal hopping. *Journal of Electromyography and Kinesiology, 22*, 37–43.

Matic, M.S., Pazin, N.R., Mrdakovic, V.D., Jankovic, N.N., Ilic, D.B., & Stefanovic, D.L.J. (2015). Optimum drop height for maximizing power output in drop jump: The effect of maximal muscle strength. *The Journal of Strength & Conditioning Research, 29*, 3300–3310.

McBride, J.M., Haines, T.L. & Kirby, T.J. (2011). Effect of loading on peak power of the bar, body, and system during power cleans, squats, and jump squats. *Journal of Sports Sciences, 29*, 1215–1221.

McBride, J.M., Triplett-McBride, T., Davie, A., & Newton, R.U. (1999). A comparison of strength and power characteristics between power lifters, Olympic lifters, and sprinters. *The Journal of Strength & Conditioning Research, 13*, 58–66.

McClymont, D. (2003). Use of the reactive strength index (RSI) as an indicator of plyometric training conditions. In T. Reilly, J. Cabri & D. Araujo (Eds.), *Science and Football V: The Proceedings of the Fifth World Congress on Sports Science and Football, 2003 Lisbon, Portugal* (pp. 408–416). Abingdon, Oxon: Routledge.

McGuigan, M.R., Cormack, S., & Newton, R.U. (2009). Long-term power performance of elite Australian rules football players. *The Journal of Strength & Conditioning Research, 23*, 26–32.

McGuigan, M.R., Cormack, S.J., & Gill, N.D. (2013). Strength and power profiling of athletes: Selecting tests and how to use the information for program design. *Strength & Conditioning Journal, 35*, 7–14.

McGuigan, M.R., La Doyle, T., Newton, M., Edwards, D.J., Nimphius, S., & Newton, R.U. (2006). Eccentric utilization ratio: Effect of sport and phase of training. *The Journal of Strength & Conditioning Research, 20*, 992–995.

McMahon, J.J., Jones, P.A., Dos'Santos, T., & Comfort, P. (2017a). Influence of dynamic strength index on countermovement jump force-, power-, velocity-, and displacement-time curves. *Sports, 5*, 72.

McMahon, J.J., Jones, P.A., Suchomel, T.J., Lake, J.P., & Comfort, P. (2017b). Influence of reactive strength index modified on force- and power-time curves. *International Journal of Sports Physiology and Performance*. Epub ahead of print.

McMahon, J.J., Suchomel, T.J., & Comfort, P. (2018). Relationship between reactive strength index variants in rugby league players. *The Journal of Strength & Conditioning Research*. In press.

Minetti, A.E. (2002). On the mechanical power of joint extensions as affected by the change in muscle force (or cross-sectional area), ceteris paribus. *European Journal of Applied Physiology, 86*, 363–369.

Morin, J.-B., & Samozino, P. (2016). Interpreting power-force-velocity profiles for individualized and specific training. *International Journal of Sports Physiology and Performance, 11*, 267–272.

Muñoz-López, M., Marchante, D., Cano-Ruiz, M.A., Chicharro, J.L., & Balsalobre-Fernández, C. (2017). Load, force and power-velocity relationships in the prone pull-up exercise. *International Journal of Sports Physiology and Performance*. Epub ahead of print, 1–22.

Nimphius, S., McGuigan, M.R., & Newton, R.U. (2010). Relationship between strength, power, speed, and change of direction performance of female softball players. *The Journal of Strength & Conditioning Research, 24*, 885–895.

Samozino, P., Edouard, P., Sangnier, S., Brughelli, M., Gimenez, P., & Morin, J.-B. (2014). Force-velocity profile: Imbalance determination and effect on lower limb ballistic performance. *International Journal of Sports Medicine, 35*, 505–510.

Samozino, P., Morin, J.-B., Hintzy, F., & Belli, A. (2008). A simple method for measuring force, velocity and power output during squat jump. *Journal of Biomechanics, 41*, 2940–2945.

Samozino, P., Rabita, G., Dorel, S., Slawinski, J., Peyrot, N., Saez De Villarreal, E., & Morin, J.B. (2016). A simple method for measuring power, force, velocity properties, and mechanical effectiveness in sprint running. *Scandinavian Journal of Medicine & Science in Sports, 26*, 648–658.

Samozino, P., Rejc, E., Di Prampero, P.E., Belli, A., & Morin, J.-B. (2012). Optimal force–velocity profile in ballistic movements—Altius: Citius or Fortius? *Medicine & Science in Sports & Exercise, 44*, 313–322.

Secomb, J.L., Nimphius, S., Farley, O.R.L., Lundgren, L.E., Tran, T.T., & Sheppard, J.M. (2015). Relationships between lower-body muscle structure and, lower-body strength, explosiveness and eccentric leg stiffness in adolescent athletes. *Journal of Sports Science and Medicine, 14*, 691.

Sheppard, J.M., Chapman, D., & Taylor, K.-L. (2011). An evaluation of a strength qualities assessment method for the lower body. *Journal of Australian Strength and Conditioning, 19*, 4–10.

Soriano, M.A., Jiménez-Reyes, P., Rhea, M.R., & Marín, P.J. (2015). The optimal load for maximal power production during lower-body resistance exercises: A meta-analysis. *Sports Medicine, 45*, 1191–1205.

Soriano, M.A., Suchomel, T.J., & Marin, P.J. (2017). The optimal load for improving maximal power production during upper-body exercises: A meta-analysis. *Sports Medicine, 47*, 757–768.

Stone, M.H., O'Bryant, H., & Garhammer, J. (1981). A hypothetical model for strength training. *Journal of Sports Medicine and Physical Fitness, 21*, 342–351.

Suchomel, T.J., Bailey, C.A., Sole, C.J., Grazer, J.L., & Beckham, G.K. (2015a). Using reactive strength index-modified as an explosive performance measurement tool in Division I athletes. *The Journal of Strength & Conditioning Research, 29*, 899–904.

Suchomel, T.J., Beckham, G.K., & Wright, G.A. (2013a). Lower body kinetics during the jump shrug: impact of load. *Journal of Trainology, 2*, 19–22.

Suchomel, T.J., Beckham, G.K., & Wright, G.A. (2014a). The impact of load on lower body performance variables during the hang power clean. *Sports Biomechanics, 13*, 87–95.

Suchomel, T.J., Beckham, G.K., & Wright, G.A. (2015b). Effect of various loads on the force-time characteristics of the hang high pull. *The Journal of Strength & Conditioning Research, 29*, 1295–1301.

Suchomel, T.J., Comfort, P., & Lake, J.P. (2017). Enhancing the force-velocity profile of athletes using weightlifting derivatives. *Strength & Conditioning Journal,, 39*, 10–20.

Suchomel, T.J., Garceau, L.R., & Ebben, W.P. (2013b). Verbal instruction effect on stretch shortening cycle duration and reactive strength index-modified during plyometrics [Abstract]. *Medicine & Science in Sports & Exercise, 45*, S428.

Suchomel, T.J., Nimphius, S., Bellon, C.R., & Stone, M.H. (2018). The importance of muscular strength: Training considerations. *Sports Medicine*. In press.

Suchomel, T.J., Nimphius, S., & Stone, M.H. (2016a). The importance of muscular strength in athletic performance. *Sports Medicine, 46*, 1419–1449.

Suchomel, T.J., & Sole, C.J. (2017). Power-time curve comparison between weightlifting derivatives. *Journal of Sports Science and Medicine, 16*, 407–413.

Suchomel, T.J., Sole, C.J., Bailey, C.A., Grazer, J.L. & Beckham, G.K. (2015c). A comparison of reactive strength index-modified between six U.S. collegiate athletic teams. *The Journal of Strength & Conditioning Research, 29*, 1310–1316.

Suchomel, T.J., Sole, C.J., & Stone, M.H. (2016b). Comparison of methods that assess lower body stretch-shortening cycle utilization. *The Journal of Strength & Conditioning Research, 30*, 547–554.

Suchomel, T.J., & Stone, M.H. (2017). The relationships between hip and knee extensor cross-sectional area, strength, power, and potentiation characteristics. *Sports, 5*, 66.

Suchomel, T.J., Wright, G.A., Kernozek, T.W., & Kline, D.E. (2014b). Kinetic comparison of the power development between power clean variations. *The Journal of Strength & Conditioning Research, 28*, 350–360.

Thomas, C., Dos'Santos, T., & Jones, P.A. (2017). A comparison of dynamic strength index between team-sport athletes. *Sports, 5*, 71.

Thomas, C., Jones, P.A., & Comfort, P. (2015). Reliability of the dynamic strength index in college athletes. *International Journal of Sports Physiology and Performance, 10*, 542–545.

Thomas, G.A., Kraemer, W.J., Spiering, B.A., Volek, J.S., Anderson, J.M., & Maresh, C.M. (2007). Maximal power at different percentages of one repetition maximum: influence of resistance and gender. *The Journal of Strength & Conditioning Research, 21*, 336–342.

Tran, Q.T., Docherty, D., & Behm, D. (2006). The effects of varying time under tension and volume load on acute neuromuscular responses. *European Journal of Applied Physiology, 98*, 402–410.

Walker, S., Davis, L., Avela, J., & Häkkinen, K. (2012). Neuromuscular fatigue during dynamic maximal strength and hypertrophic resistance loadings. *Journal of Electromyography and Kinesiology, 22*, 356–362.

Walshe, A.D., Wilson, G.J., & Murphy, A.J. (1996). The validity and reliability of a test of lower body musculotendinous stiffness. *European Journal of Applied Physiology, 73*, 332–339.

Wisløff, U., Castagna, C., Helgerud, J., Jones, R., & Hoff, J. (2004). Strong correlation of maximal squat strength with sprint performance and vertical jump height in elite soccer players. *British Journal of Sports Medicine, 38*, 285–288.

Young, K.P., Haff, G.G., Newton, R.U., & Sheppard, J.M. (2014). Reliability of a novel testing protocol to assess upper-body strength qualities in elite athletes. *International Journal of Sports Physiology and Performance, 9*, 871–875.

Young, W.B. (1995). Laboratory strength assessment of athletes. *New Studies in Athletics, 10*, 89–96.

Young, W.B., Pryor, J.F., & Wilson, G.J. (1995). Effect of instructions on characteristics of countermovement and drop jump performance. *The Journal of Strength & Conditioning Research, 9*, 232–236.

Zamparo, P., Minetti, A., & Di Prampero, P. (2002). Interplay among the changes of muscle strength, cross-sectional area and maximal explosive power: Theory and facts. *European Journal of Applied Physiology, 88*, 193–202.

Part III
Interpretation and application

15 Interpretation of results

Jeremy A. Gentles, W. Guy Hornsby and Michael H. Stone

Section I

Introduction

For the sport scientist and strength and conditioning (S&C) coach alike, it can be a daunting task to select a series of performance assessments appropriate for a given team or athlete. For some this challenge is a result of inadequate technical and analytical skills. Others may not have the personnel and instrumentation available to perform the assessments they desire. Then there are those who find it difficult to convince coaching staff there is value in testing and monitoring performance. This chapter is divided into two sections and the aim of this chapter is several-fold. The first section will include a discussion highlighting several basic considerations to make when selecting performance assessments. Most of these considerations are straightforward but often get lost in the quest to use "cutting edge gadgets" purported to be the latest and greatest. The first section will also provide a brief review of individual performance assessments. The second section of this chapter will present several published cases that provide examples of important performance assessments and their interpretation in applied and research settings.

Why test?

Assessing performance should be a key component of a larger athlete-monitoring programme (See Chapter 5). An athlete-monitoring programme should aim to achieve two broad goals: quantify both the stressors an athlete encounters and how an athlete responds to those stressors. Stressors originate from sport-related activities and training, academic demands, responsibilities to family and a variety of other non-sport-related sources.

The quantification of stressors takes many forms. Volume-load is used to quantify the magnitude of stress related to resistance training. Employing accelerometers and GPS to measure field- and court-based workloads is now routine. Questionnaires may be used to describe the extent of job- and family-related stress. Evaluating individual athlete responses to stressors may also include numerous options. Information regarding athlete soreness, feelings of frustration and cheerfulness can be collected through self-report forms using Likert scales. Training-related tissue damage and inflammation may be measured with biochemical markers such as creatine kinase (CK) and C-reactive protein (CRP). Lastly, performance testing provides information regarding adaptations to training including changes in one-repetition maximum (1-RM), jump height, sprint speed and other measures of performance.

Ultimately, an athlete-monitoring program should clarify the relationship between stressors and responses (i.e. dose-response), helping to explain how an athlete is responding/adapting to a training programme. In turn, sport scientists and S&C coaches should be able to make better decisions regarding the training and development of the athletes in their care (Stone et al., 2007).

Considerations for testing and interpretation

This text has provided a thorough treatment of a variety of performance assessments and their interpretation. However, at the most basic level there are several critical concepts that deserve reinforcement.

What are the demands of the sport? Before selecting a performance test(s), the physical abilities required of the sport should be identified. For most popular sports there is an abundance of literature addressing the key physical abilities an athlete must possess in order to excel in their sport and/or position. In some cases, these abilities have not been sufficiently identified and a needs analysis must be conducted with very little evidence from external sources.

The principal physical abilities required for a sport, also known as biomotor abilities, should be the focus of athlete assessments. There are five basic biomotor abilities: strength, endurance, speed, flexibility and coordination (Bompa & Haff, 2009). A detailed account of how to test biomotor abilities has been provided in previous chapters but will be addressed in some detail shortly.

Validity and reliability. As discussed previously in Chapter 3, it is important to select a test that is valid (it measures what it is intended to measure) and reliable (provides consistent measurements). While there are several types of validity and reliability to consider, the following guidelines can help ensure validity and reliability during performance testing.

- When possible, select tests that have been validated in previously published research.
- Calibrate instruments (if applicable) in order to reduce measurement error.
- Select tests with a low learning curve and which require movements/actions that athletes are familiar with. In many cases these actions will be similar to those performed during the sport (e.g. jumping and sprinting).
- Provide adequate familiarisation prior to testing.
- Make sure that performance testing is completed under the same conditions each time. Variables that influence testing conditions include but are not limited to location, surface, weather, time of day and testing instructions.

Comparative and normative data. Selecting tests that have been widely used (with published results) also provides advantages. Information from prior research allows practitioners to compare athletes and teams against a similar population of athletes (sport, age, sex, etc.). If enough data are available, normative values may have been established for a particular group of individuals or athletes. Keep in mind there may be cases where data for comparison are limited or do not exist. In such cases, it may be necessary to draw comparisons against similar athletes (age, sex, etc.) in a sport with like demands. Published studies or books presenting results from numerous investigations may be used for comparison (Tanner et al., 2012; Haff & Triplett, 2015).

It should also be noted that caution should be used when interpreting the results of previous research and drawing conclusions about an athlete's status using those results.

There are often a variety of methods that can be used to evaluate a given performance task, and different methods may generate different results. For instance, as discussed in detail in Chapter 7, jump height or variables used to estimate jump height can be measured via video, 3D motion analysis, force plates, jump/contact mats, optical systems, accelerometers and jump and reach assessments. Assuming several of these methods could be used to evaluate the same jump simultaneously, each one of these tools may provide a different measure of jump height. This has been demonstrated on multiple occasions, where assessments of jump height and flight time using force plates and contact mats result in jump heights that differ by $\cong$ 13–15 cm ($\cong$ 5–6 in) (McMahon et al., 2016; Whitmer et al., 2015). Including an arm-swing during countermovement jumps has also been shown to significantly increase jump height (Harman et al., 1990).

Do not take jump heights and other measures of performance reported in the literature at face value. The methods must be carefully considered before comparing an athlete's performance against previously reported values (see McMahon et al., 2017: available at https://doi.org/10.1007/s40279-017-0771-6).

Assessing change. Null hypothesis significance testing (NHST) has historically been the predominant statistic reported when assessing changes in performance. NHST involves comparing group means (e.g. time 1 vs. time 2; group A vs. group B) and includes the presentation of *P* values (a probability statistic) resulting from statistical tests such as the *T*-test and ANOVA. Although *P* values are generally presented as significant (i.e. ≤ 0.05) and non-significant (i.e. ≥ 0.05), this should not misinterpreted as "practical" and "impractical". *P* values only provide the probability of obtaining results greater than or equal to the observed results. *P* values do not provide information regarding the magnitude of effect (change or difference) and *P* values are strongly influenced by the sample size, or number of athletes being analysed (i.e. the larger the sample size, the smaller the *P* value) (see Chapter 3 for more details).

Recently the interpretation of results in sports science has shifted (and continues to) to prioritise magnitude-based inferences (MBI) over NHST. Practitioners should focus on answering two basic questions when making MBI.

(1) Was there a meaningful change?
(2) What is the magnitude of the change?

In order to determine whether changes in athlete performance are meaningful, the smallest meaningful change can be calculated (SMC; a.k.a. smallest worthwhile change). SMC is the smallest change considered important (Hopkins et al., 1999). In order to detect the SMC, it is recommended that the instrument used for measurement should be able to measure half of the calculated SMC. It is also useful to display SMC with confidence intervals (CI); this allows practitioners to visualise the overlap (or lack of) between SMC and CI. While there is no standard method to calculate SMC, a couple of acceptable methods may be used.

- For individual athletes SMC can be calculated using the following equation.
  SMC = 0.3 × (100 × (SD/mean)) or SMC = 0.3 × CV

- For team sport athletes SMC can be calculated using the following equation.
  SMC = 0.2 × between athlete SD

Effect sizes (ES) are used to illustrate the magnitude of change in the variable(s) of interest. There are a variety of methods used to calculate ES including but not limited to eta-squared, partial eta-squared and Cohen's *d*. In sport science, Cohen's *d* is generally the preferred method for ES calculations. Compared to other ES calculations, Cohen's *d* is influenced less by sample sizes; this is important as small and unequal sample sizes are frequently encountered in athletics. Calculating Cohen's *d* is straightforward using the equation below.

Cohen's *d* = (mean 2 – mean 1) / pooled SD

Pooled SD is an average of SDs from more than one group. To calculate pooled SD use the formula below, where SD_{G1} and SD_{G2} represent the SDs from each group.

$$SD_{pooled} = \frac{\sqrt{SD_{G1}^2 + SD_{G2}^2}}{2}$$

The magnitude of calculated Cohen's *d* ES can be interpreted using the following guidelines (McGuigan, 2017).

- Trivial <0.2 (This is considered the SMC.)
- Small = 0.2–0.6
- Moderate = 0.6–1.2
- Large = 1.2–2.0
- Very large = 2.0–4.0
- Extremely large = >4.0

Keep in mind there is no single standard method used to identify SMC and no single set of definitions used to describe ES strength. For instance, the ES described above is not consistent with those detailed by Rhea (2004). Rhea (2004) proposed ES that could be used to describe the magnitude of change based upon training status. This included trivial, small, moderate and large ES ranges which differ based on training status (untrained, recreationally trained and highly trained). According to Rhea (2004), the threshold for SMC is higher than those described above. These are important distinctions to be aware of because performance changes that would be classified as meaningful according to the previous description may not be classified as meaningful according to Rhea (2004). For a more detailed discussion of MBI, several resources are available (McGuigan, 2017; Buchheit, 2016; Chapter 3).

Communicating results. Considering that the primary objective of an athlete-monitoring programme is to enable better training-related decisions to be made, those making the decisions should be able to understand performance testing results. In most cases it will be the sport scientist or S&C coach who conducts performance testing. However, the head sport coach ultimately controls training at most levels of sport.

Can performance testing procedures and results be easily communicated to sport coaching staff? This is an extremely important question to ask. In order to operate a successful athlete-monitoring programme, "buy-in" from sport coaches is an element that should not be ignored. Coaches are more apt to "buy-in" to a process they understand and can clearly conceptualise how testing results may shape the training programme. This is not to suggest that performance assessments should only be selected based upon the aptitude of sport coaches. Nevertheless, selecting key performance tests that are straightforward to assess and interpret may simplify the decision-making process, particularly among groups with varying technical and analytical skills.

Testing biomotor abilities

The job of a sport scientist or S&C coach does not generally include the technical and tactical development of athletes. Their job, among other responsibilities, is to ensure athletes develop the biomotor abilities to support the technical and tactical tasks required for the sport. For sports dominated by a single biomotor ability, such as sprinting and powerlifting, the sport itself is an expression of an athlete's ability to perform that specific ability. Testing athletes of these sports may include assessments that are extremely specific to the sport (e.g. 100 m sprint and 1-RM bench press). Conversely, many team sports demand substantial contributions from several or all biomotor abilities, along with considerable technical and tactical requirements. In these cases, performance testing should focus on measuring the key biomotor abilities required for the sport, and not necessarily movements/tasks that appear only in the sport.

For example, lower-body strength and power have been shown to be indicators of throwing velocity in baseball (Chelly et al., 2010; Spaniol, 2009). As a result, among baseball players it is sensible to assume that improving lower-body strength and power will augment the ability of a baseball player to throw at higher velocities. Practitioners should focus on improving (and measuring) lower-body strength and power; the athlete and sport coach can then use the improved abilities to throw harder. In some cases, it may be valuable to illustrate that improved biomotor abilities are indeed being translated into improved sport performance. Using the example above, an S&C coach could test 1-RM squat, countermovement jump height and throwing velocity. This would allow the S&C coach to present evidence to the sport coach, demonstrating that training is having the desired effect.

For the sake of brevity, the remaining portion of Section I will present a discussion focused primarily on tests of strength, speed, endurance and their associated variables. This discussion is not intended to be an exhaustive review of performance testing. The objective of the following discussion is to concisely reintroduce options for performance testing and outline several of the performance assessments that will appear in the case examples in Section II.

Testing strength and associated variables. Stone et al. (2007) defined strength as "the ability of the neuromuscular system to produce force against an external resistance". Considering this definition of strength, it is reasonable to suggest that strength forms the foundation of all other biomotor abilities, other than flexibility perhaps. An athlete must be able to generate force in order to move quickly, move for extended periods of time and coordinate movement.

Strength and its associated variables, rate of force development (RFD), velocity and power, can be assessed a multitude of ways (See Chapters 10 and 11). Most commonly, maximum strength is assessed as a 1-RM, using isoinertial movements such as back squat, bench press and deadlift. Alternatively, multiple repetition maximum tests (e.g. 5-RM and 10-RM) can be used to estimate or predict an athlete's 1-RM (Reynolds et al., 2006). Isometric and isokinetic testing protocols can also be used to assess various force-generating characteristics. For example, isometric squats and mid-thigh pulls performed on force plates have been used to assess peak force and RFD in a variety of athletes (Nuzzo et al., 2008). In addition to jump height, static and countermovement vertical jumps (SJ and CMJ, respectively) may be used to assess RFD, take-off velocity and peak power (Cormie et al., 2009); take-off velocity and RFD require the use of force plates, while peak power can be estimated with flight time or derived from forces measured via force plates. The Wingate cycle test is also a popular option for power assessments, but is probably best reserved for cyclists.

The most useful test(s) of strength and force-generating characteristics will depend largely on the sport and the demands of specific positions within a sport. For example, in NFL football, the demands of offensive linemen and wide receivers differ greatly. Linemen do very little sprinting but must repeatedly make contact with, push and pull other athletes weighing well over 140 kg ($\cong$ 310 lbs). A wide receiver tries to avoid contact, and completes numerous sprints, jumps and changes of direction. For linemen, tests of absolute strength (1-RM squat and bench press) and/or peak force (isometric mid-thigh pull) may be good indicators of performance because their position requires high forces in order to defend against other large athletes. For wide receivers, tests of relative strength take precedence, as these tests will help identify the athlete's ability to move their own mass. Strength and force-generating characteristics can be expressed relative to body mass (e.g. load lifted/body mass) and include assessments of 1-RM, peak force and peak power (watts/kg); jump height can also be used to indicate an athlete's ability to move their own mass. Comparisons between athletes of different sexes should use alternative methods of allometric scaling (Stone et al., 2005). While absolute and relative expressions of force-generating ability are both important, the demands of the sport will dictate which may be a better indicator of performance, not the only indicator of performance.

Testing speed and associated variables. Speed is defined as distance divided by time, or, more simply put, how quickly an athlete can cover a distance. Common assessments of speed and its associated variables include tests of acceleration, average speed, peak speed and change of direction ability (COD; i.e. agility). Acceleration should be measured with running distances less than 20 m. Depending on the sport and ability of individual athletes, peak speed should be assessed using distances of 30–100 m. Keep in mind that athletes in many team sports may rarely sprint distances long enough to approach peak speed; testing should reflect typical distances covered during competition. Numerous options exist to assess COD ability. The Pro Agility Shuttle has been used to evaluate COD ability in a variety of athletes (Vescovi & McGuigan, 2008; Sierer et al., 2008), while COD tests such as the lane agility drill/test for basketball (McGill et al., 2012) have been developed for specific sports.

Testing endurance and associated variables. Endurance is described as the ability to sustain or repeat a task(s). Endurance is certainly important for an aerobically dominated sport such as marathoning (aerobic endurance), but many team sports require substantial anaerobic endurance where repeat sprints and COD are performed. Anaerobic endurance or capacity is also critical for events lasting between 30 s and 5 min such as 400–1500 m run and 2 km row.

In order to assess maximum aerobic capacity (VO_2max), respiratory gas exchange is measured during a graded exercise test (GXT; treadmill or bike) with a gas analyser. Field-based tests such as the beep test and yo-yo intermittent recovery test have been used to estimate VO_2max and may be a more appropriate choice when testing team-based sports with large groups of athletes (Krustrup et al., 2003; Thomas et al., 2006). Lactate threshold is also an important indicator of endurance performance. Other associated variables important for a variety of aerobic events include but are not limited to lactate threshold, exercise economy/efficiency and critical power (Bassett & Howley, 2000). Naturally, time trials during aerobic events also serve as indicators of aerobic ability.

Common tests of anaerobic endurance include repeat 20 m sprints (Pyne et al., 2008), the Bosco test (Urszula et al., 2014) and the Wingate test (White & Al-Dawalibi, 1986). To date, assessments of maximal accumulated oxygen deficit (MAOD) are considered the gold standard for testing anaerobic capacity. MAOD tests can be adapted for numerous events and can be performed on treadmills, bikes or rowers at a predetermined and constant power output until exhaustion (Noordhof et al., 2010).

Section II

Applied case examples

This section contains several published case examples that cover a range of athletes and assessments. These examples are intended to provide practical and meaningful examples of how results of key performance assessments are interpreted in applied and research settings. Considerations for age, training status and position are also provided where appropriate. Each case example will include the following: purpose of the study, details about selected tests and testing protocols, results and several "key concepts" that can be used to design and implement a custom athlete-testing and monitoring programme.

Applied performance assessment case example 1

The following case example examines the study "Discrepancy between exercise performance, body composition, and sex steroid response after a six-week detraining period in professional soccer players" (Koundourakis et al., 2014).

The purpose of the study presented in this first example was to investigate the effects of a 6-week detraining period on a variety of performance variables including sprint speed, jump height and aerobic capacity. Changes in body composition and several biochemical markers were also assessed. This discussion will focus largely on assessments of performance. This article is also open-access and freely available online at https://doi.org/10.1371/journal.pone.0087803.

In this study by Koundourakis et al. (2014), 55 professional male Greek soccer players participated. Each athlete was a member of one of two Superleague teams; 23 athletes were members of Team A and 22 athletes were members of Team B.

Performance testing occurred at two different times of the year. The first round of testing was conducted in May at the end of the season (Pre). The second round of testing occurred in early July after the offseason period and prior to the subsequent preseason (Post). Testing was completed over the course of 2 days and each day followed the schedule and included the assessments detailed in Table 15.1.

The 6-week offseason, or detraining period, consisted of a 2-week recuperation period and a 4-week period of light activity. During the 2-week recuperation period, all athletes were instructed to avoid any type of structured physical activity. During the remaining 4 weeks, athletes were instructed to perform low-intensity (50–60% of VO_2max) aerobic running for 20–30 min three times a week, with a rest day between each running day. This provides readers a glimpse into an interesting scenario that is not often duplicated, at least not purposely. It is rare that a coach would instruct their athletes to do absolutely no physical activity for 2 weeks, followed by very little activity for another 4 weeks. Unfortunately, this may reflect the type of break from training some athletes choose to take. For instance, in US high school and college athletics, participation in sport is tethered to the academic

Table 15.1 Daily testing schedule and details.

Day	Time	Tests	Testing instrument (performance tests only)	Test details (performance tests only)
1	08:30	Anthropometrics	See study.	See study
	09:30–10:30	Blood draws	See study.	See study
	17:00	Squat jump (SJ) Countermovement jump (CMJ)	Flight time was used to estimate jump heights using a jump mat.	For each jump type, the best of three jump attempts was used for analysis. Both jump types were complete with no arm swing (hands on hips).
		10 m sprint 20 m sprint	Sprint times were measured with timing gates.	Each sprint type was performed twice and the best of two was used for analysis. Both sprint types were performed from a standing start position.
Day 2	09:30 am	VO$_2$max	Expired gases were analysed using a metabolic cart.	VO$_2$max testing was completed on a motorised treadmill using a custom protocol.

calendar. During academic breaks such as the winter and summer breaks, athletes may not be engaged in supervised training and may choose to participate in very little to no training.

Results

What happened to fitness during this detraining period? Across the board, all measures of performance decreased in both teams. VO$_2$max decreased by 2.64 ml/kg/min (Team A) and 2.17 ml/kg/min (Team B). Team A SJ and CMJ height decreased by 2.40 cm and 1.91 cm, respectively. Team B SJ and CMJ height decreased by 2.87 cm and 2.73 cm, respectively. Since jump heights decreased, it is no surprise that sprint times also worsened. Team A saw their 10 m and 20 m sprint times increase by 0.05 sec and 0.04 sec, while 10 m and 20 m sprints for Team B both increased by 0.05 sec. Body weight and body fat percentage also increased in both teams; Team A bodyweight and body fat percentage increased by 1.53 kg and 1.73%, and Team B bodyweight and body fat percentage increased by 1.60 kg and 1.06%. Figures 15.1 and 15.2 provide a visual representation of the performance declines seen in both teams.

Discussion of key concepts

Key concept 1. It is important to recognise how testing sessions were scheduled and ordered. Due to the number and fatiguing nature of some tests, performance assessments were conducted on two separate days. The first day of testing was also divided into two sessions;

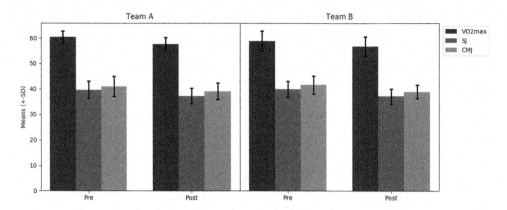

Figure 15.1 Changes in VO_2max (ml·kg·min^{-1}), squat jump height (cm) and countermovement jump height (cm) after a detraining period in Team A and Team B. **Significantly lower than Pre ($p < 0.001$).

Source: This figure has been adapted from Koundourakis et al. (2014) and has been reproduced under the terms of the Creative Commons Attribution License 4.0, which permits unrestricted use, distribution, and reproduction in any medium.

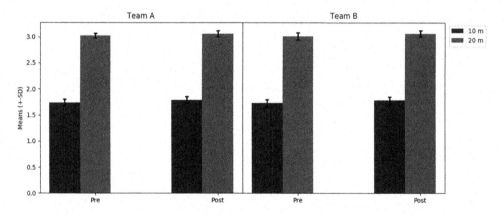

Figure 15.2 Changes in 10 m and 20 m sprint times after a detraining period in Team A and Team B. **Significantly lower than Pre ($p < 0.001$).

Source: This figure has been adapted from Koundourakis et al. (2014) and has been reproduced under the terms of the Creative Commons Attribution License 4.0, which permits unrestricted use, distribution, and reproduction in any medium.

anthropometric measures and blood draws were completed in the morning, while SJ, CMJ, 10 m sprints and 20 m sprints were completed during the afternoon. The order of performance assessments used in this study was not selected randomly; these tests are performed in order from least to most fatiguing. On the second day of testing, only VO_2max was assessed, which was also when the most fatiguing performance assessments were completed. Standardised warm-up protocols were also used prior to each testing session.

Key concept 2. The tests selected assess most of the underlying biomotor abilities that are key to the sport of soccer. In order to excel in soccer, an athlete should be able to generate high muscular power (SJ and CMJ height), accelerate quickly and run at high speed (10 and 20 m sprints) and have a substantial aerobic base (VO_2max). With this said, additional testing may have been warranted to assess other specific fitness characteristics needed in soccer. Some of the tests used could have also been eliminated, or condensed, without compromising the importance of the testing results. For instance, instead of assessing two different jump types and two different sprint distances, a CMJ and 20 m sprint with split times at 10 m and 20 m could be used. This will reduce the number of tests and allow coaching staff to come to similar conclusions. Since the number of tests has been reduced, this may provide enough time to assess other fitness characteristics such as change of direction ability (e.g. 505 change of direction, including COD deficit) and anaerobic/power endurance (e.g. repeat 20 m sprint or Bosco jump test). Instead of using a treadmill and metabolic cart to assess VO_2max, the yo-yo intermittent recovery test can be used to estimate VO_2max (Scott et al., 2013).

Key concept 3. It is certainly reasonable to expect performance to decline during extended periods of reduced (or no) training volume and/or intensity. This study helps illustrate a larger point that can be applied to any sport and level of athletics. Performance testing can be used to encourage or enforce training compliance during offseason periods where athletes may not have direct contact with coaching staff. Assessments can also be used to illustrate the importance of offseason S&C to athletes and sport coaches.

While it is beyond the scope of this chapter to address strategies to manage undertrained athletes, it is an interesting thought experiment. For instance, the first regular season game in college soccer is often during the first several days of September but athletes may not return from summer break until the first or second week of August. If athletes return undertrained, how should athletes be managed if the regular season begins less than a month after athletes return?

Applied performance assessment case example 2

The following case example examines the study, "Effect of age on anthropometric and physical performance measures in professional baseball players" (Mangine et al., 2013).

The purpose of the study presented in this second example was to investigate anthropometric and performance changes due to age (ages 16 to 35+) in Rookie, A, AA, AAA and major league baseball players. Performance assessments included isometric grip strength (IGS), countermovement vertical jump (CMJ), 300 yd shuttle, 10 yd sprint and pro agility shuttle (Pro). For the purposes of this discussion, assessments of performance will be the primary focus. This article can be found online at https://doi.org/10.1519/JSC.0b013e31825753cb.

In this study by Mangine et al. (2013), athletes from four different professional baseball organisations participated in the research. Performance assessments were completed during spring preseason training camps between 2005 and 2010. In total, data from 1157 professional baseball players were collected. All players were on the rosters of Rookie, A, AA, AAA or major league teams. Players were classified by position (position players and pitchers) and were divided into the following six age groups below.

- AG1 = 16–19 yrs (n = 82)
- AG2 = 20–22 yrs (n = 285)
- AG3 = 23–25 yrs (n = 364)
- AG4 = 26–28 yrs (n = 206)

- AG5 = 29–31 yrs (n = 112)
- AG6 = 32–34 yrs (n = 63)
- AG7 = 35+ yrs (n = 45)

Testing was completed in the order anthropometrics, ISG, CMJ, 10 yd sprint, Pro and 300 yd shuttle. Details of these assessments can be found in Table 15.2. No information regarding time of day for data collection was provided.

Before discussing the results, it is important to consider the population in this study. More specifically, take another look at the number of subjects in each age group. There is a steep change in group subject numbers from AG1 to AG2 (n = 82 and n = 285, respectively) and a sharp, continuous decline from AG3 to AG7 (n = 364 and n = 45, respectively). Figure 15.3 illustrates the number of athletes in each age group. This is important because this should shape the manner in which the results are interpreted. More on this shortly in the discussion of key concepts.

Results

The study found there was no significant decline in CMJ height in position players with age, but there was a significant decrease in CMJ height among pitchers, especially in the

Table 15.2 Performance assessment details of professional baseball players.

Tests	Testing instrument (performance tests only)	Test details (performance tests only)
Anthropometrics	See study.	See study.
Isometric grip strength	A handgrip dynamometer was used to assess grip strength in kilograms.	Handgrip strength was assessed twice in both hands. The highest score was recorded and analysed.
Countermovement jump (CMJ)	Jump and reach height was measured using a Vertec.	The CMJ was completed using an arm swing. Standing vertical reach height was subtracted from jump and reach height to estimate jump height. Three jumps were completed and the highest was recorded for analysis. Peak and average power were also estimated.
10 yd sprint	Sprint times were measured with timing gates.	The 10 yd sprint was performed three times and the best attempt was used for analysis. Timing was initiated upon player movement and players started the sprint using a two-point base running stance.
Pro agility shuttle	Agility times were measured using a hand-held stopwatch.	Timing was initiated upon player movement and players started the sprint using a two-point base running stance.
300 yd shuttle	The type of timer was not specified (assume hand-held stopwatch).	Timing was initiated upon player movement and players started the sprint using a two-point base running stance. The 300 yd shuttle was completed twice, with 5 min of rest taken between trials. The average of both attempts was analysed.

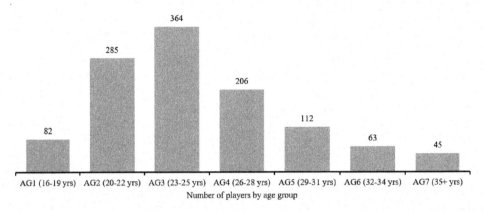

Figure 15.3 Number of players by age group.

oldest age groups (AG6 and AG7). There were no significant changes in 10 yd sprint or Pro times. Three hundred yard shuttle performance declined significantly with age (i.e. times increased), particularly for pitchers in AG5, AG6 and AG7. IGS was largely maintained throughout all age groups, but seemed to peak during the late 20s and early 30s (AG4 and AG5). As a group, body mass, lean body mass and body fat percentage increased significantly with age. Position players tend to increase both body mass and lean body mass until their early-to-mid 30s; after their mid-30s they continue to increase body mass while lean mass is maintained. Pitchers on the other hand, seem to lose both body mass and lean mass in their 30s.

Discussion of key concepts

Key concept 1. In the introduction of this published case example, the authors outline the strong relationship between baseball-specific tasks (throwing velocity, slugging percentage and stealing bases) with fitness characteristics such as strength, power, speed and agility. These fitness characteristics are the underlying abilities that support an athlete's potential to perform sport-specific tasks. As a result of this relationship, assuming an athlete has adequate skill, these fitness characteristics can be used as indicators of how well an athlete will perform, and/or to determine whether an athlete is adapting to an S&C program as expected.

Notice the performance assessments used in this study are not particularly specific to baseball, and would work equally well in many strength- and power-oriented sports. As a sport scientist or S&C coach, this reinforces a point made earlier in this chapter: it is important to select performance tests which assess the underlying biomotor abilities required for the sport, and not be overly concerned whether the test selected looks exactly like the sport or task. For instance, does a 10 yd sprint or pro agility shuttle look exactly like stealing a base or running down a fly ball? Of course not. In this example, it could be stated with confidence that those athletes who perform well in those tests will also perform well when required to steal a base or run down a fly ball because they possess the fitness characteristics that support those activities.

Key concept 2. As with the previous case example, notice that nearly all of the tests require very little equipment and the equipment that is required is rather inexpensive. There are certainly instances where expensive equipment is required for a more detailed assessment. For instance, force plates and 3D motion capture can be used to analyse a pitch. However, assessing the underlying fitness characteristics for a sport rarely requires prohibitively expensive instruments. Using tools such as jump mats to assess jump height and timing gates to measure sprint and change of direction ability are only a couple of examples. The instruments are also portable and allow for more frequent assessments to be completed.

Key concept 3. Other than CMJ height in pitchers and 300 yd shuttle times in pitchers, is performance really maintained as age increases in professional baseball players? As the discussion section of this case example eludes to, the results should be interpreted with caution.

The reason the results of this study should be approached with caution is due to the selection bias present in this investigation. This study captures a cross section of baseball players and does not follow baseball players before, during and after their career. Naturally, the only baseball players that can be tested during spring training are those still on a roster. There are two types of selection bias (there are many) encountered in this study: negative selection bias and survival bias. Now, this does not discount the results of this investigation in any way; the study simply investigated a cross section of baseball players. To illustrate both negative selection bias and survival bias in action, consider again the number of athletes in each age group. Figure 15.3 shows the number of players increased dramatically from AG1 to AG3, and then decreased dramatically from AG3 to AG7. Why does age group size change so much? More specifically, why are numbers of athletes in the youngest and oldest age groups so much lower than age groups in the middle of the age range?

It is certainly reasonable to assume there are numerous 16–19-year-old baseball players who do not yet possess the physical abilities to perform at levels required for professional baseball. This is an example of negative selection bias. It is not appropriate to conclude that performance was maintained throughout age groups because many 16–19-year-old players presumably do not perform well enough to be selected for a professional roster in the first place.

Essentially the opposite could be said for the oldest age groups. It is again reasonable to assume that as athletes enter their 30s, years of play have resulted in injury, and declining performance due to physiological changes such as decreasing testosterone (Allan & McLachlan, 2004; Leifke et al., 2000) may result in retirement from baseball. This is an example of survivor bias. Again, it is inappropriate to conclude that performance was maintained with age because many players in their 30s (or older) no longer perform well enough to remain on a professional roster.

These and other types of selection bias can influence the results and appropriate interpretation of performance assessments at all levels of athletics and in a variety of ways. For instance, due to higher training ages in senior college basketball players, more seniors may have the physical abilities to be on the team than many freshmen. In this case, seniors may outnumber lower classmen on a team for a season, but the lower classmen that were able to make the roster are high performers, particularly for their age. Does this mean that freshman typically perform at the same level as seniors? Certainly not. The reverse scenario could occur if a team largely made of seniors, and all of the senior graduates, leaving the roster filled primarily with lower classmen.

Applied performance assessment case example 3

The following case example examines the study "Strength training improves performance and pedaling characteristics in elite cyclists" (Rønnestad et al., 2015).

The purpose of the study presented in the third case example was to examine the effect of a resistance training programme on strength, pedal stroke characteristics, mean power output, cycling economy and other determinants of endurance cycling performance in elite cyclists. This article can be found online at http://dx.doi.org/10.1111/sms.12257.

In this study by Rønnestad et al. (2015), 16 elite cyclists participated in this research. Cyclists were either national- (n = 8) or international-level (n = 8) cyclists. Athletes were randomly assigned to an endurance training only group (E) or a concurrent training group (ES) that added resistance training to the endurance training that was being completed. Data were collected over a 25-week period that started 2 weeks after the end of race season. During the first 10 weeks, ES participated in two resistance training sessions a week. During the last 15 weeks, ES completed a strength maintenance period consisting of a single resistance training session every 7–10 days. The E group only participated in endurance training during the 25-week period. Testing was completed pre- and post-intervention; of the tests detailed in Table 15.3, isometric half squat was performed pre-, at 10 weeks and post-intervention. Table 15.3 summarises the testing procedures used in this case example.

Results

Respective to body mass, relative changes in isometric half-squat peak force were statistically greater in ES than in E with a very large effect size. As isometric half squat was the only assessment completed three times during this study, improvements in peak force were maintained during the 15-week maintenance phase. Peak force did not change for E. Peak Wingate power did not change significantly between groups but a moderate effect size suggest improvement favouring ES. No statistical differences for VO_2max or average Wingate power were found between groups. However, a moderate effect size was found for average Wingate power, suggesting that changes in average Wingate power was greater in ES than in E. Mean power during the last 2 min of the VO_2max test (W_{max}) was statistically greater in ES than in E, with a moderate effect size. No differences in power at lactate threshold or pedalling efficiency were found between groups.

Mean power output during the 40-min time trial increased significantly from pre-to-post in ES but no increase was found in E. The relative increase in mean power output was also statistically greater in ES compared to E, with a moderate effect size. Improvements in 40-min time trial performance, represented by mean power, were strongly correlated (r = –0.63, P < 0.01) with the ability to achieve earlier peak torque during pedal strokes.

Discussion of key concepts

Key concept 1. Improvements in performance were seen in many of the variables tested in these endurance athletes. This should come as no surprise as heavy resistance training has been shown to improve endurance performance in a variety of endurance athletes (Berryman et al., 2017). The mechanisms for this are in part due to improved muscle fibre recruitment leading to improved efficiency and higher RFD (Rønnestad & Mujika, 2014). This may explain how athletes in the ES group were able to improve important indicators of fatigue resistance and endurance performance such as W_{max} and mean power during the

Table 15.3 Performance assessment details of elite endurance cyclists.

Day	Tests	Testing instrument (performance tests only)	Test details (performance tests only)
1	Anthropometrics	See study.	See study.
2	Isometric half squat	Force plates were used to measure peak force generated during the isometric half squat.	Three trials of the isometric half squat were performed. The duration of each trial was 3 seconds and 1 min of rest was given between trials. The best of three trials was used for analysis. Position was standardised.
	30 second Wingate test	Peak and mean power were measured with a cycle ergometer.	Warm-up, loading scheme and position were all standardised. A single trial of the Wingate test was performed.
3	Incremental cycle test	A cycle ergometer was used to complete the incremental cycle test. A blood lactate analyser was used to assess blood lactate concentration at different workloads. HR monitor was used to measure HR response and a metabolic cart was used to measure gas exchange. Strain gauges were used to measure pedal force characteristics.	A standardised warm-up was completed on a cycle ergometer (5 min at 125 W). Power output was increased by 50 W every 5 min until blood lactate reached a concentration of 4 mmol/ L. Lactate was measured at the end of each 5 min stage. HR and gas exchange was measured during the last 3 min of each stage. Rotational forces (torque) were measured every 2° of crank rotation during the last 1.5–4.5 min of the stage that caused blood lactate to reach 4 mmol/L.
	VO_2max	A cycle ergometer was used to complete the VO_2max test. HR monitor was used to measure HR response and a metabolic cart was used to measure gas exchange.	After 10 min of rest, the VO_2max followed the incremental cycle test. A 10 min standardised warm-up was performed prior to testing. A 1 min rest was given between warm-up and testing. The first minute of the test was completed at a power output of 3 W/ kg. Power output was increased by 25 W each minute until exhaustion.
4	40 min all-out trial	Athletes used their own road racing bike to complete the trial. During the trial, all athletes were connected to the same electromagnetically braked roller.	A 20 min warm-up was completed. This warm-up was based upon individual needs but did conclude with two or three submaximal sprints. The electromagnetically braked roller was calibrated and adjusted during the last 5 min of the warm-up. Cyclists were instructed to complete the trial at the highest average power possible. Cyclists were allowed to change gears and change pedal frequency.

Additional details regarding the tests used in this study can be found in Rønnestad et al. (2015).
The athlete's preferred cadence was used during all cycling tests.

40-min time trial and the reduction in time required to reach peak force during each pedal stroke. It should also be emphasised that these improvements in performance occurred in the absence of statistical changes in VO_2max.

Key concept 2. If a practitioner approached a typical group of competitive endurance athletes and/or their coaches, what would their likely answer be to the following question?

"What type of resistance training would benefit endurance athletes most: light weight with high repetitions or heavy weight with low repetitions?"

On numerous occasions, heavy resistance training has been shown to be superior to lower-intensity–higher-volume resistance training for endurance performance (Berryman et al., 2017). Why then would most athletes and coaches choose to answer the above question "light weight with high repetitions"? This is likely to pertain to how endurance athletes and coaches perceive specificity. They associate higher repetitions as being more specific to endurance sport than heavy resistance training. Who can blame them though? How often do endurance athletes lift heavy loads during competition? Never.

As a practitioner, it is important to be able to explain the nuances of specificity and how it applies to testing and training. Recalling the discussion of strength testing from Section I, it was suggested that strength forms the foundation of all other biomotor abilities. The set and repetition scheme used to perform heavy resistance training is certainly not specific to endurance training. However, the abilities that are gained from improving strength and its associated characteristics (motor unit synchrony and recruitment patterns, RFD, etc.) have substantial carryover which enhances the generation of force responsible for powering every step or turn of the pedal in endurance sports.

Applied performance assessment case example 4

The following case example examines the study "Are changes in maximal squat strength during preseason training reflected in changes in sprint performance in rugby league players?" (Comfort et al., 2012).

The purpose of this study was to determine whether changes in maximal squat strength translate into changes in sprint performance during the pre-season of rugby league players. This article can be found online at http://dx.doi.org/10.1519/JSC.0b013e31822a5cbf.

In this study by Comfort et al. (2012), 19 well-trained professional rugby league players participated in the research. All athletes had previously finished an 8-week off-season hypertrophy programme. The pre-season training programme, which was of primary interest in this study, was 8 weeks in duration and consisted of a 4-week mesocycle focused on strength development, followed by a 4-week mesocycle focused on power development. A lower-body strength and conditioning programme was performed twice weekly; plyometric and agility sessions were also performed twice weekly. Core exercises during the strength mesocycle included the back squat, mid-thigh clean pull, Romanian deadlift and Nordic curl. Core exercises during the power mesocycle included the hang power clean, squat jump, back squat and Nordic curl. Testing was completed before and after the 8-week pre-season training programme. Table 15.4 summarises the testing protocol used in this case example.

Results

Absolute and relative strength increased significantly during the 8-week preseason training period. Mean absolute 1-RM squat strength increased from 170.6 kg to 200.8 kg,

Table 15.4 Performance assessment details of rugby league players.

Tests	Testing instrument (performance tests only)	Test details (performance tests only)
1RM back squat	Free weights	1-RM squat was assessed before and after the 8-week pre-season training programme at the same time of day. Post-training 1-RM squat was measured 48 h after the last training session.
		1-RM squat assessment followed a standardised protocol. Athletes were required to squat to a depth resulting in a 90° knee angle, which was established during the warm-up. A bungee cord was placed so the athlete's buttocks would touch the cord at the level indicating a 90° knee angle had been achieved. A 1-RM squat was established within four attempts. Strength was reported in absolute (kg) and relative terms (kg lifted per kg of body weight).
20 m sprint	Sprint times were measured with timing gates.	Sprint times were measured 72 hours after 1-RM squat was assessed.
		Three 20 m sprints were performed on an indoor track with 1 minute of rest between each attempt. During the 20 m sprint, 5, 10 and 20 m times were measured. The athlete's lead foot was placed 0.5 m behind the start line; this was the start position.

while relative strength, expressed as 1-RM squat divided by body mass, increased from 1.78 kg·kg^{-1} to 2.05 kg·kg^{-1}. Significant improvements in 5 m (pre, 1.05 s; post, 0.97 s), 10 m (pre, 1.78 s; post, 1.65 s) and 20 m (pre, 3.03 s; post, 2.85 s) were also seen during the 8-week preseason training period. While body composition was not assessed, a small but significant increase in body mass was seen (pre, 96.2 kg; post, 97.7 kg). Since absolute strength, relative strength and speed improved, the increase in body mass was likely to be a result of increased lean mass.

Discussion of key concepts

Key concept 1. The authors of this study implemented a block periodised programme which employs phased potentiation to guide adaptations in a specific direction. In this case, an 8-week offseason hypertrophy phase was followed by a 4-week strength phase and then a 4-week power phase. It should be noted that at no time during the strength and power phases did a phase focus on developing a singular fitness characteristic. Rather, these phases represent a changing focus but do not ignore other fitness characteristics, using a mixed-methods approach. For instance, during the strength phase, power-oriented exercises were still included (i.e. mid-thigh clean pulls and plyometrics), while the power phase also included strength-oriented exercises (i.e. back squat). Since the preseason period should be used to cause stable and sport-specific adaptations that will support the upcoming season, it is important for practitioners to understand how to sequence training phases together to direct adaptations toward a specific goal(s). A block periodised programme leveraging phased potentiation may produce superior performance gains and help manage fatigue better than other approaches to training (Hoffman et al., 2009; Painter et al., 2012).

Key concept 2. This study reinforces the importance of developing absolute and relative strength prior to the beginning of the regular season. Athletes competing in contact sports such as rugby and American football must be able to generate high absolute forces in order to tackle and block their opponents. Additionally, as this and previous research has suggested, relative strength is indicative of an athlete's ability to move their own mass during tasks such as sprinting (McBride et al., 2009), jumping and change of direction (Nimphius et al., 2010). High relative strength should therefore increase scoring opportunities and improve an athlete's chance of making and/or evading a tackle.

Key concept 3. Considering the importance of absolute and relative strength in facilitating athletic performance, efforts to maintain strength in-season should help maintain in-season performance. Since it is difficult to improve strength in-season (Baker, 2001), particularly in elite competitors and those sports with long regular seasons, it is extremely important for practitioners to develop absolute and relative strength during the preseason when stressors from competition are not an issue. Failing to develop strength prior to the beginning of the regular season may lead to performance decrements as the season continues.

Conclusion

In closing, it is important to reinforce why regular performance testing should be completed. If decisions about athlete training are made in the absence of performance testing, these decisions are better described as guesses. Performance testing should inform those responsible for developing an athlete, whether or not development is proceeding as planned. If development is not proceeding as intended, training (or other stressors) can then be adjusted or managed. In order to make quality decisions, follow the basic guidelines outlined in this chapter. Performance testing should be conducted frequently, tests must be valid and reliable, assessments should evaluate biomotor abilities important for the sport and results should be analysed and interpreted appropriately. Lastly, practitioners should ensure that testing results are easily communicable to all personnel responsible for athlete development.

References

Allan, C.A., & McLachlan, R.I. (2004). Age-related changes in testosterone and the role of replacement therapy in older men. *Clinical Endocrinology, 60*(6), 653–670.

Baker, D. (2001). The effects of an in-season of concurrent training on the maintenance of maximal strength and power in professional and college-aged rugby league football players. *Journal of Strength & Conditioning Research, 15*(2), 172–177.

Bassett Jr, D.R., and Howley, E.T. (2000). Limiting factors for maximum oxygen uptake and determinants of endurance performance. *Medicine & Science in Sports & Exercise, 32*(1), 70.

Berryman, N., et al. (2018). Strength training for middle- and long-distance performance: A meta-analysis. *International Journal of Sports Physiology and Performance, 13*(1), 57–63.

Bompa, T.O., & Haff, G. (2009). *Periodization: Theory and methodology of training.* Champaign, IL: Human Kinetics.

Buchheit, M. (2016). The numbers will love you back in return—I promise. *International Journal of Sports Physiology and Performance, 11*(4), 551–554.

Chelly, M.S., Hermassi, S., & Shephard, R.J. (2010). Relationships between power and strength of the upper and lower limb muscles and throwing velocity in male handball players. *Journal of Strength & Conditioning Research, 24*(6), 1480–1487.

Comfort, P., Haigh, A. and Matthews, M.J. (2012). Are changes in maximal squat strength during preseason training reflected in changes in sprint performance in rugby league players? *Journal of Strength & Conditioning Research, 26*(3), 772–776.

Cormie, P., McBride, J.M., & McCaulley, G.O. (2009). Power-time, force-time, and velocity-time curve analysis of the countermovement jump: impact of training. *Journal of Strength & Conditioning Research, 23*(1), 177–186.

Haff, G.G., & Triplett, N.T. (2015). *Essentials of strength training and conditioning* (4th edn.). Champaign, IL: Human Kinetics.

Harman, E.A., et al. (1990). The effects of arms and countermovement on vertical jumping. *Medicine & Science in Sports & Exercise, 22*(6), 825–833.

Hoffman, J.R., Ratamess, N.A., Klatt, M., Faigenbaum, A.D., Ross, R.E., Tranchina, N.M., McCurley, R.C., Kang, J., and Kraemer, W.J. (2009). Comparison between different off-season resistance training programs in Division III American college football players. *Journal of Strength & Conditioning Research, 23*(1), 11–19.

Hopkins, W.G., Hawley, J.A., & Burke, L.M. (1999). Design and analysis of research on sport performance enhancement. *Medicine & Science in Sports & Exercise, 31*(3), 472–485.

Koundourakis, N.E., et al. (2014). Discrepancy between exercise performance, body composition, and sex steroid response after a six-week detraining period in professional soccer players. *PloS One, 9*(2), e87803.

Krustrup, P., et al. (2003). The yo-yo intermittent recovery test: Physiological response, reliability, and validity. *Medicine & Science in Sports & Exercise, 35*(4), 697–705.

Leifke, E., et al. (2000). Age-related changes of serum sex hormones, insulin-like growth factor-1 and sex-hormone binding globulin levels in men: cross-sectional data from a healthy male cohort. *Clinical Endocrinology, 53*(6), 689–695.

Mangine, G.T., et al. (2013). Effect of age on anthropometric and physical performance measures in professional baseball players. *Journal of Strength & Conditioning Research, 27*(2), 375–381.

McBride, J.M., Blow, D., Kirby, T.J., Haines, T.L., Dayne, A.M., & Triplett, N.T. (2009). Relationship between maximal squat strength and five, ten, and forty yard sprint times. *Journal of Strength & Conditioning Research, 23*(6), 1633–1636.

McGill, S.M., Andersen, J.T., and Horne, A.D. (2012). Predicting performance and injury resilience from movement quality and fitness scores in a basketball team over 2 years. *Journal of Strength & Conditioning Research, 26*(7), 1731–1739.

McGuigan, M. (2017). *Monitoring training and performance in athletes.* Champaign, IL: Human Kinetics.

McMahon, J.J., Jones, P.A., & Comfort, P. (2016). A correction equation for jump height measured using the just jump system. *International Journal of Sports Physiology and Performance, 11*(4), 555–557.

McMahon, J.J., Jones, P.A., & Comfort, P. (2017). Comment on: "Anthropometric and physical qualities of elite male youth ruby league players". *Sports Medicine.* https://doi.org/10.1007/s40279-017-0771-6.

Nimphius, S., Mcguigan, M.R., and Newton, R.U. (2010). Relationship between strength, power, speed, and change of direction performance of female softball players. *Journal of Strength & Conditioning Research, 24*(4), 885–895.

Noordhof, D.A., de Koning, J.J., & Foster, C. (2010). The maximal accumulated oxygen deficit method. *Sports Medicine, 40*(4), 285–302.

Nuzzo, J.L., et al. (2008). Relationship between countermovement jump performance and multijoint isometric and dynamic tests of strength. *Journal of Strength & Conditioning Research, 22*(3), 699–707.

Painter, K.B., Haff, G.G., Ramsey, M.W., McBride, J., Triplett, T., Sands, W.A., Lamont, H.S., Stone, M.E., and Stone, M.H. (2012). Strength gains: Block versus daily undulating periodization weight training among track and field athletes. *International Journal of Sports Physiology and Performance, 7*(2), 161–169.

Pyne, D.B., et al. (2008). Relationships between repeated sprint testing, speed, and endurance. *Journal of Strength & Conditioning Research, 22*(5), 1633–1637.

Reynolds, J.M., Gordon, T.J., & Roberrgs, R.A. (2006). Prediction of one repetition maximum strength from multiple repetition maximum testing and anthropometry. *Journal of Strength & Conditioning Research, 20*(3), 584–592.

Rhea, M.R. (2004). Determining the magnitude of treatment effects in strength training research through the use of the effect size. *Journal of Strength & Conditioning Research, 18*(4), 918–920.

Rønnestad, B.R., et al. (2015). Strength training improves performance and pedaling characteristics in elite cyclists. *Scandinavian Journal of Medicine & Science in Sports, 25*(1), e89–98.

Rønnestad, B.R., & Mujika, I. (2014). Optimizing strength training for running and cycling endurance performance: A review. *Scandinavian Journal of Medicine & Science in Sports, 24*(4), 603–612.

Scott, B.R., et al. (2013). A comparison of methods to quantify the in-season training load of professional soccer players. *International Journal of Sports Physiology and Performance, 8*(2), 195–202.

Sierer, S.P., et al. (2008). The National Football League Combine: Performance differences between drafted and nondrafted players entering the 2004 and 2005 drafts. *Journal of Strength & Conditioning Research, 22*(1), 6–12.

Spaniol, F.J. (2009). Baseball athletic test: A baseball-specific test battery. *Strength & Conditioning Journal, 31*(2), 26.

Stone, M.H., Sands, W.A., Pierce, K.C., Carlock, J.O.N., Cardinale, M., and Newton, R.U. (2005). Relationship of maximum strength to weightlifting performance. *Medicine & Science in Sports & Exercise, 37*(6), 1037–1043.

Stone, M.H., Stone, M., & Sands, W.A. (2007). *Principles and practice of resistance training.* Champaign, IL: Human Kinetics.

Tanner, R.K., Australian Institute of Sport & Gore, C.J. (2012). *Physiological tests for elite athletes.* Champaign, IL: Human Kinetics.

Thomas, A., Dawson, B., and Goodman, C. (2006). The yo-yo test: Reliability and association with a 20-m shuttle run and VO2max. *International Journal of Sports Physiology and Performance, 1*(2), 137–149.

Urszula, S.G., Arkadiusz, S., & Tomasz, G. (2014). Applying the Kinematic Parameters From The Bosco Jump Test To Evaluate The Athlete's Preparedness And To Select Training Parameters. *Life sciences, 11*(5).

Vescovi, J.D., & McGuigan, M.R. (2008). Relationships between sprinting, agility, and jump ability in female athletes. *Journal of Sports Sciences, 26*(1), 97–107.

White, J.A., & Al-Dawalibi, M.A. (1986). Assessment of the power performance of racing cyclists. *Journal of Sports Sciences, 4*(2), 117–122.

Whitmer, T.D., et al. (2015). Accuracy of a vertical jump contact mat for determining jump height and flight time. *Journal of Strength & Conditioning Research, 29*(4), 877–881.

16 Presentation and communication of results

John J. McMahon and Peter Mundy

Introduction

There is no "gold standard" or "one size fits all" method of presenting and communicating results of performance tests to key members of an athlete's training/performance team. Rather, the precise method(s) of presentation and communication that best suits the team you are working with (and, indeed, the individual members/groups within the broader team) is likely to be determined based on several factors. Perhaps the most important factor is that although considered experts in their respective sporting/coaching domains, sports coaches are unlikely to be statistically trained (Robertson et al., 2017) or have the time available to make text-dense written reports impactful (Buchheit, 2017). The importance of presenting performance test results to sports coaches in a visual format, therefore, is clear (Buchheit, 2017; Lockie et al., 2018; McGuigan et al., 2013). It has been recommended, however, that the individual preferences of the audience to which performance test results will be presented should be considered when determining the exact mode of data visualisation to be used (Buchheit, 2017; Robertson et al., 2017). Also, particularly for performance tests included within continual athlete-monitoring batteries, there is a requirement to produce visually impactful interpretations of performance test results quickly, to enable key stakeholders to rapidly interpret their meaning and make acute adjustments to athletes' training load where necessary (Robertson et al., 2017). Thus, it is likely that different modes of visually impactful presentation of performance test results will be employed by practitioners, depending upon the target audience and relative priority (i.e. urgency) of results.

With the above in mind, this chapter will discuss some of the different visual formats in which performance test results can be presented and communicated to the key members of the athletes' training/performance team (including the athletes themselves). This chapter will also provide suggestions of how to highlight individual athlete's performance test results within squad-sized data sets. Perhaps more importantly, this chapter will complement Chapter 3 by describing methods in which "meaningful" changes in an individual athlete's performance test results (i.e. changes above normal or random error in the test scores) can be determined and then visually presented. This is imperative for the practitioner because it helps to improve the accuracy of data interpretation and visual reporting, whilst also facilitating the use of accurate language when verbally communicating the data to the athletes' key stakeholders. Only the key results of performance tests described throughout the previous chapters of this book will be discussed in the present chapter, but the included principles and presentation formats could be applied to other types of athlete performance data (i.e. those derived from competitive performances). Finally, all visual presentation formats presented in this chapter were constructed in Microsoft Excel because this is probably the most accessible and familiar software available to practitioners, but powerful visual presentation formats can also be constructed using a range of commercial software packages which may be of interest to the reader (e.g. Tableau or Microsoft Power BI [Business Intelligence]).

Forest plots

The importance of using meaningful statistics and plain language when reporting changes in performance test results (particularly for individual/small squads of athletes) to coaches has been recently stressed (Buchheit, 2016a, 2016b, 2017). Analysing changes in a performance test result using magnitude-based inferences, which consider a change in a performance test result in relation to its measurement error and then the probability of said change being "real" (i.e. greater than its measurement error) or not (i.e. less than its measurement error), is one way of achieving this. Building on the statistics presented in Chapter 3, we can present the mean change in a performance test result in relation to the associated smallest worthwhile change (SWC) and within-subject standard deviation (SD_{ws}) (also referred to as the typical error of measurement or standard error of measurement) via forest plots. This visually demonstrates whether the mean change in the performance test result is greater than the SWC (is the change meaningful), when the SD_{ws} (is the change real) is also considered. Further, reporting the probabilities (i.e. percentage chances along with associated qualitative descriptions) of the mean change in a performance test result being a "real" change, alongside the forest plots, helps to facilitate the use of plain (and consistent) language among the athletes' coaching team (Buchheit, 2016b, 2017).

Figure 16.1A contains a forest plot of the pre-season percentage change in 20 m sprint speed (black circles), SWC (grey area, calculated in this example as 0.2 times the between-athlete standard deviation, expressed as a percentage [Hopkins, 2004]) and SD_{ws} (expressed as a coefficient of variation) (error bars) for 12 rugby union players. The percentage chance of the reported percentage change in 20 m sprint speed reflecting a "real" improvement, no change or a "real" reduction in performance is also presented to the right of the forest plot. For example, 61/28/11 (reported for player 12) represents a 61%, 28% and 11% chance (probability) of the change in 20 m sprint speed being a "real" improvement, no change and a "real" reduction, respectively. If the probabilities of the change in 20 m sprint speed being a "real" improvement and a "real" reduction were both >5%, the change was reported as unclear (Haugen & Buchheit, 2016). This was the case for eight out of the 12 players' data presented in Figure 16.1A. If the probability of the change in 20 m sprint speed being a "real" reduction was ≤4%, the probability of the change in 20 m sprint speed being a "real" improvement was then qualitatively interpreted using the following scale: 25–75% = possible; 75–95% = likely; 95–99.5% = very likely; >99.5% = almost certain (Haugen & Buchheit, 2016; Hopkins, 2007). For example, the probability of the change in 20 m sprint speed being a "real" improvement was possible (74%) and very likely (95%) for players 1 and 2, respectively.

Based on the information presented above, a change in a performance test result is considered likely to be "real" when the probabilities are ≥75%, which only happens when the change is >SWC and when the coefficient of variation is ≤SWC (Haugen & Buchheit, 2016). In addition to calculating probabilities of a change in a performance test result being "real", the magnitude of the change can also be determined using Cohen's effect size principle, where changes of 1–3, 3–6, 6–9 and ≥10 times the SWC are considered small, moderate, large and very large changes, respectively (Buchheit, 2016b; Hopkins, 2004). When applied to the change in 20 m sprint speed data presented in Figure 16.1B, it can be said, for example, that player 10 demonstrated a likely small improvement whereas player 2 demonstrated very

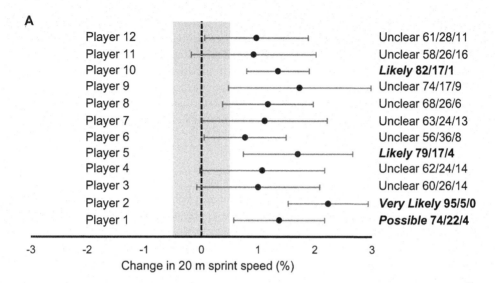

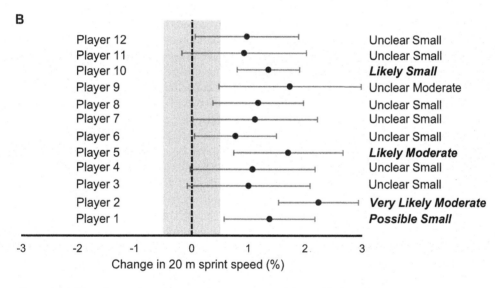

Figure 16.1 Two forest plots showing the percentage change (black circles) in 20 m sprint speed for 12 rugby union players between the start and end of pre-season training. The grey shaded area represents the associated smallest worthwhile change for the entire squad and the error bars represent the coefficient of variation for individual players (each expressed as a percentage). In top forest plot (A), the probabilities of the change in 20 m sprint speed being a "real" improvement, no change and a "real" reduction (e.g. 61/28/11 for player 12) and the associated qualitative description of the change (e.g. unclear for player 12) for each player are presented to the right of the forest plot. In bottom forest plot (B), the probabilities have been replaced with descriptions of the magnitude of the changes based on the Cohen's *d* effect size principle (e.g. a small change is reported for player 12).

likely moderate improvement. It is also worth noting that, based on the aforementioned criteria, player 9 demonstrated a moderate change in 20 m sprint speed (Figure 16.1B), but it is unclear that this change is reflective of a "real" improvement because this player's large coefficient of variation resulted in an unclear probability of this being the case. This highlights the importance of considering the associated coefficient of variation when interpreting changes in an individual's performance test result, but it is also worth noting that the coefficient of variation typically reduces when more trials of a given performance test are performed, which would increase the sensitivity of the test and thus the probability of detecting a "real" change between test occasions (Haugen & Buchheit, 2016).

Traffic-light systems

Traffic-light systems refer to the method of highlighting performance test results in either red, amber or green based on them being interpreted as negative, neutral or positive. It has been suggested that traffic-light systems are an appealing option for high-performance sport practitioners (who often work in a time/resource-constrained and fast-moving environment) because they are quick to produce (e.g. use of conditional formatting in Microsoft Excel), as well as visually appealing and easy (i.e. intuitive) to interpret (Robertson et al., 2017). Although traffic-light systems are easy to construct and interpret, determining the red, amber and green performance "bands" (i.e. the range of values obtained that would be considered negative, neutral or positive) for a given test usually requires extensive historical data to be obtained from the team you are working with, particularly in the absence of published translatable normative data sets (Robertson et al., 2017). Also, two important considerations in the utilisation of traffic-light systems in the reporting of team-sport performance test results, as suggested by Robertson et al. (2017), are to consider each individual athlete's performance within the team and to be able to identify a meaningful change in each individual athlete's performances between test occasions. Consequently, a similar approach to that described in the previous section could be utilised and then applied to the identification of red, amber and green performance test results and/or changes in performance test results between different test occasions.

For example, Table 16.1 shows one possible decision-making process in determining whether to highlight changes in 16 rugby league players' mean (of three trials) countermovement jump (CMJ) height, between the start (pre) and the end (post) of a power training mesocycle, as red, amber or green. Firstly, the percentage change in CMJ height between test occasions was calculated (using the formula: percentage change = [[test score 1 − test score 2] ÷ test score 1] × 100) for each player (fourth column) and then each player's coefficient of variation for the CMJ height test (fifth column) and the SWC of the entire squad's CMJ height (penultimate and final row of the second column) were calculated. This information was used to calculate the percentage chance of each player's change in CMJ height being reflective of a "real" improvement, no change or a "real" reduction (sixth to eighth columns), as described in the previous section. These percentage probabilities were then interpreted using the aforementioned scale (ninth column), except the term "unclear" (i.e. when the probability of both a "real" improvement and reduction was >5%) was replaced with the term "no change" for ease of understanding. Finally, different lighter shades of grey (these would be shades of green in practice) were applied to the individual player's rows depending on the scale of their improvement (i.e. likely–almost certain), while a dark grey (this would be amber in practice) was applied to cases reflective of a possible improvement in CMJ height (player 5) and black (this would be red in practice) was applied to cases reflective of a very likely reduction in CMJ height (player 8). The rows pertaining to players who were identified as demonstrating no change in CMJ height remained white.

Table 16.1 An example of the process undertaken to construct a traffic-light system for the reporting of 16 rugby league players' changes in countermovement jump height between the start (pre) and the end (post) of a power training mesocycle.

Player	Countermovement jump height				% probability of:			Interpretation
	Pre (cm)	Post (cm)	Change (%)	CV (%)	Improvement	No change	Reduction	
1	39.4	41.9	6.1	2.1	92	8	0	Likely ↑
2	32.4	36.1	10.8	3.2	97	3	0	Very likely ↑
3	40.6	40.8	0.4	2.1	30	49	21	No change
4	33.1	36.7	10.5	3.2	97	3	0	Very likely ↑
5	39.3	40.7	3.6	1.8	74	25	1	Possible ↑
6	40.5	44.8	10.1	2.9	98	2	0	Very likely ↑
7	35.0	38.2	8.7	5.3	81	12	7	Likely ↑
8	32.5	30.3	-6.9	1.9	0	5	95	Very likely ↓
9	33.5	34.4	2.5	3.1	51	36	13	No change
10	42.0	41.0	-2.3	2.3	9	35	56	No change
11	33.2	35.1	5.4	2.6	80	18	2	Likely ↑
12	32.6	37.3	13.6	3.2	99	1	0	Almost certain ↑
13	36.3	40.7	11.3	1.8	100	0	0	Almost certain ↑
14	27.0	30.0	10.8	3.4	95	5	0	Very likely ↑
15	35.1	37.3	6.1	2.1	91	9	0	Likely ↑
16	33.7	36.2	7.1	3.2	85	13	2	Likely ↑
Mean	35.4	37.6	6.1	2.8				
SD	4.0	4.0						
SWC (cm)	0.8							
SWC (%)	2.3							

CV = coefficient of variation; SD = standard deviation; SWC = smallest worthwhile change.

Showing the entire decision-making process undertaken in constructing a traffic-light system (Table 16.1) when presenting changes in performance test results to key members of the athletes' training/performance team is, of course, not advisable. Instead, we advise that just the essential data are presented in a clear and easily understood manner to such stakeholders. Because many traffic-light systems are presented in a tabulated format, we recommend that the practical advice on the production of tabulated reports provided by Buchheit (2017) is considered when constructing such systems. Other than advocating the highlighting of tabulated results in red, amber or green, presenting the important data only and removing decimal points from reported values are among the other suggestions provided by Buchheit (2017) that are thought to facilitate the construction of simple, but powerful reporting of athlete performance data in tabular form. By applying such principles to the performance test results presented in Table 16.1, we constructed the more succinct and visually appealing Table 16.2. As can be seen, the number of columns reported has been reduced by >50% by including the most important data only, the CMJ height and percentage change values have been rounded to the nearest whole number and a key has been added to the table to explain the different colours (greys and black used in the example shown) used (Table 16.2).

Table 16.2 An example of a user-friendly traffic-light system for the reporting of 16 rugby league players' changes in countermovement jump height between the start (pre) and the end (post) of a power training mesocycle.

Player	Countermovement jump height			
	Pre (cm)	Post (cm)	Change (%)	
1	39	42	6	
2	32	36	11	
3	41	41	0	
4	33	37	10	
5	39	41	4	**Key**
6	40	45	10	Almost certain ↑
7	35	38	9	Very likely ↑
8	32	30	-7	Likely ↑
9	34	34	3	Possible ↑
10	42	41	-2	Very likely ↓
11	33	35	5	
12	33	37	14	
13	36	41	11	
14	27	30	11	
15	35	37	6	
16	34	36	7	
Average	**35**	**38**	**6**	

This section provides just one example of constructing a traffic-light system (using magnitude-based inferences) to report changes in a performance test result. There are, of course, likely to be many other methods of determining a "meaningful" change in a performance test result used by practitioners and different scales applied to the interpretation of such changes. Consequently, the precise method used to construct a traffic-light system is likely to affect the interpretation of performance test results and thus the proceeding course of action taken. It is recommended, therefore, that different methods of constructing traffic-light systems are not used interchangeably, especially if applied to daily athlete performance test results (i.e. continual monitoring) whereby acute changes to the athletes' training programmes will depend on rapid and accurate interpretation of the associated results. For further discussion of the many different considerations pertaining to the construction of traffic-light systems within team-sport scenarios, the reader is referred to a recent brief review on this topic authored by Robertson et al. (2017).

Univariate scatterplots

In a research setting, univariate scatterplots have been recently advocated as a preferred alternative to bar and line graphs when presenting continuous data sets (Weissgerber et al., 2015). This is because univariate scatterplots allow for the presentation of full data sets and the distribution of said data, and any changes in the latter which may occur between testing

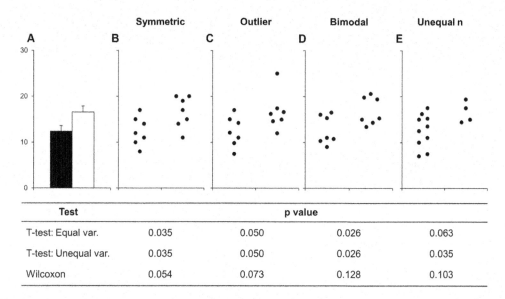

Test	p value			
T-test: Equal var.	0.035	0.050	0.026	0.063
T-test: Unequal var.	0.035	0.050	0.026	0.035
Wilcoxon	0.054	0.073	0.128	0.103

Figure 16.2 Many data sets can lead to the same bar graph.
Source: Figure adapted from Weissgerber et al. (2015) (with permission via a Creative Commons Attribution License).

occasions, rather than simply offering an overview of summary statistics such as the mean and standard deviation/standard error (and how much these changed [if at all] between testing occasions). Indeed, presenting bar or line graphs alone can be misleading due to (1) many different data distributions leading to the same bar or line graph, (2) no presentation of individual changes in test results and (3) the potential of "masking" any outliers in the data (Weissgerber et al., 2015). Examples of points 1, 2 and 3, as explained in the previous sentence, are illustrated in Figures 16.2 and 16.3.

With the above in mind, univariate scatterplots may serve as a useful visual presentation method for between-session performance test results in a team sport setting. Usefully, Weissgerber et al. (2015) published some freely downloadable Microsoft Excel templates which have been formatted to produce various univariate scatter plots (i.e. for within- and between-groups data), which can be applied to performance test data. For example, Figure 16.4A shows the average (mean of three trials) 20 m sprint times recorded for 14 academy football players on two test occasions (the start of pre-season and the end of pre-season) and Figure 16.4B shows the difference in average 20 m sprint times between these two test occasions. Figure 16.4A clearly illustrates that apart from one football player (highlighted with a thicker line and markers), all the football players demonstrated a reduction in average 20 m sprint time (i.e. an improvement) between the start and end of the pre-season training period. Figure 16.4B then provides a clearer depiction of the difference in average 20 m sprint times between these two test occasions, with the mean difference (for the 14 players) shown as the black horizontal line. In Figure 16.4B, the only football player to have demonstrated an increase in 20 m sprint time between the two test occasions is clearly visible, as his is the only data point above the zero line.

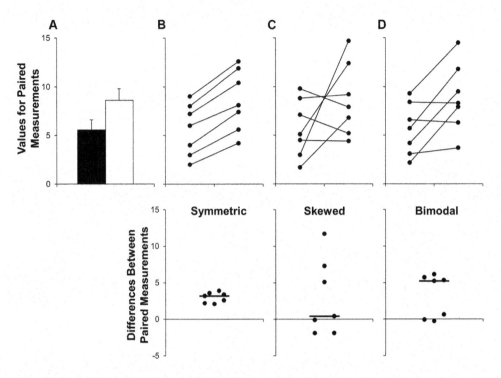

Figure 16.3 Additional problems with using bar graphs to show paired data.
Source: Figure adapted from Weissgerber et al. (2015) (with permission via a Creative Commons Attribution License).

A limitation of the univariate scatter plots showing the difference in average 20 m sprint times between the two test occasions (Figure 16.4b) is that some players' data points are not visible due to similar differences in 20 m sprint times noted for certain players (i.e. the number of visible data points shown in Figure 16.4B equals 13). The masking of individual data points due to overlapping tends to happen when the sample size is very large, and/or the differences in a test score noted between test occasions are homogeneous. A solution to this problem is to jitter the data points reflecting the similar (or identical) between-test differences in average 20 m sprint times, as shown in Figure 16.5A. This results in similar (or identical) between-test differences in average 20 m sprint times being presented parallel to one another. A further improvement to univariate scatter plots showing the between-test differences in average 20 m sprint times could be gained by adding players' squad numbers next to the individual data points. In Figure 16.5B, for example, the addition of squad numbers clearly shows that the player with squad number 15 demonstrated the sole increase in 20 m sprint time, whereas the player with squad number 14 demonstrated the greatest reduction in 20 m sprint time. Furthermore, the players with squad numbers 10 and 18 demonstrated an identical reduction in 20 m sprint time.

It is important to note that the univariate scatter plots presented in Figures 16.4 and 16.5 do not include the SWC for the squad of players or the SD_{ws} for the individual players. While the SWC for the squad of players could easily be added to these figures in the form of a shaded area or dashed line (like the mean lines presented in Figure 16.5), representing

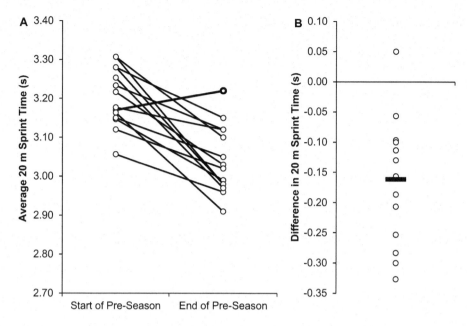

Figure 16.4 Two example univariate scatter plots. The left univariate scatter plot (A) shows the average (mean of three trials) 20 m sprint times recorded for 14 academy football players on two test occasions (the start of pre-season and the end of pre-season). The right univariate scatter plot (B) shows the individual differences in average 20 m sprint times between these two test occasions for each player (open circles) and the mean difference for the entire squad (black horizontal line).

the SD_{ws} as error bars for the individual players would be more difficult to see/interpret due to the individual data points being stacked in series with one another (i.e. some error bars would overlap each other and the individual data points). Therefore, it may be prudent to utilise forest plots in place of univariate scatter plots if the inclusion of the SWC and error bars is desirable. Additionally, the between-test differences in average 20 m sprint times shown in Figures 16.4 and 16.5 only represent absolute differences in players' scores. It may also be useful, therefore, to present between-test differences in players' scores relative to their initial score, perhaps in the form of a percentage change. This approach would account for between-player differences in absolute test scores and illustrate more fairly that (in the case of average 20 m sprint times) a given absolute difference in a test score would reflect a larger percentage difference for a faster player. For example, if the initial 20 m sprint time was 3.30 s (slower player) or 3.00 s (faster player), an absolute difference in 20 m sprint time of 0.2 s would equal a percentage difference of 6.3% and 6.9%, respectively.

Radar charts

Radar charts (sometimes referred to as spider charts) allow three or more performance test results (usually expressed as a z-score or a modified z-score) for an individual athlete to be presented on axes with an equal origin. A z-score (sometimes referred to as a standard or standardised score) represents how many standard deviations an individual athlete's score

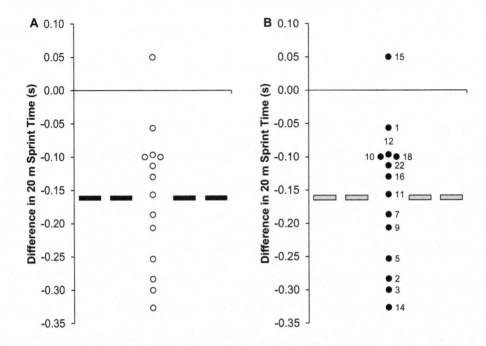

Figure 16.5 Two example univariate scatter plots. The left univariate scatter plot (A) shows the individual differences in average 20 m sprint times recorded for 14 academy football players between the start of pre-season and the end of pre-season for each player (circles) and the mean difference for the entire squad (horizontal dashed lines). The right univariate scatter plot (B) shows the same data but includes player squad numbers. In both plots, the differences in average 20 m sprint times recorded for players 10 and 18 are *jittered* to prevent overlapping of data points with identical or similar values.

is from the mean (usually the squad mean in team sport settings). It is calculated using the following formula: z-score = (the individual athlete's test score − the squad mean [average] test score) ÷ the squad standard deviation for the test score (Lockie et al., 2018; McGuigan et al., 2013). It is worth remembering at this point that ~68%, ~95% and ~99.7% of the values attained for a given performance test will fall within 1, 2 and 3 standard deviations of the mean, respectively. Consequently, if an athlete achieved a z-score of 2 or −2 for a given performance test, their score would fall within the top or bottom 5% of the associated test results attained by the entire squad, respectively. Converting z-scores into percentiles, therefore, could also be done to make their interpretation easier for some of the athletes' training team to understand.

A negative z-score was assumed to be undesirable in the previous example, but for some performance test results, such as the time taken to complete a linear sprint or change of direction task, a negative z-score is preferable (because this would represent a faster per-formance). To avoid possible confusion caused by this, it has been suggested that absolute z-scores (i.e. positive z-scores for positive outcomes) should be presented for all perform-ance test results (Lockie et al., 2018; Pettitt, 2010). A modified z-score yields similar infor-mation to the z-score but replaces the mean with the median in its calculation, but still includes the standard deviation. The modified z-score may, therefore, be more robust than the standard z-score because it is less influenced by outliers (extreme scores, which can be detected via a test of normal distribution of data [e.g. the Shapiro-Wilk test]) within a squad data set. McGuigan et al. (2013) also used the term modified z-score to describe the comparison of an individual athlete's performance test result to a predetermined "benchmark" mean and standard deviation result for the same test (using the formula modified z-score = [athlete's test score – benchmark test score] ÷ benchmark standard deviation) and more recently the modified z-score was used to describe the comparison of within-athlete data between testing occasions (McGuigan, 2017), which will be discussed in more detail later in this section. Nevertheless, either method is useful for the visual presentation of an individual athlete's results obtained for a range of performances within one radar chart, but one should understand how so-called modified z-scores have been calculated to enable them to be accurately interpreted. The utilisation of radar plots has been applied to the creation of normative profiles of individual and team sports performances (James et al., 2005; O'Donoghue, 2005), in addition to the presentation of key performance test results in line with the focus of this section (Lockie et al., 2018; McGuigan et al., 2013).

Example radar charts for two team-sport athletes (athlete A and B) containing their respective z-scores (black markers) for a range of typical performance test results can be seen in Figure 16.6. Note that the grey line presented in each radar chart represents zero on the axis, which is equivalent to the squad mean (with each black marker corresponding to the z-score which represents the number of standard deviations from the squad mean [i.e. zero] each test result was for both athletes). For example, the jump height obtained by athlete A was equal to two standard deviations higher than the mean jump height achieved by the entire squad (Figure 16.6A), whereas her 20 m sprint speed was 1 standard deviation lower, as denoted by the negative z-score. Upon closer inspection of athlete A's radar chart, it becomes evident that she was better than the squad mean in terms of jump height, isometric mid-thigh pull (IMTP) peak force and yo-yo intermittent recovery test 2 (YYIRT2) distance, but worse than the squad mean in all other performance tests (Figure 16.6A). Conversely, athlete B performed better than squad mean in all performance tests (Figure 16.6B). It can be deduced, however, that athlete A outperformed athlete B in terms of jump height, IMTP peak force and YYIRT2 distance, due to the former obtaining higher z-scores for each of these performance tests.

The radar charts presented in Figure 16.6 represent a comparison of performance test results between two athletes, but they do not consider changes in performance test results for an individual athlete between test occasions (between the start and end of pre-season training, for example). A limitation of presenting individual athlete's z-scores calculated from performance test results obtained at different test occasions is they do not highlight the associated changes to the squad mean and standard deviation. This presents a problem because an individual athlete's performance test results can remain the same between test occasions, but if the squad mean and standard deviation for each (or any) of the performance test results worsen between test occasions, the individual athlete's z-score(s) will consequently increase, thus incorrectly showing as an improvement in the radar chart. An example of this is shown in the radar chart presented as Figure 16.7A, where athlete A's result for each performance test was the same as it was for the calculation of z-scores presented in Figure 16.6A, but the squad mean and standard deviation for each test was ~5% worse. On this occasion, athlete A is highlighted as performing worse (negative value) than the squad mean in the 5 m sprint only, with superior performances noted for all other tests except for the 505 COD speed for the right leg, which was comparable to the squad

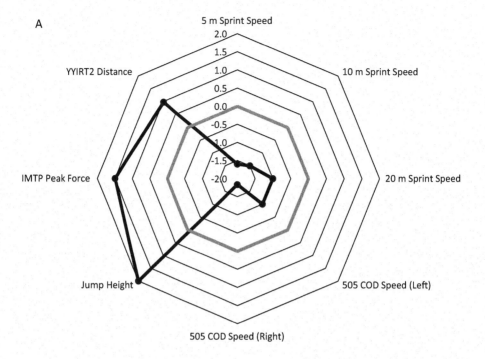

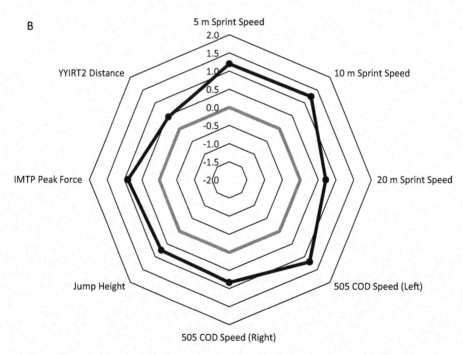

Figure 16.6 Example radar charts for two team-sport athletes (athletes A [top chart] and B [bottom chart]) containing their respective z-scores (black markers) for a range of typical performance test results. The grey line presented in each radar chart represents zero on the axis, which is equivalent to the squad mean. Left and Right represent left and right legs, respectively, COD represents change of direction, IMTP represents isometric mid-thigh pull (relative peak force is considered) and YYIRT2 represents yo-yo intermittent recovery test level 2.

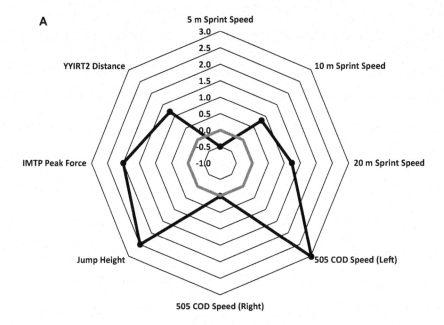

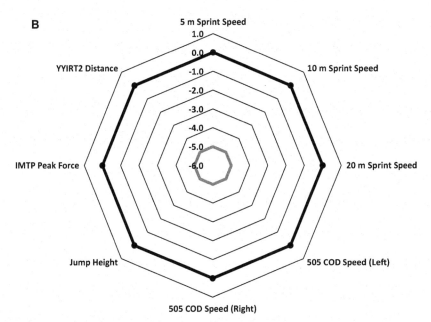

Figure 16.7 Example radar charts for one team-sport athlete (athlete A from Figure 16.6). In the top radar chart (A), the athlete's z-scores (black markers) for a range of typical performance test results are plotted along with zero on the axis (the grey line), which is equivalent to the squad mean. In this example, the athlete achieved the same performance test results as they did in the example provided in Figure 16.6A, but the squad mean performance in these tests was reduced by 5%. In the bottom radar chart (B), the athlete's and squad's performance test results are presented as a percentage change. Left and Right represent left and right legs, respectively, COD represents change of direction, IMTP represents isometric mid-thigh pull (relative peak force is considered), and YYIRT2 represents yo-yo intermittent recovery test level 2.

mean (Figure 16.7A). Presenting the performance test results for athlete A and the squad mean as a percentage change (change from the start to the end of pre-season training) in radar chart form (Figure 16.7B), reveals a different story. In Figure 16.7B, it is clear that athlete A has shown no percentage change in any performance test whereas the overall squad's performance has declined in all tests by a mean of ~5%.

In addition to presenting changes to results of performance test scores for individual athletes as percentages, z-scores associated with test occasions one and two can be presented in one radar plot alongside the squad mean derived from test one (Figure 16.8A). The results presented in Figure 16.8A show that the athlete improved in all tests on the second test occasion (black circles with dotted line) and surpassed the baseline squad mean (grey zero line) in the 20 m sprint and 505 change of direction speed tests. An alternative way of presenting these results is to calculate another type of modified z-score using the formula modified z-score = (athlete's current test score − athlete's baseline test score) ÷ athlete's baseline standard deviation (McGuigan, 2017), and then to present these modified z-scores associated with testing occasion two alongside a zero line that represents the athlete's baseline (testing occasion 1) test scores (Figure 16.8B). The latter method more clearly shows the magnitude of improvement the athlete demonstrated for each performance test between testing occasions. It has been suggested that magnitudes of 0.20, 0.60, 1.20, 2.0 and 4.0 for standardised differences in means (e.g. z-scores) between testing occasions can be interpreted as small, moderate, large, very large and extremely large, respectively (Hopkins et al., 2009). Using this scale, as mentioned in previous sections of this chapter, helps to guide consistent and accurate use of language when communicating such results to the athletes' performance team. It should be noted, however, that none of the example uses of radar plots using z-score derivatives in this section have considered the measurement error associated with each performance test, although if wanted, practitioners may amend their radar plots to include it at their own discretion. Also, it should be noted that it is important to ensure that kinetic (e.g. forces) and strength (e.g. one repetition maximum) data derived from performance tests are normalised (to body mass, for example) before they are included in z-score calculations to facilitate accurate between-sessions and between-athletes score comparisons (Pettitt, 2010).

Scatter plots

The visual presentation methods discussed in the previous sections have largely focused on the reporting of changes in performance test results between two testing occasions only. Certain performance tests are included as part of the continual athlete-monitoring process, however, whereby testing is conducted on a daily or weekly basis throughout each training cycle. Such longitudinal data sets are usually reported for individual athletes in the form of a simple scatter plot (Buchheit, 2017). The drop jump-derived reactive strength index (RSI), which is discussed in Chapter 11, is one example of a performance test that is typically included as part of a continual athlete-monitoring testing battery with results presented in a scatter plot (Beattie & Flanagan, 2015). An example of presenting weekly RSI values across an 8-week mesocycle in scatter plot-form for an individual athlete is provided in Figure 16.9. As per many of the previously discussed examples, it has been recommended that weekly changes in RSI scores are interpreted with respect to what constitutes a meaningful change (Beattie & Flanagan, 2015). In Figure 16.9, weekly mean (of three trials) RSI scores (squares) with error bars representing the week 1 RSI coefficient of variation are plotted alongside horizontal lines representing 1 (round dotted line), 3 (square dotted

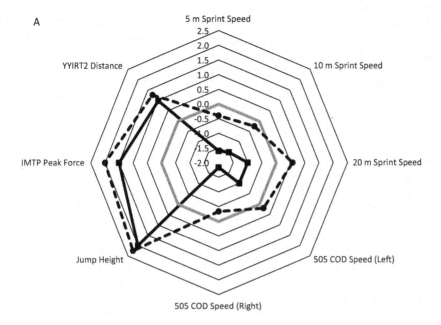

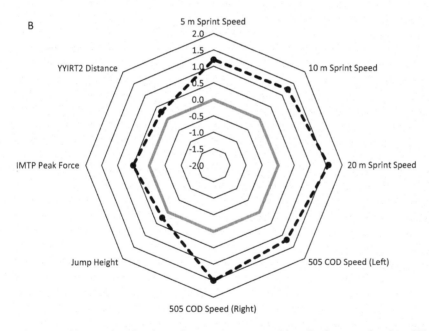

Figure 16.8 Example radar charts for one team-sport athlete. In the top radar chart (A), the athlete's z-scores for a range of typical performance test results attained on two occasions (black squares with solid line [test 1] and black circles with dotted line [test 2]) are plotted along with zero on the axis (the grey line), which is equivalent to the squad mean derived during test 1. In the bottom radar chart (B), modified z-scores for the athlete's performance results attained for test 2 (black circles with dotted line) are plotted along with a zero (grey) line that represents the athlete's results attained for test 1. Left and Right represent left and right legs, respectively, COD represents change of direction, IMTP represents isometric mid-thigh pull (relative peak force is considered), and YYIRT2 represents yo-yo intermittent recovery test level 2.

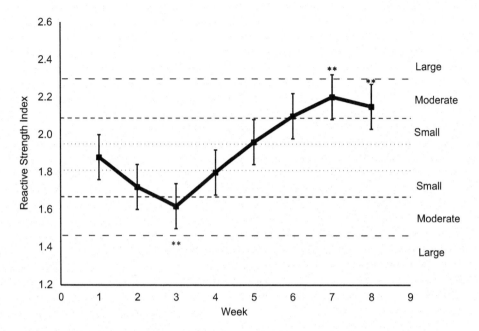

Figure 16.9 A scatter plot of weekly reactive strength index (RSI) values (squares) across an 8-week mesocycle for an individual athlete.

line line) and 6 (dashed line) times the SWC (established from week 1 data). In line with earlier discussions, mean RSI changes which exceed the aforementioned magnitudes can be considered small, moderate and large, respectively (Buchheit, 2016b; Hopkins, 2004). By taking the coefficient of variation as well as the SWC into account, the probabilities of weekly changes in mean RSI scores being "real" were also calculated and interpreted using a qualitative scale (as described in the forest plots section). Consequently, the double asterisks added to Figure 16.9 denote that likely changes (i.e. 75–95% probability) in mean RSI scores (in relation to week 1) were observed during weeks 3, 7 and 8, but changes were unclear for all other weeks.

Verbal communication of results

Once the desired method of presenting the performance test result(s) has been determined and figures have been produced, thought can then be given to the most effective way of verbally communicating the results. Indeed, as mentioned throughout the preceding sections, the selected visual presentation format (including the associated statistical analyses) will help to guide verbal communication of performance test results. This has been suggested to be the most important part of the performance data reporting process (Jeffreys, 2014), with the possession of appropriate communication skills and the capacity to efficiently deliver performance test results to the athletes' training team described as being essential (Buchheit, 2017). Acquiring such skills requires time and experience (Buchheit, 2016a), something that this book chapter cannot provide, but here we do provide some brief practical suggestions which may help to facilitate the use of accurate and plain language when reporting performance test results.

If reporting performance test results directly to athletes, who may be differentially affected (from a psychological perspective) by performing superiorly or inferiorly in a given test, then clearly communicating what the results mean from an upcoming training programming and/or squad selection standpoint is imperative (Lockie et al., 2018). Sometimes a reduction in a performance test result is better, whereas sometimes an increase in a performance test result is better (as mentioned in some of the earlier sections). For example, an improvement in sprint time over any set distance is reflected by a reduction in sprint time (i.e. a shorter sprint time). Often, however, practitioners and researchers use the term "sprint performance" to describe sprint speed when in fact they have measured sprint time. To state that sprint performance/speed has improved but produce figures for key stakeholders showing that sprint time has decreased (i.e. there is a downward trend in the presented results) would be likely to lead to confusion for those who might not understand the process that has been undertaken to acquire/interpret said data. To avoid such confusion, it is important to use accurate and familiar terminology that reflects the units of measurement included in any presented figures. For example, it would be accurate in the case of the performance test results presented in Figure 16.4 to state that sprint time decreased for most athletes, which means that these athletes became quicker. Alternatively, it might be less confusing to convert sprint times into sprint speeds before presenting such data to certain audiences. For example, the sprint speed data presented in Figure 16.10 (calculated

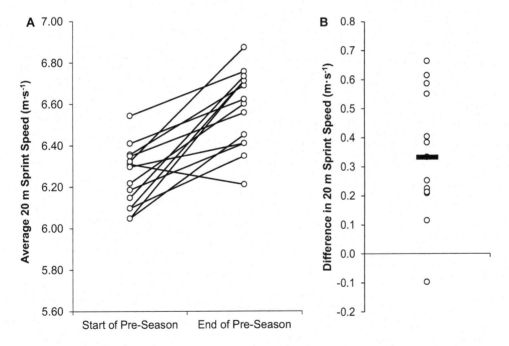

Figure 16.10 Two example univariate scatter plots. The left univariate scatter plot (A) shows the average (mean of three trials) 20 m sprint speeds recorded for 14 academy football players on two test occasions (the start of pre-season and the end of pre-season). The right univariate scatter plot (B) shows the individual differences in average 20 m sprint speeds between these two test occasions for each player (open circles) and the mean difference for the entire squad (black horizontal line).

from the sprint time data presented in Figure 16.4) show a positive trend (and perhaps a more obvious improvement) between testing occasions. As mentioned in the radar plots section, but as can be applied to any other visual presentation format that includes z-score calculations, presenting absolute z-scores (or modified z-scores) is another way of avoiding possible confusion when the change in a test score is inversely related to the desired outcome (i.e. shorter sprint time = faster sprint). Most importantly, use the chosen terminology consistently.

It has also been suggested that communication of performance test results should be completed within 3 days of conducting the testing to ensure that is has maximal impact on the athletes' training programme (McGuigan et al., 2013). However, the practitioner must also consider the relative priority (i.e. urgency) of results, and timeline communication accordingly. It is therefore suggested that practitioners confirm the timing of feedback prior to conducting the performance testing, as this ensures expectations are met, and results are impactful. For example, practitioners may consider reporting predetermined key performance indicators immediately following testing (e.g. daily monitoring), before then providing a more comprehensive report later (e.g. long-term monitoring). This becomes particularly important as the likelihood is that the performance tests conducted as part of athletes' continual and periodic performance monitoring will yield an abundance of results (i.e. many variables). As alluded to in the earlier sections of this chapter, focus should be placed on presentation of the "key" (i.e. most important) test results only. It would be wise to apply the same principle to the verbal communication of performance test results too. Indeed, a suggested effective method of facilitating a positive impact of sports science on athlete performance is to "do simple but powerful" (Buchheit, 2016a). The person (or team) who researched the performance testing protocol(s), ran the test(s), analysed the data, interpreted the results and produced the visually impactful presentation of the results will undoubtedly have many points that they could (or would like to) verbally communicate to other coaches. As mentioned earlier, however, sports coaches (and athletes) are unlikely to be statistically trained (Robertson et al., 2017), not to mention that they probably will not have a background in sports science. Therefore, less is likely to yield more when it comes to verbally communicating key performance test results to such groups. As frustrating as it sometimes can be to have performed many hours of work to then communicate just a few key points to key stakeholders, it imperative to remember your target audience and their individual preferences for receiving such information (Buchheit, 2017; Robertson et al., 2017). Perhaps this is partly why developing a strong character and demonstrating humility have been suggested as two of the most important personality traits for a strength and conditioning/sports science practitioner to possess (Buchheit, 2016a, 2017).

References

Beattie, K., & Flanagan, E. (2015). Establishing the reliability and meaningful change of the drop-jump reactive-strength index. *Journal of Australian Strength and Conditioning, 23*(5), 12–18.

Buchheit, M. (2016a). Chasing the 0.2. *International Journal of Sports Physiology and Performance, 11*(4), 417–418.

Buchheit, M. (2016b). The numbers will love you back in return – I promise. *International Journal of Sports Physiology and Performance, 11*(4), 551–554.

Buchheit, M. (2017). Want to see my report, coach? *Aspetar Sports Medicine Journal, 6*, 36–43.

Haugen, T., & Buchheit, M. (2016). Sprint running performance monitoring: Methodological and practical considerations. *Sports Medicine, 46*(5), 641–656.

Hopkins, W. (2004). How to interpret changes in an athletic performance test. *Sportscience, 8*, 1–7.

Hopkins, W. (2007). A spreadsheet for deriving a confidence interval, mechanistic inference and clinical inference from a p value. *Sportscience, 11*, 16–20.

Hopkins, W., Marshall, S., Batterham, A., & Hanin, J. (2009). Progressive statistics for studies in sports medicine and exercise science. *Medicine & Science in Sports & Exercise, 41*(1), 3.

James, N., Mellalieu, S., & Jones, N. (2005). The development of position-specific performance indicators in professional rugby union. *Journal of Sports Sciences, 23*(1), 63–72.

Jeffreys, I. (2014). The five minds of the modern strength and conditioning coach: The challenges for professional development. *Strength & Conditioning Journal, 36*, 2–8.

Lockie, R.G., Risso, F.G., Giuliano, D.V., Orjalo, A.J., & Jalilvand, F. (2018). Practical fitness profiling using field test data for female elite-level collegiate soccer players: A case analysis of a Division I team. *Strength & Conditioning Journal, 40*(3), 58–71.

McGuigan, M. (2017) Monitoring training and performance in athletes. Champaign, IL: Human Kinetics.

McGuigan, M.R., Cormack, S.J., & Gill, N.D. (2013). Strength and power profiling of athletes: Selecting tests and how to use the information for program design. *Strength & Conditioning Journal, 35*(6), 7–14.

O'Donoghue, P. (2005). Normative profiles of sports performance. *International Journal of Performance Analysis in Sport, 5*(1), 104–119.

Pettitt, R.W. (2010). Evaluating strength and conditioning tests with Z scores: Avoiding common pitfalls. *Strength & Conditioning Journal, 32*(5), 100–103.

Robertson, S., Bartlett, J., D., & Gastin, P., B. (2017). Red, amber, or green? Athlete monitoring in team sport: The need for decision-support systems. *International Journal of Sports Physiology and Performance, 12*(Suppl. 2), S2-73–S2-79.

Weissgerber, T.L., Milic, N.M., Winham, S.J., & Garovic, V.D. (2015). Beyond bar and line graphs: Time for a new data presentation paradigm. *PLOS Biology, 13*(4), e1002128.

17 Application to training

*W. Guy Hornsby, Jeremy A. Gentles
and Michael H. Stone*

Section 1

Introduction

For the purposes of this chapter "sport science" specifically refers to the planning and use of training variables (e.g. internal and external load) and performance assessment (e.g. force plate analysis, one repetition maximum [1-RM], etc.) data in an effort to optimise the recovery-adaptation process. This process involves a combination of sound planning and evidence-based coaching coupled with an integrated monitoring programme to allow for optimal "guiding" and "directing" of the adaptive process (Stone et al., 2007). Even more simply put, it is the manipulation and monitoring of fitness that leads to preparedness (Figure 17.1).

Box 17.1 The fitness-fatigue paradigm and preparedness

An athlete's performance is largely based on an athlete's preparedness (Stone et al., 2007). The fitness-fatigue paradigm involves the manipulation of two generalised after-effects from training stress; fitness and fatigue (Stone et al., 2007). An athlete's preparedness equals the difference between fitness and fatigue (Plisk and Stone, 2003; Stone et al., 2007). Preparedness is essentially the potential of an athlete to perform well. Fatigue masks the ability to express fitness, or cumulative adaptations, and thus the accumulation of fatigue can decrease preparedness. Training can be viewed as a process increasing an athlete's cumulative adaptations and then at appropriate times allowing that athlete to express those adaptations (peak) via fatigue reduction, raising preparedness. While many factors contribute to fatigue decay rates, such as genetics, training history, training status, outside stressors, etc., in trained individuals during periods of deloading fatigue has been shown to dissipate at a faster rate than fitness, thus raising preparedness (Plisk & Stone, 2003). Specifically, fitness has demonstrated a decay up to three times slower than fatigue during aggressive deloading/tapering strategies (Plisk & Stone, 2003).

Issurin (2009) has described the benefits of raising an athlete's physiological capabilities (i.e. fitness) using training phases, particularly high-volume phases, that for a given period of time decrease preparedness as a result of increased accumulative fatigue. Thus, the aim of directing preparedness should not always be to have preparedness as high as possible as this will sacrifice the development of various critical performance adaptations due to prolonged detraining; fitness will fall off.

For example, when an athlete undergoes large(r) training volumes fitness (adaptations) can increase, but so too will fatigue, thus potentially reducing preparedness (Bompa & Haff, 2009; DeWeese et al., 2015a, 2015b); if the training programme then allows fatigue to dissipate while maintaining fitness, preparedness (performance capability) may be elevated (Bompa & Haff, 2009; Stone et al., 2007). So many factors influence performance, prior to a major competition it is impossible to know exactly how an athlete is going to perform; increasing preparedness increases the likelihood that an athlete will produce a high-level performance (Sands & McNeal 2000). Thus, the management of these two training affects (fitness and fatigue) leads coaches to important training prescription and monitoring considerations (Bompa & Haff, 2009; DeWeese et al., 2015a, 2015b).

Due to acute responses in fatigue, preparedness is relatively unstable and thus an athlete's level of preparedness fluctuates constantly. Monitoring preparedness throughout the macrocycle allows a coach to be aware of alterations in preparedness. Manipulating and directing training stress and cumulative fatigue in order to elevate preparedness at the appropriate time is essential to exploit and develop cumulative training and requires achieving a balance between training stress and planned recovery and restoration (Bompa & Haff, 2009). While various monitoring factors are important, rate of force development (RFD) has been shown to be a particularly important potential indicator of fatigue management and level of preparedness due to the sensitivity of nervous systems and its role in RFD (Maffuletti et al., 2016). Rate of force development has displayed varied reliability for the IMTP, dependent upon its calculation (e.g. banding vs. peak RFD) (Chapter 10), and poor reliability has consistently been demonstrated during the propulsive phase of a CMJ (Chapter 7), thus demonstrating the importance of choosing the appropriate performance test and RFD assessment. Both RFD from IMPT measured via pre-determined time bands (e.g. 0 ms to 200 ms) (Haff et al., 2015) and RFD assessed during the propulsive phase of an SJ have demonstrated acceptable test re-test reliabilities suitable for athlete monitoring (McClellan et al. 2011).

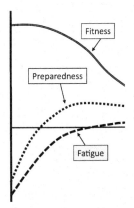

Figure 17.1 Fatigue-fitness paradigm.
Source: Modified from Stone et al. (2007).

Sport science and athlete monitoring: brief background and history

Coaches and sport scientists using data to help guide the training process is nothing new. Indeed, there is evidence of carefully documented training as far back as 1000 BC from the Roman poet Virgil in his book *The Aeneid* (Bompa & Haff, 2009). Fast forward to the twentieth century: some of the earliest published work on periodisation involved observational work in which sport scientists closely monitored highly successful athletes. For example, Leniod Matveyev's (USSR) periodisation text (1965) in which he describes what is now commonly referred to as the "classic or traditional model of periodisation", was initially developed through the monitoring of Soviet athletes as they trained for the 1952 Olympic Games in Helsinki, Finland (Bompa & Haff, 2009).

While much of the work (training and assessment data) was kept secret, due to the competitive nature of sport (as well as the work not being translated), many countries such as Hungary (1940s–1950s), the Soviet Union (1960s–1970s), East Germany (1970s–1980s), Australia (1990s–2000s) and Great Britain (mid 2000–2012) invested substantial time and money into a data-driven sport-science-based framework. Ostensibly these investments helped facilitate increases in performance (e.g. medals) on the world stage during those periods of time. Much of what drives these programmes deals specifically with monitoring loads and subsequent fatigue levels and changes in critical performance-related variables. Currently, around the word there are several institutes that incorporate high-level monitoring programmes in which data aid the coaches' and athletes' training process (AIS, INCEP, ETSU, JISS, CNIS, ASPIRE). This process often involves an integrated approach in which members of the sport performance enhancement group (SPEG), consisting of sport coaches, strength and conditioning coaches, scientists, sport medicine, dieticians and others, collaborate and share information. This approach allows for an inclusive, holistic, approach to training and provides open lines of communication amongst the SPEG members. German super-heavy weightlifter Matthias Steiner summed up the value of this scientific approach to training shortly after winning the gold medal in Beijing (2008). When asked the reason behind his victorious performance during a television interview he said, "German sport science is the best" (Sky TV, 2008).

In addition to "national" sport science programmes (e.g. Olympic training centres), which are often funded wholly or partly by national governments; private organisations, such as professional sports teams, using some form of sport science has risen exponentially over the last decade. Many of these programmes are constantly pushing the envelope for the development of better methods of quantifying training. For example: technological advances have allowed the development of tracking devices that are particularly popular in team sports. Many countries such as Great Britain, Italy and Australia began pushing this paradigm forward often through internal and external load-monitoring in part through "wearable" technology (e.g. global positioning systems, accelerometers, inertial sensors). Currently, almost every US professional sport (NHL, NBA, NFL, MLB) now employs at least one sport scientist charged with collecting and analysing various types of wearable technology data (e.g. training data, performance data, game/competition) and providing information back to the coaches and athletes. Some of these groups have taken even further steps, implementing a similar structure and framework to the national sport science programmes, and have begun developing an integrated SPEG model (e.g. Toronto Blue Jays, East Tennessee State University, LaGrange College, Texas A&M football, West Virginia University).

Research studies

Several studies have been carried out on athletes monitoring daily training variables while also periodically measuring performance outcomes (Garcia-Pallares et al., 2009; Hakkinen et al., 1987; Hornsby et al., 2013; Stone et al., 2003). Several sport scientists such as Stone, Sands and Mujika have pointed out the value of studies that better "mimic" the real world (i.e. high ecological validity) and are conducted on trained athletes who are well beyond their initial adaptations, due to differences in recovery and adaptation rates based on training status. While these studies sometimes present challenges for reviewers more accustomed to traditional research design as they are by necessity unconventional (e.g. small sample size, no control group, normative data, effect size versus *p*-value testing, etc.) these studies can lend insight into helping solve "real-world" coaching decisions. Furthermore, these "real-world" studies often do a better of job of putting training responses into a more appropriate big-picture, periodisation context.

Study Example 1: Nonfunctional overreaching during off-season training for skill position players in collegiate American football

C.A. Moore and A.C. Fry
Journal of Strength and Conditioning Research, 2007, 21(3), 793–800.

Nine skill position football players in collegiate American football (NCAA Division 1) took part in a 15-week study during a spring preparation phase. Performance and biochemical measurements were made four times throughout the 15 weeks; the week before the study began, after phase 1 (4 weeks), after phase 2 (5 weeks) and after phase 3 (4 weeks). Phase 1 involved higher weight-room volume and lower weight-room intensity (mean intensity = 75 kg to approaching 90 kg), phase 2 involved lower weight-room volume and higher intensity (all weeks above 90 kg) whilst introducing a large amount of conditioning work (high-intensity station work), phase 3 involved spring break (week 10), light conditioning (week 11) and spring football practice (weeks 12–15). Due to the large amount of conditioning coupled with the weight-training volumes the authors referred to phase 2 as an overreaching phase. The goal of the prescription was to induce gains in performance measures across phases 1 and 2 allowing for these to remain elevated after phase 3. Performance measures included physical, muscular strength (squat, power clean, bench press), sprint speed (40 yd sprint), vertical jump and change of direction (20 yard pro agility), while biochemical markers included testosterone (T) and cortisol (C) concentrations. Muscular strength, speed and change of direction performance all increased significantly after phase 1, Vertical jump increased significantly after phase 1 but remained the same for the rest of the study. It is worth noting that jump height may not be the most sensitive measure of adaptation of neuromuscular fatigue and that other variables such as the reactive strength index-modified (RSImod) may be more informative (refer to Chapter 7). The T:C ratio data displayed a decrease during phase 2, returning to baseline during phase 3. While a significant decrease in T occurred during phase 2, it did not, however, drop below a "normal" range and returned to baseline after phase 3. Cortisol levels did not change statistically throughout the course of the study. The authors concluded based on these data that the overreaching strategy used was not successful since performance was not maintained during spring football practice, referring to the training response as nonfunctional overreaching. Specifically, during phase 2, sprint speed, vertical jump height and change of direction remained either unchanged or slight decreases were observed.

As is often the case when desired outcomes do not come to fruition, the authors are left wondering what could have been done differently. The authors note that perhaps training volume during phase 2 was too high, specifically noting the large amount of conditioning that occurred during this time. They also noted that, even though anaerobic endurance may have been enhanced at this time, this high volume of non-compatible training should not be performed at the cost of the critical sport specific variables of strength, speed and change of direction speed. These observations bring into question the efficacy and efficiency of using either largely unplanned or poorly planned overreaching paradigms. This study demonstrates the importance of making multiple measurements: for example, T and C values did not suggest overtraining but based on performance data it seems fatigue was mismanaged. Considering the data in the appropriate context: compared to the observation data before the 15 weeks and the improved performance data noted after Phase 1, after going through spring practice the players were back to where they started, except now 11 weeks closer to the autumn competition season.

Study Example 2: Changes in muscle architecture, explosive ability, and track and field throwing performance throughout a competition season and following a taper

C.D. Bazyler, S. Mizuguchi, A.P. Harrison, K. Sato, A.A. Kavanaugh, B.H. DeWeese and M.H. Stone

Journal of Strength and Conditioning Research, 2017, 31(10), 2785–2793

This study followed six collegiate (NCAA Division 1) track and field throwers (three hammer, two discus, one javelin) across 12 weeks of training. The training prescription involved a block periodisation model with the last four blocks including 1 week of overreaching and a 3-week taper (ORT). The drop in training volume during the taper was statistically lower than the pre-overreaching training volume and was implemented in an effort to raise the throwers preparedness as high as possible (peak) for the conference championships. Resistance training volume load (kg·m) (VL) was recorded throughout the 12 weeks and the throwers were tested pre and post ORT. These measures included vastus lateralis size and architecture (via ultrasonography), unloaded and loaded counter-movement jump performance and in-competition throwing performance.

Increases in vastus lateralis muscle thickness (MT) (+4.5%) and pennation angle (PA) (+3.8%) occurred during the in-season training in concert with increased VL; MT and PA were maintained during the taper even though VL dropped markedly. Unloaded CMJ peak force and relative (allometrically scaled) peak power improved significantly after the ORT (PF = 4.6%, PP = 3.5%). It is possible that the planned overreaching just before the taper was instrumental in preserving muscle size. Notably, throwing performance was increased at the conference championships by 6.3%, resulting in five of the six throwers performing a personal best. Based on these data, the coaches (and the authors) declared the training prescription to have been successful, noting the advantages of the block-style periodisation scheme and ORT phase for which the major competition was targeted.

Section 2

Monitoring the training prescription: quantifying volume load

Acute and prolonged physiological disturbances from resistance training can include hormonal alterations (Haff et al., 2008; Häkkinen, 1993), increased energy expenditure

(Scott, 2011) and neuromuscular fatigue (Häkkinen et al., 1987). Häkkinen (1993) demonstrated that resistance training during a single session produced substantial physiological disturbances leading to decreases in performance. The degree of disturbance and loss of performance were related to the amount of work performed in the session. Performance decrements included decreased maximal force and neural activation (EMG) immediately post-exercise, hours post-exercise and even 2 days post-exercise (Häkkinen, 1993). This type of information provides a partial basis for altering training load (heavy and light days) to enhance fatigue management (DeWeese et al., 2015a, 2015b; Stone et al., 2007).

The quantification of training is a necessary step in understanding training outcomes. Quantification of training allows relationships to be established between the training prescription and performance-related variables as well as relationships between the training volume and the athlete's preparedness. Quantifying an athlete's external load allows the coach to evaluate (postdict) what the athlete performed in training. While an athlete's response to the given training stress is likely to differ between athletes, (idiosyncratic) a large portion of an athlete's overall stress consists of training stress and thus general trends should be expected (characteristic). Quantification of training allows for a more detailed assessment of the training prescription, including (1) evaluation of the previous training block(s) effects on performance variables, (2) reflection as to how closely the prescription matched the execution and, due to the cyclical nature of training, (3) identifying potential modifications that may be appropriate when returning to a training block of the same adaptation focus. Mujika et al. (2013) recently explained how a shortcoming of many training studies and monitoring programmes is that they lack clear, detailed reporting of training volume and that this leads to reviewers and coaches being unable to know what the athletes actually did in training as well as limiting other researchers' ability to replicate these studies.

Quantifying training variables can include training diaries (paper or electronic). Various computer programs (e.g. Excel) allow for relative easy input, storage and sharing capabilities. Given that training is a long-term process, the data should be handled as longitudinal data. Often, graphical representations of volume load and intensity aid in understanding training manipulation. There are numerous modes of training and thus numerous options for quantification. For this discussion (strength power training and adaptation), the focus on external load quantification and manipulation concerns resistance training.

Several quantification methods have been used for resistance training, such as total repetitions, time under tension, RPE (Haff, 2010). For example: the volume of training is generally considered a measure of work accomplished (Haff, 2010; Stone et al., 2007). Simply summing the repetitions together may be the easiest way to estimate volume, but it does not adequately represent the total amount of work accomplished because it does not account for training intensity (forces related to loading) or displacement (Haff, 2010). However, changes in repetitions do not necessarily correspond to changes in work accomplished (Stone & Wathen, 2001). Several methods, other than total repetitions, for estimating work (volume) of training have been used, most commonly volume load (VL). Volume load (VL), measured as sets times reps times load, has been shown to be a superior manner in which to estimate overall weight-room work accomplished, demonstrating strong relationships between work (higher VL) and fatigue (Haff, 2010; McBride et al., 2009). Researchers have also proposed including body mass or subtracting shank mass from specific lifts (e.g. squats) in VL calculations (McBride et al., 2009). This may be useful for comparison studies investigating VL from different training interventions but is probably unnecessary for most athlete-monitoring or research studies. As VL is easily calculated, it can skilfully be used for strategic planning. By using relative intensities (percentage of set-rep best or percentage of 1-RM) along with appropriate set-repetition schemes the training process can be more precisely calculated or graphed to visualise the planned fluctuations in workload. Then, through careful record-keeping, coaches and sport scientists can ascertain the degree to which the planned VL matches the actual VL experienced by the athlete. Furthermore, excessive fatigue, performance alterations, injury etc. can also be matched to reasonable workload estimates. Thus, monitoring VL in the weight room is essential to managing the recovery-adaptation process in competitive athletes since resistance training often makes up a substantial amount of an athlete's overall work (Haff, 2010).

Volume load with displacement

Stone et al. (1987) and Haff (2010) suggest that including displacement as part of the estimations of an athlete's workloads can result in a more accurate calculation of work performed in the weight room: repetitions times load times barbell displacement (VLwD). Vertical displacement for some exercises (e.g. a squat) can be measured simply (albeit less accurately) via a measuring stick or measuring tape. More complex movements can be more difficult and more time-consuming. Table 17.1 is an example: each exercise was measured using the V-scope 120 (Lipman Electronic Engineering Ltd, Ramat Hahayal, Israel). There are several other commercially available devices that can measure barbell displacement as well that are available for coaches and sport scientists to measure their own athletes with.

Table 17.1 The exercise displacement of eight (five male, three female) competitive weightlifters (Hornsby dissertation data, 2013).

Exercise	Mean displacement (m)	SD
Snatch	2.21	0.124
Clean	1.88	0.082
Power snatch	1.53	0.136
Snatch grip pull from floor	1.08	0.092
Clean grip pull from floor	1.01	0.074
Push press	0.76	0.099
Back squat	0.71	0.039
Push jerk	0.70	0.099
Jerk	0.68	0.095
Front squat	0.68	0.057
Overhead squat	0.67	0.048
Clean grip pull from knee	0.67	0.083
Snatch grip stiff-legged deadlift	0.58	0.065
Press	0.56	0.049
Clean grip stiff-legged deadlift	0.55	0.064
Behind the neck press	0.53	0.049
Mid-thigh pull – snatch grip	0.47	0.043
Mid-thigh pull – clean grip	0.39	0.051
Lockouts	0.07	0.012

Note: high intra-class correlations (ICCs >0.9) were displayed for each exercise. Reliability and validity of the V-scope (frequency of 66 Hz) was assessed by moving the V-scope cap by hand vertically through a pre-determined distance (50 cm). The total displacement difference between trials was less than 1 cm (<1%), and high ICCs were obtained (>0.99). Exercises involving two concentric portions involved measuring segments of the full movement and adding the segments together (e.g. snatch = snatch pull + overhead squat).

Two considerations explain the potential importance of including displacement in VL calculations.

(1) Exercises with greater displacements will alter the VL and VLwD relationship to a greater extent. Thus, when coaches implement training programs in which exercises such as snatch (displacement = 2.21 m) and clean and jerk (displacement = 1.88 m) constitute a large portion of the training plan, coaches may want to consider using VLwD.
(2) Partial movement exercises are commonly used for several reasons. Primary reasons include focusing on a specific portion of a full movement exercise, attempting to manage fatigue by reducing work and manipulating power output (Suchomel et al., 2017). A switch from a full movement exercise to a partial movement exercise is often used when implementing either a taper or an in-season maintenance programme. Greater training loads can be reached with partial movements (less displacement). When comparing a clean grip mid-thigh pull (CGMTP) to a clean grip pull from the floor the loading for the CGMTP is often higher but when taking into account the bar displacement the total training volume is less when compared to executing the full movement; thus using VL without displacement may be misleading. Table 17.2 and Figure 17.2 illustrate this difference.

Lastly, to be most exacting coaches or sport scientist should measure barbell displacement for each individual athlete. Although this is somewhat time-consuming it does allow for a more accurate and precise estimate of workload and estimate of relative energy expenditure. This more exacting estimate can result in much more precise postdiction analyses of training manipulation.

Monitoring adaptation(s)

Throughout training an athlete's adaptations, fatigue and thus preparedness fluctuates frequently; consequently, it is important to constantly monitor performance changes. If

Table 17.2 Hypothetical volume load and training intensity (average load) comparison of the clean grip pull from the floor and clean grip mid-thigh pull.

Sets and reps Clean grip from floor	L	VL	TI	D	VLwD
1 × 10	60	600	60	1.01	606
1 × 10	100	1000	100	1.01	1010
3 × 10	130	3900	130	1.01	3939
Total (50 reps)		5500			5555*
Mean reps per set (10)	110		110	1.01	
CGMTP	L	VL	TI	D	VLwD
1 × 10	60	600	60	0.39	234
1 × 10	150	1500	100	0.39	585
3 × 10	200	6000	130	0.39	2340
Total (50 reps)		8100			3159
Mean reps per set (10)	162		162	0.39	

L = load (kg), VL = volume load (sets × repetitions × load), TI = training intensity (VL/reps, kg), D = bar displacement (or weight displacement) in metres, VLwD = VL × displacement (kg).

Figure 17.2 Graphical illustration of vertical barbell displacement for a clean grip pull from the floor and clean grip mid-thigh pull.

measurements are only made at the beginning and end of a season or macrocycle and the information obtained by those measurements shows a decrease in performance, no improvement or much less improvement than expected, it is too late to make changes. A subpar performance at a major competition is not a good time for coaches to find out that their athlete was not adequately prepared (Sands & Stone, 2005). Thus, Banister and Wenger (1982) suggest that athlete testing should be implemented "regardless of the immediacy of a real competition" (p. 163).

There appears to not be a single variable that can completely explain whether there should be cause for concern or whether the training prescription is being fulfilled. Most likely a constellation of variables is best to capture the overall training response. Maximum strength and related variables such as relative strength, explosive strength and power output are common measures as these variables describe various aspects of an athletes "neuromuscular profile".

Neuromuscular aspects and laboratory-based monitoring options

The development of strength and power depends upon a multitude of various hypertrophic and neural adaptations. An understanding of the relationship between strength and power is vital as it has important implications in regard to the training process. Properly training various force-related variables over time can result in a shift of the force-velocity curve to the right, resulting in a more favourable athletic profile for performance (Siff, 2003; Stone et al., 2007). The manipulation of these force-related training variables in order to enhance performance should be executed by using a periodisation plan.

The neuromuscular system's ability to produce force is defined as strength (Stone et al., 2007). Neuromuscular adaptations occur through strength training such as increased muscle cross-sectional area (hypertrophy), motor neuron excitability and motor unit recruitment. With increased maximum strength, motor unit firing may become more synchronous (Van

Cutsen et al., 1998), more frequent with reduced inhibition (Van Cutsen et al., 1998) and a greater number of motor units may be activated (Van Cutsen et al., 1998). Maximum absolute strength is largely dependent on muscle cross-sectional area and volume (Balshaw et al., 2017), whereas relative strength is more dependent upon a number of factors, including fibre type, fibre II:I ratio, CSA, nervous system alterations etc. (Folland & Williams, 2007; Meijer et al., 2015). Both absolute and relative maximum strength measures are necessary in monitoring because (Stone et al., 2007; Tillin et al., 2013; Sperannza et al., 2016; Zaras et al., 2016):

(1) maximum strength and gains in maximum strength are positively associated with numerous biomechanical characteristics (e.g. impulse, RFD, power etc.) that in turn relate strongly to sports performance;
(2) maximum strength and gains in maximum strength have been consistently and positively associated with various types of sports performance.

Brief history of monitoring strength characteristics

Assessing and monitoring the training process via strength characteristics have been around for several decades. In the 1970s Dr. Yuri Verkhsoshansky utilised what he referred to as the "universal dynamometric stand", a force plate system, in which he assessed USSR athletes' maximal strength and explosive strength characteristics (Verkhsoshansky and Verkhsoshansky, 2011). In fact, it was from this work that he discovered the benefits of concentrated loading (Verkhsoshansky and Verkhsoshansky, 2011). Around the same time, Dr. Mike Stone and colleagues began experimenting with isometric strength testing at the National Strength Research Center at Auburn University. They had the athletes stand on a force plate inside a power rack with a barbell loaded beyond what the athlete could move. The athlete would attempt to accelerate the load as "hard and fast" as they could, producing a force-time curve. Initially Stone et al. began testing isometric back squat and eventually switched to the isometric clean grip mid-thigh pull (ICGMTP) in an effort to reduce spine/back stress. Currently, force plate testing along with other high-level strength power assessment is conducted throughout the world at various levels of sport.

Please refer to Chapters 7 (jumps), 10 (strength – isometric and dynamic) and 11 (power) for detailed explanations of measurement and assessment of strength characteristics. The following discussion deals with how to put strength-related assessment data into the appropriate context and subsequently apply them to training.

Monitoring ramifications for training age and history

Training age is how long an athlete has been training, while training history describes the details of that training (Balyi et al., 2013). Training is a long-term process in which, through chronic adaptation(s), an athlete's performance, capacity and response to given stimuli change. As an athlete develops, their intensity threshold(s) for a given training stimulus(i) increases, thus to induce subsequent (greater) adaptations, a greater overload is required than was previously necessary (Stone et al., 2007). For example, for highly strength-trained individuals, slightly relative intensities above 80% of 1-RM have been shown necessary to induce strength-based adaptations (Häkkinen, 1993); conversely, in untrained persons as low as 60% has been shown to produce increases in strength. This leads to both training and monitoring ramifications, suggesting that developmental athletes should be handled differently from more advanced athletes. A major benefit to possessing a greater training age for a given strength-based adaptation is a greater chronic stability of adaptation. However, a greater training age often requires decisions that can impact the monitoring process.

Greater training age (athletes being closer to their genetic ceiling for a given adaptation) typically results in the following.

(1) A greater training intensity and larger work volumes, thus a greater disruption of homeostasis, may be necessary to nudge future adaptations forward.

(2) The need for a more highly "concentrated stimulus" or concentrated loading requires "emphasis/de-emphasis" training in which a greater portion or specific phase of the overall training stress is directed towards a specific adaptation objective. Consistently performing higher intensities for a given set-rep scheme will raise the overall training volume. Thus, for advanced athletes, attempting to simultaneously develop multiple fitness characteristics can result in fatigue mismanagement or maladaptations which can be detected in the monitoring programme. Emphasis/de-emphasis training allows training variable magnitudes for specific adaptation focus to be increased due to less "competing stress".

(3) Due to advanced athletes possessing more stable adaptations a greater training percentage of the work load can be used for the "emphasis" and a lower percentage of the work load performed on the "de-emphasis". Lower training age (and less developed) athletes are likely to need to perform a somewhat greater amount of "de-emphasis" work, at the appropriate time, due to possessing less stable adaptations. A major idea of block periodisation or phase potentiation is that over time, through exploiting delayed effects, residual effects and cumulative adaptations, multiple adaptations converge (DeWeese et al., 2015a, 2015b). The more stable the adaption, the more likely the adaptation will remain "propped up" during de-emphasis periods. Certainly, the physiological nature of a given adaptation can heavily influence the decay (residual) rate. For example, adaptations that possess a greater neural component (e.g. RFD) tend to have shorter-lasting decay rates. Appropriate monitoring is vital during these periods to ascertain the degree to which the residuals and after-effects are sustained at reasonable levels. This type of information could be used to inform training programming, acutely adjust training programming or manipulate future programming.

(4) Periodisation is cyclical and when returning to a given phase of training re-establishing fitness characteristics can be the primary goal versus further development. For example, instead of setting a personal best towards the end of a given strength phase, which probably should be the goal for a developmental athlete, for an advanced athlete the goal may be to re-establish what was lost during the time spent focusing on other adaptations or from a taper. Again, careful monitoring can aid in the assessment of fitness re-establishment (or additional development).

Advanced athletes tend to respond in a much more specific fashion to training stress than less developed athletes. For example, weak athletes with very little training experience are likely to experience increases in RFD and speed during a block of higher-volume strength work (Cormie et al., 2010), while advanced athletes due to fatigue are likely to experience a decrease in RFD and other strength-related fitness characteristics (Maffiuletti et al., 2016). In this example, for the advanced athlete the primary adaptation will be strength-endurance (the ability to repeat high forces) since it is the targeted adaptation objective and where the majority of the training stress is being directed. Conversely, the weaker, less experienced athletes may derive increases in strength-endurance, maximum strength, power and increased RFD from a similar high-volume block (Cormie et al., 2010; Hornsby et al., 2013; Stone et al., 2003; Maffiuletti et al., 2016). From a training standpoint, due to lower intensity thresholds and less stable adaptations, developmental athletes may utilise less concentrated loading blocks effectively. From a monitoring standpoint, for developmental athletes the overarching goal should often be to answer the question, "is the athlete continuing to enhance their performance capabilities across the wide spectrum of strength-related adaptions?" Since advanced athletes respond in a much more specific manner coaches of such athletes should ask, "is my athlete responding to the stimulus in the expected manner?" Thus, for advanced athletes it becomes more of a process of directing and monitoring preparedness and the adaptations and fatigue that go along with it.

For many sports, peak power output, a result of impulse (force × time), is the primary characteristic that is associated with superior performance (Stone et al., 2003). Cormie et al. (2010) demonstrated that in weaker relatively untrained individuals emphasising increases in maximum strength resulted in increases in power and RFD as well or better than power training. However, among the stronger athletes higher-velocity power-oriented training was necessary to make further adaptations at the high-velocity portion of the force-velocity curve (Cormie et al., 2010). When working with less developed athletes of power sports, while both traditional strength training and high velocity may enhance power output and RFD, it is important to understand that between the two adaptations (strength and RFD) strength is much more stable and that to eventually become very powerful the athlete will likely need to become stronger (Bompa and Haff, 2009; Stone et al., 2016). Among weaker athletes, clearly an emphasis on gaining maximum strength has considerable benefit (Cormie et al., 2010; Suchomel et al., 2016). It should be noted that during this period of maximum strength emphasis, in addition to implementing heavy loads, power/velocity training can (and likely should) be included as part of the de-emphasis (DeWeese et al., 2015a, 2015b).

Among athletes in which high power outputs and higher velocities of movement are a necessity, a refocused training protocol is advantageous. Once an athlete is relatively strong (e.g. double body mass back squat for a male [Suchomel et al. 2016]) an increased emphasis on higher power and velocity movements rather can enhanced desired adaptations (Cormie et al., 2010). Again there is always combination (emphasis/de-emphasis) training taking place (Harris et al., 2000); however, a greater focus on higher-power and higher-velocity movements becomes necessary. During this re-focus, it is important that maximum strength does not decrease, as this potentially could reduce the ability to produce high power outputs

---

Box 17.2 Considerations for vertical jump testing and training age

An athlete's training age is a major consideration for jump testing and data interpretation/application. In well-trained strength power athletes it appears that underlying force characteristics (power, RFD) tell a much better story of an athlete's fatigued state compared to unloaded countermovement or static jump height data (Kraska et al., 2009). An option for coaches of well-trained athletes who do not possess a force plate is having their athletes perform vertical jumps across a wide spectrum of loads (e.g. bdm, 20%, 30%, 60%) on a switch mat (jump height estimation only) (McBride et al., 2002). Similar to how an isometric force-time curve displays alterations at different parts of the isometric force-time curve (e.g. <100 ms or >300 ms), indicating neuromuscular changes due to different types of training, a jump height-load curve can provide somewhat similar information (McBride et al., 2002). For example, during periods of high-velocity, low-force training greater adaptations may be displayed at early onset of muscle contraction (for jumps, greater jump height at the lighter loads) versus at the end of a high-force, low-velocity block, in which a greater curve shift will occur towards maximal force production (for jumps, greater jump height at the heavier loads).

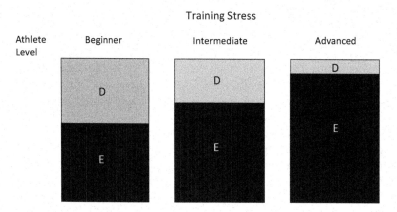

Figure 17.3 Hypothetical example of increased training concentration as an athlete develops over time. D = de-emphasis, E = emphasis.

(particularly during loaded movements) (Figure 17.3). Thus, the re-focused training may include complex and contrast training as well as periodic short phases of training in which maximum strength is again the primary emphasis.

Using data in an attempt to identify training level and age

It is often difficult for a coach to truly know how well-trained an athlete is when they begin working with that athlete. Questionnaires that ask training age and training history-related questions may be helpful; however, as one coach put it, "all athletes are very highly trained, just ask them and they will tell you". The number of years spent participating in their given sport is often different from (less than) the number of years spent on developing the important performance adaptations. Using data to discern how well-trained your athlete can be beneficial as it helps the coach conceptualise monitoring goals (e.g. develop vs. directing adaptations?) and the appropriate training prescription (the appropriate amount of training concentration). While it is certainly worthwhile to compare baseline performance measurements to other athletes (e.g. talent identification), data should more often be handled as "single subject" (see Chapter 5). For each fitness characteristic (e.g. maximal strength, power, etc.) every athlete has their own "quantitative" window of adaptation. Not only is this window of adaptation inherited, so too is the point at which the window begins, in other words an athlete's adaptation "floor" and "ceiling" (DeWeese et al., 2015a and b). Indeed, it appears that advanced and elite athletes may have two distinct genetic advantages: first are genetically linked physiological characteristics and second is a larger adaptation window (Ma et al., 2013; Klissouras, 1971; Bouchard et al., 1992). Thus, it is possible that an athlete could produce impressive performance data via strength power assessment and *not* be well trained. Using performance data longitudinally a coach can get a better understanding of how well-trained an athlete is based on the following.

(1) How specific is the adaptive response to the training stress? For example, when an athlete performs higher-volume strength work does RFD increase? This would suggest that the athlete is not highly trained.

(2) When measuring across multiple mesocycles what is the rate of gain for a given adaptation(s)? Large initial increases in strength (e.g. ≥30%) are probably indicative that (even if the athlete is relatively strong in comparison to others) the athlete is not highly trained. In the case of an individual who displays impressive absolute strength at baseline (IPF < 6 × body mass) and subsequently experiences large relative strength gains over the first several mesocycles, this suggests that the athlete has favourable genetics for strength-related performance (Bouchard et al., 1992).

Maximum strength and explosive strength: training and monitoring considerations

Explosive strength and power

This discussion on maximal strength and explosive strength is based on well-trained strength-power-based athletes. For coaches of power-based sports an understanding of maximal strength (peak force) and explosive strength (RFD) can inform the planning and practice of various aspects of both training and monitoring. Studies have shown that rate of force development (RFD) is quite sensitive to a variety of stimuli and particularly fatigue, and thus is less stable than high-force variables (1-RM back squat, isometric peak force) (Issurin, 2009; Stone et al., 2003). Thus, RFD is more sensitive to alterations in training volume and cumulative fatigue. It is possible that alterations in RFD are at least partially due to alterations in myosin heavy chains and fibre type (Andersen & Aagaard, 1998). High volumes of work can stimulate AMP kinase substantially and result in a shift away from Type IIx toward slower motor units, thus decreasing RFD (Andersen et al., 2010). Volumes large enough to result in MHC shifts would probably be accompanied by substantial fatigue. From a monitoring perspective, since isometric RFD is more sensitive to training volume it may provide a superior estimate of an athlete's preparedness.

During certain phases within a macrocycle, particularly during general preparation (e.g. strength-endurance block), inducing this fibre-type shift is likely warranted in an effort to enhance high-intensity work capacity and increase muscle cross-sectional area (hypertrophy). From a monitoring standpoint this means that during this period, explosiveness may be depressed and, *within limits*, as long as the athlete continues to develop and adapt in the desired direction fatigue, the loss of RFD can be acceptable. Conversely during subsequent periods of low volume and higher intensity (e.g. a power phase or tapering phase) diminished fatigue and an increase in RFD can be observed, indicating a rise in preparedness

(DeWeese et al., 2015a, 2015b). In part, this rise is probably due to a greater focus on explosive exercises, and a shift back toward and even a supercompensation of Type IIx fibres (Hortobagy et al., 1993; Terzis et al., 2008; Wilson et al., 2012). From a periodisation/programming standpoint this works well since, for power-based sports, explosiveness is very sport-specific and has a much faster decay rate (i.e. residual effect). Indeed, power and particularly RFD seem to fall off more quickly than maximum strength and thus should be emphasised (lower volume) closer to a major competition (Issurin, 2009).

Maximal strength

Maximal strength appears to be more resistant to fatigue, and fluctuates less than explosive strength. For example, under fatigued conditions maximal strength "hangs in there" to a much greater extent than more neural-based adaptations. Thus, maximal strength has demonstrated much slower decay rates/stronger residual effects, and from a training/development standpoint, can be de-emphasised further out from a major competition (Issurin, 2009). While perhaps as a metric for assessing preparedness it is not as robust as explosive strength, maximal strength is certainly a variable to assess and develop throughout an athlete's training.

Case study 1

An 18-year-old, male, short-distance sprinter (e.g. 55 m, 60 m, 100 m) in athletics (track and field) recently joined a higher-level club due to his current sprint ability and potential (consistently sprints a ≤10.4 second 100 m). He has around 10 years of experience in the sport and limited resistance training experience. Before his training begins with the club, he undergoes an initial performance assessment. Among his many performance variables assessed, typical values for advanced sprinters tested with an isometric mid-thigh pull (Figure 17.4) include an IPF of 5900 N, an IRFD (0–200 ms) of 24,000 N/s and a no arm-swing vertical jump (VJ) of 59 cm (Table 17.3). The new club sprinter produces an IPF of 4600 N and an IRFD (0–200 ms) of 18,000 N/s (Table 17.3). Additionally, he produces 5200 watts of peak power (PP) and a jump height (no arm swing) of 56 cm from an unweighted countermovement (Table 17.3). The coach's goal for the next several training blocks is geared towards what is in his best interest for his continued, long term development vs. what will most likley allow him to hit the best possible sprint times the quickest. After his initial testing, he performed a 4-week training block of high-volume resistance training (3 × 10) and minimal sprint work. At the end of the block they re-tested; his IPF increased (+1100 N) his IRFD remained essentially unchanged (18,300 N/s) while jump data demonstrated slight improvements (5400 W PP and 56.9 cm). These data and his previous training history suggest that his training across his next several training blocks should predominantly have a strength-based focus in the weight room before transitioning to a more a power-oriented phase(s). For example, implementing several sequential training blocks utilising high-load (>75% 1-RM), strength-oriented exercises (e.g. back squat, front squat, push press, clean pull from floor) with set-rep schemes such as 5 × 5, 3 × 5, 3 × 3. Perhaps after that transitioning to a block of maximal strength development (e.g. 3 × 3, 3 × 2, 3 × 1 often above 90% 1-RM).

Figure 17.4 An athlete preparing to perform an isometric clean grip mid-thigh pull.

Table 17.3 Performance data pre and post strength endurance block.

	Pre SE	*Post SE*
IPF (N)	4,600	5,700
IRFD (N/s)	18,000	18,300
SJ JH (cm)	56	56.9
SJ PP (W)	5,200	5,400

SE = strength endurance.

Case study 2

A 20-year-old female swimmer (50 m and 100 m freestyle) is embarking on her first national trials (qualifier for world championships) in which she has a legitimate chance of making the world team. Her lifetime best, achieved 3 months ago, puts her in fifth place coming into the trials and just a few hundredths of a second out of third place, the lowest placing necessary to land a spot on the world team. Her swim times have really improved over the last 2 years and her personal best was achieved just 3 months ago, when she was not "peaking",

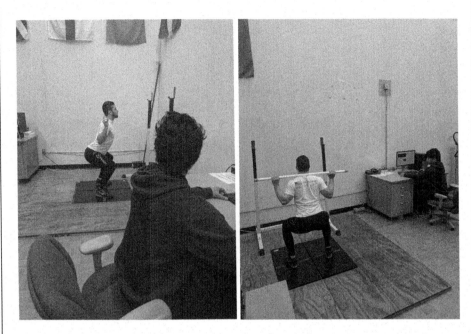

Figure 17.5 An athlete performing static vertical jumps across a spectrum of loads (0 kg, 11 kg and 20 kg).

thus her coaches are enthusiastic about her chances of making the team with a successful taper/peaking phase. In addition to daily monitoring of training volume and intensity, the coaches measured stress-related variables such as heart rate upon waking, hours of sleep, sleep disturbances, body mass, etc. During her last 6 weeks leading up to the trials her coaches assessed preparedness via static vertical jump (no arm swing) with 0 kg, 11 kg and 20 kg (Figure 17.5). Her taper involved a planned overreaching phase followed by a step-like taper in which every 2 weeks a 20% decrease in volume occurred. Across the 6 weeks of the taper her PP increased slightly from one week to the next (3600 W to eventually 4100 W) and her JH improved from 36 cm to 42 cm (a lifetime best). While these changes did not occur in a completely linear fashion (the greatest improvement occurred during the first 3 weeks) the general trend suggested that her preparedness was slowly increasing. Her time trials the last few weeks were approaching her previous lifetime best and she actually surpassed her lifetime best the week before the competition. Additionally, all of her daily stress-related variables (HR, sleep, etc.) remained in "normal ranges". Based on these data and the overall circumstance the coaches and athlete can go into the national championships focused and confident that she is prepared to do well.

Case study 3

A 26-year-old American football player (running back) who has been playing professionally for 4 years is currently entering the halfway point of the regular season (game 8 of 16). The previous 3 years his strength and conditioning coach has implemented an in-season resistance training maintenance programme consisting of three training blocks following a sequence of moderate volume (block of 3 × 5, 60–75% 1-RM), moderate to low volume (block of 3 × 5 and 3 × 3, 65–80% 1RM) and low volume (block of 3 × 3, 3 × 2). These blocks incorporate more partial movements for squat variations (e.g. half squat or 1/3 squat from safety bars) and pulling movements/weightlifting derivatives (clean grip mid-thigh pull vs. clean pull from the floor) compared to the preparation phase. Partial movements are an often utilised in-season programming strategy that, as previously mentioned, allow strength coaches to reduce the amount of work performed. Furthermore, partial movements can substantially reduce eccentric work performed and for several exercises allow for increased intensities (loads) to be performed. Additionally, interspersed throughout the season are a few brief periods (i.e. 1 week) of more full range of motion movements (e.g. full squat) and a more moderate repetition count (e.g. 5 × 5 or 3 × 5). Every Monday the S&C coach collects unloaded and loaded static vertical jump data. Across several weeks (4 – current), his PP from the loaded jumps (20 kg, 40 kg, 60 kg) continues to fall (5700 W to 4900 W) and his football performance as subjectively assessed by the coaches has slipped. Additionally, his body mass begins to drop (103 kg to 98 kg) and his resting heart rate has steadily increased (64 bpm to 69 bpm) over the 4 weeks. It is clear that there is a problem. An athlete's overall stress is a combination of both training stress and non-training stress. However, changes in an athlete's total stress (e.g. testosterone, cortisol alterations, neuromuscular fatigue, etc.) is typically due to training variable manipulation (external load) and the resultant training stress response (internal load). Sometimes issues related to "outside stressors" (e.g. lack of sleep, social stress, poor dietary habits, alcohol, etc.) versus the training prescription can lead to performance decrements and maladaptations due to the added stress as well as creating an issue of "under-recovery". How to handle this situation is much less clear and admittedly difficult. In this case there is likely to be no "perfect" answer; however, three things hopefully occur sooner rather than later: (1) the entire SPEG meets to discuss the situation, (2) members of the SPEG meet individually with the athlete and (3) even though volume is already relatively low, practice, conditioning and weight-room volume should be managed appropriately in an effort to play "damage control". While certainly not ideal, in this instance, hopefully the monitoring data can not just allow the athlete to avoid prolonged poor performance but help him avoid a serious injury or health/safety issue.

Summary

Coaching is a multifaceted process that at times can feel overwhelming. So many considerations exist within this complicated and often perplexing process. Athlete monitoring can provide insight into this process and help the coach "steer the ship" more confidently.

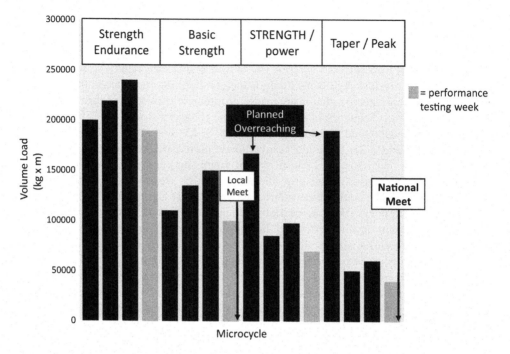

Figure 17.6 An example of a training prescription for a weightlifter displaying planned volume loads, training block objectives, testing periods and the upcoming competition schedule. Modified from, Hornsby et al., (2017). Maximum Strength, Rate of Force Development, Jump Height, and Peak Power Alterations in Weightlifters across Five Months of Training.

Using data to help plan training and monitor training is nothing new; however, over the last several years technology has provided many more options, and often advantages, to help coaches carry out their monitoring plans. Figure 17.6 is an example of a planned training prescription for a weightlifter displaying pre-determined training block objectives, with corresponding training volumes, testing periods and competition schedule. Monitoring and planning should not be viewed as two separate entities; the integration of these two incredibly important coaching tools should be viewed as complementary.

References

Andersen, L.L., & Aagaard, P. (1998). Correlation between contractile strength and myosin heavy chain isoform composition in human skeletal muscle. *Medicine & Science in Sports & Exercise, 30*(8), 1217–1222.

Andersen, L.L., Andersen, J.L., Zebis, M.K. & Aagaard, P. (2010). Early and late rate of force development: differential adaptive responses to resistance training? *Scandinavian Journal of Medicine & Science in Sports, 20*(1), 162–169.

Banister, E.W., & Wenger, H.A. (1982). Monitoring training. In J.D. MacDougall, H.A. Wenger & H.J. Green (Eds.), *Physiological testing of the elite athlete* (pp. 163–170). Ithaca, NY: Movement.

Balyi, I., Richard, W., & Higgs, C. (2013). *Long-term athlete development*. Champaigne, IL: Human Kinetics.

Balshaw, T.G., Maden-Wilkinson T., & Folland J. (2017). Muscle size and strength: debunking the "completely separate phenomena" suggestion. *European Journal of Applied Physiology, 117*(6), 1275–1276.

Bazyler, C.D., Mizuguchi, S., Harrison, A.P., Sato, K., Kavanaugh, A.A., DeWeese, B.H., & Stone, M.H. (2007). Changes in muscle architecture, explosive ability, and track and field throwing performance throughout a competition season and following a taper. *Journal of Strength and Conditioning Research, 31*(10), 2785–2793.

Bompa, T.O., & Haff, G.G. (2009). *Periodization: Theory and methodology of training* (5th edn.). Champaign, IL: Human Kinetics.

Bouchard C., Dionne FT, Simoneau J., & Bouley M. (1992). Genetics of aerobic and anaerobic performance. *Medicine & Science in Sports & Exercise, 20*, 27–58.

Cormie C., McGuigan M., & Newton R. (2010). Adaptations in athletic performance after ballistic power versus strength training. *Medicine & Science in Sports & Exercise, 42*(8), 1582–1598.

DeWeese, B.H., Hornsby, G., Stone, M., & Stone, M.H. (2015a). The training process: Planning for strength–power training in track and field. Part 1: Theoretical aspects. *Journal of Sport and Health Science, 4*(94), 308–317.

DeWeese, B.H., Hornsby, G., Stone, M., & Stone, M.H. (2015b). The training process: Planning for strength–power training in track and field. Part 2: Practical and applied aspects. *Journal of Sport and Health Science, 4*(4), 318–324.

Folland, J.P., and Williams, A.G. (2007). The adaptations to strength training: Morphological and neurological contributions to increased strength. *Sports Medicine, 37*(2), 145–168.

Garcia-Pallares, J., Sanchez-Medina, L., Carrasco, L., Diaz, A., & Izquierdo, M. (2009). Endurance and neuromuscular changes in world-class level kayakers during a periodized training cycle. *European Journal of Applied Physiology, 106*, 629–638.

Haff, G.G., Jackson, J.R., Kawamori, N., Carlock, J.M., Hartman, M.J., Kilgore, J.L., & Stone, M.H. (2008). Force-time curve characteristics and hormonal alterations during an eleven-week training period in elite women weightlifters. *Journal of Strength and Conditioning Research, 22*, 433–446.

Haff, G.G. (2010). Quantifying workloads in resistance training: A brief review. *Professional Strength and Conditioning, 19*, 31–40.

Haff, G., Ruben, R., Lider, J., Twine, C., & Cormie, P. (2015) A comparison of methods for determining the rate of force development during isometric midthigh clean pulls. *Journal of Strength and Conditioning Research, 29*(2), 38–95.

Häkkinen, K., Komi, P.V., Alen, M., & Kauhanen, H. (1987). EMG, muscle fibre and force production characteristics during a 1 year training period in elite weight-lifters. *European Journal of Applied Physiology and Occupational Physiology, 56*, 419–427.

Häkkinen, K. (1993). Neuromuscular fatigue and recovery in male and female athletes during heavy resistance exercise. *International Journal of Sports Medicine, 14*(2), 53–59.

Harris, G.R., Stone, M.H., O'Bryant, H.O., Proulx, C., & Johnson, R. (2000). Short term performance effects of high power, high force, or combined weight-training methods. *Journal of Strength and Conditioning Research, 14*, 14–20.

Hortobagyi, T., Houmard, J., Stevensen, J., Fraser, D., Johns, R., & Israel, R. (1993). The effects of detraining on power athletes. *Medicine & Science in Sports & Exercise, 25*, 929–935.

Hornsby, W.G., Haff, G.G., Sands, W.A., Ramsey, M.W., Beckham, G.K., Stone, M.E., and Stone, M.H. (2013). Alterations in strength characteristics for isometric and dynamic mid-thigh pulls in collegiate throwers across 11 weeks of training. *Gazzata Medica Italiana – Archives of Science and Medicine, 172*, 929–940.

Issurin, V.B. (2009). Generalized training effects induced by athletic preparation: A review. *Journal of Sports Medicine and Physical Fitness, 49*(4), 333–345.

Klissouras, V. (1971). Adaptability of genetic variation. *Journal of Applied Physiology, 31,* 338–344.

Kraska, J.M., Ramsey, M.W., Haff, G.G., Fethke, N., Sands, W.A., Stone, M.E., et al. (2009). Relationship between strength characteristics and unweighted and weighted vertical jump height. *International Journal of Sports Physiology and Performance, 4,* 461–473.

Ma, F., Yang, Y., Li, X., Zhou, F., Gao, C., Li, M., & Gao, L. (2013). The association of sport performance with ACE and ACTN3 genetic polymorphisms: A systematic review and meta-analysis. *PloS One, 8*(1), e54685.

Maffiuletti, N.A., et al. (2016). Rate of force development: Physiological and methodological considerations. *European Journal of Applied Physiology, 116*(6), 1091–1116.

Matveyev, L.P. (1965). *Periodization of sports training.* Moscow: Fizkultura I Sport.

McBride, J.M., McCaulley, G.O., Cormie, P., Nuzzo, J.L., Cavill, M.J., & Triplett, N.T. (2009). Comparison of methods to quantify volume during resistance exercise. *Journal of Strength and Conditioning Research, 23,* 106–110.

McBride, J.M., Triplett-McBride, T., Davie, A., & Newton, R.U. (2002). The effect of heavy- vs. light-load jump squats on the development of strength, power, and speed. *Journal of Strength and Conditioning Research, 16*(1), 75–82.

McClellan, C., Christopher, P., Lovell, D., & Gass, G. (2011). The role of rate of force development on vertical jump performance. *The Journal of Strength and Conditioning Research, 25*(2), 379–385.

Meijer, J., Jaspers, R., Rittweger, J., Seynnes, O., Kamandulis, M., Skuvydas, A., Pisot, R., Simunic, B., Narici, M., & Degens, H. (2015). Single muscle fibre contractile properties differ between body-builders, power athletes and control subjects. *Experimental Physiology, 100:* 1331–1341.

Mujika, I. (2013). The alphabet of sport science research starts with Q. *International Journal of Sports Physiology and Performance, 8,* 465–466.

Moore, C.A., & Fry, A.C. (2007). Nonfunctional overreaching during off-season training for skill position players in collegiate American football. *Journal of Strength and Conditioning Research, 21*(3), 793–800.

Plisk, S., & Stone, M.H. (2003). Periodization strategies. *Strength and Conditioning Journal, 25*(19), 37.

Sands, W.A., & McNeal, J. (2000) Predicting Athlete preparation and performance: A theoretical perspective. *Journal of Sport Behavior, 23*(3), 289–310.

Sands, W.A., & Stone, M.H. (2005). Are you progressing and how would you know? *Olympic Coach, 17,* 4–10.

Scott, B. (2011). Quantifying the immediate recovery energy expenditure of resistance training. *Journal of Strength and Conditioning Research, 25*(4), 1159–1163.

Siff, M.C. (2003). *Supertraining.* Denver, CO: Supertraining Institute.

Sperannza, M., Gabbett, T., Johnston, R., & Sheppard, J. (2016). Effect of strength and power training on tackling ability in semiprofessional rugby league players. *Journal of Strength and Conditioning Research, 30*(2), 336–343.

Stone, M.H., Pierce, K., Godsen, R., Wilson, G.D., Blessing, D., & Rozenek, R. (1987). Heart rate and lactate levels during weight training exercise in trained and untrained males. *The Physician and Sports Medicine, 15*(5), 97–106.

Stone, M.H., & Wathen, D. (2001). Letter to the editor. *Strength and Conditioning Journal, 23*(5), 7–9.

Stone, M.H., Sanborn, K., O'Bryant, H.S., Hartman, M.E., Stone, M.E., Proulx, C., Ward, B., & Hruby, J. (2003). Maximum strength-power-performance relationships in collegiate throwers. *Journal of Strength and Conditioning Research, 17,* 739–745.

Stone, M.H., Stone, M.E., & Sands, W.A. (2007). *Principles and practice of resistance training.* Champaigne, IL: Human Kinetics.

Stone, M.H., Cormie, P., Lamont, H., & Stone, M.E. (2016). Development of strength and power. In I. Jeffries (Ed.), *Strength and conditioning for sport performance* (UKSCA Strength and Conditioning Textbook). London: Routledge.

Suchomel, T., Comfort, P., & Lake, J. (2017). Enhancing the force–velocity profile of athletes using weightlifting derivatives. *Strength and Conditioning Journal, 39*(1), 10–20.

Suchomel, T., Nimphius, S., & Stone, M. (2016). The importance of muscular strength in athletic performance. *Sports Medicine, 46*(10), 1419–1449.

Terzis, G., Spengos, K., Manta, P., Sarris, N., & Georgiadis, G. (2008). Fiber type composition and capillary density in relation to submaximal number of repetitions in resistance exercise. *Journal of Strength and Conditioning Research, 22*(3), 845–850.

Tillin, N.A., Pain, M.T., & Folland, J. (2013). Explosive force production during isometric squats correlates with athletic performance in rugby union players. *Journal of Sports Science, 31*, 66–76.

Van Cutsem, M., Duchateau, J., & Hainaut, K. (1998). Changes in single motor unit behavior contribute to the increase in contraction speed after dynamic training in humans. *Journal of Physiology, 513*, 295–305.

Verkhoshansky, Y. and Verkhoshansky, N. (2011) *Special strength training: Manual for coaches.* Rome: Verkhoshansky.com.

Wilson, J., Loennek, J., Jo, E., Wilson, G., Zourdos, M., & Kim, J. (2012). The effects of endurance, strength and power training on muscle fiber type shifting. *Journal of Strength and Conditioning Research, 26*(4), 1724–1729.

Zaras, N., Stasinaki, A., Methenitis, S., Krase, A., Karampatos, G., Georgiadis, G., Spengos, K., & Terzis, G (2016). Rate of force development, muscle architecture, and performance in young competitive track and field throwers. *The Journal of Strength & Conditioning Research, 30*(1), 81–92.

Index

Note: Page numbers in **bold** refer to tables and in *italics* to figures.

1-RM (one-repetition maximum): biomotor abilities 297; isometric mid-thigh pull (IMTP) and 172; and isometric squat (ISQT) 175; muscular strength assessment 167–168, 178–179, 184–185, 298, 308–309, 342; power assessment 201, 203; prediction of 44, 46; rest period 36–37
2D (two-dimensional) motion analysis 59
3-RM (three repetition maximum) 178, 185
4 × 5 m sprint test 144, 148
30-15 IFT (30–15 intermittent fitness test) 220
95% confidence intervals 25–26, *28*
505 test 141–143, 146–150, **159**, 161; modified 143

abbreviated testing battery 37–38
absolute reliability 56; definition **57**
Achievement Goal Theory 15
ACL (anterior cruciate ligament) injury 62, 63, 65, 81
activation 14, 15, 16, 18
acute-chronic load ratio 53
adductor squeeze test 75–77
adenosine triphosphate *see* ATP
adenylate-kinase reaction 212
ADP (air displacement plethysmography) 245, 246, 264–266
"advanced cue utilisation" 151
aerobic performance assessment 212–234; aerobic capacity 213–214; critical power/critical velocity (CP/CV) 221–222; exercise economy 215–217; five × 6-second cycle test 233; incremental exercise testing 219–221; lactate threshold (LT) 217–218; lactate turnpoint (LTP) 218–219;maximal lactate steady state (MLSS) 218, 222–223; ramp incremental cycling test 224–229, *230*, 233; step incremental treadmill test 223–224; three-minute all-out test

231, 233–234; twenty-metre multi-stage shuttle run test 228–229, 232; VO_{2max} 214–216, 221; YIRT (Yo-Yo Intermittent Recovery Test) 35, 37, 232–233
air displacement plethysmography *see* ADP
agility: assessment of 150–161; definitions 140–141; human stimulus testing 153, 155; light-based systems of measurement 150, 151; perceptual-cognitive abilities 160; timing of testing 35; video-based reactive agility test (Y-agility tests) 154; video-based systems 151–153
American (NFL) football 65, 125, 129–131, 133, 142, 147, 149, 298; case studies 335–336, 350
angle of peak moment 78
anterior cruciate ligament injury *see* ACL
anthropometric tape measure 245, 254–258
anthropometry 240
anticipatory skills 151
applied model of imagery 16
Archimedes principle 245
"arousal regulation" 14
atmospheric oxygen *see* O_2
ATP (adenosine triphosphate) 212–213
attentional focusing 16–17
audience, effect of 15, 18
Australian Rules football: agility 151, 152, 153, 155, 157, 160; eccentric utilisation ratio (EUR) 277; injury risk factors 65, 77, 78, 80
automatic external defibrillator 9
autonomy 5

back squat: assessment of power **197**, 201, *202*, 203; and barbell *202*; guidelines **186**; isometric mid-thigh pull (IMTP) and 172; isometric squat (ISQT) 174, 175; maximal dynamic testing 178–179; psychological issues 17; rest periods 36–37
balance, screening test 65–67

barbell velocity assessment 46

baseball 69, 297, 302–305

baseline data 34, 37, *43*

basketball: agility 152, 155, 157; change
of direction (COD) 146, 147; injury risk
factors **60**, 62; sprinting 126; training
age 305

BD (body density) 245, *264*

bench press 14, 15, 17, 172, 178–179;
combined assessment methods
(CMAs) **276**; guidelines **186**

beneficence 5

BIA (bioelectrical impedance analysis) 247,
266–268

bilateral strength imbalance 81–83

biochemical markers 44, 293, 299, 335

biomotor abilities 294, 297–299, 302, 304

BM (body mass): body composition
243–245, 247, 254, 266, 267, 270;
case study 248–249; measurement 252;
weighing scales 244, 252

BMC (bone mineral content) 240, 242–243,
247, 248–249

BMD (bone mineral density) 242–243

BODPOD (ADP unit) 245, *265*

body composition 240–272; body mass
(BM) 243–244, 247, 254, 266, 267, 270;
bone mineral content (BMC) 240,
242–243, 247, 248–249; bone mineral
density (BMD) 242–243; case study
248–249, *250*; comparison of results
247–248; densitometry 245; fat mass (FM)
240, 241–242; fat-free mass (FFM) 240;
girth measurement 245; lean mass (LM)
240, 242, 243; skinfold assessment
245–246, 259–264; and sporting
performance 243, **244**; stature 244,
252–254; total body water (TBW) 240;
validation 240–241

body density *see* BD

body mass *see* BM

bone mineral content *see* BMC

bone mineral density *see* BMD

body volume *see* BV

Bolt, Usain 117

British Association for Sport and Exercise
Sciences 8

Brower timing gates 119, **120**, 125,
128, 133

BV (body volume) 245

CAMs (combined assessment methods)
275–284, *285*; dynamic strength deficit
(DSD) 275–277, 281; dynamic strength
index (DSI) 178, **276**, 281, 178; eccentric
utilisation ratio (EUR) 277, 281–282;
force-velocity profiles 277–279, 282, *283*;

pre-stretch augmentation percentage
(PSAP) 277; reactive strength index
(RSI) 279–280, 282–283; RSImod 280,
283–284

carbon dioxide production *see* VC_{O2}

cardiac events, risk of 6

centre of mass *see* COM

change of direction *see* COD

children 11–12

chronic loading capacity 53

circadian rhythms 35, 132–133

CKCUEST (Closed Kinetic Chain Upper-
Extremity Stability Test) 69–71

"closed-loop" tests 220

CMJ (countermovement jump) (vertical
jump) 44, 96–114; arm swing 101; braking
phase 108, 113–114; calculating mean,
peak and sum variables 110; calculation of
jump height 110–112; countermovement
technique 102; data analysis 103–112;
data interpretation 112–114;
displacement 105; equipment 96–99; field-
based equipment **100**; flight phase 109;
flight time method 110–112; force-time
curve *107*; force- time record 98–99;
forward dynamics 104–105; interpretation
of data 112–114; jump technique 102;
landing phase 109; landing position
102–103; measurement 35–36;
numerical double integration 105;
numerical integration 104; onset
of movement threshold 106; phase
identification 105–106; power 105;
propulsion phase 108, 114; protocols
99–103; standardisation of analysis 38;
starting position 101–102; take-off and
touchdown threshold 109; take-off
velocity method 112; training age
341–342; unweighting phase 106,
108, 112; variables **111**; velocity 105;
weighing phase 103–104; work 105

coaching cues 16–17, 18–19, 37

coaching feedback 55–56, 65, 119, 149, 330

co-action, effect of 15

COD (change of direction) 140–161;
and agility 150; assessment of speed
141–150, 153; Illinois test 146–147, 148;
interpretation of results 298; L-run
test 142–144, 146, 148; LAVEG laser
system 149; pro-agility test 142–143, 145,
147–149; T-test 142, 144, 148, **159**;
traditional tests 143, 148

coefficient of variation *see* CV

cognitive preparatory strategies 16

COM (centre of mass): change of direction
(COD) 150; countermovement jump
(CMJ) **100**, 101, 102–104, 105, 106,

108–110, 112; injury risk factors 78; power assessment 193, 194, 195–197, 200–204
combined assessment methods *see* CAMs
competition, effect of 15
CON:H/Q (concentric flexor (hamstrings) to concentric extensor (quadriceps) peak moment ratio) 78, 80
constant-work-rate exercise *see* CWRE
constrained action hypothesis 17
construct validity 24, 26, 56; definition **57**
continual monitoring 42, 44–47, 48, 318
contraindications for testing 10
countermovement jump *see* CMJ
CP/CV (critical power/critical velocity) 214, 218, 221–222, 233, 234
cricket 125, 127, 130, 147, 149
criterion validity, definition **57**
CV (coefficient of variation) 30, 56–57; sprint testing 119, **120–121**, 123
CWRE (constant-work-rate exercise) 215, 217, 218, 222
cycling 15, 119, 172, 219, *221*, 222, *223*, 298, 306–308; endurance cycling **307**

data analysis, standardisation of 38
data structure 27–28
DCP (dynamic control profile) 80, *81*
DCR (dynamic control ratio) 80, **82**
DCR equilibrium point *see* "point of equality"
decathlon, aerobic performance 212, 213
delayed training effect *see* DTE
densitometry 245, 246, 248
Deontology Theory 5
diagnostic accuracy, determination of 58–59
displacement: application to training 338–339, *340*; body composition 245; and countermovement jump (CMJ) 102, 104, 105, 108–110, 112, *113*; power assessment 193, 195–196, 201–204
DJ (drop jump) 59, *60*, 62–63, 279–280, 282–283; normative data **60**
Doppler effect 122
drive theory 15
drop jump (drop vertical landing test) *see* DJ
DSD (dynamic strength deficit) 178, 275, **276**, 277, 281
DSI (dynamic strength index) *see* DSD
DTE (delayed training effect) 47
dual X-ray absorptiometry *see* DXA
duty of care 6–7
DXA (dual X-ray absorptiometry) 242–243, 246–249, *250*, 251, 268–272
dynamic control profile *see* DCP
dynamic control ratio *see* DCR
dynamic strength deficit *see* DSD
dynamic strength index *see* DSI

eccentric strength 58, 78, *78*, 158
eccentric utilisation ratio *see* EUR
effect sizes *see* ES
ego-orientation 15
electromyography activity, and attentional focusing 16
electronic timing 119, 122, 122–123
electronic timing gates 37, 119, 120, 125, 128, 133
emergency communication 9
emergency resuscitation, training in 9
endurance: advanced athletes 343; case example 306–308; continual monitoring 47; intermittent sports 220; lactate threshold (LT) 218; maximal lactate steady state (MLSS) 222; oxygen consumption 214, 219, 220; and psychological issues 14, 15; strength endurance 178, 185, **348**, *351*; testing 298–299
endurance cycling **307**
ePARmed-X\+ 10
equipment selection 35–36
ES (effect sizes) 296
ethical issues 5–6
EUR (eccentric utilisation ratio) **276**, 277, 281–282
evidenced-based phase potentiation training protocol 46
exercise economy 214, 215, 216–217, 224, 226, 229
expiratory ventilation *see* VE
explosive strength 168, 178, 283, 341, 345–346
external loading 47, 194, 196, 200–204, 206, 278, 334, 337

fat mass *see* FM
fat-free mass *see* FFM
fatigue resistance, and muscular strength 166, *167*, 306
fatigue-fitness paradigm *332–333*
feedback loops 48
FFM (fat-free mass) 240, 245
"field-based" tests 220
field hockey *see* hockey
fire exits 9
first aid 9
fitness-fatigue paradigm and preparedness 332–333
five × 6-second cycle test 233
FM (fat mass) 240, 241–242, 243, **244**, 245, 246–248; case study 248–249, *251*; *see also* skinfold measurement
FMS (Functional Movement Screen) 65
football **60**, 62, 72, 75, 319, *321*, *322*, *329*

force platforms (plates) (FP): countermovement jump (CMJ) 96–99, 101, 102, 103, 105–106, **111**; drop jump (DJ) 280; historical background 341; interpretation of results 295, 297–298; muscular strength test 168, 171, 172, 174, 175, 176–177, 179, 184; power assessment 196, 197, *199*, 200–201, 203, *205*; RSImod 280; sampling frequency 36; standardisation and 35; validity of results **25**
force-velocity profiles **276**, 277–279, 282, *283*
FP *see* force platforms (plates)
FPPA (frontal plane projection angle) 59, *60*; normative data **60**
Functional Movement Screen *see* FMS
Fusion Sport timing system 121, 126, *127*

Gaelic football 75, 77
gas exchange threshold *see* GET
gender of tester, impact of 15
genetic ceiling 46–47, 342
GET (gas exchange threshold) 218, 219, 224, 226–229, *230*
GIRD (glenohumeral internal rotation deficit) 69, 70
girth 245, 254–258
glycolysis 212
goal-setting 15, 17
GRF (ground reaction force) 97, 104, 105
groin injuries 74–77
Guidelines, definition 6

hamstring strain injuries *see* HSI
hamstring strength assessment 77–83
hand-held dynamometry *see* HHD
health and safety issues 5–6
heteroscedasticity 27, *29*
HHD (hand-held dynamometers) 72–74, 77
hip adductor strength assessment 72–77
hip strength assessment 72–73
historical background 334
hockey 60, 140, 281
Hologic Horizon DXA system *269–272*
hop for distance tests 67–68; normative data **69**
HSI (hamstring strain injuries) 77–78, 78, 80–81
human stimulus 151, 153–160, *161*
hydrodensitometry 245, 246, 248

IBP (isometric bench press) 171, 177–178; protocol 184
ICC (intra-class correlation coefficient) 26, 56; sprint testing 119, **118–119**
ice hockey 74

ICGMTP (isometric clean grip mid-thigh pull) 341
Illinois test 146–147, *148*
ILP (isometric leg press) 171, 175–177; protocol 184
impulse: application to training 343; countermovement jump (CMJ) 102, 104, 105, 109, 113–114, 277; muscular strength testing 168, 169; power assessment 193, 195
impulse-momentum theorem 103, 110, 112, 195, 196
IMTP (isometric mid-thigh pull) 169, 171–172, 175, 275–276, 333; equipment selection 36; peak force (PF) 172, 275, 323, *324*, *325*, 327; protocols 181
informed consent 6–7, 10; children 11
injury risk: assessment of factors 53–84; data analysis 38; diagnostic accuracy of screening 57–59; factors associated with *54*; muscle strength assessment 71–83; reliability and validity of screening 56–57; screening tests 54–71
intensity thresholds 46, 342, 343
inter-tester reliability, definition **57**
interaction of assessment methods 44
internal load data 47
International Society for the Advancement of Kinanthropometry *see* ISAK
interpretation of results 293–310; assessment of change 295–296; comparative and normative data 294–295; reasons for testing 293–294; sport-specific abilities 294; validity and reliability 294
intra-class correlation coefficient *see* ICC
intra-tester reliability, definition **57**
ISAK (International Society for the Advancement of Kinanthropometry) 246, 258, 259, 262
isokinetic dynamometry 73, 78–78, 80, 81, 168, 297; key variables 77
isometric bench press *see* IBP
isometric clean grip mid-thigh pull *see* ICGMTP
isometric force-time curve **168**, 169, *170*, 171, 342
isometric half squat 306, **307**
isometric leg press *see* ILP
isometric mid-thigh pull *see* IMTP
isometric strength measurement 72–75, 167, 168, **169**, 275–276, 297; considerations **182**; protocols 179, 181, **183**
ISQT (isometric squat) 169, 171, 174–175, 279; protocols 181

joint position sense 55
jump mats 35–36, **100**

jumping power 193–195
justice 5

kinanthropometry 240, 243
knee valgus 62–63, 72

L-run test (three-cone drill) 142–144, 146, 148
lactate threshold *see* LT
lactate turnpoint *see* LTP
Landing Error Scoring System *see* LESS
laser devices **120**, 122–123, 149
LAVEG laser system **120**, 123, 149
lean mass *see* LM
leg-cycle ergometry 217, 219, 233
legal requirements, and risk assessment 8
LESS (Landing Error Scoring System) 63, *63*
likelihood ratios, screening tests 58, **59**
limb dissociation 55
limb length **244**, 248
limb symmetry index *see* LSI
limit of tolerance *see* Tlim
limits of agreement *see* LOA
linear position transducer *see* LPT
linear speed 117–119; *see also* sprint testing
LM (lean mass) 240, *241–243*, **244**, 247–249, *250*, 304, 309
LOA (limits of agreement) 26–27, 30
logical validity, definition **57**
LPT (linear position transducer) 101–102
LSI (limb symmetry index) 67, 83
LT (lactate threshold) 217–218
LTP (lactate turnpoint) 218–219

magnetic resonance imaging *see* MRI
magnitude-based inferences *see* MBI
manoeuvrability 141–142, 144, 146–147, 148, **159**, 161
MAOD (maximal accumulated oxygen deficit) 299
maximal accumulated oxygen deficit *see* MAOD
maximal dynamic testing 178–179, 184–185
maximal lactate steady state *see* MLSS
maximal or near maximal lifting, and risk assessment 8
maximal strength testing 178–179, 184–185, 345–350; maximal strength prediction equations **180** *see* maximal dynamic testing
MBI (magnitude-based inferences) 295
"mean response time" *see* MRT
"measured" sports 47–48
measurement error: body composition assessment 244, 245, 266; and injury screening 56–57; interpretation of results 294; presentation of results 314, 326; and reliability 23, 29, 32;

sprint timing **120–121**; standardisation of testing 34, 36
mental imagery strategies 16
Microsoft Excel 27, **31**, 38, 134
MLSS (maximal lactate steady state) 218, 222–223
morphological optimisation 243, 251
motivation 13, 15–16, 18, 220
MRI (magnetic resonance imaging) 242
MRT ("mean response time") 226
MSA (muscle strength asymmetry) 81–83
MSFT (Multi-Stage Fitness Test) 35, 37
MSRT (multi-stage 20 m shuttle run test) 220, 228–229, 232
Multi-Stage Fitness Test *see* MSFT
multi-stage 20 m shuttle run test *see* MSRT
muscle strength asymmetry *see* MSA
muscular strength: bench press, back squat and power clean 178–179; definition 166, 297; force-time curve 168–169, *170*; historical background 341; interpretation of results 297–298; isometric and dynamic testing 166–186; literature 167–169, 171–178; maximal dynamic testing 178–179, 184–185; and performance *167, 173*; protocols 179–184, **185**; reciprocal and bilateral muscle strength imbalance **82**; screening tests 71–74; sport-specificity 298
musculoskeletal injury, prevention of 6
music and activation 14, 18

National Strength and Conditioning Association 7
NBPA (Nordic Breakpoint Angle) 78, *79*
negligence claims and liability 10
net joint moment 80, *81*
neuromuscular control 54, *55*, 71–72
neuromuscular fatigue 44, 47, 279, 280, 283
neuromuscular function 44, 105
Newton's Law of Reaction 97
Newton's Laws of motion 104
Newton's Second Law 195, 200, 202, 203
Newton's Third Law 197, 200–201
NFL football *see* American football
NHL (Nordic hamstring lower) 78
NHST (null hypothesis significance testing) 295
non-maleficence 5
NordBord™ 78, *79*, 80, 81
Nordic Breakpoint Angle *see* NBPA
Nordic hamstring lower *see* NHL
null hypothesis significance testing *see* NHST

O_2 (atmospheric oxygen) 214, *216*, 217, 225, 228, *230, 231*
Optojump system **118**, 128
outside stressors 46, 350

paired sample *t*-test 24–26
PAR-Q\+ 10
participant information sheet 10
patellofemoral pain syndrome *see* PFPS
PCr (phosphocreatine) 212–213
peak force *see* PF
perceived task difficulty 13–14
perception-response times 152, 153, 155, 157, 158, 160, 161
perceptual-cognitive ability 150, 151, 153, 158, 160–161
perceptual-motor ability 150
PF (peak force): braking 114; dynamic strength deficit/index (DSD/DSI) 281; isometric assessment protocols **183**; isometric force-time curve **168**; isometric bench press (IBP) 177–178; isometric leg press (ILP) 176–177; isometric mid-thigh pull (IMTP) 172, 275, 323, *324*, *325*, *327*; isometric squat (ISQT) 175; single-point power assessment 203; strength testing 298, 306
PFPS (patellofemoral pain syndrome) 63
phosphocreatine *see* PCr
phosphorylation 212, 213, 214, 217
photoelectric cells 35, 128
piezoelectric sensors 97, 98
PJMD (portable jump monitoring device) 24–25, 29, **31**
planning process 47–48
"point of equality" (DCR equilibrium point) 80
Poisson's Law 245
portable jump monitoring device *see* PJMD
power 193–206; back-squat **197**; body segmental analysis methods 204; combined method 196, 200–202; computation method 204–206; equipment availability and processes *205*; force-platform method 196, 197, 200, 201; jumping power 193–195; methodological issues 196–206; and performance 195–196; single-point methods 202–204
power clean **46**, 178, 179; guidelines **186**
pQCT (quantitative computerised tomography) 242
pre-stretch augmentation percentage *see* PSAP
PRFD (peak RFD) 169
pro-agility test 142–143, 145, 147–149
product-moment correlation coefficient 26
proprioception 55
protocols, standardisation of 36–37
PSAP (pre-stretch augmentation percentage) **276**, 277
"psyching up" 14, 18
psychological issues 13–19; key strategies **19**

QASLS tool 60, **61**, 62
quantification of training 336–341
quantitative computerised tomography *see* pQCT

radar guns **118**, 122–123
ramp incremental cycling test 224–229, *230*, 233
random error 23–24, 26–29, 100, 123; definition **57**
range of motion *see* ROM
RAT (reactive agility tests) 151, 153–158
rate of force development *see* RFD
RCP (respiratory compensation point) 219, 224, 228, *230*
reactive strength index *see* RSI
receiver operating characteristic curve analyses 58
reciprocal knee joint muscle strength imbalance 78, 80
RED-S syndromes (relative energy deficiency in sports) 243
relative reliability 56; definition **57**
reliability 23–24, 29–32; definition **57**
repeated-measures analysis of variance 24
repetition maximum testing *see* RM
repetitions-until-failure protocol 17
research studies 335–336
respiratory compensation point *see* RCP
rest periods 36–37
results: applied performance assessment cases 299–310; assessment of change 295–296; bar graphs *319*, *320*; change in athletic performance 313; communication of 296–297, 328–330; comparative and normal data 294–295; forest plots 314–316; interpretation of 293–310; presentation of 313–330; radar charts 321–326, *327*; scatter plots 326, *328*; traffic-light systems 316–318; univariate scatterplots 318–321, *322*, *329*; verbal communication 328–330
RFD (rate of force development): application to training 333, 343–346; interpretation of results 297–298; PRFD (peak RFD) 169; strength testing 168–169, 172, 174–177, **182**, **183**, 281–282, 284
risk assessment and management 7–12; risk severity rating systems 8–9; special populations 11–12
RM (repetition maximum) testing 44, 185
ROM (range of motion) 78, 77, 80
RSI (reactive strength index) 44, **276**, 279–280, 282–283, 326, 328; RSImod **276**, 280, 283–284, *285*
rugby league: agility 157; applied performance assessment case study

308–310; change of direction (COD) 143, 152, 155; presentation of results 316; sprinting 123, 126
rugby union 78, 117, 123, 127, 281, 314, *315*
running 15, 65, 78, 214–217, 299; *see also* sprinting

safeguarding 11
safety *see* health and safety issues
sampling frequency capability, testing equipment 36
Scotland, legislation 11
screening tests: concurrent validity 56; diagnostic accuracy of 57–59; lower quadrant 59–68, **69**; negative prediction value 57; pass/fail 54; positive prediction value 57; predictive ability 58; primary/secondary 54–55; reliability 56; sensitivity 57, 59; specificity of 57, 59; upper quadrant 69–71
SDD (smallest detectable difference) 57
SDws (standard deviation) 29–30, 32, 314
SEBT (star excursion balance test) 65–67
self-confidence 13–14, 17
self-efficacy 13–14, 16, 17
self-presentation, impact of 15
self-regulatory strategies 18
self-report forms 293
self-talk 16, 18, **19**
SEM (standard error of measurement) 56–57
shoulder tests 69
Simpson's rule 104
single-leg landing *see* SLL
single-leg loading **61**
single-leg squat *see* SLS
skinfold assessment 245–246, 259–264; callipers 259, 264; pinch procedure 264
SLL (single-leg landing) 59, *60*, 62; normative data **60**
SLS (single-leg squat) 59–61; normative data **60**
SmartSpeed system 126–127
smallest detectable difference *see* SDD
SMC (smallest meaningful change) 295–296
soccer: aerobic performance assessment 220; case study 299–302; change of direction and direction (COD) 140–144, 146–147, 151, 158, 160; injury risk factors 60, **69**, 74–78, 78, 80; reactive strength index (RSI) 283; sprinting 117, 130
social facilitation 14–15
social physique anxiety 15
software/hardware updates 9
SOP (standard operating procedure) 10
special populations 11–12
speed, interpretation of results 298

SPEG (sport performance enhancement group) 334
sphygmomanometer, adductor squeeze test 75–77
split goals 16
Sport England (2004) 11–12
sport performance enhancement group *see* SPEG
sprinting 117–134; circadian rhythms 132–133; distance behind start line 130, *131*; distances, intervals and flying times 131–132; equipment *118*, 119–128; footwear 133; interpretation of results 133–134; methodological considerations 128–134; number of trials 131; protocols 37; speed curve *118*; starting position 128–130; in sports 117, 123, 126, 130, 140; surfaces 133; temperature 133; wind 133
SSC (stretch-shortening cycle) 96, 102, 112, 277, 279, 280, 282–283
stadiometers 244, 252–254, 266, 268
Stalker Radar System 123
standard deviation *see* SDws
standard error of measurement *see* SEM
standard operating procedure *see* SOP
standardisation of testing 34–38
Standards, definition 6
star excursion balance test *see* SEBT
stature 244, 252–254
step incremental treadmill test 223–224
stopwatches **118**, 119, **120**, 133
strain gauges 97, 98
stressors 44, 46, 293–294, 350
stretch-shortening cycle *see* SSC
structured testing 42–44, 47–48
subacromial impingement syndrome 70
SWC (smallest worthwhile change) 314; interpretation of results 133–134
Swift Speedlight **121**, 126
systematic bias 23, 24–29
systematic noise, definition **57**

T-test 142, 144, 148, **159**
task-orientation 15
team sports, structured testing 42, *43*
TEM (typical error of measurement), interpretation of results 133, 264
testing order, standardisation of 37–38
three-cone drill *see* L-run
three-dimensional motion analysis 59
three-minute all-out test *231*, 233–234
timing: Brower timing gates 119, **120**, 125, 128, 133; Fusion Sport timing system 121, 126, *127*; hand-held devices 119, 122; laser devices **120**, 122–123; Optojump system **118**, 128; photocell or timing gate systems

123–128; radar guns **118**, 122–123;
reliability and measurement error
120–121; stopwatches **118**, 119,
120, 133; Swift Speedlight **121**, 126
TJT (tuck jump test) 63–65
Tlim (limit of tolerance) 215, 220, 221–222,
224, 225, 228
timing of tests 34–35
training age **304**, 305, 341–345
training history 342–345
"training steering" 48
treadmill exercise 216, *218*, 219–220, 225;
step incremental treadmill test 223–224
twenty-metre multi-stage shuttle run test
228–229, 232
tuck jump test *see* TJT
typical error of measurement *see* TEM

UK: Health and Safety at Work Act 1974 7;
Health and Safety at Work Regulations
1999 7; Health and Safety Executive 7;
legislation on informed consent children 11
unfiltered data, analysis 36
"universal dynamometric stand" 341
US: legislation on informed consent
children 11; Occupational Safety and
Health Act 1970 7
Utilitarian Theory 5

V-scope 118, 338
validity 23–29; aerobic performance
assessment 229; body composition
assessment **241**; countermovement jump
(CMJ) *98*, 101; ecological 147, 150,
153, 203, 206, 220, 335; interpretation
of results 294; key terms definition **57**;
power assessment 202; psychological issues
15, 18; screening tests 56–57

VC_{O2} (carbon dioxide production) 218,
228, *230*
VE (expiratory ventilation) 218, *230*
verbal persuasion 17, **19**
vertical jump *see* CMJ
video-based reactive agility tests (Y-agility
test) 154
Virgil, *The Aeneid* 334
Virtue Theory 5
visualisation 18
VL (volume load) 336–339
VLwD (volume load with displacement)
338–341
VO_2 215, 216–218, 221, 222, 224–229, *231*
VO_{2max} (maximum aerobic capacity): aerobic
performance assessment 214–217,
219–221, 222, 223–224, **225**, 228–229,
232–234; interpretation of results 298,
299–302, 306, **307**, 308
VO_{2peak} 215, 219–221, 225, *226*,
227–228, 234
VO_2 plateau 215, 216, 225–226, 227–228
volleyball 59, 181, 284–285
volume load *see* VL
volume load with displacement *see* VLwD

weighing scales 243–244, 252
weightlifting 46, 171, 172, 174, 175, 181,
278, 338, 351
Wingate test 35, 298, 299, 306, **307**
work-energy theorem 112, 195–196

Y-agility tests *see* video-based reactive
agility test
YIET (Yo-Yo Intermittent Endurance
Test) 220
YIRT (Yo-Yo Intermittent Recovery Test) 35,
37, 220, 232–233